*Freedom Fighters of the
United States Supreme Court*

FREEDOM FIGHTERS OF THE UNITED STATES SUPREME COURT

Nine Who Championed Individual Liberty

by JAMES E. LEAHY

McFarland & Company, Inc., Publishers
Jefferson, North Carolina, and London

To those judges and justices who
have voted for, and written about,
freedom

Coventry University

British Library Cataloguing-in-Publication data are available

Library of Congress Cataloguing-in-Publication Data

Leahy, James E., 1919–
    Freedom fighters of the United States Supreme Court : nine who
championed individual liberty / by James E. Leahy.
        p.   cm.
    Includes bibliographical references and index.
    ISBN 0-7864-0206-7 (library binding : 50# alk. paper)
    1. United States.   Supreme Court—Biography.   2. Judges—
United
    States—Biography.   3. Civil rights—United States—History.
    I. Title.
    KF8744.L43   1996
    347.73'2634—dc20
    [B]
    [347.3073534]
    [B]   96-2815
                                                                 CIP

Manufactured in the United States of America

*McFarland & Company, Inc., Publishers
  Box 611, Jefferson, North Carolina 28640*

Contents

PREFACE

During the more than twenty years that I taught constitutional law at California Western School of Law, San Diego, California, it became evident to me that most Supreme Court justices voted *for* the government and *against* freedom most of the time.

In the 1920s and 1930s, when Justice Louis D. Brandeis and Chief Justice Charles Evans Hughes were on the Court, votes for and opinions about freedom became more prevalent. The pace increased in the 1940s. The Court then included justices Hugo L. Black, William O. Douglas, Frank Murphy, and Wiley B. Rutledge.

During the 1950s, when the country was looking for Communists in closets, under beds, in classrooms, in unions, and in Hollywood, a Court majority consistently voted *for* government infringement upon our rights.

The appointments of Chief Justice Earl Warren and justices William J. Brennan, Jr., Abe Fortas, Arthur J. Goldberg, and Thurgood Marshall in the fifties and sixties brought about more Court victories for freedom.

There have been biographies and articles in law reviews and other publications, as well as accolades and honors, accorded to each of the nine justices profiled herein. But I believe their contribution to securing the individual freedoms we enjoy in this country needs to be told in a way that focuses primarily upon their deep commitment to those freedoms. This book, therefore, tells how these justices voted in cases involving freedom and provides the reader with their views on the issues involved, in the justices' own words. Chapters proceed chronologically, by the justices' appointment to the Supreme Court.

The cases discussed are from the official United States Reports for the years 1863 through 1991. Few cases came to the Court involving individual freedom prior to 1863. In chronicling how these justices fought for freedom, I examined their votes and opinions about the freedoms protected by the First Amendment: freedom of religion, speech, press, association, and assembly. Also discussed are the rights "found" by the Court to be included within

1

the word *liberty* of the Due Process Clause—that is, the right to work, to travel, and of privacy.

To be really free, one must also be treated equally by government; therefore the justices' votes and opinions in equal protection cases are included.

These nine justices were chosen because each voted *for* freedom and *against* government infringement thereon, most of the time.

James E. Leahy
January 1996

PROLOGUE

So they gave their bodies to the commonwealth and received, each for his own memory, praise that will never die, and with it the grandest of all sepulchers, not that in which their mortal bones are laid, but a home in the minds of men, where their glory remains fresh to stir to speech or action as the occasion comes by. For the whole earth is the sepulcher of famous men; and their story is not graven only in stone over their native earth, but lives on far away, without visible symbol, woven into the stuff of other men's lives. For you now it remains to rival what they have done and, knowing the secret of happiness to be freedom and the secret of freedom a brave heart, not idly stand aside from the enemy's onset. —Thucydides, Funeral Oration of Pericles, 37*

As Thucydides' Oration points out, freedom fighters existed long before the birth of Jesus Christ, because people's happiness depended upon freedom, and freedom depended upon them. And as our own history tells us, we too have needed freedom fighters. For example, during the period leading up to the Revolutionary War, many spoke out that the time had come to fight for freedom from the oppressors—the British. One of those was Patrick Henry, who said:

> If we wish to be free; if we mean to preserve inviolate those inestimable privileges for which we have been so long contending; if we mean not basely to abandon the noble struggle in which we have been so long engaged, and which we have pledged ourselves never to abandon until the glorious object of our contest shall be obtained—we must fight! I repeat it, sir, we must fight!

Another patriot, who believed that the only way people were going to be free was to fight, was Thomas Paine. Paine, in an essay entitled *The Liberty Tree*, published in 1775, wrote, "We fight not to enslave, but to set a country free, and to make room upon the earth for honest men to live in."

But freedom is not won just on battlefields. "Freedom is not free," Edmond Cahn wrote.

> Shaping and preserving a new kind of society necessarily involves personal commitment, costly risk, and constant effort; the cultivation of civil liberty can be no more passive than the cultivation of a farm. A man can inherit the land on which he lives, he can even inherit the first crop of produce after he takes over from those who came before him. But then if he stops, everything stops, and begins to crumble. Nothing grows, nothing ripe and rewarding comes to him, unless he plows, plants and tends the soil and unless he keeps it fertile year after year with the chemistry of effort and forethought. Nor will he retain the harvest it yields unless, while he gathers and reaps, he exerts himself to repel trespassers and aggressors with indomitable will. It requires resolution, faith and courage to maintain what Madison called "the great rights of mankind."[1]

The "great rights of mankind," which our Constitution guarantees, are not just for the haves, but also for the have-nots—the worker, the common person, the underdog, and the downtrodden of all races and creeds. These nine justices understood that, and fought with their votes and opinions to protect these rights for all.

Each of the justices profiled herein, therefore, has earned "a home in the minds of men, where their glory remains fresh to stir to speech or action as the occasion comes by." Each, in the words of Rudyard Kipling, was "a first class fightin' man," "fightin'" for freedom. They all were *freedom fighters*.

1

JUSTICE JOHN MARSHALL HARLAN

PERSONAL LIFE

Growing Up

John Harlan's wife, Malvina (Mallie) Shanklin, first saw him when as a young woman she peeked through a crack in the window shutters of her home in 1853. In her words, she saw a "magnificent figure, his head erect, his broad shoulders well thrown back—walking as if the whole world belonged to him."[1] At that time Harlan was 20 years old, six feet two inches tall, and had red hair.

John Marshall Harlan was born in 1833 in an old stone house near Danville, Kentucky, to James and Eliza Davenport Harlan. James Harlan was a lawyer and an active member of the Whig Party. "To be a Clay Whig meant being anti–Jeffersonian and, by the same token, pro–John Marshall. John, named after the great chief justice, imbibed these views at his father's knee: belief in a government 'that would be supreme and paramount in all matters entrusted to the General Government, its powers, however, to be so exerted as not to infringe upon the rights which remained with the people of the several States.'"[2]

To be pro–John Marshal and anti–Thomas Jefferson was to be opposed to the Democratic Party and its democratic views. "It is best," Harlan wrote, "for *any* organization to control public affairs than to have the Democratic party in power. That was the kind of political meat upon which my father fed me as I grew up."[3]

During Harlan's early years, his father had a successful law practice and served as the attorney general of Kentucky. He was also appointed by President Abraham Lincoln as United States district attorney. Harlan recalled his father taking him to hear Henry Clay speak. Of this event, Harlan wrote, "I

**JUSTICE JOHN MARSHALL HARLAN (photo by Handy Studios; collection of the
Supreme Court of the United States).**

was a mere boy at the time and did not know what the occasion meant. But
I remember that during the whole time of Clay's speech I sat at his foot, and
was charmed with his magnificent bugle voice. . . ."[4]

Religion was a central part of the Harlans' family life. They were orig-
inally Quakers but later became Presbyterians. In 1892, Harlan wrote to
William Howard Taft that he had told a Scottish preacher that he was taking a trip to Scotland "in order to hear preached what I have not heard for a
long while, a little 'Hell-fire and Damnation.'"[5]

Because there were no public schools in Kentucky, John was sent to a
private school in Frankfort where the family lived. From 1848 to 1850 John
attended Centre College in Danville, Kentucky. And although his mother

wanted him to become a businessman, his father would have none of it. After graduating from college, John was sent off to law school at Transylvania University in Lexington. Recalling his law school days during a speech at that university some years later, Harlan said, "I remember when here of sitting at the feet of some of the greatest judges and lawyers that ever appeared in this or, I believe, any other country. George Robertson, Thomas A. Marshall, A.J. Woolley and Madison C. Johnson were the professors or teachers in this law school when I had the honor to be a member of it, and I undertake to say that no law school that has ever existed in this country or, in my judgment, in any other country has had at the same time as professors and teachers of the science of law four greater Lawyers than those four that I have named."[6]

Professor George Robertson's lectures on constitutional law especially had a profound effect upon Harlan. Later he recalled one of those lectures: "The Constitution should never be stringently construed like a penal statute, but always more liberally, as the charter of a great public trust for the welfare of the people, and for the maintenance of the harmony and justice of the Union; and as the best safeguard, therefore, of liberty, peace, and security."[7]

At the end of his first year of law school, Harlan obtained a position as clerk in the second auditor's office at the state capital. Governor Helm visited the office one day, and the following conversation took place. The governor said, "John, the office of Adjutant General is vacant, and I have a notion to appoint you." To which John replied, "Governor, you are jesting, I am only eighteen years of age." "No matter," answered the governor, "you can fill the place."[8] When the governor returned to his office, he signed and sent Harlan his commission as adjutant general of Kentucky. The post was mostly a ceremonial one. As adjutant, he was *ex officio* chairman of the board of visitors of the two military institutes in the state. It also made it possible for him to become acquainted with many people active in Kentucky politics.

Love, Marriage, and Family

Mallie Shanklin did not meet the "magnificent figure" she saw through the blinds until the following February. Some years later, she described how this young girl chanced to meet John Harlan. The young girl "was invited to take supper with the family of Dr. J.G. Hatchitt . . . living in the block beyond her father's residence. To her surprise, as she sat talking to her hostess, a young man—with a rope to each arm, as he 'played horsey' for the little nephew . . . (of the hostess)—suddenly pranced into the room. The young girl at once recognized him as the interesting stranger that had caught her eye six months before, as she peeped through the narrow crack of the window-shutters."[9] This chance meeting took place in Evansville, Kentucky, where Mallie was then living. John spent the following week calling on her before returning to his home in Frankfort. At the end of the week, he asked her to be his wife, a request she refused. John was not to be discouraged so easily. Upon returning to Frankfort, he wrote the Shanklins seeking their permission to marry Mallie, and referred them to some mutual friends who could attest to his character. Although Mallie was interested in marrying John, her parents sent her to a finishing school for a couple of years because she was only 16 years old. During this period, the couple corresponded and occasionally were able to be together. They were, however, married at her father's house on December 23, 1856, and moved in with John's parents in Frankfort.

This household consisted of John's parents, brother James and his wife, brother William, and sisters Laura and Sallie. Also living with the family were slaves whom John's father had inherited. This was Mallie's first direct experience with slavery, having come from a family of abolitionists.

John's law practice was not very lucrative, but with financial help from Mallie's father the couple purchased a house. John hired a black woman, Aunt Fannie, as a cook for Mallie. Aunt Fannie had a distinct mind of her own as to how food ought to be prepared, even to the point of telling Mallie that she did not know anything about cooking. Ultimately Aunt Fannie was given her freedom, and a search for a new cook was undertaken. When one could not be found, Mallie sought out one of John's mother's slaves, Aunt Emily, and inquired why it was so difficult to get someone to work for her. As Mallie later told it: "With a look on her face of mingled amusement and sorrow (lest she might hurt my feelings) she said, 'Old Fannie done gib you such a bad name, Miss Mallie, dat it's gwine to be hard for you to get a good cook. She say that Marse John is a puffect gen'leman, but dat *you'se* nuffing but a She-Debbil.'"[10]

The Harlans had a long and happy marriage during which Mallie gave birth to six children, three boys and three girls. The oldest son, Richard, had a successful career as a Presbyterian minister, and sons James and John both became successful lawyers. The daughters were Edith, Laura, and Ruth.

Harlan played golf and at age 75 hit a triple in a baseball game between lawyers and judges. He chewed tobacco and also taught Sunday school at the Presbyterian church.

Although the family lived moderately well, Harlan never made much money, and at times was in debt from his frequent political campaigns.

Lawyer and Public Servant

Harlan was admitted to the Kentucky bar in 1853 and joined his father in the practice of law. At first he worked as his father's clerk, but he gradually built up his own clientele, traveling around the area in order to do so. This often took him away from home for a week or more at a time. Having no clerk of his own, he often recruited Mallie to copy briefs for him.

Harlan was elected city attorney of Frankfort in 1854 and re-elected in 1856. "During his first year as city solicitor, Harlan prosecuted about 35 cases. The offenses consisted of breach of the peace, tippling, and selling liquor to slaves. In the vast majority of these cases Harlan secured convictions for which the penalty was always a fine, ranging from $1 to $60. Usually a jury trial was involved, but sometimes the case was simply held before a judge."[11]

Being city solicitor was not a full-time position, so John was able to continue his practice, which consisted mostly of litigation to collect debts. His fees were a meager 5 percent of the amount involved.

He was drafted to run for county judge in 1858 by the American Party, successor to the Know Nothing Party, which he had joined. The campaign was a spirited one. Harlan tried to visit every family in the county, and to shake hands with all who were willing. He was elected even though it was generally understood that the post should be filled not by lawyers but by farmers. He served as judge for two and a half years, and because it was not a full-time job, he continued to practice law.

Harlan served in two other government positions. He was elected attorney general of Kentucky, an office he held for four years, but was defeated for re-election. In 1873 he was appointed as a special federal prosecutor for federal civil rights violations in Kentucky.

Politician

Harlan was branded by his political opponents as a "political weathercock."[12] This description was apparently a reference to the fact that he was part of several different political movements, and over the years his views on many of the important issues of the day changed substantially.

The Whig Party, of which John was a member, had fallen on hard times. Nationally it was divided into Southern and Northern factions because of slavery. In Kentucky, the party went "underground," so to speak. Many, including John and his father, joined a secret organization known as the Know Nothing Society whose motto was "Put none but Americans on Guard." They were against foreigners' and Roman Catholics' holding public office and took an oath to vote only for Protestant, native Americans.

Harlan later described taking the Know Nothing Society's oath: "I was very uncomfortable when the oath was administered to me. My conscience, for a time, rebelled against it. For a moment I had the thought of retiring; for while I was intense . . . in my Protestantism, I did not relish the idea of proscribing anyone on account of his religion. But looking around the room in which the initiation occurred, I observed that the old Whig leaders of the city, including my father, were present, and I had not the boldness to repudiate the organization."[13]

Because of the secrecy of the Know Nothing Society, its candidates ran as part of the American Party. During the early 1850s, Harlan traveled the state speaking on behalf of this party's candidates. Although the American Party was successful in Kentucky in the 1855 elections, it was not so on a national level. Nevertheless, Harlan came out of that campaign with a state-wide reputation as an effective speaker and campaigner. One newspaper said of him, "He came amongst us unknown to fame, and utterly unheralded, but he left an impression behind him that will not be effaced for a long time."[14]

In 1859, the Whigs, Know Nothings, and members of the American Party joined together to form the Opposition Party, and nominated Harlan as their candidate for Congress. Harlan's opponent was Captain William E. Simms, a former Whig who had joined the Democratic Party. The campaign was long, hard-fought, and bitter. Both candidates were for slavery, but each had a different approach to its solution. Both believed that each state should be allowed to deal with the issue, but Harlan urged Congress to pass laws protecting the rights of slave owners. This campaign saw Harlan break from the philosophy of the Know Nothings which he had espoused earlier, a change that Democrats were quick to point out. He no longer spoke against foreigners and Catholics.

Although Harlan lost, he was convinced that there had been fraud in the election process. Many of his friends agreed and raised money to contest the election, but Harlan chose not to file an official protest.

Harlan's next appearance on the political scene was during the election of 1860. The remnants of the old Whig Party ran their own candidate, John Bell, for president under the label of the Constitutionalist Union Party. The party platform was: "The Union, the Constitution, and the Enforcement of the Laws." Harlan was selected as an elector for Bell. The Republican candidate was Abraham Lincoln. The Democrats, split into Northern and Southern parties, nominated Stephen A. Douglas, and John C. Breckinridge, for president and vice president, respectively. Although Lincoln was elected president, Bell carried Kentucky, Tennessee, and Virginia.

In 1861, the Harlans moved to Louisville where John joined William F. Bullock in the practice of law. By this time, South Carolina had seceded, and other Southern states were on the verge of doing so. Uppermost in the minds of the Unionists was to keep Kentucky in the Union. One writer has described Harlan's part in this endeavor as follows: "Together with other loyalists, John Harlan and his father worked both openly and secretly to keep Kentucky from secession. From May through July, John and other Louisville men held street corner rallies to persuade the public of the values of Union. By his own estimate, Harlan made at least 50 store-box speeches."[15]

Harlan played another role, although a secretive one, in espousing the Unionist cause. Through the influence of John's father and other prominent Kentuckians, arrangements were made for John to write editorials for the *Louisville Daily Journal*, all of which, of course, argued that Kentucky should remain in the Union, which it did.

Harlan served in the Union Army from 1861 until the death of his father in 1863, when he resigned and moved back to Frankfort to handle his father's estate. His wartime experiences are discussed hereafter.

Shortly after the Harlans returned to Frankfort, John's friends in the Union Party prevailed upon him to run for state attorney general. During this campaign, he vigorously attacked President Lincoln for issuing the Emancipation Proclamation and suspending the writ of *habeas corpus*. Harlan won the election but served only one term, being defeated for re-election in 1867.

The election of 1864 presented Harlan and the Unionists with a dilemma. Whom should they support for the presidency? Supporting Republican Lincoln was out of the question. But campaigning for a Democrat was just as undesirable. They finally decided to support Democrat George McClellan, and Harlan campaigned vigorously for him. Later Harlan explained his vote: "I did not vote for McClellan because I was a Democrat, or because he was a Democrat, but because I *then* believed that his mode of prosecuting the war was most likely to bring it to a speedy conclusion, with the Union preserved intact. But subsequent events satisfied me that my judgment in this particular was erroneous, . . . the defeat of Mr. Lincoln would have been the greatest calamity which could have befallen the country at that time."[16]

With little hope of being elected, Harlan became the Unionist candidate for U.S. senator from Kentucky in 1867. Senators at that time were chosen by state legislatures. Even though he had supported Democrat McClellan, he was unable to secure support from the Democratic Party and received only eight votes. He then returned to Louisville to practice law with John E. Newman, a fellow Unionist who had joined the Republican Party. Another Unionist turned Republican, Benjamin H. Bristow joined the firm in 1870.

During this period, the Ku Klux Klan was active in Kentucky and several blacks were hanged. When Harlan defended the son of a friend who had been accused of participating in the hangings, some of his black friends were dismayed. In 1873, however, he was appointed as a special prosecutor to prosecute violations of federal laws known as the Enforcement Acts.

He became a Republican and campaigned for that party's candidate, General Ulysses S. Grant, for president in 1868. At that time, it appeared that the country was gravitating toward a two-party system. Furthermore, the Unionist Party had never been successful on the national level.

Harlan became the state Republican leader and set up party organizations in most of the state's counties. It was during this period that Harlan changed his views on slavery and became a strong supporter of the Thirteenth, Fourteenth, and Fifteenth Amendments. The press, and particularly the Democratic press, did not let this change of heart go unnoticed, especially when he ran for governor on the Republican ticket in 1871. Although he lost the election, Harlan gained enough votes to allow the party thereafter to become a factor in Kentucky politics. "As one Republican observed, 'the long, dark, dreary night of Republicanism in Kentucky,' was over."[17] Harlan's activities in Kentucky brought him a second nomination for governor in 1875 but the result was the same—he was defeated. During this time, he and his law partner Ben Bristow were both beginning to be recognized on the national political scene.

One writer described their relationship as follows: "Both were ambitious, honest, and public-spirited men, and both, at times, allowed their ambitions to get the better of their good judgment. Bristow 'arrived' on the national scene earlier than Harlan, with his appointment and successful service as solicitor general. But Harlan's success in creating and leading a strong Republican campaign in Kentucky and his activities outside the state in the 1872 campaign made him, as well, a national figure."[18]

In the years leading up to the Republican National Convention in 1876, Bristow became a candidate for the presidency. Harlan vigorously campaigned for his law partner at state conventions and succeeded in leading the Kentucky delegation to the national convention pledged to him. He also made a nominating speech for Bristow. Three strong candidates emerged at the convention: Bristow, James G. Blaine of Maine, and Oliver P. Morton of Indiana. Other candidates were Roscoe Conkling of New York, Rutherford B. Hayes of Ohio, and Governor Hartrauft of Pennsylvania.

On the first ballot, Blaine received 285 votes, Morton 125, and Bristow 113. In an attempt to stop Blaine, a movement began for Hayes when Michigan switched its votes to him. When Morton conceded defeat after the sixth ballot, Harlan went to the stand and spoke, extolling Bristow's virtues. However, he had seen the handwriting on the wall, so to speak, that Bristow was not going to be nominated. Therefore he switched Kentucky's votes to Hayes, who eventually won the nomination. From that point on, the relationship between Harlan and Bristow deteriorated, although the law partnership continued for a short time.

Harlan campaigned for Hayes against the Democratic candidate, Samuel J. Tilden. Hayes was elected and took office in March 1877.

One of the tasks facing President Hayes at his inauguration was nominating someone to fill the vacancy of Justice David Davis, who had resigned just a few days before. It is rather ironic that both Bristow and Harlan were among those considered for the nomination. Because the president did not make the nomination immediately, there was much political activity throughout the summer by potential nominees and their supporters. The president finally nominated Harlan on October 16, 1877.

Soldier

When it appeared to the Unionists that Kentucky would not be spared from participating in the war, many were confronted with the question of whether to join the Confederate or the Union Army, a question that presented for some a choice between the lesser of two evils. Harlan, for example, fought very hard to keep Kentucky in the Union; thus the Confederate Army was no real option for him. However, he had also vigorously opposed Lincoln's handling of the slavery issue, so joining the Union Army meant setting aside his own views on that issue. Furthermore, Harlan and many others contemplating army service had families to consider. But Mallie made it easier for her husband when she told him, "You must do as you would if you had neither wife nor children. I could not stand between you and your duty to the country and be happy."[19]

In the fall of 1861, Harlan, calling for volunteers, formed what became the Tenth Kentucky Infantry, and he became its commander, with the rank of colonel. Author David G. Farrelly describes Harlan's military career:

> Harlan's war service was as a troop officer, a field commander, and this experience brought him into close relationships with rank and file. Indeed, it is doubtful if any other period in his long life gave him such opportunity to mix so intimately with men of all classes and creeds. Sharing the hardships of war with his soldiers, Harlan learned at first hand what it meant to suffer the privations of war; heat and dust, cold and mud, lack of food and rest, shortage of equipment. On the whole Harlan's war experience was a great leveler and his soldiers affectionately called him "Old Red." His dispatches frequently spoke in tribute of the willingness of his men to endure the sufferings of warfare. Out of this comradeship at arms Harlan developed a life-long sympathy for the common man.[20]

Being a soldier had another lasting effect upon Harlan in that it changed his views of foreigners and Catholics because he encountered both as Union soldiers and was impressed by their dedication to the war effort.

Of the war record of the Tenth Kentucky Regiment it has been written that "they marched more than they fought."[21]

Harlan resigned from the army in February 1863 upon learning of his father's death. He felt obligated to return home to handle his father's estate and take over as head of the family.

Slave Owner

James Harlan became the owner of slaves through inheritance. Although he was not an outspoken advocate of abolition, evidence indicates that he was really opposed to the continuation of slavery. His slaves, who were household servants, were well cared for and several were eventually allowed to purchase their freedom.

Mallie, in describing the family home she entered as a new bride, wrote, "In the cabins at the back of the lot, lived the slaves, who had been inherited from both sides of the Harlan family. There were almost as many slaves as there were members of 'the Family' [about a dozen] . . . . The close sympathy existing between the slaves and their Master or Mistress was a source of great wonder to me as a descendant of the Puritans, and I was often obliged to admit to myself that my former views of the 'awful Institution of Slavery' would have to be somewhat modified. . . ."[22]

When John was settling his father's estate, he gave the slaves their freedom and personally assumed the financial responsibility to the estate for them. While he may personally have been against slavery, he found it politically expedient not to call publicly for its abolition. During his campaign for Congress in 1859, he favored the slavery position, a position that his critics claimed was inconsistent with views expressed previously. The views of the Harlans, father and son, during the years before the Civil War were that slave owners had a property right in their slaves, that the federal government ought to protect this property, and that the slavery issue should be left to the individual states. Harlan did not believe in social equality for blacks, and he supported segregation in the public schools. He had also opposed the adoption of the Thirteenth, Fourteenth, and Fifteenth Amendments to the Constitution.

After the Civil War, Harlan's views changed dramatically. He became aware of the fact that blacks were attending school and working. He also learned of the lynching and harmful treatment whites were inflicting upon the newly freed blacks. And the amendments had now been adopted. Harlan expressed his change in views about slavery in a speech in 1871:

> It is true fellow citizens that almost the entire people of Kentucky, at one period in their history, were opposed to freedom, citizenship and suffrage of the Colored race. It is true that I was at one time in my life opposed to conferring these privileges upon them, but I have lived long enough to feel and declare, as I do this night, that the most perfect despotism that ever existed on this earth was the institution of African slavery. It was an enemy to free speech; it was an enemy to good government; it was an enemy to a free press.[23]

He made no attempt to excuse his past support of slavery, nor to justify his changes of views. Referring to the views just expressed, he said, "Let it be said that I am right rather than consistent."[24]

Although he now supported the amendments to the extent they protected blacks from state interference with their rights, Harlan expressed the opinion that the amendments did not give the federal government power to regulate the activities of private individuals. He subsequently changed this view also.

During his campaign for governor in 1875, his "speeches were defenses of emancipation and the War Amendments, of the Civil Rights Act of 1866 and the use of Negro testimony in state courts, of the full employment of legal rights by Negroes and the distinction between legal and social rights.

Harlan again called for an end to race-politics and anti–Negro agitation."[25] Harlan and the Republicans, however, could not stem the Democratic tide, and he was defeated.

Nomination to the Supreme Court

In the spring of 1877 Supreme Court Justice David Davis resigned, giving President Hayes his first Supreme Court appointment. Upon giving the matter considerable thought, the president "wrote to a close friend, 'Confidentially and on the whole, is not Harlan the man? Of the right age, able, of noble character, industrious, fine manners, temper and appearance. Who beats him?'"

Harlan's nomination to the Supreme Court was sent to the U.S. Senate on October 16, 1877. Due to strong opposition, he was not confirmed until November 26. He took the oath of office on December 10, and joined Chief Justice Morrison R. Waite and associate justices Ward Hunt, Nathan Clifford, William Strong, Samuel F. Miller, Joseph P. Bradley, Noah H. Swayne, and Stephen J. Field.

Professor Florian Bartosic describes Justice Harlan: a "powerful orator and a man of firm convictions and strong feelings, the Justice did not hesitate to lecture his brothers on the bench when he differed with them."[26] A vivid description of Harlan's lecturing his colleagues appeared in the *New York Tribune* concerning one of his dissents: "[Harlan] pounded the desk, shook his finger under the noses of the Chief Justice and Mr. Justice Field, turned more than once almost angrily upon his colleagues of the majority, and expressed his dissent from their conclusions in a tone and language more appropriate to a stump speech at a Populace barbecue than to an opinion on a question of law before the Supreme Court of the United States."[27]

It has also been said of him: "Harlan retires at night with one hand on the Constitution and the other on the Bible, safe and happy in a perfect faith in justice and righteousness."[28]

AS ASSOCIATE JUSTICE (1877-1911)

Equal Protection of the Law

Blacks on Juries. Shortly after Harlan joined the Court, his acceptance of the intent of the War Amendments became evident in three related cases involving the exclusion of blacks from juries. The cases were *Strauder v. West Virginia*,[29] *Virginia v. Rives*,[30] and *Ex Parte Virginia*.[31] Strauder had been indicted for murder but before trial petitioned to have his case removed to the federal court because under West Virginia law blacks were not allowed to sit on grand or petit juries. The petition was denied and the trial resulted in his conviction.

His petition to have the trial removed to the federal court was based on a federal statute that provided for such removal when it appeared that the petitioner's rights were being denied by the state. Congress enacted this law to assure to all persons the rights protected by the Fourteenth Amendment, including the right to equal protection of the law. In this case, the denial of equal protection was being tried for murder without blacks on the grand or trial jury.

The majority of the Court, including Harlan, agreed that Strauder's case should have been removed to the local federal court and reversed his conviction. Justices Field and Clifford dissented. In the opinion written by Justice Strong, the Court discussed the purposes behind the Fourteenth Amendment:

> It was designed to assure to the colored race the enjoyment of all the civil rights that under the law are enjoyed by white persons, and to give to that race the protection of the general government, in that enjoyment, whenever it should be denied by the States. It not only gave citizenship and the privileges of citizenship to persons of color, but it denied to any State the power to withhold from them the equal protection of the laws, and authorized Congress to enforce its provisions by appropriate legislation.[32]

Having concluded that the laws of West Virginia were discriminatory against blacks, the Court then addressed the question of whether Congress had the power to order cases, such as Strauder's, removed to the federal courts. Justice Strong answered for the Court that Congress did have that power, citing as authority a similar case decided by the Court that same day.

In *Rives*, the Court upheld a denial for removal to the federal court, finding that the laws of Virginia did not exclude blacks from juries. The Court did, however, affirm the meaning of the Fourteenth Amendment, as stated in *Strauder*, that "discrimination by law against the colored race, because of their color, in the selection of jurors, is a denial of the equal protection of the laws to a negro when he is put upon trial for an alleged criminal offence against a State."[33]

In *Ex Parte Virginia*, J.D. Coles, a Virginia county court judge was indicted for failing to summon blacks to serve on grand and petit juries in his court, such failure being a violation of federal law. Coles sought to be discharged from custody by a writ of *habeas corpus*, which the judge refused to grant.

Here again one of the questions to be answered by the Supreme Court was whether Congress had the power to enact a law making the acts in which Coles engaged a criminal offense. In affirming Congress's power under the Fourteenth Amendment, Justice Strong wrote, "The constitutional provision, therefore, must mean that no agency of the State, or of the officers or agents by whom its powers are exerted, shall deny to any person within its jurisdiction of the equal protection of the laws."[34]

Harlan, writing for the majority in *Neal v. Delaware*,[35] held that the law providing for the removal to federal courts cases involving an alleged civil rights violation was not the only way to secure federal review of such cases. William Neal had been indicted for rape. In his petition for removal, he alleged that blacks were not allowed to sit on juries in Delaware. This was not true, and therefore the lower court was correct in rejecting Neal's petition. But Harlan and the majority did not stop there. They were of the opinion that the state trial judge should have addressed Neal's assertion that, in spite of the law, blacks were being excluded from juries. Harlan wrote:

> The showing thus made [by Neal], including, as it did, the fact . . . that no colored citizen had ever been summoned as a juror in the courts of the State,— although its colored population exceeded twenty thousand in 1870, and in 1880 exceeded twenty-six thousand, in a total population of less than one hundred and fifty thousand,—presented a prima facie case of denial, by the officers charged with the selection of grand and petit jurors, of that equality of protection which has been secured by the Constitution and laws of the United States.[36]

On this basis, the majority reversed Neal's conviction. Chief Justice Waite and Justice Field dissented.

Justice Harlan consistently voted to reverse convictions where blacks were excluded from juries by state law.[37] However, when the claim was that the exclusion of blacks was done by those administering the jury selection process, as in *Neal*, he demanded evidence of such discrimination before reversing a conviction.

Although Harlan and the other justices were protecting the rights of blacks, they were giving a very restricted meaning to the Fourteenth Amendment's equal protection clause as applied to others. For example, in commenting upon the power of a state to restrict voting to certain members of society, Harlan wrote for a unanimous Court "that . . . a State, consistently with the purposes for which the amendment was adopted, may confine the selection of jurors to males, to freeholders, to citizens, to persons within certain ages, or to persons having educational qualifications."[38]

Separate but Equal Transportation. Harlan's initial response to state laws requiring segregation of white and black passengers on trains was that such statutes interfere with interstate commerce, and thus were a violation of Congress's power to regulate commerce under Article I, Section 8, Clause 3, of the Constitution.[39] But as the lone dissenter in *Plessy v. Ferguson*,[40] he forcefully argued that even if equal facilities on trains are furnished for whites and blacks, such segregation is a violation of equal protection.

Plessy, who was one-eighth black, took a seat in the whites-only section of a train, contrary to the laws of Louisiana where the train was traveling. He was arrested but sought a writ prohibiting the court from further proceedings on the grounds that the law was unconstitutional. The state supreme court denied relief, being of the opinion that the state law did not violate the Constitution. Plessy appealed to the U.S. Supreme Court, which agreed with the Louisiana Supreme Court.

In an opinion by Justice Henry B. Brown, the majority held that to require separate but equal facilities on trains was not involuntary servitude and therefore did not violate the Thirteenth Amendment. As to the Fourteenth Amendment, Justice Brown commented as follows:

> The object of the amendment was undoubtedly to enforce the absolute equality of the two races before the law, but in the nature of things it could not have been intended to abolish distinctions based upon color, or to enforce social, as distinguished from political equality, or a commingling of the two races upon terms unsatisfactory to either.

The only real constitutional question in the case, according to Justice Brown, was whether the law was reasonable. In finding that it was, he pointed out that "[i]n determining the question of reasonableness it [the legislature] is at liberty to act with reference to the established usages, customs and traditions of the people, and with a view to the promotion of their comfort, and the preservation of the public peace and good order."

In dissent, Harlan expressed the view that "[i]n respect of civil rights, common to all citizens, the Constitution of the United States does not, I think, permit any public authority to know the race of those entitled to be protected in the enjoyment of such rights." He then noted that the Thirteenth Amendment "not only struck down the institution of slavery . . . but it prevents the imposition of any burdens or disabilities that constitute badges of slavery or servitude."

If the Thirteenth and Fourteenth Amendments are "enforced according to their true intent and meaning," he wrote, they "will protect all the civil rights that pertain to freedom and citizenship." Harlan then discussed the intent of the Louisiana statute and pointed out that "[e]very one knows that the statute in question had its origin in the purpose, not so much to exclude white persons from railroad cars occupied by blacks, as to exclude colored persons from coaches occupied by or assigned to white persons."

He then makes the statement that is no doubt the most remembered and quoted passage from his dissent: "Our Constitution is color-blind, and neither knows nor tolerates classes among citizens." He continued: "In respect of civil rights, all citizens are equal before the law. The humblest is the peer of the most powerful. The law regards man as man, and takes no account of his surroundings or of his color when his civil rights as guaranteed by the supreme law of the land are involved."

He then chastises the Court for its decision. "It is, therefore, to be regretted," he said, "that this high tribunal, the final expositor of the fundamental law of the land, has reached the conclusion that it is competent for a State to regulate the enjoyment by citizens of their civil rights solely upon the basis of race." He predicted that this case would become as infamous as the *Dred Scott* case,[41] in which the Court held that blacks were not citizens within the meaning of the Constitution. He sums up his opinion of the law by asserting "that the statute of Louisiana is inconsistent with the personal liberty of citizens, white and black, in that State, and hostile to both the spirit and letter of the Constitution of the United States."[42]

A Private White School. Berea College, a Kentucky corporation, was indicted for permitting both black and white persons to attend as students in violation of a state law that made it "unlawful for any person, corporation or association of persons to maintain . . . any college, . . . where persons of the white and negro races are both received as pupils for instruction."[43] It was found guilty and fined $1,000. When the case reached the Supreme Court, the conviction was affirmed, with justices Harlan and William R. Day dissenting.

The majority looked only at the part of the statute relating to corporations, and held that they have no *right* to teach at all, and therefore the state could regulate whom they taught, even to the extent of prohibiting them from teaching blacks and whites together. This allowed the majority to bypass the question of the constitutionality of the state law.

Justice Harlan vigorously disagreed with this approach. He argued that it was inconceivable that the legislature intended the law to apply only to corporations and not to individuals as well. And he chided the Court for not considering the statute as a whole. "It should adjudge whether the statute, as a whole, is or is not unconstitutional, in that it makes it a crime against the State to maintain or operate a private institution of learning where white and black pupils are received, at the same time, for instruction."

The justice then expressed the opinion that the "statute is an arbitrary invasion of the rights of liberty and property guaranteed by the Fourteenth Amendment against hostile state action and is, therefore, void." If the state can prohibit teaching of blacks and whites at the same institution, he argued, could the state not also prohibit blacks and whites from assembling for religious instruction? Surely, he asserts, "that in the eye of the law the right to enjoy one's religious belief, unmolested by any human power, is no more sacred nor more fully or distinctly recognized than is the right to impart and receive instruction not harmful to the public." Harlan left for another day the question of the constitutionality of laws that require segregation of the races in public schools.

Women Cannot Practice Law or Be Barmaids. Neither Justice Harlan nor the other justices included women within the protection of the Equal Protection Clause of the Fourteenth Amendment. In 1873 the Court held that a state could prohibit a woman from practicing law because the practice of law was not a privilege or immunity of United States citizenship.[44] And in 1875 the Court upheld a ban on women voting because this too was not one of the privileges of citizenship.[45] Harlan, of course, was not on the Court when either of these cases was decided, but in 1894 he joined in a unanimous decision upholding the right of a state to prohibit a woman from practicing law.[46] And in 1904 the Court, again including Harlan, upheld a Denver city ordinance that prohibited women from working in a liquor saloon.[47]

For Chinese Laundrymen. The case of Yick Wo presented the Court with an opportunity to expand the application of the Fourteenth Amendment to include races other than blacks. Yick Wo, a citizen of China, had operated a laundry in a wooden building in San Francisco for 22 years. His application for renewal of his license was denied because he had not obtained a special permit to have his laundry in a wooden building. At the time, there were about 310 laundries in San Francisco operating in such buildings. When Yick Wo continued to operate his laundry without a permit, he was arrested. More than 150 other Chinese were arrested for the same reason. Many permits, however, had been issued to those who were not Chinese. The Supreme Court of California upheld Yick Wo's conviction, and he appealed to the U.S. Supreme Court.[48]

Justice Stanley Matthews, writing for all justices, including Justice Harlan, reversed. Justice Matthews found that the law requiring permits was fair and impartial, but the way it was administered was questionable. "Though the law itself be fair on its face and impartial in appearance," he wrote, "yet, if it is applied and administered by public authority with an evil eye and an unequal hand, so as practically to make unjust and illegal discrimination between persons in similar circumstances, material to their rights, the denial of equal justice is still within the prohibition of the Constitution." He continued, "The discrimination is, therefore, illegal, and the public administration which enforces it is a denial of equal protection of the laws and a violation of the Fourteenth Amendment of the Constitution."

The Civil Rights Acts

Because the Fourteenth Amendment protects our civil rights only from infringement by *states*, Congress in 1875 passed what has become known as the Civil Rights Act. The purpose of this Act was to prevent *individuals* from denying to any person "the full and equal enjoyment of the accommodations, advantages, facilities, and privileges of inns, public conveyances . . . theatres, and other places of public amusement."

During the October 1883 term, the Supreme Court heard appeals in several cases involving the constitutionality of this act. These cases are collectively called the Civil Rights Cases.[49] The defendants were Stanley and Nichols, who were charged with denying accommodations at an inn to blacks; Ryan, who was indicted for not allowing a black person to sit in the dress circle of a theater; and Singleton, who was charged with a similar offense. Also included was a case against a railroad brought by Robinson and his wife because the conductor refused to allow Robinson's wife, a black woman, to sit in the ladies' car. The couple sued for $500, which was the penalty allowed under the law as compensation to one who had been the victim of discrimination.

The question before the Court was whether the Thirteenth and Fourteenth Amendments gave Congress the power to enact this particular legislation. The Supreme Court, with only Justice Harlan dissenting, held that neither of the amendments gave Congress the power to control the actions of individuals, even though both amendments gave Congress the power to enforce the amendments "by appropriate legislation."

Writing for the Court, Justice Bradley said, "It is State action of a particular character that is prohibited [by the Fourteenth Amendment]. Individual invasion of individual rights is not subject-matter of the amendment." Among the concerns of the majority was that "[i]f this legislation is appropriate for enforcing the prohibitions of the amendment, it is difficult to see where it is to stop."

Referring to the Thirteenth Amendment, the majority did not believe that denying persons admission to inns, public transportation, or theaters was in any way imposing upon them a badge of slavery. The Fourteenth, however, is much broader. It deals with the "privileges and immunities of citizens of the United States," "due process of law," and "equal protection of the laws." Nevertheless, the Court concluded, "On the whole we are of the opinion, that no countenance of authority for the passage of the law in question can be found in either the Thirteenth or Fourteenth Amendment of the Constitution; and no other ground of authority for its passage being suggested, it must necessarily be declared void, at least so far as its operation in the several States is concerned."

The part that an old inkstand played in Harlan's dissenting opinion has been related by Mrs. Harlan. Harlan had noticed the inkstand in the office of the marshal of the Court and expressed an interest in it. The marshal gave it to him and explained that it was used by Chief Justice Roger B. Taney when he wrote the opinion in the *Dred Scott* case. Later, when Harlan promised to give the stand to Mrs. George Pendleton, a relative of Chief Justice Taney, Mallie took it from his study and hid it.

Mallie describes the trials and tribulations her husband was going through while working on his dissent in Civil Rights cases as follows: "His dissent (which many lawyers consider to have been one of his greatest opinions) cost him several months of absorbing labor—his interest and anxiety often disturbing his sleep. Many times he would get up in the middle of the night, in order to jot down some thought or paragraph which he feared might elude him."[50]

Noticing the struggle her husband was having with his dissent, Mallie put the inkstand on a table in his study, and upon his return home said, "I have put a bit of inspiration on your study table. I believe it is just what you need and I am sure it will help you."

Mallie concludes the story: "He was full of curiosity, which I refused to gratify. As soon as possible he went to his study. His eye lighting upon the little inkstand, he came running down to my room to ask where in the world I had found it. With mingled shame and joy I then 'fessed up.' . . . He laughed over my naughty act and freely forgave it."

That seemed to be the spark Harlan needed, and he was able to finish the dissent in a short time.

The majority opinion, Harlan wrote, "proceeds . . . upon grounds entirely too narrow and artificial."[51] Quoting from a previous case, he pointed out that the question of whether Congress has exceeded its power "is at all times . . . a question of much delicacy, which ought seldom, if ever, to be decided in the affirmative, in a doubtful case."

Harlan discusses at length events leading up to the adoption of the Thirteenth Amendment, and agrees that it was not intended to give Congress authority to legislate in the whole area of civil rights. "But," he argues, "I hold that since slavery, as the court has repeatedly declared, . . . was the moving or principal cause of the adoption of that amendment, and since that institution rested wholly upon the inferiority, as a race, of those held in bondage, their freedom necessarily involved immunity from, and protection against, all discrimination against them, because of their race, in respect of such civil rights as belong to freemen of other races."

He then makes the argument that public conveyances, inns, and places of public amusement are sort of quasi-public institutions. "I am of the opinion," he asserts, "that such discrimination practiced by corporations and individuals in the exercise of their public or quasi-public functions is a badge of servitude the imposition of which Congress may prevent under its power, by appropriate legislation, to enforce the Thirteenth Amendment."

Harlan then turns to the Fourteenth Amendment, which was adopted in 1868, and notes that the first sentence reads, "All persons born or naturalized in the United States, and subject to the jurisdiction thereof, are citizens of the United States and the State wherein they reside." This new citizenship, he reasons, "may be protected, not alone by the judicial branch of the government, but by congressional legislation of a primary direct character; this, because the power of Congress is not restricted to the enforcement of prohibitions upon State laws or State action."

Harlan concludes his dissent with a warning of what the future may hold if Congress cannot legislate to protect civil rights:

> To-day, it is the colored race which is denied, by corporations and individuals wielding public authority, rights fundamental in their freedom and citizenship. At some future time, it may be that some other race will fall under the ban of race discrimination. If the constitutional amendments be enforced, according to the intent with which, as I conceive, they were adopted, there cannot be, in this republic, any class of human beings in practical subjection to another class, with power in the latter to dole out to the former just such privileges as they may choose to grant. The supreme law of the land has decreed that no authority shall be exercised in this country upon the basis of discrimination, in respect of civil rights, against freemen and citizens because of their race, color, or previous conditions of servitude. To that decree—for the due enforcement of which, by appropriate legislation, Congress has been invested with express power—every one must bow, whatever may have been, or whatever now are, his individual views as to the wisdom or policy, either of the recent changes in the fundamental law, or of the legislation which has been enacted to give them effect.

Harlan believed that Congress had the power not only to prevent discrimination but to protect other civil rights as well. He joined the majority in upholding Congress's power to protect the right to vote,[52] the right to make a homestead,[53] and the right of persons in the custody of a U.S. marshal to be free from lawless violence.[54]

The Justice also believed that all persons had the right to contract for and sell their labor, and that such a right was within the power of Congress to protect. In *Hodges v. United States*,[55] the Court ordered dismissal of an indictment charging certain individuals with interfering with the right of Berry Winn, Dave Hinton, Percy Legg, Joe Mardis, Joe McGill, Dan Shelton, Jim Hall, and George Shelton, all blacks, to enter into contracts for their labor at a lumber mill. The majority was of the opinion that being free from interference with one's labor was not a right intended to be protected by the Thirteenth Amendment. But justices Harlan and William R. Day disagreed. Quoting from a previous case, Harlan pointed out that one of the liberties secured by the War Amendments was "the right of the citizen to be free in the enjoyment *of all his faculties; to be free to use them in all lawful ways; to live and work where he will; to earn his livelihood by any lawful calling; to pursue any livelihood or avocation, and for that purpose to enter into all contracts which may be proper, necessary and essential to the carrying out to a successful conclusion the purposes above mentioned.*" On that basis, he argues, "The interpretation now placed on the Thirteenth Amendment [by the majority] is, I think, entirely too narrow and is hostile to the freedom established by the supreme law of the land."

Harlan's deep commitment to the belief that the Thirteenth Amendment was intended to eliminate "all badges of slavery," is evident again in a case involving Robert Robertson, P.H. Olsen, John Bradley, and Morris Hansen, all seamen.[56] While in San Francisco, these seamen had signed on to work on the *Arago*, an American ship. Being dissatisfied with their work, they left the ship in Astoria, Oregon. At the request of the ship's master, they were arrested, confined to jail, and put back aboard ship when it again set sail. They refused to work, and were then taken off the ship in San Francisco, arrested, and held for trial under federal laws that permitted the procedure by which these seamen were picked up and returned to the ship. They sought release by a writ of *habeas corpus*, contending that these federal statutes were a violation of the Thirteenth Amendment.

The Court again, with only Justice Harlan dissenting, upheld the statutes and the procedure authorized thereunder as not in conflict with the Thirteenth Amendment. The majority, speaking through Justice Henry Billings Brown, concluded that a sailor's contract is not the same as other contracts and requires the sailor to "surrender his personal liberty during the life of the contract." This is true, Brown argues, because "the business of navigation could scarcely be carried on without some guaranty, beyond the ordinary civil remedies upon contract, that the sailor will not desert the ship at a critical moment." He then traces this concept back to the time of the ancient Rhodians and cites many authorities to sustain its validity. He concludes by noting that "in the face of this legislation upon the subject of desertion and absence without leave, which was in force in this country for more than sixty years before the Thirteenth Amendment was adopted, . . . it cannot be open to doubt that the provision against involuntary servitude was never intended to apply to their contracts."

In discussing the meaning of the Thirteenth Amendment, in dissent, Harlan notes, "As to involuntary servitude, it may exist in the United States; but it can only exist lawfully as a punishment for crime of which the party shall have been duly convicted. Such is the plain reading of the Constitution. A condition of enforced service, even for a limited period, in the private business of another, is a condition of involuntary servitude." And "the placing of a person, by force, on a vessel about to sail, is putting him in a condition of involuntary servitude, if the purpose is to compel him against his will to give his personal services in the private business in which the vessel is engaged." He points out that although Congress has the power to regulate interstate and foreign commerce, it cannot disregard the fundamental rights of life, liberty, and property. In answer to the majority's citation of ancient authorities, he states, "But those laws . . . were enacted at a time when no account was taken of man as man, when human life and human liberty were regarded as of little value, and when the powers of government were employed to gratify the ambition and the pleasures of despotic rulers rather than promote the welfare of the people."

Harlan argues that even though a person contracts for his labor, it "becomes a condition of involuntary servitude *from the moment he is compelled against his will* to continue in such service."[57] The laborer may be liable for damages, he notes, but forcing him to work is unconstitutional. He concludes by stating "that the statute as it now is, and under which the appellants were arrested at Astoria and placed against their will on the barkantine Arago, is null and void, and their refusal to work on such vessel after being forcibly returned to it could not be made a public offense authorizing their subsequent arrest at San Francisco."

The Pursuit of Liberty

The justices have been struggling with the meaning of *due process of law* almost since the adoption of the Bill of Rights in 1791. In 1878 Justice Samuel F. Miller wrote for the Court: "If . . . it were possible to define what it is for a State to deprive a person of life, liberty, or property without due process of law, . . . no more useful construction could be furnished by this or any other court to any part of the fundamental law."[58]

In addition to applying due process to procedural matters, Justice Harlan and others believed that due process covered substance matters as well.

As the Court struggled to give meaning to due process of law, Harlan found himself in dissent from what he thought was a very narrow definition of liberty and property. One of those cases was *Campbell v. Holt*,[59] which involved the question whether an action that was barred by a statute of limitations was revived when the legislature repealed the limitations statute. The majority held that a statute of limitations was not a right, and therefore a repeal thereof simply makes the debtor "fulfil his honest obligations." Justices Joseph P. Bradley and Harlan dissented.

Concerning the argument that vested rights are not spelled out in the Due Process Clause, Bradley responded, "The suggestion that the words 'vested rights' are not to be found in the Constitution does not prove that there are no such rights. The name of the Supreme Being does not occur in the Constitution; yet our national being is founded on a tacit recognition of His justice and goodness, and the eternal obligation of His laws."

When the Court affirmed the conviction of Mr. Geer for having in his possession certain game birds for the purpose of sending them out of state, Harlan again protested. There was no dispute that the birds were lawfully killed during an "open season." Geer's crime was that he allegedly was going to ship them out of the state contrary to state law. A majority upheld Geer's conviction, being unable to find any right of his being violated here. Harlan, however, concluded that Geer's liberty was being infringed upon by the state law. "To hold that the person receiving personal property from the owner may not receive it with the intent to send it out of the State is to recognize an arbitrary power in the government which is inconsistent with the liberty belonging to every man, as well as with the rights which inhere in the ownership of property."[60]

The justice also dissented when the Court upheld a decision of a Kentucky Board of Contests stripping William S. Taylor and John Marshall of the offices of governor and lieutenant governor, respectively. Taylor and Marshall had received the highest number of votes for their respective offices and had been awarded certificates of election by the secretary of state. Their opponents, William Goebel and J.C.W. Beckham, however, filed a contest of the election. A Board of Contests, after examining the votes, concluded that Goebel and Beckham had received the most votes for the respective offices. This decision was approved by the state legislature, and Taylor and Marshall were ousted from office. They sued, but the Kentucky Court of Appeals held that courts had no power to examine the decision of the legislature. A majority of the Supreme Court affirmed.

For Harlan, the denial of the offices to Taylor and Marshall infringed upon their liberty. "What more directly involves the liberty of the citizen," he asserted, "than to be able to enter upon the discharge of the duties of an office to which he has been lawfully elected by his fellow citizens?"[61]

Furthermore, he wrote, "Yet by the decision this day rendered, no redress can be had in the courts when a legislative body, or one recognized as such by the courts, without due process of law, by the exercise of absolute, arbitrary power, and without evidence, takes an office having a fixed salary attached thereto from one who has been lawfully elected to such office by the voters of the State at a regular election."

He concluded, "I am of the opinion . . . that the decree below took from Taylor and Marshall rights protected by the Fourteenth Amendment of the Constitution of the United States."

Harlan was again confronted with having to make the hard choice between individual liberty and interests asserted by the state in *Jacobson v. Massachusetts*.[62] During a smallpox epidemic, the city of Cambridge, Massachusetts, ordered that all its inhabitants be vaccinated. When Mr. Jacobson refused, he was convicted for violating the vaccination law, and the conviction was affirmed by the Supreme Court. Harlan wrote the opinion for the majority. Jacobson argued that his liberty was being infringed upon because of the "inherent right of every freeman to care for his own body and health in such way as to him seems best." Harlan responded, "But the liberty secured by the Constitution of the United States to every person within its jurisdiction does not import an absolute right in each person to be, at all times and in all circumstances, wholly freed from restraint." He agreed that there exists "a sphere within which the individual may assert the supremacy of his own will and rightfully dispute the authority of any human government, especially of any free government existing under a written constitution, to interfere with the exercise of that will." And he was of the opinion that the "court should guard with firmness every right appertaining to life, liberty or property as secured to the individual by the Supreme Law of the Land." But, he concluded, the safety of the people of Massachusetts outweighed Jacobson's rights in this case.

The Bill of Rights and the States

In 1947 Justice Felix Frankfurter referred to Justice Harlan as an "eccentric exception."[63] At that time, Frankfurter was discussing the question of whether the Fourteenth Amendment was "a shorthand summary of the first eight Amendments theretofore limiting only the Federal Government, and that due process incorporated those eight Amendments as restrictions upon the powers of the States." He pointed out that 43 justices had served on the Court since the adoption of the Fourteenth Amendment in 1868, and only Harlan believed that the amendment was indeed a shorthand method of making the Bill of Rights applicable to state action. While Harlan was the "eccentric exception" among those 43 justices, Justice Hugo Black, writing at the same time as Justice Frankfurter, agreed with Harlan. Justice Black stated his position on this question as follows: "My study of the historical events that culminated in the Fourteenth Amendment, and the expressions of those who sponsored and favored, as well as those who opposed its submission and passage, persuades me that one of the chief objects that the provisions of the Amendment's first section, separately, and as a whole, were intended to accomplish was to make the Bill of Rights, applicable to the states."

Justice Harlan's views were expressed in his dissent in *Hurtado v. California*.[64] When California charged Joseph Hurtado with murdering Jose Antonio Stuardo, it did not proceed by way of a grand jury indictment as the Fifth Amendment requires the federal government to do.

Hurtado was convicted and sentenced to death. His conviction was affirmed by the Supreme Court of California. In appealing to the U.S. Supreme Court, Hurtado argued that he had been denied due process under the Fourteenth Amendment because his case had not been presented to a grand jury. The Court, with only Harlan dissenting, disagreed and affirmed the California court's decision. After an exhaustive review of English and American authorities, the majority concluded that due process of law did not require a state to proceed against an individual by way of an indictment.

What disturbed Harlan about the majority's decision was that if presentment to a grand jury was not a requirement of due process, does that mean it is not a violation of due process to put a person twice in jeopardy for the same offense, or to compel a person to testify against himself? "More than that," he argued,

other amendments of the Constitution proposed at the same time, expressly recognize the right of persons to just compensation for private property taken for public use; their right, when accused of crime, to be informed of the nature and cause of the accusation against them, and to a speedy and public trial, by an impartial jury of the State and district wherein the crime was committed; to be confronted by the witnesses against them; and to have compulsory process for obtaining witnesses in their favor. Will it be claimed that these rights were not secured by the "law of the land" or by "due process of law," as declared and established at the foundation of our government? Are they to be excluded from the enumeration of the fundamental principles of liberty and justice, and, therefore, not embraced by "due process of law"?

He chastises the court for not recognizing "an immunity or right, recognized at the common law to be essential to personal security, jealously guarded by our national Constitution against violation by any tribunal or body exercising authority under the general government."

Harlan's views on why the Bill of Rights applies to the states can also be found in his dissent in *Maxwell v. Dow*.[65] Maxwell was charged with robbery and tried before a jury of only eight persons. He was convicted and sentenced to prison for 18 years. His conviction was upheld by the state supreme court and the United States Supreme Court, with only Justice Harlan dissenting. Justice Rufus W. Peckham wrote the majority opinion. He acknowledged that the right to a jury trial as guaranteed by the Sixth Amendment requires a jury of 12 in all federal courts. He concluded, however, that a state using only eight jurors does not violate either the privileges and immunities nor the due process clauses of the Fourteenth Amendment.

After discussing the history of trial by jury, and noting the various rights protected by the first ten amendments, Harlan asserted:

> I am of opinion that under the original Constitution and the Sixth Amendment, it is one of the privileges and immunities of citizens of the United States that when charged with crime they shall be tried only by a jury composed of twelve persons; consequently, a state statute authorizing the trial by a jury of eight persons of a citizen of the United States, charged with crime, is void under the Fourteenth Amendment declaring that no State shall make or enforce any law that "shall abridge the privileges or immunities of citizens of the United States."

But the justice did not stop there; he went on to argue "that the trial of the accused for the crime charged against him by a jury of eight persons was not consistent with the 'due process of law' prescribed by the Fourteenth Amendment." He closed his dissent by noting that the Court's decision did not bode well for the people's life and liberty. "But, if I do not wholly misapprehend the scope and legal effect of the present decision, the Constitution of the United States does not stand in the way of any State striking down guarantees of life and liberty that English-speaking people have for centuries regarded as vital to personal security, and which men of the Revolutionary period universally claimed as the birthright of freemen."

Throughout the rest of his time on the Court, Justice Harlan continued to assert his belief that the Fourteenth Amendment was intended to require states to abide by the Bill of Rights.[66]

Harlan was the "exception" among the 43 justices referred to by Frankfurter, and in 1947 might well have been considered "eccentric." But, looking back it is clear that while he lost many battles over this issue, the war was won by those who followed. Today almost all the provisions contained in the first eight amendments to the Constitution have been made applicable to the states by subsequent decisions of the Supreme Court. And the "fundamental principles of liberty and justice" for which he fought are now within the concept of "due process of law." The justice followed this philosophy whenever he thought that the procedure used in the trial of an accused was unjust.

Although Harlan was unsuccessful in getting his colleagues to require states to abide by the Bill of Rights, he insisted that defendants in federal courts receive the full protection guaranteed to them. For example, he wrote the opinions in two cases upholding the right of the defendants to confront the witnesses against them as required by the Sixth Amendment.[67] One of these cases involved a charge against a Mr. Kirby for receiving and having in his possession postage stamps that had allegedly been stolen from the post office at Highmore, South Dakota.

The only evidence the government had that the stamps had been stolen was the record of the trial of three others who had been convicted of breaking into the Highmore post office. In reversing Kirby's conviction, Justice Harlan pointed out that Kirby had not been present at the trial of the others, and even if he had, he would not have been permitted to confront those involved, nor the other witnesses at the trial. Further, the judge who conducted Kirby's trial charged the jury that the record of the other trial was *prima facie* evidence that the stamps were stolen, even though there was no direct evidence that the stamps that Kirby had were the same stamps.

Harlan, referring to the right of confrontation, notes that one "of the fundamental guarantees of life and liberty is found in the Sixth Amendment of the Constitution of the United States, which provides that 'in all criminal prosecutions the accused shall . . . be confronted with the witnesses against him.'"[68] He pointed out that every person charged with a crime is presumed to be innocent, and that the government bears the burden of proving the defendant's guilt beyond a reasonable doubt. "The presumption of innocence of an accused," he wrote, "attends him throughout the trial and has relation to every fact that must be established in order to prove his guilt beyond a reasonable doubt."

The Constitution Follows the Flag

Did the Constitution follow the flag to Puerto Rico, the Hawaiian Islands, the Philippine Islands, and Alaska when the United States accepted control over these territories? The Court was confronted with this question in several cases during the early 1900s. For Justice Harlan the answer was a resounding yes.

In several cases decided May 27, 1901, which dealt with taxation, the justices held that for purposes of imports from and exports to Puerto Rico, it was no longer a foreign country, and therefore the tariff laws did not apply.[69]

On that same day, however, a majority also held that "Puerto Rico is not a part of the United States within that provision of the Constitution which declares that 'all duties, imposts, and excises shall be uniform throughout the United States.'"[70] Harlan filed a vigorous dissent.

The majority concluded that there was "a clear distinction between such prohibitions of the Constitution as go to the very root of the power of Congress to act at all, . . . and such as operative only throughout the United States, or among the several States." The requirement for uniform taxes fell into the latter group, and therefore even though the taxes levied were not uniform, they were valid.

Harlan was unable to accept this interpretation of the Constitution. "In my opinion," he wrote, "Congress has no existence and can exercise no authority outside of the Constitution. Still less is it true that Congress can deal with new territories just as other nations have done or may do with their new territories. This nation is under the control of a written constitution, the supreme law of the land and the only source of the powers which our Government, . . . may exert at any time or any place." And, he continued, it "will be an evil day for American liberty if the theory of a government outside of the supreme law of the land finds lodgment in our constitutional jurisprudence."

That the Court's jurisprudence did not bode well for individual liberty was evident in the case of *Hawaii v. Mankichi*.[71] After Hawaii was formally transferred to U.S. control, Osaki Mankichi was tried and convicted of murder and sentenced to 20 years of hard labor. His case had not been presented to a grand jury, and thus he was tried without being indicted. Furthermore, the guilty verdict was agreed upon by only nine jurors rather than 12. This was in accordance with the laws of Hawaii prior to the United States' taking control. The resolution by Congress accepting the Hawaiian Islands continued in force the laws thereof "not inconsistent with this joint resolution *nor contrary to the Constitution of the United States.*"

The majority held that if the above statement were applied literally, it would nullify many of the island's laws and leave a vacuum. They therefore concluded that that could not have been the intent of Congress, and held that the Fifth and Sixth Amendments did not apply to Hawaii until Congress had adopted new criminal laws.

"I dissent altogether from any such view," Harlan wrote.

> It assumes the possession by Congress of power quite as omnipotent as that possessed by the English Parliament. It assumes that Congress, which came into existence, and exists, only by virtue of the Constitution, can withhold fundamental guarantees of life and liberty from peoples who have come under our complete jurisdiction; . . . In my judgment, neither the life, nor the liberty, nor the property of *any* person, within any territory or country over which the United States is sovereign, can be taken, under the sanction of any civil tribunal, . . . by any form of procedure inconsistent with the Constitution of the United States.

Harlan's disagreement with his colleagues on the Court on the issue of the Constitution following the flag was also evident in a series of cases involving the Philippine Islands.[72]

The First Amendment

Harlan was not a strong advocate for First Amendment rights. He and the other justices were quite willing to defer to the government when they were confronted with cases involving freedom of speech, press, religion, and assembly. Harlan joined the majority to uphold the conviction of one who had mailed literature concerning a lottery, contrary to federal law. In reference to freedom of the press, the majority conceded that "liberty of circulating is as essential to that freedom as liberty of publishing; indeed, without the circulation, the publication would be of little value."[73] Nevertheless the justices held that Congress could ban certain material from the mails so long as it did not prohibit the transportation of the material in other ways.

Harlan and a majority saw no First Amendment problem when Lew Rosen was charged with mailing an obscene, lewd, and lascivious paper in violation of federal law. Rosen had mailed a paper called "Broadway" which contained "pictures of females . . . [that] by direction of the defendant, [were] partially covered with lamp black that could be easily erased with a piece of bread. The object of sending them out in that condition was, of course, to excite a curiosity to know what was thus concealed."[74]

The Court also found no fault in the trial judge's allowing the jury to decide whether the paper was obscene. The judge charged the jury that "the test of obscenity is whether the tendency of the matter is to deprave and corrupt the morals of those whose minds are open to such influence and into whose hands a publication of this sort may fall." "'Would it,' the Court said, 'suggest or convey lewd thoughts and lascivious thoughts to the young and inexperienced?'"

Harlan voted with the majority in two cases and wrote the opinion in a third which today would raise substantial First Amendment issues. *Davis v. Massachusetts*[75] involved a Boston ordinance that prohibited the making of a speech on public grounds, except with permission of the mayor. Davis made a speech in the Boston Commons and was arrested for doing so. His conviction was upheld by the highest court of Massachusetts and by a unanimous Supreme Court. Justice Oliver W. Holmes, Jr., writing for the Court, held that Boston had the power to control the use of its parks, and in prohibiting speaking there violated no right of the defendant Davis. The defendant had argued that the ordinance violated the Fourteenth Amendment, apparently making no reference to the First Amendment.

When the Department of Immigration sought to deport John Turner because he was an anarchist, the justices again unanimously upheld the department's deportation order.[76] Turner was represented by the then prominent lawyer Clarence Darrow, who argued that the deportation violated Turner's First Amendment rights "because some anarchists are merely political philosophers, whose teachings are beneficial rather than otherwise." To this, Chief Justice Melville W. Fuller responded:

> If the word "anarchists" should be interpreted as including aliens whose anarchistic views are professed as those of political philosophers innocent of evil intent, it would follow that Congress was of the opinion that the tendency of the general exploitation of such views is so dangerous to the public weal that aliens who hold and advocate them would be undesirable additions to our population, whether permanently or temporarily, whether many or few, and, in the light of previous decisions, the act, even in this respect, would not be unconstitutional, or as applicable to any alien who is opposed to all organized government.

In the third case, with only Justice Rufus W. Peckham dissenting, the Court upheld a Nebraska statute prohibiting a representation of the U.S. flag from being used as an advertisement.[77] Halter, with several others, was charged with violating the statute by having for sale a bottle of beer upon which was printed a U.S. flag. In upholding the convictions, Harlan took note that from "earliest periods in the history of the human race, banners, standards and ensigns have been adopted as symbols of the power and history of the peoples who bore them." And for our "flag every true American has not simply an appreciation but a deep affection. No American, nor any foreign born person who enjoys the privileges of American citizenship, ever looks upon it without taking pride in the fact that he lives under this free Government." Because of this, both federal and state governments have the power to prevent desecration of the flag, and no "privilege of American citizenship or . . . any right of personal liberty is violated by a state enactment forbidding the flag to be used as an advertisement on a bottle of beer."

Harlan's most vigorous defense of the First Amendment came in a case in which Thomas M. Patterson was charged and convicted of contempt of court for publishing "certain articles and a cartoon, which, it was charged, reflected upon the motives and conduct of the Supreme Court of Colorado in cases still pending and were intended to embarrass the court in the impartial administration of justice." The Supreme Court, with Justice Holmes writing for the Court upheld Patterson's conviction.[78] In addressing the claim that the articles and cartoon were protected by freedom of the press, Holmes left "undecided the question whether there is to be found in the Fourteenth Amendment a prohibition similar to that in the First." But even assuming that the First did apply to state action, that did not mean that it would protect the defendant in this case. The purpose of the freedom of the press clause in the First Amendment, Holmes asserted, was "'to prevent all such *previous restraints* upon publications as had been practiced by other governments,' and . . . [the clause does] not prevent the subsequent punishment of such as may be deemed contrary to the public welfare."

Harlan, in a strongly worded dissent, argued that the rights to freedom of speech and of the press are "rights belonging to citizens of the United States; that is, those rights are to be deemed attributes of national citizenship or citizenship of the United States." And the Fourteenth Amendment prohibits the state from infringing upon those rights.

> As the First Amendment guaranteed the rights of free speech and of a free press against hostile action by the United States, it would seem clear that when the Fourteenth Amendment prohibited the States from impairing or abridging the privileges of citizens of the United States it necessarily prohibited the States from impairing or abridging the constitutional rights of such citizens to free speech and a free press.

And, he continued,

> I go further and hold that the privileges of free speech and of a free press, belonging to every citizen of the United States, constitute essential parts of every man's liberty, and are protected against violation by that clause of the Fourteenth Amendment forbidding a State to deprive any person of his liberty without due process of law. It is, I think, impossible to conceive of liberty, as secured by the Constitution against hostile action, whether by the Nation or by the States, which does not embrace the right to enjoy free speech and the right to have a free press.

The Court rendered the *Patterson* decision in 1907, toward the end of Harlan's long career. It is not clear, therefore, whether he would have included within those privileges of national citizenship freedom of religion.

In four cases involving the Church of Jesus Christ of Latter-Day Saints, Harlan voted with the majority to condemn polygamy even though that practice was part of the beliefs of the Church.[79] These cases involved federal interference with religion rather than state action. Harlan did not, however, show concern for the free exercise rights of the Mormons. In the first of these cases Chief Justice Morrison R. Waite, noting that plural marriages were prohibited by law, asked the question, "Can a man excuse his practices to the contrary because of his religious belief?" His answer was: "To permit this would be to make the professed doctrines of a religious belief superior to the law of the land, and in effect permit every citizen to become a law unto himself. Government could exist only in name under such circumstances."[80]

In the most egregious of these cases, a majority, which included Harlan, upheld an act of Congress repealing the incorporation of the Church and declaring that all its property escheat to the United States. This was justified, according to the majority, because "polygamy has been forbidden by the laws of the United States, under severe penalties."[81] Even the three dissenters, Chief Justice Fuller and justices Stephen J. Field and Lucius Quintus Cincinnatus Lamar, were concerned only with the power of Congress, and not with any free exercise rights of the Church and its members.

Aliens and the Constitution

The Court, in recognition of the power of Congress over immigration, has generally followed a hands-off policy with respect to the government's refusal of entry and exclusion of aliens. And the cases indicate that Justice Harlan generally agreed with this policy.[82] But he did recognize that there were cases when the alien had acquired some rights to re-entry and should not be excluded. One of those cases was *Chew Heong v. United States*.[83] Chew had come to the United States in 1880, the same year that the United States and China entered into a treaty relating, among other things, to the immigration of Chinese nationals to the United States. Chew remained in the States until 1881 when he went to Hawaii. In July 1884 Congress enacted legislation requiring Chinese laborers to have a certificate in order to enter the United States. When Chew attempted to re-enter the country in September 1884, he was prohibited from doing so because he did not have the required certificate. Because he was being detained aboard ship, he sought help from the U.S. Circuit Court, claiming that he was being denied his liberty. When the two justices of that court disagreed as to whether Chew was entitled to re-enter the country, they certified certain questions to the Supreme Court to be answered. One of those questions was, "Whether upon the record and facts herein set forth and stated the petitioner is entitled to re-enter the United States and to land from said steamship under the provisions of the said amended act?" Harlan, writing for the majority, answered that question in the affirmative. After making a thorough analysis of the treaty, he concluded that Chew, "having left before any certificate was permitted to be issued, cannot be required to produce one before re-entering, because, having resided here on the 17th day of November 1880, he was clearly entitled, under the express words of the treaty, to go from and return to the United States of his own free will—a privilege that would be destroyed, if its enjoyment depended upon a condition impossible to be performed."

Harlan joined the majority in two cases in which the actions of the government denied the aliens due process of law. In *Wong Wing v. United States,*[84] Wong Wing, Le Poy, Lee Yon Tong, and Chan Wah Dong were in the United States illegally. When they were brought before John Graves, a court commissioner, he sentenced them to 60 days at hard labor and then ordered them deported. A unanimous Supreme Court ordered the defendants released from custody. The Court held that "when Congress sees fit to promote ... [its immigration policies] by subjecting the persons of such aliens to infamous punishment at hard labor, or by confiscating their property, we think such legislation, to be valid, must provide for a judicial trial to establish the guilt of the accused."

And in *Chin Yow v. United States,*[85] in an opinion written by Justice Holmes, the court held that an alien about to be deported who alleges that he "was prevented by the officials of the Commissioner from obtaining testimony, including that of named witnesses, and that had he been given a proper opportunity he could have produced overwhelming evidence that he was born in the United States and remained there until 1904, when he departed to China on a temporary visit," is entitled to a fair hearing before being deported.

Indians, Spouses, and Inventors

John Elk, an Indian, attempted to register to vote in the Omaha city election, but his registration was refused by registrar Charles Wilkins.[86] Elk claimed that he was born in the United States, that he had severed all connections with his tribe, that he had surrendered himself to the jurisdiction of the United States, and that he was now a U.S. citizen. When he went to the polls, Wilkins refused to allow him to vote. Elk then brought an action against Wilkins, seeking $6,000 in damages for violation of his rights. The lower court dismissed the case, and the Supreme Court affirmed, Justices Harlan and William B. Woods dissenting.

The majority pointed out that in Article I, Section 2, of the Constitution and in Section 2 of the Fourteenth Amendment, "Indians not taxed" were excluded from being counted for the purposes of apportioning representatives in Congress. This led them to the conclusion that "Indians, then, not being citizens by birth, can only become citizens in the second way mentioned in the Fourteenth Amendment, by being 'naturalized in the United States,' by or under some treaty or statute."

Harlan read the phrase "Indians not taxed" differently. He argued that the phrase assumed that there were "Indians who were taxed, that is, were subject to taxation, by the laws of the State of which they were residents. Indians not taxed were those who held tribal relations, and, therefore, were not subject to the authority of any State, and were subject only to the authority of the United States." These Indians, he claimed, were intended to be included within Section 1 of the Fourteenth Amendment which reads: "All persons born or naturalized in the United States . . . are citizens of the United States and of the state in which they reside." Furthermore, "nothing in the history of the adoption of the Fourteenth Amendment . . . justifies the conclusion that only those Indians are included in its grant of national citizenship who were, at the time of their birth, subject to the complete jurisdiction of the United States." In reference to John Elk and others like him, Harlan stated that

> if he did not acquire national citizenship on abandoning his tribe and becoming, by residence in one of the States, subject to the complete jurisdiction of the United States, then the Fourteenth Amendment has wholly failed to accomplish, in respect of the Indian race, what, we think, was intended by it; and there still is in this country a despised and rejected class of persons, with no nationality whatever; who, born in our territory, owing no allegiance to any foreign power, and subject, as residents of the States, to all the burdens of government, are yet not members of any political community nor entitled to any of the rights, privileges, or immunities of citizens of the United States.

As previously pointed out, neither Harlan nor the other justices were strong proponents of women's rights. In a couple of cases, however, dealing with spousal relations, Harlan voted to sustain rights of married women. In *Baker's Executors v. Kilgore*,[87] Harlan wrote the opinion for the Court upholding a Tennessee law that exempted property of a married woman from being seized for the debts of her husband.

A creditor of William Scruggs sought to levy upon some cattle owned by Mrs. Scruggs. The creditor claimed that the law protecting Mrs. Scruggs's property denied them a right they had prior to the enactment of the law.

Harlan responded: "It was entirely competent for the legislature to change that rule in respect, at least, to the future rents and profits of the wife's estate. Such legislation is for the protection of the property of the wife, and neither impairs nor defeats any vested right of the husband."

And when the Court denied a wife the right to sue her husband for assault and battery, Justice Harlan, joined by justices Holmes and Charles Evans Hughes, protested. The majority pointed out that at common law "husband and wife were regarded as one."[88] They acknowledged that many states, including the District of Columbia, where this suit arose, had enacted laws changing the relationship between husband and wife, including giving the wife the right to bring lawsuits without the assistance of the husband. Nevertheless, the majority did not believe that the legislatures that enacted these laws intended to change the "long-established policy of the common law" which prohibited wives from suing their husbands.

Harlan argued in dissent that the District of Columbia statute permitted women "to sue separately . . . for torts committed against them, *as fully and freely as if they were unmarried.*" He also believed that the majority was making a policy decision that it would not be good for society if wives could sue husbands. He chided them for doing so, being of the opinion that it was not the province of courts to make that kind of policy decision. "If the words used by Congress lead to such result," he argued, "and if, as suggested, that result be undesirable on grounds of public policy, it is not within the functions of the court to ward off the dangers feared or the evils threatened simply by judicial construction that will defeat the plainly-expressed will of the legislative department."

The facts of the case of *International Postal Supply Company v. Bruce*[89] seem somewhat unusual, but the result seems even more so. The International Postal Supply Company owned the patent to a canceling and post-marking machine. Mr. Bruce, the postmaster at Syracuse, New York, had obtained two of these machines and put them to use in the post office in violation of the company's patent. When the company sued Bruce for patent infringement, the Supreme Court held that the suit could not be maintained because it really was a suit against the United States and not against Bruce personally, and the United States therefore was protected by sovereign immunity.

Harlan seemed appalled at the Court's simplistic way of deciding this case. "In my judgment," he asserted, "it is not possible to conceive of any case, arising under our system of constitutional government, in which the courts may not, in some effective mode, and properly, protect the rights of the citizen against illegal aggression, and to that end, if need be, stay the hands of the aggressor, even if he be a public officer, who acts in the interest or by the direction of the Government."

Privileges and Immunities

Prior to the adoption of the Constitution the 13 colonies were, in reality, 13 separate countries. A colony was under no obligation to extend to a citizen of another colony the same privileges as enjoyed by that colony's own citizens. Article IV, Section 2, of the Constitution changed that. That section simply says, "The Citizens of each State shall be entitled to all Privileges and Immunities of Citizens in the several States." The Court has said that "[the] primary purpose of this clause, like the clauses between which it is located . . . was to help fuse into one Nation a collection of independent sovereign States."[90]

When Elizabeth M. Chambers came to the Supreme Court, Harlan found himself in disagreement with the majority over the meaning of Section 2.[91] Chambers's husband, Henry, was killed in a train accident in

Pennsylvania where they lived. She commenced suit in Ohio against her husband's employer, the Baltimore & Ohio Railroad Company, for wrongful death and obtained a judgment against it. The Supreme Court of Ohio reversed, basing its decision upon an Ohio statute that permitted actions for wrongful death occurring out of state only to those cases where the decedent was an Ohio citizen. The majority was of the opinion that Chambers was being treated the same as any Ohio citizen, because had she been an Ohio citizen she could not have brought suit for the wrongful death of her husband, a noncitizen, which occurred outside of Ohio.

Harlan saw the case very differently. His focus was upon what was happening to Elizabeth Chambers, a widow. "The Ohio court," he maintained, "would have taken cognizance of this action if the decedent Chambers had been, when killed, a citizen of Ohio, while it denies relief to his widow, and puts her out of court solely because her husband was, when killed, a citizen of another State. It thus accords to the Ohio widow of a deceased Ohio citizen a privilege which it withholds from the Pennsylvania widow of a deceased Pennsylvania citizen." "This," he continued, "is an illegal discrimination against living citizens of other States, and the difficulty is not met by the suggestion that no discrimination is made against the widow of the deceased because of *her* citizenship of another State."

As a Judicial Freedom Fighter

Although Justice Frankfurter's statement that Harlan was an "eccentric exception" was not necessarily meant to be complimentary, in retrospect it does describe the justice. He surely could have been thought to be "eccentric" in his insistence that "our constitution is color-blind," especially in view of the fact that this was shortly after the Civil War, and some justices and many people did not agree with him. But 58 years later a unanimous Supreme Court did agree with him and struck down the concept of separate but equal in *Brown v. Board of Education*.[92]

And to say that Congress had the right to enact civil rights laws to protect blacks, as he did in the Civil Rights cases, set him apart from all of his colleagues on the Court.

But Harlan was not concerned only about blacks. In *Yick Wo*, for example, he voted with the majority to prevent San Francisco from closing down laundries operated by Chinese. In voting with the seamen in *Robertson v. Baldwin*[93] who were being prosecuted for refusing to work on board a ship, Harlan indicated his belief that the Thirteenth Amendment was intended to eliminate *all* "badges of slavery," for all people. "A condition of enforced service," he argued, "even for a limited period, in the private business of another, is a condition of involuntary servitude."

Harlan did not have the same concern for women, however. Because of the time in which he lived, he would not have been considered eccentric when he voted to deny women the right to practice law, to vote, or to work in a saloon. But he did write the opinion protecting the property of a married woman from the debts of her husband, and he protested when the Court denied a woman the right to sue her husband for assault and battery.

The justice had an expansive view of the words *liberty* and *property* in the Due Process Clause. He believed that *liberty* included the right to work,[94] subject only to reasonable regulation by government, and that *property* included the right to own game birds properly acquired, and to a public office for which one has been legally elected. His fellow justices did not all agree.

Harlan's opinion that the Bill of Rights applied to the states was an exception to the prevailing view, not only during his time on the Court but throughout most of our history. But despite the fact that others did not agree, he argued that "due process of law" included the rights contained in the Fourth, Fifth, and Sixth Amendments to the Constitution. He asked, "Are they to be excluded from the enumeration of the fundamental principles of liberty and justice, and therefore, not embraced by 'due process of law'?"[95] Harlan's views, of course, ultimately prevailed, as the justices have since voted to require state governments to abide by almost all provisions of the Bill of Rights.

A firm belief that Congress had no power outside of that given in the Constitution caused Harlan to disagree with his colleagues on the issue of whether the Constitution applied to territories that the United States controlled. He was concerned that persons accused of crime in the territories were being prosecuted without having the benefit of the criminal justice provisions of the Bill of Rights which were available to persons living in the United States.

He was also concerned, however, that people living in the United States receive justice when they were being accused of committing a crime. For example, he applied the Sixth Amendment right of confrontation to protect Mr. Kirby, who was not given the right to confront others involved in the alleged theft of stamps from a post office.

And when the Court upheld the conviction of Dr. Hawker for practicing medicine after the state had changed its law to make it a crime to practice medicine by anyone previously convicted of a felony, he thought that was an *ex post facto* law. He argued that to change the law after the doctor's earlier felony conviction was grossly unfair. His conviction did not take into account that the doctor might well have become a respected member of the community and able to do much good for his patients.[96]

There was not a large number of cases involving First Amendment rights to reach the Court during Harlan's term. For those in which he did participate, he generally favored the government over individual rights. But he did make a vigorous defense of Thomas M. Patterson's right to publish articles and cartoons critical of the Colorado Supreme Court. When the Court upheld Patterson's conviction, Harlan asserted that Patterson's publications were protected by freedom of the press. And he made a strong argument why the First Amendment should apply to Colorado and all the states of the Union. About 25 years later, in 1931, the Court accepted Harlan's view, and held that all states were required to abide by the freedom of the press provision of the First Amendment.

Many years after Harlan's term ended in 1911, the Court held that "aliens as a class are a prime example of a 'discrete and insular' minority . . . for whom . . . heightened judicial solicitude is appropriate."[97] During his term, Harlan extended that same kind of solicitude to aliens when he thought they were being treated unfairly by government. And he dissented when the Court refused to extend protection of one of the Civil Rights acts to aliens.

It may not be true that Harlan went to bed at night with "one hand on the Constitution and the other on the Bible." But his votes for and his opinions about freedom, justice, and equality, enshrined in those treatises, are indisputable.

2

CHIEF JUSTICE CHARLES EVANS HUGHES

PERSONAL LIFE

Growing Up

Charles Evans Hughes, age six, had spent only a few weeks in school when he decided that if he were taught at home it wosuld give him more time to play. He prepared a plan that he titled "Charles E. Hughes' Plan of Study."[1] The plan included a list of subjects he would study and the time he would give to each. His parents accepted the "Plan," and Hughes began his education studying at home early in the morning each day.

Hughes was born on April 11, 1862, to the Reverend Mr. David C. Hughes and Mary Connelly Hughes in Glens Falls, New York. After arriving in the United States from England in 1855, David Hughes studied to be a minister. During this period he met Mary Connelly. While they were attracted to one another, Mary's mother was less than enthusiastic about her daughter being courted by this Englishman. Love prevailed, however, and David and Mary were married in New York on October 5, 1860. Years later their son and only child, Charles, wrote of them,

> They were brought together in a spiritual union which held them in the closest companionship as they pursued the same aims and cherished the same hopes.... Their love for each other, which at the outset had surmounted the obstacles raised by the differences in their early environment and in temperament, grew in strength throughout the forty-nine years of their union, as they labored together in unity of spirit for a common cause and with a profound faith. I have never known any persons more sincere in what they professed or more constantly dominated by a sense of religious duty.

CHIEF JUSTICE CHARLES EVANS HUGHES (photo by Harris & Ewing; collection of the Supreme Court of the United States).

Although during these early years the Hughes family lived on the modest income of a church pastor, books were an important part of their lives. Charles received many books from his parents as gifts during the years he was being taught at home. The parents envisioned that Charles would follow his father into the ministry, and his early education was aimed at that goal.

The Reverend Hughes accepted a call to a church in Oswego, New York, and the family lived there until 1869, when they moved to Newark, New Jersey, where he became pastor of the Fifth Baptist Church. Although Charles was somewhat frail of health, he and his friends played baseball and cops and robbers, and enjoyed sledding during the winter months. When he was nine he started school, where he did very well. "In 1873, the year of his graduation, his report card bore seven marks of one hundred, two of ninety-nine, one of ninety-eight, and two of ninety-seven."

Hughes spent some happy days during the summers at his grandfather Connelly's farm in New York. In letters to his parents, he told of the fun he was having. One letter contained the following paragraph: "But I must draw to a close, I hope that you will pray earnestly for me. That, if it be possible, I may regain some of the spiritual power I once possessed and more completely obey the sentiments expressed in Ephesians 6:1." (The citation reads: "Children, obey your parents: for this is right.") Biographer Merlo J. Pusey comments that "here is the first intimation that the intense religious zeal that Charlie's parents had instilled into him was beginning to wane. The lad was starting to think for himself, and while his budding sense of differing with his parents disturbed him at first, it did not seem to interfere with his enjoyment of life."

Charles entered Newark High School in 1873, but his time there was short because the family soon moved to New York where his father became secretary of the American Bible Union. Charles entered Public School No. 35 in September 1874 and after taking an exam was assigned to the graduating class. Of this period he wrote, "Many a time I climbed up the iron fence which surrounded . . . [Columbia Law School] to see Professor Dwight, with the white pitcher of water on his table, lecturing to the law school students."

The Hugheses lived in the Greenpoint section of Brooklyn where Hughes's father was also pastor at the Union Baptist Church. Of this relationship Pusey writes, "During the Reverend Mr. Hughes' pastorate at the Union Baptist Church, more than four hundred new members were added to his congregation. His parish boasted that its Sunday school, with approximately a thousand members, was one of the largest, if not the largest, in the state. Brooklyn was a paradise for Protestant ministers."

When Hughes graduated from No. 35, he was too young to enter college, so he undertook self-study until he was old enough. When he learned about Madison University (now Colgate), he began a campaign to obtain permission from his family to go there. Hughes persevered and, after studying at home for a year, took and passed the entrance exam for Madison in June 1876. He entered the university in September. Pusey describes the living conditions at the university:

> The college's accommodations and physical equipment were primitive. The dormitories lacked central heating, lighting, running water, and, of course, bathtubs. The unfurnished rooms were in suites of two, a small study, with one large window and window seat, and an adjoining cubicle. Most of the students had small cylindrical stoves in one corner of their study. On these they heated whatever

water they used for bathing or washing—water carried from an outside pump which, in cold weather, was surrounded by ice several inches thick. Coal purchased by the students for their stoves was kept in bins lining the halls. Their toilet was a little stone outhouse at the far end of the campus, with the rudest accommodations. As there were no servants, the boys took care of their rooms—after a fashion.

During this school year, the letters that passed between the son and his parents indicated the parents' concern about their son's drift away from spirituality, and the son's dislike of the parents' constant preaching. Among the matters that concerned his parents was his joining the Delta Upsilon fraternity, taking in a roommate, and joining a boarding club. All of these, they feared, would intrude on his spiritual life. If these activities weakened his spiritual resolve, they did not hinder his academic pursuits, for he did very well scholastically.

For recreation, Madison students played the card game whist, chess, and baseball, and were able to socialize with girls from a nearby girls' school. As college students are prone to do, they also participated in some pranks, like ringing the school bell in the early hours of the morning and having snowball fights. All throughout Hughes's college career, finances were a constant problem because of his father's meager income as a pastor.

After two years at Madison, Hughes entered Brown University in Providence, Rhode Island, in September 1878. Brown opened many new vistas for him. He enjoyed the theater, played poker and whist, drank beer, and became a baseball fan.

In order to earn a little extra money, during his second year at Brown, Hughes began to write essays for his fellow students. When his mother indicated her displeasure with this "trickery," he defended himself with a long letter to her claiming, among other things, "It is no worse to write an essay for a fellow than to help him out with his lesson. And no blame could attach itself to me in any case. Hack writing, or writing for money is a perfectly legitimate business. I am not supposed to know for what it is to be used. I wrote a certain paper, received so much for it & it is the responsibility of the man himself whether he uses it for himself." When his father also criticized him for "ghost-writing," he reluctantly admitted that it might not have been "morally right," and gave it up. At the end of his junior year, Hughes was admitted to Phi Beta Kappa.

While his religious fervor weakened during this period of his life, he conceded to his parents that "whatever I may do or become, there is no danger that I ever will be able to rid myself of the truths implanted in early child-hood."

As Hughes approached the end of his senior year, he was uncertain as to his future, but he did not believe he had a call to the ministry. He contemplated studying medicine, thought about becoming a university professor, and contemplated going to law school. He began to lean toward law school, especially after one of his classmates said, "I've picked out law for myself, and if you are not a lawyer too, I'm no prophet."

While pondering his future, Charles got a job assisting property owners obtain some tax relief. He was paid six dollars per week for working six ten-hour days. Toward the end of the summer he received an offer to teach at Delaware Academy in Delhi, New York, where he taught Latin, Greek, algebra, and geometry. He also studied law in the office of a local lawyer. By the end of the year, it was clear to Hughes that studying in a law office was not the way to enter the practice of law. He turned down an offer to remain at the academy and convinced his parents to assist him in going to Columbia Law School in New York City.

Hughes entered law school in the fall of 1882. He seemed to enjoy academic pursuits and plunged into the study of law with great zeal. Not being satisfied with law school, he sought out a clerkship in one of New York's leading law firms. He was turned away, but as he was leaving the office he met Walter S. Carter, one of the senior partners, who inquired as to what he was doing there. When Charles explained his presence, Carter invited him into his office for a visit. Although Carter did not think that law students should work while going to law school, he did offer Hughes the opportunity to work during the summer. Hughes accepted, and at the end of the term went into the office to work without compensation. His work was of such caliber that as he left to return to law school for the fall term, Carter said to him, "When you get through law school, you can come back and I will put you on a salary."

The Reverend Hughes accepted a pastorate at the Summit Avenue Baptist Church, and the family moved to Jersey City Heights in the spring of 1884. Charles stayed in New York City. Upon graduation, he was the outstanding senior and was given the opportunity to tutor at the law school for the upcoming year. After passing the New York bar exam with a grade of 99 ½, he was admitted to the New York bar in June 1884.

Hughes joined the law firm of Chamberlain, Carter & Hornblower in October 1884. His salary was $30 per month, with a five-dollar raise each two-month period thereafter. He wrote briefs, assisted at trials, and helped with office work. He was still teaching part-time at Columbia. His father had accepted a position at Trinity Baptist Church in New York, and when the family moved back to the city, Hughes was able to live with them.

Love, Marriage and Family

Up to this point, love had not entered Hughes's life. His work ethic demanded most of his time. About a year after he had joined the firm, he learned that Carter had a daughter named Antoinette. Antoinette's mother had died shortly after her birth, and the girl was cared for by a nurse. Carter married again, but the new wife died shortly thereafter. A sister-in-law of Carter's then took Antoinette to Baltimore, where she lived for six years. When Carter married again, Antoinette joined the family.

Charles and Antoinette's first meeting was at a dinner party at Delmonico's restaurant in New York given for one of the firm's clerks who was leaving to teach law. They met again at the Carter home when Hughes was invited there to dinner. Although the couple dated a few times during the next few years, Hughes fought off Cupid because he did not think it wise to court the boss's daughter.

Antoinette moved to Rochester, New York, where she became part owner of a gymnasium for women and children. By the time she returned to New York City in 1887, Hughes had become a partner in the firm.

When the firm broke up in 1887, leaving only Carter, it was agreed that Hughes, Carter, and another clerk, Paul D. Cravath, would form a new firm called Carter, Hughes, and Cravath. Thus, at the age of 25 and out of law school for only about three years, Hughes became a partner in a prosperous New York City law firm.

Antoinette's return to the city and Hughes's promotion to partner in the law firm gave the couple an opportunity to begin seeing each other more often. Pusey says of Antoinette, "Antoinette proved to be not only a delightful companion but also an eager confidant and clear-headed advisor. It must have been apparent to everyone but ... [Hughes] that she loved him."

Antoinette moved back to Rochester, and the romance was carried on by mail. When Hughes proposed by letter, and Antoinette immediately accepted, he was off to Rochester with an engagement ring. The couple were married in New York City on December 5, 1887, with Hughes's father and another minister officiating. Charles and Antoinette honeymooned in Washington, D.C., and upon returning to the city set up housekeeping with Charles's parents.

Later in life, Hughes wrote of their marriage, "Our cup of happiness was full at the beginning and has been full and overflowing ever since. In all my privileges and responsibilities, in good times and bad, in success and defeat, in joy and sorrow, we have had a perfect union of minds and hearts. Whatever I have accomplished has been made possible by that strong, unselfish, ever radiant spirit, constantly by my side."

The law business demanded that Hughes be absent from home for weeks at a time. In the letters that flowed back and forth between the couple, he addressed her as "wifie," and she signed her letters the same way. A son was born in November 1889 and named after his father, and the following summer Hughes grew the beard that he wore the rest of his life.

While they were living in New York, the family became active members of the Fifth Avenue Baptist Church. Hughes taught Sunday school to young men and was elected as trustee. At a dinner of the Baptist Social Union, of which he was president, Hughes had Booker T. Washington, a noted black educator, and his wife as guests. Hughes was surprised to learn that some of the members of the union did not like this. Pusey writes, "Hughes thought this display of prejudice on the part of those who were supposed to be the least susceptible to it was ridiculous and tried to ignore it."

Despite these church activities, Hughes was not an orthodox Baptist and was often disenchanted with the ritual, which caused his parents concern. In response to a "sermonic letter" from his mother, he wrote,

> But, when we come to formal religious observances, your thinking and the circumstances of your life make it difficult for you to judge me either justly or leniently. Many things you would have me do, I cannot do with sincerity and I know that you would not wish me to act otherwise. But you grieve that I cannot enter—as you do—into certain religious exercises and this you attribute to a "religious declension." It cuts me to the heart that you should grieve and the more painfully that it should be on my account. But, while in important matters we are in entire accord, you give special prominence to certains forms which in many cases are indeed "means of grace," but which cannot be or, at least are not, in mine.

Lawyer and Professor

In 1891 Hughes was offered a position teaching law at Cornell University, which he accepted. He was then the youngest full professor at the law school. His partner, and father-in-law, could not understand why his son-in-law would give up a growing law practice and leave New York City to become a law professor. Nevertheless, the family moved to Ithaca, New York, and Hughes became Professor Hughes.

He entered into teaching with dedication and vigor, at times teaching as many as 15 hours a week. He could lecture for several hours without notes, being thoroughly familiar with the cases needing to be discussed.

Antoinette had been supportive of Hughes's leaving the firm to become a professor, and she entered into the life of a professor's wife with her usual devotion to her husband and their son. During this time she gave birth to a daughter, whom the family named Helen.

As a result of some changes in the Carter law firm, Carter urged Hughes to return to New York and take up the practice of law again. Because Hughes was enjoying teaching very much, this offer presented him with a very difficult decision. On the plus side of the return to practice was the fact that economically it would be very beneficial. The family now consisted of the parents and the two children, Charles, Jr. and Helen. The pressure from his father-in-law, plus Carter's forecast of a bright economic future for the practice, finally convinced Hughes to accept the offer. The Hugheses returned to New York in June 1893. He had, however, enjoyed his teaching experience so much that he continued to do some part-time teaching at Cornell and at New York Law School in the city.

Pusey describes Hughes as a devoted family man:

Sunday was Hughes' day with the children, who were devoted to him. It was rarely that he allowed his work to interfere with a Sunday-afternoon excursion with young Charlie and Helen. They rowed or took swan boats on Central Park lake, visited the zoo, the Museum of Natural History, and the Metropolitan Museum of Art, went coasting or took sleigh rides in the winter and victoria rides in warmer weather, took the ferries to Fort Lee or Staten Island or the "Iron Steamboats" to Coney Island, and generally availed themselves of whatever made for a companionable afternoon.

A third child, Catherine, was born on August 11, 1898.

Although Hughes and the firm had a substantial practice, he did not accumulate a lot of money. When the New York *World* wanted an opinion regarding its newsprint contract, its managing editor called Hughes. Later, the owner of the *World,* Joseph Pulitzer, consulted Hughes about his will. Sometime thereafter Pulitzer named Hughes in his will as trustee of the publishing company. After he became a Supreme Court justice, Hughes informed Pulitzer that he could no longer accept the trusteeship. Upon Pulitzer's death in 1911, his will still named Hughes trustee, with a fee of $100,000, but Hughes refused the appointment.

Hughes's participation as counsel investigating gas and electric rates and the insurance industry brought him recognition across the country and made him a potential political candidate. One newspaper described him, "Mr. Hughes is a large man, not burly, but with the appearance of one who is built on big, broad lines. He looks strong. His shoulders are square, his limbs solid, his teeth big and white and his whiskers thick and somewhat aggressive. His voice is loud, but not rasping, his manner that of one sure of himself and his position." Cartoonists had a great time with his beard.

At the completion of the investigations, Hughes helped draft legislation to control both industries which was enacted by the New York legislature.

Hughes's work in New York came to the attention of President Theodore Roosevelt, who needed someone to investigate the coal industry. When asked to undertake this investigation, Hughes accepted.

Politician

Hughes had little interest in politics. He had been urged to become more active in the Republican Party in New York County and was actually nominated for mayor of New York, but he refused to run. He also resisted the pressure to run for governor of New York, and he and son Charlie went off to Europe. But he could not escape those interested in his candidacy. Writing to his father about the "whole business," he said that he could "be of more service and far happier in my chosen profession." But that was not to be. Those urging his candidacy for governor secured the support of President Theodore Roosevelt, and the Republican Convention unanimously nominated Hughes even though he had no delegates working for him nor did he have the support of the political bosses. Hughes's Democratic opposition was William Randolph Hearst.

"When he began to campaign," Hughes's biographer Pusey has written, "people were relieved to note that he told amusing stories, that he laughed spontaneously with his whole body, that he was a good handshaker, and that he met men and women in all walks of life with friendliness and keen interest in their problems. The public began to learn what Hughes' close friends had always known—that beneath his reserve he was 'a buoyant and joyful person, fond of books of all sorts, music, golf, mountain climbing, friends, family, college and church.'"

Hughes won the election after having spent only $619 of his own money, as compared with the $500,000 Hearst spent.

Governor of New York

Hughes was a people's governor. His strength was in the people, not with the professional politicians. Early in his term he began to set aside time each morning to hear complaints and suggestions from people. Sitting behind a desk in a large room, he would listen to what the person or group had to say and would suggest what might be done about their problems. When they finished talking to him, other persons moved up to the desk. All had to take their turn, including politicians. The press was delighted with this procedure because it meant that the governor was going to conduct the state's business out in the open. One newspaper wrote, "Sly party Nicodemuses no longer go to the executive chamber by night . . . or the back door . . . . We have a governor again."

Hughes fought hard and long to clean up the state administration by replacing officials who held office because of their political standing rather than their ability. When his proposals for reform were blocked by the bosses, he turned to the people. During one speech he said, "When any proposal is made that is right . . . which the people recognize as demanded for mischiefs that exist, then let public opinion assert itself and make it impossible to defeat such a proposition upon any ground of expedience or because of the opposition of any interest."

Hughes's courting the people eventually paid off. The people began to question their legislators as to why they were not supporting the governor. Pusey writes: "Never within the memory of men had the machine been subjected to such a bombardment from so many sources. Republican bosses who had been laughing at what they called Hughes' 'babe-in-the-woods' tactics now turned and ran to cover in almost a panic of submission." Hughes was among the pioneers in promoting the creation of public service commissions rather than politically controlled boards to oversee public utilities. He also proposed workmen's compensation laws to protect workers who were injured on the job, as well as many other pieces of labor legislation. He fought for programs to conserve water, the forests, and other natural resources. But Hughes was not an "all work no play" person. During his term as governor he gave a speech entitled "Why We Want Playgrounds," which was reprinted many times.

In a speech to the Tuskegee Institute, he spoke of the black person: "We want neither slaves nor serfs, nor any body of citizens permanently below the standards which must be maintained for the preservation of the Republic. We cannot maintain our democratic ideals as to one set of our people and ignore them as to others."

Despite the demand on his time made by official duties, the family was not omitted from his daily schedule. Pusey has written of the family's routine:

> Breakfast was always served at precisely the same hour with all members of the family present. Mrs. Hughes invariably came downstairs dressed as if she were going out for the day. The Governor, too, was always fully dressed for the office before he left his room. At bedtime a cordial "Good night" went the rounds, and when their door was closed it remained closed for the night. None of the children thought of intruding or even knocking until father and mother appeared the next morning.

As governor, Hughes may have appeared to be stern and uncompromising, but to his family he was a jolly, fun-loving father. A fourth child, Elizabeth, was born on August 19, 1907, and was the first child born in the executive mansion.

Mrs. Hughes was a gracious hostess at many large and small receptions at the governor's mansion. She liked colorful clothing, and she wore her clothing well. "The tall, slender, hostess, looking beautiful in her new canary yellow or bright red dress, won the hearts of her guests by cordial greetings, by her intriguing combination of vivacity and dignity, and by her democratic practice of widely distributing the honor of acting as co-hostess."

Hughes's popularity with the people of New York did not go unnoticed within national political circles, and there began to be talk of his being a presidential candidate in the 1908 election. William Howard Taft was the most talked-about candidate at that time. At first Hughes did little either to further or to stop the talk of his entering the presidential race. When the Republican Club of New York endorsed him for president, however, he formally announced that he was a candidate.

Because he expended no effort to line up delegates for the national convention, Hughes was third in the balloting, with Taft getting more than the majority necessary for the nomination. Taft wanted Hughes to be the vice presidential candidate, an offer that Hughes refused.

Being governor was a money-losing proposition for Hughes. In addition to his family, his parents were now living with him. He was, therefore, inclined not to seek a second term. His friends, however, would not take no for an answer. One friend wrote, "The plain people understand you, love you and are for you." This, together with the urging of many others, caused him to agree to run. But not everyone supported his decision. The political professionals would have been happy if he had not been a candidate, and it did not appear that President Roosevelt would support him. Presidential candidate Taft supported Hughes's decision to be a candidate again, and through his efforts Roosevelt also got on the bandwagon. Roosevelt wrote to Taft, "Hughes is not a man I care for; he is not a man whose actions have really tended to the uplifting of political life; but he is financially an entirely honest man and one of much ability, and I am concerned that while to nominate him will do harm, not to nominate him will do more harm because I am convinced that the bulk of Republicans including the best men in the party outside the active organization, are for him." Those against Hughes were the political "insiders" because he wasn't inclined to play the political game.

Pusey describes Hughes's lack of participation in the New York State Republican Party convention in Saratoga, as follows:

> Hughes himself remained completely aloof from the convention. There were no Hughes headquarters at Saratoga, no organization representing him, no one authorized to speak for him or to promise any favor in return for support. No delegate had been importuned by him. There was no picture of him in the convention hall. When Secretary Root mentioned the Governor's name in his keynote speech, the galleries cheered and shouted but the delegates sat stonily silent. The phrase "Nobody wants Hughes but the people" was eloquently descriptive of the situation.

With the president's help, Hughes won the nomination and campaigned vigorously. Hughes was elected governor with a comfortable majority, after having spent $369 of his personal funds.

One aspect of the governorship that Hughes found very difficult was the review of applications for pardon and commutation of sentence. "It was the hardest work I ever did," he confessed to a reporter. He carefully studied each applicant's file, but felt deeply that he ought not interfere with the decisions of the courts. Hughes continued to fight for reform of the political system in New York but never succeeded in accomplishing his goals.

Early in 1910 Justice David J. Brewer of the U.S. Supreme Court died. President Taft offered the position to Hughes, and he accepted. Constant political battles had taken their toll, and warnings from his doctor told him it was time to get out of politics. His nomination was confirmed by the Senate without a negative vote.

Justice and Presidential Candidate

Hughes served as associate justice from 1910 until 1916, when he resigned to run for president on the Republican ticket. An attempt had been made to have him run in 1912, but he had firmly refused, arguing that the Court should not become involved in politics. By 1915, however, it appeared that Hughes was the only viable candidate the Republicans had, and he was flooded with requests to run. He again refused, and for the same reason. He wrote, "It seems to me very clear that, as a member of the Supreme Court, I have no right to be a candidate, either openly or passively." But this time, the people would not take no for an answer. Hughes was torn between his duty to the Court and what he saw as a duty to the country. Antoinette may have played a major part in his decision to run. She was of the opinion that if he was offered the nomination he was under an obligation to take it. Hughes's dilemma became more acute when Chief Justice Edward D. White indicated to him that he intended to retire, and that President Woodrow Wilson would name Hughes as Chief Justice. Even this, however, did not change Hughes's mind, and the Republican convention opened without an answer from him. Pusey writes, "The only real groundswell at the convention centered in the name of the silent man still wearing his judicial robe in Washington. Hughes had no headquarters at Chicago, no representative, no badges, buttons, or literature. Yet his name seemed to dominate every discussion of potential nominees."

Hughes's name was placed in nomination, along with several others, including that of former president Theodore Roosevelt. Hughes led after the first ballot but did not have a majority of the votes. After spending most of the night in negotiations, the party's professionals agreed that Hughes should be the candidate, and he was nominated overwhelmingly, even though no one knew whether he would accept.

When the word of his nomination reached Hughes, he immediately sent President Wilson his resignation from the Court and wired the convention of his acceptance.

Hughes conducted a vigorous campaign against the Democratic nominee, President Woodrow Wilson. With each candidate receiving more votes than any candidate had ever received before, Wilson won the election, with 277 electoral college votes to 254 for Hughes. Hughes took the defeat gracefully, believing that he had fought a good fight.

Lawyer and Public Servant

Hughes returned to New York and his old law firm and resumed the practice of law. He also became involved in a number of civic activities, such as the Legal Aid Society, Union League Club, the New York State Bar Association, and the Italy-American Society. He also became deeply involved in the war effort, making many speeches against isolationism and for involvement in the war.

New York Governor Charles S. Whitman appointed Hughes chairman of the District Draft Appeals Board for New York City. When he took over the job, there were hundreds of applications for exemption from service awaiting decision, but no staff to process them. He assembled an organization that began processing the cases at the rate of about 1,000 a day. This was difficult work for Hughes. A denial of an application for exemption could send a young man to battle and to his death. The strain on Hughes was made worse because his son had enlisted in the army and was sent overseas. The time at the Draft Appeals Board and his making numerous speeches concerning the war effort took a toll on his law practice, which was almost nonexistent. When the war ended with the Armistice on November 11, 1918, however, Hughes was able to resume the practice of law.

Pusey has written of Hughes's work with the Legal Aid Society: "As president of the Legal Aid Society, he attempted to give every man assurance of legal protection of his rights. 'There is no more serious menace,' he said, 'than the discontent which is fostered by a belief that one cannot enforce his legal rights because of poverty. . . . Without opportunity on the part of the poor to obtain expert legal advice, it is idle to talk of equality before the law.' "

When the New York legislature expelled five duly elected members because they were members of the Socialist Party, Hughes rushed to their defense. He succeeded in having the Bar Association appoint a committee of lawyers to intervene with the legislature on behalf of the expelled members. The committee argued that "if a majority can exclude the whole or a part of the minority because it deems the political views entertained by them hurtful, then free government is at an end." But the legislature turned a deaf ear and expelled the Socialists. It also outlawed the Socialist Party.

Hughes was still in demand as a speaker. Whenever the occasion seemed appropriate, he spoke of freedom, liberty and due process of law. "But let it also be known," he said, "as our surest protection, that with calmness and sanity we propose to maintain the guarantees of free speech, free assembly and the right of representation, and that no one, however poor, friendless or accused, shall be deprived of liberty without due process of law."

Disaster struck the family during the summer of 1919 when daughter Helen fell ill with tuberculosis. Throughout the rest of the year, Hughes worked in New York while Antoinette ministered to Helen in Glens Falls. In February 1920 they were informed that nothing further could be done for Helen. She passed away a few weeks later at the age of 28.

An attempt was made in 1920 to have Hughes run for the presidency again. He refused.

Return to Public Life

The Republicans nominated Warren G. Harding and Calvin Coolidge for president and vice president, respectively, in 1920, and they were elected. President-elect Harding then offered Hughes the position of secretary of state in his cabinet, and Hughes accepted.[2]

The Harding cabinet included Andrew Mellon, a prominent financier, as secretary of the treasury and Herbert Hoover as secretary of commerce. Hoover and Hughes worked closely together to create an atmosphere of cooperation between the State Department and the Department of Commerce.

Over the years Hughes had gained the reputation of being a tough taskmaster, but underneath the veneer he was really a pussycat. It was said of him, "Mr. Hughes never lets his dignity get thawed or his geniality get frozen." It was with this demeanor that he undertook the difficult task before him. The U.S. Senate had refused to ratify the League of Nations; a peace treaty had not been completed with Germany; questions remained concerning the German islands in the Pacific; the proliferation of arms was getting out of control; Russia was on the verge of collapse; and relations with Latin American countries needed bolstering.

Hughes immediately began to reorganize the Diplomatic Service so that it was no longer a position only for the rich. He insisted that diplomatic relations with other countries be conducted with openness and in good faith; he brought an *esprit de corps* to the department and developed cordial relations with the press.

> The Secretary could always be relied upon to attend any celebration at an embassy or legation, whether it was the wedding of a diplomat's daughter, the observance of a king's birthday, or a reception for a visiting dignitary. In addition, the Hugheses dined once a year with the heads of every diplomatic mission in Washington and entertained every chief of mission in their own home.

Antoinette was a charming and delightful hostess whenever the couple entertained.

Hughes once told the press what he thought a good public servant was: "A public officer has always got to remind himself, and he ought to say every morning as he approaches his task: 'I am a servant and it is my business to see what I can do for the American people. I am not a boss, and my little authority or great authority that I happen to have for a day, is not a personal perquisite.'"

The pressure of the office of the presidency took a toll on President Harding's health. In June 1923 he embarked upon a speaking trip across the country which ended up with a boat trip to Alaska. Upon returning to Seattle he came down with pneumonia and never recovered. He died on August 2.

Vice President Coolidge took over as president, and asked all members of the cabinet to remain with him. Hughes continued as secretary of state until March 4, 1925, when President Coolidge began his first full term, having been elected the previous November. Hughes's resignation brought many expressions of regret and acknowledgments of a job well done. Probably none touched him as much as one from a department clerk. She wrote, "I wanted you to know that not only I but every other woman in the Department appreciated more than I can tell you the unfailing generous courtesy with which you went out of your way to greet us when you saw us around the Department. It meant a great deal more to us than you have any idea of and it was quite understood that to meet you in the morning meant a happy day."

The Chicago *Tribune* carried a cartoon that depicted Uncle Sam and Hughes looking at a big book open to pages showing "Chas. E. Hughes Record." The last page was blank. The caption of the cartoon read: "Completed without a blot."

Private Citizen Once Again

The Hugheses spent the spring and summer relaxing and enjoying the opportunity to have some time together. Hughes returned to the practice of law and was elected president of the American Bar Association. He joined Newton D. Baker and S. Parkes Cadman to create the National Conference of Christians and Jews. As the election of 1928 loomed closer, pressure mounted for Hughes once again to be a candidate for president. He again refused. When Herbert Hoover was nominated by the Republican Party, Hughes offered his support and campaigned for him.

Hughes's return to the practice of law brought him many important cases, including some appeals to the U.S. Supreme Court. He was careful, however, not to allow anyone to take advantage of the fact that he had been a member of the Court. He was especially pleased when his son, Charles, was appointed solicitor general of the United States in 1929.

Nomination to the Supreme Court

Hughes served on the Permanent Court of International Justice at The Hague, Netherlands, until President Hoover appointed him chief justice of the United States Supreme Court on February 3, 1930. He was confirmed on February 13 after a somewhat acrimonious debate, which centered upon his having represented corporations and wealthy individuals during much of his legal career.

The justices on the Court at that time were Willis Van Devanter, Oliver W. Holmes, Jr., James C. McReynolds, Louis D. Brandeis, Pierce Butler, George Sutherland, Edward T. Sanford, and Harlan F. Stone.

Pusey gives this evaluation of Hughes as chief justice: "While it is true ... that Hughes was the dominant influence in the court, it was not because of any domineering attitude on his part. He 'ran the court as it was never run before.' But he did it through the thoroughness of his work, the clarity of his statements, the power of his intellect, and the considerate treatment of his colleagues. It is his fellow workers who have most frequently described him as 'the greatest of a great line of Chief Justices.'"

As Associate and Chief Justice (1910-16, 1930-41)

Hughes served on the Court as associate justice from 1910 until 1916, and as chief justice from 1930 until 1941.

The Free Exercise of Religion

Hughes participated in several free exercise of religion cases but did not write opinions in any of them. The first case involved Albert W. Hamilton and W. Alonzo Reynolds, Jr., who were suspended from the University of California at Los Angeles for refusing to participate in the Reserve Officers Training Corps.[3] Hamilton and Reynolds claimed they were religiously and conscientiously opposed to war. The Supreme Court of California and the U.S. Supreme Court upheld the suspensions.

Justice Pierce Butler, writing for the Court, acknowledged that Hamilton and Reynolds had a right to maintain their beliefs against war, but pointed out that the government also had a right to maintain peace and order and to defend itself against aggressors. "Government, federal and state," he asserted, "each in its own sphere owes a duty to the people within its jurisdiction to preserve itself in adequate strength to maintain peace and order and to assure the just enforcement of law. And every citizen owes the reciprocal duty, according to his capacity, to support and defend government against all enemies."

One may accept the premise that everyone, regardless of his or her religious beliefs, ought to participate in the defense of the country. It is more difficult, however, to agree that children can be expelled from school for refusing to salute the American flag. That was what happened in the case of *Minersville District v. Gobitis.*[4] Lillian Gobitis and her brother William, ages 12 and 10, respectively, were expelled from the public schools in Minersville, Pennsylvania, for refusing to salute the flag and recite the pledge of allegiance. Lillian and William were the children of parents who were Jehovah's Witnesses. As such they believed in strict construction of Scripture, including the Second Commandment which instructs believers "not [to] make unto thee any graven image, or any likeness of any thing that is in heaven above, or that is in the earth beneath, or that is in the water under the earth."

In upholding the suspensions, Justice Frankfurter, writing for the Court, posed this question: "When does the constitutional guarantee [of free exercise of religion] compel exemption from doing what society thinks necessary for the promotion of some great common end, or from a penalty for conduct which appears dangerous to the general good?" He believed that this was the kind of case in which the religious beliefs of the Gobitis children must give way to the "general good." The "general good," as he saw it, was the "promotion of national cohesion." Frankfurter then wrestled with the question whether "training children in patriotic impulses" by compulsion was wise. "For ourselves," he speculated, "we might be tempted to say that the deepest patriotism is best engendered by giving unfettered scope to the most crotchety beliefs. Perhaps it is best, even from the standpoint of those interests which ordinances like the one under review seek to promote, to give to the least popular sect leave from conformities like those here in issue." "But," he concluded, "the courtroom is not the arena for debating issues of educational policy." The political arena is the place to fight for the "abandonment of foolish legislation . . . [and that] is itself a training in liberty."

Four of the judicial freedom fighters profiled herein voted with the majority to sustain the expulsion of the Gobitis children. In addition to Hughes, they include Justices Hugo L. Black, William O. Douglas, and Frank Murphy. Three years later, after Hughes had left the Court, the *Gobitis* case was overruled.[5] By that time justices Black, Douglas, and Murphy had changed their minds. They now believed that the *Gobitis* decision was wrong, and that expelling children from school for refusal to salute the flag and to recite the pledge of allegiance violated those children's rights under the First Amendment.

Newton Cantwell and his sons Jesse and Russell were arrested for going door-to-door in New Haven, Connecticut, proselytizing for the Jehovah's Witnesses; Hughes joined a unanimous Court in reversing their convictions.[6] It was against Connecticut law to "solicit money, services, subscriptions or any valuable thing for any alleged religious . . . cause, unless such cause shall have been approved by the secretary of the public welfare council."

Justice Owen J. Roberts wrote the Court's opinion. He pointed out that the First Amendment "embraces two concepts,—freedom to believe and freedom to act. The first is absolute but, in the nature of things, the second cannot be. Conduct remains subject to regulation for the protection of society." Regulation of actions taken in the name of religion is permissible if such regulations are limited to setting time, place, and manner. In this case, however, there were no such regulations. The law gave the council secretary complete discretion in deciding what was an approved religious cause. "To condition the solicitation of aid for the perpetuation of religious views . . . upon a license," Roberts declared, "the grant of which rests in the exercise of a determination by state authority as to what is a religious cause, is to lay a forbidden burden upon the exercise of liberty protected by the Constitution."

In *United States v. Macintosh*,[7] the chief justice discussed the background of Douglas Clyde Macintosh as follows:

> A Canadian by birth, he first came to the United States as a graduate student at the University of Chicago, and in 1907 he was ordained as a Baptist minister. In 1909 he began to teach in Yale University and is now a member of the faculty of the Divinity School, Chaplain of the Yale Graduate School, and Dwight Professor of Theology. After the outbreak of the Great War, he voluntarily sought appointment as a chaplain with the Canadian Army and as such saw service at the front. Returning to this country, he made public addresses in 1917 in

support of the Allies. In 1918, he went again to France where he had charge of an American Y.M.C.A. hut at the front until the armistice, when he resumed his duties at Yale.

When Macintosh applied for United States citizenship, he was required to give an answer to the following question:[22] "If necessary, are you willing to take up arms in defense of this country?" He responded, "Yes; but I should want to be free to judge of the necessity." And he later filed a memorandum explaining his response to the question.

> I am willing to do what I judge to be in the best interests of my country, but only in so far as I can believe that this is not going to be against the best interests of humanity in the long run. I do not undertake to support "my country, right or wrong" in any dispute which may arise, and I am not willing to promise beforehand, and without knowing the cause for which my country may go to war, either that I will or that I will not "take up arms in defense of this country," however "necessary" the war may seem to be to the Government of the day.

Macintosh was denied citizenship and that decision was affirmed by the Supreme Court. Hughes dissented because he did not believe that Congress had intended to "exact such a promise" from one conscientiously opposed to war.

The chief justice pointed out that the president, members of Congress, the judiciary, and employees of the executive branch all have to take an oath "to support and defend the Constitution of the United States against all enemies, foreign and domestic." But, he argued, "it was not the intention of Congress in framing ... [that] oath to impose a religious test."

> When we consider the history of the struggle for religious liberty, the large number of citizens of our country, from the very beginning, who have been unwilling to sacrifice their religious convictions, and in particular, those who have been conscientiously opposed to war and who would not yield what they sincerely believed to be their allegiance to the will of God, I find it impossible to conclude that such persons are to be deemed disqualified for public office in this country because of the requirement of the oath which must be taken before they enter upon their duties.

Hughes then pointed out that the naturalization oath is substantially the same as the oath required of public employees, and we have had a "long-established practice of excusing from military service those whose religious convictions oppose it [and that] confirms the view that Congress in the terms of the [naturalization oath] did not intend to require a promise to give such service." And Hughes concluded:

> When one's belief collides with the power of the State, the latter is supreme within its sphere and submission or punishment follows. But, in the form of conscience, duty to a moral power higher than the State has always been maintained.

The reservation of that supreme obligation, as a matter of principle, would unquestionably be made by many of our conscientious and law-abiding citizens. The essence of religion is belief in a relation to God involving duties superior to those arising from any human relation.

Freedom of Speech

A Communist Flag. Yetta Stromberg, age 19, was a leader of a summer camp for children in San Bernardino, California. "Among other things, the children were taught class consciousness, the solidarity of the workers, and the theory that the workers of the world are of one blood and brothers all."[8] Each day Stromberg assisted "the children in raising a red flag, 'a camp-made reproduction of the flag of Soviet Russia, which was also the flag of the Communist Party in the United States.'"

Stromberg was charged with, and convicted of, unlawfully displaying "a red flag and banner in a public place . . . as a sign, symbol and emblem of opposition to organized government and as an invitation and stimulus to anarchist action and as an aid to propaganda that is and was of a seditious character." The California Supreme Court upheld her conviction, and she appealed to the U.S. Supreme Court, which reversed.

Chief Justice Hughes authored the opinion for the majority. Among the questions he addressed was whether California was required to abide by the free speech clause of the First Amendment. Refering to several prior cases, Hughes declared, "It has been determined that the conception of liberty under the due process clause of the Fourteenth Amendment embraces the right of free speech."

The next question that concerned the Court was whether the law could be used to punish someone who peacefully and in an orderly manner expressed opposition to government. Taking note that the California Supreme Court had said that the statute might be construed to punish such a person, Hughes responded, "The maintenance of the opportunity for free political discussion to the end that government may be responsive to the will of the people and that changes may be obtained by lawful means, an opportunity essential to the security of the Republic, is a fundamental principle of our constitutional system." He then held that "[a] statute which upon its face, and as authoritatively construed, is so vague and indefinite as to permit punishment of the fair use of this opportunity is repugnant to the guaranty of liberty contained in the Fourteenth Amendment."

The Communist Party Assemblies. Dirk De Jonge, a member of the Communist Party, spoke at a meeting in Portland, Oregon, during which he discussed conditions at the county jail, raids that had been made on the Party's headquarters, and actions taken by the police during a maritime strike, and he asked those present to recruit new members for the Party.

De Jonge was arrested and charged with criminal syndicalism, which was defined as "the doctrine which advocates crime, physical violence, sabotage or any unlawful acts or methods as a means of accomplishing or effecting industrial or political change or revolution."[9] De Jonge was convicted, and the conviction was affirmed by the Oregon Supreme Court. A unanimous U.S. Supreme Court reversed, with Chief Justice Hughes writing the Court's opinion. Hughes first pointed out that the defendant was convicted of nothing more than conducting and participating in a meeting of the Communist Party, which the State claimed was an organization that advocated criminal syndicalism. "His sole offense as charged, and for which he was convicted and sentenced to imprisonment for seven years," Hughes noted, "was that he had assisted in the conduct of a public meeting, albeit otherwise lawful, which was held under the auspices of the Communist Party." The chief justice then summed up the protection that the Constitution provides to those assembling peaceably: "It follows from these considerations that, consistently with the Federal Constitution, peaceable assembly for lawful discussion cannot be made a crime. The holding of meetings for peaceable political action cannot be proscribed. Those who assist in the conduct of such meetings cannot be branded as criminals on that score."

Advocacy of Unpopular Ideas. Before the end of the term in which *De Jonge* was decided, Hughes participated in an advocacy case. This case involved a Mr. Herndon, a member of the Kentucky Communist Party, who had gone to Atlanta to distribute Communist literature and to obtain new members for the Party. While engaged in this activity, he was arrested and charged with the crime of insurrection, which was defined as "any attempt, by persuasion or otherwise, to induce others to join in any combined resistance to the lawful authority of the State."[10] Having been convicted, and his conviction having been upheld by the Georgia Supreme Court, Herndon appealed to the U.S. Supreme Court. In an opinion written by Justice Owen J. Roberts, in which Hughes joined, the Court reversed and sent the case back to the Georgia court. Noting that Herndon was being punished for no more than being a member of the Communist Party, and soliciting new members for it, Roberts wrote, "In these circumstances to make membership in the party and solicitation of members for that party a criminal offense, punishable by death, in the discretion of a jury, is an unwarranted invasion of the right of freedom of speech." Furthermore, Roberts pointed out, "The statute, as construed and applied, amounts merely to a dragnet which may enmesh anyone who agitates for a change of government if a jury can be persuaded that he ought to have foreseen his words would have some effect in the future conduct of others.... So vague and indeterminate are the boundaries thus set to the freedom of speech and assembly that the law necessarily violates the guarantees of liberty embodied in the Fourteenth Amendment."

Hughes voted with the majority to affirm the conviction of Mr. Fox for printing and distributing material "advocating, encouraging or inciting, or having a tendency to encourage or incite the commission of any crime."[11]

Fox had written an article promoting nudity and castigating those who interfered with the freedom to be nude. "One of the liberties enjoyed by Homeites was the privilege to bathe in evening dress, or with merely the clothes nature gave them, just as they chose." He concluded his article by urging a boycott: "The boycott will be pushed until these invaders will come to see the brutal mistake of their action and so inform the people."

In affirming Fox's conviction, the justices were of the opinion that the writing was more than just an expression of opinion. It "encourages and incites a persistence in what we must assume would be a breach of the state laws against indecent exposure."

Pamphleteering. In referring to distribution of literature, Justice Stephen J. Field wrote, "Liberty of circulating is as essential to that freedom as liberty of publishing; indeed, without the circulation, the publication would be of little value."[12]

Alma Lovell was arrested for distributing Jehovah's Witnesses religious tracts on the streets of Griffin, Georgia, without a permit from the city manager. She moved to dismiss the charges, claiming that the city ordinance was invalid as an infringement upon freedom of the press and freedom of religion.[13] The trial court refused to dismiss the charges, and she was therefore convicted. The Supreme Court of Georgia affirmed, but a unanimous U.S. Supreme Court reversed. In an opinion written by the chief justice, the Court said that the Fourteenth Amendment now requires states and any subdivision thereof to abide by the First Amendment. Therefore the question before the Court was whether the city ordinance was a valid regulation of freedom of the press and of speech. The chief justice's answer was: "We think that the ordinance is invalid on its face. Whatever the motive which induced its adoption, its character is such that it strikes at the very foundation of the freedom of the press by subjecting it to license and censorship." Furthermore, he wrote, "The liberty of the press is not confined to newspapers and periodicals. It necessarily embraces pamphlets and leaflets. These indeed have been historic weapons in the defense of liberty, as the pamphlets of Thomas Paine and others in our own history abundantly attest."

Hughes participated in two subsequent cases in which the principles of Lovell's case were affirmed.[14] In one of those decisions, *Hague v. C.I.O.,*[15] the Court discussed the use of streets for First Amendment activities: "Wherever the title of streets and parks may rest, they have immemorially been held in trust for the use of the public and, time out of mind, have been used for purposes of assembly, communicating thoughts between citizens, and discussing public questions. Such use of the streets and public places has, from ancient times, been a part of the privileges, immunities, rights, and liberties of citizens."

But the Court has also pointed out that some regulation of the use of streets is necessary for the public peace and good order.

Hughes authored an opinion that upheld a New Hampshire statute requiring a license to conduct a parade or procession upon a public street.[16] The case involved the arrest of five Jehovah's Witnesses who participated in a march through downtown Manchester, New Hampshire. The Court's opinion describes what took place: "The company was divided into four or five groups, each with about fifteen to twenty persons. Each group then proceeded to a different part of the business district of the city and there 'would line up in single-file formation and then proceed to march along the sidewalk, 'single-file,' that is, following one another.' Each of the defendants carried a small staff with a sign reading 'Religion is a Snare and a Racket' and on the reverse 'Serve God and Christ the King.' "

The five were convicted, and the Supreme Court of New Hampshire affirmed. In so doing, that court held "that the regulation with respect to parades and processions was applicable only 'to organized formations of persons using the highways,' " and that if the defendants had moved separately or collectively in a way that was not a parade or procession, the law would not have applied to them. New Hampshire argued that its license requirement for parades was necessary for proper policing and fixing the time and place of a parade.

The U.S. Supreme Court unanimously affirmed. Hughes wrote for the Court, "If a municipality has authority to control the use of its public streets for parades and processions, as it undoubtedly has, it cannot be denied authority to give consideration, without unfair discrimination, to time, place and manner in relation to the other proper uses of the streets."

What the Court has been concerned about in license statutes is that the person issuing the license not be able to pick and choose among the kinds of messages to be delivered. In this case the Court did not find discrimination against the Jehovah's Witnesses because of their religion.

Peaceful Picketing. Justice Frankfurter wrote that "picketing is the poor man's [woman's] means of communication."[17] Whether Carlson was a poor man is not known, but what is known is that he was arrested for picketing at a road construction site in Shasta County, California.

> [Carlson] was one of a group of twenty-nine men engaged in "picketing" on U.S. Highway 99 in front of the Delta Tunnel Project in Shasta County. "The picketing consisted of walking [on the edge of the highway nearest the project] a distance of 50 to 100 feet in a general northerly direction, then turning around and retracing steps and continuing as before . . . all of the walking in connection with the picketing . . . was done off the paved portion of the highway and on the gravelled portion of the right-of-way, that is, on public property." . . . The sign carried by appellant [Carlson] bore the legend: "This job is unfair to CIO." These activities occurred between the hours of 7:30 and 9:00 A.M. During this period vehicles and persons passed freely without any molestation or interference through the picket line from the highway to the project and from the project to the highway, and the traffic of persons and automobiles along the highway was not obstructed. . . . The pickets committed no acts of violence, and there was no breach of the peace.[18]

Carlson was arrested and convicted of violating the Shasta County Anti-Picketing Law. In an opinion written by Justice Frank Murphy, which Hughes joined, the Court held the law to be unconstitutional. "The sweeping and inexact terms of the ordinance," Murphy declared, "disclose the threat to freedom of speech inherent in its existence. . . . The carrying of signs and banners, no less than raising of a flag, is a natural and appropriate means of conveying information on matters of public concern." And, he concluded, "The power and duty of the State to take adequate steps to preserve the peace and protect the privacy, the lives, and the property of its residents cannot be doubted. But the ordinance in question here abridges liberty of discussion under circumstances presenting no clear and present danger of substantive evils within the allowable area of state control."

On the same day that *Carlson* was decided, the chief justice joined Justice Murphy's opinion in *Thornhill v. Alabama*,[19] wherein the Court struck down Alabama's antipicketing statute.

Freedom of the Press

Prior Restraints. Thomas Jefferson said, "Were it left to me to decide whether we should have a government without newspapers, or newspapers without government, I should not hesitate for a moment to prefer the latter."[20] Chief Justice Hughes would have agreed with Jefferson as to the value of the press in a free society, for he wrote the opinion in the landmark case, *Near v. Minnesota*,[21] involving freedom of the press.

J.N. Near and Howard A. Guilford were the publishers of a periodical known as the *Saturday Press*. They used the periodical to publicize their views about the Minneapolis chief of police, the mayor, and the county attorney. "Most of the charges were directed against the Chief of Police; he was charged with gross neglect of duty, illicit relations with gangsters, and with participation in graft. The County Attorney was charged with knowing the existing conditions and with failure to take adequate measures to remedy them. The Mayor was accused of inefficiency and dereliction."

The county attorney brought an action against Near and Guilford seeking an injunction against further publication of the *Saturday Press*. He proceeded under a Minnesota statute that provided for the abatement of any "malicious, scandalous and defamatory newspaper, magazine, or other periodical." After hearing the evidence, Minnesota District Judge Mathias Baldwin "found that the defendants through these publications 'did engage in the business of regularly and customarily producing, publishing and circulating a malicious, scandalous and defamatory newspaper,' and that 'the said publication . . . under said name of The Saturday Press, or any other name, constitutes a public nuisance under the laws of the State.'" He then issued an injunction prohibiting any further publication of "any publication whatsoever which is a malicious, scandalous or defamatory newspaper, as defined by law." The Minnesota Supreme Court affirmed, but the U.S. Supreme Court reversed in a five to four decision.

The chief justice wrote the majority's opinion. "If we cut through mere details of procedure," he declared,

> the operation and effect of the statute in substance is that public authorities may bring the owner or publisher of a newspaper or periodical before a judge upon a charge of conducting a business of publishing scandalous and defamatory matter—in particular that the matter consists of charges against public officers of official dereliction—and unless the owner or publisher is able and disposed to bring competent evidence to satisfy the judge that the charges are true and are published with good motives and for justifiable ends, his newspaper or periodical is suppressed and further publication is made punishable as a contempt. This is the essence of censorship.

Hughes, noting that there have been many decisions giving the press immunity from previous restraints, points out that even though "the liberty of the press may be abused by miscreant purveyors of scandal [that] does not make any the less necessary the immunity of the press from previous restraint in dealing with official misconduct. Subsequent punishment for such abuses as may exist is the appropriate remedy, consistent with constitutional privilege."

Freedom of Association

In 1937 the chief justice wrote the Court's opinion upholding the constitutionality of the National Labor Relations Act of 1935 (NLRA):

> Thus, in its present application, the statute [NLRA] goes no further than to safeguard the right of employees to self-organization and to select representatives of their own choosing for collective bargaining or other mutual protection without restraint or coercion by their employer.
>   That is a fundamental right. Employees have as clear a right to organize and select their representatives for lawful purposes as the respondent [Jones and Laughlin Steel Corp.] has to organize its business and select its own officers and agents.[22]

In 1958 the Court held that "it is beyond debate that freedom to engage in association for the advancement of beliefs and ideas is an inseparable aspect of the 'liberty' assured by the Due Process Clause of the Fourteenth Amendment, which embraces freedom of speech."[23]

Chief Justice Hughes, however, was writing about freedom of association on a blank slate in 1937, yet he referred to it as a "fundamental right." He does not identify its source within the Bill of Rights, but there can be no doubt that he thought the right did exist, for his opinion contains several other references to "the right of employees to self-organization and to have representatives of their own choosing."[24]

Equal Protection of the Law

Blacks on Juries. The Court first held that it was a denial of equal protection to keep blacks off juries in *Strauder v. West Virginia*,[25] decided in 1880. But as the case of *Norris v. Alabama*[26] illustrates, some states were still preventing blacks from serving as late as the 1930s. Clarence Norris and eight other black youths were charged with and convicted of raping two white girls. The defendants were tried in three groups, with all trials being conducted in one day. The Supreme Court had reversed the convictions and ordered new trials. Upon retrial Norris raised a question about the composition of the jury, arguing that blacks had been systematically excluded. The trial court denied the motion, and the Alabama Supreme Court affirmed. A unanimous U.S. Supreme Court reversed. Writing for the Court, Hughes noted that "when a federal right has been specially set up and claimed in a state court, it is our province to inquire not merely whether it was denied in express terms but also whether it was denied in substance and effect." He then examined the evidence presented by the defendant which included testimony of several witnesses that "no Negro had ever served on a jury in that county or had been called for such service. Some of these witnesses were over fifty years of age and had always lived in Morgan County." Hughes then concluded, "For this long-continued, unvarying, and wholesale exclusion of negroes from jury service we find no justification consistent with the constitutional mandate." This required reversal of the defendant's conviction.

With Hughes voting with the majority, the Court reached the same result in *Hale v. Kentucky*,[27] *Pierre v. Louisiana*,[28] and *Smith v. Texas*.[29]

Separate but Equal Transportation. For a number of years after its decision in *Plessy v. Ferguson*, the Court continued to hold that separate but equal facilities on public transportation did not violate equal protection. In *McCabe v. A. T. & S. F. Ry. Co.*,[30] for example, the Court upheld an Oklahoma statute that required separate but equal coaches on trains traveling in that state. Justice Hughes, writing for the Court, acknowledged that the issue "could no longer be considered an open one, that it was not an infraction of the Fourteenth Amendment for a State to require separate, but equal, accommodations for the two races." He cited *Plessy* as authority for that statement.

There was, however, one other issue in this case. Under the state law, the railroad was not required to have separate sleeping cars, dining cars or chair cars for blacks. The railroad argued that there were not enough blacks traveling by train to make it worthwhile to have separate cars for them. Hughes, however, said that "argument . . . seems to us to be without merit." "It makes the constitutional right," he argued, "depend upon the number of persons who may be discriminated against, whereas the essence of the constitutional right is that it is a personal one. . . . It is the individual who is entitled to the equal protection of the laws, and if he is denied by a common carrier . . . a facility or convenience in the course of his journey which under substantially the same circumstances is furnished to another traveler, he may properly complain that his constitutional privilege has been invaded."

Separate but Equal Law Schools. The Supreme Court had an opportunity to dispose of the separate but equal doctrine in the case of *State of Missouri v. Canada,*[31] but it did not do so. Lloyd Gaines, who was black, graduated from Lincoln University in Missouri, a university maintained by the state for blacks. He applied to attend law school at the University of Missouri, but his application was rejected because of his race. He was advised that the state would pay his tuition at any out-of-state law school that would accept him. Had he applied to law schools at the universities of Kansas, Nebraska, Iowa, or Illinois, he might have been accepted, as those law schools did accept nonresident blacks. Gaines rejected the out-of-state alternative and brought an action seeking a court order admitting him to the University of Missouri. The writ was denied, and the denial affirmed by the state supreme court. The U.S. Supreme Court accepted the case and reversed.

The majority refused to apply the separate but equal concept in this case. "The question here," Chief Justice Hughes stated,

> is not of a duty of the State to supply legal training, or of the quality of the training which it does supply, but of its duty when it provides such training to furnish it to the residents of the State upon the basis of an equality of right. By the operation of the laws of Missouri a privilege has been created for white law students which is denied to negroes by reason of their race. The white resident is afforded legal education within the State; the negro resident having the same qualifications is refused it there and must go outside the State to obtain it. That is a denial of the equality of legal right to the enjoyment of the privilege which the State has set up, and the provision for payment of tuition fees in another State does not remove the discrimination.

In response to the state's argument that not many blacks wanted to attend law school, Hughes pointed out that "petitioner's right is a personal one. It was as an individual that he was entitled to the equal protection of the laws, and the State was bound to furnish him within its borders facilities for legal education substantially equal to those which the State there afforded persons of the white race, whether or not other negroes sought the same opportunity."

Involuntary Servitude

In the *Slaughter-House* cases,[32] the Court discussed the meaning of the phrase *involuntary servitude* as used in the Thirteenth Amendment. "The word servitude," Justice Samuel F. Miller wrote, "is of larger meaning than slavery, as the latter is popularly understood in this country, and the obvious purpose was to forbid all shades and conditions of African slavery." Justice Miller pointed out that the phrase was intended to prevent "apprenticeship for long terms," and "reducing the slaves to the conditions of serfs attached to the plantation."

Lonzo Bailey found himself in a situation from which he was rescued by Justice Hughes and the Thirteenth Amendment. Bailey had signed a contract to work as a farmhand in Alabama for $12 a month. He was given $15 at the time he signed the contract. He worked one month and a few days and refused to work thereafter without refunding the $15. He was arrested and charged with violating a statute that made it a crime to enter "into a contract in writing for the performance of any act of service, and thereby obtains money . . . from such employer, . . . and without refunding such money, . . . refuses or fails to perform such act or service."[33]

The statute also provided that refusal to perform the service or refund the money "shall be prima facie evidence of the intent to injure his employer, or to defraud him."

Bailey was convicted, ordered to refund the money, and fined $30 and costs. If he defaulted in making these payments, he would be sentenced to "twenty days (at hard labor) in lieu of said fine and one hundred and sixteen days on account of said costs." The Supreme Court of Alabama held that the statute under which Bailey was charged was constitutional and affirmed his conviction. The U.S. Supreme Court reversed, with Justices Holmes and Horace H. Lurton dissenting.

Justice Hughes authored the opinion for the majority. His first concern was with the statutory presumption of intent. "The law of the State," he noted, "did not permit him to testify that he did not intend to injure or defraud. Unless he were fortunate enough to be able to command evidence of circumstances affirmatively showing good faith, he was helpless. He stood, stripped by the statute of the presumption of innocence, and exposed to conviction for fraud upon evidence only of breach of contract and failure to pay." The statute and the presumption therefore constituted a "means of compulsion through which performance of such service may be secured." And if the statute is really a means of forcing an individual to work, the question is, is it made unconstitutional by the Thirteenth Amendment? The answer is yes, because "we must consider the natural operation of the statute here in question . . . and it is apparent that it furnishes a convenient instrument for the coercion which the Constitution and the act of Congress forbid; an instrument of compulsion peculiarly as against the poor and the ignorant, its most likely victims. There is no more important concern to safeguard the freedom of labor upon which alone can enduring prosperity be based."

The Pursuit of Liberty

The Right to Work. In 1897 the Court held that the word *liberty* in the Fourteenth Amendment protected the right to work. It protects the right of a person, the Court said, "to live and work where he will; to earn his livelihood by any lawful calling; [and] to pursue any livelihood or avocation."[34]

Justice Hughes gave recognition to the right to work in his opinion in *Truax v. Raich*.[35] That case was about Mike Raich's right to work as a cook in a restaurant owned by William Truax. Truax employed nine people; seven, including Raich, were aliens. After Arizona passed a law requiring each employer with five or more employees to employ "not less than eighty (80) percent qualified electors or native-born citizens," Truax discharged Raich.

Raich sued Truax and state attorneys who were required to enforce the law. Raich claimed that he was denied equal protection of the laws and therefore the state statute was unconstitutional as a violation of the Fourteenth Amendment. The district court issued an injunction against the attorneys prohibiting them from enforcing the law. An appeal was taken directly to the Supreme Court, which agreed that the law was a violation of equal protection, and therefore unconstitutional. Justice Hughes was assigned to write the opinion for the Court. He pointed out that in enforcing "the main purpose of the statute, . . . the complainant is to be forced out of his employment as a cook in a restaurant, simply because he is an alien." But the complainant has a right to work. "It requires no argument to show that the right to work for a living in the common occupations of the community is of the very essence of the personal freedom and opportunity that it was the purpose of the [Fourteenth] Amendment to secure." Therefore, Hughes said, "The discrimination is against aliens as such in competition with citizens in the described range of enterprises and in our opinion it clearly falls under the condemnation of the fundamental law." He and the majority then concluded that the law denied Raich and other aliens equal protection of the law.

Before Hughes joined the Court, it had upheld the right of Oregon to limit to ten the number of hours per day that women could work in laundries. The Court acknowledged that women had a right to work, but said that the right was not absolute. "Yet it is equally well settled that this liberty is not absolute . . . and that a State may, without conflicting with the provisions of the Fourteenth Amendment, restrict in many respects the individual's power of contract."[36]

Hughes participated in two subsequent cases affirming the holding in *Muller*.[37]

Hughes also participated in an unusual case coming to the Court from Texas. According to the Court's opinion,

> W.W. Smith, . . . a man 47 years of age, had spent 21 years in the railroad business. He had never been a brakeman or a conductor, but for six years he had served as fireman, for three years ran as extra engineer on a freight train, for eight years was engineer on a mixed train, hauling freight and passengers, and for four years had been an engineer on a passenger train of the Texas & Gulf Railway. On July 22, 1910, he acted as conductor of a freight train running between two Texas towns on that road. There is no claim . . . that he was not competent to perform the duties of that position.[38]

Smith was arrested for acting as a conductor in violation of Texas law making it a crime for a person to act as a conductor "without having for two (2) years prior thereto served or worked in the capacity of a brakeman or conductor on a freight train." He was convicted, and his conviction was affirmed by the Court of Criminal Appeals of Texas. The U.S. Supreme Court reversed, with Justice Joseph R. Lamar writing an opinion that Hughes joined.

To put the case in proper perspective, Justice Lamar discussed the Fourteenth Amendment. "Life, liberty, property, and the equal protection of the law, grouped together in the Constitution," he declared,

> are so related that the deprivation of any one of those separate and independent rights may lessen or extinguish the value of the other three. In so far as a man is deprived of the right to labor his liberty is restricted, his capacity to earn wages and acquire property is lessened, and he is denied the protection which the law affords those who are permitted to work. Liberty means more than freedom from servitude, and the constitutional guarantee is an assurance that the citizen shall be protected in the right to use his powers of mind and body in any lawful calling.

In concluding that the law was a violation of equal protection, Lamar wrote, "But all men are entitled to the equal protection of the law in their right to work for the support of themselves and their families. A statute which permits the brakeman to act—because he is presumptively competent—and prohibits the employment of engineers and all others who can affirmatively prove that they are likewise competent, is not confined to securing the public safety but denies to many the liberty of contract granted to brakemen and operates to establish rules of promotion in a private employment."

The Bill of Rights and the States

As chief justice, Hughes participated in *Powell v. Alabama,*[39] one of the landmark cases involving application of the Sixth Amendment's right to counsel to the states. The case grew out of the following facts:

> The record shows that on the day when the offense is said to have been committed, these defendants, together with a number of other negroes, were on a freight train on its way through Alabama. On the same train were seven white boys and two white girls. A fight took place between the negroes and the white boys, in the course of which the white boys, with the exception of one named Gilley, were thrown off the train. A message was sent ahead, reporting the fight and asking that every negro be gotten off the train. The participants in the fight, and the two girls, were in an open gondola car. The two girls testified that each of them was assaulted by six different negroes in turn, and they identified the seven defendants as having been among the number. None of the white boys was called to testify, with the exception of Gilley, who was called in rebuttal.

When the train reached Scottsboro, Alabama, the seven blacks were arrested. Because of hostility toward the defendants in the area, they were quartered in a nearby town and guarded by soldiers of the militia. Although the record indicated that the defendants were represented by counsel at their arraignment, that seems not to have been true. When the question of counsel came up at the trial, the judge said he had appointed all members of the bar to represent the defendants at arraignment and assumed that they would continue to represent them throughout the trial. They did not. The defendants were tried in three groups, with all trials being concluded in one day. The verdict was guilty for all defendants and they were sentenced to death. When the case reached the U.S. Supreme Court, it reversed, because the defendants had been denied their constitutional right to counsel as guaranteed by the Sixth Amendment.

Justice George Sutherland wrote the opinion for the majority, which included Hughes. "All that it is necessary now to decide, and we do decide," he declared,

> is that in a capital case, where the defendant is unable to employ counsel, and is incapable adequately of making his own defense because of ignorance, feeble-mindedness, illiteracy, or the like, it is the duty of the court, whether requested or not, to assign counsel for him as a necessary requisite of due process of law; and that duty is not discharged by an assignment at such a time or under such circumstances as to preclude the giving of effective aid in the preparation and trial of the case. To hold otherwise would be to ignore the fundamental postulate, already adverted to, "that there are certain immutable principles of justice which inhere in the very idea of free government which no member of the Union may disregard."

Although the Court in *Powell* held that a state was required to follow the mandates of the Sixth Amendment and provide counsel in capital cases, it reached the opposite result when it considered whether a state was bound not to put a defendant in jeopardy twice as prohibited by the Fifth Amendment. In the opinion in *Palko v. Connecticut*,[40] which Hughes joined, Justice Cardozo noted that prior to this case the Court had held that states were required to abide by the provisions of the First Amendment, and were required to furnish counsel in capital cases. In addition, he pointed out, however, that the Court had also held that states need not proceed by way of indictment in a criminal case as the Fifth Amendment requires the federal government to do. Nor does the Fifth Amendment's provision against self-incrimination apply to the states. Furthermore, the Court had said that states need not follow the commands of the Sixth and Seventh Amendments with regard to jury trials. Only those provisions of the Bill of Rights, he wrote, which are "of the essence of a scheme of ordered liberty," are applicable to state governments. Placing a defendant in double jeopardy did not fall under that mandate. "Is the kind of double jeopardy to which the statute has subjected him," Cardozo asked, "a hardship so acute and shocking that our polity will not endure it? Does it violate those 'fundamental principles of liberty and justice which lie at the base of all our civil and political institutions? ... The answer surely must be 'no'."

The fact that Hughes joined the majority in *Palko* indicates that he was aligned with those justices who were willing to apply selectively some of the provisions of the Bill of Rights to the states. They selected a particular provision to be applied to the states only if they believed that it was "of the essence of a scheme of ordered liberty."

The chief justice applied that concept when he referred to the right to assemble peaceably, in *De Jonge*. He wrote, "The First Amendment of the Federal Constitution expressly guarantees that right against abridgment by Congress. But explicit mention there does not argue exclusion elsewhere. For the right is one that cannot be denied without violating those fundamental principles of liberty and justice which lie at the base of all civil and political institutions,—principles which the Fourteenth Amendment embodies in the general terms of its due process clause."[41]

As a Judicial Freedom Fighter

While governor of New York, Hughes said, "We are under a Constitution, but the Constitution is what the judges say it is, and the judiciary is the safeguard of our liberty and our property under the Constitution."[42] Hughes did not believe, however, that judges were bound by what the Constitution might have meant at the time of its adoption.

> It is no answer to ... insist that what the provision of the Constitution [against impairment of contracts] meant to the vision of that day it must mean to the vision of our time. If by the statement that what the Constitution meant at the time of its adoption it means to-day, it is intended to say that the great clauses of the Constitution must be confined to the interpretation which the framers, with the conditions and outlook of their time, would have placed upon them, the statement carries its own refutation. It was to guard against such a narrow conception that Chief Justice Marshall uttered the memorable warning—"We must never forget that it is a *constitution* we are expounding."[43]

Hughes's record as justice and as chief justice clearly indicates that he not only believed in an expanded interpretation of the Constitution, but that he put that belief into practice with his votes and opinions.

The Court gave lip service to First Amendment rights of speech and assembly in *Gitlow v. New York*,[44] and *Whitney v. California*,[45] when Hughes was not on the Court. He, and the Court over which he presided, however, gave real substance to those rights in *Stromberg, De Jonge, Lovell,* and *Herndon*.

And the chief justice's opinion in *Near v. Minnesota* stands today as one of the landmark decisions concerning freedom of the press. It established the "principle that the constitutional guaranty of the liberty of the press gives immunity from previous restraints."[46]

Hughes made a strong defense of Douglas Clyde Macintosh's right to become a citizen even though Macintosh could not in good conscience declare that he was willing to take up arms if called upon to do so. Hughes also joined Justice Roberts in upholding the right of Jehovah's Witnesses to distribute their literature door-to-door. These cases indicate a strong commitment to the free exercise of religion.

In *Reynolds* and *Gobitis*, however, Hughes voted with the majority to infringe upon the religious beliefs of the individuals involved. Both cases seem inconsistent with the chief justice's dissenting opinion in *Macintosh*.

Hughes followed the long line of cases striking down convictions of blacks indicted by or tried before a segregated jury. Just before he retired in 1941, he joined Justice Black's majority opinion in *Smith v. Texas*[47] reversing a conviction of a black person who had been indicted by a jury from which blacks had been excluded. "What the Fourteenth Amendment prohibits," Black declared, "is racial discrimination in the selection of grand juries."

In cases involving their right to vote, black voters consistently received Hughes's vote.[48] He also voted for equal treatment of blacks in public transportation and in admission to law school, although he did accept the principle of separate but equal.

Hughes's votes reflect his belief that the Fourteenth Amendment Due Process Clause prohibited states from infringing upon First Amendment rights. For the other rights in the Bill of Rights, he was more selective.

In *De Jonge* the chief justice wrote:

> The greater the importance of safeguarding the community from incitements to the overthrow of our institutions by force and violence, the more imperative is the need to preserve inviolate the constitutional rights of free speech, free press and free assembly in order to maintain the opportunity for free political discussion, to the end that government may be responsive to the will of the people and that changes, if desired, may be obtained by peaceful means. Therein lies the security of the Republic, the very foundation of constitutional government.[49]

Whether it was in protecting the rights of free speech, press, religion, assembly, or association, or in protecting the rights of minorities and workers, Chief Justice Hughes was a staunch defender of freedom.

3

JUSTICE LOUIS DEMBITZ BRANDEIS

PERSONAL LIFE

Growing Up

> He had a slim appearance that always made him seem younger than his years. He had his father's deep-set blue eyes and straight black hair. And perhaps of greatest importance, he seemed to have inherited his father's keen intellect. He excelled in his studies, a distinction clouded only by the poor reputation of Louisville's schools at the time. At the German and English Academy, Louis continually received the highest grades and ultimately a special commendation from the principal for conduct and industry. And in 1872, when he was sixteen, he received a gold medal from the Louisville University of the Public Schools for "pre-eminence in all his studies."

That is how Lewis J. Paper describes Brandeis as a teenager in his biography *Brandeis*.[1]

Louis Brandeis was born in Louisville, Kentucky, on November 13, 1856, the son of Adolph and Frederika Brandeis. He was named Louis David Brandeis, but in later life took Dembitz as his middle name because of his admiration for his uncle Lewis Dembitz, who was a lawyer.

Adolph Brandeis came to the United States in 1848 from Prague, Bohemia, to find a place for the Brandeis, Wehle, and Dembitz families to farm, although none of them were farmers. By the time Adolph sent for the others, he had decided that farming was much too difficult and that the group should go into the grocery business instead, which they did in Madison, Indiana.

Frederika was a member of the Dembitz family. She and Adolph were married shortly after she arrived in the United States. Four children were born of this marriage: Fanny, Amy, Alfred, and Louis.

Adolph moved the family to Louisville in 1851 because he thought that there was a better future there. He went into business with Charles W. Crawford,

JUSTICE LOUIS DEMBITZ BRANDEIS (photo by Harris & Ewing; collection of the Supreme Court of the United States).

and within a few years they operated a flour mill, tobacco factory, and farm, and had a steam freighter named *Fanny Brandeis.*

Brandeis later recalled, "My earliest memories were of the war.... I remember helping my mother carry out food and coffee to the men from the North. The streets seemed full of them always. But there were times when the rebels came so near that we could hear the firing. At one time my father moved us over the river to the comparative safety of Indiana."[2]

Adolph's businesses prospered to the extent that he was able to build a home for the family in one of the exclusive sections of the city. He employed a number of blacks as servants but did not consider them to be, nor did he treat them as, slaves. The family believed that slavery should be abolished.

Louis and his brother, Alfred, enjoyed a very close personal relationship, which continued throughout their lives. "Together, they rode horseback, teased little girls, thought up pranks to frighten maids, fought with other boys, and generally enjoyed their lives as sons of a wealthy family in a border state of the mid-nineteenth century."

Although the Brandeis family was Jewish, they had little contact with the Jewish religion. Louis "did not attend temple services, did not have a bar mitzvah as induction into manhood at the age of thirteen, and had little exposure to the rituals that often bind a culture."[3]

The family observed Christmas, as Christians did, by exchanging greetings and gifts. Philippa Strum has written that Frederika "reared her children without a formal religion because she 'wanted to give them something that neither could be argued away nor would have to be given up as untenable, namely, a pure spirit and the highest ideals as to morals and love.' "[4]

The depression of 1873 saw a downturn in business, and Adolph, sensing this, closed his business and took the family to Europe. He intended to stay in Europe for 15 months, but it was not until 1875 that the family actually returned to the United States.

During their stay in Europe, Louis applied to Annen-Realschule, a school in Dresden. When the rector asked for birth and vaccination certificates Louis said, "The fact that I am here is proof of my birth; and you may look at my arm for evidence that I was vaccinated."[5] With that response, the rector agreed to admit him if he took some private lessons from some of the teachers before the beginning of the next term, which he did. His performance at the school was similar to that in Louisville: he excelled in his studies to the extent that he was awarded a prize "for his diligence and good conduct." Brandeis did not enjoy his experience at Annen-Realschule. He later said of this experience, "I was a terrible little individualist in those days, and the German paternalism got on my nerves." By this time, he had decided to enter Harvard Law School, no doubt having been influenced toward a legal career by his Uncle Lewis.

Strum writes of Brandeis at Harvard,

> There Brandeis achieved one of the great triumphs of his life. When he arrived at Harvard Law School in the fall of 1875, he was eighteen-going-on-nineteen, without a college degree, a Jew who spoke with a Kentucky accent, an almost penniless young man in one of the citadels of American aristocracy. He left Harvard three years later, having achieved the highest scholastic record of any Harvard Law School student (and this record remains unsurpassed), a special exemption from the Board of Trustees so that he could receive his degree at a younger age than the school's rules allowed, and acceptance by the Brahmin

intelligentsia and Boston society. He had even managed to save the first few dollars of what would become a multimillion-dollar fortune.[6]

Louis always referred to his law school days as "the wonderful years" and the "happiest of my life." He had some health problems while at Harvard, especially with his eyes. He was advised by an oculist that his eyes were all right but needed rest, which Louis gave them. Through the professors at Harvard, he met many of the leading citizens of Boston, including Samuel D. Warren, son of a wealthy New England family. Warren graduated second to Louis in their graduating class. Because Brandeis had enjoyed Harvard so much, he decided to stay on for another year of graduate work. In order to do this, he tutored students, and proctored exams.

Lawyer

Louis's parents wanted him to return to Louisville to practice law. His father's business was not as prosperous and needed the infusion of new blood. At the same time, his sister Fanny's husband, Charles Nagel, offered him a position in his law firm in St. Louis. But his friend Samuel Warren urged him to become his partner in Boston. The desire to be independent motivated him to reject all of these offers. Instead he accepted a position with attorney James Taussig in St. Louis. He did not, however, find the work with Taussig stimulating, nor St. Louis very exciting. During this period, his friend Samuel Warren continued to urge him to return to Boston and go into partnership with him. While Louis pondered this, he was offered a part-time position as secretary and assistant to Chief Justice Horace Gray of the Massachusetts Supreme Court at a salary of $500, which he accepted. Upon his return to Boston, Warren and Brandeis opened a law office. Lewis J. Paper reports that "the firm of Warren & Brandeis celebrated on the evening of Louis' admission to the Bar by drinking a mixture of champagne and beer in Warren's room with Oliver Wendell Holmes, Jr., who was fast becoming a renowned figure in Boston legal circles."[7]

The firm prospered. Brandeis was able to attract clients from the German-Jewish community. He also argued cases before the Massachusetts Supreme Court and in 1889 made his first appearance before the United States Supreme Court.

Brandeis had a deep affection for Harvard Law School, and when given an opportunity to teach there part-time, he accepted. Because he was an excellent teacher, he was later offered a full professorship, which he turned down. He was just beginning to enjoy and become very good at trial work. He wrote his brother: "I really long for the excitement of the contest that is a good and prolonged one covering days or weeks. There is a certain joy in the draining exhaustion and backache of a long trial, which shorter skirmishes cannot afford."[8]

During this time, Brandeis and Warren wrote several law review articles, the most noteworthy of which was entitled "The Right to Privacy," published in the *Harvard Law Review.* This article laid the foundation for the right of privacy, which the Supreme Court later held to be a constitutional right within the meaning of the word *liberty*, found in the Due Process Clauses of the Fifth and Fourteenth Amendments.

Brandeis did not believe that lawyers should be "hired guns":

> The notion that the lawyer's role was not merely to achieve whatever goal the client thought he wanted but to tell the client what to do about his problem— and to convince the client that the proposed course of action was correct—was extraordinary at a time when lawyers were increasingly becoming no more than lackeys for growing corporations, taking upon themselves whatever battles their employers were fighting and seeking to get business-oriented courts to help them win. Brandeis was not merely interested in winning cases, much as he loved litigation; he was concerned with whether or not the battle was just.[9]

It was not all work and no play, however, for Brandeis had a horse and enjoyed riding it. He also liked to go canoeing and hiking.

Warren was forced to leave the firm to take care of family business after his father died. Later Brandeis took several other lawyers into the practice and the firm was renamed Brandeis, Dunbar & Nutter in 1897. He remained with the firm until appointed to the Supreme Court in 1916.

Love, Marriage, and Family

Louis, in a letter to his sister Amy, gave a long description of a certain lady, but added: "You, of course, are very much interested in this young lady because you think I am smitten with her. But Alas! it is not so. One mistress only claims me. The 'Law' has her grip on me."

It was not until he was called back to Louisville to attend the funeral of his sister Fanny in March 1890 that Cupid touched him. His second cousin Alice Goldmark from New York was in Louisville and Louis met her there.

"Alice was a very attractive woman of twenty-four," writes Paper, "with long dark hair pulled back, beautiful eyes, and a slim build."[10]

The romance intensified when Louis joined the Goldmark and Brandeis families who were vacationing together that summer. The couple were engaged in September and married on March 23, 1891. Alice was not a physically strong person and therefore did not join Louis in horseback riding. So that they could be together, however, he obtained a buggy and trained a horse to pull it. They were then able to see the sights around Boston. Although money was not a problem, the couple throughout their married life lived frugally. Two daughters were born into the family, Susan in 1893 and Elizabeth in 1896. Paper describes a typical morning at the Brandeis home:

Mornings would begin with a breakfast with Father, or "Papsy," as he was called in those early years. Brandeis would generally get up around 5:30, do some work, and sit down for breakfast around 7:15. He would almost always have oatmeal, hot chocolate or coffee, and some kind of meat—a pork chop or steak or something similar. The girls would have shredded wheat. Because she continually suffered from headaches, Alice needed her rest and almost always had breakfast in bed—a service made possible since there were generally three servants in the house. At breakfast the girls would read aloud to their father or just chatter away about their busy lives.

Alice suffered various health problems throughout most of her life. The couple preferred to spend their time at home together talking and reading to each other. Although Alice jealously guarded her privacy, she did give a newspaper interview in 1931 strongly supporting women's suffrage.

Susan went to the University of Chicago Law School. In October 1925 she was the first woman to argue a case before the U. S. Supreme Court. She married New York attorney Jack Gilbert.

Elizabeth did her undergraduate work at Radcliffe College, in Cambridge, Massachusetts, and went to the University of Wisconsin to teach. She married Paul Raushenbush, a professor of economics there. Paul and Elizabeth were instrumental in securing passage of an unemployment compensation law in Wisconsin which became the model for similar federal legislation.

Brandeis was not a joiner. He did not belong to any men's clubs or lodges, and did not play golf or poker. He was, however, a prolific letter writer. He and Alfred corresponded almost daily. He also wrote his daughters regularly.

Public Service Lawyer

Louis describes his early public service in a letter to Alfred in 1894: "Have had a public career of late. Lecture on Taxation Sunday[,] Spoke against 'Woman Suffrage' before the Legislative Com[mit]tee yesterday & appeared before the Insurance Com[mit]tee yesterday & today."[11] He justified his opposition to women's suffrage by arguing "that the franchise was not a right but a privilege and that the duties involved in the exercise of the privilege should be imposed only upon men." He later changed his views on this issue.

There existed in Boston at this time a group called the Mugwumps, made up of some of Boston's wealthier citizens. Brandeis joined them. He also became active in the Civil Service Reform Association and the Boston American Citizenship Committee. He assisted in the organization of the Harvard Law School Alumni Association, and the *Harvard Law Review*.

The fight over control of the Boston subway system was one of the important public issues in which Brandeis became involved. When Boston Elevated Railway sought long-term franchises from the city for the subway system, and a fare no lower than five cents for 30 years, the Public Franchise league was organized to oppose private control of the system. The league proposed a bill that would provide for public construction of the subway, with a lease to Elevated for 25 years with a rental of 4.5 percent of the construction costs. After a number of years battling the railway in the legislature, the league, with Brandeis acting as its representative, won the battle with the passage of a bill including the league's proposals.

"Initially," writes Strum,

> Brandeis had given his fees for public service undertakings to charity, but he eventually decided that taking fees at all was wrong. He then went further and reimbursed his firm for the working hours he spent in public service. Brandeis believed that his partners and the nonlawyers working for the firm (all of whom participated in a profit-sharing plan) should not be "affected by [his] own feeling" about the causes he took on. He therefore substituted himself "as the client of the firm" and paid his firm as much as $25,000 on one public service matter alone. . . . By this time Brandeis had become one of the most successful lawyers in the United States, and neither he nor his family was deprived of anything because of his decision.

Brandeis became involved in many other public service issues, including reformation of the life insurance industry, regulation of natural gas sale and distribution, and the creation of a savings bank life insurance system. He was deeply involved in an attempt by the New Haven Railroad to merge with the Boston and Maine Railroad. Some of these activities did not sit well with some members of Boston society and the business community. He was no longer considered "one of the boys," and the family began to be shunned by some of their friends. He was now being referred to in newspapers as the "People's Attorney."

Realizing that success in these battles depended upon having a good organization behind him, he joined the Election Laws League, the Public School Association, People's Lobby, and the Advisory Committee of the National Municipal League's Municipal Taxation Committee, and helped organize the Good Government Association. Although he was often thought of as a potential candidate for public office, he consistently refused to run. He thought that having a political office would demand all of his time, and thus leave him no time to practice law, or become involved in other public issues.

Labor Negotiator

A "labor war" at the Carnegie Steel Works, Homestead, Pennsylvania, caused Brandeis to rethink his views about the relationship between capital and labor. When Carnegie refused to renew its contract with its workers, both sides prepared for battle. Strum describes the conflict:

> The company was clearly expecting a small war when the contract ran out. The

contract expired; wages were slashed; and the steel workers went on strike. Henry Clay Frick, Carnegie's manager, hired Pinkerton guards and sailed them up the Ohio River to protect strikebreakers. The strikers dug in on the bank of the river. As the Pinkertons arrived, and realized that the strikers would not permit them to land, they began to fire their Winchesters. The steel workers suffered most of the casualties in the ensuing battle.

Later Brandeis said that the conflict at Homestead "made him think seriously for the first time 'about the labor problem . . . it took the shock of that battle, where organized capital hired a private army to shoot at organized labor for resisting an arbitrary cut in wages, to turn my mind definitely toward a searching study of the relations of labor to industry.' "

William H. McElwain gave Brandeis an opportunity to become personally involved a labor dispute. McElwain owned a shoe factory, and when a business downturn occurred he asked his employees to accept a reduction in wages. When they refused, he asked Brandeis to intervene. Brandeis learned from McElwain that, although the workers were paid quite well, the work was seasonal. This meant that at times the workers did not work and thus received no wages. When Brandeis discussed this with his client, McElwain pointed out that the worker's average wage was pretty good. Brandeis replied: "I abhor averages. I like the individual case. A man may have six meals one day and one the next, making an average of three per day, but that is not a good way to live." He convinced his client that he should organize his business so that the employees would have work throughout the year. He suggested that the company show samples, take orders, and guarantee delivery on time. McElwain followed these suggestions and both he and the workers were satisfied with the arrangements. The success of this venture caused Brandeis to urge other employers to adopt the same method of operation. He was convinced that continuous employment was good for both labor and management.

In 1905 Brandeis assisted Edward A. Filene and Abraham Lincoln Filene, owners of a woman's clothing store in Boston, in establishing the Filene Cooperative Society. Under this agreement, Filene's employees were allowed to participate in the management of the store and the store's profits. It was through his relationship with the Filenes that Brandeis was called in to mediate the strike of the International Ladies' Garment Workers Union in New York City. The union was demanding a closed union shop, but the clothing manufacturers wanted no part of such an arrangement. Brandeis did not believe in closed shops, and therefore agreed to participate only if that demand were eliminated from the negotiations.

A settlement conference was set, presided over by Brandeis. It went well. That may have been due partly to the fact that most of those in attendance, on both sides, were Jews. "What struck me most," Brandeis said later, "was that each side had a great capacity for placing themselves in the other fellow's shoes."[12]

Despite their agreement with Brandeis, the issue of a closed shop did not die, and he recognized that a solution was necessary. Brandeis then proposed what he called "a preferential shop," later to become known as "a union shop." Under this arrangement, the employer could hire nonunion workers, if there were no qualified union workers available. The unions balked. Then Lincoln Filene entered the picture. He called in two Jewish leaders, Jacob Schiff and Louis Marshall, and the three of them met with the union representative, Julius Cohen, and the union's lawyer, Meyer London, and hammered out an acceptable agreement, which included a provision for a "union shop." This did not bring an end to the labor problems in the garment industry, but was the beginning of the use of "union shops" in labor-management contracts.

Brandeis was involved in the creation of the Industrial League, "whose purpose was 'to promote the investigation and study of economic and industrial questions and aid in improving relations between employers and employees.' "[13] He also became "vice-president of the Civic Federation of New England, which offered its services to both labor and management during a strike."

Brandeis was much sought-after as a speaker on labor-management issues. He debated Samuel Gompers, head of the American Federation of Labor, on the issue of whether unions ought to be incorporated. He argued that they should. The crux of the debate was the treatment of unions by courts. He agreed with Gompers that courts had not always treated unions fairly. But he believed that the alternative was "lawbreaking," and that the threat of legal liability and fines would make unions more cautious in their actions. Gompers disagreed. He argued, "What chance have labor and the laborers for fair play when the whole history of jurisprudence has been against the laborer? There never was a tyrant in the history of the world but who found some judge to clothe in judicial form the tyranny exercised and the cruelty imposed on the people." Although the debate was acrimonious at times, the parties did not separate as enemies, and later worked together on other labor matters.

Brandeis made legal history in the case *Muller v. Oregon.*[14] He accepted the position of cocounsel for the state of Oregon in a case involving Curt Muller, who operated a laundry in Portland. When Mrs. Elmer Gotcher was required to work more than ten hours a day in Muller's laundry, he was charged with violating an Oregon law limiting the hours of women to no more than ten. He was convicted, and the conviction was upheld by the Oregon Supreme Court. Muller then appealed to the U.S. Supreme Court. The National Consumer's League, which had been working for laws limiting women's working hours, became involved in the case. They asked Brandeis to represent them, which he agreed to do with two conditions: one, that he become an official counsel for the state, and two, that the league do extensive research and present him with facts necessary to support the claim that working long hours impaired the health of women. With those conditions agreed upon, he accepted the case *pro bono publico*—that is, for the public good.

The brief that Brandeis prepared for the case has become known as the Brandeis brief. It was over 100 pages long, with only two pages devoted to legal argument. The rest of the brief used the information gathered by the league and Brandeis to illustrate the effect upon the health and welfare of women who were required to work long hours.

At oral argument in the U.S. Supreme Court, Brandeis spent little time discussing the applicable law. Just a few years before, the Court had struck down a New York law limiting the hours of bakers.[15] He argued, however, that limiting working hours for women was entirely different. He spent the allotted time focusing the Court's attention on facts that pointed to the social problems involved in women's working long hours. The justices listened and agreed with him, and voted to uphold the Oregon law.

Politician

A friend brought Brandeis and Wisconsin Senator Robert La Follette together, and they became friends. La Follette was a progressive Republican, and his views with regard to the plight of the working man in the country's industrial revolution were shared by Brandeis. When La Follette decided to run for president in 1912, Brandeis became involved and campaigned for him. The campaign did not go well and lost steam.

Former president Theodore Roosevelt and William Howard Taft were fighting for the Republican nomination. When Taft was nominated, Roosevelt formed the Bull Moose Party and entered the campaign. The Democratic Party's nominee was Woodrow Wilson.

Brandeis believed that Wilson also shared his views concerning the problems confronting the laboring man, and he therefore urged fellow progressives to support him. When he wrote Wilson approving his position on tariffs, he immediately received an invitation to meet with the candidate. This meeting led to Brandeis's being recruited to campaign for the candidate, which he did, giving 20 speeches during the month of October 1912. Most of his progressive friends, however, stayed with Roosevelt, but Brandeis refused to let that interfere with their relationship.

After Wilson was elected president, there was much speculation that Brandeis would be given a cabinet post. He had, however, made many enemies in the business community. Ultimately his enemies prevailed, and no offer of a cabinet post was forthcoming. He did remain as an adviser to President Wilson and became a valuable part of the Wilson administration. "Woodrow Wilson owes part of his place in history to Brandeis," Philippa Strum has written.[16] She also points out, however, that "Brandeis also owed a great deal to Wilson. It was Wilson who gave him the opportunity to put some of his economic ideas into effect. The general knowledge that Brandeis was one of Wilson's trusted advisers added enormously to Brandeis' prestige and, ultimately, to his power."

Zionist

The Brandeises were not religious people in the sense of belonging to an organized religion. "I do not believe that sins can be expiated by going to divine service and observing this or that formula," Frederika once explained to Louis. "I believe that only goodness and truth and conduct that is humane and self-sacrificing towards those who need us can bring God nearer to us, and that our errors can only be atoned for by our acting in a more kindly spirit. Love, virtue and truth are the foundation upon which the education of the child must be based. They endure forever."[17] Because of this, there has been speculation how Brandeis became involved in the Zionist movement. The answer may lie in the influence that his uncle Lewis Dembitz had upon him. Dembitz, whom Brandeis held in high regard, was an Orthodox Jew and strictly observed its practices. Dembitz's involvement in Zionism was described to Brandeis by Jacob de Haas during a meeting they had at the Brandeis home. While the essence of the visit is not in dispute, whether it occurred in 1910 or 1912 is in question. Nevertheless, not only did de Haas tell about Dembitz's involvement, he also related his own participation in the movement. By 1914 Brandeis had become so interested in Zionism that he accepted the chairmanship of the new Provisional Executive Committee (PEC) for General Zionist Affairs. Some thought that Brandeis would not be an active chairman, but much to their surprise he immediately called a meeting to review the situation and create a plan of action. His take-charge attitude inspired others to action. Not only did he reorganize the PEC office, but he spoke throughout the country on the subject of Zionism. In 1915 he wrote his brother Alfred, "Things Jewish have been occupying my time largely ... Zionist affairs ... are really the important things in life now."[18]

All American Jews were not Zionists. The American Jewish Committee (AJC), for example, made up mostly of Reform Jews, was less than enthusiastic about developing a Jewish homeland. A dispute arose between the AJC and the Zionists over the organization of a conference to assist Jews in Europe, who now faced many problems because of the war going on there. Before the conflict could be resolved, Justice Joseph R. Lamar died, creating a vacancy on the Supreme Court. President Wilson nominated Brandeis to fill it.

Even after he became an associate justice, however, Brandeis continued to be active in the Zionist movement.

Nomination to the Supreme Court

Brandeis's nomination was met with shock, and it garnered much opposition. Author Strum notes: "The nomination was fought over by a subcommittee of the Senate Judiciary Committee ..., the Judiciary Committee itself, the entire Senate, the newspapers, and a host of combatants pulling one way or another behind the scenes. ... Brandeis' nomination was one of the most controversial in the history of the Supreme Court. The public charges by those opposed, the counter-charges by Brandeis supporters, the speculation about the behind-the-scenes maneuvering to affect Senators' votes—all make a lengthy and dramatic tale, which has been told elsewhere."[19]

There were several reasons the confirmation ran into trouble. If confirmed, Brandeis would be the first Jew to sit on the Court. He was considered to be a radical and against corporations because of the many cases he had against them. Even some members of the Jewish community opposed him, because, despite his Zionist activities, he had never been a part of the Jewish movement—he had never been "one of them."

Many lawyers also opposed Brandeis's confirmation, arguing that he had acted unethically in some of his cases. Seven past presidents of the American Bar Association signed a letter opposing the nomination. Nine other ABA past presidents, however, refused to sign the letter.

Despite the hearings, President Wilson did not retreat from the nomination. He received many letters, especially from labor, supporting Brandeis. One local mine union worker wrote, "Mr. Presedint, . . . at the lat regular meeting of Trades Council, a resolution was passed approving your nomenatition of attorney Brandeis for Supreme Court judge. Labor is Hartiley in favor of Mr. Brandeis and wont forget any favors wen the operunity presents itself."[20]

But the fight was far from over. Supporters urged the president to speak out, and he did by letter, giving strong support to the nominee. Charles Eliot, who had been president of Harvard at the time Brandeis received his law degree, also wrote a letter on behalf of the nominee. When the Judiciary Committee finally voted, it was strictly along party lines, ten Democrats for and eight Republicans against. The whole Senate then confirmed the nomination by a vote of 47–22. Brandeis was sworn in as justice on June 5, 1916.

Many of Brandeis's friends had mixed emotions about his appointment to the Supreme Court. Amos Pinchot wrote him that he was "sort of sorry" at losing him as an advocate for the people. "Taking it all together," Pinchot observed, "I don't think it is unfair to say that, for the last ten years, you have been the most vital and disturbing element in our public life. You have worked quietly, doing the unpopular things that reformers have talked or written about. . . . As long as you were in private life, it seemed to me that, if any monstrous injustice should be attempted upon helpless people, they would not lack protection."

Although the Brandeises were wealthy, they moved into a small apartment in Washington, and furnished it sparsely. At the beginning, they took part in the social activities to which they and the other justices and their families were invited. However, before long they began to refuse the invitations and entertained at small dinner parties at home. Alice began actively to manage her husband's time. She made and accepted his appointments, and saw to it that he got the rest he needed. Some of his clerks thought that she was overdoing it. One clerk thought that "she brooded over the justice like a mother hen."

Melvin I. Urofsky has summed up the Brandeis lifestyle:

> Certainly, the Brandeis family lived simply and far below the material style that his ample income could have provided. Brandeis just had little use for the frivolous or the merely decorative; in food, clothing, and shelter, he preferred the simple and utilitarian. He did not like telephones or automobiles and did not even want to own property; he only bought his summer home on Cape Cod because the owner, from whom he had previously rented, threatened to sell it to someone else. Dinner at the Brandeises was simple to the point of being spartan. Julian Mack, a lover of fine food, once commented that when you went to the Brandeises' for dinner you had to eat beforehand and then again afterward.[21]

Brandeis joined the Court on June 5, 1916. At the time Edward Douglas White was chief justice. The other justices were Joseph McKenna, Oliver Wendell Holmes, Jr., William R. Day, Charles Evans Hughes, Willis Van Devanter, Mahlon Pitney, and James Clark McReynolds. Hughes resigned on June 10 and was replaced by John H. Clarke.

AS ASSOCIATE JUSTICE (1916-39)

The Free Exercise of Religion

Rosika Schwimmer, a native of Hungary, petitioned to become a United States citizen in 1926.[22] One of the questions she was asked was "If necessary, are you willing to take up arms in defense of this country?" She responded, "I would not take up arms personally." By way of explanation, she testified, "If . . . the United States can compel its women citizens to take up arms in the defense of the country—something that no other civilized government has ever attempted—I would not be able to comply with this requirement of American citizenship. In this case I would recognize the right of the government to deal with me as it is dealing with its male citizens who for conscientious reasons refuse to take up arms." She said that she was "an uncompromising pacifist." A federal district court denied her citizenship, which the circuit court of appeals reversed. A majority of the Supreme Court disagreed and reinstated the decision of the district court. Justice Pierce Butler authored the Court's opinion. He said, "That it is the duty of citizens by force of arms to defend our government against all enemies whenever necessity arises is a fundamental principle of the Constitution." He was also concerned, however, that Schwimmer may be a person "who is without any sense of nationalism [and therefore] is not well bound or held by the ties of affection to any nation or government." He pointed out that during World War I some of those who were drafted into the service, and who claimed to be conscientious objectors, "were convicted and sentenced to imprisonment for offenses involving disobedience, desertion, propaganda and sedition." This led him to the conclusion that the district court was correct in denying citizenship. The free exercise of religion played no part in the Court's decision. Justices Holmes, Brandeis, and Sanford dissented.

Writing for himself and Brandeis, Holmes characterized Schwimmer as "an optimist." She "states in strong and, I do not doubt, sincere words her belief that war will disappear and that the impending destiny of mankind is to unite in peaceful leagues. I do not share that optimism nor do I think that a philosophic view of the world would regard war as absurd." Referring to her testimony, Holmes wrote, "Some of her answers might excite popular prejudice, but if there is any principle of the Constitution that more imperatively calls for attachment than any other it is the principle of free thought—not free thought for those who agree with us but freedom for the thought we hate. I think that we should adhere to that principle with regard to admission into, as well as to life within this country."

In 1931 a majority of the justices upheld the denial of citizenship of Douglas Clyde Macintosh, who said he would be willing to take up arms, "but I should want to be free to judge of the necessity."[23] This was interpreted to mean that he would be willing to take up arms only in wars he deemed morally justified.

Chief Justice Hughes dissented in an opinion that Brandeis joined. For the chief justice and Brandeis this was a case where one's belief in God should take precedence over the requirement to take up arms. "If . . . ," Hughes declared, "the mere holding of religious or conscientious scruples against all wars should not disqualify a citizen from holding office in this country, or an applicant otherwise qualified from being admitted to citizenship, there would seem to be no reason why a reservation of religious or conscientious objection to participation in wars believed to be unjust should constitute such a disqualification."

Justice Brandeis voted to deny Albert W. Hamilton and W. Alonzo Reynolds, Jr., admission to the University of California because they refused to enroll in compulsory courses in military training.[24] He joined Justice Cardozo's concurring opinion, which discussed at length the conflict between religious beliefs and the needs of government. "Instruction in military science," Cardozo asserted, "is not an interference by the state with the free exercise of religion when the liberties of the constitution are read in the light of a century and a half of history during days of peace and war."

Freedom of Speech

Pamphleteering. In 1919 Brandeis voted for the imprisonment of three persons, Schenck, Frohwerk, and Debs, for voicing their opposition to the draft, which was in effect during World War I.[25] In discussing the First Amendment rights of Schenck, Justice Holmes, who wrote the opinion in all three cases, coined a phrase that has been quoted many times since. "The most stringent protection of free speech," he declared, "would not protect a man in falsely shouting fire in a theatre and causing a panic." By this statement, Holmes was pointing out that at some point speech is no longer free and can be the subject of a criminal offense. A speech has reached that point when the words "create a clear and present danger that they will bring about the substantive evils that Congress [government] has a right to prevent."

Furthermore, when the country is at war, "many things that might be said in time of peace are such a hindrance to its effort that their utterance will not be endured so long as men fight."

Even if one agrees that there is a point at which speech may be so harmful to the public interest that the government should be able to punish the speaker, there was no evidence in these cases that the circulars and or speeches made by the defendants had disrupted or were likely to disrupt the draft.

In *Louis D. Brandeis, Justice for the People,* Philippa Strum wrote about Brandeis's concurring in the *Schenck* case: "Brandeis later regretted having voted to uphold the conviction, telling Frankfurter, 'I have never been quite happy about my concurrence . . . I had not then thought the issues of freedom of speech out—I thought at the subject, not through it.' "[26] Strum speculated that Brandeis probably thought the same about his concurrence in *Frohwerk*. Maybe he also felt that way about *Debs*.

A Mr. Abrams and four other individuals, all of whom were Russian citizens living in the United States in 1918, printed several pamphlets protesting U.S. participation in the war then going on in Europe.[27] The circulars were anti-captalism; they urged other Russian emigrants not to work in factories producing war materiel, condemned the U.S. involvement in the war, and urged the Russian workers to unite and take up arms against the government. They called themselves "Revolutionists" and "The Rebels." All were arrested and charged

> with conspiring, when the United States was at war with the Imperial Government of Germany, to unlawfully utter, write, and publish: . . . "disloyal, scurrilous and abusive language about the form of Government of the United States; . . . to bring the form of Government of the United States into contempt, scorn, contumely and disrepute;. . . to incite, provoke and encourage resistance to the United States in said war; . . . [and to] unlawfully and willfully, by utterance, writing, printing and publication, to urge, incite and advocate curtailment of production of things and products, to wit, ordnance and ammunition, necessary and essential to the prosecution of the war."

All were convicted and appealed to the Supreme Court, which upheld the convictions. Justices Holmes and Brandeis dissented. The majority summarily dismissed the argument that the defendants were protected by the First Amendment. The *Schenck* and *Frohwerk* cases, they said, "definitely negatived" any such conclusion.

Holmes and Brandeis, in dissent, were of the opinion that so long as the defendants had not committed any specific act against the government their writings were protected. "In these cases," Holmes protested, "sentences of twenty years imprisonment have been imposed for the publishing of two leaflets that I believe the defendants had as much right to publish as the Government has to publish the Constitution of the United States now vainly invoked by them."

Holmes then discusses the philosophy behind constitutional protection for speech:

> But when men have realized that time has upset many fighting faiths, they may come to believe even more than they believe the very foundations of their own conduct that the ultimate good desired is better reached by free trade in ideas— that the best test of truth is the power of thought to get itself accepted in the competition of the market, and that truth is the only ground upon which their wishes safely can be carried out. That at any rate is the theory of our Constitution.

In *Pierce v. United States*,[28] Pierce, Creo, and Zeilman were found guilty of distributing a pamphlet entitled "The Price We Pay," written by Irwin St. John Tucker, an Episcopal clergyman. The defendants were members of the Socialist Party, and had obtained the circular from that organization's national office.

Justice Mahlon Pitney, in upholding the convictions, described the pamphlet as follows: "The pamphlet—'The Price We Pay'—was a highly colored and sensational document, issued by the national office of the Socialist Party at Chicago, Illinois, and fairly to be construed as a protest against the further prosecution of the war by the United States. It contained much in the way of denunciation of war in general, the pending war in particular; something in the way of assertion that under Socialism things would be better; little or nothing in the way of fact or argument to support the assertion."

In upholding the conviction, the majority, relying upon *Schenck, Frohwerk,* and *Debs,* dismissed the defendants' First Amendment claims. This disturbed Brandeis and Holmes, who dissented. This time Brandeis wrote their dissenting opinion. He argued that the government did not prove that the information in the pamphlet was false; that even if it was false, the defendants did not know that as they did not print it; and that there was no proof that the defendants conspired to "cause insubordination, disloyalty, mutiny, or refusal of duty, in the military or naval forces." But their main concern was that the defendants were being sent to prison for the exercise of their First Amendment rights. Brandeis declared:

> The fundamental right of free men to strive for better conditions through new legislation and new institutions will not be preserved, if efforts to secure it by argument to fellow citizens may be construed as criminal incitement to disobey the existing law—merely, because the argument presented seems to those exercising judicial power to be unfair in its portrayal of existing evils, mistaken in its

assumptions, unsound in reasoning or intemperate in language. No objections more serious than these can, in my opinion, reasonably be made to the arguments presented in "The Price We Pay."

Peaceful Picketing. It was not until after Brandeis retired in 1939 that the Court held peaceful picketing to be protected by the First Amendment.[29] His opinion in *Senn v. Tile Layers Union*[30] indicates that he would have agreed with that decision. At issue in *Senn* was the validity of a Wisconsin labor law that made "peaceful picketing or patrolling" legal.

Paul Senn owned a small tile contracting business with a few employees. The Tile Layers Protective Union sought to unionize Senn's business, but because the agreement provided that he as the owner could not do tile work, he refused to sign. When the union began to picket the business, Senn brought an action against them seeking to enjoin the picketing. Relying upon the Wisconsin statute, Judge Otto H. Breidenbach held that the picketing was legal and dismissed the action. The Wisconsin Supreme Court affirmed, as did the U.S. Supreme Court.

Senn contended that forcing unionization of his business would prevent him from working and thus infringe upon his right to liberty which was protected by the Due Process Clause of the Fourteenth Amendment, and that therefore, the picketing was unconstitutional. The majority disagreed. "If the end sought by the unions," Justice Brandeis declared, "is not forbidden by the Federal Constitution the State may authorize working men to seek to attain it by combining as pickets, just as it permits capitalists and employers to combine in other ways to attain their desired economic ends." Brandeis also said that "members of a union might, without special statutory authorization by a State, make known the facts of a labor dispute, for freedom of speech is guaranteed by the Federal Constitution." He therefore recognized the First Amendment rights of the union members, but did not specifically say that picketing itself was a form of speech.

Advocacy of Unpopular Ideas. Joseph Gilbert made a speech on August 18, 1917, condemning U.S. participation in the war in Europe, and very critical of the American democratic system of government. Among the statements he made were: "We are going over to Europe to make the world safe for democracy, but I tell you we had better make America safe for democracy first"; "If this is such a great democracy, for Heaven's sake why should we not vote on conscription of men"; "I tell you if they conscripted wealth like they have conscripted men, this war would not last over forty-eight hours."[31] Gilbert was arrested and charged with violating a Minnesota statute that made it a crime for any person "to advocate or teach by word of mouth or otherwise that men should not enlist in the military or naval forces." He was convicted and his conviction was upheld by the Minnesota Supreme Court and the U.S. Supreme Court. Justice Joseph McKenna wrote the opinion for the majority. Although he did not hold that the

First Amendment was applicable to this case, he conceded that freedom of speech "is natural and inherent." But he also pointed out that "it is not absolute, [and] it is subject to restriction and limitation." In this case "restriction and limitation" was justified because "the Nation was at war with Germany, armies were recruiting, and the speech was the discouragement of that—its purpose was necessarily the discouragement of that." He concluded that it "would be a travesty on the constitutional privilege he invokes to assign him its protection."

Justice Brandeis disagreed. He was of the opinion that the statute "abridges freedom of speech and of the press, not in a particular emergency, in order to avert a clear and present danger, but under all circumstances." But the justice went further. He believed that the right to speak freely was a right "guaranteed protection by the Federal Constitution" and was "invaded by the statute in question." "The right to speak freely concerning functions of the Federal Government," he asserted, "is a privilege or immunity of every citizen of the United States which, even before the adoption of the Fourteenth Amendment, a State was powerless to curtail." He then reviews prior decisions of the Court interpreting the word *liberty* in the Due Process Clause. These included cases where the Court upheld the right to work, to conduct a business, and to contract. "I cannot believe," he concluded, "that the liberty guaranteed by the Fourteenth Amendment includes only liberty to acquire and to enjoy property."

Brandeis voted with the majority to overturn the conviction of a Mr. Herndon who was a member of the Kentucky Communist Party. Herndon had gone to Atlanta, Georgia, where he conducted meetings and distributed material about the Party. He was arrested and convicted of attempting to incite an insurrection.[32] In reversing the conviction, the Court, speaking through Justice Owen J. Roberts, said, "If the evidence fails to show that he did so incite, then, as applied to him, the statute unreasonably limits freedom of speech and freedom of assembly and violates the Fourteenth Amendment. We are of the opinion that the requisite proof is lacking."

Freedom of Association and Assembly

In 1958 the Court held that "it is beyond debate that freedom to engage in association for the advancement of beliefs and ideas is an inseparable aspect of the 'liberty' assured by the Due Process Clause of the Fourteenth Amendment, which embraces freedom of speech."[33] That was long after Brandeis had left the Court, of course, but he did have something to say about associational rights in the case of *Whitney v. California.*[34]

Charlotte Whitney, who had been a member of the Socialist Party in California, became disenchanted with the Party and left it to assist in the formation of the Communist Labor Party of America. She played an active role in the new party's organizing convention, and served on its credentials and resolutions committees. She read the following resolution at the convention: "The C.L.P. of

California proclaims and insists that the capture of political power, locally or nationally by the revolutionary working class can be of tremendous assistance to the workers in their struggle of emancipation." As a result, she was elected an alternate member of the State Executive Committee.

Whitney was arrested and charged with the crime of criminal syndicalism, a crime described as "any doctrine or precept advocating, teaching or aiding and abetting the commission of crime, sabotage . . . or unlawful acts of force and violence or unlawful methods of terrorism as a means of accomplishing a change in industrial ownership or control, or effecting any political change." A person was guilty of this crime if he or she organized or assisted in organizing any association that "assembled to advocate, teach or aid and abet criminal syndicalism." Whitney was convicted, and the conviction was upheld by the California Court of Appeal and by the United States Supreme Court. The majority opinion, written by Justice Edward T. Sanford, concluded that the statute was not a violation of the "rights of free speech, assembly, and association." "The essence of the offense denounced by the Act," he asserted, "is the combining with others in an association for accomplishment of the desired ends through the advocacy and use of criminal and unlawful methods. It partakes of the nature of a criminal conspiracy."

Justice Brandeis wrote a concurring opinion in which Justice Holmes joined. He pointed out that the "right of free speech, to teach and the right of assembly are, of course, fundamental rights. . . . These may not be denied or abridged. But, although the rights of free speech and assembly are fundamental, they are not in their nature absolute." In a very memorable way, he then philosophizes about what our forebears intended this country to be:

> Those who won our independence by revolution were not cowards. They did not fear political change. They did not exalt order at the cost of liberty. To courageous, self-reliant men, with confidence in the power of free and fearless reasoning applied through the processes of popular government, no danger flowing from speech can be deemed clear and present, unless the incidence of the evil apprehended is so imminent that it may befall before there is opportunity for full discussion. If there be time to expose through discussion the falsehood and fallacies, to avert the evil by the processes of education, the remedy to be applied is more speech, not enforced silence. Only an emergency can justify repression. Such must be the rule if authority is to be reconciled with freedom. Such, in my opinion, is the command of the Constitution. It is therefore always open to Americans to challenge a law abridging free speech and assembly by showing that there was no emergency justifying it. . . . Among free men, the deterrents ordinarily to be applied to prevent crime are education and punishment for violations of the law, not abridgment of the rights of free speech and assembly.

Brandeis took issue with the majority opinion by declaring that he was "unable to assent to the suggestion in the opinion of the Court that assembling with a political party, formed to advocate the desirability of a proletarian revolution by mass action at some date necessarily far in the future, is not a right within the protection of the Fourteenth Amendment."

The justice voted with the majority to convict Whitney, however, because "there was other testimony which tended to establish the existence of a conspiracy, on the part of members of the International Workers of the World, to commit present serious crimes; and likewise to show that such a conspiracy would be furthered by the activity of the society of which Miss Whitney was a member."

On the same day the *Whitney* case was decided, Brandeis voted to reverse the conviction of a Mr. Fiske for violating the Kansas criminal syndicalism statute. Fiske had been soliciting membership in the Workers Industrial Union, a branch of the Industrial Workers of the World. The jury had concluded "that the Industrial Workers of the World was an organization that taught criminal syndicalism."[35] But the Court could find no evidence in the record "that the organization in which he [Fiske] secured members advocated any crime, violence or other unlawful acts or methods as a means of effecting industrial or political changes or revolution."

Brandeis and the Court saw sufficient danger from the Ku Klux Klan, however, to override a Mr. Bryant's First Amendment rights when they refused to free him on a writ of *habeas corpus*.[36] Bryant, a Klan member, was charged with violating a New York statute requiring any member to file the organization's "constitution, by-laws, rules, regulations and oath of membership, together with a roster of its membership and a list of its officers for the current year."

Bryant had refused to comply with the law, arguing that the statute deprived "him of liberty in that it prevents him from exercising his right of membership in the association." The Court disagreed. It found no violation of equal protection, because the Ku Klux Klan was not the same kind of association as were the Odd Fellows, Masonic Lodge, or the Knights of Columbus.

When the Court decided *N.A.A.C.P. v. Alabama* in 1958, the justices also agreed that the Ku Klux Klan was a different kind of association from the National Association for the Advancement of Colored People.[37]

Ten years after the decision in *Whitney*, the Court decided *De Jonge v. Oregon*[38] (discussed in Chapter 2). Brandeis joined the Court in reversing De Jonge's conviction. Chief Justice Hughes wrote:

> The greater the importance of safeguarding the community from incitements to the overthrow of our institutions by force and violence, the more imperative is the need to preserve inviolate the constitutional rights of free speech, free press and free assembly in order to maintain the opportunity for free political discussion, to the end that government may be responsive to the will of the people and that changes, if desired, may be obtained by peaceful means. Therein lies the security of the Republic, the very foundation of constitutional government.

And no matter what the objectives of the Communist Party were, "the defendant [De Jonge] still enjoyed his personal right of free speech and to take part in a peaceable assembly having a lawful purpose, although called by that Party." Brandeis agreed.

Freedom of the Press

Prosecution for Publication. "To hold that such harmless additions to or omissions from news items, and such impotent expressions of editorial opinion, as were shown here, can afford the basis even of a prosecution will doubtless discourage criticism of the policies of the Government. To hold that such publications can be suppressed as false reports, subjects to new perils the constitutional liberty of the press, already seriously curtailed in practice under powers assumed to have been conferred upon the postal authorities."[39] With those words, Justices Brandeis and Holmes dissented from the Court's decision affirming the convictions of Darkow, the news editor, Werner, the editor, and Lemke, the business manager, of the *Philadelphia Tageblatt* and the *Philadelphia Sonntagsblatt.*

In justification of the affirmance of these convictions, the majority said that the "charges of the indictment were against certain articles or editorials in the newspapers published by defendants in German and intended to be circulated in families and read by persons who understood that language. The articles were adapted to the situation and, we may say, allusion and innuendo could be as effective as direct charge and 'coarse or heavy humor' when accompanied by sneering headlines and derision of America's efforts could have evil influence."

Second-Class Mail Privileges. The powers assumed by the postal authorities over the press came before the Court in *Milwaukee Pub. Co. v. Burleson.*[40] After postal authorities had revoked the second-class mail privilege of the *Milwaukee Leader,* its owner brought an action against the postmaster general seeking reinstatement of the privilege. The trial court dismissed the action, and both the court of appeals and the Supreme Court affirmed. The postal authorities justified the revocation because the *Leader* published articles critical of the war effort, calling it a "capitalistic war." The paper also opposed the draft, called the president an "autocrat" and Congress a "rubber stamp Congress."

A majority of the Court, however, agreed that the postal authorities had broad authority with regard to postal privileges, and that it was correct in its decision in this case. "Freedom of the press," Justice John H. Clarke declared, "may protect criticism and agitation for modification or repeal of laws, but it does not extend to protection of him who counsels and encourages the violation of the law as it exists. The Constitution was adopted to preserve our Government, not to serve as a protecting screen for those who while claiming its privileges seek to destroy it."

Justice Brandeis saw the matter differently and dissented. He first pointed out that the publisher of the paper had never been charged or convicted of violating the espionage law. He also argued that Congress had not given the postmaster general the authority "to deny second-class rates to future issues of a newspaper because in his opinion it had systematically violated the Espionage Act in the past." Even if Congress had given such authority, that would be unconstitutional. "Congress may not through its postal power," he asserted, "put limitations upon the freedom of the press which if directly attempted would be unconstitutional." And he quotes from *Ex Parte Jackson*,[41] an 1878 case, to the effect that "liberty of circulating is as essential to that freedom as liberty of publishing; indeed, without the circulation, the publication would be of little value." Furthermore, Brandeis argued, it would be dangerous to freedom of the press if mail rates were merely privileges that could be denied "to those whose views . . . [Congress] deems to be against public policy."

Publication of Unpopular Ideas. Benjamin Gitlow was a member of the Left Wing Section of the Socialist Party in New York. He was charged and convicted of criminal anarchy, which New York law defined as "the doctrine that organized government should be overthrown by force or violence, or by assassination of the executive head . . . of the government."[42] His conviction was upheld by the New York Court of Appeals and by a majority of the Supreme Court, with Holmes and Brandeis dissenting. As a member of the party's National Council, Gitlow assisted in the publication of "The Left Wing Manifesto" and "The Revolutionary Age." Among other things, the manifesto "advocated in plain and unequivocal language, the necessity of accomplishing the 'Communist Revolution' by a militant and 'revolutionary Socialism,' based on 'class struggle' and mobilizing the 'power of the proletariat in action,' through mass industrial revolts developing into mass political strikes and 'revolutionary mass action,' for the purpose of conquering and destroying the parliamentary state."

Gitlow argued: "1st, That the 'liberty' protected by the Fourteenth Amendment includes the liberty of speech and of the press; and 2nd, That while liberty of expression 'is not absolute,' it may be restrained 'only in circumstances where its exercise bears a causal relation with some substantive evil, consummated, attempted or likely,' and as the statute 'takes no account of circumstances,' it unduly restrains this liberty and is therefore unconstitutional."

The Court agreed that the First Amendment is included within the word *liberty* in the Fourteenth Amendment and that therefore states are prohibited from infringing upon the individual's freedom of religion, speech, press, and assembly. However, it "does not protect publications prompting the overthrow of government by force." "That utterances inciting to the overthrow of organized government by unlawful means," the Court said, "present a sufficient danger of substantive evil to bring their punishment within the range of legislative discretion, is clear. Such utterances, by their very nature, involve danger to the public peace and to the security of the State." The Court then concluded that Gitlow did not have to urge people to commit any specific or immediate act. "It was sufficient if such acts were advocated in general terms," the Court wrote, "and it was not essential that their immediate execution should have been advocated."

Holmes, writing for himself and Justice Brandeis, said that the conviction should be reversed. He pointed out that in the *Schenck* case he had written, "The question in every case is whether the words used are used in such circumstances and are of such a nature as to create a clear and present danger that they will bring about the substantive evils that [the State] has a right to prevent." Applying that test to what Gitlow had published, it was clear "that there was no present danger of an attempt to overthrow the government by force on the part of the admittedly small minority who shared the defendant's views." In response to the government's argument that the publications were an incitement, Holmes asserted:

> Every idea is an incitement. It offers itself for belief and if believed it is acted on unless some other belief outweighs it or some failure of energy stifles the movement at its birth. The only difference between the expression of an opinion and an incitement in the narrower sense is the speaker's enthusiasm for the result. Eloquence may set fire to reason. But whatever may be thought of the redundant discourse before us it had no chance of starting a present conflagration. If in the long run the beliefs expressed in proletarian dictatorship are destined to be accepted by the dominant forces of the community, the only meaning of free speech is that they should be given their chance and have their way.

Brandeis joined Chief Justice Hughes and the majority in *Near v. Minnesota*, which struck down an injunction against *The Saturday Press*, and in *Lovell v. Griffin*, wherein the Court upheld the right of Alma Lovell to distribute leaflets on a public street.

The Pursuit of Liberty

The Rights of Parents. "His right to teach and the right of parents to engage him so to instruct their children, we think, are within the liberty of the Amendment."[43] With those words the Court, with Brandeis concurring, gave birth to the meaning of the word *liberty* in the Due Process Clause of the Fourteenth Amendment, a meaning which was eventually to encompass a right of privacy, about which much more will be said later.

Robert T. Meyer, a teacher, was convicted of teaching the German language to ten-year-old Raymond Parpart in violation of a Nebraska statute that prohibited teaching any language other than English to students below the ninth grade. "The obvious purpose of this statute," the state supreme court said, "was that the English language should be and become the mother tongue of all children reared in this state." But the U.S. supreme court was concerned about the statute's effect upon "the liberty guaranteed ... by the Fourteenth Amendment." The Court noted that it had never given a precise definition to the word *liberty*. "Without doubt," Justice James Clark McReynolds declared, "it denotes not merely freedom from bodily restraint but also the right of the individual to contract, to engage in any of the common occupations of life, to acquire useful knowledge, to marry, establish a home and bring up children, to worship God according to the dictates of his own conscience, and generally enjoy those privileges long recognized at common law as essential to the orderly pursuit of happiness by free men." Liberty, therefore, includes the right of the teacher to teach, and the right of the parents to have him teach the German language to their children. Meyer's conviction, therefore, was reversed.

Shortly after the *Meyer* case, the right of parents to control the education of their children came before the Court again in a slightly different setting, in the case of *Pierce v. Society of Sisters*.[44] At issue in that case was an Oregon statute that required "every parent, guardian or other person having control or charge or custody of a child between eight and sixteen years to send him 'to a public school.'" The Sisters conducted primary schools in Oregon that taught the same courses offered in the public schools. As a result of the law, parents began to withdraw their children from the Sisters' schools. The Hill Military Academy, which conducted classes through the first 12 grades, also found its enrollment shrinking. The Sisters and the academy brought actions against Walter M. Pierce, the governor of Oregon, claiming that the statute violated their right to teach and parents' right to have their children taught in a private school setting. The case was heard by Federal District judges Charles E. Wolverton and Robert S. Bean and by Circuit Judge William B. Gilbert. Relying upon the *Meyer* case as authority, the judges ruled that the state law was unconstitutional as a violation of due process. Judge Wolverton wrote for the court that the legislature had "exceeded the limitations of its power—its purpose being to take utterly away from complainants their constitutional right and privilege to teach in the grammar grades—and has and will deprive them of their property without due process of law."[45]

The governor appealed to the Supreme Court, but the result was the same. Justice James Clark McReynolds authored the Court's opinion, which Brandeis joined. Justice McReynolds wrote, "Under the doctrine of *Meyer v. Nebraska*, ... we think it entirely plain that the Act of 1922 unreasonably interferes with the liberty of parents and guardians to direct the upbringing and education of children under their control."[46] Furthermore, the rights of the Sisters and the academy were also being infringed upon here. Taking note of the fact that the property and business of the institutions were at risk, McReynolds wrote, "These are threatened with destruction through the unwarranted compulsion which ... [the state is] exercising over present and prospective patrons of their schools."

Equal Protection of the Law

Brandeis's strong commitment to the rights of black people is found in his concurrences in the cases that came before him.

Where Blacks Live. The first of these cases is *Buchanan v. Warley.*[47] Buchanan, a white man, sold a piece of property to Warley, who was black, and who intended to build a house on it. The contract for sale provided that Warley would not have to complete the purchase unless he had a right to occupy the property as his residence. Buchanan sued Warley demanding specific performance. Warley's defense was that he would not be able to occupy the property because an ordinance of the city of Louisville, Kentucky, made it unlawful for a black person to have a home in any block where most of the houses were occupied by white persons. In the block in question, there were eight white families and two black families.

Buchanan countered with the argument that the ordinance violated the Fourteenth Amendment and therefore was unconstitutional. The Kentucky courts disagreed, upheld the ordinance, and approved judgment for Warley. A unanimous Supreme Court, including Brandeis, reversed, with Justice William R. Day writing the opinion for the Court.

Noting that the Fourteenth Amendment protects "life, liberty, and property from invasion by the States without due process of law," Justice Day wrote, "Property is more than the mere thing which a person owns. It is elementary that it includes the right to acquire, use, and dispose of it. The Constitution protects these essential attributes of property."

The Justice reviewed the enactment and purposes of the War Amendments (the Thirteenth, Fourteenth, and Fifteenth Amendments) and the cases decided by the Court since their adoption. He acknowledged that there "exists a serious and difficult problem arising from a feeling of race hostility which the law is powerless to control, and to which it must give a measure of consideration." But that's not what this case was about. "The case presented," he asserted, "does not deal with an attempt to prohibit the amalgamation of the races. The right which the ordinance annulled was the civil right of a white man to dispose of his property if he saw fit to do so to a person of color and of a colored person to make such disposition to a white person." He concluded that the ordinance was not a proper exercise of governmental power and was "in direct violation of the fundamental law enacted in the Fourteenth Amendment of the Constitution preventing state interference with property rights except by due process of law."

While Brandeis concurred in the opinion and the result in the *Buchanan* case, which struck down a law preventing black persons from buying property in a block occupied predominantly by whites, he also voted with the majority to uphold the right of a white man to enforce a restrictive covenant against another owner selling to a black person.[48] In 1948, however, the Court held that private property owners could no longer use the courts to enforce restrictive covenants. This makes such covenants virtually unenforceable today.

Blacks Have a Right to Vote. When L.A. Nixon, a black man, attempted to vote in the Democratic primary election in Texas in 1924, he was prohibited from doing so by the judges of election, who were acting pursuant to a law that declared blacks ineligible to vote.[49] Nixon brought an action against the judges, which was dismissed by the trial court. A unanimous Supreme Court reversed, with Justice Holmes writing the opinion, in which Brandeis concurred. The Court based its decision on the Fourteenth Amendment's Equal Protection Clause. "We find it unnecessary to consider the Fifteenth Amendment," Holmes argued, "because it seems to us hard to imagine a more direct and obvious infringement of the Fourteenth. That Amendment, while it applies to all, was passed, as we know, with a special intent to protect the blacks from discrimination against them." He concluded by stating that "color cannot be made the basis of a statutory classification affecting the right [to vote] set up in this case."

After this case was decided, the Texas legislature amended the law to provide that "every political party in this State through its State Executive Committee shall have the power to prescribe the qualifications of its own members and shall in its own way determine who shall be qualified to vote."[50] At the next primary election, Nixon again attempted to vote, but was again prevented from doing so because the State Executive Committee had adopted a rule that only white people could vote. Nixon brought another action against the judges of election, which action was dismissed by Judge Charles A. Boynton. He appealed to the Supreme Court, which again reversed. This time the opinion was written by Justice Cardozo, with Justice Brandeis voting with the majority.

The Democratic Party argued that, as a voluntary association separate from the state, it could choose its members and was not bound by the Constitution. The Court agreed that if the party was indeed totally free of state control, it would be free to determine its membership, and, if it desired to do so, to discriminate. But in this case, the Court pointed out, the authority of the Executive Committee to choose who shall vote was given by the state legislature; therefore, the state was involved in the discrimination. "Whatever power of exclusion has been exercised by the members of the committee," Cardozo pointed out, "has come to them, . . . not as the delegates of the party, but as the delegates of the State." Furthermore, Cardozo declared, "Whether in given circumstances parties or their committees are agencies of government within the Fourteenth or the Fifteenth Amendment is a question which this court will determine for itself." Brandeis agreed.

Blacks on Juries. Alfred Scott Aldridge, a black man, was about to be tried for murder in the first degree in the Supreme Court of the District of Columbia. His lawyer requested permission from the trial judge to ask prospective jurors whether they held any prejudice against black people. The judge refused the request, and Aldridge was convicted. The circuit court affirmed, being of the opinion that because blacks enjoyed all of the same privileges as whites in the District of Columbia, the trial judge was correct in not granting the defendant's request. The Supreme Court reversed, with Justice Brandeis voting with the majority, and only Justice George Sutherland dissenting.[51]

Chief Justice Hughes authored the majority opinion. In response to the circuit court's reference to the alleged equality of blacks in the District, he wrote, "But the question is not as to the civil privileges of the negro, or as to the dominant sentiment of the community and the general absence of any disqualifying prejudice, but as to the bias of the particular jurors who are to try the accused." The government, however, argued that "it would be detrimental to the administration of the law in the courts of the United States to allow questions to jurors as to racial or religious prejudices." Hughes's answer was: "We think that it would be far more injurious to permit it to be thought that persons entertaining a disqualifying prejudice were allowed to serve as jurors and that inquiries designed to elicit the fact of disqualification were barred."

Brandeis voted with the majority to reverse convictions in several other cases where blacks had been systematically excluded from juries.[52]

Separate but Equal Schools. As indicated in chapters 1 and 2, the Court had accepted the principle that states could fulfill their equal protection obligation by providing separate but equal facilities.[53] The Court, with all justices, including Brandeis, concurring, continued to follow that doctrine in the case of Martha Lum, a nine-year-old American citizen of Chinese descent.[54] On the opening day of school, Martha went to the white high school in the district in which she lived. Before the end of the day, she was told that she could not return to that school because she was not of the white race. Martha brought an action asking the court to order the school district to admit her, which it did. However, upon appeal, the Mississippi Supreme Court reversed. When Martha's case reached the U.S. Supreme Court, Chief Justice William Howard Taft said that the question before the Court was whether the state was according Martha "equal protection of the laws by giving her the opportunity for a common school education in a school which receives only colored children of the brown, yellow or black races." The chief justice gave an affirmative answer, concluding that as long as a state was permitted to establish separate but equal schools for white and black students, it was certainly permissible to assign Martha to the black school.

The Court had another opportunity to dispose of the separate but equal doctrine in the *Gaines* case (discussed in Chapter 2) but did not do so. "We are of the opinion," Chief Justice Hughes wrote, "that . . . [Gaines] was entitled to be admitted to the law school of the State University [of Missouri] in the absence of other and proper provision for his legal training within the State."[55]

The separate but equal doctrine was overruled in 1954 in *Brown v. Board of Education*,[56] when the Court unanimously held that segregated schools violated the Equal Protection Clause of the Fourteenth Amendment.

Citizenship and Due Process of Law

"That the government of the United States," Justice Stephen J. Field wrote, "through the action of the legislative department, can exclude aliens from its territory, is a proposition which we do not think open to controversy."[57]

Congress, in exercising the power over aliens, has passed very comprehensive legislation covering immigration into the United States, most of which has been upheld by the Supreme Court as against constitutional challenge. The Court, for example, has held that due process does not require a judicial trial before a person can be prevented from entering the country. Due process is satisfied even when the person claims U.S. citizenship, and the decision to exclude is made by an executive officer rather than by a court.[58] The Court, however, speaking through Justice Brandeis, has said that due process does require a judicial proceeding when the government attempts to exclude persons who claim citizenship, and are residing in the country at the time. Such was the case of Gin Sang Get and Gin Sang Mo.[59]

When Gin Sang Get and Gin Sang Mo arrived in San Francisco from China, and claimed U.S. citizenship, they were given a hearing before immigration officials. The officials then "ordered them admitted as citizens." Several months later, Get and Mo were arrested in Arizona, where they were living, and ordered deported by an executive officer. No other hearing was held concerning their right to remain in the United States. When the case reached the Supreme Court, it unanimously agreed that Get and Mo were entitled to a judicial trial. Justice Brandeis framed the question this way: "Does the claim of citizenship by a *resident,* so supported both before the immigration officer and upon petition for writ of habeas corpus, entitle him to a judicial trial of this claim?"[60] In giving an affirmative answer, Brandeis pointed out that to "deport one who so claims to be a citizen, obviously deprives him of liberty. . . . It may result also in loss of both property and life; or of all that makes life worth living. Against the danger of such deprivation without the sanction afforded by judicial proceedings, the Fifth Amendment affords protection in its guarantee of due process of law."

The Bill of Rights and the States

In *Palko v. Connecticut,*[61] Justice Cardozo addressed the question whether the Fourteenth Amendment required states to abide by certain provisions of the Bill of Rights. In acknowledging that the amendment does require states to abide by some parts of the Bill of Rights, he pointed out that "if the Fourteenth Amendment has absorbed them, the process of absorption has had its source in the belief that neither liberty nor justice would exist if they were sacrificed."

This "absorption process" best describes Justice Brandeis's approach to this issue. In referring to the Minnesota statute in *Gilbert's* case, which made certain kinds of advocacy a criminal offense, the Justice wrote, "It affects rights, privileges and immunities of one who is a citizen of the United States; and it deprives him of an important part of his liberty. These are rights which are guaranteed protection by the Federal Constitution; and they are invaded by the statute in question."[62] While he does not specifically say that freedom of speech is applicable to the states through the Fourteenth Amendment, he ends his dissent by stating: "I cannot believe that the liberty guaranteed by the Fourteenth Amendment includes only liberty to acquire and to enjoy property."

By the time *Whitney* came to the Court, it is clear that for Brandeis the "absorption" of the First Amendment into the Fourteenth Amendment, and thereby making it applicable to the states, was complete.

> Despite arguments to the contrary which had seemed to me persuasive, it is settled that the due process clause of the Fourteenth Amendment applies to matters of substantive law as well as to matters of procedure. Thus all fundamental rights comprised within the term liberty are protected by the Federal Constitution from invasion by the States. The right of free speech, the right to teach and the right of assembly are, of course, fundamental. . . . These may not be denied or abridged. But, although the rights of free speech and assembly are fundamental, they are not in their nature absolute. Their exercise is subject to restriction, if the particular restriction proposed is required in order to protect the State from destruction or from serious injury, political, economic or moral.[63]

The justice voted with the majority in *Powell v. Alabama* (discussed in Chapter 2), when the Court held that the Sixth Amendment requires the appointment of counsel by state courts in capital cases.

Some government action may "shock the common man's sense of decency and fair play." Those were the words Brandeis used to describe what the government had done in the case of *Burdeau v. McDowell*.[64] The government used information to convict the defendant which was stolen from the defendant by another person and given to the government.

While the majority could find no provision in the Constitution that was violated, Brandeis thought it still was not right to use the stolen information. "Still I cannot believe," he declared,

> that action of a public official is necessarily lawful, because it does not violate constitutional prohibitions and because the same result might have been attained by other and proper means. At the foundation of our civil liberty lies the principle which denies to government officials an exceptional position before the law and which subjects them to the same rules of conduct that are commands to the citizen. . . . Respect for law will not be advanced by resort, in its enforcement, to means which shock the common man's sense of decency and fair play.

Brandeis wrote a memorable dissent in *Olmstead v. United States*.[65] He tells what happened in that case.

> Before any of the persons now charged had been arrested or indicted, the telephones by means of which they habitually communicated with one another and with others had been tapped by federal officers. To this end, a lineman of long ex-

perience in wire-tapping was employed, on behalf of the Government and at its expense. He tapped eight telephones, some in the homes of the persons charged, some in their offices. Acting on behalf of the Government and in their official capacity, at least six other prohibition agents listened over the tapped wires and reported the messages taken. Their operations extended over a period of nearly five months. The type-written [sic] record of the notes of conversations overheard occupies 775 typewritten pages.

In affirming the defendants' convictions for conspiracy to violate the National Prohibition Act, the majority concluded that the Fourth Amendment did not apply to wiretapping. "The Amendment," Chief Justice William Howard Taft wrote, "does not forbid what was done here. There was no searching. There was no seizure. The evidence was secured by the use of the sense of hearing and that only. There was no entry of the houses or office of the defendants.... The language of the Amendment can not be extended and expanded to include telephone wires reaching to the whole world from the defendant's house or office."

Brandeis believed that the majority was taking an unrealistic view of a changing world. In referring to the Constitution, he wrote, "But 'time works changes, brings into existence new conditions and purposes.' Therefore a principle to be vital must be capable of wider application than the mischief which gave it birth. This is peculiarly true of constitutions." Among the changes being made are "subtler and more far-reaching means of invading privacy [which] have become available to the Government. Discovery and invention have made it possible for the Government, by means far more effective than stretching upon the rack, to obtain disclosure in court of what is whispered in the closet." He argued that the drafters of the Fourth Amendment did not intend it to be confined for all time only to the seizure of things. He then writes what has become an oft-quoted description of the intent of the makers of the Constitution.

> The makers of our constitution undertook to secure conditions favorable to the pursuit of happiness. They recognized the significance of man's spiritual nature, of his feelings and of his intellect. They knew that only a part of the pain, pleasure and satisfactions of life are to be found in material things. They sought to protect Americans in their beliefs, their thoughts, their emotions and their sensations. They conferred, as against the Government, the right to be let alone—the most comprehensive of rights and the right most valued by civilized men. To protect that right, every unjustifiable intrusion by the Government upon the privacy of the individual, whatever the means employed, must be deemed a violation of the Fourth Amendment. And the use, as evidence in a criminal proceeding, of facts ascertained by such intrusion must be deemed a violation of the Fifth.

The Justice points out that the defendant is entitled to the protection of the Constitution, even though he may have committed the crime. "The confirmed criminal is as much entitled to redress as his most virtuous fellow citizen; no record of crime, however long, makes one an outlaw." He was also disturbed by the government's action in this case.

AS A JUDICIAL FREEDOM FIGHTER

Justice Brandeis expressed his concern for government infringement upon personal freedom in his *Olmstead* dissent: "Experience should teach us to be most on our guard to protect liberty when the Government's purposes are beneficent. Men born to freedom are naturally alert to repel invasion of their liberty by evil-minded rulers. The greatest dangers to liberty lurk in insidious encroachment by men of zeal, well-meaning but without understanding."[66]

His votes and opinions on First Amendment issues indicate that after *Schenck, Frohwerk,* and *Debs* he had more deeply "thought through" those issues. For example, in dissenting in *Pierce* he wrote, "To hold that a jury may make punishable statements of conclusions or of opinion, like those here involved, by declaring them to be statements of facts and to be false would practically deny members of small political parties freedom of criticism and of discussion in times when feelings run high and the questions involved are deemed fundamental."[67]

Brandeis believed that Charlotte Whitney's activities had crossed the line between punishable and protected speech, and he voted to uphold her conviction in *Whitney v. California.* But his stirring defense of free speech is a classic. In addition to the portion of the opinion quoted above, the Justice declared:

> Those who won our independence believed that the final end of the State was to make men free to develop their faculties; and that in its government the delibera-tive forces should prevail over the arbitrary. They valued liberty both as an end and as a means. They believed liberty to be the secret of happiness and courage to be the secret of liberty. They believed that freedom to think as you will and to speak as you think are means indispensable to the discovery and spread of politi-cal truth; that without free speech and assembly discussion would be futile; that with them, discussion affords ordinarily adequate protection against the dissemi-nation of noxious doctrine; that the greatest menace to freedom is an inert peo-ple; that public discussion is a political duty; and that this should be a fundamental principle of the American Government. They recognized the risks to which all human institutions are subject. But they knew that order cannot be secured merely through fear of punishment for its infraction; that it is hazardous to discourage thought, hope and imagination; that fear breeds hate; that hate menaces stable government; that the path of safety lies in the opportunity to dis-cuss freely supposed grievances and proposed remedies; and that the fitting rem-edy for evil counsels is good ones. Believing in the power of reason as applied through public discussion, they eschewed silence coerced by law—the argument of force in its worst form. Recognizing the occasional tyrannies of government majorities, they amended the Constitution so that free speech and assembly should be guaranteed.[68]

The justice did not differentiate between freedom of speech and freedom of the press, believing that both were of equal importance to freedom. For example, in his dissent in *Schaefer v. United States,* a case involving several allegedly subversive newspaper articles, Brandeis asserted: "The constitutional right of free speech has been declared to be the same in peace and in war. In peace, too, men may differ widely as to what loyalty to our country demands; and an intolerant majority, swayed by passion or by fear, may be prone in the future, as it has often been in the past, to stamp as disloyal opinions with which it disagrees."[69]

In joining Holmes's dissent in *Schwimmer,* and that of Chief Justice Hughes in *Macintosh,* Brandeis indicates his concern for free exercise of religion.

Even in voting to deny Albert W. Hamilton and W. Alonzo Reynolds, Jr., admission to the University of California because of their refusal to take a course in military science, he did not see that requirement as having anything to do with their free exercise of religion. He joined the concurring opinion of Justice Benjamin Cardozo, who declared: "Instruction in military science, unaccompanied here by any pledge of military service, is not an interference by the state with the free exercise of religion when the liberties of the constitution are read in the light of a century and a half of history during days of peace and war."[70]

It is questionable whether it was "men of zeal" who brought about discrimination against blacks in housing and voting, and excluded them from serving on juries. It is clear, however, that in most instances Brandeis voted to strike down such discrimination.

In the early 1920s, aliens did not fare as well with the Court, Brandeis included, as they would today. The justice did, however, uphold Gin Sang Get's and Gin Sang Mo's right to have their claim of citizenship adjudicated in a judicial trial.

When Brandeis and his law partner Samuel Warren in 1890 wrote their article "The Right to Privacy," it is doubtful that either could foresee that eventually the Supreme Court, with Brandeis as one of the justices, would begin to apply that principle to protect parental rights in *Meyer v. Nebraska* and *Pierce v. Society of Sisters.* And while the Court did not expressly deal with a right of privacy in those cases, they did lay the groundwork for the Court's recognition of that right in *Griswold v. Connecticut,*[71] and the expansion of it in *Roe v. Wade.*[72]

The justice firmly believed that government officials must respect the laws of the land as citizens are required to do. And he concluded his dissent in *Olmstead* with these words:

> Decency, security and liberty alike demand that government officials shall be subjected to the same rules of conduct that are commands to the citizen. In a government of laws, existence of the government will be imperilled if it fails to observe the law scrupulously. Our Government is the potent, the omnipresent teacher. For good or for ill, it teaches the whole people by its example. Crime is contagious. If the Government becomes a law breaker, it breeds contempt for law; it invites every man to become a law unto himself; it invites anarchy. To

declare that in the administration of the criminal law the end justifies the means—to declare that the Government may commit crimes in order to secure the conviction of a private criminal—would bring terrible retribution. Against that pernicious doctrine this Court should resolutely set its face.[73]

Thus, Justice Brandeis's votes and opinions place him soundly on the side of freedom.

4

JUSTICE HUGO LAFAYETTE BLACK

PERSONAL LIFE

Growing Up

"A frequent spectator at . . . trials from the age of six, Hugo Black came to know all . . . [the] lawyers and their tactics. Seated on a courtroom bench, he fancied how he might have asked a shrewder question or more cleverly won the jury's sympathy, and dreamed of the day when he would be a lawyer, as Great-Uncle Jud Street predicted."[1]

This would-be lawyer was born in Harlan, Clay County, Alabama, on February 27, 1886, the eighth child of William LaFayette Black and Martha Toland Black. Because the family owned some of Victor Hugo's books, the newborn son was named Hugo after the writer, and LaFayette after his father. William Black, who was called Fayette, owned a small store and farmed. As the Black family grew, it was necessary to add more rooms to the one-room log cabin that was their home. Four bedrooms and a kitchen were therefore built alongside. There were also a privy and a barn out back.

In addition to doing the housework, cooking, and occasionally milking cows, Martha Black was the postmistress of Harlan. Author John P. Frank describes her as a woman who "worked her daughters hard, prayed nightly and devoutly, and kept a firm discipline over her sons."[2] There was no school in Harlan, so a makeshift one was set up in one of the buildings and the oldest child, Robert Lee, taught the other children there. This arrangement left a lot to be desired, so the family moved to nearby Ashland, population 350. Fayette and a man named Manning opened Black & Manning, a general merchandise store. The Blacks bought a five-room house, which Martha surrounded with flowerbeds.

Hugo and his sister Leora owned a cat named Dandy Jim. Leora owned the body and Hugo the tail. Hugo did odd jobs at the store, picked some cotton, and sold soda pop at celebrations. He also worked for the local paper setting type. When he was old enough, he was allowed to drive the horses 22 miles to the

JUSTICE HUGO LAFAYETTE BLACK (photo by Harris & Ewing; collection of the Supreme Court of the United States).

railroad to pick up supplies for the store. He would spend the night there sleeping on the floor of the wagonyard and return to Ashland the next day.

After elementary school, Hugo went to Ashland College, a private institution offering high school and junior college courses. Although there were not many blacks in Ashland, a couple of incidents occurred that must have made an impression on him. When one of the blacks who worked for the family came to the back door, Martha told Hugo to offer him something to eat. When he started to take the dinner out to the back step, Martha told him to ask "Uncle Dan" in and let him eat at the kitchen table. This was not the custom in the South at that time.

More dramatic is the story told by author Virginia Van der Veer Hamilton: "An ominous racial tragedy shook Ashland during one summer of Hugo's youth. Eli Sims, a friendly young Negro who had occasionally given Hugo rides in his wheelbarrow, went swimming in the same creek where the white boys swam. When one white youth ordered him to leave Eli 'sassed' him. The white boy went home, got his gun, and shot Eli dead. Because he was the son of a prominent and well-liked citizen, the white youth went free, although everyone in Ashland conceded his guilt."[3]

The Blacks ran a strict household and attended the Baptist church each Sunday. The children were not allowed to drink coffee, smoke, or play cards. But the Blacks did not believe that this made them better than anyone else. One time Fayette invited the Baptist minister and a man thought to be a "sinner" to be guests at Sunday dinner.

When Hugo became interested in local politics, he found the Democratic and Populist philosophies more to his liking. These parties seemed to be more interested in making things better for the poor.

In deference to his mother's wishes, and because his brother Orlando had become a doctor, Hugo went to Birmingham and entered medical school in 1903. In one year, he completed two years' work, and he spent the summer assisting Orlando in his practice. It soon became clear that medicine was not for him. In the fall, he and a friend set off for Birmingham and the University of Alabama. Having had one year at medical school, he thought he ought to be enrolled as a sophomore but was told that he could not do so without taking an entrance exam. Being in a hurry to get on with his education, and learning that he could enter law school immediately, he enrolled there. Later, one of the law professors said of him, "I won't say whether Black is the best student in school or not. I will say he has learned the most of any student in school. He had the most to learn."[4] And he did learn much. For the two-year term, he was among those students whose grades averaged 95 or better.

Upon graduation, Black passed the state bar examination and returned to Ashland. His father was now deceased, and, upon the death of his mother, he received some of his father's estate. He used some of the money to purchase books and open an office. Business was very slow. "To while away his time, Hugo strolled to the drugstore and made the frugal purchase of six nickel cigars for a quarter. He had strayed from Fayette's code, but cigars might make a young lawyer seem older and wiser. Those who observed him were amused to see that he took only one cigar, making separate trips to the drugstore to pick up each of the other five." When a fire destroyed the building in which he had his office, he concluded that the grass was greener in Birmingham, so he went there.

Lawyer and Public Servant

Upon arriving in Birmingham, he rented a room in a boardinghouse which he shared with three other men, and took space from another attorney, Bonner Miller, for seven dollars a month. He joined the Knights of Pythias, the Masons, and the First Baptist Church, where he taught Sunday school.

A case that was to bring Black to the attention of the community was one given to him by Miller. It was Willie Morton's case against one of the local steel companies. The companies were allowed to hire convicts to work in the mines at very low wages. Most of the convicts were black, as was Morton. When the company worked Morton 22 days beyond his release date and did not pay him, he sought legal help to secure the wages due.

When the case came before Judge A.O. Lane, W.I. Grubb, who represented the steel company, offered several motions to dismiss. But Black was well prepared and resisted. In denying the motions, Judge Lane commented to Grubb, "Well, they didn't work, did they, Billy?. . . Let's get down to the case." The judge found for Morton and gave judgment for $150. Of the $150, Morton received $75, Black $37.50, and his partner, Miller, $37.50. Black, however, gained much more. Not only did he impress Judge Lane but the company attorney as well, and new clients began to come to him.

In 1911, Lane, who was then commissioner of public safety, appointed Black as judge of the municipal court. In making the announcement Commissioner Lane said, "I have talked with a young lawyer for whom I can vouch. He is quick, enterprising, and smart. He can fill the recorder's bench well." Black's salary was to be $1,500 a year. The *Birmingham Age-Herald* reported that the new judge would be replacing three other judges, a clerk, and a number of policemen. The court's caseload was extremely heavy, with "a motley collection of drunks, petty thieves, crapshooters, dope peddlers, loafers, prostitutes, and those who the night before had been hot-tempered or careless with fists, razors or switchblades." A newspaper reporter wrote that "Judge Black was a skillful questioner and rarely raised his voice in the courtroom, pronouncing sentences with a soft, southern accent. He fined frequent offenders heavily in hopes of discouraging further visits. At times he showed a light touch, such as the day on which he handed down numerous fines for crapshooting while softly humming a popular tune, 'Everybody's doin' it, doin' it, doin' it.' One Negro was moved to protest: 'Everybody's gittin' it, gittin' it, gittin' it.'"

Black served as judge for 18 months and then resigned to practice law with a friend, David J. Davis. The firm had developed a substantial practice when Hugo decided to enter politics by running for county solicitor. There were already three candidates for the position, but the most formidable was the incumbent, Harrington P. Heflin, who had had the post for 15 years.

Black's candidacy posed a threat to a fee system by which sheriffs, justices of the peace, and clerks were paid. The more people arrested and fined, the greater the compensation of those involved in the system. A grand jury reported that the fee system "victimized poor, humble, and ignorant Negroes, forcing them to flee from arrest on trumped-up charges."

Author Hamilton describes Black's self-created campaign:

> Every day a small "teaser" advertisement appeared in the Birmingham press, containing only a picture of Black, looking young and earnest, accompanied by the words, "This is your next solicitor," or "The gamblers are against this man for solicitor." Later, his name was added and the wording changed to, "Hugo Black will make a good solicitor—ask the judges" or "ask the voters." Citizens were urged to try him as a "crime suppressor" and promised that Black, when elected, would be found at the courthouse earning his salary prosecuting criminals.[5]

Black learned a lot about what was on the people's minds as he toured the county in an old Model T Ford. He found "that citizens opposed professional gambling and bootlegging, and were tired of having their jails crowded with hundreds of Negroes who had been arrested, in the cause of enriching their persecutors, for shooting craps on payday."

Although the "establishment" was against him, Black had the support of W.I. Grubb, now a federal judge, and A.O. Lane, and he won the election handily.

The new solicitor took office and assembled a staff of young lawyers as assistants. At the time 374 prisoners were in the county jail, and 3,268 cases awaited trial, included 35 murder cases. Black dismissed about 500 petty cases of persons whom he thought were "hapless victims of the fee system."

As solicitor, Black prosecuted the rich and poor, and the gamblers and murderers. He assisted the county grand jury in investigating police beating of prisoners to obtain confessions. The jury found that such beatings were routinely given. And while the report may not have brought much change in police practices in Birmingham, police brutality made a lasting impression on the solicitor. Many years later he wrote the Supreme Court's opinion overturning the convictions of four blacks whose confessions had been coerced.[6]

When the state legislature enacted a law prohibiting liquor advertising, Black sought an injunction against the sale of newspapers containing liquor advertisements. Although the local court was of the opinion that enjoining what a newspaper could publish would be a violation of the First Amendment, the Alabama Supreme Court disagreed. Thereafter, out-of-state newspapers that carried such ads were banned from Alabama, and local newspapers were forced to discontinue them.

The Ku Klux Klan was active in Birmingham at this time. And when one of its members absconded with membership fees he had collected, Black prosecuted him.

Black lost a battle over who had the authority to appoint his assistants, causing him to think that "he was now solicitor in name only,"[7] and he resigned.

He and his assistants believed they had accomplished many things. There were now only 97 prisoners in jail and 608 cases pending.

Hugo enlisted in the army in 1917 and after three months' training was made an officer. He became an instructor and spent some time in California and Oklahoma. He was discharged in December 1919 and returned to Birmingham to begin the practice of law again.

Author John P. Frank described Black's success as a lawyer:

> From 1920 to 1925 Black's practice boomed. His practice took the usual shape of that of the liberal lawyer with some labor clientele. He represented the United Mine Workers and some other unions in their not very plentiful business. Thereby he forfeited, deliberately and cheerfully, the corporation cases; but when the working men of Birmingham suffered accidents, they regularly brought their cases to Black. He was fabulously successful as a jury lawyer; he and his partners were dissatisfied if they did not win ninety per cent of their cases.[8]

Black was listed as one of the leading lawyers in a publication of Birmingham's leading citizens. He had tried playing golf but then took up tennis instead, finding the fast pace more to his liking. He joined the Chamber of Commerce, the American Legion, and the Birmingham Bar Association, serving on its Executive Committee. He also joined the Ku Klux Klan in September 1923. There has been much speculation as to why. Noting that Black had taken almost a year to make up his mind whether to join, author Frank offers this critique:

> The reasons for staying out were the obvious ones—he had very close friends among the groups that some Klansmen condemned; he had consistently and publicly upheld fair play for Negroes; he had never in his life given evidence to anyone of a belief that Nordics had a right to rule the world. The reasons for joining were also simple: he was a poor man's lawyer, and thousands of Birmingham workmen were in the Klan; and he was ambitious for political advancement. The rationalizations were three-fold: first, that very few Klan members either practiced or approved of racial violence; second, that perhaps there was a chance to bore for decency from within; and third, that the Southern liberal in politics must do a certain amount of pretending if he is to stay in politics at all.

Black performed one other act of public service. When a number of prominent citizens in Mobile, Alabama, were indicted for violating federal liquor laws, the U.S. attorney general, Harlan Fiske Stone, was unable to find a Republican prosecutor to conduct the case. His assistant, Mable W. Willebrandt, recalling that Black had prosecuted liquor law violators when he was solicitor, asked him to take on the prosecution. Black agreed to do so, but did not want to be paid for his services. When some Republicans complained because Black was a Democrat and had campaigned for the Democratic Party's candidate, John W. Davis, during the 1924 presidential campaign, Mrs. Willebrandt summoned him to Washington. He impressed her, and that began a friendship that lasted for many years thereafter.

During Black's visit with the attorney general, Stone told him that he was pleased to have Black undertake the prosecution, but that he could not "approve of anyone working for the government without compensation."

"Black tried the case with characteristic vigor," Gerald T. Dunne has written, "and, after dropping some of the defendants in midtrial, pursued the remainder through the spring of 1924. At the end of May, the jury came back with a 'guilty' verdict, which not only operated as a great triumph for the righteous kingdom of Prohibition but yielded the previously unknown federal prosecutor a degree of fame throughout all of Alabama."[9]

Love, Marriage, and Family

Josephine Foster had been educated at Sweet Briar College in Virginia, after which she went to New York to attend Columbia University. While in New York she learned that the navy was recruiting women to serve as Yeomanettes, so she joined and spent five months working in naval intelligence.

Upon returning to Birmingham, she attended a dance, where Hugo noticed her and monopolized her time for the rest of the evening. That was the beginning of an active courtship.

Josephine was recognized by a society columnist as "an acknowledged belle of beauty and winsome personality and one of Birmingham's most popular society girls."[10] The couple was married on February 23, 1921, shortly before Hugo's thirty-fifth birthday, and when Josephine was almost 22. The Blacks had three children. Hugo, Jr., attended Yale Law School, and Sterling Foster graduated from Columbia Law School, both entering the practice of law; Josephine (Jo-Jo) went to Swarthmore and married.

Of Hugo's wife, author Hamilton writes:

> Josephine, born to southern gentility, had created in their two-story French provincial home on Altamont Road, overlooking Birmingham, an appropriate setting for a successful lawyer, his wife, and two sons, Hugo LaFayette, Jr., and Sterling Foster. It was Josephine who arranged tasteful bouquets of flowers and taught Lou, the Negro cook, to serve mint jelly with lamb. Like other young Birmingham matrons of proper background, Josephine was a member of the Junior League, but she was doubtless the only Junior Leaguer who also belonged to the American Legion. Young, impressionable Hazel, visiting her uncle, tried as best she could to emulate Josephine's flair for sewing, choosing table linens, playing Chopin preludes, and selecting clothes free from "doodads."

"Daddy never had time for appreciating the natural beauty that abounds in the world," Hugo Black, Jr., has written,

> but Mama seemed to derive inner peace from it and wanted to teach her children to love nature too. Down through the years, in places like Long Beach, Mississippi; Point Clear, Alabama; the mountains in Mentone, Alabama; Washington; and wherever we went, she taught us to enjoy sunrises and sunsets,

fireflies, blinking stars, clouds shaped like people's faces, rocks washed clean by pure creek water tumbling down a mountainside and the sunlight reflected through a dewdrop clinging to a blade of grass. She listened with me to the music of crickets and tree frogs in the night, to the waves, and the unexpected quiet of snowflakes falling to the earth.[11]

Senator from Alabama

Black began his campaign for the U.S. Senate in June 1925. The incumbent, Oscar W. Underwood, withdrew from the race one month later. Five candidates remained: Thomas E. Kilby, John Bankhead, Judge J.J. Mayfield, L. Breckenridge Musgrove, and Black, who was the youngest.

Black campaigned as the poor man's candidate, although his opponents pointed out that he was in fact fairly wealthy. But he had come from a poor area of the state and had represented the working man, rather than corporations or railroads. When one of his opponents claimed that he was worth $278,000, Black offered to sell his holdings to the candidate for half that much.

He campaigned the length and breadth of the state, wearing out two automobiles in the process. "Arriving in a county seat, Black made promptly for the courthouse square, shaking the hands of all voters from probate judge, to checker players under the shade tree, to men in overalls lounging on the steps. Not in vain had he spent a boyhood enamored of rural politics."[12]

The primary election was held in August 1926. Black won, with 32 percent of the vote. Because voters were required to list their first and second choices, his totals were 71,916 first-place votes, and 12,961 second-place.

Although he had resigned from the Klan before he began his campaign, he had its support throughout, and the Klan held a victory celebration soon after the election. Black was given a Klan "passport," which entitled him as "a citizen of the invisible empire to . . . travel unmolested throughout our beneficent domain and grant and receive the fervent fellowship of Klansmen." In accepting the "passport" Black responded, "I do not feel that it would be out of place to state to you here on this occasion that I know that without the support of this organization I would not have been called, even by my enemies, the 'Junior Senator from Alabama.' I realize that I was elected by men who believe in the principles that I have sought to advocate and which are the principles of this organization."

Black easily outdistanced his Republican challenger in the November general election, and became the junior senator from Alabama.

The Klan's support of Black followed him to Congress. William C. Bruce, senator from Maryland, said, "I have heard it said that the junior senator from Alabama owes his seat in the Senate to the Ku Klux Klan." Black quickly responded, "I got all the Ku Klux votes I could get . . . and all the Catholic votes I could get, and all the Jew votes I could get, and all the Baptist votes I could get, and all the others, and I have no apology to make for it, and I am here representing them."

Upon arriving in Washington, Black began an extensive reading campaign, believing that he needed to increase his knowledge. He read books on government, history, political theory, and economics. Frank writes:

> Among the historical works were extended excerpts from the writings of Franklin, Hamilton, and John Adams and all of Jefferson's voluminous writings; the records of the federal Constitutional Convention and of the state ratifying conventions, numerous biographies of Revolutionary and nineteenth-century American political leaders, Warren's and Myers's Supreme Court histories, most of the writings of Charles Beard, and numerous other historical works. His reading in Greek, Roman, and European history, though less comprehensive, was extended and included translations of Herodotus, Thucydides, Plutarch, Suetonius, Seneca, and Cicero.[13]

The change for the family brought about by the move from the Deep South to more cosmopolitan Washington was great. Josephine, who was 27 years old, was the youngest of the senators' wives, and had two children to care for. The family bought a house in Washington, and she turned it into a very livable home.

Black took the Senate's oath of office on December 5, 1927, and soon allied himself with the Senate liberals. He found himself in a delicate position during the 1928 presidential election campaign. The Democratic Party's candidate was Al Smith of New York, a Catholic and a "wet," which made him anathema to the Klan and many voters in Alabama. To repudiate Smith was to do the same to the Democratic Party. Black decided that his place was with the party, and although he did not take an active part in the campaign, he did urge Alabama Democrats to support Smith, which they did. Smith won the state's electoral votes by a small margin. Later Black was taken to task by a Montgomery newspaper for not taking a more active part in the campaign.

Commenting upon Black as a new senator, author Hamilton writes:

> His accent was undeniably southern, but this newcomer, reputed to be a hillbilly, surprised the Senate by displaying a scholar's acquaintance with world history and literary classics. Amid the heat of floor debate, he could momentarily stun an adversary by tossing in an apt quotation from Aristotle, a reference to the French Revolution, or advice from Thomas Jefferson. While Calvin Coolidge napped in the White House, members of the Senate were becoming acquainted with an atypical Southerner, who spoke with the assurance of a Bourbon but the fiery passion of a Populist.[14]

Black sought re-election in 1932. Four candidates filed against him in the primary election: Thomas E. Kilby, former governor; Charles McCall, former attorney general; Judge Henry L. Anderton, Birmingham attorney; and John M. Burns. Black did not wage a vigorous campaign, returning to Alabama only a few days before the primary election. In response to the charge that Josephine was on his office payroll, Black pointed out that she had been a Yeomanette in the navy during the World War. "She earned her money then," he declared. "She earned every penny she received during those few months she did temporary work." Black did not receive a majority of votes in the primary and a runoff election was required. His opponent was the former governor, Thomas E. Kilby. Although the campaign was filled with charges and countercharges, Black won the nomination, and re-election in the fall.

His legislative activity was considerably greater during his second term. He introduced a bill for a 30-hour work week, which surprisingly passed the Senate, but was waylaid in the House. The new president, Franklin D. Roosevelt, was against it. Later Black became one of the sponsors of a wage and hour bill that became the Fair Labor Standards Act.[15] The senator undertook the investigation of subsidies to the Merchant Marine, which resulted in the enactment of the Merchant Marine Act of 1936. Among other legislative investigations engaged in by Black were airline subsidies, the utility lobby, and lobbying in general.

John P. Frank writes, "The success of Black's investigations was due to his extraordinary lawyer's skill. His hard-working, detailed preparation, and his ability to get the evidence from witnesses by cross-examination, both resulted from his years as a trial lawyer. As a lawyer, Black was courteous, but it was the courtesy of a tough customer."[16] But Black had his critics, who "charged that as an investigator he was unfair and over-harsh and that he obtained evidence illegally."[17]

The senator, who steadfastly supported Roosevelt's program to cope with the Depression, campaigned for his re-election in 1936. During Roosevelt's first term, the Supreme Court had invalidated much of the legislation aimed at bringing an end to the Depression. Black and Senator Hatton Sumners introduced a bill that would have speeded up the appeal process. The senator also proposed to the president that the Court be divided into two divisions and that the number of justices be increased. It appears that Roosevelt was also thinking about ways to curb the power of the Supreme Court. He proposed that whenever a justice who was eligible to retire did not do so, the president would have the authority to appoint an additional justice. The enactment of this law would have given Roosevelt the power to appoint six new justices. Black favored the plan and spoke out for its passage. The plan was derailed, however, when the Court upheld the National Labor Relations Act and several other pieces of important New Deal legislation. This appeared to signal a change in the Court's approach to social legislation.

Nomination to the Supreme Court

On May 18, 1937, Justice Willis Van Devanter opted to retire from the Supreme Court. President Roosevelt and Attorney General Homer S. Cummings immediately began a secret search for a replacement. The list of nominees, which began with 60 names, was cut to 20, and then the president cut it to six. The list then included three federal judges, and two senators, Sherman Minton and Hugo Black, and Solicitor General Stanley Reed. "The President himself" Hamilton states, "struck off the judges as insufficiently liberal. Stanley Reed, also, was too mild for Roosevelt's taste of the moment. . . . This narrowed the field to Minton and Black."[18] When Minton refused the nomination, Black was the only viable nominee. After securing Black's acceptance, the president inserted his name on the nomination form and sent it to the Senate.

When the nomination was read in the Senate, an attempt was made to confirm immediately, as was the custom when a fellow senator had been appointed to an executive office. But because the nominee had accumulated a few political enemies, the nomination was referred to the Judiciary Committee for investigation. Although Black received approval from a subcommittee and the full Judiciary Committee, there was opposition when the nomination reached the floor of the Senate. There were rumors about Black's KKK membership, he was not liked by business, and those whom he had investigated were also against him. Much of the country's press was also opposed to the nomination.

The nominee refused to give a direct answer to questions about Klan membership, other than to say that he was not then a member. "But, he added slowly and deliberately, if any man were concerned lest he might have been a Klansman, he would ask that man to vote against his confirmation." After a few days' debate the Senate voted 63–16 to confirm.

Upon being sworn in, Black left for Europe with his family. But the Klan issue was not about to fade away. When a reporter obtained the Alabama Klan's records showing Black's membership and resignation, it made front-page headlines, and put the president on the defensive about the nomination. He emphatically denied, however, that he had had any prior knowledge about Black's membership.

Author Hamilton sums up the atmosphere that prevailed after the revelation of the Klan membership:

> But critics of Roosevelt and the New Deal—cartoonists in particular—had a field day. The President was criticized for not having sought advice before the nomination, and Black was castigated for not revealing his Klan connection to Roosevelt or the Senate. *Newsweek* said the new justice must accept responsibility for his silence during the Senate debate "and for the private advice confidentially but freely passed around Senate cloakrooms that he had no actual Klan ties, however much he owed the Klan for his first nomination and election to the Senate." But the friendly *Nation,* admitting that Black had been a political opportunist when he joined the Klan, drew a distinction between opportunism and bigotry.[19]

In Europe, the Blacks were hounded by reporters, but he refused to give them a statement. Upon his return to the United States, Black went public, giving an 11-minute radio speech, during which he devoted only a few sentences to the Klan issue. He said, "I did join the Klan. I later resigned. I have never rejoined. I have never considered and I do not now consider the unsolicited card . . . as a membership of any kind in the Ku Klux Klan, I never used it. I did not even keep it. Before becoming a Senator, I dropped the Klan. I have had nothing to do with it since that time."[20]

That closed the matter, and the new justice took his seat. At the time the other members of the Court were Chief Justice Charles Evans Hughes, and justices Benjamin N. Cardozo, James C. McReynolds, Louis D. Brandeis, Pierce Butler, George Sutherland, Owen J. Roberts, and Harlan F. Stone.

AS ASSOCIATE JUSTICE (1937-71)

The Free Exercise of Religion

In November 1935 Lillian and William Gobitis, ages 12 and 10, children of parents who were Jehovah's Witnesses, were expelled from school because they would not salute the flag of the United States. Their father, Walter, brought an action seeking to have the children reinstated, claiming that the flag salute requirement violated the free exercise of religion rights of his children. Judge Albert B. Maris agreed and ordered the school to readmit Lillian and William and not require them "to salute the national flag as a condition of their right to attend the said school."[21] The Supreme Court reversed, holding that the requirement was an "appropriate means to evoke and foster a sentiment of national unity among the children in the public schools."[22] Justice Black agreed and voted with the majority. Only Justice Harlan Fiske Stone dissented.

Three years after the *Gobitis* decision, the justices were confronted with a resolution of the West Virginia Board of Education stating "that all teachers and pupils 'shall be required to participate in the salute honoring the Nation represented by the Flag.' "[23] This time Justice Black concurred with the majority, which reversed *Gobitis* and struck down the West Virginia requirement. Black, writing for himself and Justice William O. Douglas, admitted that their votes to uphold the flag salute requirement in *Gobitis* were wrong because such a requirement "fails to accord full scope to the freedom of religion secured to the . . . [students] by the First and Fourteenth Amendments."

Black used the occasion to set forth his views on the meaning of the First Amendment's free exercise of religion clause. He wrote: "Words uttered under coercion are proof of loyalty to nothing but self-interest. Love of country must spring from willing hearts and free minds, inspired by a fair administration of wise laws enacted by the people's elected representatives within the bounds of express constitutional prohibitions. These laws must, to be consistent with the First Amendment, permit the widest toleration of conflicting viewpoints consistent with a society of free men."

When a majority voted to uphold a decision of the Illinois Supreme Court to deny Clyde Summers admission to the bar, Black vigorously dissented. Although Summers's credentials were impeccable, he could not in good conscience take an oath to support the constitution of the state of Illinois, because that Constitution required all men to serve in the militia in time of war. The justice concluded his dissent with these words: "I cannot agree that a state can lawfully bar from a semi-public position a well-qualified man of good character solely because he entertains a religious belief which might prompt him at some time in the future to violate a law which has not yet been and may never be enacted. Under our Constitution men are punished for what they do or fail to do and not for what they think and believe. Freedom to think, to believe, and to worship, has too exalted a position in our country to be penalized on such an illusory basis."[24]

Roy R. Torcaso wanted to be a notary public in the state of Maryland. He was prevented from doing so "because he would not declare his belief in God."[25] In response to the assertion that requiring a belief in God for notaries public was a religious test oath, the Maryland Supreme Court wrote that Torcaso was "not compelled to believe or disbelieve, under threat of punishment or other compulsion. True, unless he makes the declaration or belief he cannot hold public office in Maryland, but he is not compelled to hold office."

Black disagreed: "This Maryland religious test for public office unconstitutionally invades the appellant's freedom of belief and religion and therefore cannot be enforced against him."

Black and a majority of the Court turned a deaf ear to the plight of Orthodox Jews who were forced to abide by Sunday closing laws, and who were required by their faith also to close on Saturdays. For the majority, Sunday closing laws did not "make unlawful any religious practices of . . . [the Jewish merchants]; the Sunday law simply regulates a secular activity and, as applied to . . . [the merchants] operates so as to make the practice of their religious beliefs more expensive."[26]

About two years later, however, the Court upheld the right of Adell H. Sherbert, a Seventh-Day Adventist, not to be forced to work on Saturday, her Sabbath.[27]

In discussing the freedom of religion protected by the First Amendment the Court has said, "Thus the Amendment embraces two concepts,—freedom to believe and freedom to act. The first is absolute but, in the nature of things, the second cannot be."[28]

Justice Black concurred, and joined Justice Douglas's statement that "man's relation to his God was made no concern of the state. He was granted the right to worship as he pleased and to answer to no man for the verity of his religious views. The religious views espoused by . . . [the defendants] might seem incredible, if not preposterous, to most people. But if those doctrines are subject to trial before a jury charged with finding their truth or falsity, then the same can be done with the religious beliefs of any sect."[29]

When Grace Marsh's case reached the Supreme Court, Black wrote the opinion upholding her right to distribute Jehovah's Witnesses literature on the streets of Chickasaw, Alabama, a company-owned town.[30]

One of the tenets of the Jehovah's Witnesses faith was the fulfillment of Christ's command "Go ye into all the world, and preach the gospel to every creature."[31] Grace Marsh was doing just that in Chickasaw by distributing Jehovah's Witnesses' literature. When she refused to stop, she was arrested, charged, and convicted of trespassing upon private land. Marsh had argued that she was devoting "her entire life to this work. In addition to orally teaching the people concerning the Kingdom of God, she used various printed publications, such as books, booklets and magazines. Such she distributed to 'any person of good-will who desires to read them.'"

The justice framed the question before the Court as follows: "Can those people who live in or come to Chickasaw be denied freedom of the press and religion simply because a single company has legal title to all the town?" In holding that freedom of the press and religion could not be denied in this company town, Justice Black declared: "When we balance the Constitutional rights of owners of property against those of the people to enjoy freedom of press and religion, as we must here, we remain mindful of the fact that the latter occupy a preferred position. As we have stated before, the right to exercise the liberties safeguarded by the First Amendment 'lies at the foundation of free government by free men' and we must in all cases 'weigh the circumstances and . . . appraise the . . . reasons . . . in support of the regulation . . . of the rights.'"[32]

Freedom of Speech

Pamphleteering. Joseph Beauharnais was president of White Circle League, an organization that favored segregation of the races. In furtherance of the league's goals, Beauharnais caused to be distributed a leaflet "which . . . portray[ed] depravity, criminality, unchastity . . . of citizens of Negro race and color and which expose[d] . . . the Negro race . . . to contempt, derision, or obloquy."[33] Beauharnais was charged and convicted of violating a Chicago ordinance making it a crime, commonly referred to as criminal libel, to distribute such literature. The Supreme Court upheld the conviction, with Black dissenting. The majority pointed out that libelous words are not protected by the First Amendment because "such utterances are no essential part of any exposition of ideas, and are of such slight social value as a step to truth that any benefit that may be derived from them is clearly outweighed by the social interest in order and morality." Furthermore, laws such as this are necessary to ease the tension and violence that sometimes occur between racial and religious groups.

Black was not convinced. "Freedom of petition, assembly, speech and press," he argued, "could be greatly abridged by a practice of meticulously scrutinizing every editorial, speech, sermon or other printed matter to extract two or three naughty words on which to hang charges of 'group libel.' " "I think the First Amendment, with the Fourteenth," he declared, " 'absolutely' forbids such laws without any 'ifs' or 'buts' or 'whereases.' Whatever the danger, if any, in such public discussions, it is a danger the Founders deemed outweighed by the danger incident to the stifling of thought and speech."

If the First Amendment protects leaflets that promote unpopular causes, does it also protect the identity of the publisher or distributor? That was the question in *Talley v. California.*[34] The justice answered the question in the affirmative. Manuel D. Talley distributed a leaflet that "urged readers to help . . . [an] organization carry on a boycott against certain merchants and businessmen . . . [who] carried products of 'manufacturers who will not offer equal employment opportunities to Negroes, Mexicans, and Orientals.' " He was charged and convicted of violating a city ordinance that required handbills to carry the name of the "person who printed, wrote, compiled or manufactured the same." With reference to anonymous material, the justice took notice that "anonymous pamphlets, leaflets, brochures and even books have played an important role in the progress of mankind. Persecuted groups and sects from time to time throughout history have been able to criticize oppressive practices and laws either anonymously or not at all."

Furthermore, "even the Federalist Papers, written in favor of the adoption of our Constitution, were published under fictitious names. It is plain that anonymity has sometimes been assumed for the most constructive purposes."

Picketing and Parading. Justice Black agreed that peaceful picketing was speech protected by the First Amendment and voted with the majority in *Thornhill v. Alabama*[35] and *Carlson v. California*[36] to strike down state statutes making it a criminal offense to engage in labor picketing even though that picketing was peaceful.

But even if picketing is protected speech, there remains the question whether it can be enjoined when violence erupts during picketing. Frankfurter and the majority answered the question in the affirmative in *Drivers Union v. Meadowmoor Co.*[37] because there had been violence during a labor dispute involved in that case. The majority concluded that "utterance in a context of violence can lose its significance as an appeal to reason and become part of an instrument of force. Such utterance was not meant to be sheltered by the Constitution."

Black did not disagree with the general proposition that picketers may lose their right to picket if they engage in violence, but he wanted to be sure that any injunction preventing such picketing was narrowly drawn so as not to infringe on First Amendment rights. He, therefore, dissented. He acknowledged that there had been some unlawful conduct, but, he said, "It is going a long way to say that because of the acts of these few men, six thousand other members of their union can be denied the right to express their opinion to the extent accomplished by the sweeping injunction here sustained." "I am of opinion," he declared, "that the court's injunction strikes at the heart of our government, and that deprivation of these essential liberties cannot be reconciled with the rights guaranteed to the people of this Nation by their Constitution."

Thereafter whenever a majority of the justices voted to strike down an injunction against peaceful picketing, Black joined with them.[38] But when the Court upheld such injunctions, he dissented.[39] Black also voted to uphold injunctions against peaceful picketing when the picketing violated some valid state objective not directly aimed at prohibiting the right to picket peacefully.

Black stated his position on peaceful demonstrations in a concurring opinion in *Cox v. Louisiana*,[40] where he wrote, "The First and Fourteenth Amendments, I think, take away from government, state and federal, all power to restrict freedom of speech, press, and assembly *where people have a right to be for such purposes.*"[41]

A couple of places where Black did not believe people had a *right to be* for protest purposes were around courthouses and jails. "The very purpose of a court system," he declared, "is to adjudicate controversies, both criminal and civil, in the calmness and solemnity of the courtroom according to legal procedures. Justice cannot be rightly administered, nor the lives and safety of prisoners secure, where throngs of people clamor against the processes of justice right outside the courthouse or jailhouse doors. The streets are not now and never have been the proper place to administer justice."[42]

Public Employees' Right to Advocate. George P. Poole, a roller at the U.S. Mint in Philadelphia, "was politically active by aiding and assisting the Democratic Party in the capacity of worker at the polls on general election day, November 5, 1940, and assisted in the distribution of funds in paying party workers for their services on general election day, November 5, 1940."[43] Because of these activities, Poole was dismissed for violating a law that prohibits federal employees "from taking 'any active part in political management or in political campaigns.'"

The trial court upheld the dismissal, and the Supreme Court affirmed. Justice Black dissented. He asserted:

> I think the Constitution prohibits legislation which prevents millions of citizens from contributing their arguments, complaints, and suggestions to the political debates which are the essence of our democracy; prevents them from engaging in organizational activity to urge others to vote and take an interest in political affairs; bars them from performing the interested citizen's duty of insuring that his and his fellow citizens' votes are counted. Such drastic limitations on the right of all the people to express political opinions and take political action would be inconsistent with the First Amendment's guaranty of freedom of speech, press, assembly, and petition.

Advocacy of Unpopular Ideas. On March 8, 1949, Irving Feiner stood on a wooden box on a street corner in Syracuse, New York, speaking to a crowd.

Police officers who were there noticed some restlessness among the listeners. Feiner "gave the impression that he was endeavoring to arouse the Negro people against the whites, urging that they rise up in arms and fight for equal rights. The statements before such a mixed audience 'stirred up a little excitement.' Some of the onlookers made remarks to the police about the inability to handle the crowd and at least one threatened violence if the police did not act. There were others who appeared to be favoring ... [Feiner's] arguments."⁴⁴ Finally, the police asked Feiner to cease speaking, and when he refused he was arrested and charged with the crime of disorderly conduct. Feiner was later convicted, and his conviction was upheld by a majority of the justices of the Supreme Court, with Justice Black dissenting. For the majority this was a simple case where Feiner's speech presented a clear and present danger of a breach of the peace, and therefore the police were forced to act to preserve public order.

This decision disturbed Justice Black. "The record before us convinces me," he declared, "that ... [Feiner], a young college student, has been sentenced to the penitentiary for the unpopular view he expressed on matters of public interest while lawfully making a street-corner speech in Syracuse, New York." He believed that it was the duty of the police to protect the speaker. "Their duty," he argued, "was to protect ... [Feiner's] right to talk, even to the extent of arresting the man who threatened to interfere." Not protecting a speaker under these circumstances, he continued, "means that as a practical matter, minority speakers can be silenced in any city. Hereafter, despite the First and Fourteenth Amendments, the policeman's club can take heavy toll of a current administration's public critics. Criticism of public officials will be too dangerous for all but the most courageous."

Dissenting from the Court's affirmance of the convictions of 11 top officials of the Communist Party of the United States, in *Dennis v. United States*,⁴⁵ the justice concluded his dissent as follows: "Public opinion being what it now is, few will protest the conviction of these Communist petitioners. There is hope, however, that in calmer times, when present pressures, passions and fears subside, this or some later Court will restore the First Amendment liberties to the high preferred place where they belong in a free society."

After a long, hard-fought, and sometimes acrimonious trial in 1949, Eugene Dennis, Robert G. Thompson, Gus Hall, Gilbert Green, John B. Williamson, Henry Winston, Irving Potash, John Gates, Carl Winter, Jacob Stachel, and Benjamin J. Davis, Jr., all officials of the U.S. Communist Party, were convicted of violating a federal law known as the Smith Act. This law made it a crime "to knowingly or willfully advocate, ... or teach the duty, necessity, desirability, or propriety of overthrowing ... any government in the United States by force or violence." It also made it a crime to organize any group that had as its goal the overthrow of the government by force.

Judge Harold Medina, who presided at the trial, charged the jury that they "could not find the ... [defendants] guilty under the indictment unless they found that . . . [defendants] had the intent to 'overthrow . . . the Government of the United States by force and violence as speedily as circumstances would permit.' " The jury concluded that the defendants did have the intent to overthrow the government, and were going to attempt to do so as soon as possible. A majority of the Supreme Court agreed. For them the defendants' activities presented a clear and present danger to the security of the United States, and they therefore were rightly convicted. In commenting upon whether there was a clear and present danger from these defendants, Chief Justice Vinson wrote: "Obviously, the words cannot mean that before the Government may act, it must wait until the *putsch* is about to be executed, the plans have been laid and the signal is awaited. If Government is aware that a group aiming at its overthrow is attempting to indoctrinate its members and to commit them to a course whereby they will strike when the leaders feel the circumstances permit, action by the Government is required."

Justice Black responded that "a governmental policy of unfettered communication of ideas does entail dangers. To the Founders of this Nation, however, the benefits derived from free expression were worth the risk." "I have always believed," he continued, "that the First Amendment is the keystone of our Government, that the freedoms it guarantees provide the best insurance against destruction of all freedom."

The justice believed, as did Thomas Jefferson, James Madison, and George Mason, that "loyalty to the provisions of this [the First] Amendment was the best way to assure a long life for this new nation and its Government." "The First Amendment," he declared, "provides the only kind of security system that can preserve a free government—one that leaves the way wide open for people to favor, discuss, advocate, or incite causes and doctrines however obnoxious and antagonistic such views may be to the rest of us."[46]

Black, however, believed that although "the First Amendment guarantees the right of assembly and the right of petition along with the rights of speech, press, and religion, it does not guarantee to any person the right to use someone else's property, even that owned by the government and dedicated to other purposes, as a stage to express dissident ideas."[47] He dissented when the Court reversed breach of the peace convictions of five blacks who sat in at the Audubon Regional Library at Clinton, Louisiana, to protest segregation of the library.

The justice also believed that public schools were not places for uncontrolled exercise of First Amendment rights. When the Court upheld the right of students to wear black armbands to school to protest the Vietnam War, he dissented. "It is a myth," he asserted, "to say that any person has a constitutional right to say what he pleases, where he pleases, and when he pleases."[48]

Freedom of Association

Affidavits and Oaths. The hysteria abroad in the land following World War II concerning allegedly subversive activities brought forth many attempts by government to ferret out those suspected of being Communists. Among the methods used were affidavits and oaths whereby one would be required to affirm that he or she was not a member of the Communist Party, nor believed in the overthrow of the government by force or violence.

In *Communications Assn. v. Douds,*[49] the Court had before it the question of the validity of a section of the National Labor Relations Act which required each union officer to file "that he is not a member of the Communist Party or affiliated with such party, and that he does not believe in, and is not a member of or supports any organization that believes in or teaches, the overthrow of the United States Government by force or by any illegal or unconstitutional methods." When that requirement was upheld by the Supreme Court, Black vigorously protested.

In condemning "test oaths," Black wrote: "History attests the efficacy of that instrument for inflicting penalties and disabilities on obnoxious minorities. It was one of the major devices used against the Huguenots in France, and against 'heretics' during the Spanish Inquisition. It helped English rulers identify and outlaw Catholics, Quakers, Baptists, and Congregationalists—groups considered dangerous for political as well as religious reasons."

Black chided the majority for upholding the affidavit requirement because the "encroachment on liberty is just a small one" and because it "touches only a relative handful of persons." "But not the least of the virtues of the First Amendment," he argued, "is its protection of each member of the smallest and most unorthodox minority." "Fears of alien ideologies," he noted, "have frequently agitated the nation and inspired legislation aimed at suppressing advocacy of those ideologies. At such times the fog of public excitement obscures the ancient landmarks set up in our Bill of Rights. Yet then, of all times, should this Court adhere most closely to the course they mark."

Blacklisting and Punishment for Membership. In 1947 President Harry Truman issued an executive order directing the attorney general to furnish the Loyalty Review Board "the name of each foreign or domestic organization, association . . . which the Attorney General . . . designates as totalitarian, fascist, communist or subversive."[50] The attorney general thereafter designated the Joint Anti-Fascist Refugee Committee, the International Workers Order, Inc., and the National Council of American-Soviet Friendship, Inc., as Communist.

Each organization brought suit against the attorney general alleging that it was not of the type described in the executive order, and that in any event the order violated the organization's constitutional rights. The district court dismissed the suits, but the Supreme Court reversed and ordered the actions reinstated. Justice Black concurred, stating that the order "cannot be reconciled with the First Amendment as I interpret it." "In this day," he continued, "when prejudice, hate and fear are constantly invoked to justify irresponsible smears and persecution of persons even faintly suspected of entertaining unpopular views, it may be futile to suggest that the cause of internal security would be fostered, not hurt, by faithful adherence to our constitutional guarantees of individual liberty."

Although President Truman's attempt to create a list of allegedly disloyal organizations did not meet with the Court's approval, Congress got into the act and enacted the Subversive Activities Control Act of 1950. Under that act Communist-action organizations were required to register with the attorney general. When the Control Board found that the Communist Party was a Communist-action organization, it ordered the party to register. The Party turned to the courts and ultimately to the Supreme Court seeking to have the registration requirement declared unconstitutional.[51] However, a majority of the justices voted to uphold the act, agreeing with the Control Board "that the 'world Communist movement' to which its finding related the Communist Party was the same 'world Communist movement' meant by Congress," and that "the registration provisions ... [are] not repugnant to the First Amendment, insofar as they require Communist-action organizations to file a registration statement containing the names and addresses of its present officers and members."

"I do not believe," Justice Black wrote in dissent, "that it can be too often repeated that the freedoms of speech, press, petition and assembly guaranteed by the First Amendment must be accorded to the ideas we hate or sooner or later they will be denied to the ideas we cherish." He pointed out that "men and women belonging to dissenting religious, political or social groups in England before the colonization of this country were sometimes imprisoned, mutilated, degraded by humiliating pillories, exiled and even killed for their views." Black then extensively reviewed the persecution of Catholics, Puritans, and Jacobins, in England, but also in the United States in the early days of the country by the enactment of Alien and Sedition Acts. "I am compelled to say in closing," he prophesied, "that I fear that all the arguments and urgings the Communists and their sympathizers can use in trying to convert Americans to an ideology wholly foreign to our habits and our instincts are far less dangerous to the security of this Nation than laws which embark us upon a policy of repression by the outlawry of minority parties because they advocate radical changes in the structure of Government."

Associational Privacy. Although Justice Black voted with the other justices to protect the membership lists of the NAACP, in *NAACP v. Alabama,*[52] he did so without expressing his opinion on the right to associational privacy. He took the occasion to do so, however, when Florida attempted to force Theodore R. Gibson to disclose the membership of the Miami branch of the NAACP. In concurring with the Court's decision to protect the membership lists, Black stated: "In my view the constitutional right of association includes the privilege of any person to associate with Communists or anti-Communists, Socialist or anti-Socialists, or, for that matter, with people of all kinds of beliefs, popular or unpopular."[53]

One of Black's most impassioned pleas for protection of associational privacy is his dissent in *Barenblatt v. United States.*[54] Lloyd Barenblatt, a former teacher at Vassar College, had been summoned to appear before the House

Committee on Un-American Activities. He refused to answer the following questions: "Are you now a member of the Communist Party?"; "Have you ever been a member of the Communist Party?"; "Now, you have stated that you knew Francis Crowley. Did you know Francis Crowley as a member of the Communist Party?"; "Were you ever a member of the Haldane Club of the Communist Party while at the University of Michigan?"; "Were you a member while a student at the University of Michigan Council of Arts, Sciences, and Professions?"

Barenblatt was convicted for refusing to answer these questions before a congressional committee; he was then fined and sentenced to prison for six months. He appealed to the Supreme Court, which upheld the conviction.

Black took issue with the Court, balancing an assumed governmental interest in security against Barenblatt's First Amendment rights. He argued that even if a balancing of interests approach is proper, the Court is applying it wrongfully in this case. "It completely leaves out the real interest in Barenblatt's silence, the interest of the people as a whole in being able to join organizations, advocate causes and make political 'mistakes' without later being subjected to governmental penalties for having dared to think for themselves. It is this right, the right to err politically, which keeps us strong as a Nation."

The justice continued:

> History should teach us then, that in times of high emotional excitement minority parties and groups which advocate extremely unpopular social or governmental innovations will always be typed as criminal gangs and attempts will always be made to drive them out. It was knowledge of this fact, and of its great dangers, that caused the Founders of our land to enact the First Amendment as a guarantee that neither Congress nor the people would do anything to hinder or destroy the capacity of individuals and groups to seek converts and votes for any cause, however radical or unpalatable their principles might seem under the accepted notions of the time.

The extent to which a state may inquire into the associations of applicants for membership in state bar associations has been before the Court a number of times.

Raphael Konigsberg graduated from law school at the University of Southern California and passed the bar exam shortly thereafter. When called before the Committee of Bar Examiners, "Konigsberg introduced further evidence as to his good moral character [none of which was rebutted], reiterated unequivocally his disbelief in violent overthrow [of the government], and stated that he had never knowingly been a member of any organization which advocated such action. He persisted, however, in his refusals to answer any questions relating to his membership in the Communist Party."[55] The Bar Committee therefore denied him admission to the bar, and that decision was upheld by the California Supreme Court and the U.S. Supreme Court.

A majority of the justices of the U.S. Supreme Court simply relied upon the many prior cases in which it had held that the government's interest in obtaining information about a person's political associations outweighed the First Amendment associational rights of the individuals involved.

Justice Black, however, argued in dissent that this decision was contrary to the meaning of the First Amendment as the framers of that amendment intended it to be construed.

"As I have indicated many times before," he pointed out, "I do not subscribe to . . . [the balancing] doctrine for I believe that the First Amendment's unequivocal command that there shall be no abridgement of the rights of free speech and assembly shows that the men who drafted our Bill of Rights did all the 'balancing' that was to be done in this field."

Furthermore, he wrote,

> This case must take its place in the ever-lengthening line of cases in which individual liberty to think, speak, write, associate and petition is being abridged in a manner precisely contrary to the explicit commands of the First Amendment. And I believe the abridgment of liberty here, as in most of the other cases in that line, is based upon nothing more than a fear that the American people can be alienated from their allegiance to our form of government by the talk of zealots for a form of government that is hostile to everything for which this country now stands or ever has stood.

The justice's position ultimately commanded a majority of the justices in *Baird v. State Bar of Arizona.*[56]

For Advancement of Legal Goals. Justice Black participated in four cases in which associations employed a staff of lawyers that was available to the members to assist them in presenting legal claims. *N.A.A.C.P. v. Button*[57] involved the legality of the NAACP's staff of 15 lawyers assisting its members in litigating racial discrimination cases. In *Brotherhood of Railroad Trainmen v. Virginia Bar*[58] the issue was whether the union could maintain a staff of lawyers to assist its members and their families in securing compensation for injuries or death of a worker. *United Mine Workers v. Illinois Bar*[59] was a case similar to *Railroad Trainmen,* except that the Mine Workers employed a full-time lawyer to assist its members in presenting workers' compensation cases. And in *United Transportation Union v. Michigan Bar,*[60] the union recommended to its members certain lawyers who had agreed to handle damage claims under the Federal Employer's Liability Act for a fee of no more than 25 percent.

The bar associations in Virginia, Illinois, and Michigan sought to prevent these kinds of arrangements, arguing that they constituted unauthorized practice of law and violated rules against lawyers' soliciting clients. The Supreme Court disagreed and upheld associations' practices in each case.

Black summed up the previous decisions of the Court in writing the opinion in *United Transportation.* "The common thread running through our decisions in *NAACP v. Button, Trainmen,* and *United Mine Workers* is that collective activity undertaken to obtain meaningful access to the courts is a fundamental right within the protection of the First Amendment. However, that right would be a hollow promise if courts could deny associations of workers or others the means enabling their members to meet the costs of legal representation."

Freedom of the Press

Contempt of Court for Publication. Following the conviction of two union members for assaulting some nonunion truck drivers, the Times-Mirror Company published an editorial urging Judge A.A. Scott not to grant probation to the defendants. The editorial concluded, "Judge A.A. Scott will make a serious mistake if he grants probation to Matthew Shannon and Kennan Holmes. This community needs the example of their assignment to the jute mill."[61] The *Mirror* and its editor, L.D. Hotchkiss, were charged and convicted of contempt on the theory that the editorial had a "'reasonable tendency' to interfere with the orderly administration of justice." The convictions were upheld by the California Supreme Court, but reversed by the U.S. Supreme Court, with Justice Black writing the opinion.

In response to the assertion that prior to the adoption of the Bill of Rights, English judges had the power to punish for out-of-court statements, the justice declared: "The only conclusion supported by history is that the unqualified prohibitions laid down by the framers were intended to give to liberty of the press, as to other liberties, the broadest scope that could be countenanced in an orderly society."

Libel. Justice Frank Murphy wrote for the Court, "There are certain well-defined and narrowly limited classes of speech, the prevention and punishment of which have never been thought to raise any Constitutional problem. These include the lewd and obscene, the profane, *the libelous*, and the insulting or 'fighting words'—those which by their very utterance inflict injury or tend to incite an immediate breach of the peace."[62]

When an Alabama jury awarded L.B. Sullivan, commissioner of public affairs, Montgomery, Alabama, $500,000 in damages against the New York Times Co. for allegedly printing libelous material about him, Justice Black concurred in the Court's decision to reverse.[63]

Although the Court placed some limitations on libel actions against the press, it did not eliminate them entirely. Black, however, thought that they should have done so. "In my opinion," he declared, "the Federal Constitution has dealt with this deadly danger to the press in the only way possible without leaving the free press open to destruction—by granting the press an absolute immunity for criticism of the way public officials do their public duty."

The *Saturday Evening Post*, on March 23, 1963, carried a story entitled "The Story of a College Football Fix."[64] A subtitle read "A Shocking Report of

How Wally Butts and 'Bear' Bryant Rigged a Game Last Fall." Wally Butts was athletic director at the University of Georgia and "Bear" Bryant was football coach at the University of Alabama.

The story started with this comment: "Not since the Chicago White Sox threw the 1919 World Series has there been a sports story as shocking as this one. This is the story of one fixed game of college football. Before the University of Georgia played the University of Alabama last September 22, Wally Butts, athletic director of Georgia, gave Paul 'Bear' Bryant, head coach of Alabama, Georgia's plays, defensive patterns, all the significant secrets Georgia's football team possessed."

Butts sued the Curtis Publishing Co., the publisher of the *Saturday Evening Post*, for libel and was awarded $60,000 in general damages and $3 million in punitive damages, which was reduced by the trial judge to $460,000.[65] The Supreme Court upheld these awards, but Justice Black dissented.

He believed that the standards adopted in *New York Times* and in this case would lead the Court into "the same quagmire in the field of libel in which it is now helplessly struggling in the field of obscenity." "I think it is time," he argued, "for this Court to abandon *New York Times Co. v. Sullivan* and adopt the rule to the effect that the First Amendment was intended to leave the press free from the harassment of libel judgments." The justice never wavered from that position.[66]

Punishment for and Prior Restraint of Publication. Justice Black's belief that the press should be free to publish is also shown in *Mills v. Alabama*.[67] "The question here," he asked, "is whether it abridges freedom of the press for a State to punish a newspaper editor for doing no more than publishing an editorial on election day urging people to vote a particular way in the election."

James E. Mills, a newspaper editor, wrote an editorial on election day urging the people "to adopt the mayor-council form of government." For this he was arrested and charged with violating Alabama's Corrupt Practices Act, which made it a crime "to do any electioneering or to solicit any votes" on election day. Although the trial judge was of the opinion that applying the law to Mills was a violation of the First Amendment, the Alabama Supreme Court disagreed and upheld the law. A unanimous U.S. Supreme Court reversed.

"Suppression of the right of the press." Black declared, "to praise or criticize governmental agents and to clamor and contend for or against change, which is all that this editorial did, muzzles one of the very agencies the Framers of our Constitution thoughtfully and deliberately selected to improve our society and keep it free."

In June 1971, the *Washington Post* and the *New York Times* published excerpts from secret Department of Defense documents relating to the Vietnam War. The government immediately sought court orders in Washington, D.C., and New York City restraining further publication. It argued that publication of the documents would do great harm to the interests of the United States. Judge

Gerhard J. Gesell in Washington refused to enjoin publication, as did Judge Murray I. Gurfein in New York. Judge Gurfein, however, was reversed by the circuit court, which sent the case back for further proceedings.

When the cases reached the Supreme Court, it held that preventing the *Post* and the *Times* from publishing this information violated their freedom of the press guaranteed by the First Amendment. The case, which spawned ten opinions, is commonly known as the *Pentagon Papers* case.[68] Black wrote one of the concurring opinions. "I believe," he declared, "that every moment's continuance of the injunctions against these newspapers amounts to a flagrant, indefensible, and continuing violation of the First Amendment."

After reviewing the history of the adoption of the Bill of Rights, the justice pointed out: "Our Government was launched in 1789 with the adoption of the Constitution. The Bill of Rights, including the First Amendment, followed in 1791. Now, for the first time in the 182 years since the founding of the Republic, the federal courts are asked to hold that the First Amendment does not mean what it says, but rather means that the Government can halt the publication of current news of vital importance to the people of this country." But, in adopting the First Amendment, "the Founding Fathers gave the free press the protection it must have to fulfill its essential role in our democracy. The press was to serve the governed, not the governors. The Government's power to censor the press was abolished so that the press would remain forever free to censure the Government. The press was protected so that it could bare the secrets of government and inform the people. Only a free and unrestrained press can effectively expose deception in government."

Obscenity. When the New York State Regents of the university found the film *Lady Chatterley's Lover* to be immoral, and sustained the denial of a license to the distributor to distribute it, the Supreme Court unanimously reversed.[69]

In concurring, Black set forth his belief not only that is censorship contrary to the principles of the First Amendment, but that "this Court is about the most inappropriate Supreme Board of Censors that could be found." Censorship, he asserted, would require "every member of the Court . . . [to] exercise his own judgment as to how bad a picture is, a judgment which is ultimately based at least in large part on his own standard of what is immoral." It was, therefore, unnecessary for him to see *Lady Chatterley's Lover* to reach the conclusion that the distributor had a First Amendment right to show it. The justice never wavered from these views.

In *Ginzberg v. United States*,[70] the Court affirmed the conviction of Ralph Ginzberg for mailing three publications found to be obscene. The publications were (1) "EROS, a hard-cover magazine of expensive format . . . [which contained] 15 articles and photo essays on the subject of love, sex, and sexual relations," (2) "Liaison, a bi-weekly news letter . . . [which included] a prefatory 'Letter from the Editors' announcing its dedication to 'keeping sex an art and preventing it from becoming a science,' " and (3) *"The Housewife's Handbook on*

Selective Promiscuity . . . [which] purports to be a sexual autobiography dealing with complete candor the author's sexual experiences from age 3 to 36."

The justice took a dim view of the Court's approach in this and other obscenity cases decided the same day. "It is obvious," he commented,

> that the effect of the Court's decisions in the three obscenity cases handed down today is to make it exceedingly dangerous for people to discuss either orally or in writing anything about sex. Sex is a fact of life. . . . It is a subject which people are bound to consider and discuss whatever laws are passed by any government to try to suppress it. . . . I find it difficult to see how talk about sex can be placed under the kind of censorship the Court here approves without subjecting our society to more dangers than we can anticipate at the moment.

The Pursuit of Liberty

The Right to Travel. Whether the right to travel was a right protected by the Civil Rights Act of 1964 was a question to be answered in *United States v. Guest.*[71] A federal grand jury indicted Herbert Guest and five others for violating the civil rights of certain blacks in Georgia. Included in the indictment was a charge that the defendants conspired "to injure, oppress, threaten, and intimidate Negro citizens" in their "right to travel freely to and from the State of Georgia and to use highway facilities and other instrumentalities of interstate commerce within the State of Georgia."[72]

Chief District Judge William A. Bootle dismissed the indictment, asserting that the right to travel was not protected by the Civil Rights Act. The Supreme Court reversed. With regard to the existence of a right to travel, the Court wrote: "The constitutional right to travel from one State to another, and necessarily to use the highways and other instrumentalities of interstate commerce in doing so, occupies a position fundamental to the concept of our Federal Union. It is a right that has been firmly established and repeatedly recognized."[73] Black agreed.

For the justice, restricting the right to travel by denying a passport to a member of the Communist Party violated First Amendment rights. In *Aptheker v. Secretary of State,*[74] he wrote: "This case offers another appropriate occasion to point out that the Framers thought (and I agree) that the best way to promote the internal security of our people is to protect their First Amendment freedoms of speech, press, religion and assembly, and that we cannot take away the liberty of groups whose views most people detest without jeopardizing the liberty of all others whose views, though popular today, may themselves be detested tomorrow."

The Right to Work. Dr. Edward K. Barsky was a physician who had practiced medicine in New York for more than 25 years. He was subpoenaed by the House of Representatives Committee on Un-American Activities in 1954 to produce certain records of the Joint Anti-Fascist Refugee Committee, of which he was chairman. His refusal to produce the records was a violation of federal law. He was therefore convicted, fined $500, and sentenced to six months in jail.[75]

Shortly thereafter, two New York Medical Grievance Committees and the regents of the university held hearings concerning the suspension of the doctor's license. At issue was whether he should be suspended because he had "been convicted in a court of competent jurisdiction . . . of a crime." When the regents ordered the license suspended for a period of six months, Dr. Barsky appealed to the courts, but they upheld the suspension. The Supreme Court affirmed, with justices Black, Frankfurter, and Douglas dissenting.

"I have no doubt," Black pointed out, "that New York has broad power to regulate the practice of medicine. But the right to practice is . . . a very precious part of the liberty of an individual physician or surgeon. It may mean more than any property. Such a right is protected from arbitrary infringement by our Constitution, which forbids any state to deprive a person of liberty or property without due process of law."

The Right of Privacy. Justice Black did not believe that the Constitution protected a general right of privacy. He wrote a lengthy dissenting opinion in *Griswold v. Connecticut*,[76] setting forth his views. "I like my privacy as well as the next one," he declared, "but I am nevertheless compelled to admit that government has a right to invade it unless prohibited by some specific constitutional provision."

Despite Black's disagreement with the Court in *Griswold*, he did believe that people had a right to privacy in their own homes. For example, he wrote the majority opinion in *Martin v. Struthers*,[77] striking down an ordinance prohibiting door-to-door distribution of "handbills, circulars or other advertisements." In doing so, however, he recognized "the right of the individual householder to determine whether he is willing to receive . . . [the distributor's] message." He pointed out that both the distributor of the literature and the potential recipient have rights that the community may address, but this "ordinance does not safeguard these constitutional rights."

Equal Protection of the Law

Blacks on Juries. "Exclusion from Grand or Petit Jury service on account of race is forbidden by the Fourteenth Amendment."[78] With that statement the Court reversed the murder conviction of a black in the parish of St. John the Baptist, Louisiana, in 1939. Evidence indicated that no black person had served on the grand jury for 40 years, although almost half the population of the parish was black.

Justice Black, writing the majority opinion, said: "The testimony introduced by petitioner on his motion to quash created a strong *prima facie* showing that negroes had been systematically excluded—because of race—from the Grand Jury and the venire from which it was selected. Such an exclusion is a denial of equal protection of the laws, contrary to the Federal Constitution—the supreme law of the land." The justice then quoted from a prior case: "'It is a right to which every colored man is entitled, that, in the selection of jurors to pass upon his life, liberty, or property, there shall be no exclusion of his race, and no discrimination against them because of their color.'"

The justice wrote the opinions in three other cases in which the Court affirmed the constitutional rule that prohibits the exclusion of blacks from juries.[79] He also participated and voted for integration of juries in many subsequent cases.

Exclusion of Blacks from Universities. Black joined the majority in ordering Lloyd Gaines admitted to the University of Missouri Law School,[80] and Ada Lois Sipuel admitted to the University of Oklahoma Law School.[81]

When Herman Marion Sweatt, who was black, applied for admission to the University of Texas School of Law, the state sought to avoid compliance with the above cases by setting up a separate law school just for blacks.[82] This was acceptable to the Texas courts but not to any of the justices of the Supreme Court, including Black.

Chief Justice Fred M. Vinson described the new law school as follows: "The law school for Negroes which was to have opened in February 1947, would have had no independent faculty or library. The teaching was to be carried on by four members of the University of Texas Law School faculty, who were to maintain their offices at the University of Texas while teaching at both institutions. Few of the 10,000 volumes ordered for the library had arrived; nor was there any full-time librarian. The school lacked accreditation."

"In accordance with [prior] cases," the chief justice declared, " ... [Sweatt] may claim his full constitutional right: legal education equivalent to that offered by the State to students of other races. Such education is not available to him in a separate school as offered by the State."

Faced with integration of its institutions of higher education, the Oklahoma legislature decreed that black students could be admitted "upon a segregated basis."[83] In compliance with the legislative mandate, the University of Oklahoma admitted G.W. McLaurin, who was black, to its graduate program. "He was required to sit apart at a designated desk in an anteroom adjoining the classroom; to sit at a designated desk on the mezzanine floor of the library, but not to use the desks in the regular reading room; and to sit at a designated table and to eat at a different time from the other students in the school cafeteria."

When the federal court upheld these requirements, McLaurin appealed to the Supreme Court, which unanimously reversed. "We hold," Chief Justice Vinson wrote, "that under these circumstances the Fourteenth Amendment precludes differences in treatment by the state based upon race. [McLaurin], . . . having been admitted to a state-supported graduate school, must receive the same treatment at the hands of the state as students of other races."

Integration of Public Schools. In 1951 Oliver Brown and others legally challenged the validity of separate but equal schools for elementary school students in Topeka, Kansas. At that time there were 18 elementary schools for white students and four for black students. Circuit Judge Walter A. Huxman, for himself and District Judges Arthur J. Mellott and Delmas C. Hill, concluded that *Plessy v. Ferguson* and *Gong Lum v. Rice* had "not been overruled and that they still presently are authority for the maintenance of a segregated school system in the lower grades."[84]

The Supreme Court disagreed, with Chief Justice Earl Warren writing an opinion that all nine justices signed.[85]

Hugo Black, Jr., tells what happened when the news reached the South that Justice Black had voted with the majority: "All hell broke loose in the Birmingham community.... Most of the newspapers, politicians and citizens of Hugo's homestate looked on Daddy as 'a traitor to the South,' and a candidate for governor opined one day that 'Justice Black is not fit to try a chicken thief.'"[86]

The furor was so great that Hugo Black, Jr., decided to leave Birmingham and set up practice in Miami, Florida. "We were being so intimidated by the feeling against Daddy," he wrote, "that I knew my partners would be better off without me and I would be more effective somewhere else.... I felt that I did not want to live any place where my daddy, who should have been respected beyond all other Alabama public figures, living or dead, could not come without being treated like a leper."

Although the Court ordered that desegregation of public schools should take place "with all deliberate speed,"[87] resistance to doing so pervaded the South for many years. The supervisors of Prince Edward County, Virginia, for example, refused to operate schools "wherein white and colored children are taught together."[88] As a result the public schools were closed, and private segregated schools were set up in their place. Black children were without schools to attend.

The fact that ten years had elapsed since the Court had ordered desegregation of schools in *Brown* disturbed the justice. "The time for mere 'deliberate speed' has run out, and that phrase can no longer justify denying these Prince Edward County school children their constitutional rights to an education equal to that afforded by the public schools in the other parts of Virginia."

Integration of Public Facilities. Justice Black's votes on integration of public facilities are a mixed bag. Following the *Brown* case, he joined the majority in *Johnson v. Virginia*,[89] a case wherein Ford T. Johnson, Jr., who was black, was convicted for contempt because he refused to sit in the blacks-only section of a courtroom. In a *per curiam* opinion, the Court reversed, holding that "a State may not require racial segregation in a courtroom."

The justice participated in several other *per curiam* decisions striking down segregated public beaches, golf courses, and athletic contests.[90] He also joined Justice Arthur Goldberg's opinion in *Watson v. Memphis*,[91] when the Court ordered the immediate integration of the public parks in Memphis, Tennessee.

However, when the Court ordered the integration of a park created by the will of former Georgia U.S. Senator Augustus O. Bacon, he dissented. Bacon had willed the land to the city of Macon to be used as a park for whites only. When it became clear that it would be illegal for the city to maintain a segregated park, the city was removed as trustee and a group of private individuals appointed. This decision was affirmed by the Georgia Supreme Court, but reversed by the U. S. Supreme Court because the majority was of the opinion that the park had not really been disentangled from control by the city.[92] Black protested. "I find nothing in the United States Constitution that compels any city or other state subdivision to hold title to property it does not want or to act as trustee under a will when it chooses not to do so."

Because the park could no longer be for whites only, as Senator Bacon desired, the Georgia courts held that the bequest failed and the property reverted to his heirs. In an opinion written by the justice, the Supreme Court agreed. "Here," Black said, "the effect of the Georgia decision eliminated all discrimination against Negroes in the park by eliminating the park itself and the termination of the park was a loss shared equally by the white and Negro citizens of Macon since both races would have enjoyed a constitutional right of equal access to the park's facilities had it continued."[93] Douglas and Brennan dissented.

Integration of Private Facilities. In 1883 Justice Bradley, referring to the Fourteenth Amendment, said, "It nullifies and makes void all State legislation, and State action of every kind, which impairs the privileges and immunities of citizens of the United States, or which injures them in life, liberty or property without due process of law, or which denies to any of them the equal protection of the laws."[94]

Sometimes the actions of government are quite subtle. Florida, for example, had a statute that gave restaurant managers authority to remove any person they thought was " 'a person who it would be detrimental' to the restaurant to serve.' "[95] Furthermore, the Board of Health had issued regulations requiring restaurants to provide separate employee restrooms for each sex and race.

When a group of blacks went into Shell's City Restaurant in Miami, Florida, the manager asked them leave. They refused and were arrested. The individuals were convicted of violating the above statute. Their case eventually reached the Supreme Court, which reversed, with Justice Black writing the Court's opinion. "While these Florida regulations do not directly and expressly forbid restaurants to serve both white and colored people together, they certainly embody a state policy putting burdens upon any restaurant which serves both races, burdens bound to discourage the serving of the two races together." This, Black concluded, denied the blacks the equal protection of the law.

Justice Black was not ready, however, to find action by the government a violation of law when a restaurant manager called upon police for assistance in evicting blacks who had sat in at a restaurant that served whites only. When Mr. Bouie and a friend, who were black, refused to leave the restaurant, they were arrested and charged with criminal trespass.[96] A majority of the Supreme Court reversed their conviction, holding that the defendants were not given adequate warning that they were trespassing by quietly sitting in one of the booths. Thus they were denied due process of law. Justices Black, John Harlan, and Byron White dissented. They were of the opinion that the defendants had adequate warning that they were trespassing, and further that the application of the criminal trespass statute did not deny them equal protection of the laws. "We have stated today . . . ," Black declared, "our belief that the Fourteenth Amendment does not of its own force compel a restaurant owner to accept customers he does not want to serve, even though his reason for refusing to serve them may be his racial prejudice, adherence to local custom, or what he conceives to be his economic self-interest, and that the arrest and conviction of a person for trespassing in a restaurant under such circumstances is not the kind of 'state action' forbidden by the Fourteenth Amendment."

For Illegitimate Children. "These decisions can only be classified as constitutional curiosities."[97] That was the opinion of the second Justice John M. Harlan in commenting upon two decisions of the Court upholding equal protection rights of illegitimate children. It was given in a dissenting opinion in which justices Black and Stewart joined.

The first of these cases involved the five illegitimate children of Louise Levy, who were seeking damages for the wrongful death of their mother. Recovery was denied because, according to the court, the word *child* in the Louisiana wrongful death statute did not include illegitimate children.[98] The Supreme Court, however, reversed, concluding that these children were being denied equal protection of the law.

The other case was brought by Minnie Brade Glona for the wrongful death of her illegitimate son in an auto accident.[99] When the Louisiana courts also dismissed this case, she appealed to the Supreme Court, which reversed. Justices Harlan, Black, and Stewart again dissented.

Black took the opportunity to set forth his views on inheritance rights of illegitimate children when he wrote the majority opinion in *Labine v. Vincent*,[100] wherein the Court upheld the denial of such rights. The opinion recites the facts of that case: "On March 15, 1962, a baby girl, Rita Vincent, was born to Lou Bertha Patterson (now Lou Bertha Labine) in Calcasieu Parish, Louisiana. On May 10, 1962, Lou Bertha Patterson and Ezra Vincent, as authorized by Louisiana law, jointly executed before a notary a Louisiana State Board of Health form acknowledging that Ezra Vincent was the 'natural father' of Rita Vincent."

The form did not legitimize Rita Vincent or give her inheritance rights. When Ezra Vincent died without a will, Rita Vincent, acting though her guardian, brought an action claiming a right of inheritance, but the Louisiana court held that no such right existed under the law governing inheritance. Ezra Vincent's property therefore passed to his relatives, who did not include Lou Bertha Labine because she and Ezra had never married.

Black discussed at length the inheritance rights of both legitimate and illegitimate children in Louisiana. He pointed out that Rita's father could have made her legitimate by marrying Lou Bertha, or given her inheritance rights by stating his intention to do so when he acknowledged that she was his child. He could also have included her as a beneficiary in a will. In commenting upon Louisiana's laws, the justice noted that "many will think that it is unfortunate that the rules are so rigid. . . . But the choices reflected by the intestate succession statute are choices which it is within the power of the State to make." Justices Brennan, Douglas, White, and Marshall dissented.

For Aliens. Torao Takahashi, a resident alien of Japanese ancestry not entitled to citizenship, had been a commercial fisherman from 1915 until 1941 when he was evacuated from California by a military order at the beginning of World War II. When he returned in 1945, he applied for renewal of his fishing license. The application was denied because a California law prohibited the issuance of licenses to persons not eligible for citizenship. Takahashi brought an action against the state, arguing that the law was unconstitutional. Judge Henry M. Willis agreed and ordered the Fish and Game Commission to issue the license. It refused to do so and appealed to the California Supreme Court, which upheld the refusal. Takahashi then appealed to the U.S. Supreme Court, which held that California had indeed denied him equal protection of the law.[101]

In writing the Court's opinion, Justice Black noted that both federal law and the Fourteenth Amendment protect *all persons*. "The Fourteenth Amendment and the laws adopted under its authority," he wrote, "thus embody a general policy that all persons lawfully in this country shall abide 'in any state' on an equality of legal privileges with all citizens under nondiscriminatory laws."

The justice's concern for equal treatment of aliens included persons who had never been in the United States but found themselves within the grasp of the U.S. Army in China after World War II. Lothar Eisentrager and Franz Siebert were two of those persons. They were civilian employees of the German government working in China when the war ended who were arrested, tried, and convicted by a military commission for activities against the United States, and imprisoned. Eisentrager and Siebert petitioned the U.S. District Court for a writ of *habeas corpus,* claiming that they had been tried without having the benefits of the U.S. Constitution, but the court dismissed the petition.

Justice Robert H. Jackson, writing for a majority of the Supreme Court, upheld the dismissal, and pointed out that "the nonresident enemy alien, especially one who has remained in the service of the enemy, does not have . . . access to our courts, for he neither has comparable claims upon our institutions nor could his use of them fail to be helpful to the enemy."[102]

Black saw this as a denigration of the rights of those persons within the control of the United States. He wrote:

> Our Constitution has led people everywhere to hope and believe that wherever our laws control, all people, whether our citizens or not, would have an equal

chance before the bar of criminal justice. . . . Our constitutional principles are such that their mandate of equal justice under law should be applied as well when we occupy lands across the sea as when our flag flew only over thirteen colonies. Our nation proclaims a belief in the dignity of human beings as such, no matter what their nationality or where they happen to live. Habeas corpus, as an instrument to protect against illegal imprisonment, is written into the Constitution.

In Classification of Voters. When Sergeant Herbert N. Carrington, formerly of Alabama, was assigned to the army base at White Sands, New Mexico, he moved to El Paso, Texas, where he bought a home for himself, his wife, and children. He claimed El Paso as his permanent residence and commuted from there to his job at White Sands.

Carrington sought to vote in the Republican Party primary but was informed that under Texas law he could not do so. That law "prohibits '(a)ny member of the Armed Forces of the United States' who moves his home to Texas during the course of his military duty from ever voting in any election in that State 'so long as he or she is a member of the Armed Forces.' "[103]

The justification given for prohibiting service personnel from voting was that because they were subject to transfer they would not have the same interest in governmental affairs as permanent residents. Texas courts upheld the law, but the Supreme Court found it unconstitutional as a violation of the Equal Protection Clause. The majority recognized the problems connected with determining residency requirements for voting, but pointed out that "all servicemen not residents of Texas before induction come within the provision's sweep. Not one of them can ever vote in Texas, no matter how long Texas may have been his true home. '(T)he uniform of our country . . . [must not] be the badge of disfranchisement for the man or woman who wears it.' " Justice Black concurred.

The justice also concurred when the Court struck down a Louisiana law that gave "only 'property taxpayers' the right to vote in elections called to approve the issuance of revenue bonds by a municipal utility,"[104] and a Maryland law that refused to allow federal employees living on a federal reservation to vote in state elections.[105]

The justice was not sympathetic, however, with the desire of Morris H. Kramer to vote in his school district election.[106] Kramer, a bachelor, lived with his parents, had no children, and did not own or lease any real property. He therefore was not a qualified voter for school district elections. When a federal district court dismissed his lawsuit against the school district, he took his case to the Supreme Court, claiming that he was being denied equal protection of the laws. A majority of the justices agreed, but Black joined the dissenting opinion of Justice Stewart.

For New Political Parties. In order for the Ohio American Independent Party and the Socialist Labor Party to get on the 1968 Ohio election ballot, they were required to meet certain rules not applicable to the Republican or Democratic parties. The so-called established parties were automatically placed on the ballot if they received "10% of the votes in the last gubernatorial election."[107]

Furthermore, they were not required to obtain any signature petitions. New parties, however, had to "obtain petitions signed by qualified electors totaling 15% of the number of ballots cast in the last gubernatorial election and must file these petitions early in February of the election year." Although the Independent Party collected more than the required number of signatures, it was unable to meet the February deadline. The Socialist Party did not circulate petitions because it was of the opinion that it could not comply with the early filing requirement. Both parties brought suit challenging the validity of the laws. A federal district court found the laws to be a violation of equal protection. In an opinion written by Justice Black, a majority of the Supreme Court agreed. The justice noted that in "the present situation the state laws place burdens on two different, although overlapping, kinds of rights—the right of individuals to associate for the advancement of political beliefs, and the right of qualified voters, regardless of their political persuasion, to cast their votes effectively. Both of these rights, of course, rank among our most precious freedoms." "The right to form a party for the advancement of political goals," he continued, "means little if a party can be kept off the election ballot and thus denied an equal opportunity to win votes. So also, the right to vote is heavily burdened if that vote may be cast only for one of two parties at a time when other parties are clamoring for a place on the ballot."

In the Criminal Justice System. Prisoners are persons within the meaning of the Equal Protection Clause, and therefore rich and poor alike must be treated substantially equal in the administration of the criminal justice system.

It took Lawrence E. Cook, however, almost 20 years to secure equal treatment in his appeal of a murder conviction in Indiana in 1931.[108] Cook prepared an appeal within the six-month time limit for filing appeals after conviction, but prison officials refused to send the papers to the appellate court. He tried unsuccessfully in 1937 and again in 1945 to secure a review of his case. He finally brought an action in the federal district court claiming a denial of equal protection of the laws because he was not given the same right to appeal as other convicted persons. That court agreed that Cook had not received equal treatment by the Indiana courts and ordered him discharged. The state appealed to the Supreme Court, and, while all of the justices agreed that Cook had been denied equal protection, they sent the case back to Indiana, instructing it to review his case or discharge him from custody. "Under the peculiar circumstances of this case," Justice Black declared, "nothing short of an actual appellate determination of the merits of the conviction—according to the procedure prevailing in ordinary cases—would cure the original denial of equal protection of the law."

One of the essential elements of an appeal from a conviction is a stenographic transcript of the trial proceedings. After Griffin and Crenshaw were convicted of armed robbery in Illinois, they requested the state to furnish a transcript of the trial because they had no funds to pay for one. The state refused because only defendants sentenced to death were entitled to free transcripts.[109] When the appellate courts in Illinois refused to grant relief, Griffin and Crenshaw appealed to the Supreme Court, which ordered the Illinois Supreme Court to find "means of affording adequate and effective appellate review to indigent defendants." Justice Black authored the Court's opinion: "Our own constitutional guaranties of due process and equal protection both call for procedures in criminal trials which allow no invidious discriminations between persons and different groups of persons. Both equal protection and due process emphasize the central aim of our entire judicial system—all people charged with crime must, so far as the law is concerned, 'stand on an equality before the bar of justice in every American Court.'" The Court did not require the state to furnish a transcript in every case. It was permitted to "find other means of affording adequate and effective appellate review to indigent defendants."

States seemed not to have gotten Black's message that the Equal Protection Clause guarantees to indigent persons substantially the same ability to appeal as accorded those who have the means to pay. Before the justice retired, he participated in many similar cases, some of which involved denial of a free transcript.[110] The Court also voted to allow indigents to appeal without payment of a filing fee, and Black concurred.[111]

And the Court, including Black, found unconstitutional New Jersey's requirement that an incarcerated indigent whose appeal was unsuccessful was required to reimburse the state for the cost of the transcript, but one who was not in jail or prison was not required to do so.[112]

Because many states grant one appeal as a matter of right to a person convicted of a crime, the Court in *Douglas v. California*[113] held that it would be a denial of equal protection not to provide indigents with counsel without cost during such an appeal. The Court said, "There can be no equal justice where the kind of an appeal a man enjoys 'depends on the amount of money he has.'" The justice joined that opinion.

Black's one dissent came when the Court said that California must provide counsel to Charlie Anders.[114] The state had provided counsel for Anders, who, upon studying the record, concluded there were no grounds for appeal. Counsel so informed the court. Anders's request for another lawyer was denied. The appellate court then heard Anders's appeal, and upheld his conviction. Six years later Anders sought to reopen his case claiming that he had been deprived of his right to counsel during his prior appeal. California courts disagreed, but a majority of the Supreme Court concluded that the appeal should not have gone forward without new counsel being appointed. Justices Stewart, Black, and Harlan dissented, being of the opinion that Anders had not been denied equal protection because not only had counsel concluded that there were no grounds for appeal, but the appellate court had also reviewed the record and reached the same conclusion.

Justice Hugo LaFayette Black

The Bill of Rights and the States

Justice Black was of the opinion that the writers of the Fourteenth Amendment intended that states thereafter would be required to abide by _all_ provisions of the Bill of Rights. He set forth his views in a dissenting opinion in _Adamson v. California_,[115] a case in which the majority refused to require California to honor the Fifth Amendment's prohibition against self-incrimination:

> In my judgment . . . history conclusively demonstrates that the language of the first section of the Fourteenth Amendment, taken as a whole, was thought by those responsible for its submission to the people, and by those who opposed its submission, sufficiently explicit to guarantee that thereafter no state could deprive its citizens of the privileges and protections of the Bill of Rights.

The justice attached to his dissent a 32-page appendix setting forth the history to which he referred. Included were citations to the first Justice Harlan's dissenting opinions in _Hurtado v. California, Maxwell v. Dow_, and _Twining v. New Jersey_.

Black adhered to these views but was never able to convince four other justices to agree. Ultimately the Court, on a case-by-case basis, held that states must abide by most of the provisions in the Bill of Rights, and Black acquiesced in this process. For example, in 1968 the Court reversed the conviction of Gary Duncan, age 19, who had been tried and convicted for simple battery in Louisiana without a jury. Duncan had requested a jury but was informed that "the Louisiana Constitution grants jury trials only in cases in which capital punishment or imprisonment at hard labor may be imposed."[116] In reversing Duncan's conviction the Court held that thereafter states were required to abide by the Sixth Amendment's provision guaranteeing "an impartial jury." In concurring, Black pointed out that he still believed that the Fourteenth Amendment made all of the Bill of Rights applicable to the states. But taking note of the Court's "selective process" to do so, he said, "I am very happy to support this selective process through which our Court has since the _Adamson_ case held most of the specific Bill of Rights' protections applicable to the States to the same extent they are applicable to the Federal Government."

The Japanese Cases

Within months of the bombing of Pearl Harbor by the Japanese on December 7, 1941, President Franklin D. Roosevelt issued an executive order giving military commanders authority to designate "Military Areas" and to exclude persons from such areas. Acting under that executive order, Commanding General J.L. DeWitt issued an order excluding all persons of Japanese descent from the area around San Leandro, California. Fred Toyosaburo Korematsu, an American citizen of Japanese descent, was convicted of remaining within the restricted area, and his conviction was upheld by the Supreme Court, with Black writing the majority opinion. He acknowledged that "all legal restrictions which curtail the civil rights of a single racial group are immediately suspect,"[117] and that "compulsory exclusion of large groups of citizens from their homes, except under circumstances of direst emergency and peril, is inconsistent with our basic governmental institutions." But his concern for Korematsu and the other Japanese forced to leave their homes, ended there. The Japanese, and all other citizens, had to endure the effects of the war, especially "when under conditions of modern warfare our shores are threatened by hostile forces, the power to protect must be commensurate with the threatened danger." Black and the majority believed that danger from the Japanese, whether citizens or aliens, did exist. Therefore, the justices could not "by availing . . . [themselves] of the calm perspective of hindsight—now say that at that time these actions were unjustified."

Prior to *Korematsu* the justice had voted to uphold the criminal convictions of Gordon Kyoshi Hirabayashi[118] and Minoru Yasui[119] for violating curfew orders issued by the Western Defense Command, Fourth Army, for the west coastal area of the United States at the beginning of World War II.

Black did, however, vote to grant freedom to Mitsuye Endo, an admittedly loyal and law-abiding citizen who was being detained unlawfully by military authorities in 1944.[120]

As a Judicial Freedom Fighter

Justice Black saw the First Amendment in terms of absolutes. He vigorously opposed "balancing" the rights contained therein against any alleged governmental interests.

> For the principles of the First Amendment are stated in precise and mandatory terms and unless they are applied in those terms, the freedoms of religion, speech, press, assembly and petition will have no effective protection. Where these freedoms are left to depend upon a balance to be struck by this Court in each particular case, liberty cannot survive. For under such a rule, there are no constitutional rights that cannot be "balanced" away.[121]

He believed "that the men who drafted our Bill of Rights did all the 'balancing' that was to be done in this field."[122] With rare exception, the justice's votes on First Amendment issues reflected this philosophy. The one area in which he was willing to "balance" First Amendment rights was when the government was regulating conduct that indirectly affected speech as well. Those kinds of cases generally involved First Amendment activities such as solicitation, picketing, or parading. "But even such laws governing conduct. . . ," he wrote, "must be tested, though only by a balancing process, if they indirectly affect ideas."[123] Even in such cases, however, Black voted most of the time in favor of the exercise of First Amendment rights.

Black did not believe that a speaker had a right to speak at any place he or she chose. In disputing an argument that grounds around a jail were proper places to demonstrate, he asserted: "Such an argument has as its major unarticulated premise the assumption that people who want to propagandize protests or views have a constitutional right to do so whenever and however and wherever they please. That concept of constitutional law was vigorously and forthrightly rejected in two prior cases. . . . We reject it again."[124]

In discussing the free exercise of religion, the Justice acknowledged that he voted the wrong way in *Gobitis,* and, as noted earlier, he set forth his views on the free exercise of religion at some length. In his dissent in Clyde Summers's case, Black referred to the dissenting opinions of Justice Holmes in *United States v. Schwimmer* and of Chief Justice Hughes in *United States v. Macintosh.* "Dissents in both cases rested in part on the premise that religious tests are incompatible with our constitutional guarantee of freedom of thought and religion."[125] And he added, "I agree with the constitutional philosophy underlying the dissents of Mr. Justice Holmes and Mr. Chief Justice Hughes."

Black applied his belief in the absoluteness of the rights of speech, assembly, and association in the many cases involving the "witch hunt" for alleged "subversives" during the 1950s and early 1960s.

Concerning the rights of Communists, the justice declared: "Like anyone else, individual Communists who commit overt acts in violation of valid laws can and should be punished. But the postulate of the First Amendment is that our free institutions can be maintained without proscribing or penalizing political belief, speech, press, assembly, or party affiliation. This is a far bolder philosophy than despotic rulers can afford to follow. It is the heart of the system on which freedom depends."[126]

Black wrote that statement in 1950 and followed it in case after case dealing with government infringement upon First Amendment rights under the banner of ferreting out subversives. "I believe with the Framers of the First Amendment," he declared,

> that the internal security of a nation like ours does not and cannot be made to depend upon the use of force by Government to make all the beliefs and opinions of the people fit into a common mold on any single subject. Such enforced conformity of thought would tend only to deprive our people of the bold spirit of adventure and progress which has brought this Nation to its present greatness. The creation of public opinion by groups, associations, societies, clubs, and parties has been and is a necessary part of our democratic society. Such groups, like the Sons of Liberty and the American Corresponding Societies, played a large part in creating sentiment in this country that led the people of the Colonies to want a nation of their own. The Father of the Constitution—James Madison—said, in speaking of the Sedition Act aimed at crushing the Jeffersonian Party, that had

that law been in effect during the period before the Revolution, the United States might well have continued to be 'miserable colonies, groaning under a foreign yoke.' "[127]

Two other areas of communication that Justice Black believed should be free of government control were freedom of the press generally and obscenity in particular. He was especially concerned when government attempted to restrain publication. But what bothered him even more was that some justices were willing to approve such governmental action. For example, in voting to strike down the government's attempt to prevent the publication of the Pentagon Papers, he declared: "In my view it is unfortunate that some of my Brethren are apparently willing to hold that publication of news may sometimes be enjoined. Such a holding would make a shambles of the First Amendment."[128]

The right to publish was so absolute that Black refused to view films that were allegedly obscene. With regard to the film *Lady Chatterley's Lover,* he wrote, "Unlike . . . [other justices] I have not seen the picture. My view is stated by Mr. Justice Douglas, that prior censorship of moving pictures like prior censorship of newspapers and books violates the First and Fourteenth Amendments."[129]

Black recognized a right to travel and to work, neither of which is specifically referred to in the Bill of Rights, but he did not believe that there was a right of privacy.

The justice summed up his position on the exclusion of blacks from juries in *Smith v. Texas:* "It is part of the established tradition in the use of juries as instruments of public justice that the jury be a body truly representative of the community. For racial discrimination to result in the exclusion from jury service of otherwise qualified groups not only violates our Constitution and the laws enacted under it but is at war with our basic concepts of a democratic society and a representative government."[130]

The justice's position on integration of schools never wavered. And as late at 1968, three years before he retired, he voted with the majority to strike down attempts by school districts to do an end run around the requirements of *Brown v. Board of Education.*

When it came to integration of public facilities, Black voted to do so most of the time. However, he wanted to see a clear connection between the government and the owners of the private property.

As indicated earlier, Black did not have a great deal of empathy for the rights of illegitimate children. He was, however, more sympathetic to the plight of potential voters when state laws absolutely prohibited them from voting.

In the *Griffin* case Black wrote, "Providing equal justice for poor and rich, weak and powerful alike is an age-old problem. People have never ceased to hope and strive to move closer to that goal."[131] The justice certainly did his part to bring about that equality with his many votes to provide indigent defendants with transcripts and counsel on appeal. Even when Oklahoma City refused to supply a transcript to Tommie E. L. Williams so he could appeal from a conviction for drunken driving, a "petty" offense, Black joined the Court in its conclusion that this was a denial of equal protection of the law.[132]

The justice consistently argued that it was the intention of the writers of the Fourteenth Amendment that states should abide by the provisions of the first eight amendments. He was never able to convince a majority of the justices sitting at any one time of the correctness of his position. What he could not accomplish all at once, however, did eventually happen as the Court "incorporated" most of the Bill of Rights, provision by provision, into the Fourteenth Amendment, making it applicable to state governments. The justice was happy to join this process, because eventually his long-sought goal became a reality.

There is no way to justify Black's voting to sustain the military curfew and evacuation of Japanese citizens and aliens alike from the West Coast of the United States during World War II.

With the exception of those cases, however, Black's insistence upon the absoluteness of the rights contained in the First Amendment, his view that all of the Bill of Rights should be applicable to the states, and his consistent voting for the rights of minorities and indigents make him worthy of classification as a freedom fighter.

5

JUSTICE WILLIAM ORVILLE DOUGLAS

PERSONAL LIFE

Growing Up

> I have only vague memories of Maine: sawdust pitched high around the foundation of our house for winter insulation, melting snow, the first new shoots of spring, an early yellow flower, and a black cat. I called the cat Black Me, childish shorthand for "It's black and it's mine." But polio—which I had while we still lived in Minnesota—laid me low at the age of about three. In my childish associations, I somehow blamed my polio on the cat, which I had loved but which I believed also betrayed me by proving unlucky. As a result, black cats became a bad omen for me.[1]

Douglas was born in Maine, Minnesota, in 1898. His father, William Douglas, came to Maine to be its Presbyterian minister. There he met and married Julia Fisk. Two other children were born of this marriage, Martha and Art. The family moved to Estrella, California, where the Reverend Douglas had accepted a pastorate. Although Douglas was not old enough for the first grade, the school accepted him, and he remembered that as "one of the proudest days of my life."

It was in Estrella that the future justice acquired his love for the outdoors. He writes of the "dry, rolling hills dotted with oaks" in that area. "They were brown in the high heat of the day but purple at sunset. They were moody, like people, and by Easter they were covered with a nap that was a most delicate shade of green. To this day, whenever I reach the Southern California coast and see its barren hills, I feel at home. This feeling of security is rooted in Estrella, where love cemented our home into an unconquerable castle."

JUSTICE WILLIAM ORVILLE DOUGLAS (photo by Harris & Ewing; collection of the Supreme Court of the United States).

The hot California climate was too much for the Reverend Douglas, and he moved the family to cooler Cleveland, Washington. He died shortly thereafter when Douglas was not yet six years old. Later he remembered his father as "one of the few truly good men I ever knew. Like St. Francis, he loved people and went humbly among them. Spiritual reward, not monetary gain, was his desire. His values were reflected strongly in the sermons which Mother preserved and which I read as a boy."

After the death of her husband, Julia Douglas took her family to Yakima, Washington, where she used some of her husband's insurance money to build a house. A bad investment took what little was left, and the family found themselves poverty-stricken. The children helped in any way they could: sweeping out stores, washing windows, and picking berries, cherries, apricots, and peaches. The family received help from the Presbyterian Home Mission, especially at Christmastime, when they were given a box of secondhand clothing. One year the box contained "a beautiful coat with a big patch on the right elbow." Although William liked it, his pride prevented him from wearing it. This episode turned him against Christmas and people who gave to the poor only at that time rather than all throughout the year.

Martha went to college in Washington, and then worked in the personnel departments of several stores in the East and Midwest. She cared for their mother until she died in 1941, after which time Martha married. Her husband, however, died shortly thereafter.

Brother Art also went to college in Washington and then on to Columbia Law School. He practiced law in New York and later became president of Statler hotels. William and Art were close throughout their lives. Art died at the age of 56.

In his autobiography, Douglas tells about his school days in Yakima, making friends, trying to learn to play a concertina, going to the circus and to the county fair. The people who traveled with the circus and were exhibitors at the fair made an impression on him. "The people of the side shows were a sad group who lived out of suitcases, had no homes, and were drifters on a lonely sea. But they were, I thought, fine people, and the magic which they brought to Yakima will always remain a bright memory."

William's bout with polio as a young child in Minnesota left him with physical and mental scars for life. "An enervating weakness remained for years. I had no endurance in my legs. They tired easily, and when I exercised even mildly they would ache and twitch all night. I had no medical advice, no law adviser, no confidant as I was growing up, who could allay some of the worries about my legs." Other kids made fun of his skinny legs and he wanted to cover them with long pants, but his mother would not permit him to do so. This had its beneficial side, however, because Douglas took to hiking into the foothills to gain strength. "I took my early hikes into the hills to try to strengthen my legs, but they were to strengthen me in subtler ways. As I came to be on intimate terms with the hills, I learned something of their geology and botany. I heard the Indian legends associated with them. I discovered many of their secrets. I learned that they were always clothed in garments of delicate hues, though they seemed barren; though they looked dead and monotonous, they teemed with life and had many moods."

One day, while he was swimming at the YMCA, a "big bruiser of a boy" picked him up and threw him into the deep end. After going down several times, and struggling to get to the surface, he lost consciousness and awoke lying at the edge of the pool. This episode caused him to have a deep-seated fear of water, a fear he decided to conquer while a professor at Yale Law School in 1928.

During high school Douglas played basketball, and took part in track and debate. He was also in charge of the iron triangle that served as an alarm to call the students to class. "It was a coveted position, for it excused the gong-ringer from the end of every class a few minutes early, and allowed him to arrive a few minutes late. I enjoyed it immensely."

James F. Simon has written,

> In addition to being selected valedictorian, William Orville Douglas was named the student who most distinguished his class and his school. He shared with Lyndon Hassenmuller and Grace Lee the title of most brilliant member of the class. He was selected attorney to execute the class will and, in a one-act graduation play, Orville Douglas was cast in the role of the President of the United States. The inscription next to the senior picture of the gaunt, confident Orville Douglas read: "Born for success he seemed, With grace to win, with heart to hold, With shining gifts that took all eyes."[2]

While in high school, Douglas delivered papers, was pin boy at the bowling alley, and worked in an ice cream plant. But the job that probably made the most lasting impression on him was when he was hired by a local reformer to go into the red-light district to try to entrap women into soliciting him for sex or accepting a drink that he would offer to buy. He was told that if a women did either, he was to report to the police and they would move in on the woman.

Of this experience, he wrote, "In time I came to feel a warmth for all these miserable people, something I never felt for the high churchman who hired me. They were scum that society had produced—misfits, maladjusted, disturbed, and really sick. What orphanages had turned them out? What broken homes had produced them? Which of these prostitutes had first been seduced by her father, causing all standards of propriety and decency to be destroyed? Which of them had turned to prostitution and bootlegging as a result of grinding poverty?"[3]

Even though the family desperately needed the money, the future justice could stomach this job only for a few weeks.

According to sister Martha, their mother favored the boys. "Still in Martha's eyes, Julia Douglas did everything for the boys. She laughed at their jokes and cheered at their basketball games. She took the boys to the circus and brought Martha along as an afterthought. Afraid that her boys would be sissies, Julia signed Orville and Arthur up for the Boy Scouts and YMCA. Martha signed up for the YWCA herself."[4]

While William Jennings Bryan may have had some small influence on Douglas's political growth, it was his mother's politics that convinced him to be a Democrat. She was a staunch Republican. She said "that the Republicans represented the Rich, who hired the entire labor force. 'If the Rich are disenchanted, then we are all unemployed' was her comment."[5] But William had a different opinion of the rich in Yakima: "They treated labor as scum; they controlled the police; some of them even had investments in Yakima's brothels. They went to church and were 'godly' men; but I had nothing in common with them."

Although Ira Simons, who was black, was a star football player at the high school, William's contact with other blacks was minimal. On the other hand, there were many Indians in the area, and he made friends with some of them, especially one who taught him how to spear fish and told him much about Indian culture. He also worked with members of the Industrial Workers of the World, commonly referred to as the Wobblies, who were thought to be criminals. "I traveled extensively with the IWW's and came to know them as warm-hearted people who, it seemed to me even then, had higher ideals than some of the men who ran our banks and were the elders in the church. A hungry man was always welcome under the railroad bridge; not only was he offered food, but there he could feel that he was an equal with every one. And almost always, these drifters left the area cleaner than they found it."

Douglas became proficient at riding the rails when going about the area to the various jobs he had. While traveling about he encountered many Chicanos, whom he came to know as "good, hard-working, God-fearing laborers."

He tells of watching a train carrying Wobblies go through Yakima: "The train that passed through Yakima was not carrying men on display. These were sealed boxcars carrying human beings, thirty or forty in each car. The authorities were taking outcasts through our city. There were no toilets, no food, no water, just sealed boxcars with these poor bastards inside."

Douglas went to Whitman College in 1916 with a full scholarship. He rode his bicycle 165 miles to Walla Walla. There he worked part-time in a jewelry store, did janitorial work, and was a waiter in a boardinghouse; he sent much of the money he earned home to his mother.

For the first year Douglas lived in a tent but the college administration objected and he was forced to move into the dormitory. Later he lived in the Beta Theta Pi fraternity house where, as in most fraternity houses, there was much kidding. Douglas was a natural target because of his seriousness and intense work habits.

Two "powerful professors" influenced his life: Dr. Benjamin H. Brown, the physics and geology professor, and Dr. William R. Davis, who taught English. Daddy Brown, as he was called, "taught us man's small role in the universe, the immensity of the Glacial Age, the magnitude of the Pleistocene, and so on. He taught us to observe the winds and the rocks."

Of Dr. Davis, Douglas wrote, "Davis was an inspirational man who had a knack of worming his way into another's life. In a few years he became indispensable to me. He was, indeed, a second father. If I had a speech to make, Davis heard me rehearse it at the crack of dawn in the outdoor college amphitheater. If

I had a personal problem, he was my confessor. As a result, Davis became so powerful in my life, that when I graduated, I had almost decided to make English literature my career."

Woodrow Wilson's promotion of the League of Nations prompted Douglas to assist in the organization of a Woodrow Wilson Club at the college. He also participated in debates on the subject. Later in life, and looking back, he concluded that "Woodrow Wilson had done incalculable damage to our democratic idea." But, he concluded, "young men and women often go off on false trails."

Douglas became a "big man on the campus" at Whitman. He was president of the Student Congress and a member of Phi Beta Kappa, and he was honored by being one of the commencement speakers.

Although his father was a minister, and the family attended church regularly, Douglas became disenchanted with religion because he believed that "most members of the Establishment had received tickets to heaven merely by being pious on Sunday."

Although he was moving away from organized religion, he maintained his own moral code. "He refused," Simon has written, "to follow his peers who smoked or drank. He did not date. In those days, Douglas's glance at a pretty girl was usually taken covertly and sexual titillation was confined to exchange of bawdy stories on camping trips."[6]

Soldier

"I applied for service in naval aviation and passed all my examinations up to the final one, which was the color test. In those days a box of yarn was used, and I was asked to pick out Old Rose. The recruiting officer, anxious to have me, was very patient. But over and over again I picked the wrong piece of yarn, and finally I was rejected."[7]

Douglas applied for Officer's Training School and, being the first to pass the physical test, was waiting to take the color test again when the examiner sent him into another room with directions to give the color test to the other recruits. All passed, and when the examiner came to give Douglas the test, Douglas said, "You mean the guy who gives it has to take it?" The examiner responded, "Okay, put yourself down for a hundred." And the recruit was sent off to the Presidio in San Francisco. After a short training period, he returned to Whitman College to train with the ROTC. He was then ordered to Camp Taylor, Kentucky, but the Armistice came and he was discharged, his army career at an end.

Before he was mustered out, the ROTC unit participated in a victory parade in Walla Walla. "I felt for the first time," he wrote, "a mob's hysteria. The crowd was, of course, happy and relieved that the battles were over. People had lost sons and relatives, and many wept. Women broke ranks and rushed into the street to embrace us. I was sad and embarrassed. We were far from being heroes. We had never been under fire. We had never even heard the distant cannon roar.

I wanted to escape and hide, to free myself from the cheering, weeping, exultant crowd. But on we marched, and then back to the barracks."

High School Teacher

After graduating from Whitman College, Douglas returned to Yakima and accepted a position teaching English, Latin, and public speaking at the high school. He bought an old Dodge car for $40. Because of his experience in hiking and camping, the local scoutmasters recruited him to assist in their campouts, an experience he enjoyed. The high school debate team won the state championship when Douglas was their coach. He became a member of the American Legion, but concluded that because of their intolerance for foreigners and political minorities they were really un–American, and so his relationship with them was short-lived.

Douglas's interest in law was aroused by his association with O.E. Bailey, an insurance salesman in Yakima. "We sat long into the night," Douglas wrote, "in philosophical, political, and religious talk. His mind was keen. His horizons were wide. He was a man without formal education who was as eager for knowledge as anyone I have known." Bailey had also attended a session of the Supreme Court.

It was Bailey's companionship and attendance at court sessions that nurtured Douglas's desire to take up law, even though his mother wanted him to continue teaching and eventually become the high school principal. The urge to study law finally prevailed, and he sent off an application to Harvard Law School, which was accepted. But Harvard lost a potential Supreme Court justice through a chance encounter with James T. Donald, a local lawyer who had worked his way through Columbia Law School. When Donald offered to help him get into Columbia, Douglas canceled out at Harvard and applied to Columbia, where he was accepted. At the time, Harlan F. Stone, with whom Douglas later served on the Court, was the law school dean at Columbia. Donald and Douglas continued their friendship until Donald's death. They fished together, went out on pack trains, and searched for trout in the streams and lakes in the Northwest.

Law Student

The prospective law student rode the train to Chicago as shepherd for 2,000 sheep being shipped to the Chicago stockyards. He arrived in New York with little money, and, as he notes, "I had had no bath since Chicago, no change of clothes, and doubtless looked like a bum. My clothes were tattered, my hat was nondescript, my battered brown suitcase was held together by a piece of rope. I was utterly lost." Because he had been a member of Beta Theta Pi fraternity at Whitman, he sought out the New York headquarters. When he asked the clerk for a room, the reply was a firm no. As he was trying to convince the clerk that he was a fraternity brother, a friend from Whitman College came by and vouched for him. The friend also loaned him $75.

Although he was allowed to register and was assigned to a room at Columbia, he did not have enough money for tuition and board, and seemed unable to accumulate any by doing odd jobs. Finally the bursar caught up to him; he then sought help from Dean Stone, who suggested that he drop out, get a job, and return when he had saved enough money. Douglas took this advice, got a job teaching in a high school in New Jersey, but stopped at the Appointments Office just once more to see if there were any jobs listed. There was a message from a man who wanted a third-year student to help start a law program at his correspondence school. Although he wasn't even a first-year law student anymore, he prevailed upon the appointments secretary to let him try for the job. After a brief interview, he was given the job of putting together a correspondence course in business law. He convinced the owner that they should make it a "case law course" where the student would study a few pages and then be given a problem to solve. They agreed that Douglas would get a flat fee of $600 for setting up the course, with a $200 advance. He returned to the law school, paid for his tuition and room, and settled into the study of law. Douglas prepared the correspondence course, which proved to be a great success, allowing the school owner to make a substantial amount of money.

Douglas did not like living in the big city. "I needed grass and earth under my feet. But unless I traveled far—either west or north—all I found was concrete. I saw block after block of apartment houses—some standing in splendor, most in squalor—with no tree, no touch of grass to adorn them, no playground except a paved one, no nature trails."

The future justice began tutoring students for college entrance exams, charging five dollars an hour and eventually working up to 25. He also took a job in a settlement house, organizing the boys into clubs and teaching them about fishing, hiking, camping, and Indians.

He attended the theater, including the Ziegfeld Follies and the Metropolitan Opera. He saw Will Rogers, Eddie Cantor, and Enrico Caruso. Some of his classmates were Paul Robeson, Thomas E. Dewey, and Simon Rifkind. He became an editor of the Columbia Law Review after his first year.

Douglas became a research assistant for Professor Underhill Moore, "who taught courses in partnership and sales, and exhibited a violent impatience with a student's slightest intellectual fuzziness."[8] When Professor Moore was hired by the cement industry to study its sales practices, he recruited Douglas to assist him. "Moore and Douglas periodically jumped into an automobile and toured the eastern seaboard in search of cement plants. It was Douglas's introduction to expense account living, and it did not take him long to decide he liked it."

At graduation time, Douglas was crushed when one of his classmates, Al McCormack, was chosen to be a law clerk for then Supreme Court Justice Harlan F. Stone. He had expected that honor to go to him.

Lawyer and Part-time Law Professor

Upon graduating from law school, Douglas went to work for the prominent New York law firm of Cravath, deGersdorff, Swaine and Wood. He also accepted an offer to teach part-time at Columbia Law School.

The work at the firm was mainly in the fields of business and corporate law. At the end of the first year, Robert T. Swaine took him aside and said, "You've spent your life in the second balcony and I am introducing you to the orchestra."[9] He then offered a salary of $5,000 per year with rapid advancement thereafter, but Douglas refused. He had made up his mind to return to Washington. Unable to find a position in Seattle, however, Douglas became associated with James O. Cull, a lawyer in Yakima. The small-town practice barely produced $25 a month, a far cry from the income he had been accustomed to in New York. But it was not for long. He returned to New York and went to work for the Cravath firm again. He also began to teach part-time at Columbia Law School.

In the spring of 1927, Douglas was offered an assistant professorship at Columbia Law School at a salary of $5,000. After some soul-searching, he accepted and the practice of law came to an end.

Professor of Law

In the spring of 1928, when President Butler appointed a new dean of the law school without consulting the faculty, Douglas tendered his resignation.

A chance meeting with Robert M. Hutchins, dean of the Yale Law School, brought an offer to teach there, which Douglas accepted. He joined the Yale Law School faculty as an associate professor in September 1928. He describes his teaching methods: "So I bore down hard, treating each student as if it were irrelevant that his father or grandfather was a 'great man.' I tended to treat the class as the lion tamer in the circus treats his wards." Although the students protested and made a demand that he be fired, he continued to teach at Yale until 1934. The desire to "make law more relevant to life" continued as one of his goals, a goal, however, that was not realized during these teaching years.

Douglas became disenchanted with the way law was being practiced during this time. He observed that although many lawyers became very wealthy, few had done much public service, and those who had, did so to get more business. And he did not see law as an instrument for social change.

Simon wrote of Douglas as a professor, "He prepared carefully and well for his classes, but did not seem to care that his performance was not given a top rating by his students. He wrote provocative law review articles and here he took greater care, knowing that academic reputations were made in print, not in the classroom . . . . The overriding goal in all Douglas's endeavors was to impress the academic community with the quality of his mind."[10]

"Douglas made no effort to court student favor," Simon continued. "He did not linger after class or often join students for a beer at Mory's. He was indeed shy; he was also very busy" writing law review articles and books.

Summing up his years at Yale, Douglas wrote, "I enjoyed my years at Yale because they gave me great freedom. I never taught more than five hours a week, though it took me eight hours to prepare for each class. This is because I would start out each teaching year fresh, without any 'leftover' notes, teaching each course as if I had never taught it before. The light teaching schedule left much time for research."[11]

Love, Marriage and Family

Douglas married Mildred Riddle in 1924. She was then a Latin teacher at Yakima High School. "A week after he and Mildred arrived in New York with less than a dollar between them," Simon wrote, "Douglas had pocketed ninety dollars, the result of a furious tutoring spasm. In a short time, the couple had settled in a rented house in Bernardsville, New Jersey, close to the high school where Mildred taught Latin and within commuting distance of Columbia."[12]

Douglas has written of Mildred, "She was a lifelong scholar of Latin and rated high in the teaching profession for her achievements in that area. She had teacher's certificates in Oregon, Washington, New Jersey, and New York and she taught Latin for a while in a private school in Connecticut before the children were born. She was a quiet, retiring lady of beauty who liked to sit in green meadows beside purling waters; but she never really enjoyed the hard exhausting journeys into the high wilderness."[13]

After 29 years of marriage, the couple divorced in 1953. The Douglases' two children, Millie and Bill, were born in New Haven, Connecticut.

Author Simon writes, "But when he did enter the domestic world of his wife, he did so with characteristic vivacity. He was a fun-loving father, joking and kidding Millie and Bill junior, and riding them on his knee when he came home. Sometimes he would take his son for a ride around the town in their old Dodge, showing Bill junior his office and walking with him on the New Haven green."[14]

Millie went to Whitman College, married Norman Read, an Englishman, and moved to England. She and her husband had several children.

Bill, Jr., also went to Whitman College and then on to study acting in France. He became an actor, teacher, and director of plays. He married, and he and his wife had three children.

Douglas married Mercedes Davison in 1954. They were divorced in 1963. He married Joanie Martin in 1963, and they were divorced in 1966. Douglas's fourth wife, Cathy Hefferman, went to law school and became a successful Washington lawyer after they were married.

Public Service

While at Yale, Douglas had become active in Democratic Party politics, working on the senatorial campaign of Frank Maloney, who was elected and served as senator from Connecticut until 1945.

In 1934 Douglas was asked to come to Washington, D.C., by Joseph P. Kennedy, chairman of the Securities and Exchange Commission. He was asked to conduct "a study of protective and reorganization committees, which were creating new scandals in their manipulations of bankruptcies and receiverships."[15] In creating a staff, he hired Abe Fortas, who had been one of his students at Yale, and who later also served with him on the Supreme Court.

The group conducted a series of hearings in 1934 and 1935 and eventually submitted eight reports to Congress. When Kennedy resigned from the SEC in 1935, James Landis, a member of the commission, was appointed chairman, leaving a vacancy. Kennedy took Douglas to see President Franklin D. Roosevelt, who agreed to appoint him to the commission vacancy. He was confirmed in February 1936.

Although Douglas had been in Washington working at the Securities and Exchange Commission since 1934, his appointment as a member seemed to awaken the press to his existence. "With the announcement of his appointment on January 21, 1936," Simon has noted, "Douglas was suddenly 'discovered' by the national press; it was love at first sight. Rhapsodized *Time* magazine: 'Sent to the Senate for confirmation was the name of William Orville 'Bill' Douglas, 37, as brilliant a professor as the New Deal has attracted to Washington.' *Time* told the tale of Douglas's rise, from the days when 'this remarkable young man turned up in the East on the brake rods of a transcontinental freight train' to Douglas's role in the protective committee study."[16] Douglas became chairman of the commission in 1937.

John P. Frank has written of Douglas's five years on the SEC: "He ran an administration which the securities industry came to regard as strong but not destructive. He was more anxious to have the stock exchange reform itself than to use his full power to regulate it.... The combination of ... exposé and pressure from Douglas caused the Exchange to reorganize itself in 1938. The commission also took strong action to insure that purchasers of securities would have an opportunity to know the truth about what they were buying."[17]

During this period, Douglas became a member of the inner circle of the New Deal, and was able to make friends with many of the influential people in the Roosevelt administration, and in Washington. "Douglas developed a reputation among New Dealers," Frank noted, "for being a tough and effective fellow, but also for being good company, a good storyteller and a good companion on a party. In his relations with others, he was thoroughly congenial."

Conservationist

"My love of the mountains, my interest in conservation, my longing for the wilderness—all these were lifetime concerns that were established in my boyhood in the hills around Yakima and in the mountains to the west of it."[18] In his early years, Douglas hunted doves, grouse, ducks, and larger game such as elk and deer. But he became disillusioned while on a fishing trip with a friend. He describes the scene as they approached the creek where they were to fish: "Big fat men with two hundred dollars' worth of shiny new equipment, little boys with cans of worms and willow sticks, men in hip boots, with big creels, jars of salmon eggs, hats that were pincushions for flies, nets large enough to land a pickerel— all of these were headed for the run. When Hill and I reached the creek, we discovered there was standing room only, each fisherman actually being three or four feet from a neighbor on both sides . . . . The largest fish caught was eight inches long . . ."

He was also invited to go on a turkey shoot at a club in Maryland. Although he missed the actual shoot, after seeing movies showing the slaughter of turkeys that could hardly fly, he gave up hunting and took up photography.

Douglas joined conservation groups that lobbied to prohibit the construction of dams in nearby Maryland. When a proposal was made to turn the C&O Canal into a freeway, he and others marched 180 miles along the canal, urging that it be turned into a recreation area. Eventually President Dwight Eisenhower declared the area to be a national monument.

Nomination to the Supreme Court

Douglas learned of the retirement of Justice Brandeis at a friend's cocktail party the evening of the announcement, February 13, 1939. He describes the incident:

> Arthur [Krock of the *New York Times*] raised his glass and said, "To the next Justice of the Supreme Court."
> "Who has retired?" I asked.
> "Brandeis."
> "And to whom are we drinking?"
> "To you, of course," said Arthur.
> I took him aside in the hallway to find out the "facts." The "facts" were that Brandeis had retired and that a group of my friends, headed by Arthur Krock, was promoting me.

But President Roosevelt was also considering Senator Lewis Schwellenback of Washington because he thought a Westerner should be on the Court. But Douglas's many friends went to work for him. He was nominated on March 20, 1939, and confirmed by a vote of 62–4 on April 4. What little opposition there was came from senators who believed that Douglas was too closely connected to Wall Street.

John Frank has written that "when Douglas was appointed at the age of forty-one, he was the youngest Justice to have been appointed since Joseph Story in 1811. He came to the Court as the fourth New Deal appointee, following Justices Black, Reed and Frankfurter, but the entire group had been appointed within two years of each other, and clearly all were facing a brave new world of constitutional interpretation together."[19] Other members of the Court were: Chief Justice Charles Evans Hughes, and justices James McReynolds, Pierce Butler, Harlan Fiske Stone, Owen J. Roberts, Hugo Black, Stanley Reed, and Felix Frankfurter.

AS ASSOCIATE JUSTICE (1939-75)

The Free Exercise of Religion

Guy Ballard, his wife, Edna, and son, Donald, organized a movement called "I Am." The teachings of "I Am" included:

> (1) That Guy Ballard had attained a supernatural state of self-immortality, which enabled him to conquer disease, death, old age, poverty and misery.... (3) That the Ballards, by reason of their high spiritual attainments and righteous conduct, had been selected as divine messengers through whom the words of "ascended masters," including Saint Germain, would be communicated to mankind in the teachings of the "I Am" movement.... (8) That the Ballards had, by reason of divine origin, acquired a great healing power, and that followers of the "I Am" movement could acquire such power, achieve perfect bodies and heal themselves of all human ailments by giving implicit obedience to the precepts, principles, teachings and doctrines of said movement .... (11) That magazines, booklets, circulars, letters, "edicts," "decrees" and musical compositions published, circulated and sold by the Ballards were divinely inspired and dictated by supernatural entities or "ascended masters" and were a part of the medium through which salvation could be obtained.[20]

The Ballards were indicted for using the mails to defraud. At their trial, District Judge J.F.T. O'Connor charged the jury that "the religious beliefs of these defendants cannot be an issue in this court."[21] To make certain that the jury understood what he meant, Judge O'Connor said, "The issue is: Did these defendants honestly and in good faith believe these things? If they did, they should be acquitted." The defendants were convicted and appealed to the Circuit Court, which reversed, being of the opinion that the jury should have been given the opportunity to decide whether the teachings of "I Am" "were false or true." The Supreme Court disagreed and sent the case back to the lower courts. Justice Douglas explained the meaning of the Free Exercise Clause, as follows:

> Freedom of thought, which includes freedom of religious belief, is basic in a society of free men .... It embraces the right to maintain theories of life and of death

and of the hereafter which are rank heresy to followers of the orthodox faiths. Heresy trials are foreign to our Constitution. Men may believe what they cannot prove. They may not be put to the proof of their religious doctrines or beliefs. Religious experiences which are as real as life to some may be incomprehensible to others. Yet the fact that they may be beyond the ken of mortals does not mean that they can be made suspect before the law.

In *Murdock v. Pennsylvania,*[22] Douglas told how the Jehovah's Witnesses spread the word of God. "Petitioners spread their interpretations of the Bible and their religious beliefs largely through the hand distribution of literature by full or part time workers. They claim to follow the example of Paul, teaching 'publickly, and from house to house.' Acts 20:20. They take literally the mandate of the Scriptures, 'Go ye into all the world, and preach the gospel to every creature.' Mark 16:15. In doing so they believe that they are obeying a commandment of God."

The petitioners were arrested because they had not obtained a license for "canvassing or soliciting." They were convicted but appealed to the Supreme Court, which reversed, with the justice writing the majority opinion.

"The hand distribution of religious tracts," he pointed out, "is an age-old form of missionary evangelism—as old as the history of printing presses. It has been a potent force in various religious movements down through the years . . . . It is more than preaching; it is more than distribution of religious literature. It is a combination of both. Its purpose is as evangelical as the revival meeting."

The fact that the Witnesses sell their literature is of no consequence, Douglas noted, because "it should be remembered that the pamphlets of Thomas Paine were not distributed free of charge." And furthermore: "Freedom of speech, freedom of the press, freedom of religion are available to all, not merely to those who can pay their own way."

Justice Douglas was concerned about the cumulative effect of a license tax of this kind. "Itinerant evangelists moving throughout a state or from state to state," he stated, "would feel immediately the cumulative effect of such ordinances as they become fashionable. The way of the religious dissenter has long been hard. But if the formula of this type of ordinance is approved, a new device for the suppression of religious minorities will have been found."

In 1961 the Court upheld the Sunday closing laws of Maryland, Pennsylvania, and Massachusetts.[23] In one of the cases, *Braunfeld v. Brown,*[24] the question of the effect of Sunday closing on free exercise of religion was squarely raised and decided. In this case, Jewish store owners, who were required to close on Saturday because of their faith, argued that being forced to close two days a week placed a heavy burden on their free exercise of religion. A majority of the Court held that the benefits of Sunday closing laws outweighed this burden.

Justice Douglas dissented in all of these cases, and wrote an extensive dissenting opinion. For him, the question was "whether a State can impose criminal sanctions on those who, unlike the Christian majority that makes up our society, worship on a different day or do not share the religious scruples of the majority."[25]

The justice's concern was for those who did not believe in Christianity. "These laws are sustained," he argued, "because, it is said, the First Amendment is concerned with religious convictions or opinion, not with conduct. But it is a strange Bill of Rights that makes it possible for the dominant religious group to bring the minority to heel because the minority, in the doing of acts which intrinsically are wholesome and not antisocial, does not defer to the majority's religious beliefs."

Douglas was also disturbed by the impact of these laws on Jews and Sabbatarians. "When these laws are applied to Orthodox Jews . . . or to Sabbatarians their vice is accentuated. If the Sunday laws are constitutional, kosher markets are on a five-day week. Thus those laws put an economic penalty on those who observe Saturday rather than Sunday as the Sabbath." He closed his dissent with a quotation from the Reverend Allen C. Parker, Jr., a Presbyterian minister: "'I do not believe that because I have set aside Sunday as a holy day I have the right to force all men to set aside that day also. Why should my faith be favored by the State over any other man's faith.'"

Freedom of Speech

Pamphleteering. Justice Douglas joined Black's dissenting opinion in Joseph Beauharnais's case, and also wrote a dissenting opinion. There was no question that Beauharnais gave out material containing very derogatory statements about blacks. It called for the white people to unite, and added that "if persuasion and the need to prevent the white race from becoming mongrelized by the negro will not unite us, then the aggressions . . . rapes, robberies, knives, guns and marijuana of the negro, surely will."[26] But the justice believed that the material was protected by the First Amendment, and that Beauharnais's conviction should have been reversed. He wrote:

> Intemperate speech is a distinctive characteristic of man. Hotheads blow off and release destructive energy in the process. They shout and rave, exaggerating weaknesses, magnifying error, viewing with alarm. So it has been from the beginning; and so it will be throughout time. The Framers of the Constitution knew human nature as well as we do. They too had lived in dangerous days; they too knew the suffocating influence of orthodoxy and standardized thought. They weighed the compulsions for restrained speech and thought against the abuses of liberty. They chose liberty. That should be our choice today no matter how distasteful to us the pamphlet of Beauharnais may be.

Steve Ashton, "a college student from Ohio . . . [went] to Hazard [Kentucky] to help unemployed miners in that area."[27] He circulated a pamphlet that was very critical of Sam L. Luttrell, chief of police of Hazard, Charles E.

Combs, the sheriff, and Mrs. W.P. Nolan, co-owner of the Hazard *Herald*. For this he was charged and convicted of "'the offence of criminal libel' committed 'by publishing a false and malicious publication which tends to degrade or injure.' "[28] At Ashton's trial the judge "charged [the jury] that 'criminal libel is defined as any writing calculated to create disturbances of the peace, corrupt the public morals, or lead to any act, which, when done, is indictable.' " Upon appeal to the Supreme Court, the conviction was reversed by a unanimous vote of the justices. Douglas wrote the Court's opinion in which he pointed out that convictions "for breach of the peace" cannot stand where the law is "imprecisely defined," especially when dealing with First Amendment rights. "Vague laws in any area suffer a constitutional infirmity. When First Amendment rights are involved, we look even more closely lest, under the guise of regulating conduct that is reachable by the police power, freedom of speech or of the press suffer."

Picketing and Parading. "Picketing by an organized group is more than free speech, since it involves patrol of a particular locality and since the very presence of a picket line may induce action of one kind or another, quite irrespective of the nature of the ideas which are being disseminated. Hence those aspects of picketing make it the subject of restrictive regulation."[29] With these words, the justice concurred when the Court struck down an injunction that prevented union bakery truck drivers from picketing nonunion peddlers.

When Harriett Louise Adderley and others were convicted of trespass for assembling on the grounds of a county jail, Douglas protested. The group was protesting segregation and the arrest of some of their friends. Justice Black wrote for the majority: "Nothing in the Constitution of the United States prevents Florida from even-handed enforcement of its general trespass statute against those refusing to obey the sheriff's order to remove themselves from what amounted to the curtilage of the jailhouse."[30]

But Douglas saw this case in a different light. For him, this was not just another trespass case because

> the jailhouse, like an executive mansion, a legislative chamber, a courthouse, or the statehouse itself . . . is one of the seats of government, whether it be the Tower of London, the Bastille, or a small county jail. And when it houses political prisoners or those who many think are unjustly held, it is an obvious center for protest. The right to petition for the redress of grievances has an ancient history and is not limited to writing a letter or sending a telegram to a congressman; it is not confined to appearing before the local city council, or writing letters to the President or Governor or Mayor.

We do violence to the First Amendment," he declared, "when we permit this 'petition for redress of grievances' to be turned into a trespass action."

Advocacy of Unpopular Ideas. While Father Terminiello, a Catholic priest, gave a provocative, emotionally charged, anti–Communist speech, "a surging, howling mob"[31] of about 1,000 people gathered outside the auditorium.

Terminiello was arrested and charged with violating a Chicago ordinance making breach of the peace a criminal offense. At the trial, the judge charged the jury that "'breach of the peace' consists of any 'misbehavior which violates the public peace and decorum'; and that the 'misbehavior may constitute a breach of the peace if it stirs the public to anger, invites dispute, brings about a condition of unrest, or creates a disturbance, or if it molests the inhabitants in the enjoyment of peace and quiet by arousing alarm.'" The jury found the defendant guilty, and he appealed to the Supreme Court, which reversed.

Justice Douglas wrote the Court's opinion, which held that the judge's broad definition of breach of the peace conflicted with the First Amendment. "A function of free speech under our system of government," the Justice asserted,

> is to invite dispute. It may indeed best serve its high purpose when it induces a condition of unrest, creates dissatisfaction with conditions as they are, even stirs people to anger. Speech is often provocative and challenging. It may strike at prejudices and preconceptions and have profound unsettling effects as it presses for acceptance of an idea. That is why freedom of speech, though not absolute, ... is nevertheless protected against censorship or punishment, unless shown likely to produce a clear and present danger of a serious substantive evil that rises far above public inconvenience, annoyance, or unrest.

Douglas dissented when the Court upheld the conviction of Irving Feiner for giving an inflammatory speech on a street corner in Syracuse, New York.[32] (See discussion in Chapter 4.)

The justice dissented because he did not believe that Feiner's speech presented a clear and present danger of a breach of the peace. He also believed that the police had a duty to protect the speaker. "Public assemblies and public speech," Douglas argued,

> occupy an important role in American life. One high function of the police is to protect these lawful gatherings so that the speakers may exercise their constitutional rights. When unpopular causes are sponsored from the public platform, there will commonly be mutterings and unrest and heckling from the crowd. When a speaker mounts a platform it is not unusual to find him resorting to exaggeration, to vilification of ideas and men, to the making of false charges. But those extravagances . . . do not justify penalizing the speaker by depriving him of the platform or by punishing him for his conduct.

When the Court upheld the convictions of the 11 Communist Party officials in *Dennis v. United States*,[33] Douglas wrote a lengthy dissent setting forth his views on the First Amendment and unpopular speech. He first pointed out that "the teaching of methods of terror and other seditious conduct" would not be protected by the First Amendment, but "that no such evidence was introduced at the trial." "So far as the present record is concerned," he wrote, "what petitioners did was to organize people to teach and themselves teach the

Marxist-Leninist doctrine contained chiefly in four books: Stalin, Foundations of Leninism (1924); Marx and Engels, Manifesto of the Communist Party (1848); Lenin, the State and Revolution (1917); History of the Communist Party of the Soviet Union (B.) (1939) . . . . They are fervent Communists to whom these volumes are gospel. They preached the creed with the hope that some day it would be acted upon." But, he pointed out, "I repeat that we deal here with speech alone, not with speech *plus* acts of sabotage or unlawful conduct. Not a single seditious act is charged in the indictment."

Douglas argued that Communism had made few inroads in this country; that Communists had not been elected to public office; and that it was not a political force, because "free speech has destroyed it as an effective political party." He summed up his dissent by asserting, "But the command of the First Amendment is so clear that we should not allow Congress to call a halt to free speech except in the extreme case of peril from the speech itself. The First Amendment makes confidence in the common sense of our people and in their maturity of judgment the great postulate of our democracy. Its philosophy is that violence is rarely, if ever, stopped by denying civil liberties to those advocating resort to force."

Offensive Speech.

> On April 26, 1968, . . . [Paul Robert Cohen] was observed in the Los Angeles County Courthouse . . . wearing a jacket bearing the words "Fuck the Draft" which were plainly visible. There were women and children present in the corridor. The defendant was arrested. The defendant testified that he wore the jacket knowing that the words were on the jacket as a means of informing the public of the depth of his feelings against the Vietnam War and the draft.
>
> The defendant did not engage in, nor threaten to engage in, nor did anyone as the result of his conduct in fact commit or threaten to commit any act of violence. The defendant did not make any loud or unusual noise, nor was there any evidence that he uttered any sound prior to his arrest.[34]

Cohen was convicted of "maliciously and willfully disturb[ing] the peace . . . by offensive conduct" and sentenced to 30 days in jail. The Supreme Court reversed in a five-to-four decision, with Justice Douglas voting with the majority.

Justice John Harlan (grandson of the first Justice Harlan) wrote the opinion for the Court. The case presented the following question: "It is whether California can excise, as 'offensive conduct,' one particular scurrilous epithet from the public discourse, either upon the theory of the court below that its use is inherently likely to cause violent reaction or upon a more general assertion that the States, acting as guardians of public morality, may properly remove this offensive word from the public vocabulary."

Because there was no evidence that Cohen intended to incite a violent reaction or disrupt the draft, he could not be convicted on the first ground. With regard to removing this word from the public discourse, Harlan expressed concern over the ability of a state to distinguish between "offensive words" that it should punish and those that it should not. For, he said, it is "often true that one man's vulgarity is another's lyric."

Justice Douglas also voted to reverse convictions in three cases involving desecration of the United States flag.[35]

Freedom of Association

Affidavits and Oaths. Justice Douglas expressed his views that oaths are unconstitutional in a concurring opinion to *Speiser v. Randall*,[36] wherein the Court struck down an oath veterans were required to take before being eligible for a property tax exemption. Because oaths limit a person's beliefs and right to advocate unpopular ideas, Douglas wrote, "Today what one thinks or believes, what one utters and says have the full protection of the First Amendment. It is only his actions that government may examine and penalize . . . . Advocacy which is in no way brigaded with action should always be protected by the First Amendment. That protection should extend even to the ideas we despise."

Douglas was also concerned that loyalty oaths would entrap "those who join an organization, but do not share its unlawful purposes and who do not participate in its unlawful activities [because those persons] surely pose no threat, either as citizens or as public employees."[37] This statement was made in his opinion for the Court striking down an oath Arizona public employees were required to take. "This . . . [loyalty oath]," he declared, "threatens the cherished freedom of association protected by the First Amendment, made applicable to the States through the Fourteenth Amendment."

Requiring a loyalty oath from teachers was particularly odious to the justice. The case of Howard Joseph Whitehill, Jr., is a case in point. Whitehill was a teacher of creative writing and an author. He was also a member of the Society of Friends. He was offered a position as a visiting lecturer at the University of Maryland, but he refused to take an oath, declaring that he was "not engaged in one way or another in the attempt to overthrow the Government of the United States, or the State of Maryland."[38] When the courts of Maryland upheld the refusal of the university to employ Whitehill, he appealed to the Supreme Court, which reversed in an opinion written by Justice Douglas.

Because teachers should be free to investigate, study, evaluate, and criticize, "the continuing surveillance which this type of law places on teachers," Douglas argued, "is hostile to academic freedom."

Blacklisting and Punishment for Membership. The idea that government could force public employees to forgo their constitutional rights or be discharged was anathema to Douglas. When the Court upheld a New York law prohibiting employment in the school system of anyone belonging to a "subversive" organization, he protested. "I have not been able to accept the recent doctrine that a citizen who enters the public service can be forced to sacrifice his civil rights. I cannot for example find in our constitutional scheme the power of a state to place its employees in the category of second-class citizens by denying them freedom of thought and expression. The Constitution guarantees freedom of thought and expression to everyone in our society. All are entitled to it; and none needs it more than the teacher."[39]

In *Communist Party v. Control Board*,[40] the justice agreed that the Communist Party could be required to register as a "subversive" organization. If lobbyists could be required to register, he could see no reason why "a group operating under the control of a foreign power" should not also register. But when Junius Irving Scales was convicted for being a member of a "subversive" organization because he was a member of the Communist Party, Douglas dissented.

In *Scales v. United States*,[41] the justice wrote, "When we allow petitioner to be sentenced to prison for six years for being a 'member' of the Communist Party we make a sharp break with traditional concepts of First Amendment rights and make serious Mark Twain's light-hearted comment that 'It is by the goodness of God that in our country we have those three unspeakably precious things: freedom of speech, freedom of conscience, and the prudence never to practice either of them.' " What concerned Douglas, was that the Court was legalizing "guilt by association, sending a man to prison when he committed no unlawful act." He did have hope, however, that there were better times ahead. "What we lose by majority vote today," he thought, "may be reclaimed at a future time when the fear of advocacy, dissent, and nonconformity no longer casts a shadow over us."

Associational Privacy.

> On June 25, 1952, Herman A. Beilan, . . . who had been a teacher for about 22 years in the Philadelphia Public School System, presented himself at his Superintendent's office in response to the latter's request. The Superintendent said he had information which reflected adversely on petitioner's loyalty and he wanted to determine its truth or falsity . . . . The Superintendent . . . asked petitioner whether or not he had been the Press Director of the Professional Section of the Communist Political Association in 1944. [Beilan] asked permission to consult counsel before answering and the Superintendent granted his request.[42]

After consulting his attorney, Beilan refused to answer that or any similar question. For this, he was discharged by the board of education. He appealed to the Supreme Court, which upheld the board's decision.

In a companion case, the Court had before it the discharge of Lerner, a New York subway conductor who also refused to answer questions relating to his possible membership in the Communist Party.[43] In dissenting in both cases, Douglas wrote, "The holding of the Court that the teacher in the *Beilan* case and the subway conductor in the *Lerner* case could be discharged from their respective jobs because they stood silent when asked about their Communist affiliations cannot, without due deference, be squared with our constitutional principles."

Furthermore, he declared:

> Our legal system is premised on the theory that every person is innocent until he is proved guilty. In this country we have, however, been moving away from that concept. We have been generating the belief that anyone who remains silent when interrogated about his unpopular beliefs or affiliations is guilty. I would allow no inference of wrongdoing to flow from the invocation of any constitutional right. I would not let that principle bow to popular passions. For all we know we are dealing here with citizens who are wholly innocent of any wrongful action. That must indeed be our premise. When we make the contrary assumption, we part radically with our tradition.

In writing the Court's opinion upholding Herbert Schneider's right not to answer questions about his associational activities, Douglas quoted Thomas Jefferson regarding government intrusion into personal beliefs. "This is the philosophy of Jefferson," Douglas wrote, "that 'the opinions of men are not the object of civil government, nor under its jurisdiction . . . . [I]t is time enough for the rightful purposes of civil government for its officers to interfere when principles break into overt acts against peace and good order.' "[44] Schneider, who had been a merchant seaman for many years, applied to the Coast Guard for certification as a second assistant engineer. He admitted that he had once been a member of the Communist Party, but that he had become disenchanted with its tactics and quit. He also said that he did not advocate the overthrow of the government. Because he refused to answer further questions concerning his associations, his application was set aside. He brought an action to force the commandant to process the application, but the action was dismissed by the district court. The Supreme Court reversed.

When Theodore R. Gibson, president of the local branch of the NAACP, appeared before a Florida legislative committee and refused to produce the organization's membership list, he was found in contempt of the committee and sentenced to six months in jail and fined $1,200. On appeal to the Supreme Court, the decision was reversed, with Justice Douglas writing an extensive concurring opinion.[45]

"The right of association," he declared,

> has become a part of the bundle of rights protected by the First Amendment . . . , and the need for a pervasive right of privacy against government intrusion has been recognized, though not always given the recognition it deserves. Unpopular groups . . . like popular ones are protected. Unpopular groups if forced to disclose their membership lists may suffer reprisals or other forms of public hostility . . . . But whether a group is popular or unpopular, the right of privacy implicit in the First Amendment creates an area into which the Government may not enter.

Public Employees and Political Association. The federal law that prohibits political activity by federal employees is commonly referred to as the Hatch Act. Among other things, this act provides that an "employee . . . may not '(2) take an active part in political management or in political campaigns.' "[46] The National

Association of Letter Carriers and six federal employees brought an action seeking a declaration that this section of the act was unconstitutional as a violation of the First Amendment. The plaintiffs were successful in the trial court, which agreed that the section was unconstitutional. The Supreme Court reversed and upheld the act, with Justice Douglas dissenting. "We deal here," he argued, "with a First Amendment right to speak, to propose, to publish, to petition Government, to assemble," all of which a person may do in association with others. While admitting that some activities may affect the way an employee does his or her job, "his political creed, like his religion," he wrote, "is irrelevant. In the areas of speech, like religion, it is of no concern what the employee says in private to his wife or to the public in Constitution Hall."

Freedom of the Press

Contempt of Court for Publication. Several times in our history, courts have attempted to charge newspapers, their editors, and their reporters with contempt of court for publishing material critical of the actions of judges.[47] Justice Douglas wrote the Court's opinion in *Craig v. Harney,*[48] one such case. Conway C. Craig was the publisher of two newspapers in Corpus Christi, Texas, which had published several articles critical of County Judge Joe D. Browning. Without letting the jury consider the case, Browning had directed it to return a verdict for a landlord against a tenant who was a member of the armed services. One of the articles read, "Browning's behavior and attitude has brought down the wrath of public opinion upon his head, properly so . . . . American people simply don't like the idea of such going on, especially when a man in the service of his country seems to be getting a raw deal."[49]

Judge Browning charged and convicted Craig, managing editor Bob McCracken, and reporter Tom Mulvaney with contempt, and the convictions were upheld by the Texas appellate courts. The defendants appealed to the U.S. Supreme Court, which reversed. Prefacing his analysis of the published material, Justice Douglas pointed out that "the history of the power to punish for contempt . . . and the unequivocal command of the First Amendment serve as constant reminders that freedom of speech and of the press should not be impaired through the exercise of that power, unless there is no doubt that the utterances in question are a serious and imminent threat to the administration of justice."[50]

Douglas found that some of the published information was not entirely accurate but stated that "a reporter could not be laid by the heels for contempt because he missed the essential point in a trial or failed to summarize the issues to accord with the views of the judge who sat on the case." Furthermore even though an editorial accused the judge of being "high handed" and called his actions "a travesty on justice" there was no evidence that this caused a clear and present danger to the administration of justice.

Libel. In his concurring opinion in *New York Times Co. v. Sullivan,*[51] Justice Black wrote, "An unconditional right to say what one pleases about public affairs is what I consider to be the minimum guarantee of the First Amendment." Justice Douglas agreed. Both justices, therefore, had trouble with the Court's creating a rule that allowed some libel judgments against newspapers. Douglas expressed that concern in concurring in *Rosenblatt v. Baer.*[52] Baer was the supervisor of a ski resort owned by Belknap County, New Hampshire. Rosenblatt wrote an article for a local newspaper pointing out that while there had not been much snow that year, the resort's "cash income [was] simply fantastic, almost unbelievable." He then questioned what happened to the funds from the year before when skiing conditions were much better. Believing that the article defamed him, Baer sued Rosenblatt and recovered judgment for $31,500, which was upheld by the New Hampshire Supreme Court. Because the case was tried before *New York Times Co.,* a majority voted to send it back for reconsideration in accordance with the rules of that case. Douglas concurred separately, and also joined Black in arguing that the case should not be tried again because any libel judgment against Rosenblatt would violate the First Amendment. The justice was particularly concerned about the *Times* rule's applying only to certain elected public officials. "Yet if free discussion of public issues is the guide," he declared, "I see no way to draw lines that exclude the night watchman, the file clerk, the typist, or, for that matter, anyone on the public payroll." For him the proper question was "whether a public *issue,* not a public official, is involved."

Lawyer Elmer Gertz was retained by the Nelson family to represent them in an action against police officer Richard Nuccio, who had shot and killed their son. When Nuccio was tried and convicted of murder, the *American Opinion* published a long article contending that Nuccio had been framed, and that this was part of a national effort to discredit the police. Although Gertz had played no part in the trial and conviction of Nuccio, as counsel for the Nelson family he was named in the article as a "Leninist" and "Communist-fronter."[53] The article also implied that Gertz had a criminal record, which was false. Gertz sued for libel and the jury awarded him $50,000 even though there was no evidence that he had suffered any injury. District Judge Bernard M. Decker set the verdict aside and dismissed the case.

The Supreme Court reversed, with Douglas dissenting. His concern was that judgments like this would inhibit the discussion of public affairs. "There can be no doubt," he argued, "that a State impinges upon free and open discussion when it sanctions the imposition of damages for such discussion through its civil libel laws. Discussion of public affairs is often marked by highly charged emotions and jurymen, not unlike us all, are subject to those emotions. It is indeed this very type of speech which is the reason for the First Amendment since speech which arouses little emotion is little in need of protection."

Prior Restraints on Publication. New York Times Co. v. United States,[54] also known as the Pentagon Papers case, involved the publication of a classified multivolume study entitled "History of U.S. Decision-Making Process on Viet Nam Policy." When the *New York Times* and *Washington Post* obtained and published parts of this study, the government went to court, claiming that further publication would seriously impair the security of the country. In a short *per curiam* opinion, the Supreme Court disagreed. The opinion, citing prior case law, stated, "Any system of prior restraints of expression comes to this Court bearing a heavy presumption against its constitutional validity." And in this case the government has "not met that burden."

In concurring, Douglas pointed out that "secrecy in government is fundamentally anti-democratic, perpetuating bureaucratic errors. Open debate and discussion of public issues are vital to our national health. On public questions there should be 'uninhibited, robust, and wide-open' debate."

In an attempt to eliminate discrimination in employment, Pittsburgh, Pennsylvania, adopted an ordinance making it unlawful to refuse to hire a person because of his or her sex. It was also unlawful to aid in any such discrimination. Because the *Pittsburgh Press* carried help-wanted ads under columns captioned "Male Help Wanted," "Female Help Wanted," and "Male-Female Help Wanted," it was found to have violated the ordinance and ordered not to refer to sex in its want-ads thereafter. It appealed to the courts, but when they refused to lift the ban, the paper appealed to the Supreme Court, but it too found no violation of the First Amendment's freedom of the press provision.[55] The justice dissented. "But I believe that Pittsburgh Press by reason of the First Amendment may publish what it pleases about any law without censorship or restraint by Government. The First Amendment does not require the press to reflect any ideological or political creed reflecting the dominant philosophy, whether transient or fixed. It may use its pages and facilities to denounce a law and urge its repeal or, at the other extreme, denounce those who do not respect its letter and spirit."

Reporter's News Sources. Newspaper reporter Paul Branzburg wrote a story for his paper about a visit with two young men who were making hashish from marijuana. In order to get the story, he had to promise these individuals that he would not reveal their names. When summoned to appear before the county grand jury, he therefore refused to identify those possessing marijuana or those making hashish. He was found in contempt and appealed.

Earl Caldwell found himself in somewhat the same predicament. He had been assigned by his paper to cover the Black Panther Party in California. He was also ordered to appear before a grand jury and asked to bring his notes and tape recordings. He refused and was also held in contempt and appealed. A majority of the Supreme Court upheld the contempt in both cases, with Douglas dissenting.[56] Justice Byron White wrote for the majority that "we cannot seriously entertain the notion that the First Amendment protects a newsman's agreement to conceal the criminal conduct of his source, or evidence thereof, on the theory that it is better to write about crime than to do something about it."

Justice Douglas saw the reporter in an entirely different light.

> His immunity in my view is therefore quite complete, for, absent his involvement in a crime, the First Amendment protects him against an appearance before a grand jury and if he is involved in a crime, the Fifth Amendment stands as a barrier. Since in my view there is no area of inquiry not protected by a privilege, the reporter need not appear for the futile purpose of invoking one to each question. And, since in my view a newsman has an absolute right not to appear before a grand jury, it follows for me that a journalist who voluntarily appears before that body may invoke his First Amendment privilege to specific questions.

The extent to which reporters can interview prisoners was before the Court in two cases.[57] Both involved prison regulations prohibiting interview "with specific individual inmates." These restrictions were adopted because press coverage of some inmates tended to increase the disciplinary problems within the institution. The reporters argued, however, that the regulations impaired their ability to gather information that was newsworthy. The Supreme Court disagreed and upheld the ban. Justice Potter Stewart wrote that "newsmen have no constitutional right of access to prisons or their inmates beyond that afforded the general public."

Douglas believed that the majority was focusing upon the wrong issue, and therefore dissented. "In dealing with the free press guarantee, it is important to note," he argued, "that the interest it protects is not possessed by the media themselves. In enjoining enforcement of the federal regulation . . . Judge Gesell did not vindicate any right of the Washington Post, but rather the right of the people, the true sovereign under our constitutional scheme, to govern in an informed manner." The ban, he argued "is far broader than is necessary to protect any legitimate governmental interests and is an unconstitutional infringement on the public's right to know protected by the free press guarantee of the First Amendment."

Obscenity. When it came to government censorship, Douglas's position was simple and straightforward. "The First and the Fourteenth Amendments," he declared, "say that Congress and the States shall make 'no law' which abridges freedom of speech or of the press. In order to sanction a system of censorship I would have to say that 'no law' does not mean what it says, that 'no law' is qualified to mean 'some' laws. I cannot take that step." That statement was made in a concurring opinion when a unanimous Court struck down the censorship laws of Ohio and New York.[58]

When the Court in 1957 adopted a test by which government could punish the mailing, selling, or distribution of "obscene" material, the justice again protested. "The First Amendment, its prohibition in terms absolute," he asserted, "was designed to preclude courts as well as legislatures from weighing the values of speech against silence. The First Amendment puts free speech in the preferred position."[59]

In 1968 Justice John M. Harlan pointed out that only two justices, Black and Douglas, consistently argued that the First Amendment made "society powerless to protect itself against the dissemination of even the filthiest materials."[60] Harlan noted that most of the justices would "permit suppression of material that falls short of so-called 'hard-core pornography.'" But Justice Stewart would permit punishment of only "hard-core pornography." And Harlan himself believed that states should have "wider authority to deal with obnoxious matter."

Justice Douglas summed up his views on the obscenity question with this statement: "I am sure I would find offensive most of the books and movies charged with being obscene. But in a life that has not been short, I have yet to be trapped into seeing or reading something that would offend me. I never read or see the materials coming to the Court under charges of 'obscenity,' because I have thought the First Amendment made it unconstitutional for me to act as a censor."[61]

The Pursuit of Liberty

The Right of Privacy. When Estelle T. Griswold was arrested for violating a Connecticut law prohibiting the dissemination of information concerning the use of contraceptives, this gave the Court the opportunity to examine the existence of a constitutional right of privacy.[62] With Douglas writing the opinion, the Court concluded that several provisions of the Bill of Rights pointed the way to such a right.

The justice wrote:

> Various guarantees create zones of privacy. The right of association contained in the penumbra of the First Amendment is one, as we have seen. The Third Amendment in its prohibition against the quartering of soldiers "in any house" in time of peace without the consent of the owner is another facet of that privacy. The Fourth Amendment explicitly affirms the "right of the people to be secure in their persons, houses, papers, and effects, against unreasonable searches and seizures." The Fifth Amendment in its Self-Incrimination Clause enables the citizen to create a zone of privacy which the government may not force him to surrender to his detriment. The Ninth Amendment provides: "The enumeration in the Constitution, of certain rights, shall not be construed to deny or disparage others retained by the people."

The justice then applied the right of privacy to Griswold's activities. "We deal," he declared, "with a right of privacy older than the Bill of Rights—older than our political parties, older than our school system. Marriage is the coming together for better or for worse, hopefully enduring, and intimate to the degree of being sacred. It is an association that promotes a way of life, not causes; a harmony in living, not political faiths; a bilateral loyalty, not commercial or social projects. Yet it is an association for as noble a purpose as any involved in our prior decisions."

The Court has since held that the "liberty" protected by the Due Process Clause is the real source of the right of privacy, and that the right includes many family relationships.

The Court extended the right of privacy to encompass the right of a woman to choose whether to bear a child or not in *Roe v. Wade*,[63] a decision in which Douglas concurred. The justice points out that among the rights protected by the right of privacy *"is freedom of choice in the basic decisions of one's life respecting marriage, divorce, procreation, contraception, and the education and upbringing of children."*[64]

The Right to Travel. Douglas expressed his views on the existence of a right to travel in *Edwards v. California*.[65] The majority had held that the California statute making it unlawful to bring "indigent persons" into the state was an unconstitutional burden on interstate commerce. But the justice was "of the opinion that the right of persons to move freely from State to State occupies a more protected position in our constitutional system than does the movement of cattle, fruit, steel and coal across state lines."

Douglas was also concerned that allowing a state to obstruct travel by indigents "would prevent a citizen because he was poor from seeking new horizons in other States. It might thus withhold from large segments of our people that mobility which is basic to any guarantee of freedom of opportunity."

The justice had an opportunity to express his views more fully on the right to travel when Rockwell Kent brought his case to the Court. Kent's application for a passport to travel to England had been denied on two grounds: "(1) that he was a Communist and (2) that he had 'a consistent and prolonged adherence to the Communist Party line.' "[66] In holding that the secretary of state had no authority to withhold a passport for the reasons given, the justice pointed out that the "right to travel is a part of the 'liberty' of which the citizen cannot be deprived without due process of law under the Fifth Amendment." "We must remember," he declared, "that we are dealing here with citizens who have neither been accused of crimes nor found guilty. They are being denied their freedom of movement solely because of their refusal to be subjected to an inquiry into their beliefs and associations."

Equal Protection of the Law

Blacks on Juries. In cases involving the exclusion of blacks from juries, in which he participated, Justice Douglas voted to strike down the state's jury selection process in every one, but one.[67] His view that such exclusion violated equal protection coincided with that set forth by Justice Thurgood Marshall in 1972 in *Peters v. Kiff*.[68] Marshall wrote, "This Court has repeatedly held that the Constitution prohibits such selection practices, with respect to the grand jury, the petit jury, or both.

"But, where there exists a pattern of discrimination, an all-white or all-black jury commission in these times probably means that the race in power retains authority to control the community's official life, and that no jury will likely be selected that is a true cross-section of the community."[69] With those words, Douglas dissented when the majority upheld a jury selection process whereby an all-white jury commission was required to select "those persons who are 'generally reputed to be honest and intelligent . . . and . . . esteemed in the community for their integrity, good character and sound judgment.' " The justice's solution to the problem would have been to require that the jury commission system "provide for proportional representation of the two races."

Where Blacks Live and With Whom They Live. Olive B. Barrows and Leola Jackson were owners of separate pieces of property that were subject to a restriction preventing the property from "ever at any time be[ing] used or occupied by a person or persons not wholly of the white or Caucasian race."[70] Jackson gave title to her property to another person without including the restriction in the deed, thus allowing persons who were not Caucasian to move in. Barrows sued Jackson for damages claiming a breach of the restrictive covenant. Superior Court Judge Daniel N. Stevens dismissed the case, and Barrows appealed to the California Appellate Court, which affirmed. Barrows then took the case to the U.S. Supreme, which also affirmed. Justice Sherman Minton, writing for the Court, pointed out that previously the Court had held "that racial restrictive covenants could not be enforced in equity against Negro purchasers because such enforcement would constitute state action denying equal protection of the laws to the Negroes, in violation of the Fourteenth Amendment to the Federal Constitution."

The case before the Court, however, involved a Caucasian suing another Caucasian for breach of covenant. But the Court's response was the same. If courts enforced the agreement, non–Caucasians would find it difficult to purchase homes and thus would be denied equal protection. "If a state court awards damages for breach of a restrictive covenant," Minton wrote, "a prospective seller of restricted land will either refuse to sell to non-Caucasians or else will require non–Caucasians to pay a higher price to meet the damages which the seller may incur. Solely because of their race, non–Caucasians will be unable to purchase, own, and enjoy property on the same terms as Caucasians. Denial of this right by state action deprives such non–Caucasians, unidentified but identifiable, of equal protection of the laws in violation of the Fourteenth Amendment." Douglas agreed and voted with the majority.

Living together brought Dewey McLaughlin, a black man, and Connie Hoffman, a white woman, into conflict with the law. They were arrested and convicted for violating a Florida law that made it a crime for a black person and a white person to "habitually live in and occupy in the nighttime the same room."[71] The convictions were upheld by the Florida Supreme Court but reversed by a unanimous U.S. Supreme Court. Although Florida argued that the law was intended to punish "illicit extramarital and premarital promiscuity," the justices responded that there was "no suggestion that a white person and a Negro are any more likely habitually to occupy the same room together than the white or the Negro couple to engage in illicit intercourse if they do."

Justices Stewart and Douglas concurred. They could not "conceive of . . . [any] valid legislative purpose under our Constitution for a state law which makes the color of a person's skin the test of whether this conduct is a criminal offense."

Integration of Public Facilities. Justice Douglas wrote the majority opinion ordering the integration of Bacon's Park in Macon, Georgia.[72] (See Chapter 4.) The justice pointed out that what is private action as opposed to state action is not always easy to determine, but, he wrote, "when private individuals or groups are endowed by the State with powers or functions governmental in nature, they become agencies or instrumentalities of the State and subject to its constitutional limitations." And that's what had happened in this case. "Under the circumstances of this case," the justice declared, "we cannot but conclude that the public character of this park requires it to be treated as a public institution subject to the command of the Fourteenth Amendment, regardless of who now has title under state law. We may fairly assume that had the Georgia courts been of the view that even in private hands the park may not be operated for the public on a segregated basis, the resignation would not have been approved and private trustees appointed."

When Jackson, Mississippi, closed its public swimming pools rather than integrate them, and the Supreme Court upheld that decision, Douglas vigorously protested. "I conclude," he asserted, "that though a State may discontinue any of its municipal services—such as schools, parks, pools, athletic fields, and the like—it may not do so for the purpose of perpetuating or installing *apartheid* or because it finds life in a multi-racial community difficult or unpleasant. If that is its reason, then abolition of a designated public service becomes a device for perpetuating a segregated way of life. That a State may not do."[73]

Integration of Private Facilities. When three black students and one white student sat in at a lunch counter in New Orleans, Louisiana, they were arrested, charged with and convicted of taking "possession of any part . . . of a place of business, or remaining in a place of business after the person in charge . . . has ordered such person to leave the premises."[74] When the case reached the Supreme Court, the convictions were reversed even though the restaurant was privately owned. Douglas concurred. "The line between a private business and a public one," he noted, "has been long and hotly contested." But for him, the link connecting the private restaurant to the government was the fact that the restaurant was licensed by the state. "This restaurant," he argued, " needs a permit from Louisiana to operate; and during the existence of the license the State has broad powers of visitation and control. This restaurant is thus an instrumentality of the State since the State charges it with duties to the public and supervises its performance .... There is no constitutional way, as I see it, in which a State can license and supervise a business serving the public and endow it with the authority to manage that business on the basis of *apartheid,* which is foreign to our Constitution."

K. Leroy Irvis, a black man, accompanied a white friend to the Moose Lodge in Harrisburg, Pennsylvania, on Sunday, December 29, 1968. Irvis was refused service because not only did the lodge exclude non–Caucasians from membership, but only Caucasians were allowed as guests.[75] Irvis brought an action against the lodge contending that because it had a liquor license from the state, its discrimination against him was state action and a violation of the Fourteenth Amendment. The trial court agreed, but the Supreme Court did not. In the Court's opinion, Justice William Rehnquist declared that even though the state did regulate all liquor establishments, "it cannot be said to in any way foster or encourage racial discrimination. Nor can it be said to make the State in any realistic sense a partner or even a joint venturer in the club's enterprise."

Douglas dissented.

> My view of the First Amendment [freedom of association] and the related guarantees of the Bill of Rights is that they create a zone of privacy which precludes government from interfering with private clubs or groups. The associational rights which our system honors permit all white, all black, and all yellow clubs to be formed. They also permit all Catholic, all Jewish, or all agnostic clubs to be established. Government may not tell a man or woman who his or her associates must be. The individual can be as selective as he desires .... But this does not apply to this case because of Pennsylvania's liquor licensing scheme which restricts the number of licenses available, and the hours that licensees may dispense liquor. Private clubs may serve their members from 7 A.M. until 3 A.M. the next morning.

"This state-enforced scarcity of licenses," the Justice argued, "restricts the ability of blacks to obtain liquor, for liquor is commercially available *only* at private clubs for a significant portion of each week. Access by blacks to places that serve liquor is further limited by the fact that the state [license] quota is filled."

Gender Discrimination. Valentine Goesaert was the owner of a bar in Dearborn, Michigan, where she employed her daughter as a barmaid. This was in violation of a city ordinance that prohibited a female from being a barmaid unless she was "the wife or daughter of the male owner of a licensed liquor establishment."[76] Goesaert sued to restrain the enforcement of the law, but the court, with one judge dissenting, refused to do so. The Supreme Court upheld that decision, with Douglas joining Justice Wiley Rutledge's dissent. "The statute arbitrarily discriminates between male and female owners of liquor establishments. A male owner, although he himself is always absent from his bar, may employ his wife and daughter as barmaids. A female owner may neither work as a barmaid herself nor employ her daughter in that position, even if a man is always present in the establishment to keep order."

Lieutenant Sharon Frontiero attempted to secure quarters allowances and medical benefits for her husband, but these were denied because she had failed to show that he was her dependent. Had Lieutenant Frontiero been a male, such an allowance would have been granted automatically because the army assumed that a wife was a dependent. The Frontieros were successful in overturning the army's decision in the Supreme Court, where only Justice William H. Rehnquist dissented. Justice William J. Brennan wrote an opinion in which Justices Douglas, White, and Marshall joined. "We therefore conclude," Justice Brennan declared, "that, by according differential treatment to male and female members of the uniformed services for the sole purpose of achieving administrative convenience, the challenged statutes violate the Due Process Clause of the Fifth Amendment insofar as they require a female member to prove the dependency of her husband."[77]

Douglas voted with the majority in two cases dealing with family relationships. In one, the Court held that an Idaho law that gave men preference over women in the appointment of an administrator of an estate, violated equal protection. And the Court also struck down a Utah statute that required fathers to contribute to the support of sons until they were 21, but permitted a father to stop supporting daughters when they became 18.[78]

For Illegitimate Children. Ronald Bell, and Regina, Cecelia, Linda, and Austin Levy, the illegitimate children of Louise Levy, sued the state of Louisiana for the wrongful death of their mother. Judge Paul P. Garafalo gave judgment in favor of the state, concluding that only legitimate children had a right of action for wrongful death of a parent. The Louisiana appeals courts upheld Judge Garafalo's decision, but the Supreme Court reversed, with Justice Douglas delivering the opinion. "We start from the premise," he wrote, "that illegitimate children are not 'nonpersons.' They are humans, live, and have their being. They are clearly 'persons' within the meaning of the Equal Protection Clause of the Fourteenth Amendment."[79]

The justice pointed out that "legitimacy or illegitimacy of birth has no relation to the nature of the wrong allegedly inflicted on the mother. These children, though illegitimate, were dependent on her; she cared for them and nurtured them; they were indeed hers in the biological and in the spiritual sense; in her death they suffered wrong in the sense that any dependent would."

For Aliens. In 1934, when Fred Oyama, a citizen of Japanese descent, was six years old, his father, Kajiro Oyama, purchased a parcel of land in California and put the title in his son's name. Because the family was Japanese, and the United States was later at war with Japan, they were evacuated from the West Coast in 1942. Shortly thereafter, the state sought to have the land escheat to it on the grounds that Kajiro Oyama had placed the land in his son's name for the sole purpose of avoiding the Alien Land Law. That law prohibited aliens ineligible for citizenship to own land in California, but his son could own the land because he was an American citizen.

Superior Court Judge Joe L. Shell granted escheat of the land, which decision was upheld by the Supreme Court of California. The U.S. Supreme Court, in reversing the decision, concluded that the state was discriminating against the son, Fred Oyama, solely because his parents were Japanese.

Justices Black and Douglas agreed. "If there is any one purpose of the Fourteenth Amendment," Justice Black declared, "that is wholly outside the realm of doubt, it is that the Amendment was designed to bar States from denying to some groups, on account of their race or color, any rights, privileges, and opportunities accorded to other groups. I would now overrule the previous decisions of this Court that sustained state land laws which discriminate against people of Japanese origin residing in this country."[80]

> [Ephram Nestor] came to this country from Bulgaria in 1913 and was employed, so as to be covered by the Social Security Act, from December 1936 to January 1955—a period of 19 years. He became eligible for retirement and for Social Security benefits in November 1955 and was awarded $55.60 per month. In July 1956 he was deported for having been a member of the Communist Party from 1933 to 1939. Pursuant to a law, enacted September 1, 1954, he was thereupon denied payment of further Social Security benefits.[81]

When the Supreme Court upheld denial of benefits to Nestor, Douglas dissented. For him this was a bill of attainder, which "is a legislative act which inflicts punishment without a judicial trial." "The aim and purpose [of the law] are clear—to take away from a person by legislative fiat property which he has accumulated because he acted in a certain way or embraced a certain ideology. That is a modern version of the bill of attainder—as plain, as direct, as effective as those which religious passions once loosed in England and which later were employed against the Tories here."

For New Political Parties. Douglas concurred when the Court struck down Ohio's laws governing how new political parties obtain a place on the ballot.[82] "Ohio, through an entangling web of election laws," he declared, "has effectively foreclosed its presidential ballot to all but Republicans and Democrats. It has done so initially by abolishing write-in votes so as to restrict candidacy to names on the ballot; it has eliminated all independent candidates through a requirement that nominees enjoy the endorsement of a political party; it has defined 'political party' in such a way as to exclude virtually all but the two major parties."

"In our political life," he asserted, "third parties are often important channels through which political dissent is aired: All political ideas cannot and should not be channeled into the programs of our two major parties. History has amply proved the virtue of political activity by minority, dissident groups, which innumerable times have been in the vanguard of democratic thought and whose programs were ultimately accepted . . . . The absence of such voices would be a symptom of grave illness in our society."

In the Criminal Justice System. Jack T. Skinner had been convicted for stealing chickens, and twice for robbery with a firearm. Because he had committed crimes involving moral turpitude, he was adjudged to be a habitual criminal and ordered to undergo an operation to render him sexually sterile.[83] In a five-to-four decision, the order was upheld by the Oklahoma Supreme Court. Because the state law did not apply to embezzlers, the U.S. Supreme Court reversed, concluding that the statute violated the Equal Protection Clause.

Justice Douglas, writing for a unanimous Court, pointed out the inequities in the law. If, for example, a person stole chickens worth more than $20 three times, that person could be sterilized. But a bank clerk who embezzled $20 or more three times could not be. "We are dealing here," the justice declared, "with legislation which involves one of the basic civil rights of man. Marriage and procreation are fundamental to the very existence and survival of the race. The power to sterilize, if exercised, may have subtle, far-reaching and devastating effects . . . . There is no redemption for the individual whom the law touches. Any experiment which the State conducts is to his irreparable injury. He is forever deprived of a basic liberty." "Embezzlers," he continued, "are forever free. Those who steal or take in other ways are not."

"There can be no equal justice," Justice Black declared, "where the kind of trial a man gets depends on the amount of money he has. Destitute defendants must be afforded as adequate appellate review as defendants who have money enough to buy transcripts."[84] Douglas agreed. Some 13 years later, when California refused to furnish a transcript to a prisoner who had filed for a writ of *habeas corpus,* he wrote, "The State can hardly contend that a transcript is irrelevant . . . where it specifically provides one, upon request, to the appellate court and the State Attorney. So long as this system of repeated hearings exists and so long as transcripts are available for preparation of appellate hearings in habeas corpus cases, they may not be furnished those who can afford them and denied those who are paupers."[85]

In *Gideon v. Wainwright,*[86] the Court held that the Sixth Amendment required government to provide indigent criminal defendants with counsel at their trials. On the same day, the Court held that the state must also provide counsel for defendants Bennie Will Meyes and William Douglas and other defendants in the appeal of their convictions.[87] Not to do so would be a denial of equal protection. "The present case, where counsel was denied petitioners on appeal," Justice Douglas asserted,

> shows that the discrimination is not between "possibly good and obviously bad cases," but between cases where the rich man can require the court to listen to argument of counsel before deciding on the merits, but a poor man cannot. There is lacking that equality demanded by the Fourteenth Amendment which the rich man, who appeals as of right, enjoys the benefit of counsel's examination into the record, research of the law and marshalling of arguments on his behalf, while the indigent, already burdened by a preliminary determination that his case is without merit, is forced to shift for himself.

For the Poor. Annie E. Harper and several other persons sued the Virginia State Board of Elections claiming that requiring them to pay a poll tax in order to vote denied them equal protection of the laws. The trial judge wrote: "The common premise of the assault is: that the plaintiffs are financially unable to pay the tax—$1.50 for each of the three preceding years for which the elector was assessable; and that they and other State citizens similarly impecunious are thereby deprived, solely on account of their poverty, of the privilege to vote, and at the same time they are also denied a privilege accorded other citizens not so poor."[88]

The court dismissed the case, and Harper and the others appealed. The Supreme Court reversed, with Justice Douglas writing the majority opinion. "We conclude," he wrote, "that a State violates the Equal Protection Clause of the Fourteenth Amendment whenever it makes the affluence of the voter or payment of any fee an electoral standard."[89] He continued:

> Wealth, like race, creed, or color, is not germane to one's ability to participate intelligently in the electoral process. Lines drawn on the basis of wealth or property, like those of race . . . are traditionally disfavored . . . . To introduce wealth or payment of a fee as a measure of a voter's qualifications is to introduce a capricious or irrelevant factor . . . . In this context—that is, as a condition of obtaining a ballot—the requirement of fee paying causes an "invidious" discrimination . . . that runs afoul of the Equal Protection Clause.

Gladys Boddie, Bertha Barker, Ann DeNicola, Maryann Dozier, Betty Ann Perez, Catherine Strain, Mary Wierzbicki, Mamie Williams, and Mary Yeaton were all on welfare in Connecticut. They sued the state seeking to have declared unconstitutional a state law requiring payment of filing fees and costs in order to obtain a divorce. They alleged that they were unable to pay such fees and therefore were denied access to the judicial system, which denial violated their right to equal protection of the law. The court dismissed the complaint and the plaintiffs appealed to the Supreme Court, which reversed, with only Justice Black dissenting.[90]

Justice Douglas concurred. For him, the question was one of equal treatment for the poor. "Just as denying further judicial review in *Burns* and *Smith,* appellate review in *Douglas,* and a transcript in *Griffin* created an invidious distinction based on wealth, so, too, does making the grant or denial of a divorce turn on the wealth of the parties. Affluence does not pass muster under the Equal Protection Clause for determining who must remain married and who shall be allowed to separate."

The Bill of Rights and the States

> The petitioner, a farm hand, out of a job and on relief, was indicted in a Maryland state court on a charge of robbery. He was too poor to hire a lawyer.

He so informed the court and requested that counsel be appointed to defend him. His request was denied. Put to trial without a lawyer, he conducted his own defense, was found guilty, and was sentenced to eight years imprisonment. The court below found that the petitioner had at least an ordinary amount of intelligence. It is clear from his examination of witnesses that he was a man of little education.[91]

This describes what happened to a man named Betts in a case in which the Court upheld Betts's conviction for robbery, despite his claim that the Sixth Amendment required the state to appoint counsel for him. Black dissented from that decision and wrote an opinion in which Douglas and Murphy concurred. "I believe," Black declared, "that the Fourteenth Amendment made the Sixth applicable to the states. But this view, although often urged in dissents, has never been accepted by a majority of this Court and is not accepted today."

When the Court overruled the *Betts* case in *Gideon v. Wainwright*,[92] and held that the Sixth Amendment requires states to provide counsel to indigents, Douglas concurred, and wrote:

> Since the adoption of that [Fourteenth] Amendment, ten Justices have felt that it protects from infringement by the States the privileges, protections, and safeguards granted by the Bill of Rights. Justice Field, the first Justice Harlan, and probably Justice Brewer, took that position . . . as did Justices Black, Douglas, Murphy and Rutledge . . . . That view was also expressed by Justices Bradley and Swayne . . . and seemingly accepted by Justice Clifford . . . . Unfortunately it has never commanded a Court. Yet, happily, all constitutional questions are always open . . . . And what we do today does not foreclose the matter.

Because a majority of the Court never did accept that view, however, Douglas, like Black, willingly voted to require states to abide by specific provisions of the Bill of Rights on a case-by-case basis.[93]

The Japanese Cases

Douglas voted to sustain the convictions of Gordon Kiyoshi Hirabayashi and Minoru Yasui for violating the military-ordered curfew imposed upon the Japanese following the bombing of Pearl Harbor.[94] He took the position that military necessity required immediate obedience to the order. "To say that the military in such cases," he argued, "should take the time to weed out the loyal from the others would be to assume that the nation could afford to have them take the time to do it. But as the opinion of the Court makes clear, speed and dispatch may be of the essence."

Simon has reported that Vern Countryman, a Douglas law clerk at the time, was unable to convince the justice to change his vote. "I said there was nothing to support the curfew classification but race," Countryman recalled. "I also said to him: You were in the Army; you know not to believe a general. The Justice wouldn't budge."[95]

The justice also joined Black's opinion to uphold the conviction of Fred Toyosaburo Korematsu for remaining in a military area contrary to an order of the commanding general. The order prohibited persons of Japanese descent from entering certain areas along the West Coast. Here again, the justices were of the opinion that such exclusion was necessary because of the war with Japan in 1942.[96]

AS A JUDICIAL FREEDOM FIGHTER

> We are a religious people whose institutions presuppose a Supreme Being. We guarantee the freedom to worship as one chooses. We make room for as wide a variety of beliefs and creeds as the spiritual needs of man deem necessary. We sponsor an attitude on the part of the government that shows no partiality to any one group and that lets each flourish according to the zeal of its adherents and the appeal of its dogma.[97]

That sums up the Justice's views on the free exercise of religion.

In voting to reverse convictions of the 11 Communist Party officials in *Dennis,* Douglas stated:

> Free speech has occupied an exalted position because of the high service it has given our society. Its protection is essential to the very existence of a democracy. The airing of ideas releases pressures which otherwise might become destructive. When ideas compete in the market for acceptance, full and free discussion exposes the false and they gain few adherents. Full and free discussion even of ideas we hate encourages the testing of our own prejudices and preconceptions. Full and free discussion keeps a society from becoming stagnant and unprepared for the stresses and strains that work to tear all civilizations apart.
>
> Full and free discussion has indeed been the first article of our faith. We have founded our political system on it. It has been the safeguard of every religious, political, philosophical, economic, and racial group amongst us. We have counted on it to keep us from embracing what is cheap and false; we have trusted the common sense of our people to choose the doctrine true to our genius and to reject the rest. This has been the one single outstanding tenant that has made our institutions the symbol of freedom and equality. We have deemed it more costly to liberty to suppress a despised minority than to let them vent their spleen. We have above all else feared the political censor. We have wanted a land where our people can be exposed to the diverse creeds and cultures of the world.[98]

And whether it was Beauharnais's pamphleteering; Harriett Louise Adderley's picketing near the jailhouse; Terminiello's provocative statements; or

Irving Feiner's derogatory words about mayors Costello and O'Dwyer and President Truman—Douglas applied that philosophy and voted to uphold their First Amendment rights. And that was true with regard to Cohen's offensive statement on the back of his jacket, as well as the alleged desecration of an American flag to send a message, as was done by Spence.

Douglas believed that both federal and state governments far exceeded their authority in conducting investigations into allegedly subversive activities in the 1950s and 1960s. "Investigation is a part of lawmaking and the First Amendment, as well as the Fifth," he wrote, "stands as a barrier to state intrusion of privacy. . . . Lawmaking at the investigatory stage may properly probe historic events for any light that may be thrown on present conditions and problems. But the First Amendment prevents use of the power to investigate enforced by the contempt power to probe at will and without relation to existing need."[99] The justice was especially concerned about the government's punishing people for what they believed rather than for anything they might have done. "When we make the belief of a citizen the basis of government action, we move toward the concept of *total security*. Yet *total security* is possible only in a totalitarian regime—the kind of system we profess to combat."[100]

And Douglas was adamantly opposed to test oaths. He wrote: "The test oath is abhorrent to our tradition."[101] He therefore objected when the Court upheld an oath that required a person to swear that he or she would "oppose the overthrow of the government."[102] People have the right, he argued, to advocate that the government be overthrown. Thus an oath to oppose the overthrow of government is inconsistent with that right. "This oath . . . requires that appellee 'oppose' that which she has an indisputable right to advocate. Yet the majority concludes that the promise of 'opposition'—exacted as a condition of public employment—is a mere redundancy which does not impair appellee's freedom of expression."

But it was not just protection for the First Amendment rights of those who might have believed in proletarian revolution that Douglas was concerned about. He consistently voted to protect the rights of minority organizations such as the NAACP. For example, when Louisiana attempted to bar that organization from the state, he wrote, "At one extreme is criminal conduct which cannot have shelter in the First Amendment. At the other extreme are regulatory measures which, no matter how sophisticated, cannot be employed in purpose or in effect to stifle, penalize, or curb the exercise of First Amendment rights."[103]

> The press has a preferred position in our constitutional scheme, not to enable it to make money, not to set newsmen apart as a favored class, but to bring fulfillment to the public's right to know.

* * * * *

The people who govern are often far removed from the cabals that threaten the regime; the people are often remote from the sources of truth even though they live in the city where the forces that would undermine society operate. The function of the press is to explore and investigate events, inform the people what is going on, and to expose the harmful as well as the good influences at work. There is no higher function performed under our constitutional regime.[104]

Those are Justice Douglas's views of freedom of the press as set forth in his dissenting opinion in the *Caldwell* case.

The justice's views on obscenity are stated very succinctly in *Jenkins v. Georgia:* "Mr. Justice Douglas, being of the view that any ban on obscenity is prohibited by the First Amendment, made applicable to the States through the Fourteenth, concurs in the reversal of this conviction."[105]

It was Justice Douglas's opinion in *Griswold* that began the Court's development of a right of privacy. Before he retired from the Court, it had extended that right to include a woman's choice to bear a child or not,[106] the right of pregnant women to determine when to take maternity leave,[107] and the rights of the mentally ill.[108]

And what the *Griswold* decision did for the right of privacy, the justice's concurring opinion in *Edwards* did for the right to travel. Many years later he wrote:

> Free movement by the citizen is of course as dangerous to a tyrant as free expression of ideas or the right of assembly and it is therefore controlled in most countries in the interests of security. That is why riding boxcars carries extreme penalties in Communist lands. That is why the ticketing of people and the use of identification papers are routine matters under totalitarian regimes, yet abhorrent in the United States.
> Freedom of movement, at home and abroad, is important for job and business opportunities—for cultural, political and social activities—for all the commingling which gregarious man enjoys.[109]

Douglas consistently voted against discrimination against blacks in the selection of grand and petit juries. *Akins v. Texas*[110] was the one case in which he agreed with the majority that there had been no discrimination against blacks in the selection of the grand jury.

In 1971, 17 years after *Brown v. Board of Education*, Douglas joined Chief Justice Warren Burger's opinion upholding the desegregation of the schools in Charlotte, North Carolina. "The objective today," the chief justice declared,

> remains to eliminate from the public schools all vestiges of state-imposed segregation. Segregation was the evil struck down by *Brown I* as contrary to the equal protection guarantees of the Constitution. That was the violation sought to be corrected by the remedial measures of *Brown II*. That was the basis for the holding in *Green* that school authorities are "clearly charged with the affirmative duty to take whatever steps might be necessary to convert to a unitary system in which racial discrimination would be eliminated root and branch."[111]

Justice Douglas's concern for equal protection extended to the integration of public and private facilities, and with whom and where blacks live. But his interest did not stop there. He voted consistently to give equal treatment to women, illegitimate children, criminal defendants, and aliens. And while he voted in favor of the curfew and evacuation orders for the Japanese during World War II, he also voted to strike down California's alien land law and discrimination against Japanese fishermen.

In discussing the exclusion of women from jury service, Douglas wrote: "Classifications based on sex are no longer insulated from judicial scrutiny by a legislative judgment that 'woman's place is in the home,' or that woman is by her 'nature' ill-suited for a particular task . . . . But such a judgment is precisely that which underpins the absolute exemption [of women] from jury service at issue. . . . [T]his discredited stereotype . . . should be firmly disapproved."[112]

And in his opinion upholding an indigent's right to counsel on appeal, he pointed out that "absolute equality is not required; lines can be drawn and we often sustain them. . . . But where the merits of *the one and only* appeal an indigent has as of right are decided without benefit of counsel, we think an unconstitutional line has been drawn between rich and poor."[113]

In concurring in *Gideon v. Wainwright*, the justice discussed making the Bill of Rights applicable to the states. "My Brother Harlan is of the view that a guarantee of the Bill of Rights that is made applicable to the States by reason of the Fourteenth Amendment is a lesser version of that same guarantee as applied to the Federal Government. Mr. Justice Jackson shared that view. But that view has not prevailed and rights protected against state invasion by the Due Process Clause of the Fourteenth Amendment are not watered-down versions of what the Bill of Rights guarantees."[114]

The justice summed up his view of freedom in dissenting when the Court upheld the piping of music, news, and public announcements through loudspeakers onto streetcars and buses. He was of the opinion that "government should never be allowed to force the people to listen to any radio program." And he declared:

> Liberty in the constitutional sense must mean more than freedom from unlawful governmental restraint; it must include privacy as well, if it is to be a repository of freedom. The right to be let alone is indeed the beginning of all freedom. Part of our claim to privacy is in the prohibition of the Fourth Amendment against unreasonable searches and seizures. It gives the guarantee that a man's home is his castle beyond invasion either by inquisitive or by officious people. A man loses that privacy of course when he goes upon the streets or enters public places. But even in his activities outside the home he has immunities from controls bearing on privacy. He may not be compelled against his will to attend a religious service; he may not be forced to make an affirmation or observe a ritual that violates his scruples; he may not be made to accept one religious, political, or philosophical creed as against another. Freedom of religion and freedom of speech guaranteed by the First Amendment give more than the privilege to worship, to write,

to speak as one chooses; they give freedom not to do nor to act as the government chooses. The First Amendment in its respect for the conscience of the individual honors the sanctity of thought and belief. To think as one chooses, to believe what one wishes are important aspects of the constitutional right to be let alone.[115]

Not only are Justice Douglas's votes and opinions consistent with those views, but his votes indicate a deep concern for those with unorthodox ideas, minorities, including women, illegitimate children, aliens, and the poor. Thus his commitment to freedom is clear.

6

JUSTICE FRANK MURPHY

PERSONAL LIFE

Growing Up

Physically and temperamentally Murphy was richly endowed with characteristics commonly associated with the Irish. A person of medium build and sensitive features, he had the inevitable freckles and the wiry red hair, the passionate streak and the eloquence, often found among "children of the Rosaleen." He also had a revolutionary heritage. His great-grandfather was hanged by the British for rebellion in Ireland, his paternal grandparents were "forty-eighters" from County Mayo, and his own father was jailed as a youth in Canada for participating in Fenian disturbances.[1]

Murphy's father was a successful lawyer in Sand Beach (later changed to Harbor Beach), Michigan, when Frank was born in 1890. He was the third of four children born to John and Mary Murphy. The other children were Harold, Marguerite, and George.

John Murphy was a hard-drinking Irishman, active in local Democratic politics, and he served as the county prosecuting attorney. He ran unsuccessfully for Congress in 1914.

According to author Sidney Fine, "Mary Brennan Murphy was a slender woman with black hair, blue eyes, a fair complexion, and 'finely cut' features. She was a very pious woman, reserved in manner, and altogether devoted to her family—'just a sweet lady,' to use the words of a Harbor Beach resident at the time."[2]

Throughout his life, Frank was deeply devoted to his mother. "Just as the happiest moments of his youth, at least in his recollection, were those that he spent with his mother, so after Frank Murphy left home in 1908, it was to his mother alone that he addressed his daily letters." While at a Christmas Eve party in Germany in 1918, he was asked to suggest a song; he chose "I want a girl just like the girl that married dear old Dad."

JUSTICE FRANK MURPHY (photo by Pach Brothers; collection of the Supreme Court of the United States).

From his mother, Murphy inherited an abiding attachment to the Roman Catholic church and its moral universe. She also implanted in him a sense of personal destiny and an ethical code he never lost. Great moral champions like Lincoln, rather than his father, were the models which she presented for emulation. In guiding his religious education, she instilled in him the ideals that man is his brother's keeper, that salvation lies in good works, and that, in Murphy's words, the 'most precious virtue of all is the desire to serve mankind.' Christian idealism and a belief that life was a moral mission became vibrant articles of his faith at an early age.[3]

Frank learned about the law and politics from his father. He watched his father in court, at work in the office, and on the campaign trail, where Frank became impressed with his father's oratorical ability. Biographer Sidney Fine writes, "John Murphy read the Declaration of Independence and the Constitution to Frank when he was a small boy and 'indoctrinated' his son with Jeffersonian philosophy."[4]

John Murphy also passed on to the children his Catholic faith, but cautioned them not to become too involved with the clergy. "John Murphy's advice was: 'Follow the "Passion," it is sweeter to give than to receive.'" At the early age of seven, Frank became an altar boy.

> Since Harbor Beach was a small town in a rural setting, Frank "led the life of a country boy." He drove the cows to pasture and milked them in the barn in the morning and evening. He swam and fished in the summer, hunted in the woods in the autumn, and skated and went ice-fishing in the winter. As often happens in such surroundings, he found a certain excitement in observing nature that was to remain with him throughout his life.

Murphy went to public schools, was not a brilliant student, played baseball, and was quarterback on the football team. He was also elected president of his graduating class. Upon graduating from high school Frank went to the University of Michigan, where he spent six years, first as an undergraduate and then as a law student. He joined Sigma Chi fraternity, was an editor on the newspaper, "was elected a trustee of the Student Lecture Association, played the male lead in a campus dramatic production, competed in a campus singing contest, and was active in the affairs of the Michigan Union." Because of these activities, he was elected to several nonacademic societies. He did not, however, fare well in college politics, being defeated several times for student offices.

"One example of Murphy's academic work as an undergraduate survives," Sidney Fine writes, "a paper entitled 'Politics and the Laborer' that he wrote for his sociology course in 1911. The paper is of more than ordinary interest because not only does it reflect some of the ideology of progressivism, but it also correctly forecasts Murphy's later role as a champion of the workingman."

Murphy's law school grades were not much to write home about. He barely survived, but he made many lasting friendships during his college and law school days, and was always proud to be known as a Michigan alumnus.

Frank never married. Throughout his life, however, he had many women friends and enjoyed their companionship. At the time of his death, he was engaged to Joan Cuddihy. Fine suggests that the relationship with his mother may have had something to do with his remaining a bachelor. "It became evident during the early postwar years that Frank Murphy was very attractive to the opposite sex and that female companionship was very important to him. The subject of marriage, however, remained for him a 'distasteful' one. It has . . . been suggested that Murphy's failure to marry was intimately connected with his relationship to his mother, but his absorption with himself and his career was also a factor. As Norman Hill expressed it, Frank 'figured maybe he travels best who travels alone.' "

Politics and the Practice of Law

Biographer J. Woodford Howard, Jr., makes two comments that indicate the role of law and politics in Murphy's life: "Law was not his mistress," and "Politics . . . was a powerful distraction."[5]

For a short time after graduation from law school, Murphy worked for his father. The lure of politics, however, prevailed, and he became active in the campaign of Woodbridge N. Ferris, who was running for governor in 1914. This required him to spend most of his time in Detroit. Even so, the Democratic Party entered him as a candidate for county prosecuting attorney in his home county, but he was defeated. After the election, Murphy joined the law firm of Monaghan and Monaghan in Detroit at a salary of five dollars a week. He also took a job teaching English to immigrants in the Delray district of Detroit. "Murphy's experience as a teacher in Delray was the beginning of his education in the life of the big city. 'I learned more then,' he said a few years later, 'about social problems, about poverty, about the vicissitudes that breed lawlessness, than I could have learned in any other way. I grew to have an understanding of the cares and vexatious riddles of *the submerged majority*.' "[6]

Murphy handled a variety of legal matters and tried cases, which he thoroughly enjoyed. The firm was pleased with his work, much of which was representing management. He also became an instructor at the University of Detroit Law School.

But politics continued to play a major role in his life, and he accepted the position as assistant secretary of the Democratic Party's state convention. He supported Woodrow Wilson in 1912 but thought a lot of Theodore Roosevelt, from whom he acquired a concern for his physical fitness. It was not all politics and law, however, for during these years Frank led an active social life, particularly among the wealthier families of Detroit. His legal, political, and social activities were interrupted by service in the army during World War I. (More will be said about his military career later.)

Upon returning from war service, Murphy was appointed an assistant to U.S. Attorney John E. Kinnane. Because the position was a political one, Democrat Kinnane had to give up the office when the Republicans won the White House in 1921. Murphy retained his position until March 1, 1922. "Kinnane later remarked," Fine writes, "that Murphy had been 'a fearless prosecutor' and 'a match for the best lawyers who practiced in the Federal court' and that he had been 'ever mindful of the legal rights of others, particularly the poor and unfortunate.' "

Murphy and Edward G. Kemp formed a law partnership in Detroit in 1922 and within months had built up a very successful practice. In one case Murphy represented a former Detroit lawyer seeking readmission to the bar. When the lawyer refused to register for the draft, he was convicted for not doing so, sent to prison for a year, and disbarred. Murphy respected the fact that the man had followed his conscience and was successful in obtaining his readmission.

Frank continued to be active in the Democratic Party. He worked for the candidacy of A. Mitchell Palmer for the presidency. Palmer, however, was defeated in the Michigan primary election. Murphy and the other delegates to the Democratic Party's national convention carried the fight for Palmer there, but he received only 12 votes on the first ballot.

Military Service

After receiving permission from his parents, Murphy enrolled in the Reserve Officers Training Camp at Fort Sheridan, Illinois, in 1917. At the conclusion of three months' basic training, he was commissioned a first lieutenant in the army infantry. His records contained the statement "Fine mind, thorough, and will make an excellent officer." After a brief period of instruction in trench warfare at Harvard University, he was sent to Camp Custer, near Battle Creek, Michigan. "In addition to the usual duties of an officer at Camp Custer, Murphy served as an official at football games in which the Custer team played, a speaker at civilian gatherings, and an assistant judge advocate." At first, he served as defense counsel in the judge advocate's office but later was assigned to be a prosecutor. He wrote that he would much rather "defend the poor fellows who are in trouble than prosecute them." Murphy was sent to France in July 1918 where he became commanding officer of a classification camp. After being promoted to captain, and serving in several administrative posts, he learned on November 7 that he had been assigned to a battle-tested unit and was destined to go to the front. The war, however, ended with the Armistice on November 11, just as he arrived at his new post. He stayed with the army until March 2, 1919, when he was detached from service and sent to England, where he studied law at the Inns of Court, and Trinity College, Dublin, Ireland, before returning to the United States. "In his free time in Dublin," Fine writes, "Murphy gathered up and read 'all the good books' that he could find on Irish history and the struggle for Irish independence. British authorities had their eye on Murphy because he not only collected books on the independence issue but also attended Sinn Fein meetings and befriended such Sinn Fein leaders as Michael Collins and Harry Boland." As limited as it was, Murphy's time in the military served him well in later years in public service.

Public Service

"Other men have also devoted themselves to the public service," writes Sidney Fine, "but few have done so with the singleness of purpose and the 'passion' that

Murphy brought to his career. For him, government service was 'a life's vocation,' and he regarded it 'in the light of a ministry.'"[7]

Judge of the Recorder's Court. Murphy decided to run for the Recorder's Court in February 1923 and filed for the primary, to be held on March 7. There were seven judges on the court, and four of them, referred to as the "Big Four," formed a voting block and thereby controlled the court. "The . . . [Big Four] and their supporters were inclined to describe the contest that was underway as one between the forces of decency and the underworld, between the children of light and the children of darkness." Not all agreed, of course. Murphy said he was against group control as a matter of principle. "When cliques walk in," he summarized, "justice walks out." Murphy survived the primary and was one of the 12 candidates vying for six judgeships in the general election. He began a vigorous campaign. The Detroit *Times*, which was interested in the defeat of any or all of the Big Four, came out for Murphy. He also received support from many Detroit lawyers, Legionnaires, men who had served with him in the army and many alumni of the University of Michigan. The Catholic Church was also on his side. "The Reverend William J. Murphy wrote Murphy that he would see to it that everyone in church on Easter Sunday received a Murphy card. He would try to get in touch with the Sisters of St. Joseph; Father Herr, he thought, would influence the Felician Sisters; and perhaps some one could turn out the two hundred Monroe Sisters on election day. Polish, Greek, Swiss, and other ethnic organizations endorsed Murphy, . . . [also] the black electorate gravitated in his direction."

Many Protestant clergymen on Easter Sunday called attention to the "moral issue in the campaign," thus implicitly urging a vote for the Big Four. But this was to no avail, as Murphy topped the slate and two of the Big Four were defeated.

The newly elected judges took office on January 2, 1924. The court handled murder cases and mundane matters such as the size of garbage pails. It had to deal with traffic and condemnation cases, but Murphy enjoyed the work and the challenge.

Sidney Fine describes Murphy as a judge: "Murphy insisted on absolute quiet and the observance of the rules of good behavior in his courtroom—court employees called him 'Father Murphy' partly for this reason. Although he was very considerate of the attorneys appearing before him, he did not like lawyers to delay a trial by dilatory tactics or to 'translate the trial of the issue into a staged theatrical skit, so as to distract the jury from consideration of the issue.' "

Murphy believed that punishment was not the answer to crime, but rather that an attempt should be made to reform and rehabilitate a criminal. When the state house of representatives proposed to approve the use of the whipping post, he vigorously objected. The bill never did pass. He was also an ardent foe of capital punishment.

Murphy presided over "one of the major civil liberties cases of the day,"[8] a trial known as the *Sweet* case. Dr. Ossian Sweet, who was black, bought a house in a predominantly white neighborhood. Protests developed and some shots were fired, killing one person and wounding another. Eleven blacks were charged with and tried for murder, but the trial ended in a hung jury. Because he was the only one to have admitted firing a gun, Dr. Sweet was then charged with the murder. One of his attorneys, the great Clarence Darrow, argued before the jury for seven hours. "Take the hatred away," he said, "and you have nothing left."[9] Sweet was acquitted. The trial was an important step forward for blacks, and Murphy's handling of it earned him much respect and admiration, especially in the black community.

In addition to his duties on the bench, Murphy conducted a one-man investigation into corruption among city officials, and his report recommended criminal prosecution of 19 individuals. He also continued to be active in Democratic politics, attending the national convention and campaigning for Al Smith, the nominee in 1928. Because of the Depression of the late 1920s and early 1930s, Murphy was concerned about the plight of the unemployed and aged. He worked to have an unemployment compensation law and an old-age pension bill adopted but was not successful. However, he continued to work with the unemployed, assisting them to find work. He had an opportunity to become legal counsel for Chrysler but declined.

But life wasn't all work and no play. He exercised regularly and "played golf, swam a good deal, and took boxing lessons. Horseback riding became his favorite form of exercise toward the end of this period, and it remained so for the rest of his life." He led an active social life, and had friends at the bottom of the social ladder and many at the top. One of those friends was Father Charles E. Coughlin, who became a controversial activist in the fight for social justice during the Depression.

Murphy also enjoyed the company of women and had many female friends. Biographer Fine describes Murphy:

> There was the gentle, soft, compassionate, and sentimental Murphy, but there was also the Murphy who gloried in the strenuous life and was eager for combat. There was the parsimonious Murphy who was reluctant to pay his bills and the Murphy who endorsed a sizable note for a policeman on duty in his court. There was the Murphy who was at home in Grosse Point and Bloomfield Hills and the Murphy who was equally at home in Delray and in the black ghetto. There was the Murphy who loved the pomp and ceremony of high office, the vacations at Palm Beach, the yachts of the well-to-do, and the best life had to offer but also the Murphy who was content to live as simply as the average workingman.

Mayor of Detroit. When the voters recalled Mayor Charles Bowles in July 1930, Murphy became a reluctant candidate. He finally agreed to allow petitions to be circulated for his candidacy, but said he would not run unless there was a good response from the people and there was. Four others also entered the contest.

"A consummate orator," Fine writes,

> in an era when "hot" oratory was still the vogue, Murphy was especially effective
> on the hustings and was able to adjust his "mood, tempo and approach" to the
> particular audience he was addressing. "To Legionnaires and veterans' societies,"
> one writer later summarized, "he is the tough butt-and-bayonet doughboy. To
> Poles and Slovaks and hunky mill hands he is the descendant of humble immi-
> grants. To ladies' societies he is the blushing, self-deprecating sacrifice to public
> duty." Through the "idealistic ring" of his oratory and its "inspirational quality,"
> Murphy, as the *Nation* observed, was able to convert a campaign for public office
> into "a huge crusade to recapture Detroit."

Murphy won the election with 12,000 more votes than the next candidate and was sworn in on September 15, 1930. He wanted the people to know that his administration was going to be honest and nonpartisan, and his appoint-ments to the various city offices mirrored this philosophy. He was also aware of the ethnic backgrounds of the people of Detroit, and appointed many to city jobs. He continued to work for passage of unemployment insurance and old-age pension laws.

These, of course, were hard times for the whole country, but especially for the city and the people of Detroit, who depended a great deal on the ups and downs of the automobile industry. In spite of the problems, Murphy was re-elected to a two-year term in 1931. "Murphy lost no opportunity to explain to his constituents that the idle and the homeless, the people on welfare and those seeking relief, were not 'abnormal individuals' or 'bums' but 'good people' who were unemployed and destitute through no fault of their own. He was critical of the comfortable persons who seemed indifferent to suffering and want, looked disdainfully at the unemployed, and maligned the relief efforts of the city."

Detroit, like many other cities, was struggling financially during this pe-riod. Murphy organized mayors throughout the country and presented propos-als to President Herbert Hoover seeking federal help. None was forthcoming. In February 1933, Murphy organized and was elected as president of the National Conference of Mayors. The conference's proposals for unemployment relief and aid to cities were enacted into law early in the administration of the new presi-dent, Franklin D. Roosevelt.

Murphy began to support Roosevelt in early 1931 and campaigned for him in 1932. Howard describes Murphy's part in the campaign in Michigan: "At a time when President Hoover was being booed in Detroit, the friend of the un-employed drew the largest political rally in the history of Flint. It was a rugged job; the last few days, as Roosevelt said, were 'hectic.' But it was superb politics. Democrats captured Michigan's electoral votes for the first time since the GOP was born in 1852."[10] As a result of his assistance in Roosevelt's election, it was suggested that Murphy should be given a position in the new administration. Murphy's choice would have been attorney general, but that position went to

Homer Cummings. He was then offered and accepted the position as governor-general of the Philippines.

Summing up Murphy's role as mayor of Detroit, Fine notes that

> there is, of course, no entirely objective way to evaluate such a judgment, but the proposition that he was one of Detroit's great mayors is easy enough to defend. He restored faith in the city's government at a time when civic morale was at low ebb, provided Detroit with honest, economical, and generally efficient government, made excellent appointments and extended the merit system, revitalized and improved the police force, protected the rights of free speech and freedom of assembly in a time of troubles, ousted the last remaining competitor of the city-owned transportation system, initiated the process leading to lower rates for utility services, and involved blacks, white ethnic groups, and organized labor in the affairs of the city to a greater extent than any of his predecessors had. Above all, he recognized the enormity of the depression and the need to provide the unemployed with public relief, and he was one of the first public officials in the nation to press for federal aid to the cities for welfare purposes.[11]

Governor-General and High Commissioner to the Philippines. Not everyone greeted Murphy's appointment as governor-general of the Philippines with approval. "I have known Murphy for years," his former professor Joseph Ralston Hayden commented, "it is an outrageous travesty upon every principle of good government and sound judgment that he should have been sent out there."[12]

But Sidney Fine evaluates the appointment differently.

> Quite apart from what Murphy may have learned from his brief exposure to Philippine matters before he left the United States, he brought qualities to his new post that augured well for his success and that men like Hayden failed to consider in evaluating Murphy's suitability for the position: a charismatic personality, the experience of having governed a great city in time of crisis, the ability to relate successfully to persons and groups of varying backgrounds and aspirations, a lofty conception of his role as a public servant, and the capacity as an administrator to inspire aides to give the best that was in them in the performance of their duties.[13]

Murphy's sister, Marguerite, and her husband, William Teahan, accompanied the governor-general to Manila, and she acted as his official hostess. Murphy did in the Philippines what he had done as mayor of Detroit: he surrounded himself with a competent staff.

Only the president of the United States had more authority over the Philippines than did the governor-general. The governor-general appointed the cabinet and legislators and had veto power over laws passed by the legislature. If his veto was overridden, the measure went to the president for final action.

Among the attributes of the Murphy administration were the use of the merit system in hiring of public officials; keeping an open door to the press;

neutrality in dealing with the Filipino politicians; fiscal integrity; and a cautious approach to governing.

From his days as a Recorder's Court judge, Murphy had a great interest in legal reform, and his position as governor-general gave him an opportunity to implement some of his ideas. "Under his guidance Filipinos established juvenile courts, indeterminate sentences, and adult probation. The governor created a nonpartisan judicial council to recommend personnel and to watch over standards. He sponsored studies to find means of accommodating Mohammedan and national law, and caused a stir by commuting all death penalties. He even managed to install a public defender system."[14] And he never missed an opportunity to lecture on good government.

There were many lepers in the Philippines. Being made aware of their plight, the governor appointed a commission to study the matter. The commission recommended a number of improvements, and implementation of these was started immediately. Murphy also took an interest in public health, playgrounds for children, relief from typhoons, the standard of living of the urban poor and rural tenant farmers, and labor matters. When he was informed of infringements upon the right to assemble and speak, he issued an order aimed at preventing interference with those rights. "In addition to speaking out against illegal searches and seizures, Murphy was the first American governor-general to issue an executive order banning the use of the third degree by the Constabulary and the police."[15]

While Murphy adopted a policy of neutrality with regard to Philippine independence, he became involved when it appeared that women would not be given the right to vote. He intervened and convinced Filipino legislative leaders that it would be unwise not to include women as voters. A provision was then inserted into the Philippine Constitution providing for a referendum on the question of women suffrage, and if approved by a vote of 300,000 women they would have the right to vote. The referendum was held in May 1937 and approved.

President Roosevelt nominated Murphy as the first high commissioner, and he was unanimously approved by the U.S. Senate.

> The appointment of Murphy as high commissioner was hailed in the Philippines as "the best that could have been made." The legislature unanimously approved a joint resolution lauding Murphy's selection as "a fitting recognition of his able, high-minded, and statesmanlike discharge of the duties" of governor-general. Quezon, not one to speak in moderation on such occasions, declared that none of Murphy's predecessors as governor-general excelled him in "his sympathetic understanding of our problems, in his devotion to his duties, in his love of justice, in his courage to fight the wrong and to stand by the right, and in his vision as a statesman."

For Murphy, his Philippine years had been "happy years among a good people," and he retained an interest in the islands and an affection for their people for the rest of his life.

Governor of Michigan.

> Murphy embarked on a difficult task when he ran for Governor of Michigan in 1936. Drafted largely by presidential managers to bolster Democratic chances in a doubtful state, he had a strong popular base in Detroit. National acceptance of the relief principle and his public stature as an administrator in the Philippines had soothed much of the bitterness of his mayoralty. But he was untried in Michigan at large, and the circumstances of the draft, coupled with his own public resistance to it for a month after his return to the United States, complicated an already fragmented political situation. The election was an uphill fight all the way.[16]

Despite these negatives, Murphy also had many assets. Sidney Fine details some of them:

> He had an attractive personality; he was a marvelous campaigner and a superb orator—no other political figure in the state could sway an audience as he could; factory workers were solidly behind Roosevelt and the New Deal; economic conditions in the state had been improving since the beginning of the year; the state's national committeeman and most Democratic county chairmen supported him rather than Welsh (the other candidate); and the national administration, despite Roosevelt's proclaimed refusal to intervene in Democratic primaries, obviously favored Murphy and quietly aided his candidacy.[17]

After a very hard fought campaign, Murphy won an overwhelming victory in the primary. Frank D. Fitzgerald, the incumbent governor, won the Republican primary, setting the stage for the general election in November. President Roosevelt made a campaign appearance in Michigan to urge Murphy's election and was received by enthusiastic crowds. Roosevelt not only won Michigan's electoral votes in the presidential election, but he also carried Murphy to victory.

As he had done as mayor and as governor-general, Murphy brought qualified individuals into state government, not always following the recommendations of leaders of the Democratic Party. The new governor had hardly taken office when he was confronted with a sit-down strike at General Motors. He called out the National Guard to maintain order and to preserve the status quo. He also ordered relief funds to be used to help the strikers' families. This brought national condemnation for tolerating civil disobedience, but his efforts succeeded in getting the parties to come to the bargaining table.

The governor refused to break the strike despite strong pressure to do so. He believed that a negotiated end to the strike was possible and continued to work toward that end; he ultimately prevailed. Howard writes that while the results of the strike insofar as labor relations were concerned may have been uncertain, "one result appeared sure. Murphy had jumped into a vacuum of public responsibility and emerged unscathed. While Roosevelt may have called the plays, Murphy bore the responsibility and reaped the glory. A great personal gamble skyrocketed him into national prominence as a leader for sanity in industrial relations."[18]

Murphy's plans for Michigan's future came to a halt when he was defeated for re-election in 1938. His accomplishments, however, were many.[19] While Murphy surely had his critics, "to his admirers, he was the best governor Michigan had ever had, one who had 'done more' for the state in two years than his predecessors in the preceding twenty. The Murphy administration was for them a time of excitement and high purpose, a welcome change from the lackluster administrations that had generally characterized state government in Michigan."[20]

Attorney General of the United States. Frank Murphy "hit the justice department like a monsoon, a newsman observed in appraising the attorney general's performance in his cabinet post. Believing that he would remain in the position for only a brief period and anxious to recover politically from his 1938 defeat, Murphy initiated a series of actions, one rapidly following upon the other, that made the department and himself the center of public attention."[21]

President Roosevelt appointed Murphy attorney general on January 1, 1939. The appointment, however, ran into some trouble during confirmation hearings in the Senate, where the Michigan senators wanted an explanation of his conduct during the sit-down strike at General Motors. Ultimately, however, he was confirmed by the Senate in a vote of 78 to seven.

In assembling a staff, he followed the same pattern he had used in picking his previous staffs by appointing highly qualified individuals. He then moved to bring the Justice Department under a civil service merit system. He was, however, unsuccessful in having the FBI and Justice Department lawyers included. He was more successful in having well-qualified persons appointed federal judges. "With the aid of [Thomas] Corcoran's eye for talent and of Matthew F. McGuire's very able and discreet handling of senatorial relations, Murphy made surprising headway with quality selections to the federal bench."[22]

A campaign was begun against corruption and crime, with Murphy and FBI Director J. Edgar Hoover embarking upon a tour of the country.

> From a newsman's viewpoint Murphy was an ideal Attorney General. Colorful, cooperative, easy to caricature, he had a certain mystique and a sixth sense of what made effective copy. His weekly press conferences were second only to Roosevelt's in popularity. His work as Attorney General, consequently, was among the most highly publicized phenomena of the day. Behind all the hoopla, moreover, his actual performance was one of the biggest surprises of the late New Deal. As an aggressive public prosecutor, his special forte seemed to have been found. . . . Sophisticated columnists credited him with having "rejuvenated" the Department of Justice. Big-city editors hailed him for "doing one of the most remarkable jobs of public service an American has ever done in the cabinet."

In assessing Murphy's year of service as attorney general, Fine has written:

> Murphy had completed one of the most remarkable years of service in the history of the Justice Department. The record speaks for itself: quality appointments to the staff of the department and, of greater consequence, to the federal bench; expedited disposition of federal civil and criminal cases; the first national conference of United States attorneys; the first national parole conference; initiation and prosecution of major antitrust suits, especially in the building trades; prosecution of Pendergast, the Long machine, Enoch Johnson, Skidmore, Annenberg, Manton, Lepke and Bioff; investigation leading to the prosecution of Joseph Schenck; establishment of the Civil Liberties Unit and the effort to enforce long-neglected civil rights legislation; and negotiation of peace terms in Harlan County.[23]

Although some civil libertarians did not think Murphy had done enough in that area, Howard calls the creation of the Civil Liberties Unit "Murphy's single most significant contribution as Attorney General."[24]

Nomination to the Supreme Court. On November 16, 1939, Supreme Court Justice Pierce Butler died. President Roosevelt indicated to Murphy that day that he was considering appointing him to fill the vacancy. This the President did on January 4, 1940, and almost everyone thought it was a good appointment. Murphy was unanimously confirmed by the Senate on January 16 and was sworn in on February 5.

"Resignation tinged with pride was the principal reaction to the Court's newest Justice," Howard notes, "and even if it could be tacitly assumed, as Roosevelt did, that he would not remain on the bench long, Murphy could not resist taking a parting shot at the process which put him there." "'I appreciate the honor,' he told newsmen. The Court was the country's 'Great Pulpit.' 'But I consider myself unworthy of it and I think a far better selection could have been made.'"

The other justices on the Court at the time of Murphy's appointment were Chief Justice Charles Evans Hughes, and justices James C. McReynolds, Owen J. Roberts, Harlan F. Stone, Hugo L. Black, William O. Douglas, Felix Frankfurter, and Stanley F. Reed.

AS ASSOCIATE JUSTICE (1940-1949)

The Free Exercise of Religion

Rosco Jones in Opelika, Alabama, H.D. Cole, Lois Bowden, and Zada Sanders in Fort Smith, Arkansas, and Charles Jobin in Casa Grande, Arizona, all had two things in common: they were Jehovah's Witnesses and all were found guilty of distributing literature without a license. Their convictions were upheld by the supreme courts of their states, and by the U.S. Supreme Court. "The petitioners

[Bowden and Sanders], in the exercise of their beliefs concerning their duty to preach the gospel, admitted going from house to house without a license, playing phonographic transcriptions of Bible lectures, and distributing books setting forth their views to the residents in return for a contribution of twenty-five cents per book."[25] The other defendants engaged in similar activities.

Justice Stanley Reed, writing for the majority, concluded that "when proponents of religious or social theories use the ordinary commercial methods of sales of articles to raise propaganda funds, it is a natural and proper exercise of the power of the State to charge reasonable fees for the privilege of canvassing." Justice Murphy disagreed. He believed that it was unconstitutional to tax people for exercising their rights to freedom of speech, of the press, and of religion. "Important as free speech and a free press are to a free government and a free citizenry," he declared, "there is a right even more dear to many individuals—the right to worship their Maker according to their needs and the dictates of their souls and to carry their message or their gospel to every living creature. These ordinances infringe that right, which is also protected by the Fourteenth Amendment." "If this Court," he continued, "is to err in evaluating claims that freedom of speech, freedom of the press, and freedom of religion have been invaded, far better that it err in being overprotective of these precious rights."

When this case was reargued a year later, it was reversed, a decision that Murphy joined.[26] He also concurred in a companion case, *Martin v. Struthers.*[27] In this case, the appellant Martin, "espousing a religious cause in which she was interested—that of the Jehovah's Witnesses—went to the homes of strangers, knocking on doors and ringing doorbells in order to distribute to the inmates of the homes leaflets advertising a religious meeting. In doing so, she proceeded in a conventional and orderly fashion."

"I believe," Murphy declared, "that nothing enjoys a higher estate in our society than the right given by the First and Fourteenth Amendments freely to practice and proclaim one's religious convictions. . . . The right extends to the aggressive and disputatious as well as to the meek and acquiescent." "Preaching from house to house," he pointed out, "is an age-old method of proselyting, and it must be remembered that 'one is not to have the exercise of his liberty of expression in appropriate places abridged on the plea that it may be exercised in some other place.'" "The primary concern," he continued, "is with the act of canvassing as a source of inconvenience and annoyance to householders. But if the city can prohibit canvassing for the purpose of distributing religious pamphlets, it can also outlaw the door to door solicitations of religious charities, or the activities of the holy mendicant who begs alms from house to house to serve the material wants of his fellowmen and thus obtain spiritual comfort for his own soul."

Murphy dissented when the Court upheld the conviction of Sarah Prince for allowing her nine-year-old niece, Betty Simmons, to distribute Jehovah's Witnesses' literature on the streets in Brockton, Massachusetts. He was of the opinion that the state had "completely failed to sustain its burden of proving the existence of any grave or immediate danger to any interest which it may lawfully protect."[28] The state's alleged interest was Betty's welfare.

"No chapter in human history," Murphy said,

> has been so largely written in terms of persecution and intolerance as the one dealing with religious freedom. From ancient times to the present day, the ingenuity of man has known no limits in its ability to forge weapons of oppression for use against those who dare to express or practice unorthodox religious beliefs. And the Jehovah's Witnesses are living proof of the fact that even in this nation, conceived as it was in the ideals of freedom, the right to practice religion in unconventional ways is still far from secure.

The justice voted with the majority to uphold the expulsion from school of Lillian and William Gobitis, ages 12 and 10, respectively, for refusal to salute the United States flag.[29] Three years later, however, when the Court overruled *Gobitis* and upheld the right of children of Jehovah's Witnesses not to salute the flag, Murphy concurred. "The right of freedom of thought and of religion," he declared,

> as guaranteed by the Constitution against State action includes both the right to speak freely and the right to refrain from speaking at all, except insofar as essential operations of government may require it for the preservation of an orderly society,—as in the case of compulsion to give evidence in court. . . . To many it is deeply distasteful to join in a public chorus of affirmation of private belief. By some, including the members of this sect, it is apparently regarded as incompatible with a primary religious obligation and therefore a restriction on religious freedom. Official compulsion to affirm what is contrary to one's religious beliefs is the antithesis of freedom of worship which, it is well to recall, was achieved in this country only after what Jefferson characterized as the "severest contests in which I have ever been engaged."[30]

"Today another unfortunate chapter is added to the troubled history of the White Slave Traffic Act," the justice wrote when he dissented from the Court's affirmance of the convictions of Heber Kimball Cleveland and several others for transporting a woman in interstate commerce for immoral purposes.[31] Cleveland and the other defendants were Mormans who followed the tenets of their faith by having more than one wife. After going through a "celestial ceremony" in which each became married to a second woman, they went into another state to live. This allegedly violated a federal law making it a crime to transport in interstate commerce "any woman or girl for the purpose of prostitution or debauchery, or for any other immoral purpose."

In response to the defendants' argument that they "did not transport the women in interstate commerce for an immoral purpose," the majority responded that "the offense is complete if the accused intended to perform . . . the transportation of a woman for the purpose of making her his plural wife or cohabiting with her as such."

Justice Murphy protested. He was of the opinion that Congress did not intend to include polygamy within the meaning of the act. "We must recognize . . . ," he pointed out,

> that polygyny [one man with several wives], like other forms of marriage, is basically a cultural institution rooted deeply in the religious beliefs and social mores of those societies in which it appears. It is equally true that the beliefs and mores of the dominant culture of the contemporary world condemn the practice as immoral and substitute monogamy in its place. To these beliefs and mores I subscribe, but that does not alter the fact that polygyny is a form of marriage built upon a set of social and moral principles. It must be recognized and treated as such.

"It takes no elaboration here," he argued, "to point out that marriage, even when it occurs in a form which we disapprove, is not to be compared with prostitution or debauchery or other immoralities of that character."

Freedom of Speech

Picketing and Parading. "It appears that petitioner [Byron Thornhill] on the morning of his arrest was seen 'in company with six or eight other men' 'on the picket line' at the plant of Brown Wood Preserving Company. Some weeks previously a strike order had been issued by a Union. . . . Since that time a picket line with two picket posts of six to eight men each had been maintained around the plant twenty-four hours a day."[32]

Thornhill was arrested and convicted for picketing, a crime under Alabama law. He offered no evidence on his own behalf, claiming that the antipicketing law was unconstitutional under the First Amendment. The Supreme Court agreed.

Justice Murphy wrote for the Court:

> We think that . . . [the law] is invalid on its face. The freedom of speech and of the press guaranteed by the Constitution embraces at the least the liberty to discuss publicly and truthfully all matters of public concern without previous restraint or fear of subsequent punishment. The exigencies of the colonial period and the efforts to secure freedom from oppressive administration developed a broadened conception of these liberties as adequate to supply the public need for information and education with respect to the significant issues of the times.

Furthermore: "Free discussion concerning the conditions in industry and the causes of labor disputes appears to us indispensable to the effective and intelligent use of the processes of popular government to shape the destiny of modern industrial society."

Justice Murphy voted with Justice Frankfurter and the majority to uphold an injunction that prohibited picketing in a labor dispute in which there had been evidence of violence.[33]

In several subsequent cases, however, Murphy voted to strike down injunctions against peaceful picketing in labor disputes.[34]

Offensive Speech. Walter Chaplinsky's distributing religious literature on the streets of Rochester, New Hampshire, created concern among some of the people, and they complained to City Marshal Bowering. The marshal told them that Chaplinsky was doing what he had a right to do and to leave him alone. Later when a disturbance broke out, a police officer took Chaplinsky by the arm and started toward the police station. Upon meeting Bowering, a conversation took place between Chaplinsky and the marshal. Chaplinsky allegedly said: "You are a God damned racketeer" and "a damned Fascist and the whole government of Rochester are Fascists or agents of Fascists."[35] Chaplinsky was arrested and charged with the crime of addressing "offensive, derisive or annoying word[s] to any other person who is lawfully in any street or other public place." This law had been construed by the New Hampshire Supreme Court to do "no more than prohibit the face-to-face words plainly likely to cause a breach of the peace by the addressee." Chaplinsky's conviction was upheld by the Supreme Court, with Murphy writing the Court's opinion.

Chaplinsky is an important case because it guarantees the right to use "offensive" language in public except where the use thereof might prompt an addressee to fight. "We are unable to say," the justice noted, "that the limited scope of the statute as thus construed contravenes the Constitutional right of free expression. It is a statute narrowly drawn and limited to define and punish specific conduct lying within the domain of state power, the use in a public place of words likely to cause a breach of the peace."

Murphy voted with the majority to reverse the conviction of Father Terminiello, in the *Terminiello* case (discussed in Chapter 5). In pointing out that speech is free, "unless shown likely to produce a clear and present danger of a serious substantive evil," Justice Douglas wrote, "there is no room under our Constitution for a more restrictive view. For the alternative would lead to standardization of ideas either by legislatures, courts, or dominant political or community groups."[36]

Freedom of the Press

Contempt for Publication. John D. Pennekamp, associate editor, and the Miami Herald Publishing Company were adjudged in contempt for publishing two articles critical of the judges and the Dade County, Florida, criminal justice system. Among the criticisms leveled at the courts were the following: "Every accused person has a right to his day in court. But when judicial instance and interpretative procedure recognize and accept, even go out to find, every possible technicality of the law to protect the defendant, to block, thwart, hinder, embarrass and nullify prosecution, then the peoples' rights are jeopardized and the basic reason for courts stultified."[37]

The editorials then cited instances in which the editors believed that local judges had used "technicalities" to make rulings favorable to defendants.

The Supreme Court unanimously reversed. In a short opinion, Justice Murphy concurred.

> Were we to sanction the judgment rendered by the court below we would be approving, in effect, an unwarranted restriction upon the freedom of the press. That freedom covers something more than the right to approve and condone insofar as the judiciary and the judicial process are concerned. It also includes the right to criticize and disparage, even though the terms be vitriolic, scurrilous or erroneous. To talk of a clear and present danger arising out of such criticism is idle unless the criticism makes it impossible in a very real sense for a court to carry on the administration of justice. That situation is not even remotely present in this case.[38]

The justice also concurred in *Craig v. Harney*,[39] a similar case. There he wrote that a "free press lies at the heart of our democracy and its preservation is essential to the survival of liberty. Any inroad made upon the constitutional protection of a free press tends to undermine the freedom of all men to print and to read the truth." And, he concluded, "The liberties guaranteed by the First Amendment . . . are too highly prized to be subjected to the hazards of summary contempt procedure."

Justice Murphy wrote the majority opinion in an unusual freedom of the press case. Elmer Hartzel, Elmer William Soller, and one Mecartney were convicted of sedition and conspiracy to commit sedition. Soller's and Mecartney's convictions were overturned in lower courts, but Hartzel's was upheld, and he appealed to the Supreme Court.[40]

Hartzel had served in World War I, went to college thereafter, and became a "financial analyst and statistician for various banks, investment brokers and investment companies in Chicago." Prior to and during World War II he wrote several articles "containing scurrilous and vitriolic attacks on the English, the Jews and the President of the United States." He put the articles together in the form of a pamphlet and mailed it to a number of persons and organizations, including "United States Senators, representatives, bishops and other church officials; . . . the Daughters of the American Revolution and We the Mothers Mobilize . . . the Commanding General of the United States Army Air Forces . . . the United States Infantry Association . . . Northwestern University, the American Newspaper Publishers Association, the Kiwanis International, the Lions International, the Air Line Pilots Association and the American Legion, Department of Illinois." "At the trial . . . [Hartzel] testified that 'I thought there was a trend toward Communism, and I thought it was quite a dangerous position because of warfare between the white races, it would be the cause of war between the white and yellow races, and rather than have it beat into us, we might as well face the facts and know what we were facing, a certain group of Communists discussing methods, their viewpoints, I wanted to help minimize that so we could again have public standpoint established in this country.' "

A majority of the justices voted to reverse the conviction, with Murphy writing the Court's opinion. He did not believe that the pamphlets indicated that Hartzel intended "to cause insubordination, disloyalty, mutiny or refusal of duty in the military forces or to obstruct the recruiting and enlistment service." "Unless there is sufficient evidence," he continued, "from which a jury could infer beyond a reasonable doubt that he intended to bring about the specific consequences prohibited by the Act, an American citizen has the right to discuss these matters either by temperate reasoning or by immoderate and vicious invective without running afoul of the Espionage Act of 1917. Such evidence was not present in this case."

Justice Murphy parted company with Justice Black and the majority when the Court upheld the application of the Sherman Anti-Trust Act to the Associated Press.[41] The by-laws of the AP "prohibited all AP members from selling news to non-members, and . . . granted each member powers to block its non-member competitors from membership." This, the majority concluded, constituted restraint of trade.

Murphy was concerned that the Court was approving government involvement with news gathering. "The tragic history of recent years," he argued, "demonstrates far too well how despotic governments may interfere with the press and other means of communication in their efforts to corrupt public opinion and to destroy individual freedom. Experience teaches us to hesitate before creating a precedent in which might lurk even the slightest justification for such interference by the Government in these matters." He believed that the case should not have been decided in favor of the government upon a motion for summary judgment where no evidence was introduced. "The issues are too grave," he argued, "and the possible consequences are too uncertain not to require Government to prove its case by more probative and convincing evidence than it has submitted so far." "We stand," he cautioned, "at the threshold of a previously unopened door. We should pause long before opening it, lest the path be made clear for dangerous governmental interference in the future."

The Right to Life, Privacy, and Travel

The Right to Life. M. Claud Screws, sheriff of Baker County, Georgia, and others were charged with violating the civil rights of Robert Hall, who was black, whom they allegedly beat to death after taking him into custody. They were convicted, and that conviction was upheld by the circuit court of appeals but reversed by the Supreme Court, in an opinion written by Justice Douglas. The Court concluded that the jury should have been instructed, but was not, that "they must find that the defendants had the purpose to deprive the prisoner of a constitutional right."[42] The case was therefore sent back to the lower court for a new trial. Murphy vigorously protested:

> Robert Hall, a Negro citizen, has been deprived not only of the right to be tried by a court rather than by ordeal. He has been deprived of the right to life itself. That right belonged to him not because he was a Negro or a member of any particular race or creed. That right was his because he was an American citizen, because he was a human being. As such, he was entitled to all the respect and fair treatment that befits the dignity of man, a dignity that is recognized and guaranteed by the Constitution. Yet not even the semblance of due process has been accorded him. He has been cruelly and unjustifiably beaten to death by local police officers acting under color of authority derived from the state. It is difficult to believe that such an obvious and necessary right is indefinitely guaranteed by the Constitution or is foreign to the knowledge of local police officers so as to cast any reasonable doubt on the conviction under . . . [the law] of the perpetrators of this "shocking and revolting episode in law enforcement."

"It is an illusion to say," he asserted,

> that the real issue in this case is the alleged failure . . . [of the law] fully to warn the state officials that their actions were illegal. The Constitution, [the law] and their own consciences told them that. They knew that they lacked any mandate or authority to take human life unnecessarily or without due process of law in the course of their duties. They knew that their excessive and abusive use of authority would only subvert the ends of justice. The significant question, rather, is whether law enforcement officers and those entrusted with authority shall be allowed to violate with impunity the clear constitutional rights of the inarticulate and the friendless.

The Right of Privacy. The right of privacy, as we know it today, came into existence long after Justice Murphy left the Court. But he expressed the belief that such a right existed, in a dissenting opinion in *Goldman v. United States.*[43]

Martin M. Goldman, Theodore Goldman, and Jacob P. Schulman, all lawyers, were suspected of being involved in a scheme to obtain money fraudulently in a bankruptcy proceeding. Federal investigators were alerted, and they installed a listening device in the wall of Shulman's office. When this did not work, the officials used "another device, a detectaphone, having a receiver so delicate as, when placed against the partition wall, to pick up sound waves originating in Shulman's office, and means for amplifying and hearing them." This enabled the officers to hear conversations among Shulman, Martin Goldman, and another lawyer not involved in the scheme. The trial court, over the objections of the defendants, allowed into evidence a transcript of the conversations overheard on the detectaphone. The defendants were convicted, and their convictions were upheld by the Supreme Court, with Murphy dissenting.

He wrote:

One of the great boons secured to the inhabitants of this country by the Bill of Rights is the right of personal privacy guaranteed by the Fourth Amendment. In numerous ways the law protects the individual against unwarranted intrusions by others into his private affairs. It compensates him for trespass on his property or against his person. It prohibits the publication against his will of his thoughts, sentiments, and emotions, regardless of whether those are expressed in words, painting, sculpture, music, or in other modes. It may prohibit the use of his photograph for commercial purposes without his consent. These are restrictions on the activities of private persons. But the Fourth Amendment puts a restraint on the arm of the Government itself, and prevents it from invading the sanctity of a man's home or his private quarters in a chase for a suspect, except under safeguards calculated to prevent oppression and abuse of authority.

"The benefits," he declared,

that accrue from this and other articles of the Bill of Rights are characteristic of democratic rule. They are among the amenities that distinguish a free society from one in which the rights and comforts of the individual are wholly subordinated to the interests of the state. We cherish and uphold them as necessary and salutary checks on the authority of government. They provide a standard of official conduct which the courts must enforce. At a time when the nation is called upon to give freely of life and treasure to defend and preserve the institutions of democracy and freedom, we should not permit any of the essentials of freedom to lose vitality through legal interpretations that are restrictive and inadequate for the period in which we live.

The Right to Travel. When the Court held, in *Edwards v. California,*[44] that California's attempt to keep out indigent persons was an unconstitutional burden on interstate commerce, Murphy joined Douglas's concurring opinion. Douglas, Black, and Murphy were of the opinion that people had a constitutional right to travel from state to state. Referring to *Crandall v. Nevada,*[45] a case decided in 1867, Douglas wrote, "Mr. Justice Miller writing for the Court held that the right to move freely throughout the nation was a right of *national* citizenship. That the right was implied did not make it any less 'guaranteed' by the Constitution."[46]

Equal Protection of the Law

Blacks on Juries. When Henry Allen Hill, who was black, was indicted for rape, no black person had ever served on the grand jury in Dallas County, Texas. Hill moved to quash the indictment, claiming that the exclusion of blacks from the grand jury violated his right to equal protection. The motion was denied and Hill was convicted. The conviction was sustained by the court of criminal appeals, but reversed by a unanimous Supreme Court, which included Murphy.[47]

Following the *Hill* case, the procedure for selection of grand jurors in Dallas County was changed so that when L.C. Akins was indicted for murder the jury consisted of one black and 11 white men. Akins's lawyer also moved to quash the indictment, arguing that his client's constitutional right to equal protection had been violated. Judge A.R. Stout disagreed. Akins was convicted, his conviction was affirmed by the court of appeals and the United States Supreme Court. Justice Stanley Reed authored the Court's opinion. "A careful examination of . . . all the . . . evidence," he concluded, "leaves us unconvinced that the commissioners deliberately and intentionally limited the number of Negroes on the grand jury list."[48]

Justice Murphy, examining the same evidence, reached a different conclusion. He first pointed out that Akins "as a human being endowed with all the rights specified in the Constitution, can claim that no racial or religious exclusion, limitation or other form of discrimination shall enter into the selection of any jury which indicts or tries him." Turning then to what equal protection requires, he wrote:

> The equal protection clause guarantees petitioner not only the right to have Negroes considered as prospective veniremen but also the right to have them considered without numerical or proportional limitation. If a jury is to be fairly chosen from a cross section of the community it must be done without limiting the number of persons of a particular color, racial background or faith—all of which are irrelevant factors in setting qualifications for jury service. This may in a particular instance result in the selection of one, six, twelve, or even no Negroes on a jury panel. The important point, however, is that the selections must in no way be limited or restricted by such irrelevant factors.

The justice was of the opinion that the grand jury commissioners had intentionally and deliberately limited the number of blacks to one, and therefore "refused . . . to disregard the factor of color in selecting the jury personnel."

Other Discrimination Against Blacks

Traveling. Justice Murphy voted with the majority to strike down segregation on trains and busses. In *Mitchell v. United States*,[49] the Court reversed an order of the Interstate Commerce Commission which had refused to order desegregation of trains. Arthur W. Mitchell, who was black and a member of the U.S. House of Representatives, was ordered by a train conductor "to move into the car provided for colored passengers" on a trip from Memphis to Hot Springs, Arkansas. Mitchell filed a complaint against the railroad with the Interstate Commerce Commission, which the commission dismissed. "The question," Chief Justice Hughes noted,

> whether this was a discrimination forbidden by the Interstate Commerce Act is not a question of segregation but one of equality of treatment. The denial to . . . [Mitchell] of equality of accommodations because of his race would be an

invasion of a fundamental individual right which is guaranteed against state action by the Fourteenth Amendment . . . and in view of the nature of the right and of our constitutional policy it cannot be maintained that the discrimination as it was alleged was not essentially unjust. In that aspect it could not be deemed to lie outside the purview of the sweeping prohibitions of the Interstate Commerce Act.

The Court also found that a Virginia law requiring separation of the races on motor carriers was an undue burden on interstate commerce. "It seems clear to us that seating arrangements for the different races in interstate motor travel require a single, uniform rule to promote and protect national travel. Consequently, we hold the Virginia statute in controversy invalid."[50] The Court, in using the power of Congress over interstate commerce to strike down segregation on trains and motor carriers, bypassed the opportunity to declare once and for all that such segregation was a denial of equal protection guaranteed by the Fourteenth Amendment.

Voting. Lonnie E. Smith was denied the privilege of voting in the Texas Democratic primary election because he was black. He brought an action against S.E. Allwright, an election judge, seeking damages and a declaration of his right to vote. Judge Thomas M. Kennerly dismissed the action, and that decision was affirmed by the circuit court of appeals. It was reversed by the Supreme Court, with Murphy voting with the majority, and only Justice Roberts dissenting.[51] Although it was argued that the Democratic Party was a private organization not controlled by the state, the Court did not buy that argument. "The United States," Justice Stanley Reed pointed out, "is a constitutional democracy. Its organic law grants to all citizens a right to participate in the choice of elected officials without restriction by any State because of race. This grant to the people of the opportunity for choice is not to be nullified by a State through casting its electoral process in a form which permits a private organization to practice racial discrimination in the election. Constitutional rights would be of little value if they could be thus indirectly denied."

Employment, Housing, and Law School. Bester William Steele, who was black, began working as a railroad fireman in 1910. Although he and other blacks were prohibited from being members of the Brotherhood of Locomotive Firemen and Enginemen, they were forced to accept working conditions negotiated by the union because it was the exclusive bargaining agent for firemen. When the union negotiated a new agreement with the railroad, Steele and other blacks were given less favorable working arrangements, and they therefore brought an action seeking to prevent the implementation of the new agreement. Alabama Circuit Court Judge E.M. Creel dismissed the complaint, and the Alabama Supreme Court affirmed. The U.S. Supreme Court reversed, basing its decision upon the Railway Labor Act. "But we think that Congress," Chief Justice Stone noted, "in enacting the Railway Labor Act and authorizing a labor union, chosen by a majority of a craft, to represent the craft, did not intend to confer plenary power upon the union to sacrifice, for the benefit of its members, rights of the minority of the craft, without imposing on it any duty to protect the minority."[52]

While Murphy agreed with the outcome of the case, he scolded the Court for not reaching the broader constitutional issues: "The utter disregard for the dignity and the well-being of colored citizens shown by this record is so pronounced as to demand the invocation of constitutional condemnation. To decide the case and to analyze the statute solely upon the basis of legal niceties, while remaining mute and placid as to the obvious and oppressive deprivation of constitutional guarantees, is to make the judicial function something less than it should be." "No statutory interpretation," he asserted, "can erase this ugly example of economic cruelty against colored citizens of the United States. Nothing can destroy the fact that the accident of birth has been used as the basis to abuse individual rights by an organization purporting to act in conformity with its Congressional mandate."

The justice voted to prohibit courts from enforcing restrictive covenants that provided that only members of the Caucasian race could occupy certain real estate in St. Louis, Missouri.[53] He also voted to require the University of Oklahoma to provide a legal education for Ada Lois Sipuel, who was black, in the same way it provided such education to whites.[54]

For River Pilots, Women, and Political Parties. Marion B. Kotch, together with several others, brought suit against the Board of River Port Pilot Commissioners of New Orleans claiming that the method of selecting river pilots discriminated against them in violation of the Fourteenth Amendment. Kotch and the others, who had many years' experience as pilots, alleged that because the incumbent pilots controlled the selection of new pilots, "only their relatives and friends have and can become State pilots."[55] The suit was dismissed by Judge Rene Viosca, and that decision was upheld by the Louisiana Supreme Court. The U.S. Supreme Court affirmed, with justices Rutledge, Reed, Douglas, and Murphy dissenting.

"The result of the decision therefore," Rutledge declared for the dissenters, "is to approve as constitutional state regulation which makes admission to the ranks of pilots turn finally on consanguinity. Blood is, in effect, made the crux of selection. That, in my opinion, is forbidden by the Fourteenth Amendment's guaranty against denial of equal protection of the laws. The door is thereby closed to all not having blood relationship to presently licensed pilots."

Murphy also joined the dissent of Justice Rutledge in *Goesaert v. Cleary,*[56] when the Court upheld a Michigan law prohibiting women from being bartenders. And when the Court upheld the election laws of Illinois that made it very difficult for new parties to get on the ballot, the justice joined Douglas's dissenting opinion.[57] "Discrimination," Douglas argued, "against any group or class of citizens in the exercise of these constitutionally protected rights of citizenship deprives the electoral process of integrity."

In Selecting Jurors. Fay and Bove were found guilty of conspiracy to extort and extortion in connection with a large construction project in New York City. On appeal they questioned the validity of the jury selection process in New York, which resulted in the selection of two types of jurors, general jurors and special jurors. General jurors were required to be between ages 21 and 70, own $250 worth of property, be physically fit, of sound mind, good character, not convicted of a crime involving moral turpitude, be well-informed, and able to read and write. Exempted from serving were "clergymen, physicians, dentists, pharmacists, embalmers, optometrists, attorneys, members of the Army, Navy or Marine Corps, or of the National Guard or Naval Militia, firemen, policemen, ship's officers, pilots, editors, editorial writers, sub-editors, reporters and copy readers."[58] Women were also exempt, but could serve if they desired to do so.

Special jurors were those (1) not disqualified as a general juror, (2) not convicted of a crime, (3) not conscientiously opposed to the death penalty, and (4) who could hear the case and render a fair and impartial verdict. The panel of special jurors, sometimes referred to as "blue ribbon," in New York County consisted of about 3,000 individuals. Fay and Bove argued that the discrimination in the selection of special jurors, by whom they were tried, violated their right to equal protection and due process of law. The Supreme Court concluded that the process of selecting the "blue ribbon" panel was constitutional and upheld the lower court's verdicts.

Justice Murphy wrote a dissenting opinion, which justices Black, Douglas, and Rutledge joined. "The equal protection clause of the Fourteenth Amendment," he noted, "prohibits a state from convicting any person by use of a jury which is not impartially drawn from a cross-section of the community. That means that juries must be chosen without systematic and intentional exclusion of any otherwise qualified group of individuals." "Under our Constitution," he said, "the jury is not to be made the representative of the most intelligent, the most wealthy, or the most successful, nor of the least intelligent, the least wealthy, or the least successful. It is a democratic institution, representative of all qualified classes of people."

When the Court upheld the convictions of two men for murder in *Moore v. New York*,[59] Murphy again dissented because they had been tried by a special jury. "This case represents," he declared, "a tragic consequence that can flow from the use of the 'blue ribbon' jury. Two men must forfeit their lives after having been convicted of murder not by a jury of their peers, not by a jury chosen from a fair cross-section of the community, but by a jury drawn from a special group of individuals singled out in a manner inconsistent with the democratic ideals of the jury system." This he believed was a violation of the Fourteenth Amendment.

The Bill of Rights and the States

Justice Murphy joined Justice Black's dissent in *Betts v. Brady*,[60] when the Court upheld Betts's conviction even though the state would not furnish counsel for him and he had to conduct his own defense. In *Betts*, Black argued that it was the intent of the sponsors of the Fourteenth Amendment "to make secure against invasion by the states the fundamental liberties and safeguards set out in the Bill of Rights."

While Murphy agreed, he thought that the Due Process Clause of the Fourteenth Amendment guaranteed protection to the people above and beyond the provisions in the Bill of Rights. "I agree," he declared in dissent in *Adamson v. California*,[61] "that the specific guarantees of the Bill of Rights should be carried over intact into the first section of the Fourteenth Amendment. But I am not prepared to say that the latter is entirely and necessarily limited by the Bill of Rights. Occasions may arise where a proceeding falls so far short of conforming to fundamental standards of procedure as to warrant constitutional condemnation in terms of a lack of due process despite the absence of a specific provision in the Bill of Rights."

As part of an investigation concerning the performance of illegal abortions, representatives of the district attorney's office, acting without a warrant, went to the office of Dr. Julius A. Wolf, took him into custody, and seized his patient records. These records were put into evidence at the trial, which resulted in the doctor's conviction. Upon appeal, Dr. Wolf argued that because the authorities did not have a warrant for seizure of his records, their use against him in the trial was prohibited by the Fourth Amendment. The appellate court disagreed, and so did a majority of the Supreme Court.

"We hold . . . ," Justice Frankfurter wrote, "that in a prosecution in a State court for a State crime the Fourteenth Amendment does not forbid the admission of evidence obtained by an unreasonable search and seizure."[62]

This decision greatly disappointed Murphy. "It is," he said, "disheartening to find so much that is right in an opinion which seems to me so fundamentally wrong." He disagreed with the majority on the question of how to prevent police from making illegal searches and seizures. He did not believe that criminal prosecution of the police or civil actions against them were sufficient. The only sure way would be to exclude from the trial the illegally seized evidence. "The conclusion is inescapable," he asserted, "that but one remedy exists to deter violations of the search and seizure clause. That is the rule which excludes illegally obtained evidence. Only by exclusion can we impress upon the zealous prosecutor that violation of the Constitution will do him no good. And only when that point is driven home can the prosecutor be expected to emphasize the importance of observing constitutional demands in his instructions to the police."

The justice, however, did agree with the majority that the Fourteenth Amendment requires states to follow the dictates of the Fourth Amendment.

"Of course I agree with the Court," he declared, "that the Fourteenth Amendment prohibits activities [by states] which are proscribed by the search and seizure clause of the Fourth Amendment." But, he continued, "It is difficult for me to understand how the Court can go this far and yet be unwilling to make the step which can give some meaning to the pronouncements it utters."

The Japanese Cases

When the Court upheld the conviction of Gordon Kiyoshi Hirabayashi for violating the curfew imposed by military authorities along the West Coast after the bombing of Pearl Harbor, Murphy concurred. It is apparent, however, that he did so reluctantly. "We give great deference to the judgment of the Congress and of the military authorities," he noted, "as to what is necessary in the effective prosecution of the war, but we can never forget that there are constitutional boundaries which it is our duty to uphold."[63] The justice was deeply concerned that the curfew was ordered against the Japanese solely because of their race. "Distinctions based on color and ancestry are utterly inconsistent with our traditions and ideals. They are at variance with the principles for which we are now waging war.... Nothing is written more firmly into our law than the compact of the Plymouth voyagers to have just and equal laws." "Today is the first time, so far as I am aware," he noted, "that we have sustained a substantial restriction of the personal liberty of citizens of the United States based upon the accident of race or ancestry." He thought that the action of the government went "to the very brink of constitutional power."

It was the "critical military situation which prevailed on the Pacific Coast area," however, that convinced him to vote with the majority.

> In voting for affirmance of the judgment I do not wish to be understood as intimating that the military authorities in time of war are subject to no restraints whatsoever, or that they are free to impose any restrictions they may choose on the rights and liberties of individual citizens or groups of citizens in those places which may be designated as 'military areas.' While this Court sits, it has the inescapable duty of seeing that the mandates of the Constitution are obeyed. That duty exists in time of war as well as in time of peace, and in its performance we must not forget that few indeed have been the invasions upon essential liberties which have not been accompanied by pleas of urgent necessity advanced in good faith by responsible men.

Enforcement of the military-ordered curfew did not go over "the very brink of constitutional power," but for the justice the enforcement of the order evacuating the Japanese from certain areas along the West Coast surely did. In dissenting in *Korematsu v. United States,*[64] Justice Murphy declared: "This exclusion of 'all persons of Japanese ancestry, both alien and non-alien,' from the Pacific Coast area on a plea of military necessity in the absence of martial law ought not to be approved. Such exclusion goes over 'the very brink of constitutional power' and falls into the ugly abyss of racism." He was particularly disturbed because the government had made no showing why the Japanese Americans could not have been treated as individuals "by holding investigations and hearings to separate the loyal from the disloyal, as was done in the case of persons of German and Italian ancestry."

For the justice the evacuation order was "legalization of racism."

> Racial discrimination in any form and in any degree has no justifiable part whatever in our democratic way of life. It is unattractive in any setting but it is utterly revolting among a free people who have embraced the principles set forth in the Constitution of the United States. All residents of this nation are kin in some way by blood or culture to a foreign land. Yet they are primarily and necessarily a part of the new and distinct civilization of the United States. They must accordingly be treated at all times as the heirs of the American experiment and as entitled to all the rights and freedoms guaranteed by the Constitution.

Justice Murphy continued to vote against and write about discrimination against the Japanese in *Oyama v. California*[65] and *Takahashi v. Fish Comm'n.*[66] In commenting upon the California Alien Land Law in *Oyama,* he said that the "California statute in question, as I view it, is nothing more than an outright racial discrimination. As such, it deserves constitutional condemnation."[67] He then traces at some length the treatment of the Japanese who migrated to the United States after 1900 and notes that "charges of espionage, unassimilativeness, clannishness and corruption of young people were made against these 'Mongolian invaders.' "

The California Alien Land Law, which was part of that anti–Japanese feeling, he said, "was designed to effectuate a purely racial discrimination, to prohibit a Japanese alien from owning or using agricultural land solely because he is a Japanese alien." But he did not believe that most Americans subscribed to this discrimination. "Fortunately," he acknowledged, "the majority of the inhabitants of the United States, and the majority of those in California, reject racism and all of its implications. They recognize that under our Constitution all persons are entitled to the equal protection of the laws without regard to their racial ancestry. Human liberty is in too great a peril today to warrant ignoring that principle in this case."

The justice found the California law that prohibited persons ineligible for citizenship from having commercial fishing licenses to be "one more manifestation of the anti–Japanese fever which has been evident in California in varying degrees since the turn of the century."[68] For him, "legislation of that type is not entitled to wear the cloak of constitutionality." He therefore joined the Court in holding the law to be unconstitutional in *Takahashi.*

AS A JUDICIAL FREEDOM FIGHTER

"Justice Frankfurter, in a barbed effort at good humor, once listed what he called 'Frank Murphy's Clients,' among whom he included Reds, whores, crooks, Indians, and all other colored people, railroad workers, 'women, children, and most men.' "[69] While Frankfurter may have been jesting, there is a great deal of truth in that statement. Murphy was deeply concerned about the freedom and equality of all those listed, and he voted to protect those rights for them.

Murphy consistently voted to protect the rights of free exercise of religion, speech, and the press for all "women, children, and men." With regard to the free exercise of religion, the justice's concurring opinion in *Barnette*, the flag salute case, contains this statement: "Any spark of love for country which may be generated in a child or his associates by forcing him to make what is to him an empty gesture and recite words wrung from him contrary to his religious beliefs is overshadowed by the desirability of preserving freedom of conscience to the full. It is in that freedom and the example of persuasion, not in force and compulsion, that the real unity of America lies."[70]

And in *Carlson v. California*,[71] a companion case to *Thornhill*, the justice elaborated upon his understanding of free speech. "The carrying of signs and banners, no less than the raising of a flag, is a natural and appropriate means of conveying information on matters of public concern. . . . For the reasons set forth in our opinion in *Thornhill v. Alabama*, . . . publicizing the facts of a labor dispute in a peaceful way through appropriate means, whether by pamphlet, by word of mouth or by banner, must now be regarded as within that liberty of communication which is secured to every person by the Fourteenth Amendment against abridgment by a State."

Justice Murphy regularly voted for equal treatment for blacks, whether in jury selection, equal facilities on public transportation, employment, housing, or attendance at law school. When the Court upheld Texas's procedure for selecting persons to serve on the grand jury, he concluded his dissent by pointing out, "To that extent they have disregarded petitioner's right to equal protection of the laws. To that extent they have ignored the ideals of the jury system. Our affirmance of this judgment tarnishes the fact that we of this nation are one people undivided in ability or freedom by differences in race, color or creed."[72]

As noted earlier in *Adamson*, Murphy agreed that the Fourteenth Amendment carried over the Bill of Rights making it applicable to the states. But he also raised the possibility that there might be other occasions that do not conform to "fundamental standards of procedure as to warrant constitutional condemnation in terms of a lack of due process despite the absence of a specific provision in the Bill of Rights."[73]

With the exception of his vote to uphold the conviction of Gordon Hirabayashi for violating the wartime curfew along the West Coast, Murphy voted to strike down discrimination against the Japanese in all other cases in which he participated. He concurred when the Court unanimously upheld the release of Mitsuye Endo from a relocation camp in California. "I join in the opinion of the Court, but I am of the view that detention in Relocation Centers of persons of Japanese ancestry regardless of loyalty is not only unauthorized by Congress or the Executive but is another example of the unconstitutional resort to racism inherent in the entire evacuation program."[74]

Because Justice Murphy, with rare exception, voted to protect the freedom of "Reds, whores, crooks, Indians, and all other colored people, railroad workers, 'women, children, and . . . [all] men,'" he deserves to be identified as a freedom fighter.

7

CHIEF JUSTICE EARL WARREN

PERSONAL LIFE

Growing Up

When he was a schoolboy, Earl Warren asked his father, "Dad, how does it happen that all the other children have middle names and sister and I don't?" To which his father replied, "My boy, when you were born I was too poor to give you a middle name."[1]

The Warren family, father Methias, mother Christine, and sister Ethel, lived in Los Angeles when Earl was born on March 19, 1891. At the time, Methias worked for the Southern Pacific railroad as a car repairman and inspector. When Earl was four years old, the family moved to Sumner, California, near Bakersfield, where Methias continued to work as a railroad car repairman. The Warrens were Scandinavians, Methias's ancestors having come from Norway and Christine's from Sweden.

Warren describes Sumner as a town with "few cultural facilities or activities. . . . There was a small school which I later attended, a little Methodist church, and a lodge room where some social gatherings were held. But the place where the townspeople gathered most often was the railroad station." When the trains came by, "a large number of the townspeople would always be there to see if they knew anybody on the train and to visit with each other. The saloons, with their open gambling, were the only clubs. They were used extensively and sometimes tumultuously by the railroaders. My father was not a patron of them, as he never smoked or drank. Both my mother and father were total abstainers; not as prohibitionists, but merely as a matter of personal forbearance."

Warren's sister, Ethel, remembers her parents as quite young, but she said, "when I look back, I think of how much wisdom they showed in bringing us up. They didn't spoil us, but they were so self-denying. Everything was for the children."[2]

CHIEF JUSTICE EARL WARREN (photo by Robert S. Oakes, National Geography Society; collection of the Supreme Court of the United States).

"My grades were good in grammar school," Warren writes, "and I had many extra-curricular activities of my own making. I had a job every summer from the time I was nine years old, and during the school year I often had jobs in the morning before school and after school."[3] He worked as a helper on an ice wagon, for two summers drove a pair of mules pulling a grocery wagon, and did bookwork for a produce merchant.

From the time I was fifteen until I was graduated from law school, I worked every summer and Christmas vacation in some department of the Southern Pacific at Bakersfield—in the car shops, machine shops, baggage room, and as a caller of engine and train crews. I also delivered the Bakersfield *Californian* to East Bakersfield readers and at times sold the Los Angeles *Herald* early in the morning at the railroad station. While in high school, I coached a former Southern Pacific brakeman, who had become a bartender when he lost a foot, for the college entrance examinations which he was obliged to take in order to enter a medical school. To my delight, he passed the examinations and became a successful physician in Chicago.[4]

One of Warren's constant companions during these early days was a burro named Jack. "I saw nearly everything that went on in the surrounding country. My burro, Jack, would take me any place. We didn't need roads. We would go cross-country because there was very little to obstruct passage. I always rode bareback, and much of the time without a bridle. A slap on the side of the neck and pressure on his flanks with my feet were sufficient."

Jack's braying, when Warren did not come home immediately after school, did not go over too well with the neighbors. Warren's parents, therefore, insisted that Jack be sold.

When Warren entered high school, he was "the youngest and the smallest boy in the school, and to my embarrassment, I was the only one in knee pants. For an entire year, I felt humiliated, but my mother could not bear seeing me in what she considered adult clothing."

Earl learned to play the clarinet, and he and a friend were invited to become charter members of the local branch of the American Federation of Musicians. A town band was formed that played "all manner of engagements—ceremonial parades, political campaign meetings, torchlight parades, and summer concerts every Saturday night at the center of the business district."

Francis Vaughan, a high school classmate of Warren's, has said that he "was not a particularly good student. He didn't have the curiosity of a scientist. He seemed to be looking around for something to do. More interested in history, I suppose, than anything else."[5]

In his autobiography, Warren tells of the conditions of the men who worked on the railroad, the "gigantic corporation that dominated the economic and political life of the community."[6]

I saw that power exercised and the hardship that followed in its wake. I saw every man on the railroad not essential for the operation of the trains laid off without pay and without warning for weeks before the end of a fiscal year in order that the corporate stock might pay a higher dividend. I saw minority groups brought into the country for cheap labor paid a dollar a day for ten hours of work only to be fleeced out of much of that at the company store where they were obliged to trade. I helped carry men to the little room called the emergency hospital for amputation of an arm or leg that had been crushed because there were no safety appliances in the shops and yards to prevent such injuries. I knew of men who were fired for even considering a suit against the railroad for the injuries they had sustained. There was no compensation for them, and they went through life as cripples. . . . As a train caller, I saw men rush from the pay car to the gambling houses and never leave until they had lost every cent of their month's laborious earnings. . . . I saw conditions in many of the homes where the breadwinner had lost his earnings at the gaming tables. I became familiar with the ten- and even twelve-hour days, seven days a week. I worked many such hours myself.

When Warren was about to depart for the University of California, Berkeley, his father said, "Well, my boy, you are going away from home. You are a man now, and I am sure that you are going to act like one."

At a Sunday dinner attended by many students, Warren told of a suspicious high school teacher who tried to catch the students cheating. He said that it had become quite a game with the students and that they therefore did cheat whenever they thought they would not get caught. Later, he was invited to dinner by one of the seniors, who told him "that this was not the way things were done at the university. He said the university operated on the honor system; that there was no spying; that students were entrusted with self-government, and they were expected to be honorable in taking examinations as in all other things. . . . I was, of course, greatly embarrassed, but I can recall few times in my life when I appreciated advice more than this or when it did more for me. I was deeply touched by the kind manner in which he talked to me, and promised him I would never violate the honor system."

Warren was neither a great student nor active in campus politics. "My first three years at the university," he has written, "were not terribly eventful. My scholarship was fair but in no sense outstanding. I made good marks in history, political science, and English, but in the other subjects they were only passable." He played his clarinet in a dance band, joined the La Junta Club, and spent many evenings drinking beer and playing cards.

Students were allowed to enter the law school at the end of their third year at the university. Neither Warren nor biographer John D. Weaver relates much of Warren's law school career. Warren notes that he did not think much of the case method of teaching law and therefore sought and obtained a job in a law office. This apparently was against law school rules.

The future chief justice graduated on time and took the California bar examination, which he passed. He accepted a position with the Law Department of the Associated Oil Company.

The Practice of Law and Brief Military Career

Warren and his boss, Edmund Tauske, did not get along well, and after a year Warren left and joined the law firm of Robinson & Robinson in Oakland.

I kept the court calendar for the entire office, was the leg man to the courthouse on minor matters, and researched cases for the senior member of the firm, Edward C. Robinson, a kindly old gentleman who later became a respected judge of the Superior Court. I found it a pleasure to go to the Oakland courthouse. The judges were courteous and hard-working, and the attachés in the County Clerk's Office were helpful to everyone. . . . It was easy to become acquainted, particularly with young lawyers with whom I was daily thrown into contact. We developed a fine camaraderie, and because the bar association was moribund at the time, we soon formed what was called "The Young Lawyer's Club of Alameda County."

After a year and a half with the Robinson firm, Warren joined two of his law school classmates and an established lawyer, Peter J. Crosby, and formed a new partnership. Before they could find office space, the United States entered the war against Germany, and the plans for the new law firm were laid aside. Warren applied for officers' training, but hemorrhoids and pneumonia sent him to the hospital. When he was released, officers' training enlistments were closed, so instead of waiting until he was called for the draft, he enlisted in the army and sent to Camp Lewis, Washington. He describes the arrival at the camp:

When we arrived at camp, there were no army clothes for us, and we lived almost in squalor for weeks until some new issues arrived. We were little better off as far as bed clothing was concerned, with only a light canvas tick, which we filled with straw, and two thin blankets. We were immediately started on close order drill and long marches around American Lake four miles away, and through the forests which surrounded it. For guns to drill with, we had wooden objects fashioned after the general outlines of a gun. We dug trenches in which to simulate trench warfare, and improvised in many other ways to give the impression of being soldiers.

Warren was accepted to officers' training, and upon graduating as a second lieutenant was sent to Camp Lee, Virginia, where he became proficient in bayonet warfare. He was then sent to Camp McArthur, Waco, Texas, as a first lieutenant bayonet instructor. Two days later the war ended, and he was discharged on December 9.

Love, Marriage, and Family

Warren indicates in his memoirs that marriage was not a top priority for him during these early years. That all changed, however, when he attended a birthday party at the Piedmont Baths in Oakland in 1921. Biographer Weaver gives this account of what transpired.

Warren spotted a radiant face among the bathers splashing about the pool. He asked his hostess to introduce him.

"She was in the water, I could only see her head," he says, "but she looked wonderful to me."

Like Warren's mother, Nina Palmquist had been born in Sweden and brought to Iowa as a child. Her parents had moved to California seeking a mild, beneficent climate. Her mother had died when Nina was three years old, her father when she was thirteen. She had been self-supporting ever since. At the time she met Earl Warren ("I spotted him just as quickly as he spotted me"), she was the widow of a musician, Grover Meyers, who had died when their son, James, was three weeks old. She had gone back to work managing a chain of women's clothing shops.[7]

The couple's courtship was less than whirlwind, for it was two years before they were married. At the time Warren was an assistant district attorney of Alameda County. After the marriage ceremony, thanks to some friends, the couple was "serenaded" all the way to the county line with highway patrol sirens.

The Warrens had six children, including Nina's son, James, and Virginia, Earl, Jr., Dorothy, Nina Elizabeth, and Robert. Because they were all born close together, five of them were in school at the same time. They were expected to do chores and clean their rooms, for which they received 25 cents a week allowance. They were not spanked, but were given a talking to by their father.

"You were always on your honor," says Earl, Jr., a Sacramento municipal judge with four children. "If you did something wrong, the punishment was in knowing you had broken the code."

In his biography of Earl Warren, G. Edward White writes:

> *American Magazine,* in 1953, named the Warrens "Family of the Month" for their ability to "take fame in stride" and "live so normally on the political merry go round" that they merited being called "still a typical American family." Friends of Nina Warren were quoted as calling her "more domestic than the Old Woman in the Shoe"; Earl Warren was said to be "never . . . too busy to be the closest pal and confidant of his kids"; the Warrens had "done everything as a group" and "had become a single strong unit, each always ready to help the other."[8]

Public Service

Legislative Clerk. Upon returning from the army, Warren met Leon E. Gray, who had been his associate at the Robinson firm. Gray told him that he had been elected to the legislature, and asked Warren to become his attaché at a salary of five dollars a day. Warren accepted. However, when he arrived in Sacramento to begin work, he was given the opportunity to become a clerk for the Judiciary Committee for 6 dollars per day.

He comments on his first public service job: "The Legislature convened the next day, and I immediately went on the payroll, little realizing that I would from that moment, be in the public service without a break until my retirement fifty years later as Chief Justice of the United States."[9]

During the legislative session, Ezra Decoto, the district attorney for Alameda County, came to Sacramento seeking an appropriation to hire another assistant. Warren's friends told him that he could do so, provided Warren was given the job. Decoto protested because he had promised the position to Charles W. Snook. When Warren heard about Decoto's dilemma, he went to him and told him that he would like the job, but that under the circumstances Decoto should hire Snook. Decoto appreciated Warren's decision, and said that when he had another opening, he would consider hiring him.

When the job with the legislature ended, Warren accepted a part-time position with the Oakland city attorney. "I had a good general experience in the City Attorney's Office," he wrote, "advising city boards and officers, writing legal opinions and having a fair amount of contact with the courts. I was netting about one hundred fifty dollars a month in private legal work with [Leon] Gray, although I put little effort into building a practice. Still determined to become a trial lawyer, I looked forward to experience some day in the District Attorney's Office."

Assistant District Attorney. The opportunity to enter the D.A.'s office came in the spring of 1920 when Decoto offered Warren a position as an assistant. He became, as he recalls it, "a sort of Jack-of-all trades on both the criminal and civil sides. I tried criminal cases, one after another, advised Boards of Education, assisted the chief deputy in advising the Board of Supervisors, and handled lawsuits against officers of the county. It was exciting for me, every day of it, and I made quick progress."

On his first day in office, he was assigned to assist one of the deputies in trying a man for criminal syndicalism. He describes the case and his feelings at the time:

> It was part of the hysteria after World War I, and was being used throughout the state because of hostile feelings against the militant Industrial Workers of the World (IWW). In the trials, some repulsive informers were the principal witnesses, and I recall feeling squeamish about them. The defendant was an ideological radical, but I never could believe he was a terrorist. He was convicted and sentenced to prison. There was no doubt that he violated the Criminal Syndicalism Act and was, therefore, guilty. But I never liked this statute, even though its constitutionality was sustained a few years later by the United States Supreme Court, and during my many years as district attorney I never used it as a law-enforcement weapon.

Years later, when Warren was governor, the defendant in that case applied to him for executive clemency. Because he had a good record in prison, Warren granted him a full pardon.

"He [Warren] has always been a hard worker," Weaver notes, "with a prodigious capacity for accumulating, absorbing and analyzing facts. Even old friends are taken aback at times by the oddments tucked away in his memory. It is like the attic of a family that has been for some generations in the business of producing almanacs."[10]

After Warren and Nina were married, they honeymooned in Vancouver, British Columbia. Upon returning home, Nina received a present of Chinese jade jewelry from a Mr. L. Ben. Ben was "the biggest Chinese lottery operator in the county."[11] Warren gave the jewelry to the foreman of the county grand jury who returned it to Mr. Ben and obtained a receipt for its return.

District Attorney of Alameda County. Ezra Decoto resigned as district attorney in 1925, and Warren was appointed to fill the vacancy. Because Decoto's term expired in 1926, it was necessary for Warren to run for the office at that time. He did so, and was elected overwhelmingly. He writes of this campaign:

> A number of people offered campaign contributions. But I knew that in an election for such an office, some designing types would gladly contribute to both opposing candidates. It would, therefore, make little difference to them which side eventually won. I wanted no such obligations to donors hanging over me. My wife and I discussed the matter and decided that instead of buying a home we desired, I would invest one year's salary in my campaign and refuse *all* contributions. This I did, and with the exception of $150 donated by each of my top three assistants, this constituted my campaign fund.

The new district attorney ran a tight ship. Biographer White writes:

> In order to establish this new tone for his office, Warren stressed hard work, nonpartisanship, and a full-time commitment to public service as office virtues. He divided the office into five units and met each unit once a week for an hour. The meetings, he later said, were "really rugged": Warren kept very close tabs on his personnel. "We kept their feet to the fire," Warren said of his staff; "we didn't have any forty-hour week." He insisted that staff members be loyal and discreet as well as energetic; as a result he had a fairly high turnover of personnel. He tended to hire his deputies from two groups—veterans of World War I and recent law school graduates. This resulted in the district attorney's office being staffed with "young lawyers who were interested in acquiring experience," sometimes at very low or no pay. Warren was parsimonious with raises and slow with praise. His interest was in finding "a personal organization impervious to outside influences."[12]

Among the comments made by former members of Warren's staff are the following:

> He had three great qualities: The ability to make decisions, an unerring sense of timing, and an infinite capacity for remembering names.

> When he became district attorney, the office had one investigator. He built up a real investigative staff, "the crime-crushers" we used to call them. They had to read law, engage in firearm practice, study new techniques in law enforcement.

If a deputy went to him and said, "I'm not sure this man is guilty," he would be removed from the case, and we'd discuss it at our Saturday conference. If we all felt the man was not guilty, the case would be dropped. None of us was ever asked to prosecute a defendant if we weren't sure of his guilt.

Helen R. McGregor, Warren's personal secretary, relates an incident that she remembers well about Warren and the Bill of Rights. He came into her office and said: "'I've got to make a speech on the Bill of Rights.' He dictated some notes, taking each of the rights and telling how it hampered him as district attorney. But then he went on to say that he wouldn't have any one of those rights diminished in any degree 'for my sake, my children's sake, or my children's children's sake.'"

Biographer Luther A. Huston writes:

> Warren's *cause célèbre* while he was District Attorney was the "ship murder case," tried in 1936. Thugs had gone aboard the ship *Point Lobos* while it was docked in Alameda and beaten up [and killed] George Alberts, the chief engineer. Alberts had discharged a member of his engine crew without paying him overtime wages the seaman claimed were due. The seaman complained to Frank Conner, the union delegate on the *Point Lobos*, and Conner took the complaint to Earl King, secretary of the Marine Firemen, Oilers, Water Tenders and Wipers Union.
>
> King, Conner, and E.G. Ramsay, another union official, gave George Wallace and Ben Sakowitz $30 of union funds and told them to go "across the Bay and get the matter fixed up."[13]

Warren prosecuted King, Ramsay, Conner, and Wallace and obtained convictions of second-degree murder. Sakowitz escaped custody, and was later located in North Africa as a member of the French Foreign Legion. Upon being returned to the United States, he escaped and was never prosecuted.

In his memoirs, Warren notes that George Wallace had confessed to his part in the crime, and his confession was confirmed by others. "There could have been no doubt about the guilt of the persons on trial, and they were sentenced to life imprisonment for their crime."[14] Nevertheless, his handling of the case has been questioned.[15] Some have argued that Warren and his staff made unreasonable searches in violation of the Fourth Amendment, and obtained a coerced confession in violation of the Fifth Amendment Due Process Clause. Biographer White points out, however, that "under California and Supreme Court criminal procedure standards of 1936, none of the practices authorized by Warren were illegal."[16] Ironically, after Warren became Chief Justice he voted with the majority to hold some of these practices unconstitutional.

While district attorney, Warren was instrumental in getting all branches of law enforcement to work together; in reforming the bail bond system so that the county got the defaults to which it was entitled; in bringing an end to corruption in the sheriff's office; and in cleaning up the jail; he was also point person in establishing a law enforcement training school at San Jose State College.

Personal disaster struck the family when Warren's father was murdered on May 15, 1938.

> Mrs. Warren had gone to Oakland, and Methias was alone in the family home, sitting before a gas grate, reading. A tenant of one of the houses he owned had called at 8 P.M. to pay his rent.
>
> No one knows who looked in the window and saw Methias reading by the fire. Whoever it was, as the police reconstructed the story, twisted a half-buried piece of iron pipe from the back yard, entered the house quietly, and bludgeoned Methias to death.[17]

Although Warren and his staff of investigators participated in the investigation, the murderer was never found. Warren surmised that because the railroad yards were only a few blocks away, some transient had killed his father, and then took the next train out of town.

Attorney General of California. Before Warren ran for attorney general, he visited with the then attorney general, Ulysses S. Webb, and told him that he wanted to seek that office but would not do so as long as Webb was the incumbent. When Webb decided to retire at the end of 1938, he called Warren and informed him of that decision. Warren then entered the race with the financial help of friends in the Bay area. In accordance with California law, Warren was able to file as a candidate in each party, Republican, Democratic, and Progressive, and he won the nomination in all of them.

When the votes were counted in the general election, Warren won as a Republican in an election in which the state elected a Democratic governor for the first time in 30 years.

At the time, there were a number of dog racing tracks in California, all of which were operating illegally. At Warren's request, John J. Jerome, one of the operators, came to see him. Warren told him that dog track gambling was against the law and that therefore he should close the track. Jerome sent for his attorney, who, upon consulting with his client, inquired whether Warren intended to shut down all dog tracks. When Warren said he did, Jerome asked if he could operate through the coming Saturday night. Warren said that it would probably take him at least that long to get the paperwork done. The track closed that Saturday.

Shortly thereafter, Warren, together with the sheriff and the district attorney of Los Angeles County, took on Tony Cornero, the operator of the gambling ship *Rex* anchored off Long Beach. After being sure that he had legal authority to do so, Warren dispatched a group to the ship to close it down. "Some one had alerted Cornero. He barred the gangway of the *Rex* and turned a hose on Warren's armada. When the Attorney General was told his forces had been repulsed, he said, 'All right, if they won't let us on we won't let anyone off. They've got women aboard whose husbands don't know they are out gambling, and they've got husbands aboard whose wives don't know they are out with other girls. Let's see what happens.'"[18]

When the customers demanded to be allowed to go ashore, a deal was struck whereby Warren's forces would maintain a guard to see that the anchor was not raised, and the passengers were allowed to leave. After supplies aboard the ship ran low, Cornero was forced to throw in the towel. Not only was the gambling operation shut down, but Cornero was forced to pay the state's expenses for the operation.

When Governor Culbert Olson appointed Max Radin, a law professor, to the California Supreme Court, Warren played a part in Radin's being rejected by the State Commission on Judicial Qualifications. Radin was a close adviser to the governor; had apparently been critical of the prosecution of the *Point Lobos* defendants; had spoken at meetings of radicals, although he denied being a Communist; and had injected himself into a trial of individuals who had been charged with contempt for not releasing certain records to a legislative committee.

Warren makes no mention of the Radin affair in his memoirs. His son, Earl, Jr., has "suggested that the issue of Radin's nomination was 'personal' to Warren."[19] Biographer White suggests that there is evidence "that Warren acted out of passion and spite toward Radin."

Warren played a significant role in the curfew for and relocation of the Japanese to internment camps during the early part of World War II. In his memoirs, Warren describes the tension among law enforcement personnel over the presence of the Japanese along the West Coast and his participation in the relocation.

> I do not recall a single public officer responsible for the security of the state who testified against a relocation proposal. After a conference with the law officers, who agreed unanimously, I testified for a proposal which was not to intern in concentration camps *all* Japanese, but to require them to move from what was designated as the theater of operations, extending seven hundred fifty miles inland from the Pacific Ocean. Those who did not move by a certain date were to be confined to concentration camps established by the United States Government. Of course, for most of them it was the same as directing their confinement, because the limited time prescribed for removal, the fact that their businesses were turned over to the Alien Property Custodian, the problem of their having no time to look for employment in an unfamiliar part of the country, the language barrier, and the race antagonism occasioned by the war made any other alternative remote indeed.[20]

Later, in reflecting upon the Japanese issue, Warren wrote:

> I have since deeply regretted the removal order and my own testimony advocating it, because it was not in keeping with our American concept of freedom and the rights of citizens. Whenever I thought of the innocent little children who were torn from home, school friends, and congenial surroundings, I was conscience-stricken. It was wrong to react so impulsively, without positive evidence

of disloyalty, even though we felt we had a good motive in the security of our state. . . . I have always believed that I had no prejudice against the Japanese as such except that directly spawned by Pearl Harbor and its aftermath.

Governor of California. Many people had been urging Warren to run for governor. After his announcement, 65 "so-called 'moneybags' . . . convened at the Century Club in Los Angeles and solemnly decided that they would take no part in the governor's race, but would devote all their time, energy, and money to electing a conservative Legislature to curb Olson in his next term." At this meeting, a vote was taken whether this would be the action of the group and the vote was 64–1 to do so. The one negative vote was that of Gordon Campbell, a former football player at the University of Southern California, who later became Warren's campaign finance manager.

When Warren learned who had attended the meeting, he made a list of ten who had previously asked him to run for governor and went to see each one. Each was embarrassed and tried to explain, but, in Warren's words, "I told them I was not seeking an explanation. I only wanted them to know that I knew of the meeting." Warren filed for governor on both the Republican and the Democratic tickets. He won the Republican nomination easily, and received over 400,000 votes in the Democratic primary.

During the general election campaign, Campbell refused to accept contributions from any of the 64 businessmen who had chosen not to take part in the governor's race in the primary election.

Warren describes the last days of the campaign and the result: "I campaigned as diligently as possible in the final election, right up to the closing of the polls, and was rewarded with a majority of 335,000 votes. The thing that pleased me most, however, was the fact that I carried every county in the state except the little mountain county of Butte, which I lost by sixty votes because of a local school controversy in which, as attorney general, I had written an opinion which was not well received by many of its citizens."[21]

Warren served as governor of California from 1943 to 1953, being the first person to be elected three times. Following his election to a second term, the *Los Angeles Times* editorialized: "Earl Warren is an authentic leader. The people recognize him as such. In his philosophy of public service he truly represents the people as a whole. This, too, the people recognize. He is a trained, earnest, competent, successful servant of the people. He has shown a sincere concern for the welfare of the people, and in an era of political hypocrisy, cowardice, truckling and double-dealing he has stood steadfast."[22]

The Warren family was thrown into the national spotlight by his election as governor and became the focus of many magazine articles. However, they worked diligently at maintaining as much of a private family life as possible. "During Warren's first term, five of the children lived in the Governor's Mansion. Domestic affairs were handled by Nina Warren. Nina 'belonged to no clubs, committees or organizations whatsoever'; the writer for *Life* felt that 'she would be astonished if anyone asked her about her ideology.' She had had five children in six years, she told two magazines, and didn't have time for much else. Having six children, she told one reporter, was 'the wisest thing we ever did.'"[23]

Warren responded to questions about his political philosophy by pointing out that "I do not care to be categorized as either a liberal or a conservative because too many people calling themselves conservatives would consent to no change, and too many so-called liberals would also permit no change unless it was on their often unrealistic terms. . . . Also, I believed in the progressivism of Hiram Johnson, who had broken the power of predatory interests by opening up our state and local governments so the people could govern themselves through free elections."[24]

As governor, Warren required all visitors to his office to come through the reception room, and the names of those who came were available to the press at all times. And while he understood that lobbyists had a "First Amendment right '. . . to petition the Government for a redress of grievances,' . . . [this did] not include the right to debauch the Legislature or throw monkey wrenches into its machinery."

Warren became involved in a controversy over requiring faculty members of the University of California to take a loyalty oath. He opposed such an oath as *ex offico* chairman of the University Board of Regents and was successful in delaying its enactment. When it was finally approved, Warren voted against it. In explaining his vote, he argued, "I don't believe that the faculty of the University of California is Communist; I don't believe that it is soft on Communism, and neither am I. I believe that in their hearts the members of the faculty of our University are just as sincere on the things they represent against Communism as any member of this Board. . . . I have absolute confidence in the faculty of the University of California."[25]

Later, however, when the controversy did not die down, Warren proposed and the legislature enacted an oath requirement for all California state employees. Biographer White has expressed the opinion that Warren's "performance in the loyalty controversy was a confused and ambivalent one." He attributes this inconsistency to Warren's strong "emotional attachment to the University of California."

Some of the accomplishments of Warren's administration include the enactment of an "equal pay for equal work" law for women, liberalization of the old-age pension system, and reorganization of the prisons and the penal system. He also proposed a Fair Employment Practices Commission, rent control, and a limited form of compulsory health insurance.

In Politics

Biographer Huston sums up Warren's political philosophy by noting that in "state politics Warren wore a Republican hat with a Democratic hatband. In national politics he discarded the two-tone fedora and wore the solid, one-color Republican headgear, albeit Western style. Expediency and sagacity dictated that in California it was necessary to work both sides of the political street in order to win, but that formula was not adaptable to a national political race. So Warren preached Republican doctrine and belabored Democrats and their precepts and practices in the national campaigns in which he participated."[26] In reference to Warren, President Harry Truman said, "He's a Democrat and doesn't know it."[27]

The California Republican Party sent a delegation to its national convention supporting Warren's candidacy for president in 1944. They had the freedom, however, to vote for any other candidate of their choice. Warren was appointed temporary chairman of the convention and gave the keynote speech. Thomas Dewey was chosen as the Republican Party's candidate for president. Dewey attempted to have Warren become his vice presidential candidate, but Warren refused.

In 1948, when Dewey was again the Republicans' presidential candidate, Warren received the vice presidential nomination by acclamation, and he accepted.

"The vice presidential campaign, for a person as accustomed to making his own decisions and as stubborn in his beliefs as Warren," writes biographer White, "was a depressing experience."[28] He was assigned by Dewey's campaign strategists to a minor role in the campaign principally to speak where Dewey did not wish to go and to give talks reinforcing Dewey's positions on the issues. Nina apparently foresaw the problem and expressed doubts that he "could be happy with Tom Dewey directing" his affairs. To the surprise of many people, Harry Truman won the presidency in 1948. Warren then returned to California to run for a third term as governor. He overwhelmingly defeated James Roosevelt, the Democratic candidate.

Warren began to take more interest in national matters, and positioned himself for a run at the Republican presidential nomination in 1952. At the time, Robert Taft was the leading contender, but in January 1952 former general Dwight Eisenhower announced his candidacy. This pretty well sealed Warren's fate, because the battle for the nomination became one between Taft and Eisenhower, with Eisenhower the eventual winner.

Nomination to the Supreme Court

After Eisenhower was elected president, Warren received a phone call from him, the substance of which Warren relates in his memoirs.

"Governor," the new president said, "I am back here selecting my Cabinet, and I wanted to tell you I won't have a place for you in it."

I said, "General, I do not want a place on the Cabinet. I am perfectly satisfied with my job as governor, and I could not afford to move my family back to Washington for such a position."

"Well," he said, "I have been giving you serious consideration for Attorney General, but Herb Brownell has been close to me politically in the campaign, and I feel I need his political advice as well as his legal counsel."

"He will make you a splendid Attorney General," I said.

He then remarked, "But I want you to know that I intend to offer you the first vacancy on the Supreme Court."

"That is very generous of you."

"That is my personal commitment to you."[29]

President Eisenhower's recollection of this is somewhat different, as reported by biographer Houston. Eisenhower states that from conversations with Warren he had learned that they both shared views on many issues, and that during the 1952 convention they talked about a Supreme Court appointment. Eisenhower states that he told Warren that he "was definitely inclined to . . . [appoint him in the future if] a vacancy should occur. However, neither he nor I was thinking of the special post of chief justice, nor was I definitely committed to any appointment."[30]

Eisenhower's opportunity to appoint a Supreme Court justice occurred sooner than either he or Warren expected when Chief Justice Fred Vinson died unexpectedly on September 8, 1953.

Because Congress was not in session, and the Court's term was to begin early in October, Eisenhower gave Warren an interim appointment until Congress convened and he could be approved by the Senate.[31]

The other justices on the Court at the time of Warren's appointment were Hugo L. Black, William O. Douglas, Felix Frankfurter, Sherman Minton, Stanley Reed, Tom C. Clark, Harold H. Burton, and Robert H. Jackson.

AS CHIEF JUSTICE (1953-69)

The Free Exercise of Religion

Abraham Braunfeld, Isaac Friedman, Alter Diament, S. David Friedman, and Joseph R. Friedman were merchants engaged in the sale of clothing and home furnishings. They were also members of the Orthodox Jewish faith, which required them to close their businesses and refrain from work on Saturdays. They brought an action seeking to have the Pennsylvania Sunday closing laws declared unconstitutional. For them, closing on Sundays would mean the loss of two days' business each week, one day required by law, and the other by their faith.

The district court dismissed the action, and the Supreme Court upheld that decision.[32] Chief Justice Warren wrote an opinion for himself, and justices

Black, Clark, and Charles E. Whittaker. "Certain aspects of religious exercise cannot, in any way, be restricted or burdened by either federal or state legislation. Compulsion by law of the acceptance of any creed or the practice of any form of worship is strictly forbidden. The freedom to hold religious beliefs and opinions is absolute." But, he said, "The freedom to act, even when the action is in accord with one's religious convictions, is not totally free from legislative restrictions." The chief justice acknowledged that "to make accommodation between religious action and an exercise of state authority is a particularly delicate task, . . . because resolution in favor of the State results in the choice to the individual of either abandoning his religious principle or facing criminal prosecution." But he did not see the Sunday closing laws placing these petitioners in that kind of situation. "This is not the case before us," he declared, "because the statute at bar does not make unlawful any religious practices of appellants; the Sunday law simply regulates a secular activity and, as applied to appellants, operates so as to make the practice of their religious beliefs more expensive."

Justice Stewart dissented with these words: "Pennsylvania has passed a law which compels an Orthodox Jew to choose between his religious faith and his economic survival. That is a cruel choice. It is a choice which I think no State can constitutionally demand."

The chief justice voted with Justice Black and the majority to strike down Maryland's law requiring an applicant to declare his or her belief in God before becoming a notary public.[33] He also joined Justice Brennan's opinion upholding Adell H. Sherbert's right to unemployment compensation even though she could not work on Saturdays because she was a Seventh-Day Adventist.[34]

Freedom of Speech

Pamphleteering and Soliciting. Chief Justice Warren participated in several cases involving distribution of literature and soliciting, but did not write any of the opinions. In *Staub v. City of Baxley*,[35] for example, he joined Justice Whittaker's opinion striking down a city ordinance that required a license to solicit membership in any organization. The authority to issue licenses rested with the mayor and the council. "It is settled by a long line of recent decisions of this Court," Justice Whittaker pointed out, "that an ordinance which, like this one, makes the peaceful enjoyment of freedoms which the Constitution guarantees contingent upon the uncontrolled will of an official—as by requiring a permit or license which may be granted or withheld in the discretion of such official—is an unconstitutional censorship or prior restraint upon the enjoyment of those freedoms."

When the Court struck down a California law requiring personal identification upon handbills, Warren joined the majority opinion, in which Black wrote, "There can be no doubt that such identification requirement would tend to restrict freedom to distribute information and thereby freedom of expression. 'Liberty of circulating is as essential to that freedom as liberty of publishing; indeed, without the circulation, the publication would be of little value.'"[36]

Assembling, Picketing, and Parading.

> Late in the morning of March 2, 1961, the petitioners, high school and college students of the Negro race, met at the Zion Baptist Church in Columbia. From there, at about noon, they walked in separate groups of about 15 to the South Carolina State House grounds, an area of two city blocks open to the general public. Their purpose was "to submit a protest to the citizens of South Carolina, along with the Legislative Bodies of South Carolina, our feelings and our dissatisfaction with the present condition of discriminatory actions against Negroes, in general, and to let them know that we were dissatisfied and that we would like for the laws which prohibited Negro privileges in this State be removed."[37]

Although there was no evidence of violence or disruption of traffic, the police ordered them to disperse, which they refused to do. Instead they listened "to a 'religious harangue' by one of their leaders, and loudly . . . [sang] 'The Star Spangled Banner' and other patriotic and religious songs, while stamping their feet and clapping their hands." One hundred eighty-seven of them were arrested and charged with breach of the peace. All were convicted. Some received a ten-dollar fine or five days in jail, others were fined $100 or given a sentence of 30 days in jail. The Supreme Court of South Carolina upheld the convictions, but with the chief justice voting with the majority, and only Justice Clark dissenting, the U.S. Supreme Court reversed.

"It is clear to us," Justice Stewart declared, "that in arresting, convicting, and punishing the petitioners under the circumstances disclosed by this record, South Carolina infringed the petitioners' constitutionally protected rights of free speech, free assembly, and freedom to petition for redress of their grievances. . . . The circumstances in this case reflect an exercise of these basic constitutional rights in their most pristine and classic form."

Justice Abe Fortas wrote the plurality opinion when the Court struck down the convictions of five black youths who sat in at the Audubon Regional Library in Clinton, Louisiana. The chief justice and Justice Douglas joined that opinion.[38] "We are here dealing with an aspect of a basic constitutional right—," Justice Fortas argued, "the right under the First and Fourteenth Amendments guaranteeing freedom of speech and of assembly, and freedom to petition the Government for a redress of grievances." "As this Court has repeatedly stated," he continued, "these rights are not confined to verbal expression. They embrace appropriate types of action which certainly include the right in a peaceable and orderly manner to protest by silent and reproachful presence, in a place where the protestant has every right to be, the unconstitutional segregation of public facilities."

Warren also voted against the use of an injunction against peaceful labor union picketing. For example, when the Teamsters began to picket a gravel pit which employed nonunion workers, Judge Herbert A. Bundle, Jr., issued an order restraining the picketing. The Supreme Court of Wisconsin upheld the order, as did the U.S. Supreme Court.[39] Justice Douglas dissented, with the chief justice and Justice Black joining with him. Douglas pointed out that in two similar cases the Court had upheld peaceful picketing in labor disputes. And he acknowledged that sometimes speech becomes so much a part of conduct that it can be enjoined. "But where, as here, there is no rioting, no mass picketing, no violence, no disorder, no fisticuffs, no coercion—indeed nothing but speech—the principles announced . . . [in the prior cases] should give the advocacy of one side of a dispute First Amendment protection."

The chief justice cast his vote with Justice Douglas in *Adderley v. Florida*,[40] when the Court upheld the convictions of Harriett Louise Adderley and other blacks for picketing the jailhouse in Leon County, Florida. As pointed out in Chapter 5, Douglas dissented in that case. He expressed concern over the custodian of government property, in this case the county sheriff, having the power to prevent peaceful protests on the property. "That tragic consequence happens today," he said, "when a trespass law is used to bludgeon those who peacefully exercise a First Amendment right to protest to government against one of the most grievous of all modern oppressions which some of our States are inflicting on our citizens."

The Reverend Fred L. Shuttlesworth, three other ministers and over 50 people, all black, marched in Birmingham, Alabama, without first having secured a permit from the city. Permits were issued by the city commission, but could be denied if in "its judgment the public welfare, peace, safety, health, decency, good order, morals or convenience require that it be refused."[41] Shuttlesworth was arrested, convicted, given a 90-day jail sentence, and ordered to pay $99, which included a fine and costs. The court of appeals reversed, being of the opinion "that the ordinance had been applied in a discriminatory fashion, and that it was unconstitutional in imposing an 'invidious prior restraint' without ascertainable standards for the granting of permits." The Supreme Court of Alabama reversed and reinstated the conviction, but the U.S. Supreme Court unanimously reversed, with Justice Stewart writing the Court's opinion, which the chief justice joined. Stewart acknowledged that municipalities have an obligation to keep the streets open and available to the public, but also noted that "our decisions have also made clear that picketing and parading may nonetheless constitute methods of expression, entitled to First Amendment protection." What was wrong with the Birmingham ordinance, then, was that it gave the commissioners absolute discretion to pick and choose to whom they would give permits and to whom they would not. "Even when the use of its public streets and sidewalks is involved . . , " Justice Stewart pointed out, "a municipality may not empower its licensing officials to roam essentially at will, dispensing or withholding permission to speak, assemble, picket, or parade, according to their own opinions regarding the potential effect of the activity in question on the 'welfare,' 'decency,' or 'morals' of the community."

Advocacy of Unpopular Ideas. The following is a summary of the facts in the case of *Wood v. Georgia.*[42]

> In the midst of a local political campaign, a County Judge, in the presence of representatives of news media assembled at the Judge's request, issued a charge to a grand jury giving it special instructions to investigate rumors and accusations of alleged bloc voting by Negroes and the rumored use of money by political candidates to obtain their votes. The next day, while the grand jury was in session, petitioner [James I. Wood], an elected Sheriff who was a candidate for reelection, issued from his office in the same building a press statement criticizing the Judge's action and urging citizens to take notice when their judges threatened political intimidation and persecution of voters under the guise of law enforcement. Petitioner was cited in the County Court for contempt, on the ground that his statement was calculated to be contemptuous of the Court and to obstruct the grand jury in its investigation and that it constituted a "clear, present and imminent danger" to the administration of justice.

Wood was convicted, and his conviction was upheld by Georgia's appellate courts. The Supreme Court reversed, with Chief Justice Warren writing the Court's opinion. The question before the justices was whether "the exercise of the contempt power, to commit a person to jail for an utterance out of the presence of the court, has abridged the accused's liberty of free expression."

The chief justice pointed out that punishments for "out-of-court publications were to be governed by the clear and present danger standard, described as 'a working principle that the substantive evil must be extremely serious and the danger of imminence extremely high before utterances can be punished.'" Applying that standard to the statements made by Wood, the chief justice concluded that the state had failed to prove the existence of any danger whatsoever to the work of the grand jury. Therefore, "in the absence of some other showing of a substantive evil actually designed to impede the course of justice in justification of the exercise of the contempt power to silence the petitioner, his utterances are entitled to be protected." Commenting upon the freedom to speak, the chief justice stated: "Men are entitled to speak as they please on matters vital to them; errors in judgment or unsubstantiated opinions may be exposed, of course, but not through punishment for contempt for the expression. Under our system of government, counterargument and education are the weapons available to expose these matters, not abridgement of the rights of free speech and assembly."

The case of Julian Bond, who was black, presented the Court with an unusual case involving the right to hold and express unpopular ideas. In 1965, Bond was elected to the Georgia House of Representatives. At the time, he was communications director of the Student Nonviolent Coordinating Committee (SNCC), an organization involved in the civil rights movement. In January

1966, before Bond took his seat in the Georgia House, SNCC issued a statement opposing the government's policy in Vietnam and critical of the administration of the draft laws. Although Bond did not participate in writing the
statement, he agreed with it, and "added that he admired the courage of persons
who burned their draft cards; that he was a pacifist who was eager and anxious to
encourage people not to participate in the war in Viet Nam for any reason that
they might choose; and said that as a second class citizen he did not feel that he
should be required to support the war in Vietnam."[43]

A challenge was made to Bond's being seated as a member of the Georgia
legislature. His opponents claimed that his prior statements, concerning the war
in Vietnam and the draft, made him unqualified to take the oath to support the
Constitution of the United States or the Constitution of Georgia. The House
voted 184–12 to deny Bond his seat. He brought an action in the federal district
court, but that court upheld the House and dismissed the petition. The Supreme
Court reversed, with Chief Justice Warren writing an opinion in which all the
justices concurred.

Georgia argued that it had the right to demand loyalty to the Constitution
of the United States and to its own Constitution. Warren agreed, but pointed
out that "this requirement does not authorize a majority of state legislators to
test the sincerity with which another duly elected legislator can swear to uphold
the Constitution. Such a power could be utilized to restrict the right of legislators to dissent from national or state policy or that of a majority of their colleagues under the guise of judging their loyalty to the Constitution."[44] Georgia
contended that legislators should be held to a higher standard of loyalty than citizens. Warren agreed, but pointed out that the "manifest function of the First
Amendment in a representative government requires that legislators [also] be
given the widest latitude to express their views on issues of policy. The central
commitment of the First Amendment, as summarized in the opinion of the
Court in *New York Times Co. v. Sullivan*, . . . is that 'debate on public issues
should be uninhibited, robust, and wide-open.'" "We therefore hold," he continued, "that the disqualification of Bond from membership in the Georgia
House because of his statements violated Bond's right of free expression under
the First Amendment."

David Paul O'Brien did not fare as well as Julian Bond when he burned his
draft card on the steps of the South Boston courthouse in protest against the
draft. O'Brien was charged and convicted for knowingly destroying and mutilat-
ing his draft card in violation of federal law. He argued that by destroying his
registration certificate he was expressing his disagreement with the draft and
that therefore the act of burning the card was protected by the First
Amendment. Chief Justice Warren and a majority of the Court disagreed and
upheld the conviction.[45]

"We cannot accept the view," Warren asserted, "that an apparently limitless
variety of conduct can be labeled 'speech' whenever the person engaging in the

conduct intends thereby to express an idea." But even "when 'speech' and 'non-speech' elements are combined in the same course of conduct, a sufficiently important governmental interest in regulating the nonspeech element can justify incidental limitations on First Amendment freedoms." That was true in this case because the destruction of draft cards could substantially disrupt "the smooth and proper functioning of the system that Congress has established to raise armies." And "when O'Brien deliberately rendered unavailable his registration certificate, he willfully frustrated this governmental interest."

One afternoon Sidney Street heard a news report stating that noted civil rights activist James Meredith had been shot while walking along a road in Mississippi.

> Saying to himself, "They didn't protect him," . . . [Street], himself a Negro, took from his drawer a neatly folded, 48-star American flag which he formerly had displayed on national holidays. [He] left his apartment and carried the still-folded flag to the nearby intersection of St. James Place and Lafayette Avenue [Brooklyn]. [He] stood on the northeast corner of the intersection, lit the flag with a match, and dropped the flag on the pavement when it began to burn.[46]

As the flag burned, Street was heard to say, "Yes; that is my flag; I burned it. If they let that happen to Meredith we don't need an American flag." One witness thought Street had said, "We don't need no damn flag."

Street was arrested and convicted of violating a New York statute making it a crime to "publicly . . . mutilate, deface, defile, or defy, trample upon, or cast contempt upon either by words or act [any flag of the United States]." Because the Court thought there was a possibility that Street might have been convicted for what he *said*, as well as for what he *did*, it reversed the conviction. The chief justice dissented.

Addressing the question of whether flag burning as a means of protest was protected by the First Amendment, the chief justice said that such protest was not protected. "I believe that the States and the Federal Government," he declared, "do have the power to protect the flag from acts of desecration and disgrace. . . . It is difficult for me to imagine that, had the Court faced this issue, it would have concluded otherwise. Since I am satisfied that the constitutionality of appellant's conduct should be resolved in this case and am convinced that this conduct can be criminally punished, I dissent."

When John Tinker, age 15, and Mary Beth Tinker, age 13, wore black armbands to school to protest the Vietnam war, they were suspended until they agreed to return to school without the armbands. In protest of their suspension, the Tinkers brought an action against the school district seeking an injunction against enforcement of the armband rule, and damages. Judge Roy L. Stephenson gave judgment for the school district, which was affirmed by the circuit court. The Supreme Court reversed, in an opinion written by Justice Fortas, in which the chief justice concurred.[47] The majority had no problem agreeing that the "wearing of an armband for the purpose of expressing certain views is the type of symbolic act that is within the Free Speech Clause of the First Amendment." Wearing an armband, Justice Fortas said, "was closely akin to 'pure speech' which, we have repeatedly held, is entitled to comprehensive protection under the First Amendment." Furthermore, it "can hardly be argued that either students or teachers shed their constitutional rights to freedom of speech or expression at the schoolhouse gate."

The majority took issue with several of the school district's arguments made to justify the armband prohibition. The armbands, for example, did not cause any disruption at the school. Also, while armbands were banned, students were allowed to wear buttons relating to national political campaigns and even the Nazi iron cross. "Clearly," Fortas argued, "the prohibition of expression of one particular opinion, at least without evidence that it is necessary to avoid material and substantial interference with schoolwork or discipline, is not constitutionally permissible."

In summation, Fortas wrote:

> Under our Constitution, free speech is not a right that is given only to be so circumscribed that it exists in principle but not in fact. Freedom of expression would not truly exist if the right could be exercised only in an area that a benevolent government has provided as a safe haven for crackpots. The Constitution says that Congress [and the States] may not abridge the right to free speech. This provision means what it says. We properly read it to permit reasonable regulation of speech-connected activities in carefully restricted circumstances. But we do not confine the permissible exercise of First Amendment rights to a telephone booth or the four corners of a pamphlet, or to supervised and ordained discussion in a school classroom.

Chief Justice Warren agreed.

Freedom of Association

Affidavits and Oaths. Warren concurred in a number of cases in which the Court struck down loyalty oaths. One of those cases was *Baggett v. Bullitt*.[48] This case was brought by Lawrence W. Baggett, together with a number of professors and employees at the University of Washington, against the president of the university and others. Plaintiffs sought a declaration that oaths required by state law to be taken by state employees were unconstitutional as a violation of their rights to free speech and association. The employee was required to swear that he or she was not a "subversive person," as that phrase was defined at great length in the laws of the state. The federal court upheld the oath, and Baggett and the others appealed to the Supreme Court, which reversed. Justice Byron White wrote the opinion.

Justice White expressed concern that a teacher would not know what activities he or she participated in would violate the oath. "Does the statute," he asks, "reach endorsement or support for Communist candidates for office? Does it reach a lawyer who represents the Communist Party or its members or a journalist who defends constitutional rights of the Communist Party or its members or anyone who supports any cause which is likewise supported by Communists or the Communist Party?" The Court, he said, has heretofore struck down statutes that require "forswearing of an undefined variety of 'guiltless knowing behavior.' " The Washington oath, like those others, is therefore "unconstitutionally vague." Such laws are a threat to the exercise of the right to freedom of speech.

"Those with a conscientious regard for what they solemnly swear or affirm, sensitive to the perils posed by the oath's indefinite language," White noted, "avoid the risk of loss of employment, and perhaps profession, only by restricting their conduct to that which is unquestionably safe. Free speech may not be so inhibited."

Chief Justice Warren voted to strike down oaths in *Cramp v. Bd. of Public Instruction*,[49] *Keyishian v. Board of Regents*,[50] *Elfbrandt v. Russell*,[51] and *Whitehill v. Elkins*.[52] Commenting on prior oath cases, Justice Douglas wrote in *Whitehill*: "Like the other cases mentioned, we have another classic example of the need for 'narrowly drawn' legislation . . . in this sensitive and important First Amendment area."

Punishment for Associational Membership. Robel, a member of the Communist Party, worked as a machinist for Todd Shipyards in Seattle, Washington. He was convicted of violating a federal law that made it a crime to work in a defense facility while a member of a Communist-action organization not registered with the government.[53]

The trial judge dismissed the charge. The government appealed, but the Supreme Court affirmed and held that the law itself was "an unconstitutional abridgment of the right of association protected by the First Amendment."

The government argued that the law should be upheld because it was enacted by Congress pursuant to its war powers. To this the chief justice responded that "for almost two centuries, our country has taken singular pride in the democratic ideals enshrined in its Constitution, and the most cherished of those ideals have found expression in the First Amendment. It would indeed be ironic if, in the name of national defense, we would sanction the subversion of one of those liberties—the freedom of association—which makes the defense of the Nation worthwhile."

Addressing the statute itself, Warren pointed out that it "quite literally establishes guilt by association alone, without any need to establish that an individual's association poses the threat feared by the Government proscribing it. The inhibiting effect on the exercise of First Amendment rights is clear."

Associational Privacy. Chief Justice Warren was part of the unanimous Court that made freedom of association part of the First Amendment in

N.A.A.C.P. v. Alabama.[54] Thereafter he consistently voted to uphold the individual's right to choose his or her associates as against government efforts to infringe upon that right. For example, he joined the majority in *Shelton v. Tucker.*[55] B.T. Shelton, who was black and had taught for 25 years in the Little Rock, Arkansas, Special School District, brought an action against the district asserting that certain sections of Arkansas laws relating to membership were unconstitutional. One of the laws Shelton specifically targeted required all teachers to file "an affidavit listing all organizations to which he [or she] at the time belongs and to which he [or she] has belonged during the past five years." Another law made it "unlawful for any member of the National Association for the Advancement of Colored People to be employed by the State of Arkansas or any of its subdivisions." The trial court upheld the law requiring the listing of memberships, but struck down the section that made members of the NAACP ineligible for public employment. Shelton appealed the court's decision regarding listing of memberships to the Supreme Court, which reversed.

"It is not disputed," Justice Stewart wrote for the Court,

> that to compel a teacher to disclose his every associational tie is to impair that teacher's right of free association, a right closely allied to freedom of speech and a right which, like speech, lies at the foundation of a free society. . . . Such interference with personal freedom is conspicuously accented when the teacher serves at the absolute will of those to whom the disclosure must be made—those who any year can terminate the teacher's employment without bringing charges, without notice, without a hearing, without affording an opportunity to explain.

"The unlimited and indiscriminate sweep of the statute now before us," Stewart continued, "brings it within the ban of our prior cases. The statute's comprehensive interference with associational freedom goes far beyond what might be justified in the exercise of the State's legitimate inquiry into the fitness and competency of its teachers." The chief justice concurred.

Daisy Bates and Birdie Williams were each fined $25 for refusing to furnish the city of Little Rock, Arkansas, the names of members of the NAACP. Bates was state president of the NAACP, and Williams held the same office in the North Little Rock branch. The Supreme Court of Arkansas upheld the fines, being of the opinion that the requirement of disclosure of membership was not unconstitutional. The U.S. Supreme Court unanimously disagreed and reversed, with Justice Stewart writing the Court's opinion.[56]

"Like freedom of speech and a free press," Justice Stewart noted, "the right of peaceable assembly was considered by the Framers of our Constitution to lie at the foundation of a government based upon the consent of an informed citizenry—a government dedicated to the establishment of justice and the preservation of liberty. . . . And it is now beyond dispute that freedom of association for the purpose of advancing ideas and airing grievances is protected by the Due

Process Clause of the Fourteenth Amendment from invasion by the States." In this case there was no question that disclosure of the names of members of the NAACP would adversely effect that organization. And after examining the evidence offered by the city, the Court could find no reason for requiring disclosure. "We conclude," Stewart declared, "that the municipalities have failed to demonstrate a controlling justification for the deterrence of free association which compulsory disclosure of the membership lists would cause. The petitioners cannot be punished for refusing to produce information which the municipalities could not constitutionally require." Again, the chief justice agreed. He also voted to protect associational privacy in many other cases.[57] In two of those cases, *Konigsberg v. State Bar*[58] and *In re Anastaplo*,[59] the chief justice joined Black's dissents when the majority upheld a requirement that applicants to the bar be required to answer questions concerning their past associations. Justice Black's comments concerning George Anastaplo illustrate what can happen when justices follow form over substance.

> For this record shows that Anastaplo has many of the qualities that are needed in the American Bar. It shows, not only that Anastaplo has followed a high moral, ethical and patriotic course in all of the activities of his life, but also that he combines these more common virtues with the uncommon virtue of courage to stand by his principles at any cost. It is such men as these who have most greatly honored the profession of the law—men like Malsherbes, who, at the cost of his own life and the lives of his family, sprang unafraid to the defense of Louis XVI against the fanatical leaders of the Revolutionary government of France—men like Charles Evans Hughes, Sr., later Mr. Chief Justice Hughes, who stood up for the constitutional right of socialists to be socialists and public officials despite the threats and clamorous protests of self-proclaimed superpatriots—men like Charles Evans Hughes, Jr., and John W. Davis, who, while against everything for which the Communists stood, strongly advised the Congress in 1948 that it would be unconstitutional to pass the law then proposed to outlaw the Communist Party—men like Lord Erskine, James Otis, Clarence Darrow, and the multitude of others who have dared to speak in defense of causes and clients without regard to personal danger to themselves. The legal profession will lose much of its nobility and its glory if it is not constantly replenished with lawyers like these. To force the Bar to become a group of thoroughly orthodox, time-serving, government-fearing individuals is to humiliate and degrade it.

Warren voted with the majority to uphold the right of associations to use their resources to provide legal services for their members in three cases.[60] In one of these cases, Justice Black wrote for the majority: "We hold that the First and Fourteenth Amendments protect the right of the members through their Brotherhood to maintain and carry out their plan for advising workers who are injured to obtain legal advice and for recommending specific lawyers."[61]

Freedom of the Press

Libel. Chief Justice Warren expressed his views on libel and freedom of the press in the *Wally Butts* case discussed in Chapter 4. He agreed that the judgment in favor of Coach Butts should be upheld. He was also of the opinion that in libel cases "public figures" should be held to the same high standard as "public officials," which was the standard adopted by the Court in the *New York Times Co.* case. Applying that standard to "public figures," would mean that such a person could not recover damages for libel unless he or she could prove that the press acted with "actual malice"—that is, "with knowledge that the [material published] was false or with reckless disregard of whether it was false or not." "To me," the chief justice declared, "differentiation between 'public figures' and 'public officials' and adoption of separate standards of proof for each have no basis in law, logic, or First Amendment policy."[62] He pointed out that in our complex society persons who are "public figures" play a greater role "in the resolution of important questions, or, by their fame, shape events in areas of concern to society at large."

Commenting on the Curtis Publishing Company's handling of the story concerning the alleged exchange of football information between Coach Paul ("Bear") Bryant of Alabama and Coach Butts, the chief justice said that the "slipshod and sketchy investigatory techniques employed to check the veracity of the source and the inferences to be drawn from the few facts believed to be true are detailed at length in the opinion of" the Court. "I am satisfied," he continued, "that the evidence here discloses that degree of reckless disregard for the truth of which we spoke in *New York Times*. . . . Freedom of the press under the First Amendment does not include absolute license to destroy lives or careers."[63]

Versus the Right of Privacy. "[James Hill] and his wife and five children involuntarily became the subjects of a front-page news story after being held hostage by three escaped convicts in their suburban, Whitemarsh, Pennsylvania, home for 19 hours on September 11–12, 1952. The family was released unharmed. In an interview with newsmen after the convicts had departed, . . . [Hill] stressed that the convicts had treated the family courteously, had not molested them, and had not been violent at all."[64]

In 1953 Joseph Hayes wrote a novel titled *The Desperate Hours*, which was later made into a play. "The story depicted the experience of a family of four held hostage by three escaped convicts in the family's suburban home. But unlike Hill's experience, the family of the story suffer violence at the hands of the convicts; the father and son are beaten and the daughter subjected to a verbal sexual insult."

Life magazine, in its February 1955 issue, carried a story titled "True Crime Inspires Tense Play," with the subtitle, "The ordeal of a family trapped by convicts gives Broadway a new thriller, 'The Desperate Hours.'" The story referred to "the desperate ordeal of the James Hill family, who were held prisoners in their home outside Philadelphia by three escaped convicts." In addition, the magazine carried photographs of the Hill house and of some scenes in the play, including "an enactment of the son being 'roughed up' by one of the convicts, entitled 'brutish convict,' a picture of the daughter biting the hand of a convict to make him drop a gun, entitled 'daring daughter,' and one of the father throwing his gun through the door after a 'brave try' to save his family is foiled."

James Hill sued Time, Inc., the publisher of *Life*, for invasion of privacy under a New York law allowing such an action, and recovered $50,000 in compensatory damages and $25,000 in punitive damages. An appellate court reversed and sent the case back for a new trial, which was then held before a judge without a jury. The judge awarded Hill $30,000 as compensation for invasion of the family's privacy, but did not allow any punitive damages. The New York Court of Appeals affirmed, but a majority of the Supreme Court voted to reverse. "We hold," Justice Brennan said, "that the constitutional protections for speech and press preclude the application of the New York statute to redress false reports of matters of public interest in the absence of proof that the defendant published the report with knowledge of its falsity or in reckless disregard of the truth."

Furthermore, "exposure of the self to others in varying degrees is a concomitant of life in a civilized community. The risk of this exposure is an essential incident of life in a society which places a primary value on freedom of speech and of press." The majority then sent the case back for a new trial in which the jury would be instructed that "a verdict of liability could be predicated only on a finding of knowing or reckless falsity in the publication of the *Life* article."

Justice Fortas, Chief Justice Warren, and Justice Clark dissented. At the outset, the dissenters wanted it understood that a right of privacy is among the rights enjoyed by people, and the Hill family's right of privacy was involved in this case. "There are great and important values in our society," Justice Fortas noted, "none of which is greater than those reflected in the First Amendment, but which are also fundamental and entitled to this Court's careful respect and protection. Among these is the right to privacy, which has been eloquently extolled by scholars and members of this Court." Conflicts between freedom of the press and this right to privacy require "the most careful and sensitive appraisal of the total impact of the claimed tort upon the congeries of rights is required." But that does not mean that a state cannot "provide a remedy for reckless falsity in writing and publishing an article which irresponsibly and injuriously invades the privacy of a quiet family for no purpose except dramatic interest and commercial appeal."

Justice Fortas, for himself, the Chief Justice, and Justice Clark, then discusses the responsibility of courts in conflicts of this kind:

> The courts may not and must not permit either public or private action that censors or inhibits the press. But part of this responsibility is to preserve values and

procedures which assure the ordinary citizen that the press is not above the reach of the law—that its special prerogatives, granted because of its special and vital functions, are reasonably equated with its needs in the performance of these functions. For this Court totally to immunize the press—whether forthrightly or by subtle indirection—in areas far beyond the needs of news, comment on public persons and events, discussion of public issues and the like would be no service to freedom of the press, but an invitation to public hostility to that freedom. This Court cannot and should not refuse to permit under state law the private citizen who is aggrieved by the type of assault which we have here and which is not within the specially protected core of the First Amendment to recover compensatory damages for recklessly inflicted invasion of his rights.

Obscenity. David S. Alberts was convicted of "lewdly keeping for sale obscene and indecent books, and with writing, composing, and publishing an obscene advertisement of them, in violation of the California Penal Code."[65] His conviction was upheld by the Supreme Court. The chief justice concurred in the result, but approached the matter differently from the majority.

Warren noted that in obscenity cases the law has focused upon the effect the material has upon the recipient. "But," he argued, "there is more to these cases. . . . It is not the book that is on trial; it is a person. The conduct of the defendant is the central issue, not the obscenity of a book or picture." Alberts was "engaged in the business of purveying textual or graphic matter openly advertised to appeal to the erotic interest of . . . [his] customers. [He was] plainly engaged in the commercial exploitation of the morbid and shameful craving for materials with prurient effect. I believe that the State and the Federal Governments can constitutionally punish such conduct."

The chief justice expressed the same view in dissenting in another case decided the same day. In this case, the Court upheld a New York law by which officials of a municipality could obtain an injunction against a person distributing obscene material and have the materials destroyed. Warren dissented. He again thought the majority was wrong in focusing upon the obscenity of the book. "Unlike the criminal cases decided today, this New York law places the book on trial. There is totally lacking any standard in the statute for judging the book in context. The personal element basic to the criminal law is entirely absent. In my judgment, the same object may have wholly different impact depending upon the setting in which it is placed."[66] He continued: "It is the manner of use that should determine obscenity. It is the conduct of the individual that should be judged, not the quality of art or literature. To do otherwise is to impose a prior restraint and hence to violate the Constitution. Certainly in the absence of a prior judicial determination of illegal use, books, pictures and other objects of expression should not be destroyed. It savors too much of book burning."

The chief justice was concerned about "book burning" when he wrote a lengthy dissent in *Times Film Corp. v. Chicago*.[67] In that case, the Court upheld a

Chicago ordinance that required all motion pictures to be submitted to the commissioner of police for approval and a permit to exhibit. To Warren this was blatant censorship. "To me," he argued, "this case clearly presents the question of our approval of unlimited censorship of motion pictures before exhibition through a system of administrative licensing. Moreover, the decision presents a real danger of eventual censorship for every form of communication, be it newspapers, journals, books, magazines, television, radio or public speeches." "Let it be completely clear," he continued,

> what the Court's decision does. It gives official license to the censor, approving a grant of power to city officials to prevent the showing of any moving picture these officials deem unworthy of a license. It thus gives formal sanction to censorship in its purest and most far-reaching form, to a classical plan of licensing that, in our country, most closely approaches the English licensing laws of the seventeenth century which were commonly used to suppress dissent in the mother country and in the colonies.

When the Court reversed the conviction of Nico Jacobellis for possessing and exhibiting the film *Les Amants* (*The Lovers*),[68] Warren dissented. He did not, however, abandon his view that it was "the use to which various materials are put—not just the words and pictures themselves—[that] must be considered in determining whether or not the materials are obscene." Referring to the attempt of the majority to find an acceptable definition for obscenity, the chief justice wrote:

> For all the sound and fury that the *Roth* test has generated, it has not been proved unsound, and I believe that we should try to live with it—at least until a more satisfactory definition is evolved. No government—be it federal, state, or local—should be forced to choose between repressing all material, including that within the realm of decency, and allowing unrestrained licence to publish any material, no matter how vile. There must be a rule of reason in this as in other areas of the law, and we have attempted in the *Roth* case to provide such a rule.

After *Jacobellis*, and before he retired in 1969, Chief Justice Warren voted to reverse other cases where the Court found errors in the procedures used by the government in prosecuting obscenity cases.[69] He voted to uphold convictions in three cases where the defendant either mailed, possessed, or sold obscene material.[70] The chief justice also voted to reverse the convictions of two individuals for selling allegedly obscene publications.[71]

The Pursuit of Liberty

The Right to Travel, to Privacy, and to Work. The chief justice agreed with the statement in *Kent v. Dulles*[72] that "freedom to travel is, indeed, an important aspect of the citizen's 'liberty.'" And in cases dealing with the right to travel over-seas, he generally voted to uphold the right of the traveler.[73] But when the government banned most travel to Cuba, he wrote the opinion for the Court upholding that ban as against the claim of a constitutional right to travel.[74]

Louis Zemel had a valid United States passport. When the State Department refused to validate the passport for travel to Cuba, Zemel brought an action against Secretary of State Dean Rusk asking the court to order the secretary to do so. The court refused, and the Supreme Court upheld that decision.

Warren acknowledged that the right to travel was a part of the liberty protected by the Due Process Clause of the Fifth Amendment. But he pointed out that "the fact that a liberty cannot be inhibited without due process of law does not mean that it can under no circumstances be inhibited." In this case, the ban on travel was justified by two important governmental interests: (1) the potential for spread of Communism because of Cuba's Communist regime, and (2) the risk of creating an international incident were an American citizen to be detained in Cuba. The chief justice pointed out that even travel within the United States can be banned from "areas ravaged by flood, fire or pestilence." That being true, surely a ban on international travel is permissible.

In *United States v. Guest,*[75] Chief Justice Warren voted with the majority to recognize a right to travel within the United States. However, he dissented when the Court held that a one-year residency requirement before one could receive welfare payments violated the individual's right to travel.[76] "Since the congressional decision is rational," he argued, "and the restriction on travel insubstantial, I conclude that residence requirements can be imposed by Congress as an exercise of its power to control interstate commerce consistent with the constitutionally guaranteed right to travel."

Although Warren voted to uphold a right of privacy in *Griswold v. Connecticut,*[77] he did not join Justice Douglas's majority opinion. Instead, he signed on to the concurring opinion of Justice Arthur J. Goldberg. "I do agree," Justice Goldberg declared, "that the concept of liberty protects those personal rights that are fundamental, and is not confined to the specific terms of the Bill of Rights." Not being confined to the Bill of Rights means that liberty encompasses more rights than those listed, and the Ninth Amendment supports the existence of such rights. "The Ninth Amendment reads, 'The enumeration in the Constitution, of certain rights, shall not be construed to deny or disparage others retained by the people.'" Among the others retained by the people is the right of marital privacy. "To hold that a right so basic and fundamental and so deep-rooted in our society as the right of privacy in marriage," Goldberg argued, "may be infringed because that right is not guaranteed in so many words by the first eight amendments to the Constitution is to ignore the Ninth Amendment and to give it no effect whatsoever." The justice concluded his concurring opinion by stating "that the right of privacy in the marital relation is fundamental and basic—a personal right 'retained by the people' within the meaning of the Ninth

Amendment. Connecticut cannot constitutionally abridge this fundamental right, which is protected by the Fourteenth Amendment from infringement by the States. I agree with the Court that petitioners' convictions must therefore be reversed."

Despite the dissents of justices Black, Frankfurter, and Douglas, the chief justice voted with the majority to uphold the revocation of Dr. Barsky's license to practice medicine. In support of Dr. Barsky, Justice Frankfurter wrote: "It is one thing thus to recognize the freedom which the Constitution wisely leaves to the States in regulating the professions. It is quite another thing, however, to sanction a State's deprivation or partial destruction of a man's professional life on grounds having no possible relation to fitness, intellectual or moral, to pursue his profession."[78]

Equal Protection of the Law

Exclusion of Minorities from Juries. Pete Hernandez, a person of Mexican descent, was tried and convicted for the murder of Joe Espinosa. At time of trial, Hernandez, through his lawyer, objected to the impaneling of the grand jury and the jury that was to try him on the grounds that persons of Mexican descent had been excluded from both juries, and that that was a denial of equal protection of the law. Judge Frank W. Martin denied the objections, and his decision was affirmed by the Texas Court of Criminal Appeals. A unanimous Supreme Court, in an opinion written by Chief Justice Warren, reversed.[79]

The chief justice quickly disposed of Texas's argument that "there are only two classes—white and Negro—within the contemplation of the Fourteenth Amendment." "The decisions of this Court," he asserted, "do not support that view." "The exclusion of otherwise eligible persons from jury service solely because of their ancestry or national origin," he continued, "is discrimination prohibited by the Fourteenth Amendment."

Hernandez argued that the discrimination against him occurred in the administration of the jury selection laws. Commenting upon the evidence relating to jury service, Warren noted that "it taxes our credulity to say that mere chance resulted in there being no members of this class [Mexicans] among the over six thousand jurors called in the past 25 years." Summing up Hernandez's argument, Warren wrote, "The petitioner did not seek proportional representation, nor did he claim a right to have persons of Mexican descent sit on the particular juries which he faced. His only claim is the right to be indicted and tried by juries from which all members of his class are not systematically excluded—juries selected from among all qualified persons regardless of national origin or descent. To this much, he is entitled by the Constitution."

The chief justice voted with the majority in four cases wherein the Court found systematic exclusion of blacks from juries.[80] One of those cases involved Amos Reece, a black man who had been convicted and sentenced to be electrocuted for having raped a white woman. Under Georgia law, objections to the composition of a grand jury had to be made before the jury returned its indictment. Reece, who was semi-illiterate, was already in jail and an attorney was not appointed to represent him until after the indictment was given.

Before trial, Reece's attorney moved to quash the indictment. He supported the motion with uncontradicted evidence that blacks had been systemically excluded from juries in that county. The trial court denied the motion, and the Georgia Supreme Court affirmed. All the justices of the U.S. Supreme Court voted to reverse, and Justice Clark was assigned to write the Court's opinion. "This Court," Clark declared, "over the past 50 years has adhered to the view that valid grand-jury selection is a constitutionally protected right. The indictment of a defendant by a grand jury from which members of his race have been systematically excluded is a denial of his right to equal protection of the laws."[81] In commenting upon whether Reece had ample opportunity to raise the issue before the indictment was given, Clark noted, "It is utterly unrealistic to say that he had such an opportunity when counsel was not provided for him until the day after he was indicted."

Warren dissented in two cases where the majority upheld the state's jury selection procedures as against a claim of racial discrimination.[82]

Integration of Schools and Universities. Few cases have caught the public's attention as did *Brown v. Board of Education*,[83] wherein the Court unanimously ruled that separate but equal public schools violated the Equal Protection Clause. Much credit belongs to Warren for molding that unanimity.

After some comments regarding prior cases dealing with the concept of separate but equal, Chief Justice Warren framed the question in *Brown*, and gave the Court's answer: "We come then to the question presented: Does segregation of children in public schools solely on the basis of race, even though the physical facilities and other 'tangible' factors may be equal, deprive the children of the minority group of equal educational opportunities? We believe that it does."

"We conclude," Warren declared, "that in the field of public education the doctrine of 'separate but equal' has no place. Separate educational facilities are inherently unequal. Therefore, we hold that the plaintiffs and others similarly situated for whom the actions have been brought are, by reason of the segregation complained of, deprived of the equal protection of the laws guaranteed by the Fourteenth Amendment."

In four subsequent cases relating to the desegregation of public schools, the chief justice voted to require integration "with all deliberate speed."[84] He also voted to require the University of Alabama to admit Autherine J. Lucy and Polly Anne Myers, who were both black,[85] and to require the University of Florida to admit Virgil D. Hawkins, who was black, to its law school.[86]

Integration of Private Facilities. On August 9, 1960, ten black boys and girls went into the S.H. Kress store, in Greenville, South Carolina, and sat at the lunch counter. The store manager told one of the employees to call the police and then turned off the lights, indicating that the counter was closed. When the police arrived, they arrested the ten and charged them with trespass because they had refused to leave the store when requested to do so by the manager. At the time, Greenville had an ordinance that required separation of the races in restaurants. Each of the individuals was convicted and ordered to pay a fine of $100, or spend 30 days in jail. When the case reached the Supreme Court, it reversed. "It cannot be denied that here," the chief justice wrote, "the City of Greenville, an agency of the State, has provided by its ordinance that the decision as to whether a restaurant facility is to be operated on a desegregated basis is to be reserved to it."[87] And it made no difference that the manager would have acted the same without the ordinance. "When a state agency passes a law," Warren asserted, "compelling persons to discriminate against other persons because of race, and the State's criminal processes are employed in a way which enforces the discrimination mandated by that law, such a palpable violation of the Fourteenth Amendment cannot be saved by attempting to separate the mental urges of the discriminators."

Sometimes the connection between the government and the private facility is indirect. For example, in *Lombard v. Louisiana*,[88] when black students were attempting to integrate lunch counters in New Orleans, Louisiana, the superintendent of police issued a statement urging the parents of both black and white students to refrain from further sit-in demonstrations. Everyone should understand, he said, that "the police department and its personnel is ready and able to enforce the laws" of the city and the state. The mayor also made a statement in which he said that he had "directed the superintendent of police that no additional sit-in demonstrations . . . will be permitted."

Despite these warnings, three black students and one white student staged a sit-in at the McCrory Five and Ten Cent Store, and when they did not leave at the suggestion of the police they were charged with trespass. They were convicted in Judge J. Bernard Cocke's court, sentenced to 60 days in jail, and fined $350, all of which was affirmed by the Louisiana Supreme Court.

The U.S. Supreme Court reversed in an opinion written by Chief Justice Warren. Addressing the question of the city's involvement in the segregation of the lunch counter, Warren stated, "as we interpret the New Orleans city officials' statements, they here determined that the city would not permit Negroes to seek desegregated service in restaurants. Consequently, the city must be treated exactly as if it had an ordinance prohibiting such conduct." And therefore the students were denied equal protection of the law and the convictions must be reversed.

The chief justice voted to find the government involved in the enforcement of segregation in private facilities in a number of other cases.[89]

Integration of Public Facilities. During the afternoon of January 23, 1961, a group of young blacks was playing basketball in Daffin Park in Savannah,

Georgia. At the request of a white woman, two police officers went to investigate, and upon finding the blacks there arrested and charged them with breach of the peace. At their trial one of the officers testified: "I have never made previous arrests in Daffin Park because people played basketball there . . . I arrested these people for playing basketball in Daffin Park. One reason was because they were negroes. I observed the conduct of these people, when they were on the basketball court and they were doing nothing besides playing basketball, they were just normally playing basketball, and none of the children from the schools were there at that particular time."[90]

The basketball players were convicted of breach of the peace. Five were fined $100 or given a jail sentence of five months. Wright, the sixth player, was fined $125 or six months in jail. The convictions were upheld by the Georgia Supreme Court, but all justices of the U.S. Supreme voted to reverse, with the chief justice writing the Court's opinion. Georgia authorities made three arguments as to why the convictions should be upheld. "First, it is said that failure to obey the command of a police officer constitutes a traditional form of breach of the peace." Warren responded, "Obviously, however, one cannot be punished for failing to obey the command of an officer if that command is itself violative of the Constitution." In this case, it was clear that the officers intended to enforce racial segregation in the use of the park and that violated the players' right to equal protection of the law. "Second, it is argued that petitioners were guilty of a breach of the peace because their activity was likely to cause a breach of the peace by others." But there was no evidence that anyone witnessing the defendants playing basketball was disturbed by what he or she saw. Finally, the state argued that "the petitioners were guilty of a breach of the peace because a park rule reserved the playground for the use of younger people at the time." The police, however, gave the players no warning of such a rule because they themselves didn't know such a rule existed, and furthermore there were no signs setting forth times for use of the park. The chief justice concluded by pointing out that the defendants did not have adequate notice that what they were doing was a breach of the peace. "It is well established," he noted, "that a conviction under a criminal enactment which does not give adequate notice that the conduct charged is prohibited is violative of due process."

Other cases in which Chief Justice Warren voted to integrate public facilities are: *Burton v. Wilmington Parking Authority*[91] (public parking ramp), *Johnson v. Virginia*[92] (a courtroom), *Watson v. Memphis*[93] (public parks), and *Evans v. Newton*[94] (Senator Bacon's park in Macon, Georgia).

Whom Blacks Live With. Mildred Jeter, a black woman, and Richard Loving, a white man, were married in Washington, D.C., and they then moved to Virginia. Shortly thereafter they pled guilty to violating a Virginia statute prohibiting interracial marriages and were sentenced to one year in jail. The judge, however, agreed to suspend the sentence "on the condition that the Lovings leave the State and not return to Virginia for 25 years."[95] The Lovings returned to Washington and a few years later brought legal action in Virginia to vacate the prior judgment, arguing that it violated their rights to equal protection of the law. The Virginia courts refused to vacate the judgment, and the Lovings appealed to the Supreme Court, which unanimously agreed that the Virginia law discriminated against them. Virginia had argued that there was no discrimination here because both blacks and whites were treated equally—that is, both were guilty under the law. The justices, however, did not buy that argument, and concluded that there was "patently no legitimate overriding purpose independent of invidious racial discrimination which justifies this classification." Noting that the Court had previously held that marriage was one of the "basic civil rights of man," Chief Justice Warren wrote:

> To deny this fundamental freedom on so unsupportable a basis as the racial classifications embodied in these statutes, classifications so directly subversive of the principle of equality at the heart of the Fourteenth Amendment, is surely to deprive all the State's citizens of liberty without due process of law. The Fourteenth Amendment requires that the freedom of choice to marry not be restricted by invidious racial classifications. Under our Constitution, the freedom to marry, or not to marry, a person of another race resides with the individual and cannot be infringed by the State.

For Illegitimate Children. Minnie Brade Glona brought suit against the American Guarantee & Liability Insurance Company and its insured for the death of her illegitimate son in an auto accident. The company denied liability because under Louisiana law no cause of action for wrongful death could be brought for the death of illegitimate children. Judge Frederick J.R. Heebe dismissed the action, and the circuit court of appeals affirmed. A majority of the Supreme Court, including the chief justice, voted to reverse, with Justice Douglas authoring the Court's opinion.[96] Douglas pointed out that Louisiana did not condemn illegitimacy in all circumstances. "When a married woman gives birth to an illegitimate child," he noted, "he is, with a few exceptions, conclusively presumed to be legitimate. Louisiana makes no distinction between legitimate children and illegitimate children where incest is concerned. A mother may inherit from an illegitimate child whom she has acknowledged and vice versa. If the illegitimate son had a horse that was killed by the defendant and then died himself, his mother would have a right to sue for the loss of that property." Douglas thought that the Louisiana law created "an open season on illegitimates in the area of automobile accidents [and] gives a windfall to tortfeasors." He did not believe that there was any connection between denial of wrongful death for the loss of an illegitimate child and the alleged "sin" of the mother in giving birth to such a child. "To say that the test of equal protection," he asserted, "should be the 'legal' rather than the biological relationship is to avoid the issue. For the Equal Protection Clause necessarily limits the authority of a State to draw such 'legal' lines as it chooses."

For Voters.

> Morris H. Kramer, a college graduate, is a twenty-eight-year-old bachelor who resides in the private home of his parents located in Atlantic Beach, New York, within the confines of District No. 15. He has lived with his parents for many years, and he has voted in federal and state elections since 1959. He is not a property owner, a lessee or a parent with school-age children. On April 25, 1965, he attempted to register in the forthcoming school district election, but his application was rejected by defendants on the ground that he failed to meet the special voter qualifications set forth in Section 2012.[97]

Under New York State law, to be qualified to vote in school district elections, one had to be either a property owner, the spouse of a property owner, or have school-age children in the school. Kramer brought an action in the federal court challenging the constitutionality of the law, but the court dismissed the action. Kramer was successful, however, in the Supreme Court, which reversed, with the chief justice writing for the majority.[98]

The school district argued that the reason for the voting restrictions was that only those persons "primarily interested" and "directly" affected would then be voting on school matters.

The chief justice pointed out that limiting the right to vote could be sustained only by some "compelling state interest." "This careful examination is necessary," he said, "because statutes distributing the franchise constitute the foundation of our representative society. Any unjustified discrimination in determining who may participate in political affairs or in the selection of public officials undermines the legitimacy of representative government." In this case the reasons assigned for the restrictions were not compelling. "The requirements of Section 2012," he wrote, "are not sufficiently tailored to limiting the franchise to those 'primarily interested' in school affairs to justify the denial of the franchise to . . . [Kramer] and members of his class."

The chief justice joined Justice Douglas's majority opinion in *Harper v. Virginia Bd. of Elections,*[99] holding that the Virginia poll tax violated the Equal Protection Clause. And he voted with the majority to hold that a Louisiana law, which allowed only property-tax payers to vote on revenue bonds, violated equal protection.[100]

In the Criminal Justice System. In *Griffin v. Illinois,*[101] Justice Black wrote, "Providing equal justice for poor and rich, weak and powerful alike is an age-old problem. People have never ceased to hope and strive to move closer to that goal." Warren joined that opinion. He had an opportunity to state his views when he authored the opinion in *Burns v. Ohio.*[102] Burns was in an Ohio prison, sentenced to life imprisonment for burglary. He prepared and filed an appeal but did nothing for several years when he sought to perfect the appeal to the Ohio Supreme Court. With the copy of the previous notice of appeal, he filed an affidavit stating that he did not have the $20 necessary to pay the court's filing fee. The clerk of the Ohio Supreme Court returned the papers stating that the case could not be docketed without payment of the costs. Burns filed an appeal with the U.S. Supreme Court, which held that he was denied equal protection of the law, and sent the case back for reconsideration by the Ohio Supreme Court. "Here, the action of the State," the chief justice asserted, "has completely barred the petitioner from obtaining any review at all in the Supreme Court of Ohio. The imposition by the State of financial barriers restricting the availability of appellate review for indigent criminals has no place in our heritage of Equal Protection Under Law."

Chief Justice Warren voted for the indigent prisoner in a number of other cases before he retired.[103] One of those cases involved Neal Merle Smith, who was in the Iowa penitentiary for breaking and entering. When Smith sought to file a petition for writ of *habeas corpus* with the Iowa District Court, the petition was returned because Smith did not pay the four-dollar filing fee. Smith had filed with the petition an affidavit of poverty. When the Iowa Supreme Court refused to hear his appeal, he appealed to the U.S. Supreme Court, which held that he had been denied equal protection of the law. "Throughout the centuries," Justice Clark said, "the Great Writ has been the shield of personal freedom insuring liberty to persons illegally detained. Respecting the State's grant of a right to test their detention, the Fourteenth Amendment weighs the interests of rich and poor criminals in equal scale, and its hand extends as far to each. In failing to extend the privilege of the Great Writ to its indigent prisoners, Iowa denies them equal protection of the laws."[104]

Another one of those cases was *Rinaldi v. Yeager*.[105] Joseph A. Rinaldi had been convicted of several crimes, and he appealed. Because he was an indigent, the state furnished him with a transcript without cost. His appeal was unsuccessful, and he was incarcerated in the New Jersey State Prison, where he earned 20 cents a day working five days a week. His pay, however, was retained by the state to reimburse it $215 for the cost of the transcript furnished him for his appeal. Under New Jersey law, only those who had been furnished transcripts and were incarcerated were required to reimburse the state. A person who had received a free transcript and had been placed on probation need not pay for the transcript.

Rinaldi brought an action in the federal court to prevent the retention of his wages, arguing that his constitutional rights were being violated. The court disagreed, but on appeal to the Supreme Court Rinaldi was successful. In an opinion written by Justice Stewart, in which Warren joined, the Court held that the New Jersey procedures violated the Equal Protection Clause.

New Jersey argued that charging inmates for the transcripts deterred frivolous appeals. To this Justice Stewart responded: "Assuming a law enacted to perform that function to be otherwise valid, the present statutory classification is no less vulnerable under the Equal Protection Clause when viewed in relation to that function. By imposing a financial obligation only upon inmates of institutions, the statute inevitably burdens many whose appeals, though unsuccessful, were not frivolous, and leaves untouched many whose appeals may have been frivolous indeed."

The Bill of Rights and the States

In February 1964 Klopfer was tried for the crime of criminal trespass, but the jury failed to agree upon a verdict. At the April 1965 term of court, the prosecuting attorney received permission from the court to hold the case over to another term. Because Klopfer's case was not on the calendar for the August 1965 term, he filed a motion to have the case concluded as soon as possible, pointing out that 18 months had passed since he was indicted. At that time, the prosecutor requested permission from the court to take a *nolle prosequi* with leave, which was granted. This made it possible for the case to be tried at some indefinite date in the future, leaving Klopfer in limbo. Klopfer appealed to the North Carolina Supreme Court, claiming that he had been denied his right to a speedy trial. That court held that although he did have a right to a speedy trial, that right had not been violated in this case. The U.S. Supreme Court unanimously disagreed. The chief justice wrote the opinion for the Court. Commenting upon the predicament Klopfer was in, Warren wrote:

> The petitioner is not relieved of the limitations placed upon his liberty by this prosecution merely because its suspension permits him to go "whithersoever he will." The pendency of the indictment may subject him to public scorn and deprive him of employment, and almost certainly will force curtailment of his speech, associations and participation in unpopular causes. By indefinitely prolonging this oppression, . . . the criminal procedure condoned in this case by the Supreme Court of North Carolina clearly denies the petitioner the right to a speedy trial which we hold is guaranteed to him by the Sixth Amendment of the Constitution of the United States.[106]

The chief justice then noted that the justices held differing opinions about which provisions of the Bill of Rights were applicable to the states under the Fourteenth Amendment. With regard to the right to a speedy trial, however, this case would settle that question. "We hold here," Warren declared, "that the right to a speedy trial is as fundamental as any of the rights secured by the Sixth Amendment. That right has its roots at the very foundation of our English law heritage."

> Jackie Washington, was convicted in Dallas County, Texas, of murder with malice and was sentenced by a jury to 50 years in prison. The prosecution's evidence showed that petitioner, an 18-year-old youth, had dated a girl named Jean Carter until her mother had forbidden her to see him. The girl thereafter began dating another boy, the deceased. . . . [On the night of August 29, 1964, Washington, a boy named Charles Fuller, and others went to the Carter home with a shotgun in their possession.] Some of the boys threw bricks at the home and then ran back

to the car, leaving petitioner and Fuller alone in front of the house with the shotgun. At the sound of the bricks the deceased and Jean Carter's mother rushed out on the porch to investigate. The shotgun was fired by either petitioner or Fuller, and the deceased fatally wounded. Shortly afterward petitioner and Fuller came running back to the car where the other boys waited, with Fuller carrying the shotgun.

Petitioner testified in his own behalf. He claimed that Fuller, who was intoxicated, had taken the gun from him and that he had unsuccessfully tried to persuade Fuller to leave before the shooting.[107]

Fuller, who had been convicted of this murder, was not allowed to testify at Washington's trial because Texas law "provided . . . [that] persons charged or convicted as coparticipants in the same crime could not testify for one another, although there was no bar to their testifying for the State." Although the Texas Court of Appeals upheld Washington's conviction, the Supreme Court reversed.

One of the questions before the Court was "whether the right of an accused to have compulsory process for obtaining witnesses in his favor, guaranteed in federal trials by the Sixth Amendment, is so fundamental and essential to a fair trial that it is incorporated in the Due Process Clause of the Fourteenth Amendment." The chief justice answered the question in the affirmative. "The right to offer the testimony of witnesses," he declared, "and to compel their attendance, if necessary, is in plain terms the right to present a defense, the right to present the defendant's version of the facts as well as the prosecution's to the jury so it may decide where the truth lies. Just as an accused has the right to confront the prosecution's witnesses for the purpose of challenging their testimony, he has the right to present his own witnesses to establish a defense. This right is a fundamental element of due process." The Court then concluded that Washington's right to call Fuller as a witness was denied in this case.

The chief justice voted to apply sections of the Bill of Rights to the states in many other cases.[108]

AS A JUDICIAL FREEDOM FIGHTER

Chief Justice Warren voted against the claim of Orthodox Jews that Sunday-closing laws placed a heavy burden upon their free exercise of religion because they were also required by their faith to close on Saturdays, their Sabbath. In doing so, he was not oblivious to the rights of the Jews. He just could not see how Sunday closing was an infringement upon those rights. He wrote that "the statute at bar does not make unlawful any religious practice of appellants; the Sunday law simply regulates a secular activity and, as applied to appellants, operates so as to make the practice of their religious beliefs more expensive."[109] Justice Stewart called this "a cruel choice."

With the exception of the two Sunday-closing votes, Warren thereafter voted to protect the free exercise of religion. And in his book *A Republic If You Can Keep It*,[110] he quotes the following passage from an opinion by Justice Tom Clark which he joined:

> Freedom to worship was indispensable in a country whose people came from the four corners of the earth and brought with them a diversity of religious opinion. . . . The place of religion in our society is an exalted one, achieved through a long tradition of reliance on the home, the church, and the inviolable citadel of the individual heart and mind. We have come to realize through bitter experience that it is not within the power of government to invade that citadel, whether its purpose or effect be to aid or oppose, to advance or retard. In the relationship between man and religion, the state is firmly committed to a position of neutrality.

Most of the time, the chief justice voted to uphold the right to speak freely, although he wrote only a few of the Court's free speech opinions. He authored the majority opinions to uphold the right of Sheriff James I. Wood to criticize the county judge, and that of Julian Bond to make statements the Georgia legislature did not like. He also voted to protect the right of students to wear armbands on school grounds.

Warren, however, did not approve of David O'Brien's burning his draft card. He thought that was punishable conduct, not speech. And he chided the majority for not deciding whether a person who burned an American flag could be punished. He addressed that question, and concluded that burning the flag was no different from burning a draft card—it too was conduct and punishable.

Before Warren wrote the opinion for the Court upholding Robel's right to work in a defense plant, he had voted in many other cases dealing with freedom of association, and in each case he voted to uphold the associational rights of the individuals involved. He has written of this period in our history:

> In the days of the late Senator Joseph McCarthy the rights of speech and association were put in serious jeopardy through "loyalty oaths," legislative investigations solely for the sake of exposure and irresponsible speeches in Congress charging citizens with subversion or of associating with alleged subversives. Fortunately, many of the so-called loyalty oaths were invalidated, the effects of legislative exposure for the sake of exposure circumscribed either by the courts or by change of Congressional rules, and vitriolic speeches were subdued by the temper of Congress itself in response to public opinion. But the danger of repression is always present wherever and whenever men possess great power. We must guard against it constantly if we are to preserve the freedoms it would destroy.[111]

The chief justice was of the opinion that requiring both public officials and public figures to prove that the press acted with "malice," before recovering damages for libel, gave the press adequate protection. And his many votes in such cases reflect that belief.

He joined Justice White's opinion to the effect that "neither lies nor false communications serve the ends of the First Amendment, and no one suggests their desirability or further proliferation. But to insure the ascertainment and publication of the truth about public affairs, it is essential that the First Amendment protect some erroneous publications as well as true ones. We adhere to this view and to the line which our cases have drawn between false communications which are protected and those which are not."[112]

Warren generally voted against the government in obscenity cases. He was not, however, an absolutist, as were Black and Douglas. Warren believed that the focus of obscenity prosecutions ought to be upon the actions of the person involved—that is, was the person a purveyor of pornography. He applied that test to uphold the convictions of Nico Jacobellis, Ralph Ginzburg,[113] a Mr. Mishkin,[114] and Sam Ginsberg and his wife.[115]

The chief justice's views on the right of privacy are found in *Griswold* and *Time, Inc. v. Hill*, but he did not write opinions in either case. He joined Justice Goldberg's concurring opinion in *Griswold* which not only acknowledged that the Fourteenth Amendment protects a right of privacy but that the Ninth Amendment protects other rights not mentioned in the Constitution. Justice Goldberg wrote: "Rather, the Ninth Amendment shows a belief of the Constitution's authors that fundamental rights exist that are not expressly enumerated in the first eight amendments and an intent that the list of rights included there not be deemed exhaustive."[116]

And when a clash occurred between that right of privacy and freedom of the press, Warren chose to vote for the right of privacy. He joined Justice Fortas's dissenting opinion in *Time, Inc.,* where Fortas, in discussing the right of privacy, declared: "It is, simply stated, the right to be let alone; to live one's life as one chooses, free from assault, intrusion or invasion except as they can be justified by the clear needs of community living under a government of law."[117]

In seven cases involving the right to travel, Chief Justice Warren voted to protect that right in four.[118] In these cases, he draws a distinction between state infringement upon the right and one imposed by the federal government. His votes indicate that Congress's authority to regulate interstate and foreign commerce gives it greater power over interstate travel.

The chief justice's voting record to guarantee equal protection to minorities is exemplary. He deserves much of the credit for the unanimous decision in *Brown v. Board of Education,* which buried the separate but equal doctrine. He also voted consistently to integrate juries, public facilities, and private facilities, and to protect where blacks live and whom they live with.

In *Loving v. Virginia,* the chief justice declared:

The clear and central purpose of the Fourteenth Amendment was to eliminate all official state sources of invidious racial discrimination in the States. . . . At the very least, the Equal Protection Clause demands that racial classifications, especially suspect in criminal statutes, be subjected to the "most rigid scrutiny," . . . and, if they are ever to be upheld, they must be shown to be necessary to the accomplishment of some permissible state objective, independent of the racial discrimination which it was the object of the Fourteenth Amendment to eliminate.[119]

In *Harman v. Forssenius,* Warren wrote that it "has long been established that a State may not impose a penalty upon those who exercise a right guaranteed by the Constitution."[120] He applied that rule to illegitimate children, aliens, and voters.

As pointed out earlier, the chief justice joined the majority in *Griffin v. Illinois,* which extended the protection of the Equal Protection Clause to include indigent defendants in criminal cases. His commitment to assuring equal protection to such defendants is illustrated by the fact that in 11 other cases he voted to require the government to provide them with transcripts and counsel so that their ability to protect their rights would be somewhat comparable to that of the more affluent.

Whether the Fourteenth Amendment made the Bill of Rights applicable to the states seems not to have been a problem for Chief Justice Warren. In dealing with First Amendment issues, he accepted prior decisions of the Court which required states to follow the commands of that amendment. And his voting record indicates that he felt the same way about the criminal justice provisions of the Fourth, Fifth, Sixth, and Eighth Amendments.

With few exceptions, Chief Justice Warren wrote about and, more important, voted for First Amendment freedoms and equality for minorities and the less fortunate. He also voted to enforce the Bill of Rights against the states.

8

JUSTICE WILLIAM J. BRENNAN, JR.

PERSONAL LIFE

Growing Up

> On the night of April 24, his twenty-four-year-old wife Agnes, had gone into labor with their second child. Hardly calm, William ran into the street and called out in his thick Irish brogue, "I need a doctor."
>
> Riding by in a carriage was Dr. Haggarty, a physician from New Brunswick, New Jersey, passing through Newark on his way to a wedding. He postponed his wedding journey and in the early-morning hours of the following day, April 25, 1906, William Joseph Brennan, Jr., was ushered into this world by a gentleman in striped pants and morning coat.[1]

Bill, Jr., was one of eight children born to William, Sr., and Agnes McDermott Brennan. At the time, Brennan's father stoked coal at a brewery. When Bill, Sr., became disgruntled with the union, he ran for and was elected president of the firemen's local and that launched him into careers in unionism and politics. Biographer Kim Isaac Eisler describes one episode that occurred during the union activities of Bill, Sr.

> A turning point in the life of the Brennan family came in 1916 when ten-year-old Bill junior witnessed his father being carried into the house by union brothers, bloodied and beaten by city police after a particularly bitter union battle over the trolley-car drivers. Few events in his childhood affected him more. Police beatings would never be anything abstract to the Brennans. When city government is changed, the elder Brennan would say, "there will be no more police beatings."

Brennan senior then began to agitate for a change of city government, from mayor-alderman to a city-commission form. He continued to work for such change even after the city's Republican mayor appointed him commissioner of police. The movement was successful, and in 1917 the city charter was changed

JUSTICE WILLIAM J. BRENNAN, JR. (photo by Ken Heinen; collection of the Supreme Court of the United States).

to provide for a five-member commission, and Bill, Sr., was elected as one of those. He chose the portfolio of director of public safety, which included the police and fire departments.

In his capacity as public safety director, Brennan had control over the licensing of theaters. When a distributor attempted to show the film *The Naked Truth* at a local theater, Brennan threatened to revoke the theater's license. He ruled that the movie "could not be shown in Newark except without charge and either in a Y.M.C.A., a school building, or a church."[2] Later, the ruling was reversed by the New Jersey Court of Chancery in a case entitled *Public Welfare Pictures v. Brennan.*

Author Eisler writes, "Agnes was the good Irish wife, but if there was one part she would have liked to leave out of her life, it was the fishbowl of public life, the parades, the rallies, the endless speeches. Whatever you do, she said in one candid moment of exasperation, 'stay out of the headlines.' That was a piece of advice Brennan would follow until well after her death some fifty years later."[3]

Bill, Jr., worked at odd jobs while growing up, including working in a filling station, milking cows at a dairy farm, and distributing newspapers. He did not, however, have any particular hobbies, nor was he an outstanding athlete.

Kim Isaac Eisler has written, "In the evenings, Bill and his five brothers and two sisters gathered around the family's player piano or listened to the phonograph records of the great Irish tenor John McCormack. On the end table lay a stack of the magazine *Irish World.* Every aspect of his life, from church until bedtime, was absorbed with Irish feeling and the tales of Irish rebellion."[4]

Brennan was an excellent student, winning many academic prizes. "To his teachers, Bill was the perfect young man, thoughtful and polite, never a cutup. Every Sunday he held his mother's hand as they walked to Mass." By the time Bill, Jr., entered high school, his father had decided that his son was to be a lawyer.

Love, Marriage, and Family

One important event that happened to Brennan while at the University of Pennsylvania was that he met Marjorie Leonard. And this did not happen until he was about to graduate. They were married shortly thereafter. Eisler describes Marjorie: "She was much like Agnes, devoted to hearth and family. Her reading consisted mostly of detective novels, and she . . . [like her husband in later life] settled solidly into middle-class suburban life by taking up golf." The Brennans had three children, a daughter, Nancy, and two sons, Hugh and William J. Brennan III.

> Marjorie and Bill Brennan were devoted to each other and seldom socialized in the evenings. When they did, they usually just huddled with each other in a corner talking about their children and sipping a drink. But that was rare. Brennan was a constant reader and preferred to stay home. Marjorie lived the life of the busy housewife. She served on the board of the Rumson Community Appeal and the county's public health nursing organization. While Bill read, she designed and stitched her own needlepoint and watched television. In her entire career as a lawyer's wife, Marjorie had never seen her husband work. She once told New Jersey newspaper reporter Josephine Bonomo:
> "Sometimes he tells me about a case and asks me what I think. But whatever I say its always the opposite of his opinion. So we leave the legal decisions to him."

Marjorie underwent surgery for cancer in October 1969 and fought a battle against it for 13 years, passing away in December 1982. Marjorie's illness had a profound effect upon Brennan. Of her death, Eisler has written, "For the seventy-six-year-old justice, Marjorie's death came as almost a relief. She had been ill for so long. No woman had suffered more. No wife had taken her suffering with more dignity and courage. For his part, no husband had ever been more devoted."

The then-justice Brennan married his long-time secretary Mary Fowler. This marriage, although coming late in life, was a stimulant the Justice needed, and he was able to attack his work with renewed vigor.

Law School

Bill, Sr., had decided that his son should go to Harvard Law School, even though Columbia was closer. He believed that "the night spots in New York might impede his son's scholarship." Bill, Jr.'s academic record in law school the first couple of years was mediocre. By his senior year, however, his grades had improved to the extent that he was able to become a member of the Harvard Legal Aid Society. "The Legal Aid Society did what its name implies. A student organization, its lawyers were permitted to practice in the Massachusetts court system. For the most part, the legal-aid lawyers helped people with landlord-tenant problems or divorces and wills. Frequently Brennan went to the courthouse to represent indigents in civil cases. In his short tenure with the society, Brennan did little that was memorable to his colleagues."

One of his professors, in discussing obscenity, referred to the case of *Public Welfare Pictures v. Brennan* and commented how Brennan's father had tried to stop the showing of the film in Newark. When told about this, his father was not amused.

Bill, Sr., died in May 1930, leaving the family with no money. At the time, four of the children were still in school. Brennan debated whether to return to Harvard for his senior year, but decided to do so with help from the school administration. He graduated with the Harvard Law School class of 1931 and returned to Newark where he went to work for the prestigious law firm of Pitney, Hardin & Ward, a firm that represented many large corporations. While this certainly was not what his father would have wanted for him, Bill, Jr., had not only a wife to support but the other members of his family also.

Lawyer

Just as he had been at law school, the future justice was a hard-working, diligent grinder. The lights in his office rarely went out before 1 A.M. Getting home early meant arriving at his Wyoming Avenue home in South Orange between 7 P.M.

and 7:30 P.M. When he did get home, Brennan's activities were of the sedentary variety. He lit a pipe and read his cases, occasionally taking a diversion to read a biography or to pull out a copy of *Plutarch's Lives* or some Irish poetry. Marjorie would sit quietly with her husband, preferring detective stories.

Brennan became the firm's expert in labor law, representing corporate clients in their employer-employee relationships. His father's labor background was a real asset.

> The recognition gave him an instant advantage, and on numerous occasions Brennan approached the unions on behalf of Johnson & Johnson president Robert Wood Johnson. Brennan had a pleasant, winning demeanor that attracted people to him. Johnson noted his skill at dealing with people of all economic backgrounds. Brennan seemed as at home walking the floor of a factory, bantering with the workers, as he was advising the board of directors about potential labor pitfalls. While other companies fought with their unions, Johnson & Johnson's workers organized quietly and peacefully. That suited the Johnson family just fine and comported with their basic concept of a humanitarian company.

After seven years at the firm, Brennan became the first Catholic to be made a partner. The firm name became Pitney, Hardin, Ward and Brennan.

During a court hearing on a labor matter, the father of union representative Tom Dunn passed away. Upon learning of the death, Brennan asked the judge to postpone the matter. "Dunn was touched at the gesture and the genuine compassion. Brennan, he realized, was personally a gentle man. But professionally Brennan remained an unrelenting legal foe." And an unrelenting foe he was. During a strike at the Kearny Western Electric plant Brennan obtained a court order limiting the number of picketers. "When a union builds a solid line in front of individuals wanting to do business at the plant, Brennan said, it is totally defeating the purpose of the picketing in the first place." That court order ultimately brought an end to the strike, and Brennan became known as a strike-breaking lawyer.

Brennan's legal career was interrupted in July 1942 when he was asked to join the Army Ordnance Department in Washington to work on labor problems in the defense industry. He was commissioned a major but shortly thereafter was promoted to lieutenant colonel and assigned as chief of the Labor Resources Section. His work required him to work with defense plants to promote the production of weapons and other war necessities. He returned to the practice of law in September 1945.

Trial and Appellate Judge and State Supreme Court Justice

In 1944 a movement began to write a new judicial article for the New Jersey

Constitution, and . . . Brennan was one of the leaders of a younger group of lawyers fighting to consolidate New Jersey's fourteen separate courts into a more logical system. Their efforts bore fruit in the new Constitution adopted in 1947, which created, among other things, a new trial court of general jurisdiction, the New Jersey Superior Court. Because of his important role in the battle for judicial reform, Brennan was appointed to the newly-created Superior Court by Governor Driscoll in 1949.[5]

Brennan accepted the appointment reluctantly. Not only did it mean a substantial reduction in income, but most of his practice had been in chancery court before a judge sitting without a jury. One of the young lawyers who had also worked on the court reform project, Nathan L. Jacobs, had accepted a superior court appointment and wanted Brennan to do the same. "This wasn't just any judgeship, Jacobs told Brennan. It was the chance to be a part of something important, to make the long-sought changes work—to make theirs the model for court improvement throughout the states."[6] Brennan finally relented and left the practice of law in February 1949, never to return.

"Brennan's career as a state judge," Eisler writes,

> passed meteorically. He took on the Hague machine in voter fraud cases, struck down bidding procedures that allowed favoritism to Hague's pals, and eliminated city policies allowing favoritism in the dispensing of bonuses to public employees. It could hardly be said that Brennan cleaned up Hudson County—it would take federal grand juries years of effort even to make a dent on the county's deeply ingrained corruption—but by working days and nights, Brennan succeeded in getting control of the court dockets. Vanderbilt [the New Jersey chief justice] couldn't have been more pleased. He felt Brennan brought order to a situation that had been filled with chaos.

In 1950 Brennan was elevated to the New Jersey Court of Appeals, and in March 1952 he was sworn in as a justice of the New Jersey Supreme Court.

In May 1953 the case of John Henry Tune came before the New Jersey Supreme Court. Tune had been arrested for murder and had given a lengthy confession. A lawyer who had been appointed to defend Tune asked for a copy of his confession and the names of potential prosecution witnesses. The trial court allowed the lawyer to see the confession, but denied him any other information. This decision was not only upheld by the New Jersey Supreme Court, it also reversed the lower court's decision to allow the lawyer to see the confession. Brennan dissented.

"In the ordinary affairs of life we would be startled at the suggestion that we should not be entitled as a matter of course to a copy of something we signed," Brennan wrote. "To shackle counsel so that they cannot effectively seek out the truth and afford the accused the representation which is not his privilege but his absolute right seriously imperils our bedrock presumption of innocence."

It was the *Tune* case, Eisler believes, that saw Brennan change from a justice not overly committed to the rights of defendants to one who became their champion.

During this period, Senator Joseph McCarthy and his Permanent Investigations Subcommittee were running wild in their investigations of allegedly subversive activities in the country. The methods used in these investigations disturbed many people, including Brennan. In a speech before the Charitable Irish Society of Boston in 1954, he said: "'The enemy [communism] deludes himself if he thinks he detects in some practices in the contemporary scene reminiscent of the Salem witch hunts, any signs that our courage has failed us and that fear has palsied our hard-won concept of justice and fair play. These are but passing aberrations even now undergoing systematic deflation.'"[7]

And a few months later, speaking to the Monmouth Rotary Club, Brennan said, "But there are hopeful signs in recent events that we have set things aright and have become ashamed of our toleration of the barbarism which marked the procedures at some of these hearings. It is indeed reason for pure joy and relief that at long last our collective conscience has sickened of the excesses and is demanding the adoption of permanent and lasting reforms to curb investigatory abuse."[8]

Nomination to the Supreme Court

In 1953 President Dwight Eisenhower appointed Republican Earl Warren as chief justice of the U.S. Supreme Court to fill the vacancy left by the death of Chief Justice Fred Vinson. Shortly thereafter, upon the death of Justice Robert H. Jackson, the president appointed Republican John Marshall Harlan (grandson of the first Justice Harlan) to replace him. Having made two appointments from the ranks of the Republicans, Eisenhower expressed the desire to appoint a Democrat to fill the next Supreme Court vacancy. It has been reported that the president wanted that Democrat also to be a Catholic.[9]

That Catholic Democrat happened to be William J. Brennan, Jr., who was nominated to the vacancy created by the resignation of Justice Sherman Minton in 1956.

Biographer Eisler calls the choice of Brennan "An Unlikely Appointment."[10] He was practically unknown outside New Jersey, and few of his Harvard Law School classmates could even remember him. Some who did were not happy with the appointment.

"Writing in *The New York Times,* powerful columnist Arthur Krock called Brennan's appointment 'inspiring.' He went on to write: 'It is an important proof of democracy when a Supreme Court justice is representative of what an American can, with honor and industry, achieve without the birthright of social and economic privilege.'"[11]

The new justice took his seat on the Court without confirmation on October 16, 1956. When hearings were finally held in February 1957, Senator Joseph McCarthy was ready.

> It was only a matter of time before Brennan's attitudes became known to McCarthy himself: The Senator took a full day to investigate Brennan's thinking, when the Justice came before the Senate Judiciary Committee for his confirmation hearings. McCarthy badgered Brennan mostly for having expressed disapproval of the ways in which congressional committees and subcommittees, including McCarthy's, conducted hearings; harassing witnesses and causing them the loss of their livelihoods, their reputations, their friends, and, in some cases, even their lives. Although Brennan was unable to lay to rest McCarthy's concerns, his appointment to the Court was almost unanimously consented to by the Senate in a voice vote. McCarthy's was the only vote opposed: at the moment the Senator's powers were dropping to their nadir.[11]

Members of the Court at the time of Justice Brennan's appointment were Chief Justice Earl Warren, and justices Hugo L. Black, Felix Frankfurter, William O. Douglas, Tom Clark, Stanley F. Reed, Harold H. Burton, and John M. Harlan.

As Associate Justice (1956-90)

The Free Exercise of Religion

"The Court forgets, I think, a warning uttered during the congressional discussion of the First Amendment itself: '. . . the rights of conscience are, in their nature, of peculiar delicacy, and will little bear the gentlest touch of governmental hand.'"[12] With those words, Justice Brennan dissented from the majority's decision to uphold Sunday closing laws even though those laws placed a substantial economic burden on Orthodox Jews whose faith required them also to close on Saturday, their Sabbath. He took the justices to task again for their insensitivity to the concerns of S. Simcha Goldman. Goldman was an Orthodox Jewish rabbi serving as a chaplain in the navy between 1970 and 1972. In 1973, he was admitted to a graduate program in clinical psychology, from which he graduated in 1977. He was then assigned to a mental health clinic at March Air Force Base, Riverside, California, to work as a clinical psychologist. During all of this time he wore a yarmulke, the traditional head covering required to be worn by his Jewish faith. In May 1981 he was told that he could no longer wear the yarmulke because it was against air force uniform regulations. When he was unsuccessful in having the air force change its mind, he brought suit against the secretary of defense, seeking an injunction to prevent enforcement of the regulations. Judge Aubrey E. Robinson, Jr., held that preventing Goldman from wearing the head covering infringed upon his right to free exercise of religion and granted the request. The circuit court reversed. Brennan responded to the Supreme Court's affirmance with these words: "The Court's response to Goldman's request is to abdicate its role as principal expositor of the Constitution and protector of individual liberties in favor of credulous deference to unsupported assertions of military necessity."[13]

He continued his condemnation of the Court's action by stating: "If a branch of the military declares one of its rules sufficiently important to outweigh a service person's constitutional rights, it seems that the Court will accept that conclusion, no matter how absurd or unsupported it may be."

Brennan then discussed the country's commitment to the free exercise of religion.

> Through our Bill of Rights, we pledged ourselves to attain a level of human freedom and dignity that had no parallel in history. Our constitutional commitment to religious freedom and to acceptance of religious pluralism is one of our greatest achievements in that noble endeavor. Almost 200 years after the First Amendment was drafted, tolerance and respect for all religions still set us apart from most other countries and draw to our shores refugees from religious persecution from around the world.

"Although the pain the services inflict on Orthodox Jewish servicemen is clearly the result of insensitivity rather than design," he observed, "it is unworthy of our military because it is unnecessary." He then expressed the hope that "Congress will correct this wrong."

After Paula Hobbie had worked at a jewelry store in Florida for several years, she joined the Seventh-Day Adventist Church, which has Saturday as its Sabbath. When Hobbie told her supervisor at the store that she could no longer work on Saturdays, arrangements were made to have her work other hours. Upon learning of the arrangement, the manager told her that she must either work regular hours or resign. Hobbie refused and was discharged. She then filed for unemployment compensation under Florida law, which was contested by the jewelry store, which claimed that she had been "discharged for 'misconduct connected with [her] work.'"[14] The Bureau of Unemployment Compensation agreed and denied benefits. That decision was upheld by the Appeals Commission and affirmed without opinion by the Florida Fifth District Court of Appeal. The Supreme Court reversed, with only Chief Justice Rehnquist dissenting.

Referring to the very similar case of *Sherbert v. Verner,* Justice Brennan, writing for the majority, pointed out that in that case the Court had "concluded that the [state's denial of benefits] had imposed a burden upon Sherbert's free exercise rights that had not been justified by a compelling state interest." But the Appeals Commission argued that *Sherbert* was different because in this case Hobbie had become a Seventh-Day Adventist during the time she was working at the store and therefore had brought this on herself. "In effect," Brennan said, the Appeals Commission asks us to single out the religious convert for different, less favorable treatment than that given an individual whose adherence to his or her faith precedes employment. We decline to do so. The First Amendment protects the free exercise rights of employees who adopt religious beliefs or convert from one faith to another after they are hired. The timing of Hobbie's conversion is immaterial to our determination that her free exercise rights have been burdened; the salient inquiry under the Free Exercise Clause is the burden involved.

Ahmad Uthman Shabazz and Sadr-Ud-Din Mateen, members of the Muslim faith, were prisoners in a New Jersey state prison. In order to accommodate Muslim prisoners, prison officials allowed the Muslim service Jumu'ah to be held. Jumu'ah is required of all Muslims and is conducted at noon Fridays when "the sun reaches its apex and before the Asr, or mid-afternoon prayer."[15] Muslim prisoners were assigned jobs in the main building on Fridays in order to attend the services.

In March 1984 the prison rules were changed so that prisoners were no longer assigned jobs on Friday that would allow them to take part in Jumu'ah, and if they were working away from the main building they were not allowed to return. These rule changes were necessary, the officials said, to eliminate overcrowding at the main facility on Fridays, and "to reduce security and discipline problems by diminishing the burden on prison guards of accounting for and supervising inmates." Shabazz and Mateen brought suit against Edward O'Lone, administrator of the prison, claiming that the change in the rules denied them free exercise of religion. Judge John F. Gerry refused to order O'Lone to accommodate the petitioners, but the circuit court reversed and ordered prison officials to justify the infringement upon the Muslims' religious freedom. In a five-to-four decision the Supreme Court reversed, with Justice Brennan writing a dissenting opinion.

Brennan calls attention to the world of the prisoner:

> It is thus easy to think of prisoners as members of a separate netherworld, driven by its own demands, ordered by its own customs, ruled by those whose claim to power rests on raw necessity. Nothing can change the fact, however, that the society that these prisoners inhabit is our own. Prisons may exist on the margins of that society, but no act of will can sever them from the body politic. When prisoners emerge from the shadows to press a constitutional claim, they invoke no alien set of principles drawn from a distant culture. Rather, they speak the language of the charter upon which all of us rely to hold official power accountable. They ask us to acknowledge that power exercised in the shadows must be restrained at least as diligently as power that acts in the sunlight.[16]

The justice criticizes the majority for upholding the restrictions because they found them reasonable. "To deny the opportunity to affirm membership in a spiritual community . . . ," the Justice concludes, "may extinguish an inmate's last source of hope for dignity and redemption. Such a denial requires more justification than mere assertion that any other course of action is infeasible."

Freedom of Speech

Soliciting and Pamphleteering. "The question presented for review is whether a State, consistent with the First and Fourteenth Amendments, may require a religious organization desiring to distribute and sell religious literature and to solicit donations at a state fair to conduct those activities only at an assigned location within the fairgrounds even though application of the rule limits the religious practices of the organization."[17]

Minnesota State Fair rule 6.05 limits the "sale or distribution of any merchandise, including printed or written material except under license issued by . . . [the fair] and/or from a duly-licensed location." Joseph Beca, a priest of the International Society for Krishna Consciousness (ISKCON), and other members of that organization desired to distribute literature and solicit funds on the fairgrounds during the fair, but were told that they could do so only from a fixed location. ISKCON brought an action against Michael Heffron, the secretary and manager of the fair board, seeking an order allowing the organization to conduct its activities throughout the grounds. Judge Jerome Plunkett denied the request, but the Supreme Court of Minnesota reversed, holding that rule 6.05's restrictions violated the free exercise of religion rights of ISKCON. Deciding that the rule was a valid time, place, and manner regulation of First Amendment activities, the United States Supreme Court agreed with Judge Plunkett, and reversed. The majority held that the need for crowd control and the prevention of deceptive practices, annoyance, and harassment of fairgoers justified the application of the rule to ISKCON. Justice Brennan agreed that the need to prevent fraud justified restricting ISKCON's sales and solicitation of funds to a booth. He believed, however, that preventing ISKCON's members from distributing literature throughout the grounds was an unconstitutional infringement on their First Amendment right of freedom of speech. "Because of Rule 6.05," Brennan pointed out, ". . . as soon as a proselytizing member of ISKCON hands out a free copy of the BhagavadGita to an interested listener, or a political candidate distributes his campaign brochure to a potential voter, he becomes subject to arrest and removal from the fairgrounds. This constitutes a significant restriction on First Amendment rights. By prohibiting distribution of literature outside the booths, the fair officials sharply limit the number of fairgoers to whom the proselytizers and candidates can communicate their messages."

Benjamin Spock and Julius Hobson were the People's Party candidates for president and vice president, respectively, in 1972. In September they requested permission to speak and distribute campaign literature on the army base at Fort Dix, New Jersey, which request was denied by Major General Bert A. David, the base's commanding officer. He cited army regulations prohibiting political speeches on the base and allowing distribution of literature only with prior approval.

Judge Clarkson S. Fisher denied Spock and Hobson's request for a preliminary injunction against the enforcement of the regulations, but the circuit court reversed and directed Judge Fisher to grant the injunction. This allowed the candidates to hold a rally on the parking lot at Fort Dix. Later, Judge Fisher permanently enjoined the government from enforcing the regulations, and that decision was upheld by the circuit court. A majority of the Supreme Court voted to reverse. They held that because Fort Dix authorities had not opened the base to the extent of making it freely accessible to the public, the regulations did not infringe upon First Amendment rights. "What the record shows . . . ," Justice Stewart noted, "is a considered Fort Dix policy, objectively and evenhandedly applied, of keeping official military activities there wholly free of entanglement with partisan political campaigns of any kind."[18]

Justice Brennan saw Fort Dix entirely differently. He was of the opinion that because so much civilian traffic was allowed into and through the base, it no longer was a restricted area, as the majority had concluded. He pointed out that there was no sentry at the entrance; that ten paved roads, including a state highway, crossed the reservation; that civilians were welcome, came, ate, and talked to the soldiers; and that "the reservation is so open as to create a danger of muggings after payday and a problem with prostitution."

The justice acknowledged that political rallies may well present some disruption. "But," he argued, "that a rally is disruptive of the usual activities in an unrestricted area is not to say that it is necessarily disruptive so as significantly to impair training or defense, thereby requiring its prohibition. Additionally, this Court has recognized that some quite disruptive forms of public expression are protected by the First Amendment."

Turning to the requirement for prior approval of material before it could be distributed on the base, the justice declared, "requiring prior approval of expressive material before it may be distributed on base constitutes a system of prior restraint, . . . a system 'bearing a heavy presumption against its constitutional validity.'" He did not believe that the military had overcome that "heavy presumption" in this case.

"I could not agree more," he declared, "that the military should not become a political faction in this country. . . . But it borders on casuistry to contend that by evenhandedly permitting public expression to occur in unrestricted portions of a military installation, the military will be viewed as sanctioning the causes there espoused."

Albert Edward Glines, a captain in the U.S. Air Force Reserves, sought to change an air force rule regarding the length of servicemen's hair. He prepared a petition to the secretary of defense requesting the change, and began securing signatures from other military personnel. Because he did not secure approval of the base commander, he was removed from active duty and placed on standby reserve, which caused him to lose salary, retirement benefits, and flight experience. Glines brought suit in federal court, claiming that his First Amendment rights were being curtailed. After considering the matter, Judge William H. Orrick, Jr., agreed and ordered that Glines be restored to active service. The circuit court affirmed, but a majority of the Supreme Court voted to reverse, being of the opinion that the regulation requiring prior approval before circulating petitions did not violate the First Amendment.[19]

"For soldiers and sailors, as opposed to civilians," Brennan argued in dissent, "military installations *must* be the place for 'free . . . communication of thoughts' . . . Further, when service personnel are stationed abroad or at sea, the base or warship is very likely the *only* place for free communication of thoughts. Thus, in contrast to *Greer,* the regulations here permit complete foreclosure of a distinctive mode of expression by servicemen, who lack the civilian's option to depart the sphere of military authority."[20] "The Court," he asserted, "unnecessarily tramels important First Amendment rights by uncritically accepting the dubious proposition that military security requires—or is furthered by—the discretionary suppression of a classic form of peaceful group expression. Service men and women deserve better than this."

Picketing and Parading. Antiabortionists Sandra Schultz and Robert Braun joined a group picketing in front of the home of Dr. Benjamin M. Victoria in Brookfield, Wisconsin, because they opposed his performing abortions. "The picketers carried signs with a variety of inscriptions including 'Stop Abortion Now,' 'Aborted Babies Sold for Cosmetics,' 'Abortion Is Legal Murder,' 'God Bless America,' and 'Forgiveness Is Yours for the Asking.' Picketers on occasion sang and cheered or shouted other slogans that witnesses say include references to Victoria as a 'baby killer.'"[21]

Brookfield had an ordinance prohibiting "picketing before or about the residence or dwelling of any individual." When city attorney Clayton Cramer informed Schultz and Braun that the ordinance would be enforced against them if they continued to picket, they brought an action against the town requesting the court to declare the law unconstitutional as a violation of their First Amendment right to picket. Judge John W. Reynolds granted the injunction, which was upheld by an equally divided panel of the circuit court. Six justices of the Supreme Court voted to reverse, with Justices Brennan, Marshall, and Stevens dissenting.[22]

When the case was argued before the Court, the city's attorney pointed out that the "'picketing [prohibited] would be having the picket proceed on a definite course or route in front of a home.' . . . The picket need not be carrying a sign, . . . but in order to fall within the scope of the ordinance the picketing must be directed at a single residence. . . . General marching through residential neighborhoods, or even walking a route in front of an entire block of houses, is not prohibited by the ordinance."

This narrow construction of the ordinance presented the Court with the problem of balancing the privacy interests of the doctor and his family not to be forced to listen to a message they did not like, against the right of the picketers to picket for a cause in which they deeply believed. The majority concluded that the balance should be in favor of the homeowner. "Because the picketing prohibited by the Brookfield ordinance," Justice Sandra Day O'Connor pointed out, "is speech directed primarily at those who are presumptive unwilling to receive it, the State has a substantial and justifiable interest in banning it. . . . The ordinance also leaves open ample alternative channels of communication and is content neutral."

Brennan acknowledged that a municipality does have an interest in not allowing protestors "to imprison a person in his or her own house merely because they shout slogans or carry signs." "If, on the other hand," he argued, "the picketer intends to communicate generally, a carefully drafted ordinance will allow him or her to do so without intruding upon or unduly harassing the resident." This ordinance, he concluded did not do that, and the Court therefore "condones a law that suppresses substantially more speech than is necessary."

Places to Speak. Marsha Kokinda and Kevin Pearl set up a table on the sidewalk at the Bowie, Maryland, post office to solicit contributions and distribute literature for the National Democratic Policy Committee. After receiving a number of complaints, Postmaster Larry Boe told them to leave, but they refused and were arrested for soliciting on post office property contrary to postal regulations. They were tried before a U.S. magistrate and found guilty. District Judge J. Fredrick Motz upheld the convictions, but the circuit court reversed. The United States then appealed to the Supreme Court, where a majority upheld the convictions, agreeing that post office grounds were not open forums for First Amendment activities. Justices Brennan, Marshall, Stevens, and Blackmun dissented.

Writing for herself, Chief Justice Rehnquist, and justices White and Scalia, Justice O'Connor pointed out that "the postal sidewalk at issue does not have the characteristics of public sidewalks traditionally open to expressive activity. The municipal sidewalk that runs parallel to the road in this case is a public passageway. The Postal Service's sidewalk is not such a thoroughfare. Rather, it leads only from the parking area to the front door of the postoffice."[23]

Justice Kennedy voted to uphold the convictions, but did not believe that it was necessary to determine whether the sidewalk was a public forum. He concluded that "the postal regulation at issue meets the traditional standards we have applied to time, place and manner restrictions of protected expression."

The dissenters disagreed with the plurality. "It is only common sense," Brennan declared, "that a public sidewalk adjacent to a public building to which citizens are freely admitted is a natural location for speech to occur, whether that speech is critical of government generally, aimed at the particular governmental agency housed in the building, or focused upon issues unrelated to the government." This makes the post office sidewalk an open forum for the exercise of First Amendment activities just like other sidewalks.

Brennan disagreed with Kennedy that this was a neutral time, place, and manner regulation because it didn't just regulate the use of the sidewalk, it completely banned solicitation there. Furthermore, the regulation did not prohibit some other forms of expression, "such as soapbox oratory, pamphleteering, distributing literature for free, or even flag-burning." The justice concluded his dissent by noting that there would be three groups "saddened by today's decision." The first would be those who had to solicit from such "inhospitable locations as the busy four-lane highway that runs in front of the Bowie Post Office." The second group would be the people who would be "deprived of the views of the solicitors at postal locations." "The last group, unfortunately," Brennan says, "includes all of us who are conscious of the importance of the First Amendment."

When the Court upheld a zoning ordinance of Renton, Washington, "that prohibits adult motion picture theaters from locating within 1,000 feet of any residential zone, single- or multiple-family dwelling, church, park or school," Brennan and Marshall dissented.[24] "Renton's zoning ordinance," Justice Brennan argued, "selectively imposes limitations on the location of a movie theater based exclusively on the *content* of the films shown there." And just because some residents "may be offended by the *content* of the films shown at adult movie theaters [that] cannot form the basis for state regulation of speech."

Equal Access to Places to Speak.

> In 1970, petitioner, Harry J. Lehman was a candidate for the office of State Representative to the Ohio General Assembly for District 56. The district includes the city of Shaker Heights. On July 3, 1970, petitioner sought to promote his candidacy by purchasing car card space on the Shaker Heights Rapid Transit System for the months of August, September, and October. The general election was scheduled for November 3. Petitioner's proposed copy contained his picture and read:
>
> HARRY J. LEHMAN IS OLD FASHIONED!
> ABOUT HONESTY, INTEGRITY AND GOOD GOVERNMENT
> State Representative—District 56 [X] Harry J. Lehman.[25]

Lehman's proposed ad was refused because political advertisements were not permitted on the transit system. The Ohio courts turned a deaf ear to his argument that the ban on political advertising violated his right to free speech. Five justices of the Supreme Court voted to uphold the ban, but four believed that it was unconstitutional as a violation of the First Amendment.

"In my view," Brennan declared for the dissenters, "the city created a forum for the dissemination of information and expression of ideas when it accepted and displayed commercial and public service advertisements on its rapid transit vehicles. Having opened a forum for communication, the city is barred by the First and Fourteenth Amendments from discriminating among forum users solely on the basis of message content."

The justice took issue with the city's claim that its ban on political ads was necessary to shield its passengers from controversial issues. "In the eyes of many passengers," he argued, "certain commercial or public service messages are as profoundly disturbing as some political advertisements might be to other passengers." Furthermore, all passengers need to do to avoid an ad that disturbs them is to turn away their eyes. "Surely that minor inconvenience," Brennan asserts, "is a small price to pay for the continued preservation of so precious a liberty as free speech."

The Perry Education Association (PEA), as the exclusive teachers' bargaining representative at the Metropolitan School District of Perry Township, Indiana, had access to teachers' mailboxes, but another teachers' organization, the Perry Local Educator's Association (PLEA), did not.

Evelyn E. Waddell and Judith M. Dietrich brought an action for themselves and for the PLEA challenging the validity of the restriction on the use of teachers' mailboxes. They argued that by denying them access to the boxes, the school district was infringing on their First Amendment rights. Federal District Judge James E. Noland gave judgment in favor of the school district, but the circuit court held that the exclusive policy did violate the PLEA's and its members' right to equal access to the boxes. In a five-to-four decision, the Supreme Court disagreed and reversed. Justices Brennan, Marshall, Powell, and Stevens filed a dissenting opinion.

Writing for the majority, Justice White pointed out that "on government property that has not been made a public forum, not all speech is equally situated, and the State may draw distinctions which relate to the special purpose for which the property is used."[26] In this case, the mailboxes were not public forums. Therefore, giving exclusive use to the teachers' bargaining representative was permissible.

The dissenters did not believe that this was a case involving the use of a forum, public or nonpublic. This case was about "equal access" to a method of communicating with teachers. "Once the government," Brennan argued,

> permits discussion of certain subject matter, it may not impose restrictions that discriminate among viewpoints on those subjects whether a nonpublic forum is involved or not. . . . We have never held that government may allow discussion of a subject and then discriminate among viewpoints on that particular topic, even if the government for certain reasons may entirely exclude discussion of the subject from the forum. . . . Viewpoint discrimination is censorship in its purest form and government regulation that discriminates among viewpoints threatens the continued vitality of "free speech."

"In this case," he concluded, "the Board has infringed the respondent's [PLEA's] First Amendment rights by granting exclusive access to an effective channel of communication to the petitioner [PEA] and denying such access to the respondents [PLEA]."

Some Flag Desecration Is Protected Speech. Gregory Lee Johnson was a participant in a political demonstration in Dallas, Texas, during the 1984 Republican National Convention.

The demonstrators marched through the Dallas streets, chanting political slogans and stopping at several corporate locations to stage "die-ins" intended to dramatize the consequences of nuclear war. On several occasions they spray-painted the walls of buildings and overturned potted plants, but Johnson himself took no part in such activities. He did, however, accept an American flag handed to him by a fellow protestor who had taken it from a flagpole outside one of the targeted buildings.

The demonstration ended in front of Dallas City Hall, where Johnson unfurled the American flag, doused it with kerosene, and set it on fire. While the flag burned, the protestors chanted: "America, the red, white, and blue, we spit on you." After the demonstrators dispersed, a witness to the flag burning collected the flag's remains and buried them in his backyard. No one was physically injured or threatened with injury, though several witnesses testified that they had been seriously offended by the flag burning.[27]

Johnson was convicted of desecrating an American flag, and sentenced to one year in prison and fined $2,000. The Texas Court of Criminal Appeals reversed, "holding that the State could not, consistent with the First Amendment, punish Johnson for burning the flag in these circumstances." Five justices of the Supreme Court voted to affirm. "We must first determine," Justice Brennan pointed out for the majority, "whether Johnson's burning of the flag constituted expressive conduct, permitting him to invoke the First Amendment in challenging his conviction."

Several prior cases supported an affirmative answer to that question. "Especially pertinent to this case," the justice noted, "are our decisions recognizing the communicative nature of conduct relating to flags. Attaching a peace sign to the flag, . . . refusing to salute the flag, . . . and displaying a red flag, . . . we have held, all may find shelter under the First Amendment." Among the factors the Court considered were that the flag was burned as part of a larger political demonstration, and Johnson's statement, "The American flag was burned as Ronald Reagan was being nominated as President. And a more powerful statement of symbolic speech, whether you agree with it or not, couldn't have been made at that time." This led the majority to conclude that Johnson's burning of the flag "was conduct, 'sufficiently imbued with elements of communication' . . . to implicate the First Amendment."

The state had also argued that it had "an interest in preserving the flag as a symbol of nationhood and national unity." But Justice Brennen responded, "If there is a bedrock principle underlying the First Amendment, it is that the government may not prohibit the expression of an idea simply because society finds the idea itself offensive or disagreeable."

He concluded, "Johnson was convicted for engaging in expressive conduct. The State's interest in preventing breaches of the peace does not support his conviction because Johnson's conduct did not threaten to disturb the peace. Nor does the State's interest in preserving the flag as a symbol of nationhood and national unity justify his criminal conviction for engaging in political expression."

Shortly after the decision in *Johnson*, Congress enacted the flag Protection Act of 1989. "The Act criminalizes the conduct of anyone who 'knowingly mutilates, defaces, physically defiles, burns, maintains on the floor or ground, or tramples upon' a United States flag."[28] Shortly thereafter Shawn Eichman, David Blalock, and Scott Tyler burned several United States flags on the steps of the Capitol in Washington, D.C. The U.S. attorney charged the three with violating the act. Gregory Lee Johnson was with the group, but his flag failed to ignite and he therefore was not charged.

District Judge June L. Green dismissed the charges. The same five justices who voted to reverse Johnson's conviction voted to affirm Judge Green and to dismiss the charges against Eichman, Blalock, and Tyler. They were justices Brennan, Marshall, Blackmun, Scalia, and Kennedy, with Brennan writing the opinion.

The government acknowledged that flag burning was expressive conduct, but argued that it had "an interest in 'protect[ing] the physical integrity of the flag under all circumstances' in order to safeguard the flag's identity 'as the unique and unalloyed symbol of the Nation.'" But the majority did not agree that that was the real intention of Congress. They were of the opinion that Congress intended to prohibit "the communicative impact of flag destruction," and that brought the act into conflict with the First Amendment. "Punishing desecration of the flag," Brennan declared, "dilutes the very freedom that makes this emblem so revered and worth revering."

Fighting Words and Indecent Speech. Johnny C. Wilson was part of an anti–Vietnam War demonstration in front of the Army's 12th Corps Headquarters. He allegedly said to M.G. Redding, who was present at the time, "White son of a bitch, I'll kill you. . . . You son of a bitch, I'll choke you to death."[29] Wilson also spoke to T.L. Raborn and allegedly said, "You son of a bitch, if you ever put your hands on me again, I'll cut you all to pieces."

Wilson was convicted of violating Georgia Code Section 26-6303 which reads as follows: "Any person who shall, without provocation, use to or of another, and in his presence . . . opprobrious words or abusive language, tending to cause a breach of the peace . . . shall be guilty of a misdemeanor."

Wilson then brought an action in the federal district court claiming that the statute was unconstitutional as a violation of his First Amendment right to free speech. Judge Sidney O. Smith agreed and set aside the conviction. Both the circuit court and the Supreme Court affirmed Judge Smith's decision.

To focus properly on the issue in this case Justice Brennan, for the majority, pointed out, "The constitutional guarantees of freedom of speech forbid the States to punish the use of words or language not within 'narrowly limited classes of speech.'. . . Even as to such a class, however, because 'the line between speech unconditionally guaranteed and speech which may legitimately be regulated, suppressed, or punished is finely drawn,' . . . '[i]n every case the power to regulate must be so exercised as not, in attaining a permissible end, unduly to infringe the protected freedom.'"

Among those "narrowly limited classes of speech" that may be punished are those commonly referred to as "fighting words." "Fighting words" are those spoken face-to-face which "would be likely to cause an average addressee to fight." Only "face to face words plainly likely to cause a breach of peace by the addressee" are punishable as "fighting words." The question, therefore, was whether the Georgia statute fell within that definition.

Justice Brennan said it did not. By examining prior cases in which the Georgia statute had been construed, he found that it had been applied to convict individuals where the words were not spoken "face to face," nor were "likely to cause a breach of the peace."

Because the statute was not so limited, it was unconstitutional. Wilson's conviction, therefore, was set aside because a person cannot be convicted under an unconstitutional law.

Justice Brennan wrote two subsequent opinions wherein the issue before the Court was the constitutionality of laws punishing words spoken to a police officer. "Although we appreciate the difficulties of drafting precise laws," he wrote, "we have repeatedly invalidated laws that provide police with unfettered discretion to arrest individuals for words or conduct that annoy or offend them."[30] To note the potential for abuse by police officers of such laws, Brennan quotes Justice Lewis F. Powell, Jr.: "'This ordinance . . . confers on police a virtually unrestrained power to arrest and charge persons with a violation. Many arrests are made in "one-on-one" situations where the only witnesses are the arresting officer and the person charged. All that is required for conviction is that the court accept the testimony of the officer that obscene or opprobrious language had been used toward him while in the performance of his duties.'"

> A satiric humorist named George Carlin recorded a 12-minute monologue entitled "filthy Words" before a live audience in a California theater. He began by referring to his thoughts about "the words you couldn't say on the public, ah, airwaves, um, the ones you definitely wouldn't say, ever." He proceeded to list those words and repeat them over and over again in a variety of colloquialisms.[31]

Among the words Carlin used were *fuck, shit, piss, motherfucker, cocksucker, cunt,* and *tit.*

A father and his young son heard the monologue on the car radio as it was broadcast by a New York radio station. The father wrote to the Federal Communications Commission (FCC), complaining about the broadcast. "He stated that, although he could perhaps understand the 'record's being sold for private use, I certainly cannot understand the broadcast of same over the air that, supposedly, you control.'" After requesting and receiving comment from the station's owner, Pacifica Foundation, the FCC issued a warning that if additional complaints were received the station's license might be in jeopardy. The FCC called the station's attention to a federal law "which forbids the use of 'any obscene, indecent, or profane language by means of radio communication.'" The commission later indicated that it had not intended to prohibit absolutely the broadcast of such language, but "sought to channel it to times of the day when children most likely would not be exposed to it." With two judges agreeing and one dissenting, the circuit court held the commission's order to be unconstitutional. However, in a decision that brought forth four opinions, five justices voted to uphold the commission's order and four, including Brennan, dissented.

"I find the Court's misapplication of fundamental First Amendment principles so patent," Brennan declared, "and its attempt to impose *its* notions of propriety on the whole of the American people so misguided, that I am unable to remain silent." The justice acknowledged that a homeowner has a right of privacy that is invaded by radio broadcasts. "Whatever the minimal discomfort suffered by a listener," he notes, "who inadvertently tunes into a program he finds offensive during the brief interval before he can simply extend his arm and switch stations or flick the 'off' button, it is surely worth the candle to preserve the broadcaster's right to send, and the right of those interested to receive, a message entitled to full First Amendment protection."

Public Employees' Right to Advocate. "The Court correctly affirms the long-established principle that the government may not constitutionally compel persons to relinquish their First Amendment rights as a condition of public employment."[32] With that statement, Brennan dissented from the Court's decision to uphold the discharge of Sheila Myers from her position as an assistant district attorney in New Orleans.

Myers had worked in the district attorney's office for five and a half years. She objected to being transferred to another section within the department, but her objections went unheeded. She then prepared and circulated a questionnaire containing questions about "office transfer policy, office morale, the need for a grievance committee, the level of confidence in supervisors, and whether employees felt pressured to work in political campaigns." When her boss, District Attorney Harry Connick, heard about the questionnaire, he discharged her. He later said that Myers was discharged because she refused to accept the transfer to the other section, and because he did not like some of the questions on the questionnaire.

Myers filed an action against Connick claiming that her discharge violated her right to freedom of speech. Judge Jack M. Gordon agreed and ordered that Myers be reinstated and given back pay and $1,500 in damages. The circuit court affirmed, but in an opinion by Justice White the Supreme Court held that Myers's First Amendment rights were not violated and therefore reversed. "We hold," White said, "only that when a public employee speaks not as a citizen upon matters of public concern, but instead as an employee upon matters only of personal interest, absent the most unusual circumstances, a federal court is not the appropriate forum in which to review the wisdom of a personnel decision taken by a public agency allegedly in reaction to the employee's behavior."

Brennan took issue with the majority's conclusion that Myers's speech was "only of personal interest," and not of public concern. "I would hold," the justice declared, "that Myers' questionnaire addressed matters of public concern because it discussed subjects that could reasonably be expected to be of interest to persons seeking to develop informed opinions about the manner in which the Orleans Parish District Attorney, an elected official charged with managing a vital governmental agency, discharges his responsibilities." Brennan was concerned about the message the decision in this case would send to public employees, and wrote, "The Court's decision today inevitably will deter public employees from making critical statements about the manner in which government agencies are operated for fear that doing so will provoke dismissal. As a result, the public will be deprived of valuable information with which to evaluate the performance of elected officials. Because protecting the dissemination of such information is an essential function of the First Amendment, I dissent."

Commercial Speech. "I see no reason why commercial speech should be afforded less protection than other types of speech where, as here, the government seeks to suppress commercial speech in order to deprive consumers of accurate information concerning lawful activity."[33]

Justice Brennan made that statement in dissenting when the Court upheld a law of Puerto Rico which prohibited casinos from advertising "their facilities to the public of Puerto Rico." The majority was of the opinion that Puerto Rico's interest in reducing the "demand for casino gambling by the residents of Puerto Rico" justified the restriction on gambling advertising. Brennan objected to the Court's using a relaxed standard to evaluate the restriction on commercial speech. "I believe," he declared, "that where the government seeks to suppress the dissemination of nonmisleading commercial speech relating to legal activities, for fear that recipients will act on the information provided, such regulation should be subject to strict judicial scrutiny." But the law did not even meet a test of reasonableness. "In this case," he pointed out, "nothing suggests that the Puerto Rico Legislature ever considered the efficacy of measures other than suppressing protected expression. More importantly, there has been no showing that alternative measures would inadequately safeguard the Commonwealth's interest in controlling the harmful effects allegedly associated with casino gambling." Brennan concluded, "I would hold that Puerto Rico may not suppress the dissemination of truthful information about entirely lawful activity merely to keep its residents ignorant."

When New York banned the sale and advertising of contraceptives, several family planning organizations, doctors, and a minister brought an action seeking a declaration that the law was unconstitutional and requested a court order preventing enforcement of the law. The district court agreed that the law violated the right of privacy, and that the ban on advertising infringed First Amendment rights. The Supreme Court affirmed, with Brennan writing an opinion in which justices Stewart, Marshall, and Blackmun joined.

The state argued "that advertisements of contraceptive products would be offensive and embarrassing to those exposed to them, and that permitting them would legitimize sexual activity of young people."[34] Brennan responded, "We have consistently held that the fact that protected speech may be offensive to some does not justify its suppression." And he did not think that the advertisements under consideration in this case would in any way cause "illicit sexual behavior."

Richard D. Shapero, a Kentucky lawyer, wanted to send a letter "to potential clients who have had a foreclosure suit filed against them."[35] He was prevented from doing so by a bar association rule prohibiting direct mail advertising. In upholding the rule, the Kentucky Supreme Court said, "This Court is not unmindful of the serious potential for abuse inherent in direct solicitation by lawyers of potential clients known to need specific legal services. Such solicitation subjects the prospective client to pressure from a trained lawyer in a direct personal way."[36] The U.S. Supreme Court disagreed.

Writing for himself and justices Marshall, Blackmun, and Kennedy, Brennan recognized the dangers of direct mail solicitation, but nevertheless held that the Kentucky rule violated the First Amendment. The Court found this kind of solicitation to be different from "in-person solicitation by lawyers for profit," which it had previously held could be prohibited. "Unlike the potential client with a badgering advocate breathing down his neck, the recipient of a letter and the 'reader of an advertisement . . . can effectively avoid further bombardment of [his] sensibilities simply by averting [his] eyes. . . . ' A letter, like a printed advertisement (but unlike a lawyer), can readily be put in a drawer to be considered later, ignored, or discarded."

Justice Brennan acknowledged that there might be a greater potential for abuse from a letter targeting people who had a specific legal problem, as in this case, but was of the opinion that there were better ways to address the problem. "The State can regulate such abuses and minimize mistakes through far less restrictive and more precise means, the most obvious of which is to require the lawyer to file any solicitation letter with a state agency . . . giving the State ample opportunity to supervise mailings and penalize actual abuses."

The Right to Read. When the Board of Education of Island Trees Union Free School District No. 26 sought to remove several books from the school's library, students Stephen Pico, Jacqueline Gold, Russell Reiger, Glenn Yarris, and Paul Sochinski objected and filed an action seeking to prevent the removal.[37] The books at issue were *Slaughterhouse-Five,* by Kurt Vonnegut, Jr.; *The Naked Ape,* by Desmond Morris; *Down These Mean Streets,* by Piri Thomas; *Best Short Stories of Negro Writers,* edited by Langston Hughes; *Go Ask Alice,* of anonymous authorship; *Laughing Boy,* by Oliver LaFarge; *Black Boy,* by Richard Wright; *A Hero Ain't Nothin' but a Sandwich,* by Alice Childress; and *Soul on Ice,* by Eldridge Cleaver. Judge George C. Pratt granted judgment for the school board, which the circuit court reversed and sent back for trial. A splintered Supreme

Court affirmed. Justices Brennan, Marshall, Blackmun, and Stevens discussed the application of the First Amendment to the removal of books from a library. Justice White preferred to have the matter tried in the district court before addressing the First Amendment.

Brennan, writing for himself and Justices Marshall and Stevens, concluded that "the special characteristics of the school *library* make that environment especially appropriate for the recognition of the First Amendment rights of students. A school library, no less than any other public library, is 'a place dedicated to quiet, to knowledge, and to beauty.'" This led the justice to "hold that local school boards may not remove books from school library shelves simply because they dislike the ideas contained in those books and seek by their removal to 'prescribe what shall be orthodox in politics, nationalism, religion, or other matters of opinion.'" Brennan then agreed that the case should be sent back to the district court to determine whether the "decision to remove the books rested decisively upon disagreement with constitutionally protected ideas in those books, or upon a desire on the . . . [Board's] part to impose upon the students . . . a political orthodoxy to which . . . [the Board] and their constituents adhered."

Freedom of the Press

Libel. The case of *New York Times v. Sullivan*[38] marked the beginning of a new era in the Court's approach to libel and defamation cases. That case started with the publication of an advertisement placed in the *New York Times* by a group of blacks to let the public know what was happening in the civil rights movement in the South. L.B. Sullivan, commissioner of public affairs for Montgomery, Alabama, although not named in the ad, brought an action against the *Times* alleging that references in the ad to the police indirectly referred to him and were libelous. A jury awarded him $500,000, which was upheld by the Supreme Court of Alabama. All justices of the U.S. Supreme Court voted to reverse, with Justice Brennan writing an opinion for the majority.

To put the case in proper perspective, Brennan wrote, "Thus, we consider this case against the background of a profound national commitment to the principle that debate on public issues should be uninhibited, robust, and wide-open, and that it may well include vehement, caustic, and sometimes unpleasantly sharp attacks on government and public officials." Furthermore, "erroneous statement is inevitable in a free debate, and . . . it must be protected if the freedoms of expression are to have the 'breathing space' that they 'need . . . to survive.'"

Turning then to the question of whether the First Amendment requires that the press have some protection from libel actions brought by public officials, the justice answered in the affirmative. "The constitutional guarantees require, we think, a federal rule that prohibits a public official from recovering damages for a defamatory falsehood relating to his official conduct unless he proves that the statement was made with 'actual malice'—that is, with knowledge that it was false or with reckless disregard of whether it was false or not." In applying that rule to the present case, Brennan concluded that Sullivan had not proved that the *Times* or any of the other defendants had acted with "malice."

Brennan agreed with the Court that "public figures" ought to be held to the same standard as "public officials," and therefore he joined Chief Justice Warren's concurrence in *Curtis Publishing Co. v. Butts.*[39]

He would also give the same protection to the press in libel actions brought by "private" individuals when the alleged libel occurred during a media report of a matter of "public or general interest." *Rosenbloom v. Metromedia*[40] was such a case.

"We honor the commitment to robust debate on public issues, which is embodied in the First Amendment," Brennan asserted, "by extending constitutional protection to all discussion and communication involving matters of public or general concern, without regard to whether the persons involved are famous or anonymous." (The *Rosenbloom* case is discussed in detail in Chapter 9.)

When required to choose between freedom of the press and an individual's right to privacy, in *Time, Inc. v. Hill,*[41] Justice Brennan opted to protect the press. He was of the opinion that Hill's experience was a matter of public interest and therefore recovery of damages depended upon proof that Time, Inc., had acted with "actual malice." (The *Hill* case is discussed in Chapter 7.)

Brennan summed up the Court's decisions on libel actions versus freedom of the press as follows: "Our cases since *New York Times Co. v. Sullivan* have proceeded from the general premise that all libel law implicates First Amendment values to the extent it deters true speech that would otherwise be protected by the First Amendment. . . . In libel law, no less than other governmental efforts to regulate speech, States must therefore use finer instruments to ensure adequate space for protected expression."

Justice Brennan was of the opinion that by allowing unrestrained punitive damages, a state was not giving adequate protection to freedom of the press. He believed that the proper approach was to allow recovery for provable actual damages, but to restrict punitive damages only when the person defamed could prove that the allegedly defamatory material was published with "actual malice."[42]

Prior Restraints and Subsequent Punishment. Brennan concurred in the *Pentagon Papers* case.[43] He noted that the government argued that publication of the "classified study entitled 'History of U.S. Decision-Making Process on Viet Nam Policy' 'could,' or 'might,' or 'may' prejudice the national interest in various ways." "But," he declared, "the First Amendment tolerates absolutely no prior restraints of the press predicated upon surmise or conjecture that untoward consequences may result." Only in time of war might such restraints on the press be justified.

Erwin Charles Simants was arrested and charged with murdering six members of the Henry Kellie family in Sutherland, Nebraska, in October 1975. Because the crime attracted considerable attention, the county attorney requested and received a court order "prohibiting everyone in attendance [at the preliminary hearing] from 'releas[ing] or authoriz[ing] the release for public dissemination in any form or manner whatsoever any testimony given or evidence adduced.'"[44] The preliminary hearing was held and Simants was bound over for trial. Acting on behalf of the newspapers in the state, the Nebraska Press Association requested permission to intervene in the case, urging that the county court's restrictive order be lifted. After considering the matter, District Judge Hugh Stuart issued an order prohibiting the publication of certain information pending Simants's trial. The Supreme Court of Nebraska modified Judge Stuart's order, but did leave intact some restrictions on the press. This order was in effect until the trial in January 1976 when Simants was convicted. The press association petitioned the U.S. Supreme Court to review the constitutionality of the restrictive order issued in this case. Upon hearing the matter, the Court unanimously agreed that the order was unconstitutional as an infringement on freedom of the press.

Justice Brennan wrote a concurring opinion. He first pointed out that in cases such as this, two rights are at issue: the Sixth Amendment right of the defendant to a fair trial, and the First Amendment right of the press to publish freely. He acknowledged "that uninhibited prejudicial pretrial publicity may destroy the fairness of a criminal trial." On the other hand, he pointed out, the "First Amendment thus accords greater protection against prior restraints than it does against subsequent punishment for a particular speech" because prior restraints censor publication before it can occur. Furthermore, before resorting to prior restraints, judges should use other methods available to them to assure the defendant a fair trial. These include sequestration of jurors and control over the release of information by court and law enforcement personnel and attorneys involved in the case.

> To hold that courts cannot impose any prior restraints on the reporting of or commentary upon information revealed in open court proceedings, disclosed in public documents, or divulged by other sources with respect to the criminal justice system is not, I must emphasize, to countenance the sacrifice of precious Sixth Amendment rights on the altar of the First Amendment. For although there may in some instances be tension between uninhibited and robust reporting by the press and fair trials for criminal defendants, judges possess adequate tools short of injunctions against reporting for relieving the tension. To be sure, these alternatives may require greater sensitivity and effort on the part of judges conducting criminal trials than would the stifling of publicity through the simple expedient of issuing a restrictive order on the press; but that sensitivity and effort is required in order to ensure the full enjoyment and proper accommodation of both First and Sixth Amendment rights.

The case of *Globe Newspaper Co. v. Superior Court*[45] involved a closure order issued to protect the victim of a rape from exposure to the press during her testimony. During the trial of a defendant accused of raping three girls, all of whom were minors, the trial judge, acting pursuant to a Massachusetts law, closed the courtroom, although neither the prosecution nor the defendant requested such action. The defendant was acquitted, but the battle over the validity of the closure order continued. The Supreme Judicial Court of Massachusetts concluded that, while the law did not require the whole trial to be closed, it did mandate closing during the victim's testimony "to encourage young victims of sexual offenses to come forward; once they have come forward, the statute is designed to preserve their ability to testify by protecting them from undue psychological harm at trial." A majority of the U.S. Supreme Court did not accept that as sufficient reason to violate the right to freedom of the press. With Justice Brennan writing the opinion, the majority held that neither safeguarding the well-being of minors, nor trying to encourage them to report being molested justified the abridgment of the freedom of the press to report trials.

Brennan pointed out two reasons for having public trials:

> First, the criminal trial historically has been open to the press and general public. Second, the right of access to criminal trials plays a particularly significant role in the functioning of the judicial process and the government as a whole. Public scrutiny of a criminal trial enhances the quality and safeguards the integrity of the factfinding process, with benefits to both the defendant and to society as a whole. Moreover, public access to the criminal trial fosters an appearance of fairness, thereby heightening public respect for the judicial process. And in the broadest terms, public access to criminal trials permits the public to participate in and serve as a check upon the judicial process—an essential component in our structure of self-government.

Obscenity. Justice Brennan's views on obscenity changed dramatically between 1957 and 1973. In 1957 he wrote the majority opinion in *Roth v. United States,*[46] upholding convictions for the sale and distribution of obscene material. "We hold," he declared, "that obscenity is not within the area of constitutionally protected speech." Obscenity is not entitled to First Amendment protection because it is "utterly without redeeming social importance."

Having reached that conclusion, the justice was willing to allow the state to imprison a person for selling to a minor " '(a) any picture . . . which depicts nudity . . . and which is harmful to minors,' and '(b) any . . . magazine . . . which contains . . . [such pictures] . . . and which, taken as a whole, is harmful to minors.' "[47] Although scientific studies had not found a causal connection between obscenity and antisocial behavior of minors, such studies had not been able to disprove that such a link did exist. Even without scientific support, however, the New York legislature had apparently concluded that such a connection did exist and that obscenity was harmful to minors. It therefore was not for the Court to question that decision. "We therefore cannot say," Brennan concluded, "that . . . [the law] in defining the obscenity of material on the basis of its appeal to minors under 17, has no rational relation to the objective of safeguarding such minors from harm."

By 1973 it was clear to the justice that the line between material that was punishable as obscenity and that which was entitled to First Amendment protection could not be clearly drawn. "I am convinced that the approach initiated 16 years ago in *Roth v. United States*," he wrote, ". . . cannot bring stability to this area of the law without jeopardizing fundamental First Amendment values, and I have concluded that the time has come to make a significant departure from that approach."[48]

After an extensive review of the obscenity cases decided since *Roth*, Brennan concluded "that at least in the absence of distribution to juveniles or obtrusive exposure to unconsenting adults, the First and Fourteenth Amendments prohibit the State and Federal Governments from attempting wholly to suppress sexually oriented materials on the basis of their allegedly 'obscene' contents." He did not believe, however, that he had come up with the perfect solution, because "difficult questions must still be faced, notably in the areas of distribution to juveniles and offensive exposure to unconsenting adults."[49]

Freedom of Association

Affidavits and Oaths. Harry Keyishian, George Hochfield, Newton Garver, and Ralph N. Maud were teachers at the State University of New York at Buffalo. Each refused to sign "a certificate that he was not a Communist, and that if he had ever been a Communist, he had communicated that fact to the President of the State University of New York."[50] The certificate was required because a state law disqualified "from employment in the educational system any person who advocates the overthrow of government by force, violence, or any unlawful means, or publishes material advocating such overthrow or organizes or joins any society or group of persons advocating such doctrine."

When threatened with dismissal for refusing to sign the certificate, the teachers brought an action against the state Board of Regents asserting that the certificate requirement was unconstitutional. The court held that the law was not unconstitutional, but a majority of the Supreme Court reversed. Justice Brennan, writing for the majority, pointed out that "mere knowing membership without a specific intent to further the unlawful aims of an organization is not a constitutionally adequate basis for exclusion from such positions as those held by appellants." In other words, the First Amendment protects the right of a person to join an organization that has as its purpose the overthrow of the government, so long as the person does not have the specific intent to assist in carrying out that purpose. Applying this concept to the New York law, Brennan concluded that it was "invalid insofar as . . . [it proscribes] knowing membership without any showing of specific intent to further the unlawful aims of the Communist Party of the United States or of the State of New York."

The Communist Party of Indiana brought an action against the Indiana State Election Board because it was refused a place on the 1972 election ballot. Under Indiana law, access to the ballot required the political party to file "an affidavit, . . . under oath, that it does not advocate the overthrow of local, state or national government by force or violence."[51] When the case reached the Supreme Court, it held the oath requirement to be a violation of the First Amendment. "At stake," Brennan said, "are appellants' First and Fourteenth Amendment rights to associate with others for the common advancement of political beliefs and ideas. 'The right to associate with the political party of one's choice is an integral part of this basic constitutional freedom.'" The Indiana requirement, however, infringed upon the Communist Party and its members' right of association, without any proof of a specific intent to overthrow government.

Associational Privacy. "New York and Pennsylvania have publicly announced that the subway conductor and teacher are disloyal Americans. This consequence of the States' actions is devastating beside the loss of employment. In each case a man's honor and reputation are indelibly stained. . . . The petitioners thus not only lose their present jobs, but their standing in the community is so undermined as doubtless to cost them most opportunities for future jobs."[52]

It was with those words that Justice Brennan dissented from the Court's decisions to uphold the discharges of Lerner, the subway conductor, and Herman A. Beilan, the teacher, both of whom had refused to answer questions concerning their Communist affiliations. Brennan was concerned that the procedures by which the discharges were conducted did not give adequate protection to the First Amendment rights of the individuals involved. "It may be stated as a generality," he declared, "that government is never at liberty to be arbitrary in its relations with its citizens, and close judicial scrutiny is essential when state action infringes on the right of a man to be accepted in his community, to express his ideas in an atmosphere of calm decency, and to be free of the dark stain of suspicion of his loyalty on account of his political beliefs and associations."

During the 1950s when the House Committee on Un-American Activities was conducting investigations into Communist activities in the United States, New Hampshire Attorney General Louis C. Wyman was conducting a similar investigation within the state.[53] Wyman called Uphaus, the executive director of World Fellowship, Inc., which conducted a summer camp, to testify and to produce certain records of the organization. Uphaus testified concerning the group's activities but would not produce its records. He was adjudged to be in contempt and ordered to jail until the information was forthcoming. He appealed to the Supreme Court, but a majority voted to uphold the contempt order. Brennan dissented in a lengthy opinion wherein he pointed out that "where the exercise of the investigatory power collides with constitutionally guaranteed freedoms, that power too has inevitable limitations, and the delicate and always difficult accommodation of the two with minimum sacrifice of either is the hard task of the judiciary and ultimately of this Court."

After examining the record before the Court, he could find "no evidence that any activity of a sort that violates the law of New Hampshire or could in fact be constitutionally punished went on at the camp. What is clear is that there was some sort of assemblage at the camp that was oriented toward the discussion of political and other public matters. The activities going on were those of private citizens. The views expounded obviously were minority views. But the assemblage was, on its face, for purposes to which the First and Fourteenth Amendments give constitutional protection against incursion by the powers of government."

For the Advancement of Legal Goals. The Virginia Conference of the NAACP financed legal action that had as its goal bringing an end to racial segregation. The conference, however, insisted that its staff of attorneys conduct the litigation.

> The Conference defrays all expenses of litigation in an assisted case, and usually, although not always, pays each lawyer on the case a per diem fee not to exceed $60, plus out-of-pocket expenses. The assisted litigant receives no money from the Conference or the staff of lawyers. The staff member may not accept, from the litigant or any other source, any other compensation for his services in an NAACP-assisted case.[54]

When Virginia courts held that the activities of the conference violated a state law banning "the improper solicitation of any legal or professional business," the NAACP appealed to the Supreme Court. In an opinion written by Justice Brennan, a majority of the Court responded, "We hold that the activities of the NAACP, its affiliates and legal staff shown on this record are modes of expression and association protected by the First and Fourteenth Amendments which Virginia may not prohibit, under its power to regulate the legal profession."

Justice Brennan did not buy Virginia's argument "that the purpose of these regulations was merely to insure high professional standards and not to curtail free expression." "We conclude," he said, "that although the petitioner [NAACP] has amply shown that its activities fall within the First Amendment's protections, the State has failed to advance any substantial regulatory interest, in the form of substantive evils flowing from petitioner's activities which can justify the broad prohibitions which it has imposed."

Patronage Dismissals of Public Employees. One of the first things that Richard J. Elrod did when he was elected sheriff of Cook County, Illinois, was to fire John Burns and several other Sheriff Department employees because they did not belong to the Democratic Party, nor would they pledge allegiance to it. Burns and the others sought help from the federal district court, but the case was dismissed. When the circuit court ordered the case to be heard, Elrod appealed to the Supreme Court, but was not successful there either.[55] Justice Brennan, writing for himself and justices White and Marshall, set forth the question to be decided. "This case presents the question whether public employees who allege that they were discharged or threatened with discharge solely because of their partisan political affiliation or nonaffiliation state a claim for deprivation of constitutional rights secured by the First and Fourteenth Amendments." In answering the question in the affirmative, Brennan noted that "patronage practice is not new to American politics. It has existed at the federal level at least since the Presidency of Thomas Jefferson, although its popularization and legitimation primarily occurred later, in the Presidency of Andrew Jackson. . . . More recent times have witnessed a strong decline in its use, particularly with respect to public employment."

The justice then pointed out that patronage not only directly affects associational rights of the individuals involved but affects the electoral process as well.

> Conditioning public employment on partisan support prevents support of competing political interests. Existing employees are deterred from such support, as well as the multitude seeking jobs. As government employment, state or federal, becomes more pervasive, the greater the dependence on it becomes, and therefore the greater becomes the power to starve political opposition by commanding partisan support, financial and otherwise. Patronage tips the electoral process in favor of the incumbent party, and where the practice's scope is substantial relative to the size of the electorate, the impact on the process can be significant.

Once it was determined that patronage infringed upon First Amendment rights, the question remained whether there was any government interest great enough to override those rights. The state argued that having employees of similar political persuasion (1) promoted efficiency, (2) prevented obstruction of the new administrations policies, and (3) preserved the democratic process. While recognizing that these were valid interests, the justice did not find any one nor all of them combined sufficient to infringe upon the constitutional rights of the employees. He therefore concluded that "patronage dismissals severely restrict political belief and association."

Cynthia Rutan, Franklin Taylor, Rickey Standefer, Dan O'Brien, and James Moore, present, former, or would-be Illinois state employees, brought an action claiming that the hiring and promotion practices of Governor James R. Thompson violated their constitutional rights. Each of the plaintiffs claimed that he or she had been laid off, not promoted, or not hired because he or she was not a member of the Republican Party of Illinois. The Supreme Court responded: "We hold that the rule of *Elrod* . . . extends to promotion, transfer, recall, and hiring decisions based on party affiliation and support and that all of the petitioners . . . have stated claims upon which relief may be granted."[56]

The Republican Party argued that the practices followed by Governor Thompson did not violate the First Amendment because they were not punitive, as being discharged was. But Brennan and the majority did not agree. "Employees who find themselves in dead-end positions due to their political backgrounds," Brennan asserted,

> *are* adversely affected. They will feel a significant obligation to support political positions held by their superiors, and to refrain from acting on the political views they actually hold, in order to progress up the career ladder. Employees denied transfers to workplaces reasonably close to their homes until they join and work for the Republican Party will feel a daily pressure from their long commutes to do so. And employees who have been laid off may well feel compelled to engage in whatever political activity is necessary to regain regular paychecks and positions corresponding to their skill and experience.

Addressing the effect of the First Amendment upon government employment practices, Justice Brennan wrote, "The First Amendment prevents the government, except in the most compelling circumstances, from wielding its power to interfere with its employees' freedom to believe and associate, or to not believe and not associate."

Choosing a Political Party. Storer and Frommhagen wanted to run as independent candidates for election to Congress in their respective districts in 1972 but were prevented from doing so by California law. "Both men were registered Democrats until early in 1972, Storer until January and Frommhagen until March of that year. This affiliation with a qualified political party within a year prior to the 1972 primary disqualified both men."[57]

Both men challenged the constitutionality of the law, arguing that it violated their rights under the First Amendment. A majority of the Supreme Court disagreed. "It appears obvious to us," Justice White declared, "that the one-year disaffiliation provision furthers the State's interest in the stability of its political system. We also consider that interest not only permissible, but compelling and as outweighing the interest the candidate and his supporters may have in making a late rather than an early decision to seek independent ballot status."

Justice Brennan agreed with the majority that because California's law affected First Amendment rights, it needed to be "strictly scrutinized." But he disagreed that in so doing the majority had properly evaluated the burden the law placed upon Storer's and Frommhagen's rights. The law, he argued,

> plainly places a significant burden upon independent candidacy—and therefore effectively burdens as well the rights of potential supporters and voters to associate for political purposes and to vote, . . . because potential independent candidates, currently affiliated with a recognized party, are required to take affirmative action toward candidacy fully *17 months* before the general election. Thus, such candidates must make that decision at a time when, as a matter of the realities of

our political system, they cannot know either who will be the nominees of the major parties, or what the significant election issues may be. That is an impossible burden to shoulder.[58]

The justice also pointed out that the record contained no evidence whatsoever that California had attempted to accomplish its goals by less drastic means.

On the same day that *Storer* was decided, the Court, in *American Party of Texas v. White,*[59] upheld election laws by which independent candidates in Texas could get on the general election ballot. Brennan voted with the majority. "I have joined the Court's opinion in *American Party of Texas v. White, supra,*" he said, "because I agree that, although the conditions for access to the general election ballot imposed by Texas law burden constitutionally protected rights, nevertheless those laws 'are constitutionally valid measures, reasonably taken in pursuit of vital state objectives that cannot be served equally well in significantly less burdensome ways.'"[60]

The Pursuit of Liberty

The Right to Travel. "This Court long ago recognized that the nature of our Federal Union and our constitutional concepts of personal liberty unite to require that all citizens be free to travel throughout the length and breadth of our land uninhibited by statutes, rules, or regulations which unreasonably burden this movement."[61]

With those words, Justice Brennan considered the claim of Vivian Marie Thompson, an unwed mother, 19 years old and pregnant with another child, who had moved to Hartford, Connecticut, from Dorchester, Massachusetts. Thompson's application for financial aid was denied because she had not lived in Connecticut for one year as required by state law. She filed an action in the federal district court, where three judges heard her claim that the denial of aid was unconstitutional. Two of the judges, in an opinion written by Judge J. Joseph Smith, concluded that Thompson's right to travel was being abridged, that she was denied the same privileges and immunities as persons living in the state, and because she was treated differently from persons who had lived in Connecticut for more than one year, she was not accorded equal protection of the law. A majority of the justices of the Supreme Court agreed, and Brennan was assigned to write the Court's opinion. Among the arguments made by the state were (1) "to discourage those indigents who would enter the State solely to obtain larger benefits"; (2) distinguishing "between new and old residents" should be permissible because old residents have contributed more "through the payment of taxes"; (3) that the waiting period is necessary for administrative reasons to prevent fraud; and (4) the requirement would encourage "new residents to join the labor force promptly." But the majority was not convinced that these were sufficient to override Thompson's constitutional rights. "We do not doubt,"

Brennan pointed out, "that the one-year waiting-period device is well suited to discourage the influx of poor families in need of assistance. An indigent who desires to migrate, resettle, find a job, and start a new life will doubtless hesitate if he knows that he must risk making the move without the possibility of falling back on state welfare assistance during his first year of residence, when his need may be most acute. But the purpose of inhibiting migration by needy persons into the State is constitutionally impermissible."

"Philip Agee is hardly a model representative of our Nation."[62] Even so, Justice Brennan believed that Agee's constitutional right to travel was violated when his passport was revoked by the State Department.

> From 1957 to 1968 . . . [Agee] was employed by Central Intelligence Agency. He held key positions in the division of the Agency that is responsible for covert intelligence gathering in foreign countries. . . . He served in undercover assignments abroad and came to know many Government employees and other persons supplying information to the United States. The relationships of many of these people to our Government are highly confidential; many are still engaged in intelligence gathering.
>
> In 1974 Agee called a press conference in London to announce his "campaign to fight the United States CIA wherever it is operating." He declared his intent "to expose CIA officers and agents and to take the measures necessary to drive them out of the countries where they are operating."

The State Department responded by revoking Agee's passport. Agee then sued Secretary of State Cyrus Vance seeking to have the passport reinstated. Judge Gerhard A. Gesell ordered the secretary to do so, having concluded that the secretary had no legal authority to revoke the passport. The circuit court upheld Judge Gesell, but a majority of the Supreme Court reversed, with Justice Brennan dissenting. The Court acknowledged that travel abroad without a passport is difficult. Nevertheless, the majority was of the opinion that the right to travel abroad was outweighed in this case by the need "to protect the secrecy of our Government's foreign intelligence operations."

But for Brennan the case was not that simple. He wrote: "But just as the Constitution protects both popular and unpopular speech, it likewise protects both popular and unpopular travelers. And it is important to remember that this decision applies not only to Philip Agee, whose activities could be perceived as harming the national security, but also to other citizens who may merely disagree with Government foreign policy and express their views." The justice chided the majority for not following two prior passport cases: "In permitting the Secretary to stop this unpopular traveler and critic of the CIA, the Court professes to rely on, but in fact departs from, two precedents in the passport regulation area."

The Right of Privacy. Massachusetts law made it a felony for anyone to dispense contraceptives who was not a physician or pharmacist, and even when prescribing a birth control drug or article, the physician or pharmacist could do so only to married persons. After William R. Baird, who was neither a physician nor a pharmacist, had given a talk at Boston University concerning contraceptive devices, he gave a vaginal foam contraceptive to a woman in the audience. He was arrested, convicted, and sentenced to three months in jail. He applied to Federal Judge Anthony Julian for release, contending that the law was unconstitutional. Judge Julian disagreed and dismissed the petition, but the circuit court vacated the dismissal, and the Supreme Court upheld that decision. The Court found that allowing married persons to obtain contraceptives but not those who were single violated the Equal Protection Clause, as well as the right of privacy of those individuals who wished to have such devices.[63] Referring to *Griswold v. Connecticut,*[64] in which the Court developed the right of privacy, Justice Brennan wrote:

> It is true that in *Griswold* the right of privacy in question inhered in the marital relationship. Yet the marital couple is not an independent entity with a mind and heart of its own, but an association of two individuals each with a separate intellectual and emotional makeup. If the right of privacy means anything, it is the right of the *individual,* married or single, to be free from unwarranted governmental intrusion into matters so fundamentally affecting a person as the decision whether to bear or beget a child.[65]

"Appellant, Mrs. Inez Moore, lives in her East Cleveland home together with her son, Dale Moore, Sr., and her two grandsons, Dale, Jr., and John Moore, Jr. The two boys are first cousins rather than brothers; we are told that John came to live with his grandmother and with the elder and younger Dale Moores after his mother's death."[66]

When Mrs. Moore was told that under a city ordinance John was an "illegal occupant" and that he must be removed from the home, Mrs. Moore refused to comply. The ordinance in question permitted only "one dependent married or unmarried child of the nominal head of the household . . . and dependent children of such dependent child" to live together. Because John's father did not live in the home, John's presence was in conflict with the law.

Moore was convicted of violating the law, and her conviction was upheld by an Ohio appellate court but reversed by the Supreme Court. Justice Brennan wrote a concurring opinion. He acknowledged that cities have the authority to enact zoning ordinances, particularly to combat noise, traffic congestion, and overcrowding. "But," he asserted,

> the zoning power is not a license for local communities to enact senseless and arbitrary restrictions which cut deeply into private areas of protected family life. East Cleveland may not constitutionally define "family" as essentially confined to parents and the parents' own children. The plurality's opinion [which Brennan joined] conclusively demonstrates that classifying family patterns in this eccentric way is not a rational means of achieving the ends East Cleveland claims for

its ordinance, and further that the ordinance unconstitutionally abridges the "freedom of personal choice in the matters of . . . family life [that] is one of the liberties protected by the Due Process Clause of the Fourteenth Amendment."

Cora McRae, several other individuals, doctors, and Planned Parenthood of New York City, Inc., sued Joseph A. Califano, Jr., secretary of health, education, and welfare and others alleging that a law known as the Hyde Amendment infringed upon their right to liberty guaranteed by the Due Process Clause of the fifth Amendment. The Hyde Amendment prohibited the use of federal Medicaid funds for "abortions except where the life of the mother would be endangered if the fetus were carried to term; or except for such medical procedures necessary for the victims of rape or incest."[67] The Supreme Court upheld the Hyde Amendment, the majority concluding that "although government may not place obstacles in the path of a woman's exercise of her freedom of choice, it need not remove those not of its own creation. . . . The financial constraints that restrict an indigent woman's ability to enjoy the full range of constitutionally protected freedom of choice are the product not of governmental restrictions on access to abortions, but rather of her indigency."

Justice Brennan thought this was a "mischaracterization of the nature of the fundamental right recognized in *Roe v. Wade,* . . . and . . . [a] misconception of the manner in which that right is infringed by federal and state legislation withdrawing all funding for medically necessary abortions." Commenting upon the nature of the right established in *Roe,* the justice noted "that the constitutional right to personal privacy encompasses a woman's decision whether or not to terminate her pregnancy." "The Hyde Amendment's denial of public funds for medically necessary abortions," he said, "plainly intrudes upon this constitutionally protected decision, for both by design and in effect it serves to coerce indigent pregnant women to bear children that they would otherwise elect not to have." And the majority misconceives the effect that the withholding of funds really has on pregnant indigent women. "By funding all of the expenses associated with childbirth and none of the expenses incurred in terminating pregnancy," he declares, "the Government literally makes an offer that the indigent woman cannot afford to refuse. It matters not that in this instance the Government has used a carrot rather than a stick."

Edgar Paul, chief of police of Louisville, Kentucky, and Russell McDaniel, chief of police of Jefferson County, Kentucky, decided to do something about shoplifters. They put together a flyer and five pages of "mug shots" of persons who had been or were suspected to be shoplifters. A "mug shot" of Edward Charles Davis III was printed on page two. Approximately 800 copies of flyer were sent to merchants in the area.

More than a year before Davis had been arrested on suspicion of shoplifting but had not been prosecuted, and the charge against him was dismissed about the time that the flyer appeared.

Davis brought an action against both police chiefs, claiming that his constitutional rights had been violated by his picture being in the flyer. Judge Rhodes Bratcher dismissed the case; the circuit court reinstated it; but the Supreme Court, not being able to find any constitutional right that had been violated here, reversed. Although the Court acknowledged that Davis might have been injured by the publication, it concluded "that the interest in reputation asserted in this case is neither 'liberty' nor 'property' guaranteed against state deprivation without due process of law."[68]

For Brennan the "potential of today's decision . . . [was] frightening for a free people," and he dissented. After discussing several prior cases in which the Court had recognized a "liberty" interest in one's good name and reputation, he wrote:

> I have always thought that one of the Court's most important roles is to provide a formidable bulwark against governmental violation of the constitutional safeguards securing in our free society the legitimate expectations of every person to innate human dignity and sense of worth. It is a regrettable abdication of that role and a saddening denigration of our majestic Bill of Rights when the Court tolerates arbitrary and capricious official conduct branding an individual as a criminal without compliance with constitutional procedures designed to ensure the fair and impartial ascertainment of criminal culpability. Today's decision must surely be a short-lived aberration.

Equal Protection of the Law

Blacks on Juries. In *Whitus v. Georgia,*[69] Justice Tom Clark wrote, "For over fourscore years it has been federal statutory law, . . . and the law of this Court as applied to the States through the Equal Protection Clause of the Fourteenth Amendment, that a conviction cannot stand if it is based on an indictment of a grand jury or the verdict of a petit jury from which Negroes were excluded by reason of their race." Clark wrote for all the justices in *Whitus,* including Brennan, and the Court reversed Whitus's conviction.

When Batson, a black man, was being tried for burglary and receipt of stolen goods, the prosecutor, using peremptory challenges to jurors, struck off four black persons, leaving only white persons as jurors. Batson's lawyer asked the court to discharge the jury, claiming that the prosecutor's actions violated his client's constitutional rights, including a denial of equal protection of the law. The trial judge refused, and Batson was convicted. The Supreme Court of Kentucky affirmed, but eight justices of the U.S. Supreme Court, including Brennan, voted to send the case back to the trial court to determine whether striking the four black prospective jurors constituted purposeful discrimination in violation of the Equal Protection Clause.[70] While the Court has held that a person is not entitled to a jury composed only of persons of his or her race, it has also held that the "Equal Protection Clause guarantees the defendant that the State will not exclude members of his race from the jury venire on account of race . . . or on the false assumption that members of his race as a group are not qualified to serve as jurors."

Writing for the eight justices, Justice Powell pointed out that the "harm from discriminatory jury selection extends beyond that inflicted on the defendant and the excluded juror to touch the entire community. Selection procedures that purposefully exclude black persons from juries undermine public confidence in the fairness of our system of justice. . . . Discrimination within the judicial system is most pernicious because it is 'a stimulant to that race prejudice which is an impediment to securing to [black citizens] that equal justice which the law aims to secure to all others.'"

Powell responded to the state's argument that the decision would "eviscerate the fair trial values served by the peremptory challenge" as follows:

> While we recognize, of course, that the peremptory challenge occupies an important position in our trial procedures, we do not agree that our decision today will undermine the contribution the challenge generally makes to the administration of justice. The reality of the practice, amply reflected in many state- and federal-court opinions, shows that the challenge may be, and unfortunately at times has been, used to discriminate against black jurors. By requiring trial courts to be sensitive to the racially discriminatory use of peremptory challenges, our decision enforces the mandate of equal protection and furthers the ends of justice. In view of the heterogeneous population of our Nation, public respect for our criminal justice system and the rule of law will be strengthened if we ensure that no citizen is disqualified from jury service because of his race.

Where Blacks Live and Where Their Children Go to School. Nellie Hunter brought an action against the city of Akron, Ohio, claiming a violation of equal protection of the law. Hunter had asked a real estate agent to show her some houses, but when they first met, the agent, according to Hunter, told her "that she could not show me any of the houses on the list she had prepared for me because all of the owners had specified they did not wish their houses shown to negroes."[71]

When Hunter sought help from the Commission on Equal Opportunity in Housing, she was informed that the voters had repealed the fair housing law and had provided that in the future any such law would have to be adopted by a majority vote of the people. When the Ohio courts held that the action of the voters did not violate the Equal Protection Clause, Hunter appealed to the Supreme Court, which reversed, with Justice Brennan voting with the majority, and only Justice Black dissenting.

Justice White pointed out for the majority that the "automatic referendum system does not . . . [prohibit the enactment of laws against] housing discrimination on sexual or political grounds, or against those with children or dogs, nor does it affect tenants seeking more heat or better maintenance from landlords, nor those seeking rent control, urban renewal, public housing, or new building codes." The impact of the law, the justice said, "places special burdens on racial minorities within the governmental process." And he noted that burdens placed upon racial minorities are "constitutionally suspect," and "subject to the 'most rigid scrutiny.'"

Fourteen years after the Court's decision in *Brown v. Board of Education*, Justice Brennan wrote: "We [therefore] hold that . . . [the law] discriminates against minorities and constitutes a real, substantial, and invidious denial of equal protection of the laws."

"The question for decision is whether, under all the circumstances here, respondent School Board's adoption of a 'freedom-of-choice plan' which allows a pupil to choose his own public school constitutes adequate compliance with the Board's responsibility 'to achieve a system of determining admission to the public schools on a nonracial basis.'"[72]

Brennan wrote these statements in a case involving an attempt by the school board of New Kent County, Virginia, to avoid integrating its public schools. The justice described the school board's response to *Brown:*

> The pattern of separate "white" and "Negro" schools in the New Kent County school system established under compulsion of state laws is precisely the pattern of segregation to which *Brown I* and *Brown II* were particularly addressed, and which *Brown I* declared unconstitutionally denied Negro children equal protection of the laws. Racial identification of the system's schools was complete, extending not just to the composition of student bodies at the two schools but to every facet of school operations—faculty, staff, transportation, extracurricular activities and facilities. In short the State, acting through the local school board and school officials, organized and operated a dual system, part "white" and part "Negro."

Brennan did not say that "freedom-of-choice" plans were always unconstitutional, but rather might under some circumstances be an effective "tool of desegregation." But in this case it was clear that the plan was not designed to, nor did it, desegregate the schools. No white student had transferred to the all-black school, and only 115 out of 740 black students attended the former all-white school. Thus, only the white school was desegregated and that only marginally. "The Board must be required," the justice declared, "to formulate a new plan and, in light of other courses which appear open to the Board, such as zoning, fashion steps which promise realistically to convert promptly to a system without a 'white' school and a 'Negro' school, but just schools."

On the same day as the New Kent County case was decided, Brennan wrote opinions in two other desegregation cases. The Court struck down a "freedom-of-choice" plan of the Gould Schools and fields Schools in Arkansas.[73] And in commenting upon the "free transfer plan" of the school district in Jackson,

Tennessee, Brennan said that "the Board has chosen to adopt a method achieving minimal disruption of the old pattern is evident from its long delay in making any effort whatsoever to desegregate, and the deliberately discriminatory manner in which the Board administered the plan until checked by the District Court."[74]

Integration of Public and Private Facilities. "I have no doubt," Justice Brennan declared, "that a public park may constitutionally be closed down because it is too expensive to run or has become superfluous, or for some other reason, strong or weak, or for no other reason at all. But under the Equal Protection Clause a State may not close down a public facility solely to avoid its duty to desegregate that facility."[75] With those words the justice dissented from the Court's approval of the return of Bacon's park to his heirs in *Evans v. Abney*.

Brennan did not agree with the argument that the state and city were not involved in the act of returning the park to the heirs because all the state and city were doing was carrying out Bacon's wishes as expressed in his will.

> This discriminatory closing is permeated with state action: at the time Senator Bacon wrote his will Georgia statutes expressly authorized and supported the precise kind of discrimination provided for by him; in accepting title to the park, public officials of the City of Macon entered into an arrangement vesting in private persons the power to enforce a reversion if the city should ever incur a constitutional obligation to desegregate the park; it is a *public* park that is being closed for a discriminatory reason after having been operated for nearly half a century as a segregated *public* facility; and it is a state court that is enforcing the racial restriction that keeps apparently willing parties of different races from coming together in the park. That is state action in overwhelming abundance.[76]

"This, then," he argued, "is not a case of private discrimination. It is rather discrimination in which the State of Georgia is 'significantly involved,' and enforcement of the reverter is unconstitutional."

Sandra Adickes, a schoolteacher from New York conducting a "Freedom School"[77] in Hattiesburg, Mississippi, was refused service at a lunch counter operated by S.H. Kress & Co. With her at the time were six of her black students, who were served. When Adickes left the store, she was arrested and charged with vagrancy and jailed. Adickes then sued Kress & Co., alleging a violation of her civil rights and claiming that she had been refused service "because she was a 'Caucasian in the company of Negroes.'" In order to recover damages, Adickes needed to prove that Kress & Co. acted under color of law—that is, that somehow the state of Mississippi and or the city of Hattiesburg were connected to the discrimination she received from Kress & Co. The trial court granted judgment for Kress & Co., which was upheld by the circuit court, both courts being of the opinion that Adickes had not offered sufficient proof to connect the government to the action taken by Kress & Co.'s manager. The Supreme Court reversed and remanded the case for further proceedings. Justice Brennan concurred in a lengthy opinion wherein he reviewed the Court's approach to finding state involvement in private discrimination.

> The state-action doctrine reflects the profound judgment that denials of equal treatment, and particularly denials on account of race or color, are singularly grave when government has or shares responsibility for them. Government is the social organ to which all in our society look for the promotion of liberty, justice, fair and equal treatment, and the setting of worthy norms and goals for social conduct. Therefore something is uniquely amiss in a society where the government, the authoritative oracle of community values, involves itself in racial discrimination. Accordingly, in the cases that have come before us this Court has condemned significant state involvement in racial discrimination, however subtle and indirect it may have been and whatever form it may have taken. . . . These decisions represent vigilant fidelity to the constitutional principle that no State shall in any significant way lend its authority to the sordid business of racial discrimination.

He then agreed that Adickes's case should not have been dismissed, and that she was entitled to another opportunity to prove that the government, state, and or city were behind the discrimination she suffered at the lunch counter.

The justice dissented when the Court dismissed K. Leroy Irvis's case against the Moose Lodge because it did not find state involvement in the lodge's refusal to serve Irvis, who was black.[78] Brennan found state action by the fact that it had granted the lodge a liquor license. "Liquor licensing laws," he argued,

> are only incidentally revenue measures; they are primarily pervasive regulatory schemes under which the State dictates and continually supervises virtually every detail of the operation of the licensee's business. Very few, if any, other licensed businesses experience such complete state involvement. Yet the Court holds that such involvement does not constitute "state action" making the Lodge's refusal to serve a guest liquor solely because of his race a violation of the Fourteenth Amendment. The vital flaw in the Court's reasoning is its complete disregard of the fundamental value underlying the "state action" concept.

Gender Discrimination.

> Sharron Frontiero, a lieutenant in the United States Air Force, sought increased quarters allowances, and housing and medical benefits for her husband, . . . Joseph Frontiero, on the ground that he was her "dependent." Although such benefits would automatically have been granted with respect to the wife of a male member of the uniformed services, . . . [Frontiero's] application was denied because she failed to demonstrate that her husband was dependent on her for more than one-half of his support.[79]

The Frontieros brought suit against the secretary of defense claiming that they were denied equal protection of the law by the air force regulations. The case was heard before a three-judge district court, which found no denial of equal protection, with one judge dissenting. Justices Brennan, Douglas, White, Marshall, and Stewart voted to reverse, with Brennan writing an opinion that all joined, except Stewart.

Commenting upon the different treatment of women, Brennan pointed out,

> There can be no doubt that our Nation has had a long and unfortunate history of sex discrimination. Traditionally, such discrimination was rationalized by an attitude of "romantic paternalism" which, in practical effect, put women, not on a pedestal, but in a cage. . . . As a result of notions such as these, our statute books gradually became laden with gross, stereotyped distinctions between the sexes and, indeed, throughout much of the 19th century the position of women in our society was, in many respects, comparable to that of blacks under the pre–Civil War slave codes. Neither slaves nor women could hold office, serve on juries, or bring suit in their own names, and married women traditionally were denied the legal capacity to hold or convey property or to serve as legal guardians of their own children.

These "statutory distinctions between the sexes," he continued, "often have the effect of invidiously relegating the entire class of females to inferior legal status without regard to the actual capabilities of its individual members."

In *Craig v. Boren*,[80] Justice Brennan wrote: "The question to be decided is whether such a gender-based differential constitutes a denial to males 18–20 years of age of the equal protection of the law in violation of the Fourteenth Amendment."

The gender-based discrimination was that females 18 years of age and older could purchase 3.2 percent beer, but males had to wait until they were 21 years old. The majority answered the question by holding that the law was a denial of equal protection and therefore unconstitutional.

The state attempted to justify this disparity of treatment with statistics relating to the use of alcohol and traffic accidents, and driving under the influence. But the Court was unimpressed, particularly because none of the studies specifically related to the use of 3.2 percent beer, which the state had labeled "nonintoxicating." "But this merely illustrates that proving broad sociological propositions by statistics," the justice declared, "is in tension with the normative philosophy that underlies the Equal Protection Clause. . . . We hold, therefore, that . . . Oklahoma's 3.2% beer statute invidiously discriminates against males 18–20 years of age."

Lillian M. Orr sued her former husband, William H. Orr, for back alimony. Justice Richard L. Jones of the Alabama Supreme Court describes the issue in the case: "Here, we have a needy wife who qualifies for alimony and a husband who has the property and earnings from which alimony can be paid. . . . The husband, however, complains that the statutes are unconstitutional because they place an obligation upon male spouses which is not reciprocally impressed upon female spouses."[81] The Alabama Supreme Court refused to hold the state laws unconstitutional, and Justice Jones dissented. In an opinion written by Justice Brennan, the U.S. Supreme Court agreed with Justice Jones and reversed.[82]

In looking at the state's justification for the gender classification, Justice Brennan found two "legislative objectives." "One is a legislative purpose to provide help for needy spouses, using sex as a proxy for need. The other is a goal of compensating women for past discrimination during marriage, which assertedly has left them unprepared to fend for themselves in the working world following a divorce." Insofar as assisting needy spouses, Brennan pointed out that "individualized hearings" into the needs of either party would solve that problem. "There is no reason, therefore," he declared, "to use sex as a proxy for need. Needy males could be helped along with needy females with little if any additional burden on the State." Furthermore, "individualized hearings can determine which women were in fact discriminated against vis-a-vis their husbands, as well as which family units defied the stereotype and left the husband dependent on the wife."

The justice then concluded that since "the State's compensatory and ameliorative purposes are as well served by a gender-neutral classification as one that gender classifies and therefore carries with it the baggage of sexual stereotypes, the State cannot be permitted to classify on the basis of sex."

Justice Brennan dissented in *Michael M. v. Sonoma County Superior Court,*[83] when the Court upheld the California "statutory rape" statute that made it a crime for a male to have sexual intercourse with a female under the age of 18. He believed that the statute was based on the outmoded idea "that young women, in contrast to young men, were to be deemed legally incapable of consenting to an act of sexual intercourse. Because their chastity was considered particularly precious those young women were felt to be uniquely in need of the State's protection. In contrast, young men were assumed to be capable of making such decisions for themselves; the law therefore did not offer them any special protection." And because the law was based on this outmoded sexual stereotype, and the state was unable to present any other reason for its existence, it was unconstitutional as a violation of equal protection.

For Illegitimate Children. "The Court nowhere mentions the central reality of this case: Louisiana punishes illegitimate children for the misdeeds of their parents." That is how Brennan, in dissent, characterized the Court's decision in *Labine v. Vincent,*[84] which upheld the laws of Louisiana excluding illegitimate children from their father's inheritance. "I think," he wrote, "the Supreme Court of North Dakota stated the correct principle in invalidating an analogous discrimination in that State's inheritance laws: 'This statute, which punishes innocent children for their parents' transgressions has no place in our system of government which has as one of its basic tenets equal protection for all.'"

Justice Brennan also dissented in another case involving disinheritance of an illegitimate child. He describes the case: "All interested parties concede that Robert Lalli is the son of Mario Lalli. Mario Lalli supported Robert during his son's youth. Mario Lalli formally acknowledged Robert Lalli as his son. . . . Yet, for want of a judicial order of filiation entered during Mario's lifetime, Robert Lalli is denied his intestate share of his father's estate."[85]

In condemning the Court's decision, Brennan argued that it was not necessary to require a court order of paternity in order to protect an estate from fraudulent claims by illegitimate children. He believed "that the state interest in the speedy and efficient determination of paternity 'is completely served by public acknowledgement of parentage.'" And that was true in this case because "there is no factual dispute as to the relationship between Robert and Mario Lalli, [and therefore] there is no justification for denying Robert Lalli his intestate share."

Justice Brennan wrote the opinion in *Pickett v. Brown*,[86] when the Court unanimously struck down a Tennessee law requiring that an action for paternity and support be brought within two years of the birth of the child.

> Frances Annette Pickett filed an action . . . seeking to establish that Braxton Brown was the father of her son, Jeffrey Lee Pickett, who was born on November 1, 1968. . . . Frances Pickett also sought an order from the court requiring Brown to contribute to the support and maintenance of the child. Brown denied that he was the father of the child. . . . It is uncontested that he had never acknowledged the child as his own or contributed to the child's support. . . . Brown moved to dismiss the suit on the ground that it was barred by the 2-year limitations period. . . . Frances Pickett responded with a motion challenging the constitutionality of the limitations period.

The juvenile court concluded that the statute was unconstitutional, but the Tennessee Supreme Court upheld the law and reversed.

Brennan pointed out in his opinion that "in view of the history of treating illegitimate children less favorably than legitimate ones, we have subjected statutory classifications based on illegitimacy to a heightened level of [judicial] scrutiny." The justice then noted the effect the two-year limitation period might have upon the mother: "The mother may experience financial difficulties caused not only by the child's birth, but also by a loss of income attributable to the need to care for the child. Moreover, 'continuing affection for the child's father, a desire to avoid disapproval of family and community, or the emotional strain and confusion that often attend the birth of an illegitimate child,' . . . may inhibit a mother from filing a paternity suit on behalf of a child within two years after the child's birth."

This brought the justice to the conclusion that the law denied "certain illegitimate children [those whose mothers did not bring suit within two years] the equal protection of the laws guaranteed by the Fourteenth Amendment."

For Aliens. Federal District Judge William Wayne Justice of the Eastern District of Texas described the case before him as follows:

> This civil action began in September, 1977, when plaintiffs, a group of Mexican

children who had entered the United States illegally and currently reside in Smith County, Texas, sought injunctive and declaratory relief from this court by and through their parents, as next friends, against their exclusion from the public schools in the Tyler Independent School District. . . . The defendant Board of Trustees of Tyler I.S.D. had refused to enroll any undocumented child, absent a tuition fee of $1,000 per year, pursuant to . . . [Texas] law.[87]

After hearing the evidence, including the board's assertion that giving free education to illegal alien children would place a substantial drain on its funds, Judge Justice concluded that the children were being denied equal protection of the law and ordered that they be admitted to school without payment of any fee. The circuit court affirmed, as did the Supreme Court, with Justice Brennan writing the majority opinion.

The school board argued that the Equal Protection Clause protects only persons within the jurisdiction of the state, and that persons who are here illegally do not fit that description. Brennan responded, "Neither our cases nor the logic of the Fourteenth Amendment supports that constricting construction of the phrase 'within its jurisdiction.'"[88] "To permit a State," he continued,

to employ the phrase 'within its jurisdiction' in order to identify subclasses of persons whom it would define as beyond its jurisdiction, thereby relieving itself of the obligation to assure that its laws are designed and applied equally to those persons, would undermine the principal purpose for which the Equal Protection Clause was incorporated in the Fourteenth Amendment. The Equal Protection Clause was intended to work nothing less than the abolition of all caste-based and invidious class-based legislation. That objective is fundamentally at odds with the power the State asserts here to classify persons subject to its laws as nonetheless excepted from its protection.

The justice took note of the fact that there is "a substantial 'shadow population' of illegal migrants—numbering in the millions—within our borders." "The children who are plaintiffs in these cases," he continued,

are special members of this underclass. Persuasive arguments support the view that a State may withhold its beneficence from those whose very presence within the United States is the product of their own unlawful conduct. These arguments do not apply with the same force to classifications imposing disabilities on the minor *children* of such illegal entrants. At least, those who elect to enter our territory by stealth and in violation of our law should be prepared to bear the consequences, including, but not limited to, deportation. But the children of those illegal entrants are not comparably situated. Their "parents have the ability to conform their conduct to societal norms," and presumably the ability to remove themselves from the State's jurisdiction; but the children who are the plaintiffs in these cases "can affect neither their parents' conduct nor their own status."[89]

In responding to the state's desire to conserve its funds for the education of those lawfully in the state and likely to remain there, the justice wrote, "Even assuming that such an interest is legitimate, it is an interest that is most difficult to quantify. The State has no assurance that any child, citizen or not, will employ the education provided by the State within the confines of the State's borders."

Brennan concluded his opinion with these words: "If the State is to deny a discrete group of innocent children the free public education that it offers to other children residing within its borders, that denial must be justified by a showing that it furthers some substantial state interest. No such showing was made here."

For Voters and New Political Parties. While *Holt Civic Club v. Tuscaloosa*[90] is not exactly a "taxation without representation" case, Brennan thought it to be very similar, and dissented. Holt, a small community near Tuscaloosa, is "subject to Tuscaloosa's police and sanitary ordinances, to the jurisdiction of its municipal court, and to the requirements of its licensing fees, . . . [but the citizens of Holt] are not permitted to vote in Tuscaloosa's municipal elections, or to participate in or to initiate Tuscaloosa's referenda or recall elections." All of this, which was in accordance with Alabama state law, was approved by a majority of the Supreme Court, which found no violation of equal protection.

Justice Brennan thought this decision was contrary to previous cases that have protected the right to vote. He was also concerned that the result constituted a fracturing of the relationship between the governed and the government. "At the heart of our basic conception of a 'political community' . . . ," he argued, "is the notion of a reciprocal relationship between the process of government and those who subject themselves to that process by choosing to live within the area of its authoritative application." Extending Tuscaloosa's jurisdiction over activities outside its boundaries creates two types of citizens, those in Tuscaloosa, who can vote in municipal elections, and, in this case, citizens of Holt, who cannot. Because the law allowing this result distinguishes between "otherwise qualified voters without a compelling justification," Justice Brennan concluded that "the challenged statutes . . . [are a] violation of the Equal Protection Clause."[91]

> On April 24, 1980, petitioner John Anderson announced that he was an independent candidate for the office of President of the United States. Thereafter, his supporters—by gathering the signatures of registered voters, filing required documents, and submitting filing fees—were able to meet the substantive requirements for having his name placed on the ballot for the general election in November 1980 in all 50 States and the District of Columbia. On April 24, however, it was already too late for Anderson to qualify for a position on the ballot in Ohio and certain other States because the statutory deadlines for filing a statement of candidacy had already passed. The question presented in this case is whether Ohio's early filing deadline placed an unconstitutional burden on the voting and associational rights of Anderson's supporters.[92]

Among the important constitutional issues presented by Anderson's case was whether Ohio's early filing requirement was an undue burden upon the First Amendment associational rights of Anderson and his supporters, and whether the fact that national parties are not required to meet that deadline constitutes a violation of equal protection. The Court, with Brennan joining the majority, held that Ohio's filing deadline was unconstitutional on all counts.

Addressing the disparity in treatment between independent candidates and national party candidates, Justice Stevens wrote:

> The name of the nominees of the Democratic and Republican Parties will appear on the Ohio ballot in November even if they did not decide to run until after Ohio's March deadline had passed, but the independent is simply denied a position on the ballot if he waits too long. Thus, under Ohio's scheme, the major parties may include all events preceding their national conventions in the calculus that produces their respective nominees and campaign platforms, but the independent's judgment must be based on a history that ends in March.

For Fundamental Rights. Ron Brown and other members of the Committee Against Racism were picketing the home of Michael Bilandic, the mayor of Chicago, when they were arrested and charged with violating an Illinois law prohibiting picketing in front of another person's residence. The picketers were calling attention to the fact that the mayor had not supported busing as a means of achieving racial integration. They pled guilty to the charge and were sentenced, but they then brought an action in the federal district court asserting that the law was unconstitutional and that therefore their convictions were void. Judge John F. Grady dismissed the action, being of the opinion that the law was valid. The circuit court reversed, and the Supreme Court affirmed.[93]

Brown and his companions argued that because the law did not prohibit picketing if done during a labor dispute, it did not treat all picketers equally and therefore was a denial of equal protection of the law. Justice Brennan, writing for the majority, agreed. He pointed out that peaceful picketing, even in a residential neighborhood, is "expressive conduct that falls within the First Amendment's preserve." And "under the guise of preserving residential privacy, Illinois has flatly prohibited all nonlabor picketing even though it permits labor picketing that is equally likely to intrude on the tranquility of the home."

"The State's interest in protecting the well-being, tranquility, and privacy of the home," Brennan noted, "is certainly of the highest order in a free and civilized society. 'The crucial question, however, is whether [the Illinois statute] advances that objective in a manner consistent with the command of the Equal Protection Clause.' . . . And because the statute discriminates among pickets based on the subject matter of their expression, the answer must be 'No.'"

Eduardo Soto-Lopez and Eliezer Baez-Hernandez, citizens of the United States living in Puerto Rico, were inducted into the U.S. Army. Both were honorably discharged and eventually moved to New York, where both took the New York Civil Service examination. Under the law, both would have been entitled to have points added to their examination scores had they been residents of New York at the time they entered the service. They commenced an action against the New York Civil Service Commission, claiming that the statute infringed upon their right to travel and denied them equal protection of the law. Judge Richard Owen dismissed the case, but the circuit court reversed, and the Supreme Court upheld that decision.

To put the case in its proper focus, Brennan wrote, "Our task in this case, then, is first to determine whether New York's restriction of its civil service preference to veterans who entered the Armed Forces while residing in New York operates to penalize those persons who have exercised their right to migrate. If we find that it does, . . . [Soto-Lopez and Baez-Hernandez] must prevail unless New York can demonstrate that its classification is necessary to accomplish a compelling state interest."[94]

New York offered four reasons for giving preference only to those who lived in the state at the time they entered service: "(1) the encouragement of New York residents to join the Armed Services; (2) the compensation of residents for service in time of war by helping these veterans reestablish themselves upon coming home; (3) the inducement of veterans to return to New York after wartime service; and (4) the employment of a 'uniquely valuable class of public servants' who possess useful experience acquired through their military service."

Brennan did not find any, nor all, of these reasons to be sufficient to overcome the infringement upon the right of others to migrate to New York. After discussing each of the reasons given, the justice concluded:

> In sum, [New York's laws], which limit the award of a civil service employment preference to resident veterans who lived in New York at the time they entered the Armed Forces, effectively penalize otherwise qualified resident veterans who do not meet the prior residence requirement for their exercise of the right to migrate. The State has not met its heavy burden of proving that it has selected a means of pursuing a compelling state interest which does not impinge unnecessarily on constitutionally protected interests. Consequently, we conclude that New York's veterans' preference violates appellees' constitutionally protected rights to migrate and to equal protection of the law.

Connecticut Welfare Department regulations required a woman seeking welfare assistance for an abortion to submit a certificate from a doctor "that the abortion is 'recommended as medically or psychiatrically necessary.'"[95] Acting in accordance with this regulation, the department refused to pay for Susan Roe's abortion because it was not medically necessary.

Roe, and several other women, believing that the law denied them equal protection, brought an action seeking a court order that the law was unconstitutional. The trial court agreed, but a majority of the Supreme Court reversed, with Justice Brennan dissenting.[96] The majority acknowledged "that the Fourteenth Amendment's concept of personal liberty affords constitutional protection against state interference with certain aspects of an individual's personal 'privacy,' including a woman's decision to terminate her pregnancy," but concluded that the Connecticut regulation prohibiting payment for nontherapeutic abortions did not infringe upon any rights of indigent women.

Brennan saw the matter in an entirely different light. He criticized the majority for its "distressing insensitivity to the plight of impoverished pregnant women." "The stark reality for too many, not just for 'some,' indigent pregnant women," he argued, "is that indigency makes access to competent licensed physicians not merely 'difficult' but 'impossible.' . . . This disparity in funding by the State clearly operates to coerce indigent pregnant women to bear children they would not otherwise choose to have, and just as clearly, this coercion can only operate upon the poor, who are uniquely the victims of this form of financial pressure."

Justice Brennan saw this decision as a retreat from *Roe v. Wade.* "Until today," he asserted, "I had not thought the nature of the fundamental right established in *Roe* was open to question, let alone susceptible of the interpretation advanced by the Court. The fact that the Connecticut scheme may not operate as an absolute bar preventing all indigent women from having abortions is not critical. What is critical is that the State has inhibited their fundamental right to make that choice free from state interference."

In *Fashing v. Moore,*[97] "Fashing . . . a Judge of the County Court-at-Law; Baca and McGhee . . . Justices of the Peace; and Ybara . . . Constable. . . . All . . . [sought] to enjoin . . . [Texas government officials] from enforcing the provisions of the Texas Constitution. . . ."

What Fashing, Baca, McGhee, and Ybarra were complaining about were provisions of the Texas constitution that barred them from being candidates for the state legislature, and automatically terminated them from their official positions if they announced or filed for "any office of profit or trust under the laws" of Texas or the United States. Texas's justification for these restrictions was "its interest in discouraging abuse of office and neglect of duties by current officeholders campaigning for higher office during their terms."[98]

Judge Harry Lee Hudspeth held that these provisions were unconstitutional as a violation of the First Amendment's right to engage in political activities, and a denial of the constitutional guarantee of equal protection under the Fourteenth Amendment. The circuit court affirmed, but the Supreme Court reversed, with Brennan dissenting.

The justice's disagreement with the Court centered on the fact that many Texas state officeholders were exempt from the law's prohibitions, and "neither the State nor . . . [the Court] offers any justification for *differential* treatment of various classes of officeholders, and the search for such justification makes clear that the classifications embodied in these provisions lack any meaningful relationship to the State's asserted or supposed interests."

Justice Brennan was also of the opinion that restricting judges from running for the legislature infringed upon the First Amendment rights of the petitioners. Restricting the pursuit of political office by government employees "is clearly protected by the First Amendment and [such] restrictions . . . must be justified by the State's interest in ensuring the continued proper performance of current public duties." He could find "no substantial way any of the asserted state interests [could be] said to support . . . [the provision], and . . . [it was] not narrowly tailored to avoid unnecessary interference with the First Amendment interests of government employees."

In the Criminal Justice System. Preston A. Tate found himself on the "horns of a dilemma." He had been convicted nine times for various traffic offenses and fined a total of $425. Because he had no money to pay the fines, he was imprisoned for 85 days, the time required to satisfy the $425 fine at the rate of five dollars per day. He petitioned the court for release, stating, "Because I am too poor, I am, therefore, unable to pay the accumulated fine of $425."[99] He was not released, and the "Court of Criminal Appeals of Texas affirmed, stating: 'We overrule appellant's contention that because he is too poor to pay the fines his imprisonment is unconstitutional.'"

Justice Brennan, writing for all justices, reversed. "Since Texas has legislated a 'fines only' policy for traffic offenses," the justice declared,

> that statutory ceiling cannot, consistently with the Equal Protection Clause, limit the punishment to payment of the fine if one is able to pay, yet convert the fine into a prison term for an indigent defendant without the means to pay his fine. Imprisonment in such a case is not imposed to further any penal objective of the State. It is imposed to augment the State's revenues but obviously does not serve that purpose; the defendant cannot pay because he is indigent and his imprisonment, rather than aiding collection of the revenue, saddles the State with the cost of feeding and housing him for the period of his imprisonment.

The facts of the case of *Mayer v. City of Chicago*[100] are:

> A jury in the Circuit Court of Cook County, Illinois, convicted . . . [Mayer] on nonfelony charges of disorderly conduct and interference with a police officer in violation of ordinances of the city of Chicago. He was sentenced to a $250 fine in each offense; . . . Desiring to appeal, he petitioned the Circuit Court for a free transcript of the proceedings of his trial to support his grounds of appeal that the evidence was insufficient for conviction and that misconduct of the prosecutor denied him a fair trial. The Circuit Court found that he was indigent, but denied his application, stating "that defendant was found guilty of ordinance violations and . . . rule 607 of the Illinois Supreme Court applies only to felony cases."

If Mayer had been convicted of a *felony*, a report of the trial would have been provided because of his indigency.

The U.S. Supreme Court unanimously reversed, being of the opinion that refusal to provide transcripts to nonfelony defendants denied them equal protection of the law. Justice Brennan was assigned to write the Court's opinion.

"*Griffin v. Illinois* . . . ," he wrote, "is the watershed of our transcript decisions. We held there that '[d]estitute defendants must be afforded as adequate appellate review as defendants who have money enough to buy transcripts.' . . . This holding rested on the 'constitutional guarantees of due process and equal protection both [of which] call for procedures in criminal trials which allow no invidious discriminations between persons and different groups of persons.'"

In applying *Griffin* to Mayer's case, the justice did not buy the state's argument that there was a difference between felony and nonfelony cases. "The size of the defendant's pocketbook bears no more relationship to his guilt or innocence in a nonfelony than a felony case." Nor was there any reason for not providing transcripts when a defendant had been fined but not incarcerated. "*Griffin,*" Brennan pointed out, "does not represent a balance between the needs of the accused and the interests of society; its principle is a flat prohibition against pricing indigent defendants out of as effective an appeal as would be available to others able to pay their own way. The invidiousness of the discrimination that exists when criminal procedures are made available only to those who can pay is not erased by any differences in the sentences that may be imposed."

Justice Brennan vigorously protested when the Court upheld the denial of a transcript to MacCollom, a prisoner in a federal penitentiary. Two years passed after MacCollom had been convicted before he sought to have his sentence vacated. In his petition to the court, he indicated that he could not afford a transcript and requested that one be supplied to him. At the time federal law gave the court authority to order transcripts if the judge "certifies that the suit or appeal is not frivolous and that the transcript is needed to decide the issue presented by the suit or appeal."[101] The trial court denied the request, and the Supreme Court affirmed.

According to the Court, had MacCollom appealed at the time of his conviction he would have been furnished a transcript, but, because he was now proceeding by a motion to vacate the sentence, he had lost his constitutional right to one and was entitled to it only if his claim was "not frivolous" or was "needed to decide the issue."

Brennan was disturbed by the distinction the Court was making between a direct appeal at the time of conviction, when a transcript would have been provided, versus applying for relief at a later date by motion and leaving the question of a transcript to the discretion of the trial court. "The Constitution," he argued, "demands that respondent [MacCollom], despite his indigency, be afforded the same opportunity for collateral review of his conviction as the nonindigent." "I reject," he continued, "as wholly fallacious the argument that adequacy of opportunity to present claims at trial and on direct appeal so far diminishes the importance of collateral review [by motion], that discrimination between indigent and nonindigent in post-conviction proceedings is constitutionally tolerable."

The Bill of Rights and the States

"The Court has not hesitated to re-examine past decisions according the Fourteenth Amendment a less central role in the preservation of basic liberties than that which was contemplated by its Framers when they added the Amendment to our constitutional scheme."[102]

With those words, Justice Brennan approached the question of whether the fifth Amendment's protection against compelled self-incrimination prohibited states from forcing a person to testify against himself.

When Malloy was called before a court-appointed referee conducting an investigation into gambling in Hartford County, Connecticut, he "refused to answer any question 'on the grounds it may tend to incriminate me.'" He was adjudged to be in contempt and committed to prison. On appeal he argued that he had been denied his constitutional right to remain silent, but the Connecticut Supreme Court of Errors held that the Fifth Amendment Self-Incrimination Clause did not apply to the states. The U.S. Supreme Court reversed. "We hold today," Brennan declared for the majority, "that the Fifth Amendment's exception from compulsory self-incrimination is also protected by the Fourteenth Amendment against abridgment by the States." The justice then explained what the Fifth Amendment prohibits governments from doing.

> Governments, state and federal, are thus constitutionally compelled to establish guilt by evidence independently and freely secured, and may not by coercion prove a charge against an accused out of his own mouth. Since the Fourteenth Amendment prohibits the States from inducing a person to confess through "sympathy falsely aroused," . . . or other like inducement far short of "compulsion by torture," . . . it follows *a fortiori* that it also forbids the States to resort to imprisonment, as here, to compel him to answer questions that might incriminate him. The Fourteenth Amendment secures against state invasion the same privilege that the Fifth Amendment guarantees against federal infringement— the right of a person to remain silent unless he chooses to speak in the unfettered exercise of his own will, and to suffer no penalty . . . for such silence.

Prior to Malloy's case, and subsequent thereto, Brennan voted to require states to abide by many other provisions of the Bill of Rights.[103]

AS A JUDICIAL FREEDOM FIGHTER

Whether it was the Jewish merchants in *Braunfeld,* navy chaplain Goldman, Seventh-Day Adventists Hobbie, Sherbert, and Thomas, Muslims Shabazz and Mateen, or Native Americans made no difference to Justice Brennan. For him, all were entitled to protection of the Free Exercise Clause of the First Amendment. Not only did he believe that the government should not interfere with people's religious beliefs, he was of the opinion that sometimes government should assist the individual in the free exercise of his or her religion. He wrote that "our cases recognize that, in one important respect, the Constitution is *not* neutral on the subject of religion: Under the Free Exercise Clause, religiously motivated claims of conscience may give rise to constitutional rights that other strongly held beliefs do not. . . . Moreover, even when the government is not compelled to do so by the Free Exercise Clause, it may to some extent act to facilitate the opportunities of individuals to practice their religion."[104]

The justice's commitment to protection for freedom of speech ranged over the whole spectrum of speech activities. And it made no difference that the public might not have approved the type of speech involved. For example, in the flag-burning case *United States v. Eichman,* the government urged the Court to reconsider its holding in *Texas v. Johnson,* that burning a flag was speech. "We decline the Government's invitation to reassess this conclusion in light of Congress' recent recognition of a purported 'national consensus' favoring a prohibition of flag-burning," Brennan declared. ". . . Even assuming such a consensus exists, any suggestion that the Government's interest in suppressing speech becomes more weighty as popular opposition to that speech grows is foreign to the First Amendment."[105]

Even Mallie Lewis's vulgar speech could not be punished just because it was "opprobrious." Lewis became very upset when the police came to arrest her son and verbally expressed her displeasure. A police officer "testified that . . . [Lewis] 'started yelling and screaming that I had her son or did something to her son and she wanted to know where he was. . . . She said, 'you god damn m. f. police—I am going to [the superintendent of police] about this.'"[106] Lewis denied using any vulgarity, but nevertheless was convicted under an ordinance making it a crime "to use obscene or opprobrious language toward . . . any member of the city police." In holding the ordinance unconstitutional, Brennan wrote, "Since Section 49-7 . . . is susceptible of application to protected speech, the section is constitutionally overbroad and therefore is facially invalid."

Brennan especially believed that speech in the political arena and the academic community must be protected. "The free exchange of ideas provides special vitality to the process traditionally at the heart of American constitutional democracy—the political campaign. . . . The political candidate does not lose the protection of the First Amendment when he declares himself for public office."[107]

And when the Court upheld a Minnesota statute prohibiting some teachers from meeting and conferring with their superiors, Brennan protested. He believed that the restriction implicated both the right to speak freely and to associate freely with others.

> The first right is rooted in our common understanding that the First Amendment safeguards the free exchange of ideas at institutions of higher learning. This Court's decisions acknowledge unequivocally that academic freedom is "a special concern of the First Amendment," . . . and that protecting the free exchange of ideas within our schools is of profound importance in promoting an

open society. . . . The basis of the second right—the right to be free from compelled associations—is found in our conviction that individuals may not be
forced to join or support positions or views which they find objectionable on
moral, ideological, or personal grounds. . . . This right is especially worthy of respect in the academic setting, for the denial of associational freedom threatens
that cherished spirit of our schools and universities "to inquire, to study and to
evaluate," . . . which the First Amendment seeks to preserve.[108]

For Justice Brennan, freedom of the press was as important as freedom to
speak. Both were necessary to protect the free exchange of ideas. And restrictions upon the press, whether in the form of prior restraint, or licensing of, or
subjecting the press to damages for libel, were all anathema to him. When
Stevenson was being tried for murder for the fourth time, there having been one
reversal of conviction and two mistrials, he asked the court to exclude all persons
from the courtroom, and the presiding judge did so. Excluded were members of
the press who immediately sought to have the judge's order reversed. Not being
successful in the Ohio courts, they took an appeal to the Supreme Court, which
reversed. The Court held that the First Amendment required trials to be open to
the public, and that included the press. Brennan concurred. "The Court's approach in right-of-access cases simply reflects the special nature of a claim of
First Amendment right to gather information. Customarily, First Amendment
guarantees are interposed to protect communication between speaker and listener. When so employed against prior restraints, free speech protections are almost insurmountable."[109]

When the city of Lakewood, Ohio, enacted an ordinance requiring a permit to place a newsrack on a city street, and giving the mayor the authority to
issue permits, the Supreme Court struck it down. Brennan wrote the Court's decision. "At the root of this long line of precedent is the time-tested knowledge
that in the area of free expression a licensing statute placing unbridled discretion
in the hands of a government official or agency constitutes a prior restraint and
may result in censorship."[110]

The justice was particularly concerned about the impact upon the press of
potential liability for defamation. He believed that public officials and public
figures should not be allowed to recover damages for alleged defamation unless
they were able to prove that the press acted with malice, or with reckless disregard of the truth. He also believed that standard ought to prevent the ordinary
citizen from recovering damages if the alleged libel occurred when the press was
reporting "events of public or general interest," or when involved in a judicial
proceeding.[111]

Brennan summed up his position on the values protected by freedom of
speech and of the press as follows: "The Court has emphasized that the central
meaning of the free expression guarantee is that the body politic of this Nation
shall be entitled to the communications necessary for self-governance, and that
to place restraints on the exercise of expression is to deny the instrumental means

required in order that the citizenry exercise that ultimate sovereignty reposed in its collective judgment by the Constitution."[112]

In *Sable Communications of Cal., Inc. v. FCC,*[113] the Court held unconstitutional a federal law that prohibited "indecent as well as obscene interstate commercial telephone messages." Justice Brennan concurred, and restated his views with regard to punishment for selling or distributing obscene material. "I have long been convinced that the exaction of criminal penalties for the distribution of obscene materials to consenting adults is constitutionally intolerable. In my judgment, 'the concept of "obscenity" cannot be defined with sufficient specificity and clarity to provide fair notice to persons who create and distribute sexually oriented materials, to prevent substantial erosion of protected speech as a by-product of the attempt to suppress unprotected speech, and to avoid very costly institutional harms.'"

Brennan's deep commitment to the right of privacy is illustrated in his dissents in two cases in which the Court upheld laws that prohibit payment for nontherapeutic abortions for indigent women.[114] In *Maher v. Doe,* the justice criticized the majority for backtracking from *Roe v. Wade.* "Indeed," he declared, "it cannot be gainsaid that today's decision seriously erodes the principles of *Roe* . . . announced to guide the determination of what constitutes an unconstitutional infringement on the fundamental right of pregnant women to be free to decide whether to have an abortion." He took exception to the Court's conclusion that the law does not place any obstacle in the way of a woman's securing an abortion. "The fact that the Connecticut scheme may not operate as an absolute bar preventing all indigent women from having abortions is not critical. What is critical is that the State has inhibited their fundamental right to make that choice free from state interference." Furthermore, he wrote, "We have repeatedly found that infringements of fundamental rights are not limited to outright denials of those rights. First Amendment decisions have consistently held in a wide variety of contexts that the compelling-state-interest test is applicable not only to outright denials but also to restraints that make the exercise of those rights more difficult."

Justice Brennan did not write many opinions dealing with integration. He did, however, consistently vote to require it. He also voted to strike down a Florida law making it a criminal offense for an unmarried, mixed racial couple to live together. In that case, Justice White authored the majority opinion, which Brennan joined.

> But we deal here with a classification based upon the race of the participants, which must be viewed in light of the historical fact that the central purpose of the Fourteenth Amendment was to eliminate racial discrimination emanating from official sources in the States. This strong policy renders racial classifications "constitutionally suspect," . . . and subject to the "most rigid scrutiny," . . . and "in most circumstances irrelevant" to any constitutionally acceptable legislative purpose.[115]

When Jackson, Mississippi, closed all its swimming pools rather than operate them on an integrated basis, Brennan joined Justice White's dissent.

> As stated at the outset of this opinion, by closing the pools solely because of the order to desegregate, the city is expressing its official view that Negroes are so inferior that they are unfit to share with whites this particular type of public facility, though pools were long a feature of the city's segregated recreation program. . . . Closing the pools without a colorable nondiscriminatory reason was every bit as much an official endorsement of the notion that Negroes are not equal to whites as was the use of state National Guard troops in 1957 to bar the entry of nine Negro students into Little Rock's Central High school, a public facility that was ordered desegregated in the wake of *Brown*.[116]

Justice Brennan expressed the same concern for equal treatment for illegitimate children, aliens, and voters, and for males and females when the classifications were based on gender.

And when the government had made a classification that affected a fundamental right, Brennan consistently voted to hold such classification a violation of equal protection. For example, in *Eisenstadt v. Baird*,[117] William Baird had been convicted of giving a contraceptive to an unmarried woman in violation of Massachusetts law. With Justice Brennan writing the opinion, the Court held that the law discriminated against single people and their right to privacy, and declared it unconstitutional. "It is true," he wrote, "that in *Griswold* the right of privacy in question inhered in the marital relationship. Yet the marital couple is not an independent entity with a mind and heart of its own, but an association of two individuals each with a separate intellectual and emotional makeup. If the right of privacy means anything, it is the right of the *individual*, married or single, to be free from unwarranted governmental intrusion into matters so fundamentally affecting a person as the decision whether to bear or beget a child."

The justice's votes in cases involving classifications made in the administration of the criminal justice system indicate his deep concern that all criminal defendants be treated substantially equally. For example, in referring to the *Griffin* and *Douglas* cases, Brennan pointed out that in denial of transcripts and or counsel to indigent defendants who wanted to appeal their convictions, both due process and equal protection issues were involved. "In cases like *Griffin* and *Douglas*," he noted, "due process concerns were involved because the States involved had set up a system of appeals as of right but had refused to offer each defendant a fair opportunity to obtain an adjudication on the merits of his appeal. Equal protection concerns were involved because the State treated a class of defendants—indigent ones—differently for purposes of offering them a meaningful appeal."[118]

Brennan's record as a judicial freedom fighter can be described in no way other than superb, whether he was upholding First Amendment rights, guaranteeing equal protection of the law, or pursuing liberty.

Justice Thurgood Marshall

Personal Life

Growing Up

Thurgood was high-spirited and rambunctious, traits that often got him into trouble. A *New York Times Magazine* story quotes Thurgood Marshall as saying, "We lived on a respectable street, but behind us were back alleys where rough-necks and the tough kids hung out. When it was time for dinner, my mother used to go to the front door to call my older brother. Then she'd go to the back door and call me."

His elementary school principal would send recalcitrant students to the school's basement with a copy of the Constitution and orders to memorize a passage before returning to the classroom. Thurgood spent many hours in the basement. "Before I left that school," he later told a reporter, "I knew the entire Constitution by heart."[1]

Thurgood Marshall was born to Norma and William Canfield Marshall on July 2, 1908, in Baltimore, Maryland. Shortly thereafter, the family moved to the Harlem area of New York City so that Thurgood's mother could attend graduate school at Columbia University.

The Marshalls returned to Baltimore five years later. His father had worked as a railroad dining-car waiter, but because that frequently required him to be away from home, he gave that up to become a waiter at an exclusive, whites-only club, on Chesapeake Bay.

When . . . [William] served on a grand jury—the first black man to do so in Baltimore—he became angry because jurors always asked whether the person under investigation was white or black and blacks were far more likely to be indicted than whites. On the third day of service he suggested the panel abandon the practice of determining an individual's race before deciding whether or not to return an indictment. To Marshall's surprise the white jury foreman agreed with him, and the race question was never again raised by that jury.

JUSTICE THURGOOD MARSHALL (photo by Joseph Lavenburg, National Geographic Society; collection of the Supreme Court of the United States).

Although his mother wanted him to become a dentist, Thurgood credited his father for his becoming a lawyer, not because he told him to become one, "but he turned me into one," Thurgood said. "He taught me how to argue, challenged my logic on every point, by making me prove every statement I made, even if we were discussing the weather." And it was from his father that Thurgood learned that the Constitution recognized slavery and that the Supreme Court had approved separate but equal facilities in *Plessy v. Ferguson.*

Norma Marshall monitored her children's education because, as a teacher, she believed that was important. When Thurgood had not earned enough money to go to college, his mother "pawned her wedding and engagement rings and gave him the money. She never redeemed them."

Biographers Michael D. Davis and Hunter R. Clark recount several incidents in which Thurgood became aware of the racism that existed as he grew up.

> "I heard a kid call a Jewish boy I knew a 'kike' to his face," Marshall explained. "I was about seven. I asked him why he didn't fight the kid. He asked me what would I do if someone called me 'nigger'—would I fight? That was a new one on me. I knew 'kike' was a dirty word, but I hadn't known about 'nigger.' I went home and wanted to know right that minute what all this meant. That's not easy for a parent to explain so it makes any sense to a kid, you know."
>
> Will Marshall indeed had difficulty defining the racial slur, but he had no problem telling young Thurgood how he should respond when anyone called him "nigger." "Anyone calls you 'nigger,' you not only got my permission to fight him—you got my orders to fight him." It was an order Thurgood Marshall would follow physically and legally for the rest of his life.

Another incident that etched racism indelibly on his mind was when Thurgood "discovered there were no public restrooms for black people, not even in the department stores where their patronage and dollars were welcomed. He hopped aboard the trolley, hoping it would carry him quickly to his home. He made it as far as the front door. It was an indignity he would never forget."

Thurgood entered Lincoln University, Chester, Pennsylvania, in 1925. This was an all-black, all-male university with an all-white faculty. "During his first semester at Lincoln, the seventeen-year-old Marshall, no longer under the guidance of his parents, continued his pranks. He was a founding member of the school's Weekend Club, a group of happy-go-lucky, party-going students who proudly boasted they never opened a book or could be found studying on the Lincoln campus on weekends. He played pinochle and poker frequently and later confided to friends that he played well enough to keep himself in spending money."

Marshall tells of going to a theater with some other black students and being told to sit in the balcony. When they took seats in the whites-only section, they were ordered to move, but they refused to do so.

> Thurgood recalled hearing a bitter voice in the theater's darkness saying, "Nigger, why don't you just get out of here and sit where you belong?"
>
> Marshall told the man that he had paid for his ticket and did not intend to move from his comfortable orchestra seat. Recalling the incident in a letter to his parents, he wrote, "You can't really tell what a person like that looks like because it's just an ugly feeling that's looking at you, not a real face. . . . But the amazing thing was that when we were leaving, we just walked out with all those other people and they didn't do anything, didn't say anything, didn't even look at us—at

least, not as far as I know. I'm not sure I like being invisible, but maybe it's better than being put to shame and not able to respect yourself."

Thurgood said the Oxford movie theater incident started his civil rights career. "The leader of that group at Lincoln was a guy named U.S. Tate. He was the leader who said we ought to do something about it. We desegregated the theater in the little town of Oxford. I guess that's what started the whole thing in my life."

Marshall became a debater while at Lincoln, and a good one. "His oratorical skills and fiery delivery earned him the nickname 'the Wrathful Marshall.' 'If I were taking debate for credit I would be the biggest honor student they ever had around here,' he wrote in a 1929 letter to his father."

Love, Marriage, and Law School

"We went there [Cherry Street Memorial Church] because we learned that's where all the cute chicks went." It was there that Marshall met Vivian "Buster" Burey, one of the "cute chicks." They began dating and were married on September 24, 1929. "His days of campus carousing and drinking with classmates came to an abrupt end. It was time to get down to the hard and serious business of supporting a wife and paving the financial path for his continuing education. He took part-time jobs as waiter and bellhop to meet the rent on the small apartment, pay tuition, and buy textbooks for his last semester at Lincoln. Vivian worked full-time as a secretary."

After Thurgood graduated, he and Vivian moved in with his parents in Baltimore, and Thurgood applied for admission to the law school at the University of Maryland, which was denied because he was black. He then enrolled at Howard University Law School in Washington, D.C. Some years later, Marshall participated in legal action against the University of Maryland seeking the admission of Donald Gaines Murray, who was black, to the law school. After hearing the evidence, Judge O'Dunne issued an order requiring the university to admit Murray. "In January 1936 the Maryland Court of Appeals upheld O'Dunne's decision: 'Compliance with the Constitution cannot be deferred at the will of the State. Whatever system it adopts for legal education now must furnish equality of treatment now.'"

Going to Howard Law School required Thurgood to travel from Baltimore to Washington in segregated railroad cars twice a day. "During his first year in law school Thurgood left Baltimore every weekday at 5:30 A.M., attended classes until 3:00 P.M., then returned to his part-time jobs as a waiter, a bellhop, and a baker at Preece's Bakery on Pennsylvania Avenue. Then he studied until midnight. 'I heard law books were to dig in,' he said, 'so I dug deep. I got through simply by overwhelming the job, and I was at it twenty hours a day, seven days a week.'"

When Thurgood started law school, Charles Hamilton Houston was the school's vice dean. "Houston was the man who transformed Howard's law school into a fully accredited institution and then used it as the NAACP's 'legal laboratory' to plan strategies for important civil rights cases. Houston became Marshall's teacher, his mentor, his colleague, and his friend."

> In a speech to Howard law students many years later, Marshall said, "[What] Charlie beat into our heads was excellence." He said that Houston told his students, "When you get in a courtroom, you can't just say, 'Please, Mr. Court, have mercy on me because I'm a Negro.' You are in competition with a well-trained white lawyer, and you better be at least as good as he is; and if you expect to win, you better be better. If I give you five cases to read overnight, you better read eight. And if I say eight, you read ten. You go that step further, and you might make it."

Because Marshall was first in his class at the end of the first year, he was given a job in the library and he earned enough to cover his law school expenses. He was therefore able to give up his part-time jobs. Washington was a racist city at this time. Blacks could not attend the National Theatre or go to Constitution Hall.

During his second year, Marshall was asked to assist William Henry Hastie in a legal action to integrate the law school at the University of North Carolina. They were unsuccessful and Thurgood was deeply disappointed. In 1949 Hastie became the first black federal judge.

Marshall graduated from law school in 1933, first in his class, and set up practice in Baltimore.

Civil Rights Lawyer

"Marshall began earning a reputation as 'the little man's' lawyer. He spent a lot of time in Baltimore courtrooms, not unfamiliar territory, because he had often been there as a child with his father. He honed his courtroom skills on everyday, mundane legal work, from traffic offenses to eviction cases and some minor criminal matters. He had very few paying clients the first year, and his expenses exceeded his income by a thousand dollars."

It was during this period that Thurgood was recruited to help revitalize the NAACP in Baltimore. When he organized a boycott of stores near his home, hoping to force them to hire black workers, he was met with a lawsuit by the store owners. He sought the help of his former teacher Charles Houston, and together they were able to convince the judge that blacks had a legal right to boycott the merchants.

Marshall then took on the plight of black teachers in Baltimore, who were paid salaries similar to those of the school janitors. After a two-year battle, Marshall won an increase in pay for the teachers. However, he was not successful in having a black student admitted to an all-white high school in Baltimore.

Marshall was successful in having Donald Gaines Murray admitted to the University of Maryland Law School. Winning the *Murray* case prevented Marshall and Houston from taking the question of segregated educational facilities to the United States Supreme Court. That opportunity came when the University of Missouri Law School refused to admit Lloyd Gaines, who was black. Gaines, with the assistance of Marshall and Houston, brought an action against the state seeking to force the law school to admit him. The case, *State of Missouri v. Canada*,[2] is discussed in Chapter 2, and, as noted there, Chief Justice Hughes wrote the majority opinion, which resulted in Gaines's admission to law school. The case did not, however, settle the question of the constitutionality of separate but equal facilities.

Shortly after Charles Houston accepted a position as legal counsel for the NAACP in Harlem, New York, he prevailed upon Thurgood to join him there.

> The Marshalls enjoyed Harlem's nightlife, with its supper clubs and cabarets. On weekends the Marshalls frequently joined Walter White, Roy Wilkins, and other NAACP officials at Arthur "Happy" Rhone's club, on the corner of 143rd Street and Lenox Avenue. Rhone's, the NAACP's unofficial "after-hours headquarters," was a popular nightclub with white linen tablecloths and fine English bone china. Winthrop Rockefeller, Wall Street banker Robert Lehman and his wife, Kitty, and other wealthy white liberals "tipped uptown" in gowns, tuxedos, and limousines to get a taste of black culture and ample helpings of Rhone's well-known chitterlings, spare ribs, and pigs' feet, served with champagne.[3]

Thurgood spent a couple of years working in New York, frequently returning to Baltimore to take care of clients. These years brought disappointment to the Marshalls as Buster lost three children through miscarriages.

In addition to trying cases, Thurgood traveled throughout the South carrying the NAACP's message and recruiting black and white lawyers who were willing to take integration cases. He had an old 1929 Ford Model T.

> When Marshall and Houston traveled together filing suits, the old Ford was turned into a legal office on wheels. "Charlie would sit in my car—I had a little old beat-up '29 Ford—and type out the briefs. And he could type up a storm—faster than any secretary—and not just with two fingers going, I mean he used 'em all. We'd stay at friends' homes in those days—for free, you understand. I think the whole budget for the legal office then was maybe $8,000—that was for two lawyers and a secretary."

In 1938, Houston resigned as legal counsel of the NAACP and Marshall was appointed in his place. When a couple of white court employees in Dallas threw an elderly black man down the courthouse steps as he came to serve on the grand jury, Marshall immediately went to Dallas to intervene. He was able to secure a meeting with Governor James Allred which resulted in a proclamation from the governor "that prospective black jurors would no longer be harassed."

Walter White, who was the executive director of the NAACP, created the Legal Defense and Education Fund, Inc. (The Fund) in 1939 and appointed Marshall its director, a position he held for 21 years. "To NAACP branch members and thousands of other blacks in the South, Thurgood Marshall was their knight in shining armor who came to town to fight their legal battles. To them he *was* the NAACP. 'Thurgood is coming' was whispered among people anxiously awaiting his arrival to hear their complaints and file civil rights cases."

Justice John Marshall Harlan's dissent in *Plessy v. Ferguson* was one of Marshall's favorites. Constance Baker Motley, one of Marshall's associates at The Fund has written: "I do not believe we ever filed a brief in the pre–*Brown* days in which a portion of that opinion was not quoted. Marshall's favorite quotation was, 'Our Constitution is color-blind.' It became our basic legal creed. Marshall admired the courage of Harlan more than any Justice who has ever sat on the Supreme Court."[4] Motley later became a judge of the United States District Court.

In 1944, Marshall hired Robert L. Carter as his assistant.

Carter, who also became a judge of the Unites States District Court, describes his interview with his prospective boss: "What I remember about that first encounter was his plain-speaking, down-to-earth persona and his studied attempt to put me at ease. He was already a prominent lawyer and civil rights personality by then, but he put himself out to help relieve whatever nervous tension I might have been experiencing."[5]

A few of the cases that Marshall took to the Supreme Court and won include *Sipuel v. Board of Regents* (discussed in chapters 4 and 6), *Sweatt v. Painter*, and *McLauren v. Oklahoma State Regents* (both discussed in Chapter 4).

In *Smith v. Allwright*,[6] Marshall succeeded in convincing the Court that the exclusion of blacks from voting in the Democratic primary election in Texas violated the Fifteenth Amendment. But the biggest challenge was yet to come—the integration of public schools—because even though Marshall had succeeded in having Ada Sipuel and Herman Sweatt admitted to law school, and George McLauren to a doctoral program, the Court had not directly overruled the separate but equal doctrine of *Plessy*. "Marshall and Houston decided to attack the separate-but-equal doctrine by establishing in a court of law, by a preponderance of scientific, biological, and sociological evidence, that there was no rational basis for race-based distinctions. After all, the law, like most fields, was interdisciplinary. The considerations that shaped judicial opinions were economic, social, and moral, as well as legal."[7]

But the road to abolishing the doctrine was not to be easy. By the time the issue was squarely presented to the Supreme Court, it included five separate cases, one from Clarendon County, South Carolina, involving the children of Harry Briggs, Sr., and Liza Briggs. "Over half the public school funds in Clarendon went to white schools, although the school system enrolled three times as many blacks as whites. In addition, Clarendon's annual per capita outlay for white students was almost a hundred times more than for blacks. Teachers' salaries were disparate, too, although the Briggses had won an earlier ruling that black teachers' pay be brought up to that of the white teachers in Clarendon." After a number of legal skirmishes in an attempt to integrate the Clarendon County schools, including a hearing before the Supreme Court, Marshall had not realized his goal. And when District Court Judge John J. Parker ruled that the county was proceeding promptly to integrate the schools, "one of the attorneys for South Carolina looked at Marshall, seated across the counsel table. In a voice loud enough for everyone in the courtroom to hear, he told him, 'If you show your black ass in Clarendon County again you'll be dead.'"

The *Briggs* case was ultimately combined with *Brown v. Board of Education,* discussed in Chapter 7. *Brown* was argued twice, first in December 1952. "In his closing remarks, Marshall . . .[said] 'It seems to me . . . that the significant factor running through all these arguments up to this point is that for some reason, which is still unexplained, Negroes are taken out of the mainstream of American life in these states [that have segregated public education].' He continued, 'There is nothing involved in this case other than race and color.'" Marshall concluded, "'It seems to me that in a case like this that the only way that South Carolina, under the test set forth in this case, can sustain that statute is to show that Negroes as Negroes—all Negroes—are different from everybody else.' This Marshall insisted, had not and could not be done."[8]

The Court, being unable to arrive at a satisfactory decision, ordered *Brown* to be argued again in October 1953; however, the death of Chief Justice Fred Vinson in September delayed the argument until Earl Warren was appointed and had taken his seat as chief justice. The second hearing took place on December 7, 1953.

> "The only way that this Court can decide this case in opposition to our position," . . . [Marshall] told the justices, "is that there must be some reason which gives the state the right to make a classification . . . in regard to Negroes, and we submit the only way to arrive at this decision is to find that for some reason Negroes are inferior to all other human beings." . . .
>
> He concluded, "The only thing it can be is an inherent determination that the people who were formerly in slavery, regardless of anything else, shall be kept as near that stage as is possible, and now is the time, we submit, that this Court should make it clear that that is not what our Constitution stands for."[9]

When the decision in *Brown* was announced, Marshall said, "I was so happy I was numb."

While getting the Court to throw out the separate but equal doctrine was a great victory, disaster struck the Marshall family with the death of Vivian from cancer in February 1955. In December of that year, Thurgood married Cecilia (Cissy) Suyat, a secretary at the NAACP headquarters. Cissy was of Filipino ancestry, born and raised in Hawaii. Two children, Thurgood, Jr., and John, were born of this marriage.

The *Brown* decision did not bring an immediate end to segregated schools. Southern senators and congressmen and school boards did everything they possibly could to prevent or at least delay integration. These delaying tactics were met by lawsuits brought on behalf of black children, some of which continue to this day. "By the end of the decade, Marshall had argued seven major [desegregation] cases before the Supreme Court that resulted from resistance to, or unwillingness to enforce, *Brown*. He won all of them. In addition the Court used the *Brown* ruling as the basis for requiring the desegregation of public parks and recreational facilities, local transportation, and professional athletics."

Richard L. Revesz, who served as one of Marshall's Supreme Court clerks, has written about Thurgood's dream: "At a reunion of law clerks a few years ago, Justice Marshall stated with great emotion that his dream was for the poorest black child in Mississippi to have access to the same quality of education as a child born into the Rockefeller family. He observed that this dream was unattainable, but that progress had been made and would continue to be made. Moreover, he said, even if we never quite get there, it is still a wonderful dream to have."[10]

Following *Brown*, the civil rights movement turned to segregation wherever it existed, including on buses, at lunch counters, and other in public and private facilities. Street demonstrations, sit-ins, and boycotts became the methods of attack. The Reverend Martin Luther King, Jr., who urged civil disobedience and nonviolence, became involved in the struggle. Not all blacks, however, approved of King's approach, including Marshall and the "old guard" at the NAACP.

> Marshall bluntly told King the NAACP had marched, boycotted, and picketed since 1917, but none of its protest involved deliberately breaking laws or staging mass sit-ins that resulted in the arrests of hundreds of its members. He reminded King that the NAACP had just months earlier won a landmark U.S. Supreme Court decision, *Brown v. Board of Education*. Marshall asked King if he believed his tactics of civil disobedience and nonviolence could win some of the major battles the NAACP had painstakingly fought in the courts since King was a child. King quietly told Marshall he did not know.[11]

Although Marshall did not approve of the demonstrations, he and the NAACP lawyers were willing to defend the protestors, which eventually brought Marshall and the NAACP into the fray. They succeeded in having the Supreme Court reverse the convictions of 15 students who had peacefully sat in at a Kress department store in Baton Rouge, Louisiana.[12]

Judge of the Circuit Court of Appeals

Marshall was nominated to be judge of the Second Circuit Court of Appeals by President John F. Kennedy in September 1961. He was to be the second black circuit court judge in U.S. history. His confirmation, however, was not to be an easy one. Senator James Eastland of Mississippi, chairman of the Judiciary Committee, appointed a subcommittee to conduct an investigation of Marshall's fitness to serve. That subcommittee consisted of senators Olin Johnston of South Carolina, John McClellan of Arkansas, and Roman Hruska of Nebraska. Although the subcommittee finally conducted hearings over a period of six days, they delayed taking any action until New York Senator Jacob Javits declared that he would take the matter to the full Senate. The Judiciary Committee, on September 7, voted 11–4 for confirmation, and the full Senate agreed in a vote of 54–16.[13]

Biographers Davis and Clark point out that "Thurgood Marshall found himself in the judicial mainstream on the U.S. Second Circuit Court of Appeals in New York City. During his four-year tenure, he wrote ninety-eight majority opinions, none of which was reversed by the U.S. Supreme Court, and contributed eight concurrences. He wrote only twelve dissents."[14]

Solicitor General of the United States

"On the evening of Friday, July 2, 1965, President Lyndon Baines Johnson's wife, Lady Bird, made an entry in her personal diary. 'Lyndon admires Thurgood Marshall and spoke [today] of the possibility of asking him to be solicitor general, and if he proved himself outstanding, perhaps when a vacancy on the Supreme Court opened up he might nominate him as a justice—the first of his race.'"

President Johnson did nominate Thurgood as solicitor general in July 1965, and he reluctantly accepted. He was concerned about leaving a lifetime appointment with a better salary to take a government job with no guarantee and a lesser salary. Marshall was approved by the Senate Judiciary Committee in 29 minutes, and the Senate voted to confirm by a 69–11 vote. For the swearing-in ceremony:

> President Johnson stood at his nominee's right. Next came Cissy, Thurgood Jr., and John. Cissy wore a demure pink dress with a short jacket, white gloves, a single strand of pearls, and double pearl earrings. The four-foot-one inch Cissy Marshall was dwarfed by the two six-footers, Johnson and Thurgood. The Marshall boys wore fresh summer cord suits, which they probably appreciated because of the swamplike mugginess of Washington summers. Thurgood wore a dark blue three-button suit that pinched his spreading paunch. The Marshall boys would have to wait to see their father in his cutaway.

When the University of Maryland dedicated its new law library to Justice Thurgood Marshall in 1980, Justice Brennan gave the dedicatory address. Discussing Marshall's tenure as solicitor general, Brennan said: "As Solicitor General of the United States Thurgood Marshall personally argued eighteen cases and prevailed in fourteen. The range of issues was extraordinarily wide and his success again attested to his high skill in advocacy. The high quality of his advocacy richly earned him his reputation as one of the great advocates in the history of the Court."[15]

Among the cases Marshall argued before the Supreme Court were *United States v. Guest* (discussed in Chapter 4), *Evans v. Newton*, and *Harper v. Virginia Bd. of Elections* (discussed in Chapter 5).

After Marshall had argued his first case before the Court, "*Washington Star* reporter Mary McGrory was impressed with his performance. 'Thurgood Marshall was, predictably, in excellent form as he argued his first major case before the Supreme Court. He was at ease, quick with the law, and able to command the acceptable joke.'"[16] And those who knew him well speak of those "acceptable jokes." "I have in mind the edge of his indefatigable humor," Scott Brewer, one of Justice Marshall's former clerks, wrote, "his skill at wielding the samurai sword of sarcasm or even the unsubtle sabre of silliness to poke fun at everybody: at those who worked for him, at members of the Court, at his family, at himself and, most deliciously, at hapless attorneys making what appeared to him to be arguments in the disservice of justice."[17]

Nomination to the Supreme Court

On June 13, 1967, Marshall was called to the White House to meet President Johnson. He later described the meeting with the president.

> "Oh, hi, Thurgood. Sit down. Sit down."
> So we chatted a few minutes, and I didn't ask him what was on his mind. I let him speak. And all of a sudden, he just looked at me and said, "You know something, Thurgood?"
> I said, "No, sir, what's that?"
> He said, "I'm going to put you on the Supreme Court."
> I said: "Oh, yipe! What did you say?"
> He said, "That's it."
> I said, "O.K., sir."[18]

After an introduction to the press, and back in the Oval Office again, the president and Marshall concluded their meeting with the following conversation.

> Then he said, very interesting, "I guess this is the end of our friendship."
> I said: "Yep. Just about. Be no more of that."
> I said: "Well, I'll tell you this, Mr. President. You know, . . . Tom Clark and Harry Truman were close as anybody, but when that steel case came up, Tom had to sock it to him." . . .
> He said, "Well, you wouldn't do like that to me?"
> I said, "No sooner than."
> He said, "Well, that's the way I want it." And that's the way it was.

Thurgood called Cissy from the President's office. "Take a deep breath and sit down slowly," Thurgood told her. "Now, wait just a minute." The next voice on the line was that of President Johnson, telling her that he had asked her husband to join the Supreme Court.

"Mr. President, I am simply speechless," said the wife of the justice designate. She was glad she had sat down and taken a deep breath. "Thank you for having so much faith in my husband."[19]

Although Marshall was confirmed by the Senate with a comfortable margin of 69–11, the Southern senators were not about to let that happen without having their day in court. "The confirmation hearings wore on for five days, July 13, 14, 18, 19, and 24, 1967. The questioning ranged from the penetrating to the absurd, from the philosophical to the kind of esoterica found in a law school exam."

After the Senate had voted on the confirmation, "Senate majority leader Mike Mansfield of Montana called the action 'a confirmation of the vitality of the democratic system.' He added, 'Thurgood Marshall's rise to the Supreme Court reaffirms the American ideal that what counts is what you are and not who you are, or whom your antecedents may have been.'"

Members of the Court at the time of Justice Marshall's appointment were Chief Justice Earl Warren, justices Hugo L. Black, William O. Douglas, William J. Brennan, Jr., Byron R. White, Abe Fortas, Potter Stewart, and John M. Harlan.

AS ASSOCIATE JUSTICE (1967-91)

The Free Exercise of Religion

Larry G. Hardison started to work for Trans World Airlines, Inc., as a stores clerk in June 1967. During the spring of 1968, he became a member of the Worldwide Church of God, whose Sabbath commenced at sundown Friday evening and ended at sundown Saturday. Hardison and his union, the International Association of Machinists and Aero Space Workers, attempted to work out an arrangement whereby he would not work during this Sabbath period, but they were not successful. Because Hardison did not report to work on two successive Saturdays in March, he was found guilty of insubordination and discharged. He brought an action against TWA and the union, claiming that he had been unlawfully discharged in violation of the Civil Rights Act of 1964, which prohibited discrimination against employees because of their religion. District Judge John W. Oliver gave judgment for the defendants, concluding that TWA had made a reasonable attempt to accommodate Hardison and that the union did not have to alter its seniority system for him. The circuit court did not agree and reversed. The Supreme Court, however, upheld Judge Oliver's conclusion that TWA had made reasonable accommodation for Hardison, and it reversed the circuit court. Justice Marshall dissented.[20]

Justice Marshall found the decision "deeply troubling."

> An employer, the Court concludes, need not grant even the most minor special
> privilege to religious observers to enable them to follow their faith. As a question
> of social policy, this result is deeply troubling, for a society that truly values reli-
> gious pluralism cannot compel adherents of minority religions to make the cruel
> choice of surrendering their religion or their job. And as a matter of law today's
> result is intolerable, for the Court adopts the very position that Congress ex-
> pressly rejected in 1972, as if we were free to disregard congressional choices that
> a majority of this Court thinks unwise.

The justice then summed up his concern for Hardison, other members of
minority religions, and the American people:

> What makes today's decision most tragic, however, is not that respondent
> Hardison has been needlessly deprived of his livelihood simply because he chose
> to follow the dictates of his conscience. Nor is the tragedy exhausted by the im-
> pact it will have on thousands of Americans like Hardison who could be forced to
> live on welfare as the price they must pay for worshiping their God. The ultimate
> tragedy is that despite Congress' best efforts, one of this Nation's pillars of
> strength—our hospitality to religious diversity—has been seriously eroded. All
> Americans will be a little poorer until today's decision is erased.[21]

When the Court reversed the conviction of Elliott Ashton Welsh II for refusing to be inducted into the armed forces, Justice Marshall joined the plurality
opinion. Although Welsh asserted that he was conscientiously opposed to war,
he was not a member of any particular religious group. There was, however, no
doubt as to his sincerity. The plurality concluded that the law exempting conscientious objectors "exempts from military service all those whose consciences,
spurred by deeply held, moral, ethical, or religious beliefs, would give them no
rest or peace if they allowed themselves to become a part of an instrument of
war."[22] Justice Marshall wrote the decision in *Gillette v. United States*,[23] another
conscientious objector case. In that case, the Court considered "the question
whether conscientious objection to a particular war, rather than objection to war
as such, relieves the objector from responsibilities of military training and service." With only Justice Douglas dissenting, the Court responded to the question by concluding that neither Guy Porter Gillette nor Louis A. Negre were
entitled to be classified as conscientious objectors.

Gillette was willing to "participate in a war of national defense or a war
sponsored by the United Nations as a peace-keeping measure, but declared his
opposition to American military operations in Vietnam, which he characterized
as 'unjust.'" Negre also objected to the war in Vietnam, which he too considered
unjust. He believed that "it was his duty as a faithful Catholic to discriminate between 'just' and 'unjust' wars, and to foreswear participation in the latter."

In justification for affirming the denial of conscientious objector status to

Gillette and Negre, Marshall pointed out, "Our cases do not at their farthest reach support the proposition that a stance of conscientious opposition relieves an objector from any colliding duty fixed by a democratic government."

Freedom of Speech

The Place to Speak. "This case presents the question whether peaceful picketing of a business enterprise located within a shopping center can be enjoined on the ground that it constitutes an unconsented invasion of the property rights of the land on which the center is located."[24]

That was the question Justice Marshall sought to answer in a case involving picketing of the Weiss market by the Amalgamated Food Employees Union, Local 590, Altoona, Pennsylvania. Weiss had opened a supermarket with nonunion employees, and to voice their objection union members began to picket in the parking lot and parcel pickup area of the store. Weiss, and the center's owner, obtained an injunction against the picketing, and the union appealed. The Pennsylvania Supreme Court upheld the injunction "on the sole ground that . . . [picketers] conduct constituted a trespass" on the shopping center's property. The Supreme Court reversed, on the ground that the center was an open area similar to other commercial areas of the town and therefore the picketing was protected by the First Amendment.

"We start with the premise," Marshall pointed out, "that peaceful picketing carried on in a location open generally to the public is, absent other factors involving the purpose or the manner of the picketing, protected by the First Amendment."

Marshall then recalled the Court's decision in *Marsh v. Alabama*, wherein the Court held that the First Amendment protected Grace Marsh when she distributed religious literature on the streets of a company-owned town. The justice discussed the physical aspects of the mall, and noted that there were roads near it, and sidewalks and parking spaces on it, and the public had unlimited access to it. "The shopping center here," he concluded, "is clearly the functional equivalent of the business district of Chicasaw involved in *Marsh*." Marshall did not accept the center's argument that it had an absolute right to control the use of its property.

Quoting from *Marsh*, the justice pointed out that "'ownership does not always mean absolute dominion. The more an owner, for his advantage, opens up his property for use by the public in general, the more do his rights become circumscribed by the statutory and constitutional rights of those who use it.' Logan Valley Mall is the functional equivalent of a 'business block' and for First Amendment purposes must be treated in substantially the same manner."

While Marshall and the justices who voted with him in this case won a temporary battle to keep shopping centers open as a place to exercise First Amendment rights, they eventually lost the war. Over Justice Marshall's dissent, the Court held that a shopping center was not open for distribution of handbills that were "unrelated to any activity within the center and where respondents had adequate alternative means of communication."[25] In response to the argument that hand-billing would disturb a center's customers, the justice responded:

> It is undisputed that some patrons will be disturbed by any First Amendment activity that goes on, regardless of its object. But, there is no evidence to indicate that speech directed to topics unrelated to the shopping center would be more likely to impair the motivation of customers to buy than speech directed to the uses to which the Center is put, which petitioner concedes is constitutionally protected under *Logan Valley*. On the contrary, common sense would indicate that speech that is critical of a shopping center or one or more of its stores is more likely to deter consumers from purchasing goods or services than speech on any other subject.

The Court finally closed the door even to labor picketing on a mall when it held "that warehouse employees of company which operated retail store in shopping center had no First Amendment right to enter the shopping center for the purpose of advertising their strike against the employer; and that the rights and liabilities of the parties were dependent exclusively upon the National Labor Relations Act."[26] Marshall did not let the issue rest without expressing his dismay at the Court's decision.

> In the final analysis, the Court's rejection of any role for the First Amendment in the privately owned shopping center complex stems, I believe, from an overly formalistic view of the relationship between the institution of private ownership of property and the First Amendment's guarantee of freedom of speech. No one would seriously question the legitimacy of the values of privacy and individual autonomy traditionally associated with privately owned property. But property that is privately owned is not always held for private use, and when a property owner opens his property to public use the force of those values diminishes. A degree of privacy is necessarily surrendered; thus, the privacy interest that petitioner retains when he leases space to 60 retail businesses and invites the public onto his land for the transaction of business with other members of the public is small indeed.

The Court, with Justice Marshall concurring, left the way open for *states* to declare malls open for First Amendment activities when it affirmed a decision of the California Supreme Court which held "that the California Constitution protects 'speech and petitioning, reasonable exercised, in shopping centers even when the centers are privately owned.'"[27]

Federal law makes it a criminal offense to put any mailable material in another person's mailbox. The Postal Service offers three reasons for the law. It "(1) protects mail revenues; (2) . . . it facilitates efficient and secure delivery of the mails; and (3) . . . it protects the privacy of mail patrons."[28]

When a group of civic organizations in Westchester County, New York,

challenged the validity of the law, District Judge William C. Conner held it unconstitutional as a violation of First Amendment rights to communicate. A majority of the Supreme Court disagreed and reversed, being of the opinion that
mailboxes were not proper places to conduct First Amendment activities. Justice
Marshall did not see that as the issue in the case. "The question, . . . " he argued,
"is whether this statute burdens any First Amendment rights enjoyed by . . . [the
civic groups]." "We have long recognized," he pointed out, "the constitutional
rights of groups which seek, as appellees do, to 'communicate ideas, positions on
local issues, and civic information to their constituents' through written handouts and thereby to promote the free discussion of governmental affairs so central to our democracy."

While groups can take their handouts door-to-door, if no one is home the
law prevents them from delivering the material even though "by placing their
circulars in the letterboxes . . . appellees [can be] certain that their messages will
be secure from wind, rain or snow, and at the same time will alert the attention of
the residents without notifying would-be burglars that no one has returned
home to remove items from doorways or stoops."

Marshall also took the Court to task for giving the government control over
mailboxes and proceeding with its analysis as if it were government property.
"Instead of starting with the scope of government control," he argued,

> I would adhere to our usual analysis which looks to whether the exercise of a First
> Amendment right is burdened by the challenged governmental action, and then
> upholds that action only where it is necessary to advance a substantial and legiti-
> mate governmental interest. In my view, the statute criminalizing the placement
> of hand-delivered civic association notices in letterboxes fails this test. The brute
> force of the criminal sanction and other powers of the Government, I believe,
> may be deployed to restrict free expression only with greater justification.

Can people sleep in a public park to call attention to the plight of the homeless? That was the legal question raised by the Community for Creative Non-
Violence.

> The Community for Creative Non-Violence (CCNV) applied for and was
> granted a renewable seven-day permit to conduct a round-the-clock demonstra-
> tion, commencing on the first day of winter, on the Mall and in Lafayette Park in
> Washington, D.C. The declared purpose of the demonstration was to impress
> upon the Reagan Administration, the Congress, and the public the plight of the
> poor and the homeless. The National Park Service (Park Service) granted
> CCNV a permit to set up two symbolic campsites, one on Mall with a maximum
> of one hundred participants and forty tents, and one in Lafayette Park with ap-
> proximately fifty participants and twenty tents.
>
>   Although the permit allowed the demonstration participants to maintain a
> twenty-four hour presence at their symbolic campsites, the Park Service denied
> the participants a permit to sleep. . . . CCNV claims that this prohibition strikes

at the core message the demonstrators wish to convey—that homeless people have no permanent place to sleep.[29]

In a lawsuit brought by CCNV protesting the antisleep rule, Judge John H. Pratt granted summary judgment for the government, but the circuit court reversed, being of the opinion that in this case sleeping was expressive conduct and entitled to First Amendment protection, and that "the government has failed to show how the prohibition of sleep, in the context of round-the-clock demonstrations . . . furthers any of its legitimate interests." The Supreme Court disagreed and reversed with Justice Marshall dissenting. Justice White, writing for the majority, assumed that the Mall and the park were proper places for the exercise of First Amendment rights, but concluded that the antisleeping rule was a reasonable regulation of the use of the government's property.[30]

Marshall saw the Court's decision as one in which the majority did not really understand the messenger's message. "[T]he majority," he wrote,

> is either unwilling or unable to take seriously the First Amendment claims advanced by respondents [CCNV]. Contrary to the impression given by the majority, respondents are not supplicants seeking to wheedle an undeserved favor from the Government. They are citizens raising issues of profound public importance who have properly turned to the courts for the vindication of their constitutional rights. . . . The majority's approach denatures respondents' asserted right and thus makes all too easy identification of a Government interest sufficient to warrant its abridgment.

The justice agreed that the government had a substantial "interest in 'maintaining the parks in the heart of our Capital in an attractive and intact condition, readily available to the millions of people who wish to see and enjoy them by their presence.'" But he could find no evidence that sleeping in the park and on the Mall in any way conflicted with that interest. "The First Amendment," he argued, "requires the Government to justify *every* instance of abridgment. That requirement stems from our oft-stated recognition that the First Amendment was designed to secure 'the widest possible dissemination of information from diverse and antagonistic sources,' . . . and 'to assure unfettered interchange of ideas for the bringing about of political and social changes desired by the people.'"[31]

Thaddeus Zywicki, wanting to distribute a newspaper article about unfit judges, chose the sidewalk in front of the Supreme Court building as the place to do so. He discontinued the distribution when a police officer informed him that he was violating a federal law prohibiting such activity on the grounds of the Court, and that if he continued he would be arrested.

When Mary Terese Grace heard about Zywicki's experience, she prepared a sign containing the words of the First Amendment and stood alone on the sidewalk adjacent to the Supreme Court building. She too was informed that it was unlawful to display the sign there and that she would be arrested if she did not leave.

Grace and Zywicki brought an action in the district court claiming that the law was unconstitutional, but Judge Louis F. Oberdorfer dismissed the case because he thought that the plaintiffs should have applied first to the Supreme Court marshal for a permit to use the sidewalk for First Amendment activities. The circuit court, however, concluded that the law prohibiting speech activities on the grounds of the Supreme Court was unconstitutional and therefore reversed. The Supreme Court affirmed the circuit court's decision, but held that although the law itself was constitutional, it did not apply to Grace and Zywicki, because the sidewalk was not part of the grounds of the Supreme Court and therefore was a proper place for them to protest.[32]

Marshall agreed that Grace and Zywicki had a right to speak on the sidewalk near the Court, but he also agreed with the circuit court that the law was unconstitutional. "The statute in no way distinguishes the sidewalks from the rest of the premises," he argued, "and excising the sidewalks from its purview does not bring it into conformity with the First Amendment. Visitors to this Court do not lose their First Amendment rights at the edge of the sidewalks any more than 'students and teachers shed their constitutional rights to freedom of speech or expression at the schoolhouse gate.'"

Justice Marshall was concerned that by leaving the law in place, First Amendment activities could be prohibited on the grounds of the Court. "Every citizen lawfully present in a public place," he declared, "has a right to engage in peaceable and orderly expression that is not incompatible with the primary activity of the place in question, whether that place is a school, a library, a private lunch counter, the grounds of a statehouse, the grounds of the United States Capitol, a bus terminal, an airport or a welfare center." "I see no reason," he continued, "why the premises of this Court should be exempt from this basic principle. It would be ironic indeed if an exception to the Constitution were to be recognized for the very institution that has the chief responsibility for protecting constitutional rights. I would apply to the premises of this Court the same principles that this Court has applied to other public places."

Public Employees' Right to Advocate.

> On March 30, 1981, President Reagan was shot. After hearing a radio report of the attempted assassination, Ardith McPherson, a clerical worker in a Houston, Texas constable's office, said to a co-worker: "[I]f they go for him again, I hope they get him." A deputy constable overheard the statement and reported it to Constable Rankin, who immediately summoned McPherson to his office to question her about the remark. When McPherson acknowledged both that she had made the statement and that she meant it, Rankin fired her.[33]

McPherson brought a civil rights action against Rankin and Harris County claiming that the discharge violated her right to freedom of speech. Judge

Norman W. Black did not agree and dismissed the case. The circuit court held that McPherson's speech was protected by the First Amendment and that therefore her discharge was unlawful. A majority of the Supreme Court affirmed, with Justice Marshall writing the Court's opinion. "The issue in this case," Marshall wrote, "is whether a clerical employee in a county Constable's office was properly discharged for remarking, after hearing of an attempt on the life of the President, 'If they go for him again, I hope they get him.'"[34]

The rule of law to be applied to this case, the justice noted, is "clearly established." That law is "that a State may not discharge an employee on a basis that infringes that employee's constitutionally protected interest in freedom of speech." And the proper solution to such cases, is to balance the employee's right to speak about matters of public concern against the need of government to maintain efficiency in the service it provides to the public.

Marshall agreed that McPherson's statement related to a matter of public concern. "The statement was made in the course of a conversation addressing the policies of the President's administration. It came on the heels of a news bulletin regarding what is certainly a matter of heightened public attention: an attempt on the life of the President."

In examining the record, Marshall could find no evidence that McPherson's statement had any effect upon the operation of the constable's office, and in fact Rankin had testified that that had nothing to do with his decision to discharge her. "McPherson's employment-related interaction with the Constable," the justice noted, "was apparently negligible. Her duties were purely clerical and were limited solely to the civil process function of the Constable's office. There is no indication that she would ever be in a position to further—or indeed to have any involvement with—the minimal law enforcement activity engaged in by the Constable's office. Given the function of the agency, McPherson's position in the office, the nature of her statement, we are not persuaded that Rankin's interest in discharging her outweighed her rights under the First Amendment."

Aaron Finkel and Alan Tabakman, Republicans, were employed as assistant public defenders in the office of the public defender, Rockland County, New York. When Peter Branti, Jr., a Democrat, was appointed public defender, he immediately sent termination notices to six of nine assistants, including Finkel and Tabakman. Finkel and Tabakman then commenced legal action against Branti asserting that their discharge on the grounds of their political beliefs violated their First Amendment rights. Judge Vincent L. Broderick concluded that because neither Finkel or Tabakman was a policy-making employee their discharge was unconstitutional. The circuit court affirmed, and the Supreme Court agreed, with Marshall voting with the majority.

"If the First Amendment protects a public employee from discharge based on what he has said," Justice John Paul Stevens declared, "it must also protect him from discharge based on what he believes. Under this line of analysis, unless the government can demonstrate 'an overriding interest,' . . . requiring that a person's private beliefs conform to those of the hiring authority, his beliefs cannot be the sole basis for depriving him of continued employment."[35]

Commercial Speech. "This case presents the question whether the First Amendment permits a municipality to prohibit the posting of 'For Sale' or 'Sold' signs when the municipality acts to stem what it perceives as the flight of white homeowners from a racially integrated community."[36] Justice Marshall stated his opinion in the case of *Linmark Associates, Inc. v. Willingboro*[37] with that question. He went on to explain that while Willingboro, New Jersey, was experiencing a slow growth in population, the white population was decreasing and the reason for the decline appeared to be " 'panic selling'—that is, selling by whites who feared that the township was becoming all black and that property values would decline." In order to counteract this, the city enacted an ordinance that severely limited the size and location of "For Sale" and "Sold" signs.

Linmark Associates, the owner of land in Willingboro that it wanted to sell, brought an action challenging the constitutionality of the law. Judge Clarkson S. Fisher held the ordinance to be unconstitutional, but the circuit court reversed. It was of the opinion that the law was a reasonable regulation of commercial speech in view of the municipality's desire to prevent panic selling. The Supreme Court unanimously disagreed. Marshall acknowledged that speech that conveys a commercial message is entitled to some protection of the First Amendment. "Persons desiring to sell their homes are just as interested in communicating that fact as are sellers of other goods and services. Similarly, would-be purchasers of realty are no less interested in receiving information about available property than are purchasers of other commodities in receiving like information about those commodities." What concerned the justice, then, was the effect that the ordinance would have upon the free flow of that information.

> That information, which pertains to sales activity in Willingboro, is of vital interest to Willingboro residents, since it may bear on one of the most important decisions they have a right to make: where to live and raise their families. The Council has sought to restrict the free flow of these data because it fears that otherwise homeowners will make decisions inimical to what the Council views as the homeowners' self-interest and the corporate interest of the township: they will choose to leave town. . . . If dissemination of this information can be restricted, then every locality in the country can suppress any facts that reflect poorly on the locality, so long as a plausible claim can be made that disclosure would cause the recipients of that information to act "irrationally."

Federal law provides that "any unsolicited advertisement of matter which is designed, adapted, or intended for preventing conception is nonmailable matter, shall not be carried or delivered by mail and shall be disposed of as the Postal Service directs."[38]

Youngs Drug Products Corporation, which manufactures and sells contraceptives, desired to do some mass mailing for their products, but before doing so the company submitted the material to the Postal Service for approval. Youngs desired to mail three types of material:

> One type . . .[was] informational pamphlets promoting the desirability and availability of prophylactics in general, and Youngs' products in particular. The second type . . . [was] flyers exclusively or substantially devoted to promoting prophylactics in general, those made by Youngs, and/or those stocked . . . by a particular drugstore or chain of drugstores. The third type . . .[was] multi-page, multi-item flyers promoting a large variety of products available and perhaps on discount there, including prophylactics.

When the Postal Service informed Youngs that the material was not acceptable, Youngs brought an action in the federal district court alleging that the law was an unconstitutional infringement upon their First Amendment rights.

District Judge John Garrett Penn agreed. He held that "the statute was constitutionally impermissible because it was more extensive than necessary to serve governmental interest in protecting privacy of individuals in their homes." All justices of the Supreme Court agreed, with Marshall writing the Court's opinion. Brennan did not participate in the case.

The Court concluded that all of the material fell within the classification of commercial speech, which is not entitled to the same high degree of protection as other speech.

Nevertheless, because commercial speech does enjoy First Amendment protection, the burden then fell upon the Postal Service to justify the statute. It argued "that the statute (1) shields recipients of mail from materials that they are likely to find offensive and (2) aids parents' efforts to control the manner in which their children become informed about sensitive and important subjects such as birth control."[39]

Justice Marshall held that these asserted interests were insufficient to override First Amendment rights. "[W]e have never held," he asserted,

> that the Government itself can shut off the flow of mailings to protect those recipients who might potentially be offended. The First Amendment "does not permit the government to prohibit speech as intrusive unless the 'captive' audience cannot avoid objectionable speech." . . . Recipients of objectionable mailings, however, may "effectively avoid further bombardment of their sensibilities by averting their eyes." . . . Consequently, the "short, though regular journey from mail box to trash can . . . is an acceptable burden, at least so far as the Constitution is concerned."

Marshall acknowledged that the statute under consideration might help some parents—that is, "those parents who desire to keep their children from confronting such mailings, who are otherwise unable to do so, and whose children have remained relatively free from such stimuli." "This marginal degree of protection," he notes, "is achieved by purging all mailboxes of unsolicited material that is entirely suitable for adults. We have previously made clear that a restriction of this scope is more extensive than the Constitution permits, for the government may not 'reduce the adult population to reading only what is fit for children.'"

Prisoners' Mail and Loud Music in the Park. Robert Martinez and Wayne Earley, for themselves and other prisoners in California prisons, brought an action in federal district court alleging that the rules regulating prisoners' mail violated their constitutional rights. Prisoners' mail, both outgoing and incoming, was opened by prison staff and examined for material that prison rules considered to be contraband.

Contraband included "writings 'expressing inflammatory political, racial, religious or other views or beliefs.'"[40] Inmates were also prohibited from sending or receiving "letters that pertain to criminal activity; are lewd, obscene, defamatory; contain foreign matter, or are otherwise inappropriate." The district court held that these restrictions were unconstitutional as a violation of the prisoners' First Amendment right to communicate.

Although the Supreme Court affirmed, it did so by focusing on the rights of the nonprisoner who sends or is the recipient of the mail. "Whatever the status of a prisoner's claim to uncensored correspondence with an outsider," Justice Powell declared, "it is plain that the latter's interest is grounded in the First Amendment's guarantee of freedom of speech. And this does not depend on whether the nonprisoner correspondent is the author or intended recipient of a particular letter, for the addressee as well as the sender of direct personal correspondence derives from the First and Fourteenth Amendments a protection against unjustified governmental interference with the intended communication."

Although concurring in the Court's decision, Justice Marshall objected to the Court's bypassing the question of the First Amendment rights of prisoners. "I write separately," he asserted, "only to emphasize my view that prison authorities do not have a general right to open and read all incoming and outgoing prisoner mail. A prisoner does not shed such basic First Amendment rights at the prison gate. Rather, he 'retains all the rights of an ordinary citizen except those expressly, or by necessary implication, taken from him by law.' . . . Accordingly, prisoners are, in my view, entitled to use the mails as a medium of free expression not as a privilege, but rather as a constitutionally guaranteed right."

Commenting on the needs of prisoners for self-expression, Justice Marshall wrote:

> The First Amendment serves not only the needs of the polity but also those of the human spirit—a spirit that demands self-expression. Such expression is an integral part of the development of ideas and a sense of identity. To suppress

expression is to reject the basic human desire for recognition and affront the individual's worth and dignity. . . . When the prison gates slam behind an inmate, he does not lose his human quality; his mind does not become closed to ideas; his intellect does not cease to feed on a free and open interchange of opinions; his yearning for self-respect does not end; nor is his quest for self-realization concluded. If anything, the needs for identity and self-respect are more compelling in the dehumanizing prison environment. Whether an O. Henry writing his short stories in a jail cell or a frightened young inmate writing his family, a prisoner needs a medium for self-expression. It is the role of the First Amendment and this Court to protect those precious personal rights by which we satisfy such basic yearnings of the human spirit.

"No one can doubt that government has a substantial interest in regulating the barrage of excessive sound that can plague urban life."[41] With those words, Justice Marshall opened his dissent in the case of *Ward v. Rock Against Racism*, a case questioning the validity of New York's solution to excessive noise in Central Park. In an attempt to balance the interests of the performers at the bandshell with those of other users of the park and those living in the vicinity, the city decided that it would furnish the amplification equipment and employ a sound technician to operate it.

Rock Against Racism, which for many years had used the bandshell for speeches and concerts, sued Benjamin R. Ward, the New York police commissioner, and other city officials, challenging the constitutionality of the new guideline. Judge Charles S. Haight, Jr., upheld the regulation, but the circuit court reversed, concluding that alternative methods for controlling the sound should be pursued. The Supreme Court, however, found the guideline valid, and reversed. Marshall dissented because he was of the opinion that the guidelines were "not narrowly tailored to serve . . . [the city's] interest in regulating loud noise, and because they constitute an impermissible prior restraint."

The justice believed that the majority was not adhering to prior rules established by the Court for testing regulations affecting speech. "A time, place and manner regulation of expression," he argued, "must be content neutral, serve a significant interest, and leave open ample alternative channels of communication." In approving the guideline, the Court was not adhering to that standard. "Today," he said, "the majority enshrines efficacy but sacrifices free speech."

The fact that sound volume was to be under the control of the city through its employment of a sound engineer also troubled Marshall. He saw this as a prior restraint upon performers and censorship of their performance. "But whether the city denies a performer a bandshell permit," he argued, "or grants the permit and then silences or distorts the performer's music, the result is the same—the city censors speech." The justice expressed his dismay with the Court's decision in a concluding paragraph to his dissent: "Today's decision has significance far beyond the world of rock music. Government no longer need balance the effectiveness of regulation with the burdens on free speech. After today, government need only assert that it is most effective to control speech in advance of its expression. Because such a result eviscerates the First Amendment, I dissent."

Freedom of the Press

Libel. While the police were at a newsstand investigating the sale of obscene material, George Rosenbloom arrived to deliver some nudist magazines to the dealer. He was immediately arrested for selling and distributing obscene material. Subsequently, the police, armed with a search warrant, searched Rosenbloom's home and barn where they found a number of magazines and books, which they seized. Rosenbloom, who had been released on bail, was arrested again. Shortly thereafter, radio station WIP, owned by Metromedia, carried a story about the raid and Rosenbloom's arrest. The broadcast led off with the words "City Cracks Down on Smut Merchants."[42] The broadcast named Rosenbloom, and stated that he had been arrested for possession of obscene material and that "3,000 obscene books" had been seized.

Rosenbloom brought suit in the federal district court seeking an injunction against the police to prevent them from interfering with his business. He claimed that the magazines he was distributing were not obscene. Before the matter could be heard, the station broadcast another story about the case. Although Rosenbloom was not named, the station's report said, "The girlie-book peddlers say the police crack-down and continued reference to their borderline literature as smut or filth is hurting their business."

Rosenbloom was later acquitted of all charges by a jury acting under instructions from the judge that the material was not obscene as a matter of law. Rosenbloom then brought an action against WIP claiming that the stories about him were libelous. The jury agreed and awarded him $25,000 in general damages and $750,000 in punitive damages. The circuit court reversed, holding that the investigation into the sale and possession of obscene material was a matter of public concern and that therefore Rosenbloom could not recover unless he was able to prove that WIP had acted with "actual malice." And because the circuit court concluded that the evidence did not show "actual malice," the case must be dismissed. The Supreme Court affirmed, with Justice Marshall dissenting.

To begin with, Justice Marshall pointed out that Rosenbloom was "an individual who held no public office, who had not taken part in any public controversy, and who lived an obscure private life. George Rosenbloom, before the events and reports of the events involved here, was just one of the millions of Americans who live their lives in obscurity." Thus, he noted, there were two conflicting interests at stake in this controversy: the protection of the Rosenbloom's reputation, and the freedom of the press.

The justice was of the opinion that these two interests were best served by restricting the complainant to actual damages in libel actions.

The threats to society's interest in freedom of the press that are involved in punitive and presumed damages can largely be eliminated by restricting the award of damages to proved, actual injuries. The jury's wide-ranging discretion will largely be eliminated since the award will be based on essentially objective, discernible factors. And the self-censorship that results from the uncertainty created by the discretion as well as the self-censorship resulting from the fear of large judgments themselves would be reduced. At the same time, society's interest in protecting individuals from defamation will be fostered. The victims of defamation will be compensated for their real injuries. They will not be, however, assuaged far beyond their wounds. And, there will be substantial although imprecise and imperfect admonition to avoid future defamation by imposing the requirement that there be compensation for actual damages.

Time, Inc. v. Firestone[43] is a case about the rich but maybe not so famous people. "Mary Alice Firestone, married Russell Firestone, the scion of one of America's wealthier industrial families, in 1961." The couple separated in 1964, and Mrs. Firestone sought separate maintenance. Russell counterclaimed for divorce, claiming extreme cruelty and adultery on the part of his wife. In granting the request for divorce to Russell, the trial court's judgment reads:

> According to certain testimony in behalf of the defendant [Russell], extramarital escapades of the plaintiff were bizarre and of an amatory nature which would have made Dr. Freud's hair curl. Other testimony, in plaintiff's [Mary's] behalf, would indicate that defendant was guilty of bounding from one bedpartner to another with the erotic zest of a satyr. The court is inclined to discount much of this testimony as unreliable. Nevertheless, it is the conclusion and finding of the court that neither party is domesticated, within meaning of that term as used by the Supreme Court of Florida.

The trial court also awarded Mary Firestone $3,000 per month alimony.

Shortly thereafter, *Time,* in its "Milestones" column, published the following paragraph:

> DIVORCED. By Russell A. Firestone, Jr. 41, heir to the tire fortune: Mary Alice Sullivan Firestone, 32, his third wife; onetime Palm Beach schoolteacher; on grounds of extreme cruelty and adultery; after six years of marriage, one son; in West Palm Beach, Fla. The 17-month intermittent trial produced enough testimony of extramarital adventures on both sides, said the judge, "to make Dr. Freud's hair curl."

Mary Firestone demanded a retraction from Time, Inc., pointing out that the divorce was granted on the grounds of extreme cruelty, not on the grounds of adultery. When no retraction was forthcoming, she brought an action against Time, Inc., for libel, and the jury awarded her $100,000. The verdict was upheld by the Supreme Court of Florida.

In a decision that spawned five opinions, the U.S. Supreme Court vacated the judgment and sent the case back to the Florida courts. Marshall dissented, because he did not think that the Court was giving sufficient protection to Time, Inc.'s freedom to publish.

"Mary Alice Firestone," the Justice noted, "was not a person 'first brought to public attention by the defamation that is the subject of this lawsuit.' . . . On the contrary, she was 'prominent among the "400" of Palm Beach society,' and an 'active [member] of the sporting set,' . . . whose activities predictably attracted the attention of a sizable portion of the public. Indeed, Mrs. Firestone's appearances in the press were evidently frequent enough to warrant her subscribing to a press-clipping service."

Because the plaintiff was a public figure, the justice concluded that she should not recover in this case. "I would hold that, for purposes of this case, Mrs. Firestone is a public figure," he wrote, "who must demonstrate that the report in question was published with 'actual malice'—that is, with knowledge that it was false or with reckless disregard of whether it was false or not." No showing had been made that Time, Inc., had, in any way, acted with malice toward Mrs. Firestone.

Marshall continued to express his concern for freedom of the press in a dissent in *Herbert v. Lando.*[44]

> Petitioner, Anthony Herbert, is a retired Army officer who had extended wartime service in Vietnam and who received wide-spread media attention in 1969–1970 when he accused his superior officers of covering up reports of atrocities and other war crimes. Three years later, on February 4, 1973, respondent Columbia Broadcasting System, Inc. (CBS), broadcast a report on petitioner and his accusations. The program was produced and edited by respondent Barry Lando and was narrated by respondent Mike Wallace. Lando later published a related article in Atlantic Monthly magazine. Herbert then sued Lando, Wallace, CBS, and Atlantic Monthly for defamation. . . . In his complaint, Herbert alleged that the program and article falsely and maliciously portrayed him as a liar and a person who had made war-crimes charges to explain his relief from command. . . .

Before trial, Herbert's lawyers examined Lando by way of deposition, but he refused to answer questions relating to the "state of mind of those who edit, produce, or publish, and into the editorial process," claiming that that information was protected from discovery by the First Amendment. Judge Charles S. Haight, Jr., held that the questions were proper and ordered discovery to proceed. The circuit court, with one judge dissenting, reversed, concluding that the media was protected from such disclosure by the First Amendment. The Supreme Court reversed, being of the opinion that "an absolute privilege to the editorial process of a media defendant in a libel case is not required, authorized, or presaged by our prior cases."

Justice Marshall's starting point, in dissent, was in acknowledging the two interests at stake in defamation actions.

States undeniably have an interest in affording individuals some measure of protection from unwarranted defamatory attacks. Libel actions serve that end, not only by assuring a forum in which reputations can be publicly vindicated and dignitary injuries compensated, but also by creating incentives for the press to exercise considered judgment before publishing material that compromises personal integrity. . . . Against these objections must be balanced society's interest in promoting unfettered debate on matters of public importance.

Marshall, however, was also aware of the abuses of discovery procedures, and he believed that the opportunity for such abuse was particularly present in libel actions. "Given the circumstances under which libel actions arise," he declared, "plaintiff's pretrial maneuvers may be fashioned more with an eye to deterrence or retaliation than to unearthing germane material." And he expressed concern that the possibility of long and expensive discovery proceedings could adversely effect editorial decisions. He concluded that in order to protect "uninhibited, robust, and wide-open" debate on public issues, "some constraints on roving discovery" were necessary. "I would require," he concluded, "that district courts superintend pretrial disclosure in such litigation so as to protect the press from unnecessarily protracted or tangential inquiry. To that end, discovery requests should be measured against strict standard of relevance. Further, because the threat of disclosure may intrude with special force on certain aspects of the editorial process, I believe some additional protection in the form of an evidentiary privilege is warranted."

Prior Restraints and Punishment for Publication.

Albert Greenwood Brown, Jr. was tried and convicted of rape and murder of a teenage girl, and sentenced to death in California Superior Court. Before the *voir dire* examination of prospective jurors began, petitioner, Press-Enterprise Co., moved that the *voir dire* be open to the public and the press. Petitioner contended that the public had an absolute right to attend the trial, and asserted that the trial commenced with the *voir dire* proceedings. The State opposed petitioner's motion, arguing that if the press were present, jurors' responses would lack the candor necessary to assure a fair trial.

The trial judge agreed and permitted petitioner to attend only the "general voir dire." He stated that counsel would conduct the "individual voir dire with regard to death qualifications and any other special areas that counsel may feel some problem with regard to . . . in private." . . . The *voir dire* consumed *six weeks* and all but approximately three days was closed to the public.[45]

After the jury was impaneled, and again at the conclusion of the trial, the newspaper attempted to secure a transcript of the questions and answers of the prospective jurors. The request was denied. The California Court of Appeals and the California Supreme Court upheld the denial, but the United States Supreme Court reversed.

Chief Justice Burger wrote for the majority:

The open trial thus plays as important a role in the administration of justice today as it did for centuries before our separation from England. The value of openness lies in the fact that people not actually attending trials can have confidence that standards of fairness are being observed; the sure knowledge that *anyone* is free to attend gives assurance that established procedures are being followed and that deviations will become known. Openness thus enhances both the basic fairness of the criminal trial and the appearance of fairness so essential to public confidence in the system.

Justice Marshall concurred, but he wanted to make clear that the constitutional right of the public and press to attend trials is not limited just because some "deeply personal matters" might be disclosed. "Indeed," he declared, "the policies underlying those rights . . . are most severely jeopardized when courts conceal from the public sensitive information that bears upon the ability of jurors impartially to weigh the evidence presented to them." He suggested that in those cases where closure may be necessary,

> the constitutionally preferable method for reconciling the First Amendment interests of the public and the press with the legitimate privacy interests of jurors and the interests of defendants in fair trials is to redact transcripts in such a way as to preserve the anonymity of jurors while disclosing the substance of their responses. Only in the most extraordinary circumstances can the substance of a juror's response to questioning at *voir dire* be permanently excluded from the salutary scrutiny of the public and the press.

> [B.J.F.] reported on Thursday, October 20, she was crossing Brentwood Park, which is in the 500 block of Golfair Boulevard, enroute to her bus stop, when an unknown black man ran up behind the lady and placed a knife to her neck and told her not to yell. The suspect undressed the lady and had sexual intercourse with her before fleeing the scene with her 60 cents, Timex watch and gold necklace. Patrol efforts have been suspended concerning this incident because of a lack of evidence.[46]

The above report appeared in the *Star*, a newspaper in Jacksonville, Florida, and had been obtained from the police report of the incident. The article contained the actual name of the victim where the letters "B.J.F." appear above. Because Florida law made it a criminal offense to publish the name of a victim of a sexual offense, B.J.F. brought an action against the *Star* for damages, and recovered $75,000 in actual damages and an additional $25,000 in punitive damages. The trial court overruled the *Star*'s argument that the law violated its right to freedom of the press, and that ruling was upheld by Florida appellate courts. With Justice Marshall writing the opinion, the Supreme Court reversed.

The justice summed up the positions of the *Star*, on the one hand, and of B.J.F., on the other. The *Star* argued "that the press may never be punished civilly or criminally, for publishing the truth." Attorneys for B.J.F., however, urged the Court to establish a rule "that publication of the name of a rape victim never enjoys constitutional protection." Marshall did not accept either argument. Instead, he said, the rule with regard to cases of this kind should be: "If a newspaper lawfully obtains truthful information about a matter of public significance then state officials may not constitutionally punish publication of the information, absent a need to further a state interest of the highest order."

In applying that rule to this case, the justice noted that the *Star* had obtained the information from the government itself, and "if liability were to be imposed, self-censorship would result." Also, the law imposes liability for publication without the newspaper being given any opportunity to respond. "This is so," Marshall noted, "regardless of whether the identity of the victim is already known throughout the community; whether the victim has voluntarily called public attention to the offense; or whether the identity of the victim has otherwise become a reasonable subject of public concern—because, perhaps, questions have arisen whether the victim fabricated an assault by a particular person." And finally, the statute punishes only publication by "an instrument of mass communication" and does not prevent anyone else from dissemination of the information.

Justice Marshall concluded his opinion with a summary of the decision:

> We do not hold that truthful publication is automatically constitutionally protected, or that there is no zone of personal privacy within which the State may protect the individual from intrusion by the press, or even that a State may never punish publication of the name of a victim of a sexual offense. We hold only that where a newspaper publishes truthful information which it has lawfully obtained, punishment may lawfully be imposed, if at all, only when narrowly tailored to a state interest of the highest order, and that no such interest is satisfactorily served by imposing liability under . . . [this law] to appellant under the facts of this case.

Obscenity. In 1965 the city of Dallas, Texas, enacted an ordinance requiring motion pictures to be classified by a board as "'suitable for young persons,' or as 'not suitable for young persons.'"[47] Pictures that are "not suitable for young persons" include those "describing or portraying nudity beyond the customary limits of candor in the community, or sexual promiscuity or extra-martial or abnormal sexual relations in such a manner as to be, in the judgment of the Board, likely to incite or encourage delinquency or sexual promiscuity on the part of young persons or to appeal to their prurient interest." In making that decision, the board was to consider whether the conduct portrayed in the film would "create the impression on young persons that such conduct is profitable, desirable, acceptable, respectable, praiseworthy, or commonly accepted."

The board classified the picture *Viva Maria* as "not suitable for young persons," and the exhibitor, Interstate Circuit, appealed. The board's decision was upheld by the appellate courts of Texas, but reversed by the Supreme Court. Of particular concern to the Court was the vagueness of the ordinance's provisions, which were to guide the board in making its decision. "The vice of vagueness," Justice Marshall declared, "is particularly pronounced where expression is sought to be subjected to licensing." Vague licensing laws may cause film producers to act as a self-censor. "If he is unable to determine what the ordinance means," Marshall asserted, "he runs the risk of being foreclosed, in practical effect, from a significant portion of the movie-going public. Rather than run that risk, he might choose nothing but the innocuous, perhaps save for the so-called 'adult' picture."

Turning attention to the criteria set forth in the ordinance, Marshall noted that the phrase "sexual promiscuity" was not defined thus leaving it to the board to determine whether the picture "would encourage delinquency or sexual promiscuity on the part of young persons." The problem with this approach, he pointed out, was that what "may be to one viewer the glorification of an idea as being 'desirable, acceptable, or proper,' may to the notions of another be entirely devoid of such a teaching. The only limits on the censor's discretion is his understanding of what is included within the term 'desirable, acceptable or proper.' This is nothing less than a roving commission."

The facts of the case of *Stanley v. Georgia*[48] are as follows:

> An investigation of appellant's [Stanley's] alleged bookmaking activities led to the issuance of a search warrant for appellant's home. Under authority of this warrant, federal and state agents secured entrance. They found very little evidence of bookmaking activity, but while looking through a desk drawer in an upstairs bedroom, one of the federal agents, accompanied by a state officer, found three reels of eight-millimeter film. Using a projector and screen found in an upstairs living room, they viewed the films. The state officer concluded that they were obscene and seized them. Since further examination of the bedroom indicated that appellant occupied it, he was charged with possession of obscene matter and placed under arrest. He was later indicted for "knowingly hav[ing] possession of . . . obscene matter" in violation of Georgia law. Appellant was tried before a jury and convicted. The Supreme Court of Georgia affirmed.

On appeal to the U.S. Supreme Court, Stanley argued "that the Georgia obscenity statute, insofar as it punishes mere private possession of obscene matter, violates the First Amendment." The Supreme Court agreed.

After commenting on prior obscenity cases, Marshall concluded for the majority that this was a different kind of case, and needed to be put in proper perspective.

"It is now well established," he observed,

> that the Constitution protects the right to receive information and ideas. . . . This right to receive information and ideas, regardless of their social worth, . . . is fundamental to our free society. Moreover, in the context of this case—prosecution for mere possession of printed or filmed matter in the privacy of a person's own

home—that right takes on an added dimension. For also fundamental is the right to be free, except in very limited circumstances, from unwanted governmental intrusions into one's privacy.

"These are the rights that appellant is asserting," the justice declared, "in the case before us. He is asserting the right to read or observe what he pleases—the right to satisfy his intellectual and emotional needs in the privacy of his own home. He is asserting the right to be free from state inquiry into the contents of his library." But, Georgia argued, these films were obscene. That did not impress the justice. "If the First Amendment means anything," he wrote, "it means that a State has no business telling a man, sitting alone in his own house, what books he may read or what films he may watch. Our whole constitutional heritage rebels at the thought of giving government the power to control men's minds."

"We hold," Marshall concluded, "that the First and Fourteenth Amendments prohibit making mere private possession of obscene material a crime."

About two years after Stanley's case, the Court considered whether the ruling in that case protected Milton Luros. When Luros returned to Los Angeles from a trip to Europe, he had 37 photographs that the government seized as obscene.

In an action by the government to have the photos forfeited, Luros argued that they were not obscene and that even if they were, he was entitled to carry them to the privacy of his home. The district court agreed, but the Supreme Court did not. "That the private user under *Stanley* may not be prosecuted for possession of obscenity in his home," Justice White wrote, "does not mean that he is entitled to import it from abroad free from the power of Congress to exclude noxious articles from commerce. *Stanley*'s emphasis was on the freedom of thought and mind in the privacy of the home. But the port of entry is not a traveler's home."[49]

Justice Marshall would have applied the rationale of *Stanley* and allowed Luros to keep the photographs. "Although claimant stipulated that he intended to use some of the photographs to illustrate a book which would be later distributed commercially," he argued, "the seized items were then in his purely private possession and threatened neither children nor anyone else. In my view, the Government has ample opportunity to protect its interest if and when commercial distribution should take place."

Freedom of Association

Oaths and Associational Privacy.

[Mrs.] Richardson, was hired as a research sociologist by the Boston State Hospital. Appellant Cole is superintendent of the hospital. Soon after she entered on duty Mrs. Richardson was asked to subscribe to the oath required of all public employees in Massachusetts. The oath is as follows:

> I do solemnly swear (or affirm) that I will uphold and defend the Constitution of the United States of America and the Commonwealth of Massachusetts and that I will oppose the overthrow of the government of the United States of America or of this Commonwealth by force, violence or by any illegal or unconstitutional method.

> Mrs. Richardson informed the hospital's personnel department that she could not take the oath as ordered because of her belief that it was in violation of the United States Constitution. Approximately 10 days later, appellant Cole personally informed Mrs. Richardson that under state law she could not continue as an employee of the Boston State Hospital unless she subscribed to the oath. Again she refused. On November 25, 1968, Mrs. Richardson's employment was terminated and she was paid through that date.
> In March 1969, Mrs. Richardson filed a complaint in the United States District Court for the District of Massachusetts. The complaint alleged the unconstitutionality of the statute, sought damages and an injunction against its continued enforcement.[50]

The district court concluded that the first part of the oath was constitutional, but "that the 'oppose and overthrow' clause was 'fatally vague and unspecific,' and therefore a violation of First Amendment rights."

The Supreme Court disagreed, and held "that the Massachusetts oath is constitutionally permissible."

Marshall dissented. He found "the language 'I will oppose the overthrow of the government of the United States or of this Commonwealth by force, violence or by any illegal or unconstitutional method' to be impermissibly vague and overbroad." The justice was particularly concerned that the oath would require persons taking it to refrain from speech and associational activities that they had a right to engage in and that were protected by the First Amendment. "The Constitution," he declared, "severely circumscribes the power of government to force its citizens to perform symbolic gestures of loyalty. . . . Since the overbreadth of the oath tends to infringe areas of speech and conduct that may be protected by the Constitution, I believe that it cannot stand." Marshall listed the many instances in which people are required to take an oath, such "as a condition of government employment, . . . as a prerequisite to entering military service, to obtaining citizenship, to securing a passport or an educational loan or countless other government offerings." "Perhaps," he continues, "we have become so inundated with a variety of these oaths that we tend to ignore the difficult constitutional issues that they present. It is the duty of judges, however, to endeavor to remain sensitive to these issues and not to 'encourage the casual taking of oaths by upholding the discharge or exclusion from public employment of those with a conscientious and scrupulous regard for such undertakings.'"

Justice Marshall concluded his dissent with these words of warning: "Loyalty oaths do not have a very pleasant history in this country. Whereas they may be developed initially as a means of fostering power and confidence in government, there is a danger that they will swell 'into an instrument of thought control and a means of enforcing complete political conformity.'"

In order for a person to be admitted to the bar of New York, he or she is required to "furnish satisfactory proof to the effect: 1. that he (she) believes in the form of the government of the United States and is loyal to such government."[51] Proof of an applicant's loyalty is obtained by requiring the applicant to answer the following questions:

> 26. (a) Have you ever organized or helped to organize or become a member of any organization or group of persons which, during the period of your membership or association, you knew was advocating or teaching that the government of the United States or any state or political subdivision thereof should be overthrown or overturned by force, violence or any unlawful means? . . .
>
> (b) If your answer to (a) is in the affirmative, did you, during the period of such membership or association, have the specific intent to further the aims of such organization or group of persons to overthrow or overturn the government of the United States or any state or political subdivision thereof by force, violence or any unlawful means?[52]

Several applicants for the bar filed an action in the U.S. District Court seeking a declaration that requiring answers to the above questions infringed upon their constitutional rights of free speech and association. The district court upheld the rule and the questions, and that decision was affirmed by the Supreme Court. In dissenting, Marshall summarized the complaint of the applicants. "The underlying complaint, strenuously and consistently urged, is that New York's screening system focuses impermissibly on the political activities and viewpoints of Bar applicants, that the scheme thereby operates to inhibit the exercise of protected expressive and associational freedoms by law students and others, and that this chilling effect is not justified as the necessary impact of a system designed to winnow out those applicants demonstrably unfit to practice law."

Justice Marshall then turned to Question 26 (a) and pointed out why he thought it was unconstitutional.

> Question 26 (a) asks whether the applicant has "ever organized or helped to organize or become a member of" any association that he knew was "advocating or teaching" that any local, state, or federal governmental institution "should be overthrown or overturned by force, violence or any unlawful means." Plainly this language covers a wide range of associational activities fully protected by the First Amendment, along with some conduct that may not be privileged. The question is not aimed at concerted activity of whatever sort oriented to the doing of illegal acts, but at affiliations with political associations that "advocate" or "teach" certain political ideas. All kinds and degrees of affiliation are covered; indifferent and energetic members alike, in well-disciplined organizations or in any transitory "group of persons." There is no specificity in the phrase, "overthrown or overturned by force, violence or any unlawful means." The language covers all

advocacy of thorough-going political change to be brought about partly through unlawful acts—acts to be done now, or at some hypothetical future moment which may or may not occur—acts of bloody and atrocious terror, or conscientious action involving nonviolent disobedience to law. "Advocating or teaching" includes the most abstract sort of doctrinal discourse, and ideological utterances altogether ancillary to the political program of a given association.

Marshall concluded that the "overintrusive probing for details about an applicant's associational affiliations, creates an obvious *in terrorem* effect on the exercise of First Amendment freedoms by law students and others."

Getting on the ballot is sometimes difficult for small political parties.

The Socialist Workers Party (SWP) is a small political party with approximately 60 members in the State of Ohio. The Party states in its constitution that its aim is "the abolition of capitalism and the establishment of a workers' government to achieve socialism." As the District Court found, the SWP does not advocate the use of violence. It seeks instead to achieve social change through the political process, and its members regularly run for public office. The SWP's candidates have had little success at the polls. In 1980, for example, the Ohio SWP's candidate for the United States Senate received fewer than 77,000 votes, less than 1.9% of the total vote. Campaign contributions and expenditures in Ohio have averaged about $15,000 annually since 1974.[53]

The SWP filed a complaint with the U.S. District Court alleging the unconstitutionality of an Ohio law that required "every candidate for political office to file a statement identifying each contributor and each recipient of a disbursement of campaign funds." The court agreed that application of the disclosure requirement to the SWP would violate members' freedom of association rights, and the Supreme Court affirmed. Marshall wrote the Court's opinion. He first set forth the ground rules for evaluating infringement upon associational rights.

The Constitution protects against the compelled disclosure of political associations and beliefs. Such disclosure "can seriously infringe on privacy of association and belief guaranteed by the First Amendment." . . . The right to privacy in one's political associations and beliefs will yield only to a "subordinating interest of the State [that is] compelling," . . . and then only if there is a "substantial relation between the information sought and [an] overriding and compelling state interest."

The application of those rules to the SWP led him to one conclusion.

The First Amendment prohibits a State from compelling disclosures by a minor party that will subject those persons identified to the reasonable probability of threats, harassment, or reprisals. Such disclosures would infringe the First Amendment rights of the party and its members and supporters. In light of the substantial evidence of past and present hostility from private persons and Government officials against the SWP, Ohio's campaign disclosure requirements cannot be constitutionally applied to the Ohio SWP.

Political Parties: Ballot Access and New Members. Justice Marshall commenced his dissent in *Munro v. Socialist Workers Party*[54] by noting that "limitations on ballot access burden two fundamental rights: 'the right of individuals to associate for the advancement of political beliefs, and the right of qualified voters, regardless of their political persuasion, to cast their votes effectively.' . . . These fundamental rights are implicated most clearly where minor-party access to the ballot is restricted."

In *Munro*, the majority upheld a requirement of the state of Washington that a minor-party candidate's name not be placed on the general election ballot if the candidate received less than 1 percent of the votes cast for the office in the primary. Dean Peoples's name appeared on the primary ballot as a senatorial candidate of the Social Workers Party, but he received only 596 votes out of a total of 681,690 cast. After the election, he challenged the validity of the law, but it was upheld by the district court. The circuit court, however, decided that the law was unconstitutional and reversed.

Justice Marshall did not buy the state's argument that the law was necessary to eliminate cluttering the ballot with too many candidates. "The only purpose this statute seems narrowly tailored to advance," he argued, "is the impermissible one of protecting the major political parties from competition when that competition would be most meaningful. Because the statute burdens appellees' [SWP's] First Amendment interests, it must be subjected to strict scrutiny; because it fails to pass such scrutiny, it is unconstitutional."

The Republican Party of Connecticut, in order to attract more voters, opened its primary election to independent voters—that is, those not registered with any other party. This was contrary to state law, which prohibited a person from voting in a party primary "unless he is on the last-completed enrollment list of such party."[55]

The party challenged the law in the district court, which held the law unconstitutional, a decision that was affirmed by both the circuit court and the Supreme Court.

Connecticut argued that the law was necessary to ensure "the administrability of the primary system, preventing raiding, avoiding voter confusion, and protecting the responsibility of party government." Marshall, for the majority, did not find any, nor all, of these sufficient to outweigh the associational rights of the party and he responded to each.

Even acknowledging that the Party's invitation to independents would add to administration of the primary, the justice pointed out that the state "can no more restrain the Republican Party's freedom of association for reasons of its own administrative convenience than it could on the same ground limit the ballot access of a new major party." With regard to party raiding, there was none here because the party was trying to attract independents, not raid the Democratic Party.

"We conclude," Justice Marshall declared, "that the State's enforcement, under these circumstances, of its closed primary system burdens the First Amendment rights of the Party. The interests which the appellant [State] adduces in support of the statute is insubstantial, and accordingly the statute as applied to the Party in this case, is unconstitutional."

The Pursuit of Liberty

The Right of Privacy. Thomas Dwen, for himself and as president of the Suffolk County Patrolmen's Benevolent Association, brought an action against the Suffolk County Police Department alleging that its hair-grooming regulation violated patrolmen's constitutional rights. "The regulation was directed at the style and length of hair, sideburns, and mustaches; beards and goatees were prohibited, except for medical reasons; and wigs conforming to the regulation could be worn for cosmetic reasons."[56] "The District Court held that '[n]o proof' was offered to support any claim of the need for the protection of the police officer, and that while 'proper grooming' is an ingredient of a good police department's esprit de corps, . . . [the police department's] standards did not establish a public need because they ultimately reduced to '[u]niformity for uniformity's sake.'"

The Supreme Court, assuming that an individual does have a "liberty" interest in his or her personal appearance, nevertheless reversed. The majority concluded that "similarity in appearance of police officers is desirable. This choice may be based on a desire to make police officers readily recognizable to the members of the public, or a desire for the esprit de corps which such similarity is felt to inculcate within the police force itself."

Justice Marshall did not think that the majority gave the right to one's personal appearance the attention and respect it deserved, and he therefore dissented. He set forth his views on the meaning of "liberty."

> An individual's personal appearance may reflect, sustain, and nourish his personality and may well be used as a means of expressing his attitude and lifestyle. In taking over control of a citizen's personal appearance, the government forces him to sacrifice substantial elements of his integrity and identity as well. To say that the liberty guarantee of the Fourteenth Amendment does not encompass matters of personal appearance would be fundamentally inconsistent with the values of privacy, self-identity, autonomy, and personal integrity that I have always assumed the Constitution was designed to protect.

Having said that, the justice considered the arguments in support of the regulation. He did not think much of the Court's conclusion that similarity in appearance would promote esprit de corps. He pointed out that "as long as their hair does not go below their collars, two police officers, one with an 'Afro' hair style and the other with a crewcut could both be in full compliance with the regulation." And he could find no rational relationship between hairstyles and easy identification of police officers.

"In the spring of 1978, . . . [H.L.] was an unmarried 15-year-old girl living with her parents in Utah and dependent on them for her support. She discovered she was pregnant. She consulted with a social worker and a physician. The physician advised . . . [her] that an abortion would be in her best medical interest. However, because of Utah . . . [law] he refused to perform the abortion without first notifying . . . [her] parents."[57]

H.L. brought an action in the Utah District Court requesting the court to declare the law unconstitutional. The trial judge, however, concluded that the law was constitutional and dismissed the complaint. The Utah Supreme Court and the U.S. Supreme Court affirmed.

"As applied to immature and dependent minors," Chief Justice Burger said,

> the statute plainly serves the important considerations of family integrity and protecting adolescents. . . . In addition, . . . the statute serves a significant state interest by providing an opportunity for parents to supply essential medical and other information to a physician. The medical, emotional, and psychological consequences of an abortion are serious and can be lasting; this is particularly so when the patient is immature. An adequate medical and psychological case history is important to the physician.

"Our cases have established," Marshall asserted in dissent, "that a pregnant woman has a fundamental right to choose whether to obtain an abortion or carry the pregnancy to term. . . . Her choice, like the deeply intimate decisions to marry, to procreate, and to use contraceptives, is guarded from unwarranted state intervention by the right of privacy." Minors also have this right of privacy, and for those minors who have a good relationship with their parents, this law poses no obstacle. It is for those minors who do not enjoy a solid parental relationship "that the parental notification requirement creates a problem."

Although acknowledging the role that most parents play in the upbringing of their children, Justice Marshall concluded that the "Court must join the state courts and legislatures which have acknowledged the undoubted social reality: some minors, in some circumstances, have the capacity and need to determine their health needs without involving their parents."

"I am persuaded," he concluded, "that the Utah notice requirement is not necessary to assure parents . . . [their] traditional child-rearing role, and that it burdens the minor's fundamental right to choose with her physician whether to terminate her pregnancy."

The justice continued his concern for the minor's right of privacy when he argued that a minor who did not wish to notify her parents of an abortion should not be required to obtain the consent of a judge to have one. The Court upheld such a requirement in *Hodgson v. Minnesota*,[58] with Marshall dissenting.

He explained the Minnesota requirement: "Minnesota's bypass provision allows a judge to authorize an abortion if he determines either that a woman is sufficiently mature to make the decision on her own or, if she is not sufficiently mature, that an abortion without parental notification would serve her best interests."

The fault of this procedure, Justice Marshall argued, was that it gives a judge "an absolute veto over the decision of the physician and his patient." Furthermore, it placed a significant burden upon the woman's right to choose. "This scheme forces a young woman in an already dire situation to choose between two fundamentally unacceptable alternatives: notifying a possibly dictatorial or even abusive parent and justifying her profoundly personal decision in an intimidating judicial proceeding to a black-robed stranger. For such a woman, this dilemma is more likely to result in trauma and pain than in an informed and voluntary decision."

The laws of Nebraska provide a method by which inmates of its penal institutions may obtain parole. Each year the Board of Parole is required to examine the record of every prisoner to determine whether he or she is eligible to be released. "At the initial review hearing, the Board examines the inmate's entire preconfinement and postconfinement record. Following that examination it provides an informal hearing; no evidence as such is introduced, but the Board interviews the inmate and considers any letters or statements that he wishes to present in support of a claim for release."[59]

Only if the board determines that the inmate is "a likely candidate for release," is a more formal hearing held, and even then the inmate "is not permitted to hear adverse testimony or cross-examine witnesses who present such evidence."

In an action brought by inmates, the district court held that the state's parole system created "a constitutionally protected 'conditional liberty' interest" for the inmates, and that Nebraska's parole procedures did not satisfy the requirements of due process. The circuit court affirmed, but the Supreme Court reversed, holding that there "is no constitutional or inherent right of a convicted person to be conditionally released before the expiration of a valid sentence."

Marshall's position was just the opposite.

> It is self-evident that all individuals possess a liberty interest in being free from physical restraint. Upon conviction for a crime, of course, an individual may be deprived of this liberty to the extent authorized by penal statutes. But when a State enacts a parole system, and creates the possibility of release from incarceration upon satisfaction of certain conditions, it necessarily qualifies that initial deprivation. In my judgment, it is the existence of this system which allows prison inmates to retain their protected interest in securing freedoms available outside prison. Because parole release proceedings clearly implicate this retained liberty interest, the Fourteenth Amendment requires that due process be observed, irrespective of the specific provisions in the applicable parole statute.

The justice then concluded that "substantially more procedural protection is necessary in parole release proceedings than the Court requires."

Equal Protection of the Law

Blacks on Juries.

> In 1962, the grand jury of Kings County, California, indicted respondent, Booker T. Hillery, for a brutal murder. Before trial in Superior Court, respondent [Hillery] moved to quash the indictment on the ground that it had been issued by a grand jury from which blacks had been systematically excluded. A hearing on respondent's motion was held by Judge Meredith Wingrove, who was the sole Superior Court Judge in the county and had personally selected all grand juries, including the one that indicted respondent, for the previous seven years. Absolving himself of any discriminatory intent, Judge Wingrove refused to quash the indictment. Respondent was subsequently convicted of first-degree murder.
>
> For the next 16 years, respondent pursued appeals and collateral relief in state courts, raising at every opportunity his equal protection challenge to the grand jury that indicted him.[60]

Hillery finally sought help from the U.S. District Court, again arguing discrimination in the selection of the grand jury. After hearing the evidence, Judge Lawrence K. Karlton found that there had been discrimination. The court of appeals and the Supreme Court both affirmed.

Justice Marshall, for the majority, pointed out that in "1880, this Court reversed a state conviction on the ground that the indictment charging the offense had been issued by a grand jury from which blacks had been excluded. We reasoned that deliberate exclusion of blacks 'is practically a brand upon them, affixed by the law, an assertion of their inferiority, and a stimulant to that race prejudice which is an impediment to securing to individuals of the race that equal justice which the law aims to secure to all others.'"

The state argued that a retrial after all these years would impose "on it an unduly harsh penalty for a constitutional defect bearing no relation to the fundamental fairness of the trial." But Justice Marshall would have none of that. "Yet, intentional discrimination in the selection of grand jurors," he responded, "is a grave constitutional trespass, possible only under color of state authority, and wholly within the power of the State to prevent." Once a state prevents the exclusion of any race from serving on the grand jury, "no conviction will ever again be lost on account of it."

Furthermore: "Once having found discrimination in the selection of a grand jury, we simply cannot know that the need to indict would have been assessed in the same way by a grand jury properly constituted. The overriding imperative to eliminate this systemic flaw in the charging process, as well as the difficulty in assessing its effect on any given defendant, requires our continued adherence to a rule of mandatory reversal."

Justice Marshall concurred in *Batson v. Kentucky*[61] (discussed in Chapter 8), where the Court held that a prosecutor's use of peremptory challenges is subject to equal protection scrutiny. Justice Marshall agreed with the Court's decision that discriminatory use of peremptory challenges violates equal protection, but he did not agree with its solution. "The inherent potential of peremptory challenges to distort the jury process by permitting the exclusion of jurors on racial grounds," he argued, "should ideally lead the Court to ban them entirely from the criminal justice system."

When Daniel Holland, a white man, was being tried for "aggravated kidnaping, rape, deviate sexual assault, armed robbery, and aggravated battery,"[62] the prosecutor used his peremptory challenges to strike the only two black persons on the venire. Holland's counsel's objection was overruled, and Holland was convicted. His conviction was upheld by both the Illinois and the U.S. Supreme Courts. The constitutional question before the Court was whether this was a denial of Holland's "Sixth Amendment right to 'be tried by a representative cross section of the community.'" The majority said it was not, but Marshall disagreed and dissented. "To reach this startling result, the majority misrepresents the values underlying the fair-cross-section requirement, overstates the difficulties associated with the elimination of racial discrimination in jury selection, and ignores the clear import of well-grounded precedents."

After a lengthy analysis of precedent and the Court's reasoning, the justice concluded:

> The majority today insulates an especially invidious form of racial discrimination in the selection of petit juries from Sixth Amendment scrutiny. To reach this result, the majority chooses to pretend that it writes on a blank slate, ignoring precedent after precedent. The majority then conjures up specters—of the dreaded "representative jury" requirement and of the destruction of our "venerable" system of peremptory challenges—as though they were real sources of concern. Our recent refusal in *Batson* to permit such fantastic fears to override our constitutional duty in the equal protection context makes clear, however, that these apparitions vanish on close examination.

Integration of Public Schools. Justice Marshall's concern for the effect of segregated schools upon black children brought a dissent in *Bd. of Ed. of Oklahoma City v. Dowell*.[63] That case involved a desegregation decree entered in 1972, 18 years after the *Brown* decision. In Justice Marshall's words, the precise question before the Court was whether "13 years after that injunction was imposed, the same Board should have been allowed to return many of its elementary schools to their one-race status."

The majority sent the case back to the district court "for further evaluation of whether the purposes of the injunctive decree were achieved sufficient to justify the decree's dissolution."

Marshall protested. "I believe a desegregation decree cannot be lifted so long as conditions likely to inflict the stigmatic injury condemned in *Brown I* persist and there remain feasible methods of eliminating such conditions.

Because the record here shows, and the Court of Appeals found, that feasible steps could be taken to avoid one-race schools, it is clear that the purposes of the decree have not been achieved."

The justice did not believe that the majority really understood the impact of segregation. "By focusing heavily on present and future compliance with the Equal Protection Clause," he declared, "the majority's standard ignores how the stigmatic harm identified in *Brown I* can persist even after the State ceases actively to enforce segregation." And, he continued, "Our jurisprudence requires . . . that the job of school desegregation be fully completed and maintained so that the stigmatic harm identified in *Brown I* will not recur upon lifting the decree. Any doubt on the issue whether the School Board has fulfilled its remedial obligations should be resolved in favor of the Afro-American children affected by this litigation."

Miscellaneous Racial Discrimination Cases. Linda Sidoti Palmore was awarded custody of her three-year-old daughter, Melanie, when she divorced the child's father, Anthony J. Sidoti. All were Caucasians and lived in Florida. Shortly thereafter, Linda began to live with Clarence Palmore, Jr., who was black, whom she later married. Anthony then sought and was awarded custody of Melanie. One of the issues in the case, was whether it was in Melanie's best interests to be removed from the Palmore's biracial family. The trial judge concluded that Melanie's interests would be better served if she were to live with her father, Anthony.

In making that decision, the judge said: "*This Court feels that despite the strides that have been made in bettering relations between the races in this country, it is inevitable that Melanie will, if allowed to remain in her present situation and attains school age and thus more vulnerable to peer pressures, suffer from the social stigmatization that is sure to come.*"[64] When an appeals court upheld the judge's decision, Linda appealed to the Supreme Court, which reversed, in an opinion by Chief Justice Burger which all justices, including Marshall, joined.

The chief justice acknowledged "that racial and ethnic prejudices" do exist, and that there "is a risk that a child living with a stepparent of a different race may be subject to a variety of pressures and stresses not present if the child were living with parents of the same racial or ethnic origin."

But the real question "is whether the reality of private biases and the possible injury they might inflict are permissible considerations for removal of an infant child from the custody of its natural mother. We have little difficulty concluding that they are not." And the chief justice concluded, "The effects of racial prejudice, however real, cannot justify a racial classification removing an infant child from the custody of its natural mother found to be an appropriate person to have such custody."

In *Memphis v. Greene*,[65] the Court wrote,

The question presented is whether a decision of the city of Memphis to close the north end of West Drive, a street that traverses a white residential community, violated . . . [the Civil Rights Act] or the Thirteenth Amendment to the United States Constitution. The city's action was challenged by respondents, who resided in a predominantly black area to the north. The Court of Appeals ultimately held the street closing invalid because it adversely affected respondents' ability to hold and enjoy their property. . . . We reverse because the record does not support that holding.

Dissenting justices Marshall, Brennan, and Blackmun, however, were of the opinion that the majority was simply giving its blessing to a case of racial discrimination couched in nonracial terms.

Justice Marshall wrote for the dissenters:

The stated explanation for the closing is of a sort all too familiar: "protecting the safety and tranquility of a residential neighborhood" by preventing "undesirable traffic" from entering it. Too often in our Nation's history, statements such as these have been little more than code phrases for racial discrimination. These words may still signify racial discrimination, but apparently not, after today's decision, forbidden discrimination. The majority, purporting to rely on the evidence developed at trial, concludes that the city's stated interests are sufficient to justify erection of the barrier. Because I do not believe that either the Constitution or federal law permits a city to carve out racial enclaves, I dissent.

After examining the evidence, and noting that the intent of the Civil Rights Act was to give recourse to those who were victims of discrimination, Marshall concluded;

Given the majority's decision to characterize this case as a mere policy decision on the part of the city of Memphis to close a street for valid municipal reasons, the conclusion that it reaches follows inevitably. But the evidence in this case, combined with a dab of common sense, paints a far different picture from the one emerging from the majority's opinion. In this picture a group of white citizens has decided to act to keep Negro citizens from traveling through their urban "utopia," and the city has placed its seal of approval on the scheme. It is this action that I believe is forbidden, and it is for that reason that I dissent.

Justice Black wrote the majority opinion in *Palmer v. Thompson*,[66] wherein the Court upheld the decision of the city council of Jackson, Mississippi, to close its swimming pools because it concluded that they "could not be operated safely or economically on an integrated basis." Dissenting opinions were filed by Justices Douglas, White, and Marshall, with Brennan joining both White's and Marshall's opinions.

"By effectively removing public owned swimming pools from the protection of the Fourteenth Amendment—at least if the pools are outside school buildings,—" Marshall declared, "the majority and concurring opinions turn the clock back 17 years (to a time prior to *Brown I*). After losing a hard fought legal battle to maintain segregation in public facilities, the Jackson, Mississippi, authorities now seek to pick and choose which of the existing facilities will be kept open. Their choice is rationalized on the basis of economic need and is even more transparent than putting the matter to a referendum vote."

Gender Discrimination. "During her 12-year tenure as a state employee, . . . [Helen B. Feeney], who is not a veteran, had passed a number of open competitive civil service examinations for better jobs, but because of Massachusetts' veterans' preference statute, she was ranked in each instance below male veterans who had achieved lower test scores."[67]

Feeney "brought an action, alleging that the absolute-preference formula . . . inevitably operates to exclude women from consideration for the best state civil service jobs and thus discriminates against women in violation of the Equal Protection Clause of the Fourteenth Amendment." The district court agreed, but the Supreme Court reversed.

The majority saw the law as "a preference for veterans of either sex over nonveterans of either sex, not for men over women." But Justice Marshall saw the law as "an absolute veterans' preference system [which] evinces purposeful gender-based discrimination," and he dissented. He did not accept the majority's conclusion that this was simply a veteran versus nonveteran law. He pointed out that statistically the law gave preference to 47 percent of the men and 0.8 percent of the women who were veterans, over the 53 percent of the men and 99.2 percent of the women who were not.

"In its present unqualified form," Marshall concluded, "the veterans' preference statute precludes all but a small fraction of Massachusetts women from obtaining any civil service position also of interest to men. . . . Given the range of alternatives available, this degree of preference is not constitutionally permissible."

Joan Feenstra found herself confronted with a Louisiana statute that one can only describe as a throwback to the days when men had control over their spouses' property. That law provided: "The husband is the head and master of the partnership or community of gains; he administers its effects, disposes of the revenues which they produce, and may alienate them by an onerous title, without the consent and permission of his wife."[68]

During marital difficulties, the husband, Harold, sought legal advice from attorney Karl Kirchberg. In order to pay Kirchberg, Harold executed a note to him in the amount of $3,000, secured by a mortgage on the home that he and Joan owned jointly. When Harold moved out of state, Kirchberg sought to collect the amount of the note from Joan, and it was then that she first became aware of the mortgage.

In an action brought by attorney Kirchberg against Joan Feenstra, District Judge Morey L. Sear wrote: "Equity would seem to require that the complaint here presented be resolved in favor of the wife whose husband mortgaged her home to raise funds for the defense of criminal charges brought against him by the wife and who then defaulted on the obligation which it secured. But at stake here is the bedrock of Louisiana's community property system."[69] Judge Sear then upheld the statute. The circuit court reversed, on the ground that the law violated equal protection. The Supreme Court unanimously agreed.

"By granting the husband exclusive control over the disposition of community property," Marshall wrote, " . . . [the law] clearly embodies the type of express gender-based discrimination that we have found unconstitutional absent a showing that the classification is tailored to further an important governmental interest. In defending the constitutionality . . . [of the law] Kirchberg does not claim that the provision serves any such interest."[70]

Robert Goldberg, together with others, filed suit contesting the validity of the selective service requirement that they register for the draft, claiming that the law violated equal protection because it did not include women. The district court held that because the draft applied only to males it was unconstitutional as a denial of equal protection.

Justice Rehnquist, writing for a majority of the Supreme Court, concluded that it was within the power of Congress to determine whether women should be included or not. And furthermore, women are excluded from combat by law, and therefore would not be needed in the event a draft actually took place. Marshall wrote a dissenting opinion, which Brennan joined.

Justice Marshall made an extensive examination of congressional hearings that included considerable testimony by Defense Department personnel. His dissent then contains the following statements: "The Government does not defend the exclusion of women from registration on the ground that preventing women from serving in the military is substantially related to the effectiveness of the Armed Forces. Indeed, the successful experience of women serving in all branches of the Armed Services would belie any such claim."[71]

Furthermore, he wrote;

> In this case, the Government makes no claim that preparing for a draft of combat troops cannot be accomplished just as effectively by *registering* both men and women but *drafting* only men if only men turn out to be needed. . . .
>
> All four Service Chiefs agreed that there are no military reasons for refusing to register women, and uniformly advocated requiring registration of women. . . .
>
> Congressional enactments in the area of military affairs must, like all other laws, be *judged* by the standards of the Constitution. . . .
>
> In an attempt to avoid its constitutional obligation, the Court today "pushes back the limits of the Constitution" to accommodate an Act of Congress. . . .

For Illegitimate Children.

The reason why the United States Government should not add to the burdens that illegitimate children inevitably acquire at birth is radiantly clear: We are committed to the proposition that all persons are created equal. The Court's reason for approving discrimination against this class—"administrative convenience"—is opaque and insufficient: opaque because the difference between this justification and the argument rejected in *Jimeniz v. Weinberger* . . . is so difficult to discern; insufficient because it unfairly evaluates the competing interests at stake.[72]

With those words, Justices Stevens, Brennan, and Marshall dissented when the Court upheld the denial of Social Security benefits to the children of Robert Cuffee, deceased.

Robert Cuffee, now deceased, lived with Belmira Lucas during the years 1948 through 1966, but they were never married. Two children were born to them during these years; Ruby M. Lucas, in 1953, and Darin E. Lucas, in 1960. In 1966 Cuffee and Lucas separated. Cuffee died in Providence, R.I., his home, in 1968. He died without ever having acknowledged in writing his paternity of either Ruby or Darin, and it was never determined in any judicial proceeding during his lifetime that he was the father of either child. After Cuffee's death, Mrs. Lucas filed an application on behalf of Ruby and Darin for surviving children's benefits under . . . [the Social Security Act] based upon Cuffee's earnings.

Benefits were denied by the Social Security Administration because Cuffee had not legitimatized Ruby and Darin and they were unable to prove that he was contributing to their support at the time of his death. If Ruby and Darin had been legitimate, they would have been presumed dependent upon their father and entitled to benefits without actually having to prove he was supporting them.

In an action filed by Mrs. Lucas, District Judge Raymond J. Pettine held that the treatment accorded illegitimate children was a violation of equal protection.

A majority of the justices of the Supreme Court, however, concluded that "in failing to extend any presumption of dependency to . . . [Ruby and Darin] and others like them, the Act does not impermissibly discriminate against them as compared with legitimate children or those illegitimate children who are statutorily deemed dependent."[74]

But the dissenters were not convinced. "I am persuaded," Stevens argued,

that the classification which is sustained today in the name of "administrative convenience" is more probably the product of a tradition of thinking of illegitimates as less deserving persons than legitimates. The sovereign should firmly reject that tradition. The fact that illegitimacy is not as apparent to the observer as sex or race does not make this governmental classification any less odious. It cannot be denied that it is a source of social opprobrium, even if wholly unmerited, or that it is a circumstance for which the individual has no responsibility whatsoever.

The following three scenarios illustrate Congress's views on illegitimate children:

> Ramon Fiallo, an infant and an American citizen by birth, applied ... to have his alien father officially declared to be his parent under the immigration laws, so that the latter might remain in the United States. Ramon Fiallo's petition was rejected, the Counsel stating that Fiallo senior could not be declared the parent of an American citizen since his child was illegitimate."[75]

> Cleophus Warner, a naturalized American citizen, attempted to have his illegitimate son Serge, a citizen of the West Indies, officially declared to be his child ... so that the boy might remain permanently with his father in this country. The petition was rejected since the boy was neither the father's legitimate nor legitimated offspring...

> Trevor and Arthur Wilson are two brothers under twenty-one years of age who are permanent residents of the United States. After the death of their biological mother they sought to have their father, a citizen of Jamaica, officially classified as their parent so that he might qualify for permanent residency in this country. It is not clear whether their petition has already been denied, but denial is certain since the boys were never legitimized and hence their father cannot qualify as a parent...

The denial of permission to enter and live in the United States was upheld by a federal district court in each of these cases and by the Supreme Court. Justice Marshall thought the discrimination in these cases "invidious and irrational" and dissented.

> Until today I thought it clear that when Congress grants benefits to some citizens, but not to others, it is our duty to insure that the decision comports with ... [the] principles of due process and equal protection. Today, however, the Court appears to hold that discrimination among citizens, however invidious and irrational, must be tolerated if it occurs in the context of the immigration laws. Since I cannot agree that Congress has license to deny fundamental rights to citizens according to the most disfavored criteria simply because the Immigration and Nationality Act is involved, I dissent.[76]

What puzzled the justice was that Congress had granted preferred status to almost every type of relationship, except for some illegitimate children. "Fathers cannot obtain preferred status for their illegitimate children," he pointed out, "but mothers can. Conversely, every child except illegitimate—legitimate, legitimated, step-, adopted—can obtain preferred status for his or her alien father."

For Aliens. Edmond Foley applied for a position as a New York State trooper but was denied permission to take the examination because he was a citizen of Ireland. Foley sued William G. Connelie, superintendent of New York State Police, alleging a violation of equal protection of the law. The district court granted summary judgment for the state, and Foley appealed to the Supreme Court, which affirmed. "The police function," Chief Justice Burger declared, "fulfills a most fundamental obligation of government to its constituency. Police officers in the ranks do not formulate policy, *per se*, but they are clothed with authority to exercise an almost infinite variety of discretionary powers. The execution of the broad powers vested in them affect members of the public significantly and often in the most sensitive areas of daily life."[77] And he concluded that in "the enforcement and execution of the laws the police function is one where citizenship bears a rational relationship to the special demands of the particular position. A State may, therefore, consonant with the Constitution, confine the performance of this important public responsibility to citizens of the United States."

In dissent, Marshall took issue with the Court's implication that police officers had much to do with making public policy: "Just as firefighters execute the public policy that fires should be extinguished, and sanitation workers execute the public policy that streets should be kept clean, state troopers execute the public policy that persons believed to have committed crimes should be arrested."

Having disposed of the public policy issue, Justice Marshall found it easy to conclude that "[s]ince no other rational reason, . . . has been advanced in support of the statute here at issue, I would hold that the statute's exclusion of aliens from state trooper position violates the Equal Protection Clause of the Fourteenth Amendment."

Two individuals, Margareta M. Vargas and Efrem Bernal, applied to become notaries public in Texas, but both applications were denied because neither was a citizen of the United States. Vargas was a legal secretary for a real estate firm in Brownsville, and Bernal worked for the Texas Rural Legal Aid, Inc., as a paralegal. Vargas and Bernal filed an action with the federal district court seeking a judgment that the citizenship requirement was unconstitutional under the Equal Protection Clause. Judge Filemon B. Vela agreed that the law was unconstitutional, but the circuit court reversed. Justice Marshall, for himself and seven other justices, agreed with Judge Vela and reinstated his decision.[78]

Although Texas argued that notaries are officers whose duties "go to the heart of representative government," Marshall was not convinced. "Texas does not require court reporters to be United States citizens," he pointed out, "even though they perform some of the same services as notaries. Nor does Texas require that its Secretary of State be a citizen, even though he holds the highest appointive position in the State and performs many important functions, including supervision of the licensing of all notaries public."

Texas also argued that the law "serves its 'legitimate concern that notaries be reasonably familiar with state law and institutions' and 'that notaries may be called upon years later to testify to acts they have performed.'" But Justice Marshall could find "nothing in the record that indicates that resident aliens, as a class, are so incapable of familiarizing themselves with Texas law as to justify the State's absolute and classwide exclusion. The possibility that some resident aliens are unsuitable for the position cannot justify a wholesale ban against all resident aliens." Furthermore, if that were a real concern of the state, it could administer a test to applicants before certifying them.

For Voters and New Political Parties. James F. Blumstein "moved to Tennessee on June 12, 1970, to begin employment as an assistant professor of law at Vanderbilt University in Nashville. With an eye toward voting in the upcoming August and November elections, he attempted to register to vote on July 1, 1970. The county registrar refused to register him, on the ground that Tennessee law authorized registration of only those persons who, at the time of the next election, will have been residents of the State for a year and residents of the county three months."[79]

Blumstein challenged the validity of the residency requirements in the federal district court. With District Judge Frank Gray, Jr., writing the opinion, the district court held that Tennessee's law denied Blumstein equal protection. The Supreme Court, with Justice Marshall writing the opinion, affirmed. "There is no need to repeat now the labors undertaken in earlier cases to analyze this right to vote," he said, "and to explain in detail the judicial role in reviewing state statutes that selectively distribute the franchise. In decision after decision, this Court has made clear that a citizen has a constitutionally protected right to participate in elections on an equal basis with other citizens in the jurisdiction."

Tennessee offered two reasons for its requirements: (1) to ensure purity of the ballot box, and (2) to have knowledgeable voters. After carefully examining these and other sections of the state's laws, Marshall concluded "that Tennessee has at its disposal a variety of criminal laws that are more than adequate to detect and deter whatever fraud may be feared."

Turning to the second justification for the law, the justice simply did not believe and could find "nothing in the record to support the conclusive presumption that residents who have lived in the State for less than a year and their county for less than three months are uninformed about elections."

It seemed that just about everybody in New York was entitled to vote by absentee ballot except those in jail awaiting trial or serving time for misdemeanor convictions. When some inmates were refused a mobile registration unit, they requested to be taken to the polls or to be allowed to vote by absentee ballot. Both requests were denied. To vote by absentee ballot, any person "confined at home or in a hospital or institution, . . . because of illness or physical disability or because his duties, occupation, or business require him to be outside the county of residence, or if a resident of the city of New York, outside said city, on such days, may be registered."[80] The law also allowed "absentee voting . . . if the voters are vacationing away from their residence on election day." The law, therefore, permitted "a New York resident eligible to vote [who] is confined in a county jail in a county in which he does not reside, . . . [to] secure an absentee ballot and vote . . . because he is 'unavoidably absent the county of his residence.'" Thus, for example, "two citizens awaiting to be charged—sitting side by side in the same cell, may receive different treatment as to voting rights." If one of the inmates in the cell is from the county in which the jail is located, he cannot vote, whereas if his cellmate is from another county, he can do so.

Despite this unusual situation, New York courts did not find the law violated the Equal Protection Clause. The Supreme Court reversed, with Justice Marshall concurring. When New York attempted to justify the discrimination against the pretrial detainees and convicted misdemeanants because "without protection of the voting booth, local officials might be too tempted to try to influence the local vote of in-county inmates," Justice Marshall did not buy it. "Though protection of the integrity of the ballot box is surely a legitimate state concern, I frankly find something a bit disturbing about this approach to the problem. It is hard to conceive how the State can possibly justify denying any person his right to vote on the ground that his vote might afford a state official the opportunity to abuse his position of authority. . . . There are surely less burdensome means to protect inmate voters against attempts to influence their votes."

The Socialist Workers Party in Chicago desired to offer a candidate for mayor in a special election to fill the vacancy created by the death of Mayor Richard J. Daley in 1977. In order to get on the ballot, however, the party was required to obtain 35,947 signatures, which was 5 percent of the number of votes for the office of mayor at the last mayoralty election. In elections for statewide offices, however, new and independent parties were only required to obtain 25,000 voters throughout the state to qualify for a ballot position.

The party sued the Chicago Board of Election commissioners arguing that the disparity between the number of signatures required for statewide elections and the number for city elections discriminated against them, making it considerably more difficult to get on the ballot for the mayoralty election. District Judge Bernard M. Decker agreed. "The court cannot find any rational reason," he declared, "why a petition with identical signatures can satisfy legitimate state interests for restricting ballot access in state elections, and yet fail to do the same in a lesser unit. Any greater requirement than 25,000 signatures cannot be said to be the least drastic means of accomplishing the state's goals, and must be found to unduly impinge the constitutional rights of independents, new political parties, and their adherents."[81] The circuit court affirmed, as did the Supreme Court.

Justice Marshall pointed out, for the majority, that this case involved some very important fundamental rights:

> Restrictions on access to the ballot burden two distinct and fundamental rights, "the right of individuals to associate for the advancement of political beliefs, and the right of qualified voters, regardless of their political persuasion, to cast their

votes effectively." . . . The freedom to associate as a political party, a right we have recognized as fundamental, . . . has diminished practical value if the party can be kept off the ballot. Access restrictions also implicate the right to vote because, absent recourse to referendums, "voters can assert their preferences only through candidates or parties or both." . . . By limiting the choices available to voters, the State impairs the voters' ability to express their political preferences.[82]

Addressing Illinois's ballot requirements, Marshall wrote that the state "has advanced no reason, much less a compelling one, why the State needs a more stringent requirement for Chicago." And finding no justification, he concluded "that the Illinois Election Code is unconstitutional insofar as it requires independent candidates and new political parties to obtain more than 25,000 signatures in Chicago."

For Fundamental Rights.

Earl Mosley, a federal postal employee, [had] for seven months . . . frequently picketed Jones Commercial High School in Chicago. During school hours and usually by himself, Mosley would walk the public sidewalk adjoining the school, carrying a sign that read: "Jones High School practices black discrimination. Jones High School has a black quota." His lonely crusade was always peaceful, orderly, and quiet, and was conceded to be so by the city of Chicago.[83]

As a result of Mosley's picketing, the city enacted an anti-picketing ordinance that required picketers to be at least 150 feet away from the school while it was in session. One who picketed within the limit committed the criminal offense of disorderly conduct. The ordinance, however, did not apply if the picketing was related to a labor dispute.

Upon learning of the ordinance, Mosley contacted the Chicago Police Department and was told that he would be arrested if he continued to picket the school after the ordinance went into effect. He discontinued picketing the day before the ordinance's effective date and filed an action against the Police Department. "He alleged a violation of constitutional rights in that (1) the statute punished activity protected by the First Amendment; and (2) by exempting only peaceful labor picketing from its general prohibition against picketing, the statute denied him 'equal protection of the law in violation of the First and Fourteenth Amendments.'" Judge Joseph Samuel Perry dismissed the case, but the circuit court reversed, those judges being of the opinion that the ordinance infringed upon the First Amendment right to picket. The Supreme Court affirmed, but chose to rely upon the Equal Protection Clause.

Chicago argued that there was no intent to censor here, but to prevent disruption of the school. Marshall, for the Court, acknowledged that that was an important interest, but that it wasn't the question. "The crucial question, however, is whether [Chicago's ordinance] advances that objective in a manner consistent with the command of the Equal Protection Clause." And he answered: "It does not."

The justice did not agree that "nonlabor picketing is more prone to produce violence than labor picketing." "Some labor picketing is peaceful, some disorderly; the same is true of picketing on other themes. No labor picketing could be more peaceful or less prone to violence than Mosley's solitary vigil." This brought Marshall to the conclusion that the ordinance was not supported by a substantial governmental interest and therefore "the discrimination among pickets is based on the content of their expression, . . . [and] under the Equal Protection Clause, it may not stand."

Robert D. Murgia, a lieutenant colonel in the Massachusetts State Police, had been a police officer for more than 20 years when he was forced to retire at the age of 50. At that time, he was in good health and fully capable of performing the duties of a state police officer. Murgia brought an action against the State Board of Retirement contending that the forced retirement violated his right to due process and equal protection. The court concluded that the law was arbitrary and irrational and therefore violated due process. The Supreme Court reversed, stating that

> the Massachusetts statute clearly meets the requirements of the Equal Protection Clause, for the State's classification rationally furthers the purpose identified by the State: Through mandatory retirement at age 50, the legislature seeks to protect the public by assuring physical preparedness of its uniformed police. Since physical ability generally declines with age, mandatory retirement at 50 serves to remove from police service those whose fitness for uniformed work presumptively has diminished with age. This clearly is rationally related to the State's objective.[84]

Justice Marshall took the Court to task for its conclusion that the law is valid because it is rationally related to the government's goal. "There is simply no reason why a statute that tells able-bodied police officers, ready and willing to work," he asserted, "that they no longer have the right to earn a living in their chosen profession merely because they are 50 years old should be judged by the same minimal standards of rationality that we use to test economic legislation that discriminates against business interests."

Without deciding whether the right to work was a "fundamental" right or not, the justice believed that when legislating with regard to employment of the elderly, the state "must show a reasonably substantial interest and a scheme reasonably closely tailored to achieving that interest." And even though he agreed that the need for healthy and physically fit officers was compelling, the state had not chosen the least restrictive method of achieving its goal. He pointed out that the commonwealth already required physical fitness tests for its officers, and relied upon them when making employment decisions. "I conclude," Marshall wrote, "that the Commonwealth's mandatory retirement law cannot stand when measured against the significant deprivation of the Commonwealth's action works upon the terminated employees."

Roger Redhail, while a high school student and not married, admitted that he was the father of a baby girl. He was therefore required to pay support for the child until she became 18 years of age. Because Redhail was unable to make payments as required, the child became a public charge. Several years later Redhail applied for a marriage license, which County Clerk Thomas E. Zablocki refused to issue because Redhail did not have a court order granting him permission to marry. Zablocki relied on a Wisconsin statute that required persons who were under an obligation to support a minor, as Redhail was, to secure a court's permission to marry.

Redhail, for himself and others similarly situated, filed an action with the federal district court seeking a declaration that the law was unconstitutional and an injunction against its enforcement. District judges John W. Reynolds and Robert W. Warren, and Circuit Judge Philip W. Stone concluded that marriage was included within the right of privacy, and that requiring some persons to obtain a court order to marry and not others violated equal protection. The Supreme Court affirmed.

Commenting upon the marriage as being under the umbrella of the right of privacy, Justice Marshall declared: "It is not surprising that the decision to marry has been placed on the same level of importance as decisions relating to procreation, childbirth, child rearing, and family relationships. As the facts of this case illustrate, it would make little sense to recognize a right of privacy with respect to other matters of family life and not with respect to the decision to enter the relationship that is the foundation of the family in our society."[85]

After noting that the law creates two classes, persons who can and persons who cannot marry without a court order, the justice then restated the rule that must be applied to classifications affecting fundamental rights.

In this case, Wisconsin offered two interests to support the law: "The permission-to-marry proceedings furnishes an opportunity to counsel the applicant as to the necessity of fulfilling his prior support obligations; and the welfare of the out-of-custody children is protected." Marshall agreed that these were important state interests, but pointed out that the statute does not require counseling before the order to marry is given. Furthermore even if counseling did take place, "this counseling obviously cannot support the withholding of court permission to marry once counseling is completed." Insofar as the interest of the child is concerned, the justice could not see how the law provided any financial assistance because the only thing the law did was prevent a father from getting married, and other methods of securing financial help for the child were available to the state. This brought Marshall to the conclusion that the statutory classification "cannot be justified by the interests advanced in support of it."

In the Criminal Justice System. From the time he was arrested for burglary and grand larceny, James Royster spent 404 days in the Nassau County, New York, jail before being convicted and transferred to prison.

For Percy Rutherford, the time was 242 days before he was convicted of robbery and sent to prison. Royster and Rutherford brought an action against prison officials seeking a court order requiring them to give *good time* credit for the time spent in jail, in computing their release dates. Prison officials had refused to give *good time* credit because state law did not provide such credit for *jail* time prior to entering prison.

Royster and Rutherford argued that because they were unable to make bail they spent more time being incarcerated (jail time plus prison time) than those who were fortunate to have funds for bail and thus were allowed their freedom until convicted and incarcerated. This, they claimed, denied them equal protection of the law, and Judge Morris E. Lasker agreed. The Supreme Court reversed, however, with Justice Marshall joining Justice Douglas's dissent.[86]

Douglas agreed with the petitioner's argument that of two inmates who have committed the same crime and received the same sentence, the one who has been out on bail pending trial will ultimately spend less time being incarcerated than the one who was confined to the county jail. "The important issue involved in this case," he argued, "is not when and whether a prisoner is released. It concerns only the time when the Parole Board may give a hearing. To speed up the time of that hearing for those rich or influential enough to get bail or release on personal recognizance and to delay the time of the hearing for those without means to buy a bail bond or the influence or prestige that will give release on personal recognizance emphasizes the invidious discrimination at work."

Oregon's requirement that an indigent defendant reimburse the state for the costs of counsel provided to him for his defense came before the Court in *Fuller v. Oregon*.[87] Oregon provided Prince Eric Fuller with counsel and paid for an investigator for him when he was charged with sodomy. Counsel represented him when he pleaded guilty and was sentenced to five years' probation. One of the conditions of probation was that Fuller reimburse the county for the costs expended for both the counsel and the investigator if and when he was able to do so. He appealed, claiming that this arrangement denied him equal protection of the law. The Supreme Court of Oregon affirmed Fuller's conviction, with one justice dissenting. The U.S. Supreme Court also affirmed, with justices Marshall and Brennan dissenting.

After examining Oregon's procedures for recoupment of costs involved in indigent defense, Justice Stewart concluded that "Oregon's legislation is tailored to impose an obligation only upon those with a foreseeable ability to meet it, and to enforce that obligation only against those who actually become able to meet it without hardship."

But Justice Marshall believed that the Court was overlooking a crucial fact. "The important fact," he declared, "which the majority ignores is that under Oregon law, the repayment of the indigent defendant's debt to the State can be made a condition of his probation, as it was in this case. Petitioner's failure to pay his debt can result in his being sent to prison." He then compares Fuller's situation with that of a well-heeled defendant who retains counsel but does not pay him. If counsel sues for his money, the well-heeled defendant will not go to prison for nonpayment. This led the justice to conclude: "Since Oregon chooses not to provide imprisonment for debt for well-heeled defendants who do not pay their retained counsel, I do not believe it can, consistent with the Equal Protection Clause, imprison an indigent defendant for his failure to pay the costs of his appointed counsel."

For the Poor. Robert William Kras filed a petition for bankruptcy in May 1971, and petitioned the court to be relieved of paying the $50 filing fee. The Kras household consisted of himself, his wife, two children, his mother, and his mother's child.

> The Kras household subsists entirely on $210 per month public assistance received for Kras' own family and $156 per month public assistance received for his mother and her daughter. These benefits are all expended for rent and day-to-day necessities. The rent is $102 per month. Kras owns no automobile and no asset that is non-exempt under the bankruptcy law. He receives no unemployment or disability benefit. His sole assets are wearing apparel and $50 worth of essential household goods that are exempt under . . . [New York law]. He has a couch of negligible value in storage on which a $6 payment is due monthly.[88]

Judge Anthony J. Travia concluded that requiring indigents to pay the filing fee denied them equal protection of the law, and ordered the petition for bankruptcy to be filed.

The Supreme Court reversed. In an opinion written by Justice Harry Blackmun, the Court held

> that the filing fee requirement does not deny Kras the equal protection of the laws. Bankruptcy is hardly akin to free speech or marriage or to those other rights, so many of which are imbedded in the First Amendment, that the Court has come to regard as fundamental and that the lofty requirement of a compelling governmental interest before they may be significantly regulated. . . . Neither does it touch upon what have been said to be suspect criteria of race, nationality, or alienage. Instead, bankruptcy legislation is in the area of economics and social welfare.

Furthermore, the justice pointed out, the fee could be paid in weekly installments of $1.92 if spread over a six-month period, or $1.28 per week if the period of payment were nine months.

Justice Marshall dissented and criticized the majority for its lack of understanding of how the poor must live.

> It may be easy for some people to think that weekly savings of less than $2 are no burden. But no one who has had close contact with poor people can fail to understand how close to the margin of survival many of them are. A sudden illness, for example, may destroy whatever savings they may have accumulated, and by eliminating a sense of security may destroy the incentive to save in the future. A pack

or two of cigarettes may be, for them, not a routine purchase but a luxury indulged in only rarely. The desperately poor almost never go to see a movie, which the majority seems to believe is an almost weekly activity. They have more important things to do with what little money they have—like attempting to provide some comforts for a gravely ill child, as Kras must do.

"It is perfectly proper," he continued, "for judges to disagree about what the Constitution requires. But it is disgraceful for an interpretation of the Constitution to be premised upon unfounded assumptions about how people live."

The inequities in school financing came before the Court in *San Antonio School District v. Rodriguez.*[89]

"In sum, to the extent that the Texas system of school financing results in unequal expenditures between children who happen to reside in different districts, we cannot say that such disparities are the product of a system that is so irrational as to be invidiously discriminatory." That is the conclusion that Justice Lewis F. Powell, Jr., and a majority of the Court reached when considering the constitutionality of Texas's system of funding education which resulted in wealthier districts having more funds available than the not-so-wealthy districts.

Justice Marshall responded in a dissenting opinion that should be required reading for all persons interested in funding for public education. He not only discussed the constitutional issues, but the effect underfunding has upon the quality of education children receive. Marshall did not agree that "there ... [was] simply no denial of equal educational opportunity to any Texas schoolchildren as a result of the widely varying per-pupil spending power provided districts under the current financing scheme." "In my view," he asserted,

> ... even an unadorned statement of this contention is sufficient to reveal its absurdity. ... Indeed, conflicting expert testimony was presented to the District Court in this case concerning the effect of spending variations on educational achievement. We sit, however, not to resolve disputes over educational theory but to enforce our Constitution. It is an inescapable fact that if one district has more funds available per pupil than another district, the former will have greater choice in educational planning than will the latter. In this regard, I believe the question of discrimination in educational quality must be deemed to be an objective one that looks to what the State provides its children, not to what the children are able to do with what they receive. That a child forced to attend an underfunded school with poorer physical facilities, less experienced teachers, larger classes, and a narrower range of courses than a school with substantially more funds—and thus with greater choice in educational planning—may nevertheless excel is to the credit of the child, not the State. ... Indeed, who can ever measure for such a child the opportunities lost and the talents wasted for want of a broader, more enriched education? Discrimination in the opportunity to learn that is afforded a child must be our standard.

Marshall also dissented when the Court upheld a requirement of the

Dickinson, North Dakota, School District that all students must pay a fee in order to ride the school bus. "This case," he wrote,

> involves state action that places a special burden on poor families in their pursuit of education. Children living far from school can receive a public education only if they have access to transportation; as the state court noted in this case, "a child must reach the schoolhouse door as a prerequisite to receiving the educational opportunity offered therein." . . . Indeed, for children in Sarita's position, imposing a fee for transportation is no different in practical effect from imposing a fee directly for education. Moreover, the fee involved in this case discriminated against Sarita's family because it necessarily fell more heavily upon the poor than upon wealthier members of the community.[90]

The Bill of Rights and the States

> In August 1965, petitioner [Benton] was tried in a Maryland state court on charges of burglary and larceny. The jury found petitioner not guilty of larceny but convicted him on the burglary count. He was sentenced to 10 years in prison. [Shortly thereafter the Maryland Court of Appeals held that it was unconstitutional to require] jurors to swear their belief in the existence of God. As a result of this decision, petitioner's case was remanded to the trial court. Because both the grand and petit juries in petitioner's case had been selected under the invalid constitutional provision, petitioner was given the option of demanding re-indictment and retrial. He chose to have his conviction set aside, and a new indictment and new trial followed. At the second trial, petitioner was again charged with both larceny and burglary. Petitioner objected to retrial on the larceny count, arguing that because the first jury found him not guilty of larceny, retrial would violate the constitutional prohibition against subjecting persons to double jeopardy for the same offense. The trial judge denied petitioner's motion to dismiss the larceny charge, and petitioner was tried for both larceny and burglary. This time the jury found petitioner guilty of both offenses, and the judge sentenced him to 15 years on the burglary count and 5 years for larceny, the sentences to run concurrently. On appeal to the newly created Maryland Court of Special Appeals, petitioner's double jeopardy claim was rejected on the merits.[91]

On appeal to the Supreme Court, Justice Marshall and a majority held "that the Double Jeopardy Clause of the Fifth Amendment is applicable to the States through the Fourteenth Amendment, and we reverse petitioner's conviction for larceny."

In 1937, in the case of *Palko v. Connecticut*,[92] the Court had held that putting a person in double jeopardy is not one of "those 'fundamental principles of liberty and justice which lie at the base of all our civil and political institutions,'" and therefore states are not prohibited from trying a defendant a second time. But, Marshall noted, things have changed substantially since that case, and he wrote:

Recently, . . . this Court has "increasingly looked to the specific guarantees of the [Bill of Rights] to determine whether a state criminal trial was conducted with due process of law." . . . In an increasing number of cases, the Court "has rejected the notion that the Fourteenth Amendment applies to the States only a 'watered-down, subjective version of the individual guarantees of the Bill of Rights. . . .'" Only last term we found that the right to trial by jury in criminal cases was "fundamental to the American scheme of justice," . . . and held that the Sixth Amendment right to a jury trial was applicable to the States through the Fourteenth Amendment. For the same reasons, we today find that the double jeopardy prohibition of the Fifth Amendment represents a fundamental ideal of our constitutional heritage, and that it should apply to the States through the Fourteenth Amendment. Insofar as it is inconsistent with this holding, *Palko v. Connecticut* is overruled.[93]

AS A JUDICIAL FREEDOM FIGHTER

Justice Marshall's views on the free exercise of religion are revealed in his dissent in Larry G. Hardison's case. Another indication is found in his joining Justice Blackmun's dissenting opinion in *Employment Div., Dept. of Human Res. v. Smith.*[94] At issue in that case was whether Native Americans could be punished for using peyote as a part of a religious ceremony. A majority of the Court held that they could. Blackmun, Brennan, and Marshall dissented. Blackmun wrote: "This Court over the years painstakingly has developed a consistent and exacting standard to test the constitutionality of a state statute that burdens the free exercise of religion. Such a statute may stand only if the law in general, and the State's refusal to allow a religious exemption in particular, are justified by a compelling interest that cannot be served by less restrictive means."

In the opinions Marshall wrote on freedom of speech, it is clear that he was in favor of free speech not only in the abstract, but also for particular people in particular places. Among those whose speech rights he voted to protect were the demonstrators who wanted to sleep in Lafayette Park and on the Mall in Washington, D.C.; Mary Grace and Thaddeus Zywicki, who picketed near the Supreme Court; public employees like Ardith McPherson; and prisoners, and even those held in jail awaiting trial. In the latter case, Marshall objected when the Court upheld a rule of the Metropolitan Correctional Center in New York City that the pretrial detainees could receive books and magazines only if sent by the publisher or a book club. In discussing the so-called publisher-only rule, Justice Marshall stated that "individuals have a fundamental First Amendment right to receive information and ideas is beyond dispute. Under the balancing test . . . the Government must therefore demonstrate that its rule infringing on that interest serves a compelling necessity. As the courts below found, the Government failed to make such a showing."[95]

372 Justice Thurgood Marshall

Marshall also expressed concern that rules that restrict lawyer solicitation of clients can too severely restrict the free flow of information.

> I do not mean to belittle those obviously substantial interests that the State has in regulating attorneys to protect the public from fraud, deceit, misrepresentation, overreaching, undue influence, and invasions of privacy. But where honest, un-pressured "commercial" solicitation is involved . . . I believe it is open to doubt whether the State's interests are sufficiently compelling to warrant the restriction on the free flow of information which results from a sweeping nonsolicitation rule and against which the First Amendment ordinarily protects."[96]

> Although the Free Press Clause does not guarantee the press a preferred position over other speakers, the Free Press Clause does "protec[t] [members of press] from invidious discrimination." . . . Selective taxation is precisely that. In light of the Framers' specific intent "to preserve an untrammeled press as a vital source of public information," . . . our precedents recognize that the Free Press Clause imposes a special obligation on government to avoid disrupting the in-tegrity of the information market.[97]

With those words, Marshall dissented when the Court upheld the Arkansas gross receipts tax, which applied to cable television gross receipts but not to newspaper and magazine sales.

The justice's views on obscenity changed over the years, as had Justice Brennan's. Both abandoned the approach taken in *Roth v. United States*, in dissenting in *Paris Adult Theatre I*. Both affirmed their new approach in a concurring and dissenting opinion, written by Justice Brennan, in *Sable Communications of Ca., Inc. v. FCC*.[98] In that case, the Court affirmed a lower court ruling that "upheld the prohibition against obscene interstate telephone communications for commercial purposes, but enjoined the enforcement of the statute insofar as it applied to indecent messages." Brennan wrote for himself and Justice Marshall:

> I have long been convinced that the exaction of criminal penalties for the distri-bution of obscene materials to consenting adults is constitutionally intolerable. In my judgment, "the concept of 'obscenity' cannot be defined with sufficient specificity and clarity to provide fair notice to persons who create and distribute sexually oriented materials, to prevent substantial erosion of protected speech as a by-product of the attempt to suppress unprotected speech, and to avoid very costly institutional harms." . . . To be sure, the Government has a strong interest in protecting children against exposure to pornographic material that might be harmful to them. . . . But a complete criminal ban on obscene telephonic mes-sages for profit is "unconstitutionally overbroad, and therefore invalid on its face," as a means for achieving this end.

Justice Marshall gave voice to his concern for freedom of association in dissenting when the Court upheld prison rules that "prohibited prisoners from soliciting other inmates to join the Union and barred Union meetings and bulk mailings concerning the Union from outside sources."[99] He started his analysis of the question whether these rules violated First Amendment rights of prisoners by noting: "A prisoner does not shed ... basic First Amendment rights at the prison gate. Rather he 'retains all the rights of an ordinary citizen except those expressly, or by necessary implication, taken from him by law.'" With that premise in mind, Marshall attacked the prison's rules, pointing out that the lower court "not only found that there was 'not one scintilla of evidence to suggest that the Union had been utilized to disrupt the operation of the penal institutions,' ... it also found no evidence 'that the inmates intend to operate [the Union] to hamper and interfere with the proper interests of government,' ... or that the Union posed a 'present danger to security and order.'" But even if there were some risks involved in allowing the Union to meet, solicit members, and have bulk-mailing privileges, that would not justify the infringement upon the prisoners' right of association. "The central lesson of over a half century of First Amendment adjudication," Marshall declared, "is that freedom is sometimes a hazardous enterprise, and that the Constitution requires the State to bear certain risks to preserve our liberty."

Because of Marshall's long record of voting to protect the right of personal privacy, no one should have been surprised that he dissented when the Court upheld the application of Georgia's sodomy laws to homosexuals. Justice Blackmun wrote the dissent on behalf of himself and justices Brennan, Marshall, and Stevens. In response to the majority's assertion that many of the prior cases upholding a right of privacy have dealt with family relationships, Blackmun said that there was more to privacy than that. He quoted from a prior case: "The concept of privacy embodies the 'moral fact that a person belongs to himself and not others nor to society as a whole.'"[100] He continued:

> Only the most willful blindness could obscure the fact that sexual intimacy is "a sensitive, key relationship of human existence, central to family life, community welfare, and the development of human personality,". . . . The fact that individuals define themselves in a significant way through their intimate sexual relationships with others suggests, in a Nation as diverse as ours, that there may be many "right" ways of conducting those relationships, and that much of the richness of a relationship will come from the freedom an individual has to *choose* the form and nature of these intensely personal bonds.

In *University of California Regents v. Bakke,*[101] the Court considered the constitutionality of "the special admissions program of ... the Medical School of the University of California at Davis, which ... [was] designed to assure the admission of a specified number of students from certain minority groups." In a very splintered decision, the Court invalidated the admissions policy, but concluded that race could be taken into account as one factor in making medical school admissions decisions. Marshall agreed, but would have upheld the policy as it was being administered at the medical school. In an extended opinion, the justice traced the history of black people since they were "dragged to this country in chains to be sold into slavery." And he pointed out that the "position of the Negro today in America is the tragic but inevitable consequence of centuries of unequal treatment. Measured by any benchmark of comfort or achievement, meaningful equality remains a distant dream for the Negro." He therefore did not believe that the Fourteenth Amendment's Equal Protection Clause should stand in the way of the attempt of the state to bring more minorities into the mainstream. "Neither its history nor our past cases lend any support to the conclusion that a university may not remedy cumulative effects of society's discrimination by giving consideration to race in an effort to increase the number and percentage of Negro doctors." And, he concluded:

> It is because of a legacy of unequal treatment that we now must permit the institutions of this society to give consideration to race in making decisions about who will hold the positions of influence, affluence, and prestige in America. For far too long, the doors to those positions have been shut to Negroes. If we are ever to become a fully integrated society, one in which the color of a person's skin will not determine the opportunities available to him or her, we must be willing to take steps to open those doors. I do not believe that anyone can truly look into America's past and still find that a remedy for the effects of that past is impermissible.

Justice Marshall voted consistently to strike down classifications based on gender and discrimination against illegitimate children and aliens. He believed that classifications affecting illegitimate children were "invidious and irrational," and that "aliens are 'persons' within the meaning of the Fourteenth Amendment"[102] and are thus entitled to its protection.

Classifications affecting the right to vote were also anathema to Marshall. "The State has the heavy burden of showing, first, that the challenged disenfranchisement is necessary to a legitimate and substantial state interest; second, that the classification is drawn with precision—that it does not exclude too many people who should not and need not be excluded; and, third, that there are no other reasonable ways to achieve the State's goal with a lesser burden on the constitutionally protected interest."[103] The justice wrote those words in dissenting when the Court upheld a California law disenfranchising ex-felons.

Edwin and Judith Dickman owned a house in Belle Terre, New York, which they rented to college students Bruce Boraas, Anne Parish, Michael Truman, and three other unrelated students. Because of the number of people involved, this living arrangement did not qualify as a "family" under the village's zoning ordinance. When the Dickmans were ordered to remedy the violation, they and the students brought an action seeking a declaration that the ordinance was unconstitutional. An appeals court held that the ordinance had no rational basis and struck it down. The Supreme Court reversed, with Justice Marshall dissenting. "My disagreement with the Court today is based upon my view that the ordinance in this case unnecessarily burdens appellee's First Amendment freedom of association and their constitutionally guaranteed right to privacy."[104] Furthermore, he wrote:

> The instant ordinance discriminates on the basis of . . . a personal lifestyle choice as to household companions. It permits any number of persons related by blood or marriage, be it two or twenty, to live in a single household, but it limits to two the number of unrelated persons bound by profession, love, friendship, religious or political affiliation, or mere economics who can occupy a single home. Belle Terre imposes upon those who deviate from the community norm in their choice of living companions significantly greater restrictions than are applied to residential groups who are related by blood or marriage, and compose the established order within the community. The village has, in effect, acted to fence out those individuals whose choice of lifestyle differs from that of its current residents.

Justice Marshall voted consistently to guarantee equal protection to rich and poor alike within the criminal justice system. Justice Brennan expressed his and Marshall's beliefs as follows: "Equal protection demands that States eliminate unfair disparities between classes of individuals. There is no rational basis for assuming that petitions submitted by indigents for collateral review will be less meritorious than those of other defendants. . . . Since an impoverished prisoner must take whatever a State affords, it is imperative that the court-appointed counsel be scrutinized so that the indigent receives adequate representation."[105]

Justice Marshall fought vigorously for equal rights and equal opportunity for all minorities, before and after he became a justice. But his fight for freedom did not end there. As a justice, he consistently voted to protect freedom of religion, speech, the press, and association, and the right of privacy as well.

EPILOGUE

"I believe there are more instances of the abridgment of the freedom of the people by gradual and silent encroachments of those in power than by violent and sudden usurpations."

Those are the words James Madison spoke on June 16, 1788, at the Virginia Convention to ratify the proposed Constitution.

Silent encroachments upon our rights occur by actions of government, federal, state, and local. When laws are passed or actions taken by government that curtail freedom, we look to judges and justices for protection. Madison assured us that these "independent tribunals of justice will consider themselves in a peculiar manner the guardians of those rights; they will be an impenetrable bulwark against every assumption of power in the Legislative or Executive; they will be naturally led to resist every encroachment upon rights expressly stipulated for in the Constitution by the declaration of rights."

There are many instances in which judges and justices have not been the "impenetrable bulwark" Madison assured us they would be. If there is one theme, however, that runs through the votes and opinions of the justices profiled in this book, it is their fight to prevent the "gradual and silent encroachment" upon the freedoms guaranteed by our Constitution.

But we cannot and should not depend upon judges and justices alone to preserve our freedom. We need to do more than just give lip service to freedom, as we do on the Fourth of July. Commitment to freedom must be for us a "fighting faith." And we need to heed the words of Carl Sandburg: Freedom is baffling:/men having it often/know not they have it/till it is gone and/they no longer have it.

NOTES

A note regarding citations of court cases. "X v. Y, 25 U.S. 372, 376 (19nn)" means that the X v. Y opinion appears in volume 25 of the *United States* reports at page 372, and that quotation appears at page 376, and that case was decided in 19nn.

Quotations without notes are taken from the same source as the next preceding numbered quotation.

Prologue

1. *The Great Rights*, edited by Edmond Cahn (New York: Macmillan, 1963), pp. 11–12.

1. Justice John Marshall Harlan

1. Loren P. Beth, *John Marshall Harlan, The Last Whig Justice* (Lexington: University Press of Kentucky, 1992), p. 21.
2. Ibid., p. 8. A Clay Whig was one who subscribed to the views of Henry Clay.
3. "John Marshall Harlan," 10 *Vanderbilt Law Review* 209, 212 (1957).
4. "John Marshall Harlan," 46 *Kentucky Law Journal* 321, 324 (1958).
5. Ibid., p. 351.
6. Beth, note 1, pp. 17–18.
7. 46 *Kentucky Law Journal*, p. 377.
8. Ibid., p. 378.
9. Beth, note 1, pp. 21–22.
10. Beth, note 1, p. 23.
11. 46 *Kentucky Law Journal*, p. 379.
12. Allison Dunham and Philip B. Kurland, eds., *Mr. Justice*, "Mr. Justice Harlan," *Mr. Justice Harlan*, article by Alan F. Westin (Chicago: University of Chicago Press, 1964), p. 111.
13. 46 *Kentucky Law Journal*, p. 382.
14. Ibid., p. 385.
15. 10 *Vanderbilt Law Review*, p. 214.
16. Ibid., p. 219.
17. Dunham and Kurland, note 12, p. 111.
18. Beth, note 1, p. 98.
19. Ibid., p. 51.
20. 10 *Vanderbilt Law Review*, p. 215.
21. Ibid., p. 215.
22. 46 *Kentucky Law Journal*, p. 331.
23. Dunham and Kurland, note 12, p. 108.
24. Ibid., p. 109.
25. Ibid., p. 113.
26. 46 *Kentucky Law Journal*, p. 414.
27. Leon Friedman and Fred L. Israel, *The Justices of the United States Supreme Court 1789–1969, Their Lives and Major Opinions*, vol. 5 (New York: Chelsea House, 1969), p. 1287.
28. Farnum, "John Marshall Harlan," 30 *American Bar Association Journal* 576–577 (1944).
29. 100 U.S. 303 (1880).
30. 100 U.S. 313 (1880).
31. 100 U.S. 339 (1880).
32. 100 U.S. at 306.
33. 100 U.S. at 321.
34. 100 U.S. at 347.
35. 103 U.S. 370 (1881).
36. 103 at 397. See Bush v. Kentucky, 107 U.S. 110 (1882), for a similar result.
37. See Appendix.
38. Gibson v. Mississippi, 162 U.S. 565, 580 (1890).
39. Louisville & Nashville R.R. Co. v. Mississippi, 133 U.S. 587 (1890).
40. 163 U.S. 537 (1896).
41. 60 U.S. 393 (1857).
42. 163 U.S. at 563.
43. Berea College v. Kentucky, 211 U.S. 45 (1903).
44. Bradwell v. Illinois, 83 U.S. 130 (1873).
45. Minor v. Happersett, 85 U.S. 162 (1875).
46. In re Lockwood, 154 U.S. 116 (1894).
47. Cronin v. Adams, 192 U.S. 108 (1904).

48. Yick Wo v. Hopkins, 118 U.S. 356, 373–74 (1886).

49. 109 U.S. 3 (1883).

50. 46 *Kentucky Law Journal*, pp. 348–49.

51. 109 U.S. at 26.

52. Ex parte Yarbrough, 110 U.S. 651 (1884). See Appendix.

53. United States v. Waddell, 112 U.S. 76 (1884).

54. Logan v. United States, 144 U.S. 263 (1892).

55. 203 U.S. 1 (1906).

56. Robertson v. Baldwin, 165 U.S. 275 (1897).

57. Ibid., at 301. Italics in original. See Clyatt v. United States, 199 U.S. 207 (1905), where Harlan concurred in a decision upholding a federal law making it a crime to hold a person in "peonage."

58. Davidson v. New Orleans, 96 U.S. 97, 104 (1878).

59. 115 U.S. 620 (1885).

60. Geer v. Connecticut, 161 U.S. 519, 543 (1896).

61. Taylor v. Beckham, 178 U.S. 548, 603–4 (1900).

62. 197 U.S. 11 (1905).

63. Adamson v. California, 332 U.S. 46, 62 (1947).

64. 110 U.S. 516 (1884).

65. 176 U.S. 581 (1900).

66. See Appendix. Harlan voted with the majority in several cases in which the Court made statements to the effect that the first eight amendments to the Constitution did not apply to the states. He gives no explanation for his votes.

67. Kirby v. United States, 174 U.S. 47 (1899); and Motes v. United States, 178 U.S. 458 (1900).

68. 174 U.S. at 55.

69. DeLima v. Bidwell, 182 U.S. 1 (1901), imports from Puerto Rico. Dooley v. United States, 182 U.S. 222 (1901), exports to Puerto Rico.

70. Downes v. Bidwell, 182 U.S. 244 (1901).

71. 190 U.S. 197 (1903).

72. See Appendix.

73. Ex Parte Jackson, 96 U.S. 727 (1878). This decision was approved in In re Rapier, 143 U.S. 110 (1892).

74. Rosen v. United States, 161 U.S. 29, 31 (1896).

75. 167 U.S. 43 (1897).

76. Turner v. Williams, 194 U.S. 279 (1904).

77. Halter v. Nebraska, 205 U.S. 34 (1907).

78. Patterson v. Colorado, 205 U.S. 454 (1907).

79. Reynolds v. United States, 98 U.S. 145 (1879); Murphy v. Ramsey, 114 U.S. 15 (1885); Davis v. Beason, 133 U.S. 333 (1890); Mormon Church v. United States, 136 U.S. 1 (1890).

80. 98 U.S. at 167.

81. Mormon Church, 136 U.S. at 50.

82. See Appendix.

83. 112 U.S. 536 (1884). See United States v. Jung Ah Lung, 124 U.S. 621 (1888), a case in which Harlan dissented from an order allowing re-entry to a Chinese alien whose certificate had been stolen. Harlan thought that that was the alien's "misfortune." In Lau Ow Bew v. United States, 144 U.S. 47 (1892), the justice voted with the majority to allow re-entry of a Chinese alien who had left the country temporarily, always having the intention to return.

84. 163 U.S. 228 (1896).

85. 208 U.S. 8 (1908).

86. Elk v. Wilkins, 112 U.S. 94 (1884). In Talton v. Mayes, 163 U.S. 376 (1896), Harlan dissented from a holding that the Fifth Amendment did not apply to criminal proceedings on the Cherokee Nation.

87. 145 U.S. 487 (1892).

88. Thompson v. Thompson, 218 U.S. 611 (1910).

89. 194 U.S. 601 (1904).

90. Toomer v. Witsell, 334 U.S. 385, 395 (1949).

91. Chambers v. Baltimore & Ohio, Railroad, 207 U.S. 142 (1907).

92. 347 U.S. 483 (1954).

93. 165 U.S. 275 (1897).

94. See Appendix.

95. 110 U.S. at 548.

96. Hawker v. New York, 170 U.S. 189 (1898).

97. Graham v. Richardson, 403 U.S. 365, 372 (1971).

2. Chief Justice Charles Evans Hughes

1. Merlo J. Pusey, *Charles Evans Hughes*, vol. 1 (New York: Columbia University Press, 1963), p. 7.

2. For a detailed account of Hughes's tenure as secretary of state, see Pusey, note 1, chapters 39–59.

3. Hamilton v. Regents, 293 U.S. 245 (1934).

4. 310 U.S. 586 (1940).

5. Board of Education v. Barnette, 319 U.S. 624 (1943).

6. Cantwell v. Connecticut, 310 U.S. 296 (1940).

7. 283 U.S. 605 (1931).

8. Stromberg v. California, 283 U.S. 359, 362 (1931).

9. De Jonge v. Oregon, 299 U.S. 353, 357 (1937).

10. Herndon v. Lowry, 301 U.S. 242, 246 (1937).

11. Fox v. Washington, 236 U.S. 273, 275 (1915).

12. Ex Parte Jackson, 96 U.S. 727, 733 (1878).

13. Lovell v. Griffin, 303 U.S. 444 (1938).

14. Hague v. C.I.O., 307 U.S. 496 (1939); Schneider v. State, 308 U.S. 147 (1939).

15. 307 U.S. 496 (1939).

16. Cox v. New Hampshire, 312 U.S. 569 (1941).

17. Driver's Union v. Meadowmoor, 312 U.S. 287, 293 (1941).

18. Carlson v. California, 310 U.S. 106, 110 (1940).

19. 310 U.S. 88 (1940).

20. 1992 Almanac, p. 248.

21. 283 U.S. 697 (1931).

22. Labor Board v. Jones & Laughlin, 301 U.S. 1, 33 (1937).

23. NAACP v. Alabama, 357 U.S. 449, 460 (1958).

24. 301 U.S. at 42, 43.

25. 100 U.S. 303 (1880).

26. 294 U.S. 587 (1935).

27. 303 U.S. 613 (1938).

28. 306 U.S. 354 (1939).

29. 311 U.S. 128 (1940).

30. 235 U.S. 151 (1914).

31. 305 U.S. 337 (1938).

32. 83 U.S. 36 (1873).

33. 219 U.S. 219, 227–228 (1941).

34. Allgeyer v. Louisiana, 165 U.S. 578, 589 (1897).

35. 239 U.S. 33 (1915).

36. Muller v. Oregon, 208 U.S. 412 (1908).

37. Riley v. Massachusetts, 232 U.S. 671 (1914); Miller v. Wilson, 236 U.S. 373 (1915).

38. Smith v. Texas, 233 U.S. 630, 635 (1914).

39. 287 U.S. 45 (1932).

40. 302 U.S. 319 (1937).

41. 299 U.S. at 364.

42. Pusey, note 1, p. 204.

43. Home Building & Loan Assn. v. Blaisdell, 290 U.S. 398, 442–443 (1934). Italics in original.

44. 268 U.S. 652, 666 (1925).

45. 274 U.S. 357, 371 (1927).

46. 283 U.S. at 719.

47. 311 U.S. 128 (1940).

48. See Appendix.

49. 299 U.S. at 365

3. Justice Louis Dembitz Brandeis

1. Lewis J. Paper, *Brandeis* (Englewood Cliffs, N.J.: Prentice-Hall, 1983), p. 11.

2. Philippa Strum, *Louis D. Brandeis, Justice for the People* (Cambridge, Mass.: Harvard University Press, 1984), p. 6.

3. Paper, note 1, p. 199.

4. Strum, note 2, p. 10.

5. Paper, note 1, pp. 12–13.

6. Strum, note 2, p. 18.

7. Paper, note 1, p. 24.

8. Ibid., note 1, p. 27.

9. Strum, note 2, pp. 39–40.

10. Paper, note 1, p. 43.

11. Strum, note 2, p. 54.

12. Paper, note 1, p. 139.

13. Strum, note 2, p. 103.

14. 208 U.S. 412 (1908).

15. Lochner v. New York, 198 U.S. 45 (1905).

16. Strum, note 2, p. 221.

17. Paper, note 1, p. 199.

18. Strum, note 2, p. 256.

19. For detailed accounts of Brandeis's confirmation, see Paper, note 1, pp. 209–40, and Strum, note 2, pp. 290–301.

20. Paper, note 1, p. 234.

21. Nelson L. Dawson, *Brandeis and America* (Lexington: University Press of Kentucky, 1989), pp. 146–47.

22. United States v. Schwimmer, 279 U.S. 644 (1929).

23. United States v. Macintosh, 283 U.S. 605, 617–18 (1931).

24. Hamilton v. Regents, 293 U.S. 245 (1934).

25. Schenck v. United States, 249 U.S. 47 (1919); Frohwerk v. United States, 249 U.S. 204 (1919); Debs v. United States, 249 U.S. 211 (1919).

26. Strum, note 2, p. 316.

27. Abrams v. United States, 250 U.S. 616 (1919).

28. 252 U.S. 239, 253 (1920).

29. Thornhill v. Alabama, 310 U.S. 88 (1940).

30. 301 U.S. 468 (1937).
31. Gilbert v. Minnesota, 254 U.S. 325 (1920).
32. Herndon v. Lowry, 301 U.S. 242 (1937).
33. N.A.A.C.P. v. Alabama, 357 U.S. 449 (1958).
34. 274 U.S. 357 (1927).
35. Fiske v. Kansas, 274 U.S. 380, 384 (1927).
36. Bryant v. Zimmerman, 278 U.S. 63 (1928).
37. N.A.A.C.P. v. Alabama, note 33, p. 465.
38. 299 U.S. 353 (1937).
39. Schaefer v. United States, 251 U.S. 466, 493–94 (1920).
40. 255 U.S. 407 (1921).
41. 96 U.S. 727 (1878).
42. Gitlow v. New York, 268 U.S. 652, 654 (1925).
43. Meyer v. Nebraska, 262 U.S. 390, 400 (1923).
44. 268 U.S. 510 (1925).
45. Society of Sisters v. Pierce, 296 Fed. 928, 938 (1924).
46. 268 U.S. 510, note 44 at pp. 534–35.
47. 245 U.S. 60 (1917).
48. Corrigan v. Buckley, 271 U.S. 323 (1926).
49. Nixon v. Herndon, 273 U.S. 536 (1927).
50. Nixon v. Condon, 286 U.S. 73, 82 (1932).
51. Aldridge v. United States, 283 U.S. 308 (1931).
52. See Appendix.
53. Plessy v. Ferguson, 163 U. S. 537 (1896); South Covington and Cincinnati Street Railway Co. v. Kentucky, 252 U.S. 399 (1920).
54. Gong Lum v. Rice, 275 U.S. 78 (1927).
55. Missouri ex. rel. Gaines v. Canada, 305 U.S. 337 (1938).
56. 347 U.S. 483 (1954).
57. The Chinese Exclusion Case, 130 U.S. 581, 603 (1889).
58. United States v. Ju Toy, 198 U.S. 253 (1905).
59. Ng Fung Ho v. White, 259 U.S. 276 (1922).
60. Ibid., at 282. Italics supplied.
61. 302 U.S. 319 (1937).
62. 254 U.S. at 336.
63. 274 U.S. at 373.
64. 256 U.S. 465, 477 (1921).
65. 277 U.S. 438 (1928).
66. 277 U.S. at 479.
67. 252 U. S. at 269.
68. 274 U.S. at 375–76.
69. 251 U.S. at 495.
70. 293 U.S. at 266.
71. 381 U.S. 479, 482–83 (1965).
72. 410 U.S. 113, 152–54 (1973).
73. 277 U.S. at 485.

4. Justice Hugo LaFayette Black

1. Virginia Van der Veer Hamilton, *Hugo Black: The Alabama Years* (Baton Rouge: Louisiana State University Press, 1972), p. 18.
2. John P. Frank, *Mr. Justice Black: The Man and His Opinions* (New York: Alfred A. Knopf, 1949), p. 4.
3. Hamilton, note 1, at pp. 21–22.
4. Frank, note 2, p. 13.
5. Hamilton, note 1, p. 51.
6. Chambers v. Florida, 309 U.S. 227 (1940).
7. Hamilton, note 1, p. 68.
8. Frank, note 2, p. 34.
9. Gerald T. Dunne, *Hugo Black and the Judicial Revolution* (New York: Simon and Schuster, 1977), p. 108.
10. Hamilton, note 1, p. 82.
11. Hugo Black, Jr., *My Father, A Remembrance* (New York: Random House, 1975), pp. 168–69. This book contains an interesting and informative description of life in the Black family as experienced by Hugo Black, Jr.
12. Hamilton, note 1, p. 121.
13. Frank, note 2, p. 46.
14. Hamilton, note 1, p. 158.
15. Leon Friedman and Fred L. Israel, *The Justices of the United States Supreme Court 1789–1969*, vol. 3 (New York: Chelsea House, 1969), article by John P. Frank, p. 2327.
16. Ibid., p. 2329.
17. Frank, note 2, p. 88.
18. Hamilton, note 1, pp. 273–74.
19. Ibid., p. 289.
20. Dunne, note 9, p. 73.
21. Gobitis v. Minersville, 24 F. Supp. 271, 275 (1938).
22. Minersville District v. Gobitis, 310 U.S. 586 (1940).
23. Board of Education v. Barnette, 319 U.S. 624, 626 (1943).
24. In re Summers, 325 U.S. 561, 573 (1945).
25. Torcaso v. Watkins, 367 U.S. 488 (1961).
26. Braunfeld v. Brown, 366 U.S. 599, 605 (1961).

27. Sherbert v. Verner, 374 U.S. 398 (1963).

28. Cantwell v. Connecticut, 310 U.S. 296, 303–4 (1940).

29. United States v. Ballard, 322 U.S. 78, 87 (1944).

30. Marsh v. Alabama, 326 U.S. 501 (1946).

31. Marsh v. State, 21 So. 2d 558, 560 (1945).

32. 326 U.S. at 509.

33. Beauharnais v. Illinois, 343 U.S. 250, 252 (1952).

34. 362 U.S. 60 (1960).

35. 310 U. S. 88 (1940).

36. 310 U.S. 106 (1941).

37. 312 U.S. 287 (1941).

38. Bakery Drivers Union v. Wohl, 315 U.S. 769 (1942).

39. Carpenter's Union v. Ritter's Cafe, 315 U.S. 722 (1942). See Appendix.

40. 379 U.S. 559 (1965).

41. Ibid., at 578. Italics in original.

42. Cox v. Louisiana, 379 U.S. 583 (1965); Adderley v. Florida, 385 U.S. 39 (1966).

43. United Public Workers v. Mitchell, 330 U.S. 75, 92 (1947).

44. Feiner v. New York, 340 U.S. 315, 317 (1951).

45. 341 U.S. 494 (1951).

46. Yates v. United States, 354 U.S. 298, 344 (1957).

47. Brown v. Louisiana, 383 U.S. 131, 166 (1966).

48. Tinker v. Des Moines School District, 393 U.S. 503, 522 (1969).

49. 339 U.S. 382 (1950).

50. Anti-Fascist Committee v. McGrath, 341 U.S. 123, 125 (1951).

51. Communist Party v. Control Board, 367 U.S. 1 (1961).

52. N.A.A.C.P. v. Alabama, 357 U.S. 449 (1958).

53. Gibson v. Florida Legislative Comm., 372 U.S. 539, 559 (1963).

54. 360 U.S. 109, 135 (1959).

55. Konigsberg v. State Bar, 366 U.S. 36, 39 (1961).

56. 401 U.S. 1 (1971).

57. 371 U.S. 415 (1963).

58. 377 U.S. 1 (1964).

59. 389 U.S. 217 (1967).

60. 401 U.S. 576 (1971).

61. Bridges v. California, 314 U.S. 252, 272 (1941).

62. Chaplinsky v. New Hampshire, 315 U.S. 568, 571–72 (1942). Italics supplied.

63. New York Times Co. v. Sullivan, 376 U.S. 254 (1964).

64. Curtis Publishing Company v. Butts, 351 F. 2d 702, 705 (1965).

65. Curtis Publishing Co. v. Butts, 388 U.S. 130, 138 (1967).

66. See Appendix.

67. 384 U.S. 214 (1966).

68. New York Times Co. v. United States, 403 U.S. 713 (1971).

69. Kingsley Pictures Corp. v. Regents, 360 U.S. 684 (1959).

70. 383 U.S. 463 (1966).

71. 383 U.S. 745 (1966).

72. United States v. Guest, 246 F. Supp. 475, 477 (1964).

73. 383 U.S. at 757.

74. Aptheker v. Secretary of State, 378 U.S. 500 (1964).

75. Barsky v. Board of Regents, 347 U.S. 442 (1954).

76. Griswold v. Connecticut, 381 U.S. 479 (1965).

77. 319 U.S. 141 (1943).

78. Pierre v. Louisiana, 306 U.S. 354, 357 (1939).

79. See Appendix.

80. Missouri ex rel Gaines v. Canada, 305 U.S. 337 (1938).

81. Sipuel v. Board of Regents, 332 U.S. 631 (1948).

82. Sweatt v. Painter, 339 U.S. 629 (1950).

83. McLauren v. Oklahoma State Regents, 339 U.S. 637, 639 (1950).

84. Brown v. Board of Education, 98 F. Supp. 797, 800 (1951).

85. Brown v. Board of Education, 347 U.S. 483 (1954).

86. Black, note 11, p. 209.

87. Brown v. Board of Education, 349 U.S. 294, 301 (1955).

88. Griffin v. School Board, 377 U.S. 218, 222 (1964). When the Court decided to hear this case, it took notice of "the long delay in the case since our decision in the *Brown* case" (p. 225).

89. 373 U.S. 61, 62 (1963).

90. See Appendix.

91. 373 U.S. 526 (1963).

92. Evans v. Newton, 382 U.S. 296 (1966).

93. Evans v. Abney, 396 U.S. 435 (1970).

94. Civil Rights Cases, 109 U.S. 3, 11 (1883).

95. Robinson v. Florida, 378 U.S. 153, 154 (1964).

96. Bouie v. City of Columbia, 378 U.S. 347 (1964).

97. Glona v. American Guarantee Co., 391 U.S. 73, 76 (1968).

98. Levy v. Louisiana, 391 U.S. 68 (1968).

99. Glona, note 97.

100. 401 U.S. 532 (1971).

101. Takahashi v. Fish Comm'n., 334 U.S. 410 (1948).

102. Johnson v. Eisentrager, 339 U.S. 763, 776 (1950).

103. Carrington v. Rash, 380 U.S. 89 (1965).

104. Cipriano v. City of Houma, 395 U.S. 701, 702 (1969).

105. Evans v. Cornman, 398 U.S. 419 (1970).

106. Kramer v. Union School District, 395 U.S. 621 (1969).

107. Williams v. Rhodes, 393 U.S. 23, 26 (1968).

108. Doud v. Cook, 340 U.S. 206 (1951).

109. Griffin v. Illinois, 351 U.S. 12 (1956).

110. See Appendix.

111. Burns v. Ohio, 360 U. S. 252 (1959); Smith v. Bennett, 365 U.S. 708 (1961).

112. Rinaldi v. Yeager, 384 U.S. 305 (1966).

113. 372 U.S. 353 (1963).

114. Anders v. California, 386 U.S. 738 (1967).

115. 332 U.S. 46 (1947).

116. Duncan v. Louisiana, 391 U.S. 145, 146 (1968).

117. Korematsu v. United States, 323 U.S. 214, 216 (1944).

118. Hirabayashi v. United States, 320 U.S. 81 (1943).

119. Yasui v. United States, 320 U.S. 115 (1943).

120. Ex parte Endo, 323 U.S. 283 (1944).

121. Wilkinson v. United States, 365 U.S. 399, 422–23 (1961).

122. Konigsberg v. State Bar, 366 U.S. 36, 61 (1961).

123. Barenblatt v. United States, 360 U.S. 109, 142 (1959).

124. Adderley v. Florida, 385 U.S. 39, 47–48 (1966).

125. 325 U.S. at 577.

126. 339 U.S. at 452–53.

127. 367 U. S. 1 (1961).

128. 403 U.S. at 715. At this point in Black's concurrence he recalls the events leading up to the adoption of the Bill of Rights.

129. 360 U.S. at 690.

130. 311 U.S. 128 (1940).

131. 351 U.S. at 16.

132. Williams v. Oklahoma City, 395 U.S. 458 (1969).

5. Justice William O. Douglas

1. William O. Douglas, *Go East, Young Man: The Early Years* (New York: Random House, 1974), p. 8.

2. James F. Simon, *Independent Journey: The Life of William O. Douglas* (New York: Harper and Row, 1980), p. 35.

3. Douglas, note 1, p. 61.

4. Simon, note 2, p. 38.

5. Douglas, note 1, p. 7.

6. Simon, note 2, pp. 45–46.

7. Douglas, note 1, p. 91.

8. Simon, note 2, p. 68.

9. Douglas, note 1, p. 156.

10. Simon, note 2, pp. 108–9.

11. Douglas, note 1, p. 174.

12. Simon, note 2, p. 73.

13. Douglas, note 1, p. 144.

14. Simon, note 2, p. 115.

15. Douglas, note 1, p. 258.

16. Simon, note 2, p. 153.

17. Leon Friedman and Fred L. Israel, *The Justices of the United States Supreme Court 1789–1969*, vol 4 (New York: Chelsea House, 1969), article by John P. Frank, p. 2452.

18. Douglas, note 1, p. 55.

19. Friedman and Israel, note 17, pp. 2454–55.

20. Ballard v. United States, 138 F. 2d 540, 542–43 (1943). Guy Ballard, who was the husband of Edna and father of Donald, died before the case was commenced.

21. United States v. Ballard, 322 U.S. 78, 81 (1944).

22. 319 U.S. 105 (1943).

23. McGowan v. Maryland, 366 U.S. 420 (1961); Two Guys v. McGinley, 366 U.S. 582 (1961); Braunfeld v. Brown, 366 U.S. 599 (1961); Gallagher v. Crown Kosher Market, 366 U.S. 617 (1961).

24. 366 U.S. 599 (1961).

25. 366 U.S. at 561.

26. Beauharnais v. Illinois, 343 U.S. 250, 252 (1952).

27. Ashton v. Commonwealth, 405 S. W. 2d 562, 564 (1966).

28. Ashton v. Kentucky, 384 U.S. 195, 197 (1966).

29. Bakery Drivers Local v. Wohl, 315 U.S. 769, 776 (1942).

30. Adderley v. Florida, 385 U.S. 39, 47 (1966).

31. Terminiello v. Chicago, 337 U.S. 1, 16 (1949).

32. Feiner v. New York, 340 U.S. 315, 330 (1951).

33. 341 U.S. 494 (1951).

34. Cohen v. California, 403 U.S. 15, 16 (1971).

35. Street v. New York, 394 U.S. 576, 579 (1969); Smith v. Goguen, 415 U.S. 566, 571 (1974); Spence v. Washington, 418 U.S. 405 (1974).

36. 357 U.S. 513 (1958).

37. Elfbrandt v. Russell, 384 U.S. 11, 17 (1966).

38. Whitehill v. Elkins, 389 U.S. 54, 55 (1967).

39. Adler v. Board of Education, 342 U.S. 485, 508 (1952).

40. 367 U.S. 1, 174–75 (1961).

41. Scales v. United States, 367 U.S. 203 (1961).

42. Beilan v. Board of Education, 357 U.S. 399, 400–401 (1958).

43. Lerner v. Casey, 357 U.S. 468 (1958).

44. Schneider v. Smith, 390 U.S. 17, 25 (1968).

45. Gibson v. Florida Legislative Comm., 372 U.S. 531, 561 (1963).

46. C.S.C. v. Letter Carriers, 413 U.S. 548, 550 (1973).

47. Bridges v. California, 314 U.S. 252 (1941); Pennekamp v. Florida, 328 U.S. 331 (1946).

48. 331 U.S. 367 (1947).

49. Ex parte Craig, 193 S.W. 2d 178, 181 (1946).

50. 331 U.S. at 373.

51. 376 U.S. 254 (1964).

52. 383 U.S. 75 (1966).

53. Gertz v. Robert Welch, Inc., 418 U.S. 323, 326 (1974).

54. 403 U.S. 713 (1971).

55. Pittsburgh Press Co. v. Human Rel. Comm'n., 413 U.S. 376 (1973).

56. Branzburg v. Hayes, 408 U.S. 665 (1972).

57. Pell v. Procunier, 417 U.S. 817 (1974); Saxbe v. Washington Post Co., 417 U.S. 843 (1974).

58. Superior Films v. Dept. of Education, 346 U.S. 587, 589 (1954).

59. Roth v. United States, 354 U.S. 476, 514 (1957).

60. Interstate Circuit v. Dallas, 390 U.S. 676, 705 (1968).

61. Paris Adult Theatre I v. Slaton, 413 U.S. 49, 71 (1973).

62. Griswold v. Connecticut, 381 U.S. 479 (1965).

63. 410 U.S. 179 (1973).

64. Ibid., at 211. Italics in original.

65. 314 U.S. 160 (1941).

66. Kent v. Dulles, 357 U.S. 116, 117–18 (1958).

67. See Appendix.

68. 407 U.S. 493 (1972).

69. Carter v. Jury Commission, 396 U.S. 320, 342–43 (1970).

70. Barrows v. Jackson, 346 U.S. 249, 251 (1953).

71. McLaughlin v. Florida, 379 U.S. 184 (1964).

72. Evans v. Newton, 382 U.S. 296, (1966). In Evans v. Abney, 396 U.S. 435 (1970), the Court upheld the transfer of the park to Bacon's heirs because integrating the park would be inconsistent with Bacon's intentions as expressed in his will. Douglas dissented.

73. Palmer v. Thompson, 403 U.S. 217, 239 (1971).

74. Lombard v. Louisiana, 373 U.S. 267, 269, note 1 (1963).

75. Moose Lodge No. 107 v. Irvis, 407 U.S. 163 (1972).

76. Goesaert v. Cleary, 335 U.S. 464, 465 (1948).

77. Frontiero v. Richardson, 411 U.S. 677, 690–91 (1973). In Bolling v. Sharpe, 347 U.S. 497 (1954), the Court held that the Fifth Amendment Due Process Clause includes the concept of equal protection and therefore the federal government is also bound to give equal protection of the law.

78. Reed v. Reed, 404 U.S. 71 (1971); Stanton v. Stanton, 421 U.S. 7 (1975).

79. Levy v. Louisiana, 391 U.S. 68, 70 (1968).

80. Oyama v. California, 332 U.S. 633, 647 (1948).

81. Fleming v. Nestor, 363 U.S. 603, 628–29 (1960).

82. Williams v. Rhodes, 393 U.S. 23, 35 (1968).

83. Skinner v. Oklahoma, 316 U.S. 535 (1942).

84. Griffin v. Illinois, 351 U.S. 12, 1956).

85. Gardner v. California, 393 U.S. 367, 370 (1969).

86. 372 U.S. 335 (1963).

87. Douglas v. California, 372 U.S. 353 (1963).

88. Harper v. Virginia State Board of Elections, 240 F. Supp. 270, 271 (1964).

89. Harper v. Virginia Board of Elections, 383 U.S. 663, 666 (1966).

90. Boddie v. Connecticut, 401 U.S. 371, 380 (1971)

91. Betts v. Brady, 316 U.S. 455, 474 (1942).

92. 372 U.S. 335 (1963).

93. Douglas concurred in Justice Black's spirited defense of the position that the Fourteenth Amendment was intended to make all of the Bill of Rights applicable to the states. See Douglas v. Louisiana, 391 U.S. 145, 162 (1968).

94. Hirabayashi v. United States, 320 U.S. 81 (1943); Yasui v. United States, 320 U.S. 115 (1943).

95. Simon, note 2, p. 242.

96. Korematsu v. United States, 323 U. S. 214 (1944).

97. Zorach v. Clausen, 343 U.S. 306, 314–15 (1952).

98. 341 U.S. at 584–85.

99. DeGregory v. New Hampshire, 383 U.S. 825, 829 (1966).

100. Beilan v. Board of Education, 357 U.S. 399, 416 (1958). Italics in original.

101. Girouard v. United States, 328 U.S. 61, 69 (1946).

102. Cole v. Richardson, 405 U.S. 676, 677 (1972).

103. Louisiana v. NAACP, 366 U.S. 293, 297 (1961).

104. United States v. Caldwell, 408 U.S. 665, 722, 723 (1972).

105. 419 U.S. 153 (1974).

106. Roe v. Wade, 410 U.S. 179 (1973); Doe v. Bolton, 410 U.S. 179 (1973).

107. Cleveland Board of Education v. La Fleur, 414 U.S. 632 (1974).

108. O'Connor v. Donaldson, 422 U.S. 563 (1975).

109. Aptheker v. Secretary of State, 378 U.S. 500, 519–20 (1964).

110. 325 U.S. 398 (1945).

111. Swann v. Board of Education, 402 U.S. 1, 15 (1971).

112. Alexander v. Louisiana, 405 U.S. 625, 641–42 (1972).

113. Douglas v. California, 372 U. S. 353, 357 (1963). Italics in original.

114. 372 U.S. at 346–47.

115. Public Utilities Comm'n. v. Pollak, 343 U.S. 451, 469 (1952).

6. Justice Frank Murphy

1. J. Woodward Howard, Jr., *Mr. Justice Murphy: A Political Biography* (Princeton N.J.: Princeton University Press, 1968), pp. 3–4.

2. Sidney Fine, *Frank Murphy: The Detroit Years* (Ann Arbor: University of Michigan Press, 1975), p. 4.

3. Howard, note 1, p. 5.

4. Fine, note 2, p. 10.

5. Howard, note 1, p. 12.

6. Fine, note 2, pp. 34–35. Italics in original.

7. Ibid., pp. 89–90.

8. Howard, note 1, p. 26.

9. Fine, note 2, p. 166.

10. Howard, note 1, p. 56.

11. Fine, note 2, p. 455.

12. Howard, note 1, p. 60.

13. Sidney Fine, *Frank Murphy: The New Deal Years* (Chicago: University of Chicago Press, 1979), p. 3.

14. Howard, note 1, p. 76.

15. Fine, note 13, p. 88.

16. Howard, note 1, p. 118.

17. Fine, note 13, p. 235.

18. Howard, note 1, pp. 143–44.

19. Fine, note 13, pp. 522–24.

20. Ibid., p. 524.

21. Sidney Fine, *Frank Murphy: The Washington Years* (Ann Arbor: University of Michigan Press, 1984), p. 32.

22. Howard, note 1, p. 192.

23. Fine, note 21, p. 141.

24. Howard, note 1, p. 206.

25. Jones v. Opelika, 316 U.S. 584, 589 (1942).

26. Ibid.

27. 319 U.S. 141 (1943).

28. Prince v. Massachusetts, 321 U.S. 158, 174 (1944).

29. Minersville District v. Gobitis, 310 U.S. 586 (1940).

30. Board of Education v. Barnette, 319 U.S. 624, 645–46 (1943).

31. Cleveland v. United States, 329 U.S. 14, 24 (1946).

32. Thornhill v. Alabama, 310 U.S. 88, 93–94 (1940).

33. Drivers Union v. Meadowmoor Co., 312 U.S. 287 (1941).

34. See Appendix.

35. Chaplinsky v. New Hampshire, 315 U.S. 568, 569 (1942).

36. Terminiello v. Chicago, 337 U.S. 1, 4–5 (1949).

37. Pennekamp v. State, 22 So. 2d 875, 878 (1948).
38. Pennekamp v. Florida, 328 U. S. 331, 369–70 (1946).
39. 331 U.S. 367 (1947). This case is discussed more fully in Chapter 5.
40. Hartzel v. United States, 322 U.S. 680 (1944).
41. Associated Press v. United States, 326 U.S. 1 (1945).
42. Screws v. United States, 325 U.S. 91 (1945).
43. 316 U.S. 129, 136 (1942).
44. 314 U.S. 160 (1941).
45. 73 U.S. 35 (1867).
46. 314 U.S. at 178. Italics in original.
47. Hill v. Texas, 316 U.S. 400, 406 (1942).
48. Akins v. Texas, 325 U.S. 398, 407 (1945).
49. 313 U.S. 80 (1941).
50. Morgan v. Virginia, 328 U.S. 373, 386 (1946).
51. Smith v. Allwright, 321 U.S. 649 (1944).
52. Steele v. L. & N. R. Co., 323 U.S. 192, 199 (1944).
53. Shelley v. Kraemer, 334 U.S. 1 (1948).
54. Sipuel v. Board of Regents, 332 U.S. 631 (1948).
55. Kotch v. Pilot Comm'rs., 330 U.S. 552, 555 (1947).
56. 335 U.S. 464, 467 (1948).
57. MacDougall v. Green, 335 U.S. 281 (1948).
58. Fay v. New York, 332 U.S. 261 (1947).
59. 333 U.S. 565 (1948).
60. 316 U.S. 455 (1942).
61. 332 U.S. 46 (1947).
62. Wolf v. Colorado, 338 U.S. 25, 33 (1949).
63. Hirabayashi v. United States, 320 U.S. 81, 110 (1943).
64. 323 U.S. 214 (1944).
65. 332 U.S. 633 (1948).
66. 334 U.S. 410 (1948).
67. 332 U.S. note 65, at 656.
68. 334 U.S. note 66, at 422.
69. Leon Friedman and Fred L. Israel, *The Justices of the United States Supreme Court 1789–1969, Their Lives and Major Opinions*, vol. 4, (New York: Chelsea House, 1969), p. 2496.
70. 319 U.S. at 646.
71. 310 U.S. 106 (1940).
72. 325 U.S. at 410.
73. 332 U.S. at 124.
74. Ex parte Endo, 323 U.S. 283, 307 (1944).

7. Chief Justice Earl Warren

1. Earl Warren, *The Memoirs of Earl Warren, by Chief Justice Earl Warren* (Garden City, N.Y.: Doubleday, 1977), p. 15.
2. John D. Weaver, *Warren: The Man, the Court, the Era* (Boston: Little, Brown: 1967), p. 21.
3. Warren, note 1, p. 19.
4. Ibid., p. 21. Italics in original.
5. Weaver, note 2, p. 27.
6. Warren, note 1, p. 30.
7. Weaver, note 2, pp. 39–40.
8. G. Edward White, *Earl Warren: A Public Life* (New York: Oxford University Press, 1982), p. 88.
9. Warren, note 1, p. 52.
10. Weaver, note 2, p. 37.
11. Warren, note 1, p. 66.
12. White, note 8, p. 30.
13. Luther A. Huston, *Pathway to Judgment: A Study of Earl Warren* (Philadelphia and New York: Chilton Books, 1966), p. 46.
14. Warren, note 1, p. 115.
15. White, note 8, pp. 34–35. See also White, notes 30, 37, p. 385, and note 71, p. 387.
16. Ibid., p. 44.
17. Huston, note 13, p. 14.
18. Ibid., pp. 55–56.
19. White, note 8, pp. 18–19.
20. Warren, note 1, p. 148.
21. Ibid., p. 165.
22. Huston, note 13, p. 69.
23. White, note 8, p. 88.
24. Warren, note 1, p. 171.
25. White, note 8, p. 119. For a detailed discussion of the oath controversy, see White, pp. 112–26.
26. Huston, note 13, p. 81.
27. Weaver, note 2, p. 55.
28. White, note 8, p. 134.
29. Warren, note 1, p. 260. See Warren, p. 261, wherein the chief justice states that his recollection of this conversation is not the same as President Eisenhower's.
30. Huston, note 13, p. 96.
31. Warren, note 1, p. 274.
32. Braunfeld v. Brown, 366 U.S. 599 (1961).
33. Torcaso v. Watkins, 367 U.S. 488 (1961).
34. Sherbert v. Verner, 374 U.S. 398 (1963).
35. 355 U.S. 313 (1958).
36. Talley v. California, 362 U.S. 60, 64 (1960).

37. Edwards v. South Carolina, 372 U.S. 229, 230 (1963).
38. Brown v. Louisiana, 383 U.S. 131 (1961).
39. Teamsters Union v. Vogt, Inc., 354 U.S. 284 (1957).
40. 385 U.S. 39 (1966).
41. Shuttlesworth v. Birmingham, 394 U.S. 147, 149–50 (1969).
42. 370 U.S. 375 (1962).
43. Bond v. Floyd, 251 F. Supp. 333, 336 (1966).
44. Bond v. Floyd, 385 U.S. 116 (1966).
45. United States v. O'Brien, 391 U. S. 367 (1968). See James E. Leahy, "Flamboyant Protest, The First Amendment and the Boston Tea Party," 36 *Brooklyn Law Review* 185 (1970).
46. Street v. New York, 394 U.S. 576, 579 (1969).
47. Tinker v. Des Moines School District, 393 U.S. 503 (1969).
48. 377 U.S. 360 (1964).
49. 368 U.S. 278 (1961).
50. 385 U.S. 589 (1967).
51. 384 U.S. 11 (1966).
52. 389 U.S. 54 (1967).
53. United States v. Robel, 389 U.S. 258 (1967).
54. 357 U.S. 449 (1958).
55. 364 U.S. 479 (1960).
56. Bates v. Little Rock, 361 U.S. 516 (1960).
57. See Appendix.
58. 366 U.S. 36 (1961).
59. 366 U.S. 82 (1961).
60. See Appendix.
61. Railroad Trainmen v. Virginia Bar, 377 U.S. 1, 8 (1964).
62. Curtis Publishing Co. v. Butts, 388 U.S. 130, 162 (1967).
63. See Appendix.
64. Time, Inc. v. Hill, 385 U.S. 374, 378 (1967).
65. Roth v. United States, 354 U.S. 476, 481 (1957).
66. Kingsley Books, Inc. v. Brown, 354 U.S. 436, 445–46 (1957).
67. 365 U.S. 43 (1961).
68. Jacobellis v. Ohio, 378 U.S. 184, 186 (1964).
69. See Appendix.
70. See Appendix.
71. Redrup v. New York, 386 U.S. 767 (1967).
72. 357 U.S. 116 (1958).
73. Ibid.

74. Zemel v. Rusk, 381 U.S. 1 (1965).
75. 383 U.S. 745 (1966).
76. 394 U.S. 618 (1968).
77. 381 U.S. 479 (1965).
78. Barsky v. Board of Regents, 347 U.S. 442, 470 (1954).
79. Hernandez v. Texas, 347 U.S. 475 (1954).
80. See Appendix.
81. Reece v. Georgia, 350 U.S. 85, 87 (1955).
82. Michel v. Louisiana, 350 U.S. 91 (1955), and Swain v. Alabama, 380 U.S. 202, 228 (1965).
83. 347 U.S. 483 (1954).
84. See Appendix.
85. Lucy v. Adams, 350 U.S. 1 (1955).
86. Hawkins v. Board of Control, 350 U.S. 413 (1956).
87. Peterson v. Greenville, 373 U.S. 244, 247–48 (1963).
88. 373 U.S. 267 (1963).
89. See Appendix.
90. Wright v. Georgia, 373 U.S. 284, 286 (1963).
91. Burton v. Wilmington Parking Auth., 365 U.S. 715, 717 (1961).
92. 373 U.S. 61 (1963).
93. 373 U.S. 526 (1963).
94. 382 U.S. 296 (1966).
95. Loving v. Virginia, 388 U.S. 1, 3 (1967).
96. Glona v. American Guarantee Co., 391 U.S. 73 (1968).
97. Kramer v. Union Free School Dist., No. 15, 282 F. Supp. 70, 71 (1968).
98. Kramer v. Union Free School Dist., 395 U.S. 621 (1969).
99. 383 U.S. 663 (1966).
100. Cipriano v. City of Houma, 395 U.S. 701 (1969).
101. 351 U.S. 12, 16 (1956).
102. 360 U.S. 252 (1959).
103. See Appendix.
104. Smith v. Bennett, 365 U.S. 708, 714 (1961).
105. 384 U.S. 305 (1966).
106. Klopfer v. North Carolina, 386 U.S. 213, 221–22 (1967).
107. Washington v. Texas, 388 U.S. 14, 15–16 (1967).
108. See Appendix.
109. 366 U.S. at 605.
110. Earl Warren, *A Republic If You Can Keep It* (New York: Quandrangle Books, A New York Times Company, 1972), pp. 119–20; Abbington School District v. Schempp, 374 U.S. 203, 226 (1963).

111. Warren, at 124–25.

112. St. Amant v. Thompson, 390 U.S. 727, 732 (1968).

113. Ginzburg v. United States, 383 U.S. 463 (1966).

114. Mishkin v. New York, 383 U.S. 502 (1966).

115. Ginsberg v. New York, 390 U.S. 629 (1968).

116. 381 U.S. at 492.

117. 385 U.S. at 413.

118. See Appendix.

119. 388 U.S. at 10–11.

120. 380 U.S. 528, 540 (1965).

8. Justice William J. Brennan, Jr.

1. Kim Isaac Eisler, *A Justice for All, William J. Brennan, Jr., and the Decisions That Transformed America* (New York: Simon and Schuster, 1993), p. 17.

2. Edward de Grazia, "Freeing Literary and Artistic Expression During the Sixties: The Role of Justice William J. Brennan, Jr.," 13 *Cardozo Law Review* 103, 114 (Oct. 1991).

3. Eisler, note 1, p. 22.

4. Ibid., note 1, p. 23.

5. Leon Friedman and Fred L. Israel, *The Justices of the United States Supreme Court 1789–1969, Their Lives and Major Opinions*, vol. 4 (New York: Chelsea House, 1969), p. 2851.

6. Eisler, note 1, p. 65.

7. Friedman and Israel, note 5, p. 2852.

8. Eisler, note 1, p. 82.

9. de Grazia, note 2, at pp. 118–19. And see note 1, p. 89.

10. Eisler, note 1, at pp. 86–96.

11. de Grazia, note 2, at pp. 119–20.

12. 366 U.S. 599, 616 (1961).

13. Goldman v. Weinberger, 475 U.S. 503, 513–14 (1986).

14. Hobbie v. Unemployment Appeals Comm'n. of Florida, 480 U.S. 136, 138 (1987).

15. Shabazz v. O'Lone, 782 F. 2d 416, 417 (1986).

16. O'Lone v. Shabazz, 482 U.S. 342, 355 (1987).

17. Heffron v. Int. Society for Krishna Consc., 452 U.S. 640 (1981).

18. Greer v. Spock, 424 U.S. 828, 839 (1976).

19. Brown v. Glines, 444 U.S. 348, 353 (1980).

20. Ibid., p. 372. Italics in original.

21. Schultz v. Frisby, 619 F. Supp. 792, 795 (1985).

22. Frisby v. Schultz, 487 U.S. 474 (1988).

23. United States v. Kokinda, 110 S. Ct. 3115, 3120 (1991).

24. Renton v. Playtime Theatres, Inc., 475 U.S. 41 (1986).

25. Lehman v. City of Shaker Heights, 418 U.S. 298 (1974).

26. Perry Ed. Assn. v. Perry Local Educator's Assn., 460 U.S. 37, 55 (1983).

27. Texas v. Johnson, 491 U.S. 397, 399 (1989).

28. United States v. Eichman, 110 S. Ct. 2404, 2405 (1990).

29. Gooding v. Wilson, 405 U.S. 518, 520, note 1 (1972).

30. Houston v. Hill, 482 U.S. 451, 465 (1987); Lewis v. New Orleans, 415 U.S. 130 (1974).

31. FCC v. Pacifica Foundation, 438 U.S. 726, 729 (1978).

32. Connick v. Myers, 461 U.S. 138, 156 (1983).

33. Posadas de Puerto Rico Assoc. v. Tourism Co., 478 U.S. 328, 350 (1986).

34. Carey v. Population Services International, 431 U.S. 678, 701 (1977).

35. Shapero v. Kentucky Bar Assn., 486 U.S. 466, 469 (1988).

36. Shapero v. Kentucky Bar Assn., 727 S. W. 2d 299, 301 (1987).

37. Board of Education v. Pico, 457 U.S. 853 (1982).

38. 376 U.S. 254 (1964).

39. 388 U.S. 130, 172 (1967).

40. 403 U.S. 29 (1971).

41. 385 U.S. 374 (1967).

42. 403 U.S. at 54–55.

43. New York Times Co. v. United States, 403 U.S. 713, 724 (1971).

44. Nebraska Press Assn. v. Stuart, 427 U.S. 539, 542 (1976).

45. 457 U.S. 596 (1982).

46. 354 U.S. 476 (1957).

47. Ginsberg v. New York, 390 U.S. 629, 633 (1968).

48. Paris Adult Theatre I v. Slaton, 413 U.S. 49, 73–74 (1973).

49. See Appendix.

50. Keyishian v. Board of Regents, 385 U.S. 589, 592 (1967).

51. Communist Party of Indiana v. Whitcomb, 414 U.S. 441, 442–43 (1974).

52. Beilan v. Board of Education, 357 U.S. 399, 418 (1958).

53. Uphaus v. Wyman, 360 U.S. 72 (1959).

54. NAACP v. Button, 371 U.S. 415, 420 (1963).

55. Elrod v. Burns, 427 U.S. 347 (1976).
56. Rutan v. Republican Party of Illinois, 110 S. Ct. 2729, 2739 (1990).
57. Storer v. Brown, 415 U.S. 724, 728 (1974).
58. Ibid., p. 758. Italics in original.
59. 415 U.S. 767 (1974).
60. Ibid., p. 757.
61. Shapero v. Thompson, 394 U.S. 618, 629 (1969).
62. Haig v. Agee, 453 U.S. 280, 319 (1981).
63. Eisenstadt v. Baird, 405 U.S. 438 (1972).
64. 381 U.S. 479 (1965).
65. 405 U.S. at 453. Italics in original.
66. Moore v. East Cleveland, 431 U.S. 494, 496–97 (1977).
67. Harris v. McRae, 448 U.S. 297, 302 (1980).
68. Paul v. Davis, 424 U.S. 693, 712 (1976).
69. 385 U.S. 545 (1967).
70. Batson v. Kentucky, 476 U.S. 79 (1986).
71. Hunter v. Erickson, 393 U.S. 385, 387 (1969).
72. Green v. County School Board, 391 U.S. 430, 431–32 (1968).
73. Raney v. Board of Education 391 U.S. 443 (1968).
74. Monroe v. Board of Commissioners, 391 U.S. 450, 458 (1968).
75. Evans v. Abney, 396 U.S. 435, 453 (1970).
76. Ibid., at 454–55. Italics in original.
77. Adickes v. Kress & Co., 398 U.S. 144, 146 (1970).
78. Moose Lodge No. 107 v. Irvis, 407 U.S. 163, 184 (1972).
79. Frontiero v. Richardson, 411 U.S. 677, 680 (1973).
80. 429 U.S. 190 (1976).
81. Orr v. Orr, 351 So. 2d 906, 907 (1977).
82. Orr v. Orr, 440 U.S. 268 (1979).
83. 450 U.S. 464 (1981).
84. 401 U.S. 532 (1971).
85. Lalli v. Lalli, 439 U.S. 259, 277 (1978).
86. 462 U.S. 1 (1983).
87. Doe v. Plyler, 458 F. Supp. 569, 571 (1978).
88. Plyler v. Doe, 457 U.S. 202, 211 (1982).
89. Ibid. at 219-20. Italics in original.
90. 439 U.S. 60 (1978).
91. See Appendix.
92. Anderson v. Celebrezze, 460 U.S. 780, 782 (1983).
93. Carey v. Brown, 447 U.S. 455 (1980).
94. Attorney General of New York v. Soto-Lopez, 476 U.S. 898, 906 (1986).
95. Roe v. Norton, 408 F. Supp. 661, 662 (1975).
96. Maher v. Roe, 432 U.S. 464 (1977).
97. Fashing v. Moore, 489 F. Supp. 471, 472 (1980).
98. Clements v. Fashing, 457 U.S. 957, 978 (1982).
99. Tate v. Short, 401 U.S. 395, 397 (1971).
100. 404 U.S. 189 (1971).
101. United States v. MacCollom, 426 U.S. 317, 320 (1976).
102. Malloy v. Hogan, 378 U.S. 1, 5 (1964).
103. See Appendix.
104. Marsh v. Chambers, 463 U.S. 783, 812 (1983).
105. United States v. Eichman, 110 S. Ct. 2404, 2409 (1990).
106. Lewis v. City of New Orleans, 415 U.S. 130, 131 (1974).
107. Brown v. Hartledge, 465 U.S. 45, 54 (1982).
108. Minnesota Bd. of Com. Colleges v. Knight, 465 U.S. 271, 296–97 (1984).
109. Richmond Newspapers, Inc. v. Virginia, 448 U.S. 555, 586–87 (1980).
110. Lakewood v. Plain Dealer Publishing Co., 486 U.S. 750, 757 (1988).
111. Gertz v. Robert Welch, Inc., 418 U.S. 323, 361 (1974).
112. Time, Inc. v. Firestone, 424 U.S. 448, 471 (1976).
113. 492 U.S. 115 (1989).
114. Beal v. Doe, 432 U.S. 438 (1977), Maher v. Roe, 432 U.S. 464 (1977).
115. McLaughlin v. Florida, 379 U.S. 184, 191–92 (1964).
116. Palmer v. Thompson, 403 U.S. 217, 266–67 (1971).
117. 405 U.S. 438 (1972).
118. Evitts v. Lucey, 469 U.S. 387, 405 (1985).

9. Justice Thurgood Marshall

1. Michael D. Davis and Hunter R. Clark, *Thurgood Marshall: Warrior at the Bar, Rebel on the Bench* (New York: Birch Lane Press, Carol Publishing Group, 1992), p. 37.
2. 305 U.S. 337 (1938).
3. Davis and Clark, note 1, p. 101.
4. Constance Baker Motley, "Thurgood Marshall," 68 *New York University Law Review* 208, 210 (1993).
5. Ibid., p. 205.
6. 321 U.S. 649 (1944).

7. Davis and Clark, note 1, p. 138.

8. Ibid., pp. 164–65. For a review of Marshall's arguments before the Supreme Court, see Anthony G. Amsterdam, "Thurgood Marshall's Image of the Blue-eyed Child in Brown," 68 *New York University Law Review*, 226–36 (1993).

9. Davis and Clark, note 1, p. 172.

10. Richard L. Revesz, "Thurgood Marshall's Struggle," 68 *New York University Law Review* 237, 263 (1993).

11. Davis and Clark, note 1, p. 202.

12. Garner v. Louisiana, 368 U.S. 157 (1961). As a civil rights lawyer, Marshall argued 16 cases before the Supreme Court. For a summary, see statement by Attorney General Janet Reno, 114 S. Ct. CXXVIII, CXXIX (1993).

13. For a detailed account of Marshall's confirmation hearings, see Revesz, note 10, pp. 237–67, and Davis and Clark, note 1, pp. 223–43.

14. Davis and Clark, note 1, p. 240.

15. William J. Brennan, Jr., "Justice Thurgood Marshall: Advocate for Human Need in American Jurisprudence," 40 *Maryland Law Review* 390, 395–96 (1993).

16. Davis and Clark, note 1, p. 256.

17. Scott Brewer, "Justice Marshall's Justice Martial," 71 *Texas Law Review* 1121 (1993).

18. Louis H. Pollak, "Thurgood Marshall," 71 *Texas Law Review* 1115, 1117 (1993).

19. Davis and Clark, note 1, p. 265.

20. Trans World Airlines, Inc. v. Hardison, 432 U.S. 63 (1977).

21. See Appendix.

22. Welsh v. United States, 398 U.S. 333 (1970).

23. Gillette v. United States, 401 U.S. 437 (1971).

24. Amalgamated Food Employees Union v. Logan Valley Plaza, 391 U.S. 308, 309 (1968).

25. Lloyd Corp. v. Tanner, 407 U.S. 551 (1972).

26. Hudgens v. NLRB, 424 U.S. 507 (1976).

27. Pruneyard Shopping Center v. Robbins, 447 U.S. 74, 78 (1980).

28. U.S. Postal Service v. Greenburgh Civic Assns., 453 U.S. 114, 117 (1981).

29. Community for Creative Non-Violence v. Watt, 703 F. 2d 586, 587 (1983).

30. Clark v. Community for Creative Non-Violence, 468 U.S. 288 (1984).

31. Ibid., at 309. Italics in original.

32. United States v. Grace, 461 U.S. 171 (1983).

33. McPherson v. Rankin, 786 F. 2d 1233, 1234 (1986).

34. Rankin v. McPherson, 483 U.S. 378, 379–80 (1987).

35. Branti v. Finkel, 445 U.S. 507, 515–16 (1980).

36. Linmark Associates, Inc. v. Willingboro, 431 U.S. 85, 86 (1977).

37. Ibid.

38. Youngs Drug Products Corp. v. Bolger, 526 F. Supp. 823, 825 (1981).

39. Bolger v. Youngs Drug Products Corp., 463 U.S. 60, 71 (1983).

40. Procunier v. Martinez, 416 U.S. 396, 399 (1974).

41. Ward v. Rock Against Racism, 491 U.S. 781, 803 (1989).

42. Rosenbloom v. Metromedia, 403 U.S. 29, 33 (1971).

43. 424 U.S. 448 (1976).

44. 441 U.S. 153 (1979).

45. Press-Enterprise Co. v. Superior Court of Cal., 464 U.S. 501, 503 (1984).

46. The Florida Star v. B.J.F., 491 U.S. 524, 527 (1989).

47. Interstate Circuit v. Dallas, 390 U.S. 676, 678 (1968).

48. Stanley v. Georgia, 394 U.S. 557, 559 (1969).

49. United States v. Thirty-seven Photographs, 402 U.S. 363, 376 (1971).

50. Cole v. Richardson, 405 U.S. 676, 677–79 (1972).

51. Law Students Civil Rights Research Council, Inc. v. Wadmond, 299 F. Supp. 117, 122 (1969).

52. Law Students Civil Rights Research Council, Inc. v. Wadmond, 401 U.S. 154, 164–65 (1971).

53. Brown v. Socialist Workers' '74 Campaign Comm., 459 U.S. 87, 88–89 (1982).

54. 479 U.S. 189 (1986).

55. Tashjian v. Republican Party of Connecticut, 479 U.S. 208, 211, note 1 (1986).

56. Kelley v. Johnson, 425 U.S. 238, 239–40 (1976).

57. H.L. v. Matheson, 450 U.S. 398, 400 (1981).

58. 497 U.S. 417 (1990).

59. Greenholtz v. Nebraska Penal Inmates, 442 U.S. 1, 4 (1979).

60. Vasquez v. Hillery, 474 U.S. 254, 255–56 (1986).

61. 476 U.S. 79 (1986).

62. Holland v. Illinois, 493 U.S. 474, 476 (1990).

63. 498 U.S. 237 (1991).

64. Palmore v. Sidoti, 466 U.S. 429, 431 (1984). Italics in original.

65. Memphis v. Greene, 451 U.S. 100, 102 (1981).

66. 403 U.S. 217 (1971).

67. Personnel Adm'r. of Massachusetts v. Feeney, 442 U.S. 256, 257 (1979).

68. Kirchberg v. Feenstra, 450 U.S. 455, 457, note 1 (1981).

69. Kirchberg v. Feenstra, 430 F. Supp. 642, 644 (1977).

70. Kirchberg v. Feenstra, note 68, 459–60.

71. Rostker v. Goldberg, 453 U.S. 57, 90 (1981).

72. Mathews v. Lucas, 427 U.S. 495, 516–17 (1976).

73. Lucas v. Secretary, Dept. Health, Education and Welfare, 390 F. Supp. 1310 (1975).

74. 427 U.S. at 516.

75. Fiallo v. Bell, 406 F. Supp. 162, 164 (1975).

76. Fiallo v. Bell, 430 U.S. 787, 800 (1977).

77. Foley v. Connelie, 435 U.S. 291, 297 (1978).

78. Bernal v. Fainter, 467 U.S. 216 (1984).

79. Dunn v. Blumstein, 405 U.S. 330, 331 (1972).

80. O'Brien v. Skinner, 414 U.S. 524 (1974).

81. Socialist Workers Party v. Chicago Board of Election, 433 F. Supp. 11, 20 (1977).

82. Illinois Board of Elections v. Socialist Workers Party, 440 U.S. 173, 184 (1979).

83. Police Dept. of Chicago v. Mosley, 408 U.S. 92, 93 (1972).

84. Massachusetts Bd. of Retirement v. Murgia, 427 U.S. 307, 314–15 (1976).

85. Zablocki v. Redhail, 434 U.S. 374, 386 (1978).

86. McGinnis v. Royster, 410 U.S. 263 (1973).

87. 417 U.S. 40 (1974).

88. United States v. Kras, 409 U. S. 434, 438 (1983).

89. San Antonio School District v. Rodriguez, 411 U.S. 1 (1973).

90. Kadramas v. Dickinson Public Schools, 487 U.S. 450, 467 (1988).

91. Benton v. Maryland, 395 U.S. 784, 785 (1969).

92. 302 U.S. 319 (1937).

93. 395 U.S. at 794.

94. 494 U.S. 872 (1990).

95. Bell v. Wolfish, 441 U.S. 520, 573 (1979).

96. Ohralick v. Ohio State Bar Assn., 436 U.S. 447, 476 (1978).

97. Leathers v. Medlack, 499 U.S. 439, 464–65 (1991).

98. 492 U.S. 115, 117 (1989).

99. Jones v. North Carolina Prisoners' Union, 433 U.S. 119 (1977).

100. Bowers v. Hardwick, 478 U.S. 186, 204 (1986).

101. 438 U.S. 265 (1978).

102. 435 U.S. at 302.

103. Richardson v. Ramirez, 418 U.S. 24, 78 (1974).

104. Village of Belle Terre v. Boraas, 416 U.S. 1, 15 (1974).

105. Pennsylvania v. Finley, 481 U.S. 551, 569 (1987).

APPENDIX: VOTING RECORDS IN ADDITIONAL FREEDOM CASES

Column numbers correspond to chapter numbers; i.e., 1 is Justice John M. Harlan; 2 is Chief Justice Charles Evans Hughes; and 3 is Justice Louis D. Brandeis.
    F indicates a vote For and A indicates a vote Against freedom.

	1	2	3

EQUAL PROTECTION OF THE LAW

Blacks on Juries

	1	2	3
In re Wood, 140 U.S. 278 (1891)	A		
Smith v. Mississippi, 162 U.S. 592 (1896)	A		
Williams v. Mississippi, 170 U.S. 213 (1898)	A		
Carter v. Texas, 177 U.S. 442 (1900)	F		
Brownfield v. South Carolina, 189 U.S. 426 (1903)	A		
Rogers v. Alabama, 192 U.S. 226 (1904)	F		
Martin v. Texas, 200 U.S. 316 (1906)	A		
Thomas v. Texas, 212 U.S. 278 (1909)	A		
Aldridge v. United States, 283 U.S. 308 (1931)		F	
Norris v. Alabama, 294 U.S. 587 (1935)			F
Patterson v. Alabama, 294 U.S. 600 (1935)			F
Hollins v. Oklahoma, 295 U.S. 394 (1935)		F	F
Hale v. Kentucky, 303 U.S. 613 (1938)			F

Blacks' Right to Vote

	1	2	3
Giles v. Harris, 189 U.S. 475 (1903)	F		
Guinn v. United States, 238 U.S. 347 (1915)		F	
Nixon v. Condon, 286 U.S. 73 (1932)		F	F
Grovey v. Townsend, 295 U.S. 45 (1935)		A	A
Lane v. Wilson, 307 U.S. 268 (1939)		F	F

	1	2	3
Separate but Equal			
Chesapeake and Ohio Ry. Co. v. Kentucky, 179 U.S. 388 (1900)	F		
Mitchell v. United States, 313 U.S. 80 (1941)			F
A Private White School			
Cumming v. Board of Education, 175 U.S. 528 (1894)	A		
Where Blacks Live			
Buchanan v. Warley, 245 U.S. 60 (1917)			F
Gender			
Mackenzie v. Hare, 239 U.S. 299 (1915)		A	
Breedlove v. Suttles, 302 U.S. 277 (1937)		A	A
Aliens			
Truax v. Raich, 239 U.S. 33 (1915)		F	
Heim v. McCall, 239 U.S. 175 (1915)		A	
Crane v. New York, 239 U.S. 195 (1915)		A	
Terrace v. Thompson, 263 U.S. 197 (1923)			A
Porterfield v. Webb, 263 U.S. 225 (1923)			A
Webb v. O'Brien, 263 U.S. 313 (1923)			A
Frick v. Webb, 263 U.S. 326 (1923)			A
Cockrill v. California, 268 U.S. 258 (1925)			A
Civil Rights Acts			
In re Quarles and Butler, 158 U.S. 532 (1895)	F		
Swafford v. Templeton, 185 U.S. 487 (1902).	F		
James v. Bowman, 190 U.S. 127 (1903)	F		
Giles v. Teasley, 193 U.S. 146 (1904)	F		

THE PURSUIT OF LIBERTY

	1		
Butchers Union Co. v. Crescent City Co., 111 U.S. 746 (1884)	F		
Crowley v. Christensen, 137 U.S. 86 (1890)	A		
Hooper v. California, 155 U.S. 648 (1895)	F		
Allgeyer v. Louisiana, 165 U.S. 578 (1897)	F		
Holden v. Hardy, 169 U.S. 366 (1898)	A		
Hawker v. New York, 170 U.S. 189 (1898)	F		
Nutting v. Massachusetts, 183 U.S. 553 (1902)	F		
Atkins v. Kansas, 191 U.S. 207 (1903)	A		

	1	2	3
Lochner v. New York, 198 U.S. 45 (1905)	A		
Adair v. United States, 208 U.S. 161 (1908)	F		
Muller v. Oregon, 208 U.S. 412 (1908)	A		
Smith v. Texas, 233 U.S. 630 (1914)		F	
Coppage v. Kansas, 236 U. S. 1 (1915)		A	
Adams v. Tanner, 244 U.S. 590 (1917)			A
Yu Cong v. Trinidad, 271 U.S. 500 (1926)			F
Farrington v. Tokushige, 273 U.S. 254 (1927)			F
Buck v. Bell, 274 U.S. 200 (1927)			A

ALIENS AND THE CONSTITUTION

	1	2	3
The Chinese Exclusion Case, 130 U.S. 581 (1889)	A		
Lem Sing v. United States, 158 U.S. 538 (1895)	A		

THE BILL OF RIGHTS AND THE STATES

	1	2	3
Baldwin v. Kansas, 129 U.S. 52 (1889)	F		
Eitenbecker v. Plymouth County, 134 U.S. 31 (1890)	A		
In re Kemmler, 136 U.S. 436 (1890)	A		
Chicago, B. & Q. R. Co. v. Chicago, 166 U.S. 226 (1897)	F		
Hodgson v. Vermont, 168 U.S. 262 (1897)	A		
Bollen v. Nebraska, 176 U.S. 83 (1900)	F		
West v. Louisiana, 194 U.S. 258 (1904)	F		
Lloyd v. Dollison, 194 U.S. 445 (1904)	A		
Patterson v. Colorado, 205 U.S. 454 (1907)	F		
Twining v. New Jersey, 211 U.S. 78 (1908)	F		
Ensign v. Pennsylvania, 227 U.S. 592 (1913)		A	
Minneapolis & St. Louis R. Co., v. Bombolis, 241 U.S. 211 (1916)		A	
Prudential Ins. Co. v. Cheek, 259 U.S. 530 (1922)			A
Gitlow v. New York, 268 U.S. 652 (1925)			F
Fiske v. Kansas, 274 U.S. 380 (1927)			F
Gaines v. Washington, 277 U.S. 81 (1928)			A
Stromberg v. Carlson, 283 U.S. 359 (1931)		F	
Near v. Minnesota, 283 U.S. 697 (1931)			F
Hamilton v. Regents, 293 U.S. 245 (1934)		F	F
Grosjean v. American Press Co., 297 U.S. 233 (1936)			F
DeJonge v. Oregon, 299 U.S. 353 (1937)			F
Herndon v. Lowry, 301 U.S. 242 (1937)			F
Senn v. Tile Layers Union, 301 U.S. 468 (1937)			F
Schneider v. State, 308 U.S. 147 (1939)		F	
Cantwell v. Connecticut, 310 U.S. 296 (1940)		F	

THE CONSTITUTION FOLLOWS THE FLAG

	1	2	3
Hawaii v. Mankichi, 190 U.S. 197 (1903)	F		
Kepner v. United States, 195 U.S. 100 (1904)	F		

	1	2	3
Dorr v. United States, 195 U.S. 138 (1904)	F		
Trono v. United States, 199 U.S. 521 (1905)	F		
Weems v. United States, 217 U.S. 349 (1910)	F		
Dowdell v. United States, 221 U.S. 325 (1911)	F		
Rassmussen v. United States, 197 U.S. 516 (1905)	F		

THE FREE EXERCISE OF RELIGION

	1	2	3
Selective Service Draft Law Cases, 245 U.S. 366 (1918)			F

FREEDOM OF SPEECH

Pamphleteering

	1	2	3
Lovell v. Griffin, 303 U.S. 444 (1938)		F	F
Schneider v. State, 308 U.S. 147 (1939)		F	

Peaceful Picketing

	1	2	3
Senn v. Tile Layers Union, 301 U.S. 468 (1937)		F	
Lauf v. E. G. Skinner Co., 303 U.S. 323 (1938)		F	F
New Negro Alliance v. Grocery Co., 303 U.S. 552 (1938)		F	F
Drivers' Union v. Meadowmoor, 312 U.S. 287 (1941)		A	
A. F. of L. v. Swing, 312 U.S. 321 (1941)		A	

Advocacy of Unpopular Ideas

	1	2	3
Stromberg v. Carlson, 283 U.S. 359 (1931)			F
Herndon v. Georgia, 295 U.S. 441 (1935)		A	F
DeJonge v. Oregon, 299 U.S. 353 (1937)			F

Miscellaneous Speech Cases

	1	2	3
Semler v. Dental Examiners, 294 U.S. 608 (1935)		A	A

FREEDOM OF THE PRESS

	1	2	3
Mutual Film Corp. v. Ohio Industrial Comm'n., 236 U.S. 230 (1915)		A	
Toledo Newspaper Co. v. United States, 247 U.S. 402 (1918)			F
Near v. Minnesota, 283 U.S. 697 (1931)			F
Grosjean v. Am. Press Co., 297 U.S. 233 (1936)		F	

	1	2	3

FREEDOM OF ASSOCIATION

	1	2	3
Waugh v. Mississippi, 237 U.S. 589 (1915)		A	
Texas & N. O. Ry. Co. v. Ry. Clerks, 281 U.S. 548 (1930)		F	F

INVOLUNTARY SERVITUDE

	1	2	3
Bailey v. Alabama, 211 U.S. 452 (1908)	F		
Bailey v. Alabama, 219 U.S. 219 (1911)	F		
United States v. Reynolds, 235 U.S. 133 (1914)		F	
Butler v. Perry, 240 U.S. 328 (1916)		A	

For the columns that follow, 4 is Justice Hugo L. Black; 5 is Justice William O. Douglas; 6 is Justice Frank Murphy; 7 is Chief Justice Earl Warren; 8 is Justice William J. Brennan, Jr; and 9 is Justice Thurgood Marshall.

	4	5	6	7	8	9

THE FREE EXERCISE OF RELIGION

	4	5	6	7	8	9
Schneider v. State, 308 U.S. 147 (1939)	F	F				
Cantwell v. Connecticut, 310 U.S. 296 (1940)	F	F	F			
Minersville District v. Gobitis, 310 U.S. 586 (1940)	A	A	A			
Jones v. Opelika, 316 U.S. 584 (1942)		F				
Jamison v. Texas, 318 U.S. 413 (1943)	F	F	F			
Largent v. Texas, 318 U.S. 418 (1943)	F	F	F			
Murdock v. Pennsylvania, 319 U.S. 105 (1943)	F		F			
Jones v. Opelika, 319 U.S. 103 (1943)	F	F	F			
Douglas v. Jeannette, 319 U.S. 157 (1943)	A	A	A			
Board of Education v. Barnette, 319 U.S. 624 (1943)	F	F	F			
Falbo v. New York, 320 U.S. 549 (1944)	A	A	F			
Prince v. Massachusetts, 321 U.S. 158 (1944)			F			
Follett v. McCormick, 321 U.S. 565 (1944)	F	F				
United States v. Ballard, 322 U.S. 78 (1944)			F			
In re Summers, 325 U.S. 561 (1945)	F	F	F			
Marsh v. Alabama, 326 U.S. 501 (1946)	F		F			
Tucker v. Texas, 326 U.S. 517 (1946)	F	F	F			
Esstep v. United States, 327 U.S. 114 (1946)	F	F	F			
Girouard v. United States, 328 U.S. 61 (1946)	F		F			
Cleveland v. United States, 329 U.S. 14 (1946)	F		F			
Niemotko v. Maryland, 340 U.S. 268 (1951)	F	F				
Kunz v. New York, 340 U.S. 290 (1951)	F	F				
Kredroff v. St. Nicholas Cathedral, 344 U.S. 94 (1952)	F	F				
Fowler v. Rhode Island, 345 U.S. 67 (1953)	F	F				
Poulos v. New Hampshire, 345 U.S. 396 (1953)	F	F				

	4	5	6	7	8	9
Dickinson v. United States, 346 U.S. 389 (1953)	F	F	F			
Witmer v. United States, 348 U.S. 375 (1955)	F	F	A			
Sicurella v. United States, 348 U.S. 385 (1955)	F	F	F			
First United Church v. Los Angeles, 357 U.S. 545 (1958)	F	F	F	F		
Kreshik v. St. Nicholas Cathedral, 363 U.S. 190 (1960)	F	F	F	F		
Braunfeld v. Brown, 366 U.S. 599 (1961)		F		F		
Gallagher v. Crown Kosher Market, 366 U.S. 617 (1961)	A		A	F		
Torcaso v. Watkins, 367 U.S. 488 (1961)		F		F		
Sherbert v. Verner, 374 U.S. 398 (1964)		F		F		
United States v. Seeger, 380 U.S. 163 (1965)	F	F	F	F		
Presbyterian Church v. Hull Church, 393 U.S. 440 (1969)	F	F	F	F	F	
Welsh v. United States, 398 U.S. 333 (1970)	F	F		F	F	
Gillette v. United States, 401 U.S. 437 (1971)	A	F		A	A	
Cruz v. Beto, 405 U.S. 319 (1972)		F		F	F	
Wisconsin v. Yoder, 406 U.S. 205 (1972)		F		F	F	
Johnson v. Robison, 415 U.S. 361 (1974)		F		A	A	
Serbian Eastern Orthodox Church v. Milivojevich, 426 U.S.696 (1976)				F	F	
Wooley v. Maynard, 430 U.S. 705 (1977)				F	F	
Trans World Airlines, Inc. v. Hardison, 432 U.S. 63 (1977)				F		
McDaniel v. Paty, 435 U.S. 618 (1978)				F	F	
Jones v. Wolf, 443 U.S. 595 (1979)					A	
Thomas v. Rev. Bd. Ind. Emp. Sec. Div., 450 U.S. 707 (1981)					F	
United States v. Lee, 455 U.S. 252 (1982).				A	A	
Bob Jones University v. United States, 461 U.S. 574 (1983)				A	A	
Goldman v. Weinberger, 475 U.S. 503 (1986)					F	
Bowen v. Roy, 476 U.S. 693 (1986)				F	F	
Hobbie v. Unemployment App. Comm'n., 480 U.S. 136 (1987)				F		
O'Lone v. Estate of Shabazz, 482 U.S. 342 (1987)					F	
Lyng v. N.W. Indian Cemetery Prot. Assn., 485 U.S. 439 (1988)						F
Frazee v. Illinois Empl. Sec. Dept., 489 U.S. 829 (1989)					F	F
Employment Div. v. Smith, 485 U.S. 660 (1988)					F	F
Employment Div. v. Smith, 494 U.S. 872 (1990)					F	F

FREEDOM OF SPEECH

Pamphleteering and Solicitation

	4	5	6	7	8	9
Martin v. Struthers, 319 U.S. 141 (1943)		F				
Hartzel v. United States, 322 U.S. 680 (1944)	F	A				
Staub v. City of Baxley, 355 U.S. 313 (1958)	F	F		F	F	
Talley v. California, 362 U.S. 60 (1960)	F	F		F	F	
Ashton v. Kentucky, 384 U.S. 195 (1966)	F			F	F	
Organization for a Better Austin v. Keefe, 402 U.S. 415 (1971)		F			F	F
Hynes v. Mayor of Oradell, 425 U.S. 610 (1976)					F	F
Brown v. Glines, 444 U.S. 348 (1980)					F	
Sec. of Navy v. Huff, 444 U.S. 453 (1980)					F	

	4	5	6	7	8	9
Schaumberg, Village of, v. Citizens for Better Environment, 444 U.S. 620 (1980)					F	F
Heffron v. Int. Soc. for Krishna Consc., Inc., 452 U.S. 640 (1981)					F	F
Sec. of State, Md. v. J. H. Munson Co., Inc., 467 U.S. 947 (1988)					F	F
Riley v. Nat. Fed. of Blind, 487 U.S. 781 (1988)						F
United States v. Kokinda, 497 U.S. 720 (1990)						F

Picketing and Parading

	4	5	6	7	8	9
Thornhill v. Alabama, 310 U.S. 88 (1940)		F				
Carlson v. California, 310 U.S. 106 (1940)		F				
Drivers Union v. Meadowmoor, Co., 312 U.S. 287 (1941)		F				
A. F. of L. v. Swing, 312 U.S. 321 (1941)	F	F	F			
Cox v. New Hampshire, 312 U.S. 569 (1941)	A	A	A			
Carpenters Union v. Ritter's Cafe, 315 U.S. 722 (1942)		F	F			
Bakery Drivers Local v. Wohl, 315 U.S. 769 (1942)			F			
Cafeteria Wkrs. Union v. Angelos, 320 U.S. 293 (1943)	F	F	F			
Giboney v. Empire Storage & Ice, 336 U.S. 490 (1949)		A	A			
Hughes v. Superior Court, 339 U.S. 460 (1950)	A					
Teamsters Union v. Hanke, 339 U.S. 470 (1950)	F					
Building and Service Union v. Gazzam, 339 U.S. 532 (1950)	A					
Plumbers Union v. Graham, 345 U.S. 192 (1953)	F	F				
Teamsters Union v. Vogt, Inc., 354 U.S. 284 (1957)	F	F		A		
Edwards v. South Carolina, 372 U.S. 229 (1963)		F		F		
Henry v. Rock Hill, 376 U.S. 776 (1964)	F	F		F	F	
Cox v. Louisiana, 379 U.S. 536 (1965)	F	F		F	F	
Cox v. Louisiana, 379 U.S. 559 (1965)		F		F		
Adderley v. Florida, 385 U.S. 39 (1966)	A			F		
Cameron v. Johnson, 390 U.S. 611 (1968)	A	A		A	A	A
Shuttlesworth v. Birmingham, 394 U.S. 147 (1969)	F	F			F	F
Grayned v. City of Rockford, 408 U.S. 104 (1972)		F			A	A
Am. Radio Assoc., Inc. v. Mobile S. S. Assn., 419 U.S. 215 (1974)					F	F
Nationalist Socialist Party v. Skokie, 432 U.S. 43 (1977)					F	F
N.A.A.C.P. v. Claiborne Hdwe. Co., 458 U.S. 886 (1982)					F	F
United States v. Grace, 461 U.S. 171 (1983)					F	F
Frisby v. Schultz, 487 U.S. 474 (1988)					F	F

Public Employees' Right to Advocate

	4	5	6	7	8	9
United Public Workers v. Mitchell, 330 U.S. 75 (1947)	F	F				
Pickering v. Board of Education, 391 U.S. 563 (1968)	F	F		F	F	F
C. S. C. v. Letter Carriers, 413 U.S. 548 (1973)		F			F	F
Broadrick v. Oklahoma, 413 U.S. 601 (1973)		F			F	F
Mt. Healthy Cty. Bd. of Education v. Doyle, 429 U.S. 274 (1977)					F	F
Givhan v. Western Line Consol. Sch. Dist., 439 U.S. 410 (1979)					F	F
Connick v. Myers, 461 U.S. 138 (1983)					F	F

	4	5	6	7	8	9
Minn. Bd. for Comm. Colleges v. Knight, 465 U.S. 271 (1984)					F	A
Rankin v. McPherson, 483 U.S. 378 (1987)					F	F

Advocacy of Unpopular Ideas (Offensive Speech)

	4	5	6	7	8	9
Taylor v. Mississippi, 319 U.S. 583 (1943)	F	F	F			
Bridges v. Wixon, 326 U.S. 135 (1945)	F	F	F			
Terminiello v. Chicago, 337 U.S. 1 (1949)	F					
Yates v. United States, 354 U.S. 298 (1957)	F	F		F		
Wood v. Georgia, 370 U.S. 375 (1962)	F	F			F	
Brown v. Louisiana, 383 U.S. 131 (1966)		F		F	F	
Bond v. Floyd, 385 U.S. 116 (1966)	F	F		F		
United States v. O'Brien, 391 U.S. 367 (1968)	A	F		A	A	
Tinker v. Des Moines Sch. District, 393 U.S. 503 (1969)		F		F	F	F
Street v. New York, 394 U.S. 576 (1969)	A				F	F
Watts v. United States, 394 U.S. 705 (1969)	F	F		F	F	F
Brandenburg v. Ohio, 395 U.S. 444 (1969)	F	F		F	F	F
Bachellar v. Maryland, 397 U.S. 564 (1970)	F	F			F	F
Cohen v. California, 403 U.S. 15 (1971)	A					F
Gooding v. Wilson, 405 U.S. 518 (1972)			F			F
Colton v. Kentucky, 407 U.S. 104 (1972)			F	A		
Plummer v. City of Columbus, 414 U.S. 2 (1973)			F		F	F
Norwell v. City of Cincinnati, 414 U.S. 14 (1973)			F		F	F
Hess v. Indiana, 414 U.S. 105 (1973)					F	F
Lewis v. New Orleans, 415 U.S. 130 (1974)			F		F	F
Smith v. Goguen, 415 U.S. 566 (1974)					F	F
Eaton v. City of Tulsa, 415 U.S. 697 (1974)			F		F	F
Parker v. Levy, 417 U.S. 733 (1974)			F		F	
Spence v. Washington, 418 U.S. 405 (1974)			F		F	F
F. C. C. v. Pacifica Foundation, 438 U.S. 726 (1978)						F
Consolidated Edison v. PSC., 447 U.S. 531 (1980)					F	F
Bethel School Dist. v. Fraser, 478 U.S. 675 (1986)					A	F
Houston v. Hill, 482 U.S. 451 (1987)					F	F
Texas v. Johnson, 491 U.S. 397 (1989)						F
United States v. Eichman, 496 U.S. 310 (1990)						F

Commercial Speech

	4	5	6	7	8	9
Valentime v. Chrestensen, 316 U.S. 52 (1942)	A	A	A			
Railway Express v. New York, 336 U.S. 106 (1949)	A	A	A			
Bigelow v. Virginia, 421 U.S. 809 (1975)					F	F
Va. Pharmacy Bd. v. Va. Cit. Consumer Council, 425 U.S. 748 (1976)					F	F
Linmark Assoc., Inc. v. Willingboro, 431 U.S. 85 (1977)					F	
Bates v. State Bar of Arizona, 433 U.S. 350 (1977)					F	F
In re Primus, 436 U.S. 412 (1978)						F
Friedman v. Rogers, 440 U.S. 1 (1979)					A	F
Central Hudson G. and E. v. Pub. Ser. Com., 447 U.S. 557 (1980)					F	F
Metromedia, Inc. v. San Diego, 453 U.S. 490 (1981)					F	F

	4	5	6	7	8	9
In re R. M. J., 455 U.S. 191 (1982)					F	F
Zauderer v. Off. of Disc. Counsel, 471 U.S. 626 (1985)					F	F
Posadas de Puerto Rico Assoc. v. Tourism Co.,						
478 U.S. 328 (1986)						F
Shapero v. Kentucky Bar Assn., 486 U.S. 466 (1988)					F	
Bd. of Trustees, St. Univ. of N. Y. v. Fox,						
492 U.S. 469 (1989)					F	F
Peel v. Atty. Reg. & Disc. Com., 496 U.S. 91 (1990)					F	F

Places to Speak

	4	5	6	7	8	9
Amalg. Food Empl. Union v. Logan Valley Plaza,						
391 U.S. 308 (1968)	A	F		F	F	
Flower v. United States, 407 U.S. 197 (1972)		F			F	F
Lloyd Corp. v Tanner, 407 U.S. 551 (1972)		F			F	
Lehman v. Shaker Heights, 418 U.S. 298 (1974)						F
S. E. Promotions, Ltd. v. Conrad, 420 U.S. 546 (1975)					F	F
Greer v. Spock, 424 U.S. 828 (1976)					F	F
Young v. American Mini Theatres, 427 U.S. 50 (1976)					F	F
Madison Sch. Dist. v. Wisc. Empl. Rel. Comm'n.,						
429 U.S. 167 (1976)					F	F
Pruneyard Shopping Center v. Robbins, 447 U.S. 74 (1980)					F	
Shad v. Mount Ephraim, 452 U.S. 61 (1981)					F	F
U.S. Postal Service v. Greenburgh Civic Assn.,						
453 U.S. 114 (1981)					A	
Widmar v. Vincent, 454 U.S. 263 (1981)					F	F
Perry Ed. Assn. v. Perry Local Ed. Assn.,						
460 U.S. 37 (1983)						F
City Council v. Taxpayers for Vincent, 466 U.S. 789 (1984)					F	F
Clark v. Comm. for Creative Non-Violence,						
468 U.S. 288 (1984)					F	
United States v. Albertini, 472 U.S. 675 (1985)					F	F
Cornelius v. NAACP Leg. Def. & Ed. Fund,						
473 U.S. 788 (1985)					F	
Renton v. Playtime Theatres, 475 U.S. 41 (1986)					F	F
Airport Comm'rs v. Jews for Jesus, Inc., 482 U.S. 569 (1987)					F	F
Boos v. Barry, 485 U.S. 312 (1988)					A	A
United States v. Kokinda, 497 U.S. 720 (1990)					F	F

Miscellaneous Speech Cases

	4	5	6	7	8	9
Thomas v. Collins, 323 U.S. 516 (1945)	F	F	F			
Saia v. New York, 334 U.S. 558 (1948)	F	F	F			
Kovacs v. Cooper, 336 U.S. 77 (1949)	F	F	F			
Public Utilities Comm'n. v. Pollak, 343 U.S. 451 (1952)	A					
United States v. Harriss, 347 U.S. 612 (1954)	F	F		A		
Garrison v. Louisiana, 379 U.S. 64 (1964)	F	F		F	F	
Stanford v. Texas, 379 U.S. 476 (1965)	F	F		F	F	
Lamont v. Postmaster General, 381 U.S. 301 (1965)	F	F		F		
Carroll v. Pres. & Comrs. of Princess Anne,						
393 U.S. 175 (1968)	F	F		F	F	F
Schacht v. United States, 398 U.S. 58 (1970)	F	F			F	F

	4	5	6	7	8	9
California v. LaRue, 409 U.S. 109 (1972)					F	F
Procunier v. Martinez, 416 U.S. 396 (1974)				F	F	
Doran v. Salem Inn., 422 U.S. 922 (1975)					F	F
Buckley v. Valeo, 424 U.S. 1 (1976)					F	F
Abood v. Det. Bd. of Ed., 431 U.S. 209 (1977)					F	F
First Nat. Bank of Boston v. Bellotti, 435 U.S. 765 (1978)					A	A
Bell v. Wolfish, 441 U.S. 520 (1979)					F	
Cons. Edison Co. v. Pub. Ser. Comm'n. 447 U.S. 530 (1980)					F	F
Brown v. Hartlage, 456 U.S. 45 (1982)					F	F
Board of Ed. v. Pico, 457 U.S. 853 (1982)						F
FEC v. Nat. Conservative PAC., 470 U.S. 480 (1985)					F	A
Wayte v. United States, 470 U.S. 598 (1985)					F	F
Pacific G. & E. Co. v. Pub. Util. Comm'n., 475 U.S. 1 (1986)					F	F
F. E. C. v. Massachusetts Citizens for Life, 479 U.S. 238 (1986)					F	F
Meese v. Keene, 481 U.S. 465 (1987)					F	F
Turner v. Safley, 482 U.S. 78 (1987)					F	F
Keller v. State Bar of California, 496 U.S. 1 (1990)					F	F
Rust v. Sullivan, 500 U.S. 173 (1991)						F
Lehnert v. Ferris Faculty Assn., 500 U.S. 507 (1991)						A
Barnes v. Glen Theatre, Inc., 501 U.S. 560 (1991)						F

FREEDOM OF ASSOCIATION

Affidavits and Oaths

	4	5	6	7	8	9
Communications Assn. v. Douds, 339 U.S. 382 (1950)	F					
Garner v. Los Angeles Board, 341 U.S. 716 (1951)	F	F				
Wieman v. Updegraff, 344 U.S. 183 (1952)	F	F				
First Unit. Church v. Los Angeles, 357 U.S. 545 (1958)	F	F		F		
Cramp v. Bd. of Pub. Instr., 368 U.S. 278 (1961)	F	F		F		
Baggett v. Bullitt, 377 U.S. 360 (1964)	F	F		F		
Elfbrandt v. Russell, 384 U.S. 11 (1966)	F			F		
Keyishian v. Board of Regents, 385 U.S. 589 (1967)	F	F				
Whitehill v. Elkins, 389 U.S. 54 (1967)	F				F	F
Schneider v. Smith, 390 U.S. 17 (1968)	F		F	F		
Cole v. Richardson, 405 U.S. 676 (1972)				F		
Socialist Labor Party v. Gilligan, 406 U.S. 583 (1972)			F		F	F
Communist Pty. of Indiana v. Whitcomb, 414 U.S. 441 (1974)			F			F

Blacklisting and Punishment for Membership

	4	5	6	7	8	9
Anti-Facist Committee v. McGrath, 341 U.S. 123 (1951)		F				
Adler v. Bd. of Education, 342 U.S. 485 (1952)	F	F				
Carlson v. Landon, 342 U.S. 524 (1952)	F	F				
Harisiades v. Shaughnessy, 342 U.S. 580 (1952)	F	F				

	4	5	6	7	8	9
Galvan v. Press, 347 U.S. 522 (1954)	F	F	A			
Fleming v. Nestor, 363 U.S. 603 (1960)	F			F	F	
Communist Party v. Control Board, 367 U.S. 1 (1961)		F		F	F	
Scales v. United States, 367 U.S. 203 (1961)				F	F	
Noto v. United States, 367 U.S. 290 (1961)	F	F		F	F	
United States v. Robel, 389 U.S. 258 (1967)	F	F		F		
Kleindienst v. Mandel, 408 U.S. 753 (1972)			F		F	F

Associational Privacy

	4	5	6	7	8	9
United States v. Rumely, 345 U.S. 41 (1953)	F	F				
Schware v. Bd. of Bar Examiners, 353 U.S. 232 (1957)	F	F		F	F	
Konigsberg v. State Bar, 353 U.S. 252 (1957)	F	F		F	F	
Watkins v. United States, 354 U.S. 178 (1957)	F	F		F	F	
Sweezy v. New Hampshire, 354 U.S. 234 (1957)	F	F		F	F	
Beilan v. Board of Education, 357 U.S. 399 (1958)				F		
NAACP v. Alabama, 357 U.S. 449 (1958)		F		F		
Barenblatt v. United States, 360 U.S. 109 (1959)		F		F	F	
Uphaus v. Wyman, 360 U.S. 72 (1959)					F	
Bates v. Little Rock, 361 U.S. 516 (1960)	F	F		F		
Uphaus v. Wyman, 364 U.S. 388 (1960)	F	F		F	A	
Shelton v. Tucker, 364 U.S. 479 (1960)		F		F		
Wilkinson v. United States, 365 U.S. 399 (1961)		F		F	F	
Braden v. United States, 365 U.S. 431 (1961)	F	F		F	F	
Konigsberg v. State Bar, 366 U.S. 36 (1961)		F		F	F	
In re Anastaplo, 366 U.S. 82 (1961)	F	F		F		
Louisiana v. NAACP, 366 U.S. 293 (1961)	F			F	F	
Gibson v. Florida Leg. Committee, 372 U.S. 539 (1963)				F	F	
NAACP v. Alabama, 377 U.S. 288 (1964)	F	F		F	F	
DeGregory v. New Hampshire Atty. Gen., 383 U.S. 825 (1966)	F			F	F	
Baird v. State Bar of Arizona, 401 U.S. 1 (1971)		F			F	F
In re Stolar, 401 U.S. 23 (1971)	F	F			F	F
Law Students Res. Council v. Wadmond, 401 U.S. 154 (1971)		F			F	
Brown v. Socialist Workers Party, 459 U.S. 87 (1982)					F	
Seattle Times Co. v. Rhinehart, 467 U.S. 20 (1984)					F	F

For Advancement of Legal Goals

	4	5	6	7	8	9
NAACP v. Button, 371 U.S. 415 (1963)			F	F		
Railroad Trainmen v. Virginia Bar, 377 U.S. 1 (1964)			F	F	F	
United Mine Workers v. Illinois Bar, 389 U.S. 217 (1967)			F	F	F	F
United Transp. Union v. Michigan Bar, 401 U.S. 576 (1971)			F		F	F

Public Employees and Political Association

	4	5	6	7	8	9
Elrod v. Burns, 427 U.S. 347 (1976)						F
Branti v. Finkel, 445 U.S. 507 (1980)					F	F
Rutan v. Republican Pty. of Illinois, 497 U.S. 62 (1990)						F

4 5 6 7 8 9

Political Parties: Ballot Access and New Members

	4	5	6	7	8	9
Williams v. Rhodes, 393 U.S. 23 (1968)			F		A	F
Rosario v. Rockefeller, 410 U.S. 752 (1973)			F		F	F
Kusper v. Pontikes, 414 U.S. 51 (1973)			F		F	F
Storer v. Brown, 415 U.S. 724 (1974)			F		F	F
Cousins v. Wigoda, 419 U.S. 477 (1975)					F	F
Democratic Pty. of U.S. v. Wisconsin, 450 U.S. 107 (1981)					F	F
Anderson v. Celebrezze, 460 U.S. 780 (1983)					F	F
Munro v. Socialist Wkrs. Party, 479 U.S. 189 (1986)					F	
Tashjian v. Republican Pty. of Conn., 479 U.S. 208 (1986)					F	
Eu v. San Francisco Dem. County Cent. Committee, 489 U.S. 214 (1989)					F	F

Miscellaneous Association Cases

	4	5	6	7	8	9
United States v. Auto Workers, 352 U.S. 567 (1957)	F	F		F	A	
Lathrop v. Donohue, 367 U.S. 820 (1961)		F				
Stanford v. Texas, 379 U.S. 476 (1965)	F	F		F	F	
Coates v. Cincinnati, 402 U.S. 611 (1971)	F	F			F	F
Healy v. James, 408 U.S. 169 (1972)		F			F	F
Jones v. N.C. Prisoners' Union, 433 U.S. 119 (1977)					F	
Citizens Against Rent Control v. Berkeley, 454 U.S. 290 (1981)					F	F
FEC v. Nat. Right to Work Com., 459 U.S. 197 (1982)					A	A
Roberts v. United States Jaycees, 468 U.S. 609 (1984)					A	A
Chicago Teachers Union v. Hudson, 475 U.S. 292 (1986)					F	F
Bd. of Dir. of Rotary Intl. v. Rotary Club, 481 U.S. 537 (1987)					A	A
Lyng v. UAW, 485 U.S. 360 (1988)					F	F
New York State Club Assn. v. New York City, 487 U.S. 1 (1988)					A	A
Dallas v. Stanglin, 490 U.S. 19 (1989)					A	A

FREEDOM OF THE PRESS

Contempt of Court

	4	5	6	7	8	9
Bridges v. California, 314 U.S. 252 (1941)			F			
Pennekamp v. Florida, 328 U.S. 331 (1946)	F					
Craig v. Harney, 331 U.S. 367 (1947)	F					

Libel

	4	5	6	7	8	9
New York Times v. Sullivan, 376 U.S. 254 (1964)				F		
Linn v. Plant Guard Workers, 383 U.S. 53 (1966)	F	F		F	A	

	4	5	6	7	8	9
Rosenblatt v. Baer, 383 U.S. 75 (1966)	F			F	F	
Time, Inc. v. Hill, 385 U.S. 374 (1967)	F	F		A		
Curtis Pub. Co. v. Butts, 388 U.S. 130 (1967)			F	F		
Beckley Newspapers v. Hanks, 389 U.S. 81 (1967)	F	F		F	F	F
St. Amant v. Thompson, 390 U.S. 727 (1968)	F	F		F	F	F
Greenbelt Pub. Assn. v. Bresler, 398 U.S. 6 (1970)	F	F		F	F	F
Monitor Patriot Co. v. Roy, 401 U.S. 265 (1971)	F	F			F	F
Time, Inc. v. Pape, 401 U.S. 279 (1971)	F	F			F	F
Ocala Star-Banner Co. v. Damron, 401 U.S. 295 (1971)	F	F			F	F
Rosenbloom v. Metromedia, 403 U.S. 29 (1971)	F					
Letter Carriers v. Austin, 418 U.S. 264 (1974)			F		F	F
Gertz v. Robert Welch, Inc., 418 U.S. 323 (1974)					F	A
Time, Inc. v. Firestone, 424 U.S. 448 (1976)					F	
Herbert v. Lando, 441 U.S. 153 (1979)					F	
Bose Corp. v. Consumers Union, 466 U.S. 485 (1984)					F	F
McDonald v. Smith, 472 U.S. 479 (1985)					F	F
Dun and Bradstreet, Inc. v. Greenmoss Bldrs., Inc., 472 U.S. 749 (1985)					F	F
Philadelphia Newspapers, Inc. v. Hepps, 475 U.S. 767 (1986)					F	F
Hustler Magazine v. Falwell, 485 U.S. 46 (1988)					F	F
Harte-Hanks Comm. v. Connaughton, 491 U.S. 657 (1989)					F	F
Milkovich v. Lorain Journal Co., 497 U.S.1 (1990)					F	F
Masson v. New Yorker Magazine, Inc., 501 U.S. 496 (1991)						A

Punishment for and Prior Restraint of Publication

	4	5	6	7	8	9
Mills v. Alabama, 384 U.S. 214 (1966)	F		F	F		
New York Times Co. v. United States, 403 U.S. 713 (1971)						F
Pitsburgh Press Co. v. Human Rel. Comm'n., 413 U.S. 376 (1973)					A	A
Pell v. Procunier, 417 U.S. 817 (1974)					F	F
Saxbe v. Washington Post, 417 U.S. 843 (1974)					F	F
Miami Herald Pub. Co. v. Tornillo, 418 U.S. 241 (1974)	F				F	F
Cox Broadcasting Corp. v. Cohn, 420 U.S. 469 (1975)	F				F	F
Nebraska Press Assn. v. Stuart, 427 U.S. 539 (1976)						F
Oklahoma Publishing Co. v. District Court, 430 U.S. 308 (1977)					F	F
Zacchini v. Scrips-Howard Broadcasting Co., 433 U.S. 562 (1977)					F	F
Landmark Com., Inc. v. Virginia, 435 U.S. 829 (1978)						F
Houchins v. KQED. Inc, 438 U.S. 1 (1978)					F	
Smith v. Daily Mail Pub. Co., 443 U.S. 97 (1979)					F	F
Snepp v. United States, 444 U.S. 507 (1980)					F	F
Richmond Newspapers, Inc. v. Virginia, 448 U.S. 555 (1980)					F	F
Globe Newspaper Co. v. Superior Court, 457 U.S. 596 (1982)						F
Press-Enterprise Co. v. Superior Ct., 464 U.S. 501 (1984)					F	F
Seattle Times Co. v. Rhinehart, 467 U.S. 20 (1984)					A	A
FCC v. League of Women Voters, 468 U.S. 364 (1984)					F	F

	4	5	6	7	8	9
Regan v. Time, Inc., 468 U.S. 641 (1984)					F	F
Press-Enterprise Co. v. Superior Ct., 478 U.S. 1 (1986)					F	F
Hazelwood Sch. Dist. v. Kuhlmeier, 484 U.S. 260 (1988)					F	F
City of Lakewood v. Plain Dealer Pub., 486 U.S. 750 (1988)					F	F
The Florida Star v. B. J. F., 491 U.S. 524 (1989)					F	
Butterworth v. Smith, 494 U.S. 625 (1990)					F	F

Obscenity

	4	5	6	7	8	9
Gelling v. Texas, 343 U.S. 960 (1952)	F	F				
Butler v. Michigan, 352 U.S. 380 (1957)	F	F	F	F		
Kingsley Books, Inc. v. Brown, 354 U.S. 436 (1957)	F	F	F	F		
Roth v. United States, 354 U.S. 476 (1957)	F		A	A		
Kingsley Pictures Corp. v. Regents, 360 U.S. 684 (1959)		F	F	F		
Smith v. California, 361 U.S. 147 (1959)		F	F	F		
Times Film Corp. v. Chicago, 365 U.S. 43 (1961)	F	F	F	F		
Marcus v. Search Warrant, 367 U.S. 717 (1961)	F	F	F	F		
Bantam Books, Inc. v. Sullivan, 372 U.S. 58 (1963)	F	F	F	F		
Jacobellis v. Ohio, 378 U.S. 184 (1964)	F	F	A	F		
A Quantity of Books v. Kansas, 378 U.S. 205 (1964)	F	F	F	F		
Freedman v. Maryland, 380 U.S. 51 (1965)	F	F	F	F		
Memoirs v. Massachusetts, 383 U.S. 413 (1966)	F	F	F	F		
Miskin v. New York, 383 U.S. 502 (1966)	F	F	A	A		
Ginzburg v. United States, 383 U.S. 463 (1966)		F	A	A		
Redrup v. New York, 386 U.S. 767 (1967)	F	F	F	F		
Teitel Film Corp. v. Cusack, 390 U.S. 139 (1968)	F	F	F	F	F	
Ginsberg v. New York, 390 U.S. 629 (1968)	F	F	A	A	A	
Interstate Circuit v. Dallas, 390 U.S. 676 (1968)	F		F	F		
Rabeck v. New York, 391 U.S. 462 (1968)	F	F	F	F	F	
Lee Art Theatre v. Virginia, 392 U.S. 636 (1968)	F	F	F	F	F	
Stanley v. Georgia, 394 U.S. 557 (1969)	F		F	F		
Blount v. Rizzi, 400 U.S. 410 1971)	F	F			F	F
United States v. Reidel, 402 U.S. 351 (1971)	F	F			A	A
United States v. Thirty-seven Photographs, 402 U.S. 363 (1971)	F	F			A	
Kois v. Wisconsin, 408 U.S. 229 (1972)		F			F	F
Miller v. California, 413 U.S. 15 (1973)		F			F	F
Paris Adult Theatre I v. Slaton, 413 U.S. 49 (1973)					F	F
Kaplan v. California, 413 U.S. 115 (1973)		F			F	F
United States v. 12-200 ft Reels of Film, 413 U.S. 123 (1973)		F			F	F
United States v. Orito, 413 U.S. 139 (1973)		F			F	F
Heller v. New York, 413 U.S. 483 (1973)		F			F	F
Roaden v. Kentucky, 413 U.S. 496 (1973)		F			F	F
Hamling v. United States, 418 U.S. 87 (1974)		F			F	F
Jenkins v. Georgia, 418 U.S. 153 (1974)					F	F
Erznoznik v. City of Jacksonville, 422 U.S. 205 (1975)		F			F	F
McKinney v. Alabama, 424 U.S. 669 (1976)					F	F
Marks v. United States, 430 U.S. 188 (1977)					F	F
Smith v. United States, 431 U.S. 291 (1977)					F	F
Splawn v. California, 431 U.S. 595 (1977)					F	F
Ward v. Illinois, 431 U.S. 767 (1977)					F	F
Vance v. Universal Amusement Co., 445 U.S. 308 (1980)					F	F

	4	5	6	7	8	9
Flynt v. Ohio, 451 U.S. 619 (1981)					F	F
California v. Mitchell Bros. Santa Anna Theater, 454 U.S. 90 (1981)					F	F
New York v. Ferber, 458 U.S. 747 (1982)					A	A
Maryland v. Macon, 472 U.S. 463 (1985)					F	F
Brockett v. Spokane Arcades, Inc., 472 U.S. 491 (1985)					F	F
New York v. P. J. Video, Inc., 475 U.S. 868 (1986)					F	F
Acara v. Cloud Books, Inc., 478 U.S. 697 (1986)					F	F
Pope v. Illinois, 481 U.S. 497 (1987)					F	F
Massachusetts v. Oakes, 491 U.S. 576 (1989)					F	F
Sable Comm. of Cal. Inc v. FCC., 492 U.S. 115 (1989)					F	F
FW/PBS, Inc. v. Dallas, 493 U.S. 215 (1990)					F	F
Osborne v. Ohio, 495 U.S. 103 (1990)					F	F

Miscellaneous Press Cases

	4	5	6	7	8	9
Associated Press v. United States, 326 U.S. 1 (1945)	A	A				
Winters v. New York, 333 U.S. 507 (1948)	F	F	F			
Red Lion Broadcasting Co. v. F. C. S., 395 U.S. 367 (1969)	A	A		A	A	A
Breard v. Alexandria, 341 U.S. 622 (1951)	F	F				
Joseph Burstyn, Inc. v. Wilson, 343 U.S. 495 (1952)	F	F				
Branzburg v. Hayes, 408 U.S. 665 (1972)					F	F
Papish v. Univ. of Missouri Curators, 410 U.S. 667 (1973)			F		F	F
C. B. S. v. Democratic Party, 412 U.S. 94 (1973)			F		A	A
Zurcher v. Stanford Daily, 436 U.S. 547 (1978)						F
Minneapolis Star v. Minnesota Comm'r. of Revenue, 460 U.S. 575 (1983).					F	F
Arkansas Writer's Proj., Inc. v. Ragland, 481 U.S. 221 (1987)					F	F
Cohen v. Cowles Media Co., 501 U.S. 663 (1991)					F	
Leathers v. Medlock, 111 S. Ct. 1438 (1991)					F	

THE PURSUIT OF LIBERTY

The Right to Travel

	4	5	6	7	8	9
Edwards v. California, 314 U.S. 160 (1941)	F		F			
Kent v. Dulles, 357 U.S. 116 (1958)				F	F	
Dayton v. Dulles, 357 U.S. 144 (1958)	F	F		F	F	
New York v. O'Neill, 359 U.S. 1 (1958)	F	F		A	A	
Aptheker v. Secretary of State, 378 U.S. 500 (1964)				F	F	
Zemel v. Rusk, 381 U.S. 1 (1965)	F	F		A	A	
United States v. Guest, 383 U.S. 745 (1966)			F	F	F	
Shapiro v. Thompson, 394 U.S. 618 (1969)			F	A	F	F
Sosna v. Iowa, 419 U.S. 393 (1975)				A	F	F
California v. Torres, 435 U.S. 1 (1978)					F	
California v. Azavorian, 439 U. S 170 (1978)					A	A
Haig v. Agee, 453 U.S. 280 (1981)					F	F
Zobel v. Williams, 457 U.S. 55 (1982)					F	F
Atty. General of N. Y. v. Soto-Lopez, 476 U.S. 898 (1986)					F	F

The Right to Work

The Right of Privacy

	4	5	6	7	8	9
The Right to Work						
Barsky v. Regents, 347 U.S. 442 (1954)				F	F	
The Right of Privacy						
Armstrong v. Manzo, 380 U.S. 545 (1965)	F	F			F	F
Griswold v. Connecticut, 381 U.S. 479 (1965)					F	F
Wisconsin v. Constantineau, 400 U.S. 433 (1971)	A	F			F	F
Stanley v. Illinois, 405 U.S. 645 (1972)		F			F	F
Morrissey v. Brewer, 408 U.S. 471 (1972)		F			F	F
Roe v. Wade, 410 U.S. 113 (1973)					F	F
U.S. Dept. Agriculture v. Moreno, 413 U.S. 528 (1973)		F			F	F
Cleveland Bd. of Ed. v. La Fleur, 414 U.S. 632 (1974)					F	F
Wolff v. McDonnell, 418 U.S. 539 (1974)		F			F	F
O'Connor v. Donaldson, 422 U.S. 563 (1975)		A			F	F
Turner v. Dept. Employ. Security, 423 U.S. 44 (1975)					F	F
Paul v. Davis, 424 U.S. 696 (1976)					F	F
Kelly v. Johnson, 425 U.S. 238 (1976)		F				
Meachum v. Fano, 427 U.S. 215 (1976)					F	F
Planned Parenthood of Missouri v. Danforth, 428 U.S. 52 (1976)					F	F
Whalen v. Roe, 429 U.S. 589 (1977)					F	F
Moore v. East Cleveland, 431 U.S. 494 (1977)					F	F
Carey v. Population Ser. Int., 431 U.S. 678 (1977)					F	F
Beal v. Doe, 432 U.S. 438 (1977)					F	F
Maher v. Doe, 432 U.S. 464 (1977)					F	F
Bellotti v. Baird, 443 U.S. 622 (1979)					F	F
Vitek v. Jones, 445 U.S. 480 (1980)					F	F
Harris v. McRae, 448 U.S. 297 (1980)					F	F
H. L. v. Matheson, 450 U.S. 398 (1981)					F	
Santosky v. Kramer, 455 U.S. 745 (1982)					F	F
Youngberg v. Romeo, 457 U.S. 307 (1982)					F	F
Akron v. Akron Center, 462 U.S. 416 (1983)					F	F
Planned Parenthood Assn. v. Ashcroft 462 U.S. 476 (1983)					F	F
Simpoulos v. Virginia, 462 U.S. 506 (1983)					A	A
Lehr v. Robertson, 463 U.S. 248 (1983)					A	F
Thornburgh v. Am. Coll. of Obst. & Gyn., 476 U.S. 747 (1986)					F	F
Bowers v. Hardwick, 478 U.S. 186 (1986)					F	
Turner v. Safley, 482 U.S. 78 (1987)					F	F
DeShaney v. Winnebago Co. Soc. Ser. Dept., 489 U.S. 189 (1989)					F	F
Michael H. v. Gerald D., 491 U.S. 110 (1989)					F	F
Webster v. Reproductive Health Ser., 492 U.S. 490 (1989)					F	F
Washington v. Harper, 494 U.S. 210 (1990)					F	F
Cruzan v. Dir., Missouri Dept. of Health, 497 U.S. 261 (1990)					F	F
Hodgson v. Minnesota, 497 U.S. 417 (1990)					F	
Ohio v. Akron Center, 497 U.S. 502 (1990)					F	F

EQUAL PROTECTION OF THE LAW

Blacks on Juries

Case	4	5	6	7	8	9
Hale v. Kentucky, 303 U.S. 613 (1938)	F					
Smith v. Texas, 311 U.S. 128 (1940)	F	F	F			
Hill v. Texas, 316 U.S. 400 (1942)	F	F				
Akins v. Texas, 325 U.S. 398 (1945)	F	A				
Patton v. Mississippi, 332 U.S. 463 (1947)	F	F	F			
Cassell v. Texas, 339 U.S. 282 (1950)	F					
Brown v. Allen, 344 U.S. 443 (1953)	F	F				
Avery v. Georgia, 345 U.S. 559 (1953)	F	F				
Reece v. Georgia, 350 U.S. 85 (1955)	F	F	F			
Michel v. Louisiana, 350 U.S. 91 (1955)	F	F	F			
Eubanks v. Louisiana, 356 U.S. 584 (1958)	F	F	F	F		
Arnold v. North Carolina, 376 U.S. 773 (1964)	F	F	F	F		
Swain v. Alabama, 380 U.S. 202 (1965)	A	F	F	A		
Whitus v. Georgia, 385 U.S. 545 (1967)	F	F	F	F		
Jones v. Georgia, 389 U.S. 24 (1967)	F	F	F	F	F	
Coleman v. Alabama, 389 U.S. 22 (1967)	F	F	F	F	F	
Carter v. Jury Com., 396 U.S. 320 (1970)	F			F	F	
Turner v. Fouche, 396 U.S. 346 (1970)	F	F		F	F	
Alexander v. Louisiana, 405 U.S. 625 (1972)			F	F	F	
Rose v. Mitchell, 443 U.S. 545 (1979)				A	A	
Vazquez v. Hillery, 474 U.S. 254 (1986)				F		
Batson v. Kentucky, 476 U.S. 79 (1986)				F		
Allen v. Hardy, 478 U.S. 255 (1986)				A	F	
Holland v. Illinois, 493 U.S. 474 (1990)				F		
Powers v. Ohio, 499 U.S. 400 (1991)						F
Ford v. Georgia, 498 U.S. 411 (1991)						F
Edmonson v. Leesville Concrete Co., 111 S. Ct. 2077 (1991)						F

Hispanics on Juries

Case	4	5	6	7	8	9
Hernandez v. Texas, 347 U.S. 475 (1954)	F	F		F		
Castaneda v. Partida, 430 U.S. 482 (1977)					F	F
Hernandez v. New York, 500 U.S. 352 (1991)						F

Exclusion of Blacks from Universities

Case	4	5	6	7	8	9
Sipuel v. Regents, 332 U.S. 631 (1948)			F	F		
Sweatt v. Painter, 339 U.S. 629 (1950)			F			
McLaurin v. Oklahoma State Regents, 339 U.S. 637 (1950)			F			
Lucy v. Adams, 350 U.S. 1 (1955)	F	F		F		
Hawkins v. Board of Control, 350 U.S. 413 (1956)	F	F		F		

Integration of Public Schools

Case	4	5	6	7	8	9
Brown v. Bd. of Education, 347 U.S. 483 (1954)		F	F			
Bolling v. Sharp, 347 U.S. 497 (1954)	F	F	F			
Brown v. Bd. of Education, 349 U.S. 294 (1955)		F	F			
Cooper v. Aaron, 358 U.S. 1 (1958)	F	F	F	F		
Goss v. Bd. of Education, 373 U.S. 683 (1963)	F	F	F	F		
Griffin v. School Board, 377 U.S. 218 (1964)	F	F	F	F		
Rogers v. Paul, 382 U.S. 198 (1965)	F	F	F	F		
Green v. County School Board, 391 U.S. 430 (1968)	F	F	F			F
Raney v. Bd. of Education, 391 U.S. 443 (1968)	F	F	F			F
Monroe v. Bd. of Commissioners, 391 U.S. 450 (1968)	F	F	F			F
United States v. Montgomery County, 395 U.S. 225 (1969)	F	F	F	F	F	
Swann v. Bd. of Education, 402 U.S. 1 (1971)	F	F		F	F	
Davis v. School Comm'rs., 402 U.S. 33 (1971)	F	F		F	F	
Bd. of Education v. Swann, 402 U.S. 43 (1971)	F	F		F	F	
Wright v. Coun. of City of Emporia, 407 U.S. 451 (1972)		F		F	F	
United States v. Scotland Neck, Bd. of Ed., 407 U.S. 484 (1972)		F		F	F	
Norwood v. Harrison, 413 U.S. 455 (1973)		F		F	F	
Washington v. Seattle School Dist. No. 1, 458 U.S. 457 (1982)				F	F	
Crawford v. Los Angeles Bd. of Ed., 458 U.S. 527 (1982)				A	F	

Integration of Public Facilities

Case	4	5	6	7	8	9
Muir v. Louisville Park Theatrical Assoc., 347 U.S. 971 (1954)	F	F	F			
Mayor, et al v. Dawson, 350 U.S. 877 (1955)	F	F	F			
Holmes v. City of Atlanta, 350 U.S. 879 (1955)	F	F	F			
Gayle v. Members of Bd. of Comm., 352 U.S. 903 (1956)	F	F	F	F		
New Orleans City Park Imp. Assoc. v. Detiege, 358 U.S. 54 (1958)	F	F		F	F	
State Athletic Com. v. Dorsey, 359 U.S. 533 (1959)	F	F		F	F	
Johnson v. Virginia, 373 U.S. 61 (1963)		F		F	F	
Wright v. Georgia, 373 U.S. 284 (1963)	F	F		F		
Watson v. Memphis, 373 U.S. 526 (1963)		F		F	F	
Schiro v. Bynum, 375 U.S. 395 (1964)	F	F		F	F	
Evans v. Newton, 382 U.S. 296 (1966)				F	F	
Evans v. Abney, 396 U.S. 435 (1970)					F	
Palmer v. Thompson, 403 U.S. 217 (1971)	A				F	
Gilmore v. City of Montgomery, 417 U.S. 556 (1974)		F			F	F

Integration of Private Facilities

Case	4	5	6	7	8	9
Burton v. Wilmington Pkg. Authority, 365 U.S. 715 (1961)	F	F		F	F	
Turner v. City of Memphis, 369 U.S. 350 (1962)	F	F		F	F	
Peterson v. Greenville, 373 U.S. 244 (1963)	F	F		F	F	
Shuttlesworth v. Birmingham, 373 U.S. 262 (1963)	F	F		F	F	
Lombard v. Louisiana, 373 U.S. 267 (1963)	F			F	F	
Gober v. City of Birmingham, 373 U.S. 374 (1963)	F	F		F	F	
Avent v. North Carolina, 373 U.S. 375 (1963)	F	F		F	F	

	4	5	6	7	8	9
Griffin v. Maryland, 378 U.S. 130 (1964)	A	F		F	F	
Robinson v. Florida, 378 U.S. 153 (1964)	F	F		F	F	
Bell v. Maryland, 378 U.S. 226 (1964)	A	F		F	F	
Hamm v. Rock Hill, 379 U.S. 306 (1964)	A	F		F	F	
Adickes v. Kress & Co., 398 U.S. 144 (1970)	F			F		
Moose Lodge #107 v. Irvis, 407 U.S. 163 (1972)				F	F	

Where and with Whom Blacks Live

	4	5	6	7	8	9
Shelley v. Kramer, 334 U.S. 1 (1948)	F	F				
Hurd v. Hodge, 334 U.S. 24 (1948)	F	F	F			
Barrows v. Jackson, 346 U.S. 249 (1953)	F					
McLaughlin v. Florida, 379 U.S. 184 (1964)	F			F	F	
Reitman v. Mulkey, 387 U.S. 369 (1967)	A	F		F	F	
Loving v. Virginia, 388 U.S. 1, (1967)	F	F		F	F	
Jones v. Mayer Co., 392 U.S. 409 (1968)	F	F		F	F	F
Hunter v. Erickson, 393 U.S. 385 (1969)	A	F		F	F	F
James v. Valtierra, 402 U.S. 137 (1971)	A				F	F
Palmore v. Sidoti, 466 U.S. 429 (1984)					F	

Gender Discrimination

	4	5	6	7	8	9
Breedlove v. Suttles, 302 U.S. 277 (1937	A					
Ballard v. United States, 329 U.S. 187 (1946)	F	F	F			
Goesaert v. Cleary, 335 U.S. 464 (1948)	A	F	F			
Reed v. Reed, 404 U.S. 71 (1971)					F	F
Frontiero v. Richardson, 411 U.S. 677 (1973)					F	F
Kahn v. Shevin, 416 U.S. 351 (1974)			A		F	F
Geduldig v. Aiello, 417 U.S. 484 (1974)			F		F	F
Schlesinger v. Ballard, 419 U.S. 498 (1975)			F		F	F
Weinberger v. Wiesenfeld, 420 U.S. 636 (1975)					F	F
Stanton v. Stanton, 421 U.S. 7 (1975)			F		F	F
Craig v. Boren, 429 U.S. 190 (1976)					F	F
Califano v. Goldfarb, 430 U.S. 199 (1977)					F	F
Quillion v. Walcott, 434 U.S. 246 (1978)					A	A
Orr v. Orr, 440 U.S. 268 (1979)					F	F
Parham v. Hughes, 441 U.S. 347 (1979)					F	F
Caban v. Mohammed, 441 U.S. 380 (1979)					F	F
Davis v. Passman, 442 U.S. 228 (1979)					F	F
Personnel Adm. of Massachusetts v. Feeney, 442 U.S. 256 (1979)					F	
Califano v. Westcott, 443 U.S. 76 (1979)					F	F
Wengler v. Druggists Mutual Ins. Co., 446 U.S. 142 (1980)					F	F
Kirchberg v. Feenstra, 450 U.S. 455 (1981)					F	
Michael M. v. Sonoma Co. Sup. Ct., 450 U.S. 464 (1981)					F	F
Rostker v. Goldberg, 453 U.S. 57 (1981)					F	
Mississippi Univ. for Women v. Hogan, 458 U.S. 718 (1982)					F	F
Roberts v. United States Jaycees, 468 U.S. 609 (1984)					F	F
Bd. of Dir. Rotary, Intl. v. Rotary Club, 481 U.S. 537 (1987)					F	F

Equal Protection for Illegitimate Children

Case	4	5	6	7	8	9
Levy v. Louisiana, 391 U.S. 68 (1968)				F	F	F
Glona v. Am. Guarantee & Liab. Co., 391 U.S. 73 (1968)		F		F	F	F
Labine v. Vincent, 401 U.S. 532 (1971)		F			F	F
Weber v. Aetna Cas. & Sur. Co., 406 U.S. 164 (1972)		F			F	F
Gomez v. Perez, 409 U.S. 535 (1973)		F			F	F
Linda R. S. v. Richard D., 410 U.S. 614 (1973)		F			F	A
New Jersey Welfare Rights Org. v. Cahill, 411 U.S. 619 (1973)		F			F	F
Jimenez v. Weinberger, 417 U.S. 628 (1974)		F			F	F
Mathews v. Lucas, 427 U.S. 495 (1976)					F	
Norton v. Mathews, 427 U.S. 524 (1976)					F	F
Trimble v. Gordon, 430 U.S. 762 (1977)					F	F
Fiallo v. Bell, 430 U.S. 787 (1977)					F	
Lalli v. Lalli, 439 U.S. 259 (1978)						F
Califano v. Boles, 443 U.S. 282 (1979)					F	F
Mills v. Habluetzel, 456 U.S. 91 (1982)					F	F
Pickett v. Brown, 462 U.S. 1 (1983)					F	F
Reed v. Campbell, 476 U.S. 852 (1986)					F	F
Clark v. Jeter, 486 U.S. 456 (1988)					F	F

Equal Protection for Aliens

Case	4	5	6	7	8	9
Oyama v. California, 332 U.S. 633 (1948)	F		F			
Takashi v. Fish Comm'n., 334 U.S. 410 (1948)		F				
Johnson v. Eisentrager, 339 U.S. 763 (1950)		F				
Graham v. Richardson, 403 U.S. 365 (1971)	F	F			F	F
Sugarman v. Dougal, 413 U.S. 634 (1973)		F			F	F
In re Griffiths, 413 U.S. 717 (1973)		F			F	F
Hampton v. Mow Sun Wong, 426 U.S. 88 (1976)					F	F
Examining Board v. Flores de Otero, 426 U.S. 572 (1976)					F	F
Nyquist v. Mauclet, 432 U.S. 1 (1977)					F	F
Foley v. Connelie, 435 U.S. 291 (1978)					F	
Ambach v. Norwick, 441 U.S. 68 (1979)					F	F
Cabell v. Chavez-Salido, 454 U.S. 432 (1982)					F	F
Plyler v. Doe, 457 U.S. 202 (1982)					F	F
Bernal v. Fainter, 467 U.S. 216 (1984)					F	

Equality in Classification of Voters

Case	4	5	6	7	8	9
Smith v. Allwright, 321 U.S. 649 (1944). (15th Amend.)	F	F				
Butler v. Thompson, 341 U.S. 937 (1951)	A	F				
Terry v. Adams, 345 U.S. 461 (1953)	F	F				
Lassiter v. Northampton Elections Bd., 360 U.S. 45 (1959)	A	A		A	A	
Carrington v. Rash, 380 U.S. 89 (1965)		F		F		
Harper v. Virginia Bd. of Elections, 383 U.S. 663 (1966)	A		F	F		
McDonald v. Bd. of Elections, 394 U.S. 802 (1969)	A	A		A	A	A
Kramer v. Union Sch. District, 395 U.S. 621 (1969)		F		F	F	F
Cipriano v. City of Houma, 395 U.S. 701 (1969)		F		F	F	F
Evans v. Cornman, 398 U.S. 419 (1970)					F	F

	4	5	6	7	8	9
Phoenix v. Kolodziejski, 399 U.S. 204 (1970)	F	F			F	F
Goosby v. Osser, 409 U.S. 512 (1972)		F			F	F
Marston v. Lewis, 410 U.S. 679 (1973)		F			F	F
Burns v. Fortson, 410 U.S. 686 (1973)		F			F	F
O'Brien v. Skinner, 414 U.S. 524 (1974)		F			F	
Hill v. Stone, 421 U.S. 289 (1975)					F	F
Holt Civic Club v. Tuscaloosa, 439 U.S. 60 (1978)					F	F
Hunter v. Underwood, 471 U.S. 222 (1985)					F	F
Quinn v. Millsap, 491 U.S. 95 (1989)					F	F

Protection for New Political Parties

	4	5	6	7	8	9
MacDougall v. Green, 335 U.S. 281 (1948)	F	F				
Williams v. Rhodes, 393 U.S. 23 (1968)				A	F	F
Hadnott v. Amos, 394 U.S. 358 (1969)		F		F	F	F
Moore v. Ogilvie, 394 U.S. 814 (1969)	F	F		F	F	F
Jenness v. Fortson, 403 U.S. 431 (1971)	A	A			A	A
American Party of Texas v. White, 415 U.S. 767 (1974)		F			A	A
Illinois Election Bd. v. Socialist Wkrs. Party, 440 U.S. 173 (1979)					F	

Equal Protection for the Poor

	4	5	6	7	8	9
Dandridge v. Williams, 397 U.S. 471 (1970)	A				F	F
Boddie v. Connecticut, 401 U.S. 371 (1971)	A				F	F
Bullock v. Carter, 405 U.S. 134 (1972)			F		F	F
Jefferson v. Hackney, 406 U.S. 535 (1972)			F		F	
United States v. Kras, 409 U.S. 434 (1973)			F		F	
Ortwein v. Schwab, 410 U.S. 656 (1973)			F		F	F
San Antonio Sch. Dist. v. Rodriquez, 411 U.S. 1 (1973)			F		F	F
U.S. Dept. of Agric. v. Moreno, 413 U.S. 528 (1973)			F		F	F
Memorial Hospital v. Maricopa Co., 415 U.S. 250 (1974)			F		F	F
Lubin v. Panish, 415 U.S. 709 (1974)			F		F	F
Beal v. Doe, 432 U.S. 438 (1977)					F	F
Maher v. Doe, 432 U.S. 464 (1977)					F	F
Harris v. Rosario, 446 U.S. 651 (1980)						F
Little v. Streater, 452 U.S. 1 (1981)					F	F
Lassiter v. Dept. Soc. Services, 452 U.S. 18 (1981)					F	F
Lyng v. Castillo, 477 U.S. 635 (1986)					F	F
Kadramas v. Dickinson Sch. Dist., 487 U.S. 450 (1988)					F	

Equal Protection in the Criminal Justice System

	4	5	6	7	8	9
Skinner v. Oklahoma, 316 U.S. 535 (1942)	F	F				
Fay v. New York, 332 U.S. 261 (1947)	F	F	F			
Moore v. New York, 333 U.S. 565 (1948)	F	F	F			
Dowd v. Cook, 340 U.S. 206 (1951)	F					
Griffin v. Illinois, 351 U.S. 12 (1956)				F		
Johnson v. United States, 352 U.S. 565 (1957)	F	F		F		

	4	5	6	7	8	9
Eskridge v. Washington Prison Board, 357 U.S. 214 (1958)	F	F		F	F	
Burns v. Ohio, 360 U.S. 252 (1959)		F		F	F	
McCrary v. Indiana, 364 U.S. 277 (1960)	F	F		F	F	
Smith v. Bennett, 365 U.S. 708 (1961)		F		F	F	
Beck v. Washington, 369 U.S. 541 (1962)	F	F		F	A	
Douglas v. California, 372 U.S. 353 (1963)				F	F	
Lane v. Brown, 372 U.S. 477 (1963)	F	F		F	F	
Draper v. Washington, 372 U.S. 487 (1963)	F	F		F	F	
Rinaldi v. Yeager, 384 U.S. 305 (1966)		F		F	F	
Long v. Dist. Ct. of Iowa, 385 U.S. 192 (1966)	F	F		F	F	
Swenson v. Bosler, 386 U.S. 258 (1967)	F	F		F	F	
Anders v. California, 386 U.S. 738 (1967)		F		F	F	
Entsminger v. Iowa, 386 U.S. 748 (1967)	F	F		F	F	
Roberts v. LaValle, 389 U.S. 40 (1967)	F	F		F	F	F
Gardner v. California, 393 U.S. 367 (1969)		F		F	F	F
Williams v. Oklahoma, 395 U.S. 458 (1969)	F	F		F	F	F
Williams v. Illinois, 399 U.S. 235 (1970)	F	F			F	F
Tate v. Short, 401 U.S. 395 (1971)	F	F			F	F
Mayer v. City of Chicago, 404 U.S. 189 (1971)		F			F	F
Britt v. North Carolina, 404 U.S. 226 (1971)		F			F	A
Lindsey v. Normet, 405 U.S. 56 (1972)		F			F	F
James v. Strange, 407 U.S. 128 (1972)		F			F	F
McGinnis v. Royster, 410 U.S. 263 (1973)		F			A	
Fuller v. Oregon, 417 U.S. 40 (1974)		A			F	F
Ross v. Moffit, 417 U.S. 600 (1974)		F			F	F
Richardson v. Ramirez, 418 U.S. 24 (1974)		A			F	F
Estelle v. Dorrough, 420 U.S. 534 (1975)		F			F	F
United States v. MacCollom, 426 U.S. 317 (1976)					F	F
McClesky v. Kemp, 481 U.S. 279 (1987)					F	F
Pennsylvania, v. Finley, 481 U.S. 551 (1987)					F	F

Equal Protection for Fundamental Rights

	4	5	6	7	8	9
Marton v. Walton, 368 U.S. 25 (1961)	F	F		A	A	
Baxstrom v. Herold, 383 U.S. 107 (1966)	F	F		F	F	
Dunn v. Blumstein, 405 U.S. 330 (1972)		F			F	F
Eisenstadt v. Baird, 405 U.S. 438 (1972)		F			F	F
Police Dept. of Chicago v. Mosley, 408 U.S. 92 (1972)		F			F	
Grayned v. City of Rockford, 408 U.S. 104 (1972)		F			F	F
Village of Belle Terre v. Borass, 416 U.S. 1 (1974)		A				F
Califano v. Jobst, 434 U.S. 47 (1977)					A	A
Zablocki v. Redhail, 434 U.S. 374 (1978)					F	F
Carey v. Brown, 447 U.S. 455 (1980)					F	F
Hooper v. Bernalillo Co., 472 U.S. 612 (1985)					F	F

Miscellaneous Equal Protection Cases

	4	5	6	7	8	9
Anderson v. Martin, 375 U.S. 399 (1964)	F	F		F	F	
Richardson v. Belcher, 404 U.S. 78 (1971)		F			F	F
Massachusetts Bd. of Retirement v. Murgia, 427 U.S. 307 (1976)					A	
Vance v. Bradley, 440 U.S. 93 (1979)					A	F

	4	5	6	7	8	9
New York Transit Auth. v. Beazer, 440 U.S. 568 (1979)					F	F
Schweiker v. Wilson, 450 U.S. 221 (1981)					F	F
Memphis v. Greene, 451 U.S. 100 (1981)					F	
Martinez v. Bynum, 461 U.S. 321 (1983)					A	
Williams v. Vermont, 472 U.S. 14 (1985)					F	F
Bowen v. Owens, 476 U.S. 340 (1986)					F	F

THE BILL OF RIGHTS AND THE STATES

	4	5	6	7	8	9
Palko v. Connecticut, 302 U.S. 319 (1937)	A					
Lovell v. Griffin, 303 U.S. 444 (1938)	F					
Betts v. Brady, 316 U.S. 455 (1942)	F					
Francis v. Resweber, 329 U.S. 459 (1947)	F	F	F			
Everson v. Bd. of Education, 330 U.S. 1 (1947)	F	F	F			
Adamson v. California, 332 U.S. 46 (1947)		F				
Foster v. Illinois, 332 U.S. 134 (1947)	F	F	F			
Wolf v. Colorado, 338 U.S. 25 (1949)	F	F				
Cuicci v. Illinois, 356 U.S. 571 (1958)	F					
Bartkus v. Illinois, 359 U.S. 121 (1959)	F			F	F	
Mapp v. Ohio, 367 U.S. 643 (1961)	F	F		F	F	
Robinson v. California, 370 U.S. 660 (1962)	F	F		F	F	
Gideon v. Wainwright, 372 U.S. 335 (1963)	F			F	F	
Malloy v. Hogan, 378 U.S. 1 (1964)	F	F		F	F	
Pointer v. Texas, 380 U.S. 400 (1965)	F	F		F	F	
Klopfer v. North Carolina, 386 U.S. 213 (1967)	F	F			F	
Washington v. Texas, 388 U.S. 14 (1967)	F	F			F	
Duncan v. Louisiana, 391 U.S. 145 (1968)		F		F	F	F
Benton v. Maryland, 395 U.S. 784 (1969)	F	F		F	F	

THE JAPANESE CASES

	4	5	6	7	8	9
Yasui v. United States, 320 U.S. 115 (1943)				A		
Ex parte Endo, 323 U.S. 283 (1944)			F			

INDEX